DISCIPLINES AND DOCUMENTATION STYLES **D**

Chapter 12
Writing about Literature lit
12a Literature and its genres
12b Reading and interpretation
12c Vocabulary for literature
12d Approaches to literature
12e Conventions for writing about literature
12f Sample literary interpretation

Chapter 13
MLA Documentation mla
13a MLA-style in-text citations
13b MLA list of works cited
13c Sample MLA-style paper

Chapter 14
Writing in the Social Sciences soc
14a Audience, purpose, and the research question
14b Evidence, sources, and reasoning
14c Conventions of language and organization
14d Samples of writing

Chapter 15
APA Documentation apa
15a APA-style in-text citations
15b APA-style reference list
15c Sample APA-style paper

Chapter 16
Writing in the Humanities hum
16a Audience, purpose, and the research question
16b Evidence, sources, and reasoning
16c Conventions of language and organization
16d Samples of writing

Chapter 17
CMS Documentation cms
17a CMS note and bibliographic forms
17b Sample CMS-style paper

Chapter 18
Writing in the Natural Sciences nat
18a Audience, purpose, and the research question
18b Evidence, sources, and reasoning
18c Conventions of language and organization
18d Samples of writing

Chapter 19
CSE Documentation cse
19a CSE citation systems
19b Sample CSE-style paper

Chapter 20
Writing in Business bus
20a Conventions of language and organization
20b Business letters
20c Business memos and e-mails
20d Résumés
20e Letters of application
20f Business plans
20g Oral presentations with PowerPoint
20h Business reports

GRAMMAR **G**

Chapter 21
Sentence Essentials
21a Parts of speech
21b Subjects and predicates
21c Complements
21d Basic sentence patterns

Chapter 22
Phrases and Clauses in Sentences ph/cl
22a Phrases
22b Clauses
22c Conjunctions and conjunctive adverbs
22d Sentence forms
22e Sentence functions

Chapter 23
Sentence Fragments frag
23a Recognizing sentence fragments
23b Phrases as sentence fragments
23c Dependent clauses as sentence fragments

Chapter 24
Comma Splices and Fused Sentences cs/fs
24a Punctuating independent clauses
24b Recognizing comma splices and fused sentences
24c Revising comma splices and fused sentences
24d Divided quotations

Chapter 25
Modifiers mod
25a Recognizing modifiers
25b Comparatives and superlatives
25c Placement of modifiers
25d Double negatives

Chapter 26
Pronouns pro
26a Recognizing pronouns
26b Pronoun case
26c Pronoun-antecedent agreement
26d Clear pronoun reference

Chapter 27
Verbs vb
27a Verb forms
27b Verb tenses
27c Verb tense consistency
27d Voice
27e Mood
27f Subject-verb agreement

EFFECTIVE **S**

28 ... su
... arranging details
28c including necessary words
28c Revising mixed metaphors
28d Relating sentence parts
28e Completing comparisons
28f Completing intensifiers

Chapter 29
Consistency cst
29a Verb tense
29b Point of view
29c Tone

Chapter 30
Subordination and Coordination sub/coor
30a Using subordination
30b Using coordination
30c Avoiding faulty or excessive subordination and coordination

Chapter 31
Parallelism //
31a Recognizing parallel elements
31b Repeating words and grammatical forms
31c Linking two or more sentences
31d Correlative conjunctions
31e Emphasizing key ideas

Chapter 32
Emphasis emp
32a Placement of words
32b Cumulative and periodic sentences
32c Ordering ideas from least to most important
32d Repeating important words
32e Choosing active voice or passive voice
32f Inverting word order
32g Using an occasional short sentence

Chapter 33
Variety var
33a Sentence length and form
33b Sentence openings
33c Questions, exclamations, and commands

W9-BAH-607

USAGE U

Chapter 34
Good Usage   usg
34a Usage and the rhetorical situation
34b Clear style
34c Word choice
34d Inclusive language
34e Dictionaries
34f Thesauruses

Chapter 35
Exactness   ex
35a Accurate and precise word choice
35b Evocative language
35c Idioms and collocations
35d First-person and second-person pronouns
35e Clear definitions

Chapter 36
Conciseness   con
36a Eliminating wordiness
36b Unnecessary repetition
36c Elliptical constructions

PUNCTUATION P

Chapter 37
The Comma   ,
37a Before a coordinating conjunction linking independent clauses
37b After introductory clauses, phrases, or words
37c Separating elements in a series
37d With nonessential elements
37e With geographical names and items in dates and addresses
37f With direct quotations
37g Unnecessary or misplaced commas

Chapter 38
The Semicolon   ;
38a Connecting independent clauses
38b Separating elements that contain commas
36c Revising common semicolon errors

Chapter 39
The Apostrophe   ’
39a Indicating ownership
39b Marking omissions of letters or numbers
39c Forming certain plurals

Chapter 40
Quotation Marks   " "
40a Direct quotations
40b Titles of short works
40c For tone or unusual usage
40d With other punctuation marks

Chapter 41
The Period and Other Punctuation Marks
41a Period
41b Question mark   ?
41c Exclamation point   !
41d Colon   :
41e Dash   —
41f Parentheses   ( )
41g Square brackets   [ ]
41h Ellipsis points   . . .
41i Slash   /

MECHANICS M

Chapter 42
Spelling, the Spell Checker, and Hyphenation sp
42a Spell checker
42b Spelling and pronunciation
42c Words that sound alike
42d Prefixes and suffixes
42e Confusion of *ei* and *ie*
42f Hyphens

Chapter 43
Capitals   cap
43a Proper names
43b Titles and subtitles
43c Beginning a sentence
43d Computer terms
43e Unnecessary capitals

Chapter 44
Italics   ital
44a Works published or produced separately
44b Foreign words
44c Legal cases
44d Names of ships, aircraft, etc.
44e Words, letters, or figures referred to as such
44f Emphasizing words

Chapter 45
Abbreviations, Acronyms, and Numbers   ab/ac/n
45a Abbreviations with names
45b Addresses in correspondence
45c Abbreviations in source documentation
45d Abbreviations in academic and professional writing
45e Acronyms
45f General uses of numbers
45g Special uses of numbers

Glossary of Usage   gu
Glossary of Terms   gt
Credits
Index

THE WRITER'S HARBRACE HANDBOOK

 **FOURTH EDITION**

THE **WRITER'S**
HARBRACE
HANDBOOK

CHERYL GLENN

The Pennsylvania State University

LORETTA GRAY

Central Washington University

 WADSWORTH
CENGAGE Learning·

Australia · Brazil · Japan · Korea · Mexico · Singapore · Spain · United Kingdom · United States

WADSWORTH
CENGAGE Learning™

The Writer's Harbrace Handbook, **Fourth Edition**
Cheryl Glenn, Loretta Gray

Acquiring Sponsoring Editor:
Kate Derrick

Senior Development Editor:
Michell Phifer

Assistant Editor: Kelli Strieby

Editorial Assistant: Jake Zucker

Senior Technology Project
Manager: Cara Douglass-Graff

Marketing Manager:
Jenn Zourdos

Marketing Assistant:
Ryan Ahern

Senior Marketing
Communications Manager:
Stacey Purviance Taylor

Senior Project Manager,
Editorial Production:
Lianne Ames

Senior Art Director: Cate Barr

Senior Print Buyer:
Betsy Donaghey

Permissions Editor:
Mollika Basu

Text Researcher:
Karyn Morrison

Production Service:
Lifland et al., Bookmakers

Text Designer: Anne Carter

Photo Manager: John Hill

Photo Researcher: Billie Porter

Cover Designer: Anne Carter

Compositor: Pre-PressPMG

For product information and
technology assistance, contact us at **Cengage Learning
Customer & Sales Support, 1-800-354-9706**

For permission to use material from this text or product,
submit all requests online at **cengage.com/permissions**
Further permissions questions can be emailed to
permissionrequest@cengage.com

Library of Congress Control Number: 2008943958

ISBN-13: 978-1-4282-3022-4

ISBN-10: 1-4282-3022-X

Wadsworth
20 Channel Center Street
Boston, MA 02210
USA

Cengage Learning products are represented in Canada by
Nelson Education, Ltd.

For your course and learning solutions, visit
www.cengage.com

Purchase any of our products at your local college store or
at our preferred online store **www.ichapters.com**

Printed in the United States of America
1 2 3 4 5 6 7 13 12 11 10 09

Contents

Preface   **xvii**

 PART I   **WRITING and the RHETORICAL SITUATION**

CHAPTER 1   **The Rhetorical Situation**   **3**   rhet
1a   Understanding the rhetorical situation   4
1b   Writing to an exigence   5
1c   Writing with a specific purpose   6
1d   Considering audience   9
1e   Sending and receiving a message within
         a context   15

CHAPTER 2   **Reading Rhetorically**   **18**   read
2a   Previewing for an initial impression   19
2b   Reading for content   25
2c   Rereading for understanding   28
2d   Recognizing a personal response   28
2e   Writing daily about your reading   29

CHAPTER 3   **Planning and Drafting Essays**   **30**   pln/dft
3a   Selecting worthwhile subjects for writing   31
3b   Focusing a subject idea into a specific topic   34
3c   Conveying a clearly stated thesis   37
3d   Arranging or outlining ideas   41
3e   Getting your ideas into a first draft   43
3f   Drafting well-developed paragraphs   44
3g   Employing rhetorical methods of development   47

CHAPTER 4	**Revising and Editing Essays** 55	rev/ed
4a	The essentials of revision 56	
4b	Guiding readers with your introduction and conclusion 59	
4c	Revising for unified and coherent paragraphs 65	
4d	Transitions within and between paragraphs 71	
4e	The benefits of peer review 74	
4f	Editing for clearer ideas, sentences, and paragraphs 87	
4g	Proofreading for an error-free essay 89	
4h	The final draft 90	

CHAPTER 5	**Planning for Academic Success** 96	acad
5a	Easing the pressures of academic reading and writing 96	
5b	Taking advantage of academic support opportunities 100	
5c	Managing deadlines 102	
5d	Abbreviating the writing process 103	
5e	Taking essay examinations 105	

CHAPTER 6	**Online Writing** 110	online
6a	Assessing the online rhetorical situation 110	
6b	Participating in online discussion communities 112	
6c	Netiquette and online writing 116	
6d	Composing Web documents 117	
6e	Visual elements and rhetorical purpose 126	

CHAPTER 7	**Composing with Visuals** 130	vis
7a	Visual documents and the rhetorical situation 131	
7b	The design principles of visual rhetoric 134	
7c	Combining visual and verbal elements 137	
7d	Common genres and effective features of visual documents 144	

CHAPTER 8	**Writing Arguments**	**154**	arg
8a	Determining the purpose of your argument	155	
8b	Considering differing viewpoints	156	
8c	Distinguishing between fact and opinion	158	
8d	Taking a position or making a claim	160	
8e	Providing evidence for an effective argument	163	
8f	Using the rhetorical appeals to ground your argument	167	
8g	Purposefully arranging an effective argument	170	
8h	Using logic to argue effectively and ethically	174	
8i	Avoiding rhetorical fallacies	177	
8j	Sample argument	184	

R　PART II　RESEARCH

CHAPTER 9	**Finding Sources in Print, Online, and in the Field**	**193**	find
9a	Research and the rhetorical situation	193	
9b	Finding books	198	
9c	Finding articles	202	
9d	Finding online sources	207	
9e	Field research	211	

CHAPTER 10	**Evaluating Print and Online Sources**	**216**	eval
10a	Credibility of authors	216	
10b	Credibility of publishers	221	
10c	Online sources	223	
10d	Relevance and timeliness	227	

CHAPTER 11	**Using Sources Effectively and Responsibly**	**229**	src
11a	The rhetorical situation and the research paper	229	
11b	Organizing notes	231	
11c	Working bibliography and annotated bibliography	234	

11d   Integrating sources   235
11e   Avoiding plagiarism   241
11f   Responding to sources   244

D   PART III   **DISCIPLINES and DOCUMENTATION STYLES**

CHAPTER 12   **Writing about Literature   249**   lit
12a   Literature and its genres   249
12b   Active reading and literary interpretation   251
12c   Vocabulary for discussing literature   254
12d   Approaches to interpreting literature   259
12e   Conventions for writing about literature   263
12f   Sample literary interpretation   266

CHAPTER 13   **MLA Documentation   273**   mla
13a   MLA-style in-text citations   273
13b   MLA list of works cited   281
13c   Sample MLA-style paper   315

CHAPTER 14   **Writing in the Social Sciences   329**   soc
14a   Audience, purpose, and the research question   331
14b   Evidence, sources, and reasoning   332
14c   Conventions of language and organization   334
14d   Samples of writing in the social sciences   338

CHAPTER 15   **APA Documentation   346**   apa
15a   APA-style in-text citations   346
15b   APA-style reference list   349
15c   Sample APA-style paper   368

CHAPTER 16   **Writing in the Humanities   378**   hum
16a   Audience, purpose, and the research question   380
16b   Evidence, sources, and reasoning   382
16c   Conventions of language and organization   384
16d   Samples of writing in the humanities   386

CHAPTER 17 **CMS Documentation**   **400**   cms
  17a   CMS note and bibliographic forms   400
  17b   Sample CMS-style paper   415

CHAPTER 18 **Writing in the Natural Sciences**   **430**   nat
  18a   Audience, purpose, and the research question   431
  18b   Evidence, sources, and reasoning   434
  18c   Conventions of language and organization   435
  18d   Samples of writing in the natural sciences   437

CHAPTER 19 **CSE Documentation**   **450**   cse
  19a   CSE citation-sequence, name-year,
            and citation-name systems   450
  19b   Sample CSE-style paper   461

CHAPTER 20 **Writing in Business**   **467**   bus
  20a   Conventions of language and organization   467
  20b   Business letters   469
  20c   Business memos and e-mails   472
  20d   Résumés   475
  20e   Letters of application   480
  20f   Business plans   482
  20g   Oral presentations with PowerPoint   487
  20h   Business reports   491

G PART IV **GRAMMAR**

CHAPTER 21 **Sentence Essentials**   **508**   se
  21a   Parts of speech   508
  21b   Subjects and predicates   517
  21c   Complements   521
  21d   Basic sentence patterns   523

CHAPTER 22 **Phrases and Clauses in Sentences**   **528** ph/cl
  22a   Phrases   528
  22b   Clauses   538

22c   Conjunctions and conjunctive adverbs   543
22d   Sentence forms   547
22e   Sentence functions   550

CHAPTER 23   **Sentence Fragments   553**   frag
23a   Recognizing sentence fragments   553
23b   Phrases as sentence fragments   556
23c   Dependent clauses as sentence fragments   558

CHAPTER 24   **Comma Splices and Fused**   cs/fs
                    Sentences   562
24a   Punctuating independent clauses   563
24b   Recognizing comma splices and fused
             sentences   565
24c   Revising comma splices and fused
             sentences   567
24d   Divided quotations   570

CHAPTER 25   **Modifiers   572**   mod
25a   Recognizing modifiers   572
25b   Comparatives and superlatives   577
25c   Placement of modifiers   580
25d   Double negatives   585

CHAPTER 26   **Pronouns   588**   pro
26a   Recognizing pronouns   588
26b   Pronoun case   593
26c   Pronoun-antecedent agreement   599
26d   Clear pronoun reference   603

CHAPTER 27   **Verbs   607**   vb
27a   Verb forms   607
27b   Verb tenses   616
27c   Verb tense consistency   627
27d   Voice   628
27e   Mood   631
27f   Subject-verb agreement   634

S PART V   **EFFECTIVE SENTENCES**

CHAPTER 28   **Sentence Unity   646**   su
28a   Choosing and arranging details   646
28b   Including necessary words   648
28c   Revising mixed metaphors   649
28d   Relating sentence parts   650
28e   Completing comparisons   653
28f   Completing intensifiers   654

CHAPTER 29   **Consistency   655**   cst
29a   Verb tense   655
29b   Point of view   658
29c   Tone   659

CHAPTER 30   **Subordination and Coordination   662**   sub/coor
30a   Using subordination effectively   662
30b   Using coordination effectively   664
30c   Avoiding faulty or excessive subordination
        and coordination   666

CHAPTER 31   **Parallelism   668**   //
31a   Recognizing parallel elements   668
31b   Repeating words and grammatical forms   669
31c   Linking two or more sentences   670
31d   Using correlative conjunctions   671
31e   Emphasizing key ideas in introductions
        and conclusions   672

CHAPTER 32   **Emphasis   674**   emp
32a   Placing words for emphasis   674
32b   Using cumulative and periodic sentences   676
32c   Ordering ideas from least to most important   676
32d   Repeating important words   677
32e   Choosing between the active voice
        and the passive voice   677
32f   Inverting word order   679
32g   Using an occasional short sentence   680

CHAPTER 33   **Variety   682**   var
33a   Revising sentence length and form   683
33b   Varying sentence openings   687
33c   Using questions, exclamations,
         and commands   689

U **PART VI** **USAGE**

CHAPTER 34   **Good Usage   693**   usg
34a   Usage and the rhetorical situation   693
34b   Clear style   694
34c   Appropriate word choice   695
34d   Inclusive language   696
34e   Dictionaries   702
34f   Thesauruses   706

CHAPTER 35   **Exactness   707**   ex
35a   Accurate and precise word choice   707
35b   Evocative language   712
35c   Idioms and collocations   713
35d   First-person and second-person pronouns   715
35e   Clear definitions   717

CHAPTER 36   **Conciseness   719**   con
36a   Eliminating wordiness and other
         redundancies   719
36b   Avoiding unnecessary repetition   723
36c   Using elliptical constructions   723

P PART VII **PUNCTUATION**

CHAPTER 37 **The Comma   727**   ,

37a   Before a coordinating conjunction linking independent clauses   728

37b   After introductory clauses, phrases, or words   729

37c   Separating elements in a series   732

37d   With nonessential elements   733

37e   With geographical names and items in dates and addresses   737

37f   With direct quotations   738

37g   Unnecessary or misplaced commas   738

CHAPTER 38 **The Semicolon   741**   ;

38a   Connecting independent clauses   741

38b   Separating elements that contain commas   742

38c   Revising common semicolon errors   743

CHAPTER 39 **The Apostrophe   745**   '

39a   Indicating ownership and other relationships   745

39b   Marking omissions of letters or numbers   751

39c   Forming certain plurals   752

CHAPTER 40 **Quotation Marks   753**   " "

40a   Direct quotations   753

40b   Titles of short works   755

40c   For ironic tone or unusual usage   756

40d   With other punctuation marks   757

CHAPTER 41 **The Period and Other Punctuation Marks   760**

41a   The period   761   .

41b   The question mark   761   ?

41c   The exclamation point   763   !

41d   The colon   763   :

41e   The dash   766   —

41f   Parentheses   767   ( )

41g   Square brackets   768   [ ]

41h   Ellipsis points   769   . . .

41i   The slash   772   /

M PART VIII MECHANICS

CHAPTER 42   **Spelling, the Spell Checker,**   **sp**
                          and Hyphenation   **777**

42a   Spell checker   777

42b   Spelling and pronunciation   778

42c   Words that sound alike   779

42d   Prefixes and suffixes   780

42e   Confusion of *ei* and *ie*   783

42f   Hyphens   784

CHAPTER 43   **Capitals**   **787**   **cap**

43a   Proper names   788

43b   Titles and subtitles   792

43c   Beginning a sentence   793

43d   Computer keys, menu items, and icon names   795

43e   Unnecessary capitals   796

CHAPTER 44   **Italics**   **798**   **ital**

44a   Titles of works published or produced
        separately   799

44b   Foreign words   800

44c   Legal cases   801

44d   Names of ships, submarines, aircraft, spacecraft,
        and satellites   801

44e   Words, letters, or figures referred to as such
        and letters used in mathematical expressions   802

44f   Words receiving emphasis   802

CHAPTER 45   **Abbreviations, Acronyms,**   **ab/ac/n**
                          and Numbers   **804**

45a   Abbreviations with names   805

45b   Addresses in correspondence   805

45c   Abbreviations in source documentation   806

45d   Acceptable abbreviations in academic and
            professional writing   807
45e   Acronyms   809
45f   General uses of numbers   810
45g   Special uses of numbers   811

Glossary of Usage   **815**   gu

Glossary of Terms   **831**   gt

Credits   **843**

Index   **847**

Preface

Welcome! This fourth edition of *The Writer's Harbrace Handbook* builds on two important innovations made to the previous edition. First, we have focused even more closely on the rhetorical demands of writing in a digital age; we provide students with guidance for completing assignments—delivered online or on paper—that require clear writing as well as effective graphics and images. Many students appear in our classrooms already fluent in the uses of technology, ready to learn about the rhetorical situation and the ways it can help them make decisions about choosing the most effective words and visuals and arranging those in the best way to achieve their purpose. Second, to prepare students for writing successfully in a wide range of disciplines, we have significantly enhanced the coverage of academic writing and added a number of assignments in a variety of genres. These two major improvements further our commitment to helping students use the rhetorical situation to inform their interpretation and production of textual and visual documents—in whatever the medium or genre.

The History

The book you have in your hands has the richest—and longest—history of any handbook in the United States. First published in 1941 by University of Tennessee English professor John C. Hodges, the handbook was initially a direct result of Hodges's own classroom experience and his federally funded research, an analysis of twenty thousand student papers. Sixteen English professors of rhetoric from various regions of the United States marked those thousands of papers, after which Hodges worked with a cadre of graduate students to create a taxonomy of writing issues (from punctuation and grammar to style and usage) that would organize the first writing manual for American college students and teachers. This taxonomy, developed nearly seventy years ago, still underpins the overall design and organization of nearly every handbook on the market today. No other handbook or handbook author has yet devised a better means for providing students and teachers with easy access to the information they need.

Hodges's original *Harbrace Handbook of English* eventually evolved into *The Writer's Harbrace Handbook,* Fourth Edition, which continues the tradition of up-to-date reliability and practicality. Like John Hodges, we have used our classroom experience and our research to respond to the needs of teachers and students. In our classrooms, we have kept track of the questions students ask and the problems they have with their writing, and we have noted the specific issues that pose difficulties, both for them as they write and for us as we teach. We have revised this handbook accordingly, taking special care to respond to students' concerns (including concerns about the use of technology and about writing in the disciplines). We have also moved far beyond our individual classrooms, collaborating on a nationwide study that examines what exactly students consider to be the rewards and challenges of college-level writing. Preliminary results of that study influenced many of the decisions we made in producing this handbook—a handbook dedicated to providing both teachers and students with the ease of reference and attention to detail that have made the Harbrace handbooks the standard of reliability.

New to This Edition

■ **Chapter 7, "Composing with Visuals,"** introduces students to the design principles underpinning the effective use of visuals in many kinds of documents. The principles of alignment, proximity, contrast, and repetition can support students in their selection and arrangement of visuals, helping them make their visual and verbal texts work together to reach their audience and fulfill their purpose.

■ **Chapter 16, "Writing in the Humanities,"** transcends the traditional focus on English courses by including conventions for writing across the humanities, whether in philosophy, art history, history, foreign languages, religion, comparative literature, cultural studies, or women's and gender studies. This chapter introduces students to the types of assignments they will be expected to fulfill in their humanities courses and guides them in determining the audience and purpose for these assignments. The chapter also supports students as they choose the most appropriate evidence and reasoning to employ in their writing assignments. Finally, the chapter provides style, formatting, and documentation conventions specific to writing in the humanities.

■ **Chapter 29, "Consistency,"** encourages students to use a consistent tone, point of view, and time frame. By examining sample paragraphs, students learn to edit their essays with an eye for shifts in expression that may distract their readers. Students practice locating unnecessary shifts and revising sentences to fit the overall context of their essays.

■ **New Student Papers** This edition features approximately twenty full-length and excerpted student papers on wide-ranging topics, ranging from learning a foreign language to changing forms of business communication. The revised chapters on academic writing highlight student papers or extended excerpts that illustrate responses to a variety of assignments, including case studies, lab reports, reviews, business letters, and résumés. We have also added new research papers to the chapters devoted to style guides. A research paper on whether genetically modified crops will benefit developing countries follows MLA guidelines; a co-authored sociology paper on trends in tattooing is written and formatted according to APA standards.

Revised for This Edition
Attention to the rhetorical situation continues to invigorate all the writing and research chapters and most of the grammar chapters, whether the chapters are thoroughly redesigned or completely new. Several chapters have been extensively revised in light of contemporary composition pedagogy, while maintaining those features of traditional rhetorical theory that are still widely respected.

■ **Chapter 6, "Online Writing,"** helps students assess the rhetorical situation in the online environment, whether they are participating in electronic messaging or a discussion forum or composing documents for online presentation. This extensively revised chapter explains the value of netiquette, visual elements that fulfill a rhetorical purpose, and hyperlinks that enhance online documents. Most important is the focus on composing effective, well-designed Web documents.

▪ **Chapters 12 through 20,** constituting part III, are the chapters dedicated to writing across the disciplines and the major documentation styles integral to those disciplines. Significantly expanded and reorganized, this part of the book supports students as they write in various academic areas, encountering diverse rhetorical situations across the curriculum. With a strong emphasis on academic writing, the discipline-specific chapters provide students with guidance for successfully fulfilling approximately four different kinds of assignments in each chapter. We have rearranged the order of these chapters so that each documentation chapter (MLA, APA, CMS, or CSE) follows the academic-writing chapter to which it corresponds. This improved arrangement embodies a logical progression from a discipline-specific chapter that explains the conventions and genres of academic writing within a discipline to a chapter that presents the corresponding documentation and formatting conventions and culminates with a student-written paper in the pertinent style. For example, chapter 14, "Writing in the Social Sciences," is followed by chapter 15, "APA Documentation," and chapter 16, "Writing in the Humanities," a completely new chapter (described above), is followed by chapter 17, "CMS Documentation." Having the documentation chapters paired with their respective discipline chapters enables students to locate more easily the appropriate documentation guidelines to use for their papers. Chapter 14, "Writing in the Social Sciences," and chapter 18, "Writing in the Natural Sciences," emphasize the kinds of graphics (tables, charts, and photographs) expected in scientific writing as well as the objective presentation of research methodology and results. Chapter 20, "Writing in Business," has been expanded to include a discussion of using PowerPoint for oral presentations, which includes example slides. All of these discipline-specific chapters include directions for and examples of the kinds of academic writing students are expected to master in their courses, including literary analyses, research papers, field reports, position papers, laboratory reports, literature reviews, business letters and reports, letters of application, and résumés.

▪ In this edition, we continue our thorough coverage of the guidelines from the **style manuals for academic writing** published by the Modern Language Association (MLA), the American Psychological Association (APA), *The Chicago Manual of Style* (CMS), and the Council of Science Editors (CSE). *The Writer's Harbrace Handbook* itself follows *The Chicago Manual of Style*, which is the style guide used by most publishers, although we note the other style guides' preferences for punctuation and mechanics when they differ from those listed in CMS. Each documentation chapter opens with general guidelines that help students understand the patterns inherent in the particular documentation system. By studying these patterns, students become more efficient and accurate at creating bibiliographies. All the documentation chapters have easy-to-follow, color-coded examples of each type of citation (for a book, an article, and an online source), displaying the major components and their exact arrangement. In addition, tip boxes remind students of all the steps they need to follow as they compose their bibliographies.

The forthcoming updated version of *The Writer's Harbace Handbook,* Fourth Edition, will include a completely revised chapter on MLA documentation, based on the 2009 publication of the *MLA Handbook for Writers of Research Papers,* Seventh Edition. All MLA-style student papers in this updated version will also be revised to reflect the changes to the style guide.

■ **Chapters 21 through 27,** the grammar chapters, have been revised to make concepts more accessible for those students with little background in writing in English. The exercises in these chapters continue to give students practice in areas they frequently find difficult.

Other Features

■ **Instructive visuals** are featured in most chapters. For instance, in chapter 8, "Writing Arguments," cartoons illustrate several rhetorical fallacies. In the research and documentation chapters, annotated visuals, such as screen shots of databases and Web sites, help students learn how to locate in these kinds of sources the information they need for their bibliographies. Most of the student-generated papers in this handbook include some kind of visual—photograph, table, or figure. In the process of referring to the visuals in this book, students will come to understand the specific ways these features communicate meaning to an audience, meaning that supplements and enhances the information conveyed by words.

■ **Thinking Rhetorically** boxes prompt students to consider the impact on their purpose and target audience of the choices they make in grammar, style, and punctuation. Many of the boxes present situations in which a writer has multiple options or in which a conventional rule may be broken, creating opportunities for students to determine which choice is the most effective one in terms of purpose and audience. These possibilities move students away from thinking that one rule fits all toward gauging the rhetorical effect of the sentence-level decisions they make.

■ **Multilingual Writers** boxes identify common areas of confusion for English language learners, whether English is their first or second (or third) language. In addition, these boxes address concerns that may arise for all students as they draft, revise, and edit their work.

■ **Checklists** in most chapters provide tips for accomplishing a task (e.g., finding a research question) or prompts that remind students of the steps they need to follow in order to complete a project (e.g., designing an online document).

■ **Tech Savvy** boxes help students use their word processors to produce documents for a variety of courses. The boxes cover topics ranging from the creation of dashes to the insertion of tables and graphs to advice for attaching files to e-mail messages.

Supplements
Technology Supplements

InSite™ for Writing and Research   This all-in-one online writing and research tool includes electronic peer review, an originality checker, an assignment library, help with common errors, and access to InfoTrac® College Edition. InSite makes course management practically automatic. Visit **http://insite.wadsworth.com**.

InfoTrac® College Edition   Students can do in-depth research right from their desktop or laptop computer or catch up on the latest news online—using four months of access to InfoTrac College Edition. They can search this virtual university library's more than 18 million reliable, full-length articles from five thousand academic and popular periodicals (including the *New York Times, Newsweek, Science, Forbes,* and *USA Today*) and retrieve results almost instantly. They can also use InfoMarks—stable URLs that can be linked to articles, journals, and searches to save time when doing research—and access the InfoWrite online resource center for guides to writing research papers, grammar help, critical thinking guidelines, and much more.

Turnitin®   This online plagiarism-prevention program promotes fairness in the classroom by helping students learn to cite sources correctly and allowing instructors to check for originality before reading and grading papers. Turnitin checks student papers against billions of pages of Internet content, millions of published works, and millions of other student papers and generates a comprehensive originality report within seconds.

English21   The largest compilation of online resources ever organized for composition and literature courses, English21 is a complete online support system that weaves robust, self-paced instruction with interactive assignments. English 21 engages students as they become better-prepared and successful writers and supports them through every step of the writing process, from assignment to final draft. English21 includes carefully crafted multimedia assignments; a collection of essays that amounts to a full-sized thematic reader; a full interactive handbook including hundreds of animations, exercises, and activities; a complete research guide with animated tutorials and a link to Gale's InfoTrac database; and a rich multimedia library with hand-selected images, audio clips, video clips, stories, poems, and plays. Access to **Personal Tutor**, an online environment with one-on-one tutoring and on-demand help from experienced tutors, is included with English21. To learn more, visit **http://academic.cengage.com/english21.**

English21 Plus   Access to English21 Plus is available for a nominal fee when packaged with new copies of the text. English21 Plus includes all of the features mentioned above as well as access to Wadsworth's **InSite for Writing and Research™.** InSite features an electronic peer review system, an originality checker, a rich assignment library, and electronic grade marking. To learn more, visit **http://academic.cengage.com/english21.**

The Writer's Harbrace eBook   A completely interactive experience, the eBook version of *The Writer's Harbrace Handbook* presents the entire handbook online, with integrated links that give students access to a wide variety of resources with the click of a mouse. The **integrated online College Workbook** covers grammar, punctuation, usage, style, and writing. A variety of exercises with clear examples and explanations supplement the exercises found in the handbook. The Answer Key to the workbook is found in the Instructor's Resource Manual on the companion Web site for the handbook.

The Writer's Harbrace Handbook Web Site   The free companion Web site provides links, sample syllabi, quizzes and tests, and interactive exercises on the fundamentals of writing, including grammar, mechanics, and punctuation. A student paper library includes sample papers with accompanying editing and revising activities.

■ The **Diagnostic Test Package** allows comprehensive evaluation of students' writing skills through pre- and post-tests covering a variety of concepts in grammar, mechanics, usage, and spelling. The Diagnostic Test Package includes practice versions of the TAKS and CLAST tests as well as general diagnostic tests and writing prompts for essays—all designed to help instructors evaluate students' skill level.

■ The **Instructor's Resource Manual** gives instructors maximum flexibility in planning and customizing a course. Available on the instructor's companion Web site as well as on the PowerLecture CD-ROM, its pedagogically rich materials are organized into two main sections. "Part One: Questions for Teachers" raises a variety of pedagogical questions (and gives possible solutions) for you to consider when teaching your course with this handbook; "Part Two: Sample Syllabi and Activities" offers sample syllabi with possible assignments for a semester-long course and for a quarter-long course. Additionally, this section contains sample in-class collaborative learning activities, technology-oriented activities, and critical thinking and writing activities. The Instructor's Resource Manual also includes the following supplementary materials: (1) an ESL insert aimed at helping mainstream instructors teach writing effectively to their ESL students, (2) an insert on disability issues as they relate to teaching first-year composition, (3) the Answer Key for the exercises in the handbook, and (4) the Answer Key for the online handbook.

CengageNOW™ for Writing   Students can boost their writing skills with CengageNOW, a Web-based, multimedia, writing assessment and learning program. This study system helps students understand what they know, as well as identify what they don't know, and helps them build study strategies to fill in the gaps and master the crucial rudimentary concepts of writing. Using a variety of technologies to accommodate many learning styles, CengageNOW covers all aspects of writing. Its interactive learning tools, such as Diagnostic Quizzes, Personalized Study Plans, and Multimedia Tutorials, will help students master the fundamentals of writing and build their confidence as they become more effective writers.

PowerLecture   A course preparation tool on CD-ROM, PowerLecture includes the Writer's Harbrace PowerPoints, the Diagnostic Test Package, and the Instructor's Resource Manual. The PowerPoint component of PowerLecture is a set of slides designed to help instructors guide their students through the features, content, and organization of *The Writer's Harbrace Handbook*. These slides, which have been carefully created to help your students get the most out of their handbook, illustrate the major features that will aid students in grasping important concepts.

Toolbox   Harness the power of the Internet and bring your course to life with Toolbox, a course management program. You can use its wealth of interactive resources along with those on the handbook's companion Web site to supplement the classroom experience and ensure that students have the resources they need to succeed in today's business world. You can even use this effective resource as an integrated solution for distance learning or a Web-enhanced course.

Printed Supplements
Instructor's Correction Chart   To make marking your students' papers easier, you can prop up on your desk this oversized, laminated chart, which lists all of the sections of the handbook and shows the editing symbols correlated to them.

Dictionaries   The following dictionaries are available for a nominal price when bundled with the handbook: *The Merriam-Webster Dictionary,* Second Edition; *Merriam-Webster's Collegiate® Dictionary,* Eleventh Edition; *Merriam-Webster Pocket Thesaurus;* and *Heinle's Newbury House Dictionary of American English with Integrated Thesaurus.* The latter was created especially for ESL students.

Acknowledgments

We would like to thank our colleagues who reviewed this handbook throughout the course of development. Their astute comments, frank responses, and thoughtful suggestions helped shape what is the final version—until the next edition. We thank them for taking the time out of their already busy schedules to help us.

Handbook Reviewers

Mary Adams, Steven Brehe, and Joyce Stavick, North Georgia College and State University; Jesse Airaudi, Baylor University; Cathryn Amdahl, Harrisburg Area Community College; Karen Cajka, East Tennessee State University; Mechel Camp, Jackson State Community College; Joyce Cottonham, Southern University-Shreveport; Nancy Cox, Arkansas Tech University; Christopher Ervin, University of South Dakota; Maryanne Garbowsky, County College of Morris; Kim Gunter, University of North Carolina, Pembroke; David James, Houston Community College; Joseph Jones, University of Memphis; Bryan Moore, Arkansas State University; David Murdock, Gadsden State Community College; Robert Spirko, University of Tennesee, Knoxville; Eula Thompson, Jefferson State Community College; Linda Weeks, Dyersburg State Community College; Stephen Whited, Piedmont College; and Marla Wiley, Hinds Community College.

Focus Group Participants

Pat Belanoff, SUNY, Stony Brook; Laura Carroll, Abilene Christian University; Elyse Fields, Red Rocks Community College; Lynee Gaillet, Georgia State University; Patricia Jenkins, University of Alaska, Anchorage; Maureen Jonason, Concordia University; Rachel Robinson, Middle Tennessee State University; Michelle Sidler, Auburn University; and Christa Teston, Kent State University.

The fourth edition of this handbook took shape through extensive conversations and correspondence between the authors as well as with a number of members of the Cengage Learning/Wadsworth editorial staff. For their collective ideas, enthusiasm, support, and wise counsel, we remain grateful. In particular, we thank Lyn Uhl, Publisher, Kate Derrick, Acquisitions Editor, and Jennifer Zourdos, Marketing Manager, whose unwavering enthusiasm and encouragment supported us through many months of work. Lianne Ames, Senior Production Project Manager, helped to bring this huge project to completion, and Jane Hoover carried out the copyediting with style and care. Anne

Carter gave the book its clear and aesthetically pleasing interior design and cover. Without the help and support of these imaginative people, we simply could not have produced *The Writer's Harbrace Handbook.*

But it is Michell Phifer, Senior Development Editor Extraordinaire as well as friend—to whom we owe a special thanks. A scrupulously careful editor—and our constant intellectual companion—Michell successfully helped us balance our writing and research deadlines with our other professional commitments (teaching, for instance!). She regularly prodded us to think critically about each chapter, about our choice of images or textual examples, and especially about the project as an intellectual whole. Michell has been on our team for three editions, guiding our collaboration until the very last minute, when the presses rolled.

The successful completion of our work would not have been possible without the research assistance of Rebecca Wilson Lundin, Rosalyn Collings Eves, Michelle Smith, and Brandy Scalise, all from The Pennsylvania State University. Consummate professionals, they helped us envision and frame chapter 6, "Online Documents," chapter 7, "Composing with Visuals," chapter 16 "Writing in the Humanities," and chapter 20 "Business Writing," providing more good information than we could possibly use. We want to thank Richard Petraglia, Faith Haney, Anna Seitz, Kaitlyn Andrews-Rice, Marianna Suslin, Jason Wallin, Rachel L. Pinter, Sarah M. Cronin, Matthew Marusek, Kaycee Hulet, Carla Spohn, Nicole Hester, Mike Demmon, Heather Jensen, Michelle Tebbe, and Joe Delaney, whose academic writing samples bring this handbook to life. We're also grateful for the help of the many colleagues and students whose conversations about writing enriched our understanding of composition pedagogy.

Finally, we are grateful to our friends and families. Although our faces toward the screen meant our backs toward you, you were never far from our thoughts. After all, without you, our work would be neither possible nor worthwhile.

To all of you reading this preface and using or considering using this handbook for the first time, know that we are grateful to you too. In fact, if you have advice for how we might improve the next edition or if we can help you in any way, write us c/o Cengage Learning, English Editorial Department, 20 Channel Center Street, Boston, MA 02210.

Cheryl Glenn
Loretta Gray
December 2008

W

WRITING and the RHETORICAL SITUATION

Elements of the rhetorical situation.

1 The Rhetorical Situation 3

2 Reading Rhetorically 18

3 Planning and Drafting Essays 30

4 Revising and Editing Essays 55

5 Planning for Academic Success 96

6 Online Writing 110

7 Composing with Visuals 130

8 Writing Arguments 154

CHAPTER 1
The Rhetorical Situation 3

1a Understanding the rhetorical situation 4
1b Writing to an exigence 5
1c Writing with a specific purpose 6
1d Considering audience 9
1e Sending and receiving a message within a context 15

CHAPTER 2
Reading Rhetorically 18

2a Previewing for an initial impression 19
2b Reading for content 25
2c Rereading for understanding 28
2d Recognizing a personal response 28
2e Writing daily about your reading 29

CHAPTER 3
Planning and Drafting Essays 30

3a Selecting worthwhile subjects for writing 31
3b Focusing a subject idea into a specific topic 34
3c Conveying a clearly stated thesis 37
3d Arranging or outlining ideas 41
3e Getting your ideas into a first draft 43
3f Drafting well-developed paragraphs 44
3g Employing rhetorical methods of development 47

CHAPTER 4
Revising and Editing Essays 55

4a The essentials of revision 56
4b Guiding readers with your introduction and conclusion 59
4c Revising for unified and coherent paragraphs 65
4d Transitions within and between paragraphs 71
4e The benefits of peer review 74
4f Editing for clearer ideas, sentences, and paragraphs 87
4g Proofreading for an error-free essay 89
4h The final draft 90

CHAPTER 5
Planning for Academic Success 96

5a Easing the pressures of academic reading and writing 96
5b Taking advantage of academic support opportunities 100
5c Managing deadlines 102
5d Abbreviating the writing process 103
5e Taking essay examinations 105

CHAPTER 6
Online Writing 110

6a Assessing the online rhetorical situation 110
6b Participating in online discussion communities 112
6c Netiquette and online writing 116
6d Composing Web documents 117
6e Visual elements and rhetorical purpose 126

CHAPTER 7
Composing with Visuals 130

7a Visual documents and the rhetorical situation 131
7b The design principles of visual rhetoric 134
7c Combining visual and verbal elements 137
7d Common genres and effective features of visual documents 144

CHAPTER 8
Writing Arguments 154

8a Determining the purpose of your argument 155
8b Considering differing viewpoints 156
8c Distinguishing between fact and opinion 158
8d Taking a position or making a claim 160
8e Providing evidence for an effective argument 163
8f Using the rhetorical appeals to ground your argument 167
8g Purposefully arranging an effective argument 170
8h Using logic to argue effectively and ethically 174
8i Avoiding rhetorical fallacies 177
8j Sample argument 183

1 The Rhetorical Situation

Rhetoric, the purposeful use of language, pervades your daily activities. You cannot read your mail, fill out an employment application, or answer an exam question without using rhetoric to analyze what you are reading or to produce language that others will understand. Every day, you use rhetoric as you read and write—whether you are reading class assignments, course syllabi, e-mails, or directions for your MP3 player or are submitting written assignments, creating a résumé, or text messaging with your friends. Every day, you are surrounded by rhetoric and rhetorical opportunities, and you have been reading and writing rhetorically for most of your life.

This chapter explains reading and writing rhetorically as processes, each a series of sometimes overlapping steps that help you understand these four elements of the rhetorical situation (**1a**):

- exigence (**1b**),
- purpose (**1c**),
- audience (**1d**), and
- context (**1e**).

Writing rhetorically helps you to fulfill a variety of class assignments, some of which are discussed in this handbook:

- an essay from personal experience (**4h**),
- an argument from personal experience and research (**8j**),
- an argument based on research (chapters **9–11**),
- an interpretation of a literary text (**16g**),
- a field report and a lab report (**17d, 18d**),
- a Web page for an organization (**6d, 6e**),
- a business letter and a résumé (**19b, 19d**), and
- a business plan (**19f**).

1a   Understanding the rhetorical situation

As a communicator, you use visual and verbal language purposefully, every day, in terms of a **rhetorical situation** (fig. 1.1), the circumstances in which you are interpreting a reading or composing a piece of writing or even a visual. When you read and write rhetorically—whether in or out of school, as the sender or the receiver—you have a clear sense of the rhetorical situation and the specific elements that constitute it.

The **writer** in a rhetorical situation is the person who identifies the **exigence,** the reason or problem that impels that person to write or speak in the first place. When purposeful language can resolve the exigence, the situation is rhetorical. The writer then prepares a **message** (information delivered through visual or verbal means) with the purpose of resolving that exigence. But to fulfill that purpose, the writer must gauge the message in terms of the intended **audience,** the reader who has the capability of resolving the exigence or problem. Whether or not that audience works to resolve the exigence, the audience reads, hears, or sees the message within a specific **context,** the constraints (obstacles) and resources (positive influences) in the environment of the rhetorical situation. Those constraints and resources include whatever else has already been said on

Fig. 1.1. The rhetorical situation.

the subject; when, where, and through what medium the transaction between writer and audience takes place; and the writer's relationship with the audience, the writer's credibility (or believability), and the appropriateness of the message in terms of both content and means of delivery (electronic, print, visual, or oral).

Reading and writing rhetorically offer you the opportunity to consider each of these elements separately as well as in combination. You can actively engage a text by establishing the writer's credibility, intended audience, context, purpose, and overall message and by establishing the interdependence of these elements. For instance, a writer's purpose, whether stated or implied, should be appropriate for the intended audience and the context. The writer's choice of audience might change depending on purpose or context; the context affects the audience and the writer's purpose (1e).

By reading and writing rhetorically, you can also evaluate the thesis statement (3c), the key points, and the amount of support each point merits, as well as what needs to be said and what is purposefully left unsaid. Therefore, when you *read* rhetorically, you read more efficiently and effectively—and you can talk knowledgeably about what you have read (chapter 2). When you *write* rhetorically, you generate new ideas and communicate them clearly and concisely to your audience (chapters 3 and 4)—and you improve your understanding of what you have read.

1b Writing to an exigence

The exigence is the particular problem or situation that calls for words. A parking violation, a birth, a college application, an engagement—these are all events that compel people to write. Words—either spoken or written—can resolve the problem of fining a parking violator, announcing a birth, awarding college admission, or inviting wedding guests. Once you determine the exigence for your writing—the reason that impels you to write—you will be better able to gauge all the elements of your writing (from word choice to organizational pattern) in terms of your overall purpose.

Natural disasters provide exigencies for writing and speaking, often with the purpose of stimulating fundraising and relief efforts.

THINKING RHETORICALLY

⁂ EXIGENCE

Historical events of varying significance often serve as the exigencies for writing. In 2005, Hurricane Katrina scoured the Louisiana coast, leaving in its wake a prolonged disaster that politicians, humanitarian groups, celebrities, and local individuals have addressed continuously since then. When NFL quarterback Michael Vick was suspended from the Atlanta Falcons in 2007 after being charged with involvement with dogfighting, animal rights activists across the nation raised their collective voice in calls for further investigation. And the 2007 Malibu wildfires sparked responses—written and spoken—from homeowners, journalists, schoolchildren, and California's Governor Arnold Schwarzenegger.

1c Writing with a specific purpose

As soon as you know that words can resolve an exigence or address a particular need or situation, you can concentrate on the general purpose of those words. Writers must clarify their purpose, and readers should be influenced according to that purpose—whether the writer wants to express feelings about something, amuse or entertain, report information, explain or evaluate the significance of information, analyze a situation, clarify a point, invite the audience to consider alternative points of view, or argue for or against a course of action.

Depending on the writer's overall purpose, then, the message (whether composed or received) can be classified as expressive, expository, or argumentative. Any of these types of writing can help a writer fulfill an overall purpose.

(1) Expressive writing emphasizes the writer's feelings and reactions to people, objects, events, or ideas.

Personal letters and journals are often expressive, as are many essays and short stories. The following example (paragraph 1) comes from an essay designed to convey the excitement of a mother-to-be as she imagines telling her husband the happy news. (For ease of reference, each of the sample paragraphs in this chapter is numbered.)

1   I haven't breathed a word to him yet, about having this baby, and I won't until he arrives. I won't blurt out such special news on the telephone. I won't write it in an e-mail. I want to be there standing in front of him—the best seat in the house—to watch the smile break across his face. I want to share the joy of that first moment of knowledge, of all that this baby will mean to our lives. I feel jealously possessive about this moment to come. He arrives this evening and, impatient as I am, I am hanging on, savouring the scene, playing it out in my head, over and over again.

—CAROL DRINKWATER, "The Fruits of Spring"

(2) Expository writing focuses more on objects, events, or ideas than on the writer's feelings about them.

Textbooks, news accounts, scientific reports, and encyclopedia articles are generally expository, as are many of the essays students are expected to write in college. When you report, explain, clarify, or assess, you are practicing exposition. Paragraph 2 is excerpted from a book that explains how paleoanthropologists—specifically, a paleoanthropologist named Mac—discover their prizes.

2   Searching only in the most promising areas isn't the key to [Mac's] success; perseverance is. He walks the same territory over and over again, changing courses around obstacles, and he tells his people to do the same. If you walked to the left around this bush yesterday, then walk to the right today. If you walked into the sun yesterday, then walk with the

sun at your back today. And most of all, walk, and walk, and walk, and *look* while you are doing it. Don't daydream; don't scan the horizon for shade; ignore the burning sun even when the temperature reaches 135°F. Keep your eyes on the ground searching for that elusive sliver of bone or gleaming tooth that is not just any old animal, fossilized and turning to rubble, but a hominid. Those are the prizes we seek; those are the messengers from the past.

—ALAN WALKER AND PAT SHIPMAN, *The Wisdom of the Bones*

(3) Argumentative writing is intended to influence the reader's attitudes and actions.

Most writing is to some extent an argument. Through the choice and arrangement of material, even something as apparently straightforward as a résumé can be an argument for an interview. However, writing is usually called argumentative if it clearly supports a specific position (chapter 8). In paragraph 3, note how the writer calls for people to take a winning stance.

3   I warn you, a winning stance is never achieved by *trying.* I hear some say, "I will try as hard as I can." Trying is for losers. Trying implies the possibility of losing. I will *try* to win. I will *try* not to lose. If after trying they have lost, well, they *tried,* did they not? *Losers always try.* Winners never try. Winners only win.   —GERRY SPENCE, "The Unbeatable Power Argument"

Writers need to identify their overall purpose for each piece of writing, knowing that they can tap various methods of development (such as narration, description, and cause-and-effect analysis; see 3g) to work toward that goal. Whether you are the reader or the writer, you must assess the rhetorical purpose. For instance, when you are the reader, you want to assess the overall purpose of the writing in order to know how best to respond. If you can identify specific words or passages that convey the writer's purpose, you can discern whether the writer wants you to be entertained, informed, or persuaded. When you are the writer, you want to compose a message that responds to an exigence and fulfills a purpose while also alerting your intended audience to that purpose. If you are writing in response to a specific assignment, talk with your instructor or check your assignment sheet to review which elements of the rhetorical situation (exigence, audience, context, purpose) have already been set for you (5a(2)).

CHECKLIST for Assessing Purpose

- Has your instructor provided a purpose for your writing, or are you defining a purpose on your own?

- Are you trying primarily to express how you feel? Are you writing to improve your self-understanding or trying to help others understand you better?

- Are you trying to be entertaining or inspiring? How easily does your topic lend itself to your purpose? What examples or choice of words will help you fulfill that purpose?

- Are you writing primarily to convey information? Are you trying to teach others something they do not know or to demonstrate that you have knowledge in common?

- Are you writing primarily to argue for or against a course of action? Do you want your readers to stop a certain behavior, to undertake a specific action, or to consider alternative points of view?

- Do you have more than one purpose in writing? Which purpose is primary? How can the other purposes help you achieve that primary one? Or are some of your purposes in conflict?

Exercise 1

Select one of the following subjects; write two paragraphs that begin to develop an expressive, expository, or argumentative essay on that subject.

1. your finances
2. your generation
3. your career goals
4. your computer expertise
5. your favorite musical group
6. volunteer work
7. academic pressures
8. music or dance performances
9. student housing
10. your closest relative

1d   Considering audience

A clear understanding of the audience—its values, concerns, and knowledge—helps writers tailor their writing in terms of length, quality and quantity of details, the kind of language used, and the examples that will be most effective. Of course, the audience is anyone who reads the text, but that broader audience includes the writer's intended audience, those people whom the writer considers capable of being influenced by the words or who are capable of bringing about change. Some writers like to plan and draft essays with their purpose and their audience clearly in mind; others like to focus first on purpose and attend to their audience when they are revising (chapters 3 and 4). As a writer, you will need to think clearly, at some point, about who exactly will be reading what you write and ask yourself whether your choices are appropriate for that audience.

(1) A specialized audience is predisposed to the message.

A **specialized audience** has a demonstrated interest in the subject. If a relative died as the result of drunk driving, you might become a member of a specialized audience: people whose lives have been affected by alcohol abuse. You would probably be interested in alcohol-abuse information that is specifically geared to people who have had experiences

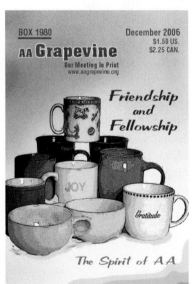

When writing to a specialized audience, take into account the needs, interests, and values of its members.

like yours. And if you decided to write about the harm done through alcohol abuse, you would probably direct your text to members of an organization such as Alcoholics Anonymous or Mothers Against Drunk Driving, who constitute a specialized audience.

Any group of people (such as nutritionists, police officers, or social workers) who have an area of expertise, an agenda, or a specific interest can form a specialized audience, one that you will want to address accordingly. Depending on the topic, you can usually assume that every member of a specialized audience has an interest in your subject and some knowledge of it.

You will want to consider the members of your specialized audience— what they know that you do not, how much and what sorts of information you might provide them, and how best to develop your information—in terms of your overall purpose. You will be writing to readers with some degree of expertise, so you will need to establish common ground with them by mentioning areas of agreement, acknowledging their expertise, and adjusting your tone and language choices to their knowledge and attitudes (4a(3) and chapter 32). You will also benefit your readers by providing them with new information—or a new way of understanding information with which they are already familiar.

A general reader might be surprised by the emotional content of the following excerpt, which was created for a specialized audience, one already familiar with the dire consequences of drunk driving.

4   Early on Sunday morning, September 18, 1999, Jacqueline Saburido, 20, and four friends were on their way home from a birthday party. Reggie Stephey, an 18-year-old star football player, was on his way home from drinking beer with some buddies. On a dark road on the outskirts of Austin, Texas, Reggie's SUV veered into the Oldsmobile carrying Jacqui and the others. Two passengers in the car were killed at the scene and two were rescued. Within minutes, the car caught fire. Jacqui was pinned in the front seat on the passenger side. She was burned over 60% of her body; no one thought she could survive. But Jacqui lived. Her hands were so badly burned that her fingers had to be amputated. She lost her hair, her ears, her nose, her left eyelid and much of her vision. She has had more than 50 operations since the crash and has many more to go.

In June 2001 Reggie Stephey was convicted of two counts of intoxication manslaughter for the deaths of Jacqui's two friends. He was sentenced to seven years in prison and fined $20,000.

—TEXAS DEPARTMENT OF TRANSPORTATION, "Jacqui's Story"

This passage was not written for a general audience. Instead, it is aimed at a specialized audience, most of whose members are educators who are committed to ending drunk driving. These educators can tell Jacqui's story to discourage people from driving while intoxicated.

Many of the essays you will be assigned to write in college—in English, history, economics, psychology, and the sciences, for example—will be aimed at a specialized audience. That audience will often be an instructor, who is already familiar with the subject matter. For example, if you are writing an essay about molecular mapping for your biology instructor, it is not necessary to define *chromosomes*. Instead, your essay needs to communicate your understanding of the overall process and its applications.

Writing for a specialized audience does not mean that you have to know more than the members of that audience, nor does it mean that you have to impress them with your interpretation. Since no one knows everything about a subject, members of a specialized audience will usually appreciate thinking about their subject in a new way, even if they are not learning new information.

(2) A diverse audience represents a range of expertise and interest.

A **diverse audience** consists of readers with differing levels of expertise and varying interest in your subject. For example, if you are writing about upgrading computer software in a report that will be read by all the department heads of a company, you should be aware that some of your readers probably know more about software than others, and some may know more than you. But you can also assume that all of your readers share a willingness to learn about new material if it is presented clearly and respectfully by someone who is establishing common ground with them.

Paragraph 5 helps a diverse audience of readers understand an unusual illness that put a young man in the hospital.

5   I first met Greg in April 1977, when he arrived at Williamsbridge Hospital. Lacking facial hair, and childlike in manner, he seemed younger than his twenty-five years. He was fat, Buddha-like, with a vacant, bland face, his blind eyes roving at random in their orbits, while he sat motionless in his wheelchair. If he lacked spontaneity and initiated no exchanges, he responded promptly and appropriately when I spoke to him, though odd words would sometimes catch his fancy and give rise to associative tangents or snatches of song and rhyme. Between questions, if the time was not filled, there tended to be a deepening silence; though if this lasted for more than a minute, he might fall into Hare Krishna chants or a soft muttering of mantras. He was still, he said, "a total believer," devoted to the group's doctrines and aims. —OLIVER SACKS, "The Last Hippie"

Oliver Sacks writes for a diverse audience. Although its members share an interest in science writing, and medical stories in particular, they bring varying levels of expertise to Sacks's essay. Therefore, Sacks describes a medical condition in words easily understood by a wide audience. When you are writing for a diverse audience, you too need to establish what the members are likely to have in common in order to make appropriate word choices (chapters 34–36) and include appropriate details (3f(1)).

There will be times when you simply will not know much about your audience, even though your purpose for writing might be to evaluate a product or argue for a course of action. When this is the case, it may help you to imagine a thoughtful audience of educated adults, with whom you may share some common ground. Such an audience is likely to include people with different backgrounds and cultural values (8e(2)), so be careful not to assume that you are writing for readers who are exactly like you (34d). To a considerable extent, the language you use will determine whether diverse readers feel included in or excluded from your work. Be careful to avoid jargon or technical terms that would be understood only by a specialized audience. If you must use a specialized term, explain what it means (34c and 34e).

(3) Multiple audiences read for different reasons.

Writers often need to consider multiple audiences, a task related to—yet different from—addressing a diverse audience. When you address a diverse audience, you try to reach everyone. When you consider multiple audiences, you gauge your choice of words and tone according to your primary audience, knowing that a secondary audience might have access to your text. At work, for instance, you address your research report, employee evaluation, or proposal to your boss. But if you know that she will circulate the text among your colleagues, you adjust your words and tone accordingly. You might not be as frank in writing as you would be speaking in person; you might omit potentially hurtful information or temper your words. If you are asked to evaluate the performance of an employee under your supervision, you might be asked to send the evaluation to your boss, who is looking to see whether you are a competent supervisor, and a copy of it to the employee, who is looking for praise. When you know that your rhetorical situation includes multiple audiences, you can better select your words.

The use of e-mail for communication (6b) has increased the likelihood of writing for multiple audiences because messages can be forwarded easily—and not always with the writer's permission. Other electronic texts, such as those generated by listserv dialogues or online conversations through a Web site, also reach multiple audiences. When writing for electronic submission, consider whether anyone outside your primary audience might read your work.

While writing essays in college, you may also find yourself addressing multiple audiences. For example, you may use research you have done in your history class as the starting point for developing an essay for a class in literature or economics. You may take a linked or team-taught course in which you submit written work for evaluation by two instructors (your two primary audiences). Or you may write an essay for a general audience (which constitutes your secondary audience) and submit it to an instructor who is a specialist in your subject (and your primary audience). In each of these cases, you are writing for multiple audiences. This kind of writing requires that you consider a variety of attitudes and positions (**8d** and **8e**). Considering different points of view is helpful when planning an essay and also when reading what you have drafted as you prepare to revise it (chapter **4**). The following checklist may also help you assess your audience.

CHECKLIST for Assessing Audience

- Who is going to be reading what you write?
- What do you know about the members of your audience? What characteristics can you safely assume they have? What do they have in common? How are they different?
- What values do you share with them? How do you differ from them?
- How much do they already know about your topic?
- What kind of language is appropriate or inappropriate for this audience?
- How open are the members of this audience to views that may be different from their own?
- What level of expertise will they expect from you?
- What do you not know about this audience? What assumptions would be risky?
- Are you writing with a primary audience in mind but expecting a secondary audience to also read what you have written? If so, have you clearly identified the primary audience so that you can address that audience specifically, while recognizing the expectations of the secondary audience?

Exercise 2

Examine an introductory and an advanced textbook in a discipline of your choice, and locate a passage in each devoted to the same issue or concept. Photocopy these passages, and prepare a class presentation in which you explain how they reveal differences in audience.

1e Sending and receiving a message within a context

Context includes time and place, writer and audience, and the medium of delivery—the circumstances under which writer and reader communicate. Social, political, religious, and other cultural factors influence context, as do the constraints and resources of the rhetorical situation. Therefore, what you are able to produce in writing is always influenced (positively or negatively) by the context.

Your background and beliefs often shape the stance (or attitude) you take when writing. An essay written shortly before your school's winter break, for example, could be influenced by both your anticipation of a combined religious holiday and family reunion and your uncertainty about whether your audience shares that anticipation. Or an international crisis, such as the war in Iraq or the prolonged disaster in Darfur, might prompt you to reconsider the purpose of an essay you are drafting for your international economics course. Writers who consider the time, the place, and other factors of the context in which they are writing, as well as their audience, are more likely to communicate their ideas effectively.

The medium in which you are writing is also part of the context. Writing material for a Web page or another online medium requires you to think differently about organization, design, and style than does writing a traditional academic essay or business letter. Depending on your familiarity with and aptitude in using the technology, writing in an electronic medium may demand a good deal more time from you, too. Considering the method of delivery for a Web page, for example, requires making different kinds of rhetorical decisions than you would make for a text in a wholly static print medium (chapter 6).

Context shapes how messages are sent and received.

When you read the work of other writers, you will sometimes find that the context is explicitly stated, as in paragraph 6.

6   Katrina tore up lives as well as landscapes. A city below sea level was churned suddenly and convulsively by the hurricane that struck New Orleans in late August 2005. Rich people died along with the indigent. The pricey homes of the professional classes, both black and white, were destroyed, as were rickety cottages owned or rented by the poor. Millionaires and high-flying politicians were undone by Katrina, while other survivors found opportunity in the ruins of the city. That did not make Katrina an "equal opportunity destroyer," as some hastened to call it. Poor blacks did disproportionately more of the dying. And as the engines of recovery creaked into gear, people of means enjoyed advantages that had been theirs all along.

—**JED HORNE,** *Breach of Faith: Hurricane Katrina and the Near Death of a Great American City*

Often, however, the context must be inferred. Whether the context is announced or not, it is important that writers and readers identify and consider it.

CHECKLIST for Assessing the Context

■ Under what circumstances of time and place are you writing?

■ Under what circumstances will your writing probably be read? Will it be one among many texts or documents being received, or is your particular message eagerly awaited? In either case, how can you help your reader quickly see the purpose and thrust of your work under these circumstances?

■ How has your response to the task been influenced by other events in your life, your country, or the world?

■ Have you been asked to write a text of a specific length? If length has not been specified, what seems appropriate for your purpose and audience?

■ What document design (chapter 7) is appropriate given the context for your writing?

2   Reading Rhetorically

Reading is more pleasurable and profitable when undertaken as a series of steps. Every time you pick up a newspaper, glance over the headlines, turn to the sports section, skim over the first page, and then go back to read the story that most intrigues you, you are reading rhetorically. Sometimes, as with an article about Marion Jones, who agreed to return her five Olympic gold medals after admitting to taking steroids, you find yourself rereading the text to make sure that you understand the differences between what the sportswriter is reporting and what Marion Jones is actually admitting.

Whether you are reading the sports pages, a church bulletin, or your biology assignment, you are reading rhetorically every time you find yourself previewing a text, reading for content, responding, and rereading. When you follow these steps, you can more easily determine how difficult the text will be to understand, what you are likely to learn from it, and how useful it will be to you—assessments that will improve your comprehension. In addition, you can use these steps to consider the features of the rhetorical situation (writer, audience, exigence, context, and meaning).

This chapter explains the process of reading rhetorically and describes ways you can monitor your personal and intellectual responses to a text. Whether **chronological** (in order of occurrence) or **recursive** (alternating between moving forward and looping back), reading rhetorically is a process of

- previewing (**2a**),
- reading for content (**2b**), and
- rereading (**2c**).

This chapter will not only help you carry out this process but will also

- help you distinguish between actual content and your personal response to that content (**2d**) and
- encourage you to write daily about your reading (**2e**).

2a   Previewing for an initial impression

You often preview reading material—when you thumb through a newspaper or a magazine looking for articles that stir your interest. A systematic preview, though, gives you more reliable results and makes your

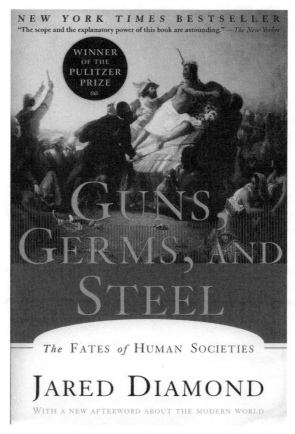

The title of Jared Diamond's book—*Guns, Germs, and Steel: The Fates of Human Societies*—accurately reflects the contents.

reading more efficient. When reading rhetorically, you systematically preview a text by reading the author's name and the title, then skimming the entire text to get a sense of how the information is organized and what you can expect from reading the text.

You will also want to assess what the reading demands of you in terms of time, effort, and previous knowledge. By previewing the length of a text, you can estimate how much time you need to set aside for reading. By reading the summary (often located in the preface or introductory chapter) or the abstract (usually preceding a scholarly article), you can decide whether the text will be useful. If the text is difficult, you can preview the major points, often found in headings (14c and 18c).

FEATURES OF A TEXT FOR PREVIEWING

Title

The title (and subtitle, if any) often reveals the focus of a text and sometimes its thesis (3c). When a title does not provide much information, look at the chapter titles or section headings to get a clearer sense of the work as a whole as well as to gauge how much you may already know about the subject.

Author

If you know anything about the author, you may have an idea about the expertise or tone being brought to the topic. If David Sedaris is the author, you can expect the essay to be humorous, but if Ellen Goodman is the author, you can expect the essay to be timely and political. Jared Diamond's science writing is highly respected and widely read, for he has earned a Pulitzer Prize (for *Guns, Germs, and Steel*), a MacArthur Foundation fellowship (otherwise known as a "genius award"), and a National Medal of Science.

Length

Considering a text's length allows you to estimate how much time you should set aside for reading. By checking length, you can also estimate whether a work is long enough to include useful content or so short that it might only skim the surface of the subject it addresses.

Directories

In addition to previewing title and author, you will also want to examine various directories within the text. The **table of contents**, for example, identifies the chapters and main sections within a book, and the **index,** at the back, lists in alphabetical order the specific topics covered. A **bibliography**, or list of research sources and related works, indicates how much research was involved in writing the book and can also direct you to additional sources. Checking these directories can help you determine whether the book has the kind of information you are looking for, where you can find it, and how much or what sections of the book you want to read.

Visual Aids

The extent to which visual aids are useful varies, but a quick check for graphs and other illustrations can help you decide whether the work has the kind of information you need, depending on the topic you are researching.

Summaries

Both books and articles often contain summaries. Reading a summary can help you decide whether the work as a whole will be helpful; a summary can also help you follow a difficult text because it highlights the major points. Summaries can often be found in the preface of a book as well as in introductory and concluding chapters. Scholarly articles often begin with a summary identified as an abstract (9c). Within other kinds of articles, the introductory and concluding paragraphs often include summaries. Sometimes, book summaries are provided on the inside cover or the back cover.

In addition to assessing the title, author, length, directories, visual aids, and summary of a text you are previewing, assess how much you already know about the subject. If you are unfamiliar with the subject matter, you might want to start with a less demanding treatment of the topic, either in print or online. Finally, if you know that your values or opinions differ greatly from those of the author, you will want to pay close attention to

CONTENTS

Preface to the Paperback Edition   9

PROLOGUE   YALI'S QUESTION
  The regionally differing courses of history   1 3

PART ONE   FROM EDEN TO CAJAMARCA   3 3

  CHAPTER 1 UP TO THE STARTING LINE
  What happened on all the continents before 11,000 B.C.?   3 5

  CHAPTER 2 A NATURAL EXPERIMENT
  OF HISTORY
  How geography molded societies on Polynesian islands   5 3

  CHAPTER 3 COLLISION AT CAJAMARCA
  Why the Inca emperor Atahuallpa did not capture
  King Charles I of Spain   6 7

PART TWO   THE RISE AND SPREAD OF FOOD
PRODUCTION   8 3

  CHAPTER 4 FARMER POWER
  The roots of guns, germs, and steel   8 5

                                      5

The table of contents shows how the material in Diamond's book is arranged and indicates how fully that material is developed.

passages in the text that you might be tempted to dismiss without reading carefully.

Previewing helps make your reading easier and helps you select appropriate research materials (chapter 9). But remember that previewing a text is not the same as reading it for understanding.

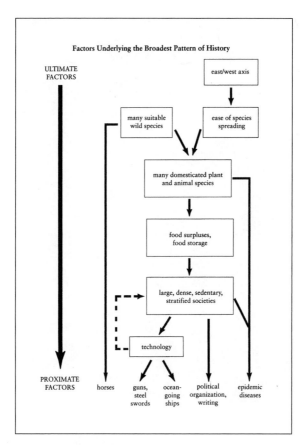

Factors Underlying the Broadest Pattern of History

ULTIMATE FACTORS

east/west axis

many suitable wild species

ease of species spreading

many domesticated plant and animal species

food surpluses, food storage

large, dense, sedentary, stratified societies

technology

PROXIMATE FACTORS

horses

guns, steel swords

ocean-going ships

political organization, writing

epidemic diseases

In chapter 4, Diamond uses a visual aid to map out the causal chain of factors that he believes underlies patterns of history—especially the development of steel and guns and the spread of germs.

SCIENCE

OVER 1 MILLION COPIES SOLD

"Fascinating. . . . Lays a foundation for understanding human history."
—Bill Gates

"Artful, informative, and delightful. . . . There is nothing like a radically new angle of vision for bringing out unsuspected dimensions of a subject, and that is what Jared Diamond has done." —William H. McNeill, *New York Review of Books*

"This is a brilliantly written, passionate, whirlwind tour through 13,000 years of history on all the continents—a short history of everything about everybody. The origins of empires, religion, writing, crops, and guns are all here. By at last providing a convincing explanation for the differing developments of human societies on different continents, the book demolishes the grounds for racist theories of history. Its account of how the modern world was formed is full of lessons for our own future. After reading the first two pages, you won't be able to put it down." —Paul R. Ehrlich, Bing Professor of Population Studies, Stanford University

"An ambitious, highly important book." —James Shreeve, *New York Times Book Review*

"A book of remarkable scope, a history of the world in less than 500 pages which succeeds admirably, where so many others have failed, in analyzing some of the basic workings of culture process. . . . One of the most important and readable works on the human past published in recent years." —Colin Renfrew, *Nature*

WINNER OF THE PHI BETA KAPPA AWARD IN SCIENCE

JARED DIAMOND is professor of geography at UCLA and author of the best-selling and award-winning *The Third Chimpanzee*. He is a recipient of a MacArthur Foundation fellowship and has been awarded a 1999 National Medal of Science.

With a new afterword extending the book's significance to today's economies and geopolitics

Cover design by Calvin Chu

Cover painting: Sir John Everett Millais, *Pizarro seizing the Inca of Peru*, 1845. Victoria & Albert Museum, London/Art Resource, NY

W. W. NORTON
NEW YORK • LONDON

ISBN 0-393-31755-2
51695
9 780393 317558
$16.95 USA $24.99 CAN.
www.wwnorton.com

The reviewers have summarized Diamond's book as well as evaluated its importance.

CHECKLIST for Previewing a Reading Selection

- What do you already know about this subject that you can use to connect with the text?
- What do the title and subtitle reveal about the way the subject is being treated?
- How long is this work, and how is it organized? What do the major divisions indicate to you?
- What information do the table of contents and the index provide about the book?
- Does the article include an abstract, or does the book include a summary?
- What do you know about this author that contributes to his or her credibility? If the author is unfamiliar, what biographical information could help you assess that credibility (**8c** and **10a**)?
- If there are graphs, figures, or other visuals in the text, what do they illustrate?
- Is there a bibliography that indicates how extensive and current the research is?
- Is the text suited to your level of understanding, or should you start with a simpler (or more sophisticated) treatment of the same subject?
- Do you have strong feelings about this subject that could interfere with your ability to understand how it is treated in this text (**2d**)?

2b Reading for content

Effective readers pay close attention to the words on the page and develop specific strategies for increasing their comprehension as well as for working through misunderstandings. After previewing a text, you should be able to determine what the author wants to communicate, to whom, and for what specific purpose. In other words, you can begin to read for content.

As you read, you will want to note the author's major points, perhaps by underlining or highlighting them. Particular words and key phrases often signal those important points: "There are *three* advantages to this proposal. . . . The *first* is . . . . The *second* is . . . ." The phrase *in other words* signals that the author is about to paraphrase a point—because it is important. And *in this article* (or *chapter*) introduces a statement of the author's focus or purpose, whereas *in summary, in conclusion,* and *the point I am making* place a significant emphasis on the information just presented. Thus, transitional words or phrases indicating sequencing (**4d**) or movement within a text help you grasp content. Transitional expressions—especially those indicating purpose, result, summary, repetition, exemplification, and intensification (see page 73)—alert you to important points. Such phrases identify opportunities for you to talk back to the text itself, as though you were carrying on a conversation with the author.

When reading from a book or periodical (a magazine or professional journal) that you own, you can underline, highlight, or add comments to passages that interest or confuse you, or that you question. Write in the margins and annotate key passages whenever you have something to say or a question to pose. If you have borrowed a book, you can use sticky notes to highlight and annotate the text. With an electronic text, you can print out a hard copy and annotate it or use your word-processing program to respond directly on the screen.

Reading for content means making sure you understand the words on the page. When you encounter a word that is new to you, the meaning may be defined in the text itself, or you may be able to infer the meaning from the way the word has been used. Whenever a new term appears in a critically important position such as a thesis statement (**3c**) or a conclusion (**4b(2)**), look it up in a college-appropriate dictionary (**34e**). But even language that is well chosen can sometimes be misleading because words have different specific meanings (**denotations**) as well as strong associations (**connotations**) that vary from reader to reader (**35a**) and culture to culture (chapter **34**)—depending on the rhetorical situation.

Your challenge as a reader, then, is to try to understand what exactly the author wanted the words to mean within the particular rhetorical situation, to understand as much as you can but to keep that understanding flexible enough to accommodate what will come. If you are reading a twenty-page chapter, you probably need a preliminary understanding of the first ten pages if you are going to understand the next

HEMISPHERES COLLIDING • 3 5 7

Eurasia's diverse and protein-rich cereals; hand planting of individual seeds, instead of broadcast sowing; tilling by hand instead of plowing by animals, which enables one person to cultivate a much larger area, and which also permits cultivation of some fertile but tough soils and sods that are difficult to till by hand (such as those of the North American Great Plains); lack of animal manuring to increase soil fertility; and just human muscle power, instead of animal power, for agricultural tasks such as threshing, grinding, and irrigation. These differences suggest that Eurasian agriculture as of 1492 may have yielded on the average more calories and protein per person-hour of labor than Native American agriculture did.

amazing— all by hand

interesting

SUCH DIFFERENCES IN food production constituted a major ultimate cause of the disparities between Eurasian and Native American societies. Among the resulting proximate factors behind the conquest, the most important included differences in germs, technology, political organization, and writing. Of these, the one linked most directly to the differences in food production was germs. The infectious diseases that regularly visited crowded Eurasian societies, and to which many Eurasians consequently developed immune or genetic resistance, included all of history's most lethal killers: smallpox, measles, influenza, plague, tuberculosis, typhus, cholera, malaria, and others. Against that grim list, the sole crowd infectious diseases that can be attributed with certainty to pre-Columbian Native American societies were nonsyphilitic treponemas. (As I explained in Chapter 11, it remains uncertain whether syphilis arose in Eurasia or in the Americas, and the claim that human tuberculosis was present in the Americas before Columbus is in my opinion unproven.)

oh! I want to hear more

This continental difference in harmful germs resulted paradoxically from the difference in useful livestock. Most of the microbes responsible for the infectious diseases of crowded human societies evolved from very similar ancestral microbes causing infectious diseases of the domestic animals with which food producers began coming into daily close contact around 10,000 years ago. Eurasia harbored many domestic animal species and hence developed many such microbes, while the Americas had very few of each. Other reasons why Native American societies evolved so few lethal microbes were that villages, which provide ideal breeding grounds for epidemic diseases, arose thousands of years later in the Americas than in Eurasia; and that the three regions of the New World supporting urban

So contact w/livestock/ animals was a major factor w/ disease

When you annotate a printed text—that is, talk back to it—you read it actively and rhetorically.

ten. But if you later reread the entire chapter, your understanding of all the material is likely to deepen. Accordingly, effective readers usually reread texts that are important to them in order to master the content.

2c Rereading for understanding

Rereading is the easiest way to check your understanding of the content. Effective readers use their second pass through the material to determine the author's specific purpose and to note how the information is organized and how supporting ideas are developed (chapter 3 and 6e). In addition to noting these general features, you can also scan the first and last sentences in every paragraph. The central idea of a paragraph, which suggests a sense of content and overall organization, can occur anywhere in the paragraph (4c), but it often appears in one of those two sentences.

2d Recognizing a personal response

Critical readers consciously work to keep their personal responses from interfering with their ability to understand. So, in addition to reading for content, they also keep track of what they think about or how they are reacting to this content. That is, critical readers are not passive readers. Reading rhetorically means reading actively, noting where you agree or disagree, become frustrated or intrigued, sympathetic or annoyed—and keeping track of what feature of the writing (or of yourself) triggered each response: was it the writer's tone (4a(3)), an example that evoked a personal memory, a lapse in the organization (3d), the topic itself (3b), or a visual element such as a photo or an illustration?

As you read, try to determine what the author thinks and why he or she holds that opinion. Then determine what *you* think and why *you* hold your opinion. In other words, what information do you agree or disagree with—and why? What passages brought to mind your own experience or expertise? What have you learned from your reading? What about this text confuses you? What would you like to know more about?

By noting personal responses and recognizing that they are independent of a work's content even if they are inspired by it, you can increase your understanding of the purposeful choices writers make when communicating with readers. Personal responses often serve as the basis for your own writing (2e). Often, good readers and writers use techniques from the following list.

TIPS FOR RECORDING PERSONAL RESPONSES

- Note passages that capture your attention. Underline or highlight your own copy; highlight with color when reading on a computer screen.

- Put a question mark in the margin when you do not understand a passage—or if you question its accuracy.

- Put an exclamation point in the margin when a statement or an example surprises you.

- Write *yes* or *no* in the margin when you agree or disagree. When a passage reminds you of another passage (or something else you have read), note that association in the margin. Keep a reading journal (3a(1)). Include at least one question or reservation about something you read each day.

- Correspond by e-mail with other people who are reading the same material (chapter 6).

2e Writing daily about your reading

Effective readers write daily about their reading. Whether you keep a personal journal, a writer's notebook, or a reading journal (or, in some classes, participate in an online discussion forum; see 6c), you are taking the opportunity to write about your reading in terms of content and personal response. When you respond to a text by listening to it, arguing with it, extending it, and connecting it with your own experience, you are engaging with that text and will be more likely to understand and remember it. Writing regularly about your reading, then, helps you increase your comprehension and identify responses that could be the seeds from which larger pieces of writing subsequently grow. Whatever form your journal takes, writing about your reading will benefit both your comprehension and your creativity.

3 Planning and Drafting Essays

Experienced writers understand that writing is a process. Think of the writing you do out of school, and you will realize how experienced you already are at the process. When you compose an e-mail, for instance, you consider the audience, the message, and the tone you wish to convey in order to fulfill your purpose. Even though you are writing quickly, you often cut and paste or delete—just as you do when you are writing more slowly to fulfill an academic assignment. Whether you are writing in or out of school, you do so in terms of your audience, context, and purpose (**1c–e**), revising and editing all along the way.

This chapter will help you understand writing as a process and

- find good topics (**3a**),
- focus your ideas (**3b**),
- write a clear thesis statement (**3c**),
- organize your ideas (**3d**),
- express your ideas in a first draft (**3e**), and
- use various strategies to develop effective paragraphs (**3f**) and essays (**3g**).

Effective writers know they cannot do everything at once, so they generate, organize, develop, and clarify their ideas as well as polish their prose during a series of sometimes separate—but often overlapping—steps.

The writing process is **recursive,** which means that as you plan and draft an essay, you may need to return to a specific activity several times. For example, drafting may help you see that you need to go back and collect more ideas, modify your thesis, or even start over with a new one. Experienced writers expect the writing process to lead to new ideas as well as uncover passages in need of improvement.

Despite the infinite variations of the writing process, writing usually involves four basic, recursive stages, described in the following box.

STAGES OF THE WRITING PROCESS

- **Prewriting** is the initial stage of the writing process. As soon as you begin thinking about a specific writing task, consider what is expected of you in terms of your intended audience, context, and overall purpose. Then start exploring your topic by talking with others working on the same assignment, keeping a journal, freewriting, or questioning. You might research your general subject either online or in the library. In short, do whatever it takes to energize your thinking and jump-start your writing.

- **Drafting** involves writing down your ideas quickly, writing as much as you can, without worrying about being perfect or staying on topic. The more ideas you get down on paper, the more options you will have as you begin to clarify your thesis and purpose for writing, organizing, and revising. Progress is your goal at this stage, not perfection.

- **Revising** offers you the opportunity to focus your purpose for writing, establish a clear thesis statement (**3c**), and organize your ideas toward those ends (**3d**). This is the time to start stabilizing the overall structure of your essay as well as the structure of the individual paragraphs (**3f** and **4c**) and to reconsider your introduction and conclusion (**4b**). Remember that revising means producing another draft for further revision and editing.

- **Editing** focuses on surface features: punctuation, spelling, word choice, grammar, sentence structure, and all the rest of the details of Standardized English (**4f**). As you prepare your work for final submission, consider reading it aloud to discover which sentence structures and word choices could be improved.

3a Selecting worthwhile subjects for writing

Whether you are assigned a subject or are free to respond to an exigence of your own choosing, you must consider what you already know—or would like to learn about—and what is likely to interest your audience (**1d**). The first step toward engaging an audience is to be interested in the subject yourself, so consider your interests and experience. Often the best subject is one drawn from your specific knowledge of hobbies, sports, jobs, or places. When subjects are important to you, they usually interest readers, especially when you write with a clear purpose and well-chosen details (**1c** and **3f(1)**).

More often, however, you will be asked to write essays about subjects outside your personal experience but within your academic coursework. If, for instance, you are assigned an essay for a course in ancient history, you may be responsible for choosing your topic—but it will have to be related to the course. In order to find material that interests you, look in your textbook, particularly in the sections listing suggestions for further reading. Go through your lecture notes, your reading journal, or any marginal annotations you have made in your textbook (**2d**). Ask yourself whether any details of the subject have surprised, annoyed, or pleased you—if there is something you feel strongly about and would like to explore further. Writing about a subject is one of the best ways to learn about it, so use a writing assignment not only to impart information to your audience but also to satisfy yourself.

(1) Keeping a journal is one way to explore a subject.

Keeping a journal is a good way to generate subjects for essays. In a **personal journal,** you reflect on your experiences, using writing as a means to explore how you feel about what is happening in your life or in the world around you. You might focus on external events, such as what you think about a book or a film, or on your inner life, such as changes in your moods or attitudes. Writers who keep personal journals usually write for their own benefit, but in the process of writing a journal—or reading it—they may discover subjects and exigencies they can use for essays.

Other writers prefer to keep a reading journal (**2e**), where they record and explore material for future projects, list quotations and observations that invite development, draft the introduction to an essay, outline an idea for a story, or experiment with writing a poem. You may find it convenient to keep your journal in a word-processing file on your computer, especially if you use a laptop. Whichever type of journal you keep or method you use to record your thoughts, feel free to write quickly, without worrying about spelling or grammar.

(2) Freewriting offers a risk-free way to explore a subject.

When **freewriting,** writers record whatever occurs to them, without stopping, for a limited period of time—often no more than ten minutes. They do not worry about whether they are repeating themselves or getting off track; they simply write to see what comes out. Freewriting is another good way to generate ideas for a writing assignment because no matter what you write, it will contain ideas and information you did not realize you had. Some writers use colored marking pens (or change the font or color in their word-processing program) to identify different topics generated by this activity.

In **directed freewriting,** you begin with a general subject and record whatever occurs to you about this subject during the time available. When Richard Petraglia's English instructor asked him to write for five minutes, assessing the reasons for studying a foreign language, Richard produced the following freewriting. (This freewriting represents the first step toward Richard's essay, three different versions of which appear in chapter 4.)

> Why am I taking German? When I'm happiest about my progress, I think I'm taking German so I can travel all around Germany and speak with the natives. Most Americans think that "everyone can speak English," but I know that's not true. At my lowest moments, I think I'm memorizing all this German vocabulary and verb conjugations because I'm fulfilling the foreign language requirement of my major. I read some statistics that show that students who pursue several years of foreign language study in high school tend to score higher on standardized tests. I did. And I did, probably because when I was learning Spanish, I learned so much vocabulary. I also learned a great deal about my native language, English. Maybe that's why I did so well. Or maybe the reason I did so well on those tests was that I've always been a motivated student!

Richard's freewriting generated a number of possibilities for developing an essay about why he is taking German: because it is a requirement, because he is a motivated student, because he wants to speak German and travel to Germany, because he's learning more about English. But perhaps his freewriting is taking him in a completely different direction. Instead of writing about *why* he is taking German, he may write about the positive consequences of taking German. Notice how his freewriting becomes more animated when he refers to his success as a student.

(3) Questioning pushes the boundaries of your subject.
You can also explore a subject by asking yourself some questions. The simplest questioning strategy for helping you explore a subject comes

from journalism. **Journalists' questions**—*Who? What? When? Where? Why?* and *How?*—are easy to use and can help you discover ideas about any subject. Using journalists' questions to explore the reasons for taking a foreign language could lead you to think about this subject in a number of ways: *Who* typically has to take a foreign language while in college? *What* foreign language should a college student study? *When* should students fulfill their foreign language requirement? *Where* should students use their foreign language? *Why* is taking a foreign language an important part of the college experience? And *how* might students make the most of what they learn about a foreign language?

3b   Focusing a subject idea into a specific topic

By exploring your subject, you can discover productive strategies for development as well as a specific focus for your topic. As you prewrite, you will decide that some ideas seem worth pursuing, but others seem inappropriate for your purpose, audience, or context. You will find yourself discarding ideas even as you develop new ones and determine your topic.

A simple analogy helps explain focus: When you take a picture of a landscape, you cannot photograph all that your eye can take in. You must focus on just part of it. As you aim the camera, you look through the viewfinder to make sure the subject is correctly framed and in focus. At this point, you may wish to move in closer and focus on one part of the scene, or you may decide to change the angle, using light and shadow to emphasize certain features of the landscape. You can think of your writing the same way—you focus and direct your ideas just as you focus and direct the lens of a camera, moving from a general subject to a more specific topic.

Like photographers, writers need to focus their ideas, moving from a general subject to a more specific topic.

In addition to reviewing the ideas you have generated through strategies such as freewriting and questioning, you can also focus by thinking in terms of how the various rhetorical methods you could use for developing your ideas (3g) might take you in different directions. Responding to the exigence of assessing the reasons for studying a foreign language, Richard needed to focus his subject into a narrow topic. Thus, he considered the subject in terms of the following rhetorical methods of development:

- *Narration.* What kind of story can I tell about learning German?
- *Description.* What kind of German class am I taking? What do we do? What is the teacher like? What are my classmates like?
- *Process analysis.* How have I gone about learning German, from memorizing vocabulary and verb conjugations to actually carrying on conversations?
- *Cause-and-consequence analysis.* What have been the causes of my success in my German class? Concentration? Commitment? The fact that I already know Spanish fairly well? What are some of the consequences of my learning German? Some conversational skill? Less time in my schedule for other classes? Feeling successful?
- *Comparison and contrast.* How does learning German compare with learning English or with learning some other foreign language? How does taking German differ from taking history or another type of course?
- *Classification and division.* How can I classify the types of language courses that college students take? How can I divide up the desirable consequences of those courses?
- *Definition.* How do I define good reasons for taking German? Are those reasons defined by immediate or long-term benefits, by German's significance in the context of my entire college education, or by its contribution to my professional success?

The following sentence suggests a focus on comparison and contrast:

Studying German seems to be mostly memorization whereas studying English seems to be mostly reading and writing.

This sentence focuses on cause and consequence:

Now that I'm taking second-year German, I'll have a chance to talk and write more in German.

A combination of strategies soon led Richard toward a focus:

> When I think of how much time I have spent memorizing German vocabulary and verb conjugations, I am really proud of myself. Back in high school I didn't take the time to memorize Spanish the way I should have (and the way other students were), so my Spanish isn't as good as I wish it were. But, then, neither is my English. Now that I've been concentrating on learning another language, all the grammar and parts of speech, I've found that my English is much better. I write better and with more confidence because I'm making conscious choices about how to use language. I have gained a much better understanding of English grammar while learning German grammar.

Because writing is a form of thinking and discovering, your focus might not emerge until after you have written your first draft. When you compare the draft of Richard's essay on learning German (pages 78–82) with the final version of it (pages 91–94), you will see how drafting and revising can sharpen a writer's focus.

Whatever method you use to bring a topic into focus, your choice should be determined not only by your interests but also by your purpose, the needs of your audience, and the time and space available. The following checklist may help you assess your topic.

CHECKLIST for Assessing a Topic

- Are you interested in the topic?
- Is the topic appropriate for your audience?
- Can you interest the audience in your topic?
- What is your purpose in writing about this topic?
- Can you do justice to the topic in the time and space available to you? Or should you narrow it down or expand it?
- Do you know enough about the topic to write a paper of the required length? If not, how will you get additional information?
- Are you willing to learn more about the topic?

Use the journalists' questions to generate more ideas about a subject that interests you. Then consider how you might focus that general subject into a specific topic appropriate for an essay.

3c Conveying a clearly stated thesis

Once you have focused your subject into a topic, you have come a long way toward developing the main idea you want to convey. By this point, you have probably also established your purpose for writing, whether it is to explain, teach, analyze, argue, or compare. Your subject, purpose, supporting information, and focus all come together in a controlling idea, or **thesis,** which is appropriate for your audience and context (chapter 1) and helps you achieve your purpose. In the first draft or two, your thesis may be only tentative. By your final draft, however, you will have developed a clear thesis statement.

Most pieces of writing have a **thesis statement,** an explicit declaration (usually in one sentence) of the main idea. Your thesis statement, then, will convey a single idea, clearly focused and specifically stated. A thesis can be thought of as a central idea stated in the form of an assertion, or **claim** (8d), which indicates what you believe to be true, interesting, or valuable about your topic.

An explicitly formulated thesis statement helps keep your writing on target. It identifies the topic, the purpose, and, in some cases, the plan of development. Notice how the following thesis statements fulfill their purpose. The first is from a descriptive essay.

> If Lynne Truss were Catholic, I'd nominate her for sainthood.
>
> —FRANK McCOURT, Foreword, *Eats, Shoots & Leaves*

With this simple statement, McCourt establishes that the topic is Lynne Truss and indicates that he will describe why she should be a saint. He conveys enthusiasm and awe toward Truss's work.

The following thesis statement for a cause-and-consequence essay sets the stage for an analysis of what happened when refugees from Cuba were redefined by the U.S. Government as illegal aliens:

> At 10:30 p.m. on the night of August 18, 1994, Attorney General Janet Reno strode into the White House press room and in her practiced monotone announced new measures to halt the thousands of Cubans who were launching themselves into the Florida Straits aboard flimsy rafts every day that summer.
> —ROBERTO SURO, "Looking North"

The main idea in an argumentative essay usually carries a strong point of view, as in the following, which unmistakably argues for a specific course of action:

> Amnesty International opposes the death penalty in all cases without exception. —AMNESTY INTERNATIONAL, "The Death Penalty: Questions and Answers"

It is just as important to allow your thesis statement to remain tentative in the early stages of writing as it is to allow your essay to remain flexible through the first and second drafts. Rather than starting with a preconceived thesis, which you must struggle to support, you should let your final thesis statement grow out of your thinking and discovery process as you draft and revise. The following tips might help you develop a thesis statement that is neither too obvious nor too general.

TIPS FOR DEVELOPING A THESIS STATEMENT

- Decide which feature of the topic interests you most.
- Write down your point of view or assertion about that feature.
- Mark the passages in your freewriting, journal, or rough draft that support your position.
- Draft a thesis statement, and consider whether you can address the full scope of this tentative thesis in your essay or whether it is still too broad to be developed sufficiently.
- After your first or second draft, ask yourself whether your thesis is too broad for your essay (or vice versa). Revise your thesis to widen or narrow its scope in the direction your essay has taken.
- If you are unhappy with the results, start again with the first tip, and be even more specific.

A clear, precise thesis statement helps unify what you write; it directs your readers to the writing that follows. Therefore, as you write and revise, check your thesis statement frequently to see whether you have drifted away from it. It should inform your decisions about which details to keep and which to toss out as well as guide your search for appropriate additional information to support your assertions. All of your supporting material should pertain to the thesis statement.

A thesis is usually stated in a declarative sentence with a single main clause—that is, in either a simple or a complex sentence (22d). If your thesis statement presents two or more coordinate ideas, as a compound sentence does (22d), be sure that you are not losing direction and focus. For example, the following thesis statement, composed of two sentences, coordinates and focuses two ideas, indicating a discussion that will contrast men's and women's use of language:

> Male students are more likely to be comfortable attacking the readings and might find the inclusion of personal anecdotes irrelevant and "soft." Women are more likely to resist discussion they perceive as hostile, and, indeed, it is women in my classes who are most likely to offer personal anecdotes.
> —DEBORAH TANNEN, "How Male and Female Students Use Language Differently"

If you wish to sharpen a thesis statement by adding information that qualifies or supports it, subordinate such material to the main idea:

> I experienced many different trials when I first came to this country due to the fact that I did not speak English, and also because of my skin color.
> —ORLANDO CEPEDA, "Baseball Taught Me English"

As you clarify your thesis statement, resist using such vague qualifiers as *interesting, important,* and *unusual,* which can signal that the topic lacks interest or focus. For example, in the thesis statement "My education has been very unusual," the vague word *unusual* may indicate that the idea itself is weak and that the writer needs to find a sharper focus. However, this kind of vague thesis may disguise an idea of real interest that simply needs to be made specific: "Our family grew closer after my parents decided to teach me at home." The following examples show how vague thesis statements can be clarified and sharpened:

Vague thesis   It is hard to balance work with school.

Better thesis   Hardworking students who balance a part-time job with success in schoolwork can grow in maturity and self-confidence.

Vague thesis	Genetically modified foods are highly controversial.
Better thesis	Developed responsibly, genetically modified foods may be able to ameliorate current food shortages sooner rather than later.
Vague thesis	In "Everyday Use," Alice Walker emphasizes the different ways three women use their heritage.
Better thesis	In "Everyday Use," Alice Walker shows that an authentic appreciation of heritage does not come from showcasing fashionable artifacts or practices; rather, it comes from embracing that heritage every day.

The thesis statement most often appears in the first paragraph of an essay, although you can put yours anywhere that suits your purpose (occasionally even in the conclusion). The advantage of putting the thesis statement in the first paragraph is that readers know from the beginning what you are writing about and where the essay is going. Especially appropriate in academic writing, this technique helps readers who are searching for specific information to locate it easily. If the thesis statement begins the introductory paragraph, the rest of the sentences in the paragraph usually support or clarify it, as is the case in paragraph 1. (For ease of reference, each of the sample paragraphs in this chapter is numbered.)

1   [*Eats, Shoots & Leaves* is] a *book about punctuation*. Punctuation, if you don't mind! (I hesitated over that exclamation mark, and it's all her doing.) The book is so spirited, so scholarly, those English teachers will sweep all other topics aside to get to, you guessed it, punctuation. Parents and children will gather by the fire many an evening to read passages on the history of the semicolon and the terrible things being done to the apostrophe. Once the poor stepchild of grammar (is that comma OK here?), punctuation will emerge as the Cinderella of the English language.

—FRANK McCOURT, Foreword, *Eats, Shoots & Leaves*

If the thesis statement is the last sentence of the opening paragraph, the preceding sentences will build toward it, as in paragraph 2.

2   The story of zero is an ancient one. Its roots stretch back to the dawn of mathematics, in the time thousands of years before the first civilization, long before humans could read and write. But as natural as zero seems to us today, for ancient peoples zero was a foreign—and frightening—idea. An Eastern

concept, born in the Fertile Crescent a few centuries before the birth of Christ, zero not only evoked images of a primal void, it also had dangerous mathematical properties. *Within zero there is the power to shatter the framework of logic.*
—CHARLES SEIFE, *Zero: The Biography of a Dangerous Idea*

Most of the writing done for college courses contains an obvious thesis statement. The following checklist may help you assess the thesis of your essay.

CHECKLIST for Assessing a Thesis

- Does your thesis make a clear comment about your topic?
- Is your thesis an accurate reflection of what you believe to be true about your topic?
- Does your thesis match your essay in terms of focus and coverage?
- What two assertions can you make to support your thesis?
- What specific examples, illustrations, or experiences support your assertions?
- How does your thesis relate to the interests of your audience? To your purpose? To the context of your essay?
- Where is your thesis located in your essay? Would your readers benefit from having it stated earlier or later?

3d Arranging or outlining ideas

Many writers need a working plan to direct their ideas and keep their writing on course. Various plans of arrangement might be determined for them by their instructor, by the discipline in which they are writing, or by tradition.

Some writers quickly compose informal lists, which grow out of a collection of ideas. The ideas in these lists can overlap, be discarded, or lead to a tentative thesis statement, conclusions, and the beginning of an overall organizational plan. Other writers, however, rely on outlines. Either method (list or outline) can be especially helpful when you are writing lengthy papers and when you are writing under pressure (chapter 5). Whatever method you choose for arranging your ideas, remember that you can always alter your arrangement to accommodate any changes your writing undergoes during the process.

You can simplify your thinking about arrangement if you accept Aristotle's claim that every speech needs "a beginning, a middle, and an end." Even the simplest outline offers an essay a structure, much like the basic framework of a house. And, like the framework of a house, a simple outline can quickly become more elaborate and detailed. As you work and think, you might introduce indentations, letters, and numbers into your rough outline to indicate various levels of subordination and coordination in your material. Thus, an outline becomes a visual map of your thinking. The main points form the major headings, and the supporting ideas form the subheadings. An outline of Richard's essay might look something like the following:

TENTATIVE THESIS STATEMENT: Studying a foreign language is the best way to learn about English.

I. Many Americans don't think they need to learn another language.
   A. English is the language of global communication.
   B. English speakers always have an advantage in intercultural communication.
II. English-only speakers miss out on benefits of learning another language.
   A. Learning another language is not just about being able to talk to people in different countries.
   B. Studying another language increases a student's knowledge of another culture and so promotes tolerance and understanding.
   C. Knowing the language enriches a student's stay in a foreign country.
III. Students who take a foreign language do better on standardized tests.
   A. Students can compare grammars to better remember the rules of their own language.
   B. Studying a foreign language opens up a student's mind to different ways of speaking and expressing ideas.
   C. Studying a foreign language helps students acquire better reading skills.

IV. Learning a language teaches students to learn in a combination of ways.

    A. Students practice learning intuitively.

    B. Students practice following complex rules.

    C. Learning a language teaches students to be better learners in general.

    D. Studying a language teaches students subtle ways to better express themselves.

V. Learning German grammar improves students' knowledge of English.

    A. Students who learn German grammar also learn English grammar.

    B. Students who study German begin to understand how English really works.

    C. Learning German helps students understand the subtle changes of meaning that can happen with changes in grammar.

    D. Students who study German feel more confident writing in English because they know the grammar better.

    E. Studying German allows a student to see English from a different perspective.

    F. Students learn about how language can be used in different ways to express ideas.

However streamlined or detailed an outline you create, you need enough headings to develop your topic fully within the boundaries stated in your thesis. The important thing to remember, though, is that your final essay does not have to follow your outline. As you write, you may find yourself moving ideas around, deleting some, or adding others. An outline is simply a tool to help you get started.

3e   Getting your ideas into a first draft

When writing a first draft, get your ideas down quickly. Spelling, punctuation, and correct usage are not important in the first draft; ideas are. Experienced writers know that the most important thing about a first draft is to have done it, for it gives them something to work on—and against. If you are not sure how to begin, look over some of the journal writing, listing, or outlining you have already done, and try to state a tentative thesis. Then write out some main points you would like to develop, along with some of the supporting information for that development. Keep your overall plan in mind as you draft. If you find yourself losing track of where you want to go, stop writing and reread what you have already done. Talk with someone working on the same assignment, or write in your journal. You may find that you need to revise your plan—or you may need to rethink your topic. Experienced writers expect a change in plan as they write and revise.

If you feel stuck, move to another part of your essay and draft paragraphs that might appear later. Doing so may help you restart your engine, for when you are actually writing (rather than worrying), you think more efficiently. You can then move on to another part that is easier to write, such as sentences that develop another supporting idea, an introduction, or a conclusion. Do not worry about writing a provocative introduction or a sensible conclusion at this point. Later, when you are revising, you can experiment with ways of polishing those sections of an essay (4b). What is important at this stage is to begin writing and then keep writing as quickly as you can. Save this early work so that you can refer to it as you revise (chapter 4).

Finally, remember that writing is a form of discovering, understanding, and thinking. As you draft, you are likely to discover that you have more to say than you ever thought you would. So, whenever drafting leads you in a direction you did not intend, allow yourself to explore if you sense that this side trip may lead to a useful discovery. You can consider whether to integrate or suppress this new material when you prepare to revise.

3f   Drafting well-developed paragraphs

You compose a draft by developing the information that will constitute the paragraphs of your essay. If you are working from an informal list (3d), you will have a sense of where you want to take your ideas but may be uncertain about the number and nature of the paragraphs you will need. If you are working from an outline (3d), you can anticipate the number of paragraphs you will probably write and what you hope to accomplish in each paragraph. In the first case, you enjoy the freedom to pursue new ideas that occur as you draft. In the second, you enjoy the security of a clear direction. In both cases, however, you need to develop each paragraph fully and then ask yourself whether any additional paragraphs (or additional supporting information within any paragraph) would help your audience understand the main idea of your essay.

Paragraphs have no set length. Typically, they range from 50 to 250 words, and paragraphs in books are usually longer than those in newspapers and magazines. There are certainly times when a long paragraph makes for rich reading, as well as times when a long paragraph exhausts a single minor point, combines too many points, or becomes repetitive. On the other hand, short, one-sentence paragraphs can be effectively used for emphasis (chapter 34) or to establish transition (4d). Short paragraphs can also, however, indicate inadequate development. There will be times when you can combine two short paragraphs as you revise (chapter 4), but there will be many more occasions when you need to lengthen a short paragraph by developing it with specific details or examples.

Experienced writers do not worry much about paragraph length; rather, they concentrate on getting words on the paper or on the screen, knowing that all paragraphs can be shortened, lengthened, merged, or otherwise improved later in the writing process. So think of revising and developing your paragraphs as a luxury, an opportunity to articulate exactly what you want to say without anyone interrupting you—or changing the subject.

(1) You can develop a paragraph with details.

A good paragraph developed with details brings your idea to life. Consider the following well-developed paragraph by Alice Walker:

3   I stood in front of the mirror and looked at myself and laughed. *My hair was one of those odd, amazing, unbelievable, stop-you-in-your-tracks creations— not unlike a zebra's stripes, an armadillo's ears, or the feet of the electric-bluefooted boobie—that the Universe makes for no reason other than to express its own limit- less imagination.* I realized I had never been given the opportunity to appreci- ate hair for its true self. That it did, in fact, have one. I remembered years of enduring hairdressers—from my mother onward—doing missionary work on my hair. They dominated, suppressed, controlled. Now, more or less free, it stood this way and that. I would call up my friends around the country to report on its antics. It never thought of lying down. Flatness, the missionary position, did not interest it. It grew. Being short, cropped off near the root,

another missionary "solution," did not interest it either. It sought more and more space, more light, more of itself. It loved to be washed; but that was it.

—ALICE WALKER, "Oppressed Hair Puts a Ceiling on the Brain"

Notice how the series of details in paragraph 3 supports the main idea, or topic sentence (4c), which is italicized. Readers can easily see how one sentence leads into the next, creating a clear picture of the hair being described.

(2) You can develop a paragraph by providing examples.

Like details, examples contribute to paragraph development by making specific what otherwise might seem general and hard to grasp. **Details** describe a person, place, or thing; **examples** illustrate an idea with information that can come from different times and places. Both details and examples support your idea in terms of the rhetorical situation.

The author of paragraph 4 uses several closely related examples (as well as details) to support the main idea with which she begins.

4   *It began with coveting our neighbor's chickens.* Lily would volunteer to collect the eggs, and then she offered to move in with them. Not the neighbors, the chickens. She said if she could have some of her own, she would be the happiest girl on earth. What parent could resist this bait? Our lifestyle could accommodate a laying flock; my husband and I had kept poultry before, so we knew it was a project we could manage, and a responsibility Lily could handle largely by herself. I understood how much that meant to her when I heard her tell her grandmother, "They're going to be just *my* chickens, grandma. Not even one of them will be my sister's." To be five years old and have some other life form entirely under your control—not counting goldfish or parents—is a majestic state of affairs.   —BARBARA KINGSOLVER, "Lily's Chickens"

Exercise 2

Examine some of your own writing—such as an essay you have recently drafted, e-mail messages still on file, or entries in your journal—and select one paragraph that holds potential interest. Write out (by hand) the original paragraph. Then rewrite it, developing it with additional details or examples.

3g Employing rhetorical methods of development

When drafting essays, you can develop a variety of paragraphs using **rhetorical methods,** mental operations that help you think through various types of rhetorical problems—having to do with establishing boundaries (definition), making sense of a person, place, or event (description and narration), organizing concepts (classification and division), understanding or thinking critically about a process (process or cause-and-consequence analysis), or needing to convince someone (argumentation). The strategies used for generating ideas, focusing your topic (3b), developing paragraphs and essays, and arranging ideas are already second nature to you. Every day, you use one or more of them to define a concept, narrate a significant incident, supply examples for an assertion, classify or divide information into specific parts, compare two or more things, analyze a process, or identify a cause or consequence. When drafting an essay, you may discover that you need to define a term or explain a process before you can take your readers further into your topic. Writers have the option of tapping one, two, or several rhetorical methods to fulfill their overall purpose, which might be to explain, entertain, argue, or evaluate.

(1) Narrating a series of events tells readers what happened.

A **narrative** discusses a sequence of events, normally in **chronological order** (the order in which they occur), to develop a particular point or set a mood. This rhetorical method, which often includes a setting, characters, dialogue, and description, usually uses transition words or phrases such as *first, then, later, that evening, the following week,* and so forth to guide readers from one incident to the next. Whatever its length, a narrative must remain focused on the main idea. Drawn from an interview with Ben Harper conducted by Austin Scaggs, the narrative in paragraph 5 traces the development of Harper's music.

5   Growing up in the verdant Los Angeles suburb of Claremont, Harper was drawn to the blues and folk—"everything from Woody Guthrie to Son House to Ry Cooder." He also developed an early love for soul music: He remembers sitting on his dad's lap listening to Stevie Wonder's *Talking Book.* At age seven he scored his first acoustic guitar, from the Folk Music Center, a store in Claremont owned by his maternal grandparents, that to this day

features a dizzying array of international instruments. In his teens Harper was sidetracked by the rebelliousness of hip-hop—his black friends sneered at his deep knowledge of traditional music, nicknaming him Mr. Ukulele man—but after high school, Harper rekindled his first musical love. "As much as I loved hip-hop, I knew that wasn't going to be my route," he says. "I was just too connected with the music I grew up with."

—AUSTIN SCAGGS, "Ben Harper's European Vacation"

(2) Describing how something looks, sounds, smells, or feels adds useful detail.

By describing a person, place, object, or sensation, you can make your material come alive. Often descriptions are predominantly visual, but even visual descriptions can include the details of what you hear, smell, taste, or touch; that is, descriptions appeal to the senses.

Description should suit your purpose and audience. In describing your car, for example, you would emphasize certain features to a potential buyer, others to a mechanic who was going to repair it, and still others to a friend whom you wished to impress. In paragraph 6, Judith Ortiz Cofer employs vivid descriptive details to convey her ideas about cultural influences on adolescent striving and embarrassment.

Combining appeals to several senses, this ad's photograph and descriptive words bring information alive for the reader (and potential buyer).

6   I came to remember Career Day in our high school, when teachers told us to come dressed as if for a job interview. It quickly became obvious that to the barrio girls, "dressing up" sometimes meant wearing ornate jewelry and clothing that would be more appropriate (by mainstream standards) for the company Christmas party than as daily office attire. That morning I had agonized in front of my closet, trying to figure out what a "career girl" would wear because, essentially, except for

Marlo Thomas on TV, I had no models on which to base my decision. I knew how to dress for school: at the Catholic school I attended we all wore uniforms; I knew how to dress for Sunday mass, and I knew what dresses to wear for parties at my relatives' homes. Though I do not recall the precise details of my Career Day outfit, it must have been a composite of the above choices. But I remember a comment my friend (an Italian-American) made in later years that coalesced my impressions of that day. She said that at the business school she was attending the Puerto Rican girls always stood out for wearing "everything at once." She meant, of course, too much jewelry, too many accessories. On that day at school, we were simply made the negative models by the nuns who were themselves not credible fashion experts to any of us. But it was painfully obvious to me that to the others, in their tailored skirts and silk blouses, we must have seemed "hopeless" and "vulgar." Though I now know that most adolescents feel out of step much of the time, I also know that for the Puerto Rican girls of my generation that sense was intensified. The way our teachers and classmates looked at us that day in school was just a taste of the culture clash that awaited us in the real world, where prospective employers and men on the street would often misinterpret our tight skirts and jingling bracelets as a come-on.

—JUDITH ORTIZ COFER, "The Myth of the Latin Woman: I Just Met a Girl Named María"

(3) Explaining a process shows readers how something happens.
Process paragraphs, in explaining how something is done or made, often use both description and narration. You might describe the items used in a process and then narrate the steps of the process chronologically. By adding an explanation of a process to a draft, you could illustrate a concept that might otherwise be hard for your audience to grasp. In paragraph 7, Sam Swope explains the process by which an elementary school assistant principal tried (unsuccessfully) to intimidate students into "ratting on" a fellow student who stole report cards.

7   Later that day, a frowning assistant principal appeared in the doorway, and the room went hush. Everyone knew why he was there. I'd known Mr. Ziegler only as a friendly, mild-mannered fellow with a comb-over, so I was shocked to see him play the heavy. His performance began calmly, reasonably, solemnly. He

Explanations of a process, such as learning sign langauge, often combine description and narration.

told the class that the administration was deeply disappointed, that this theft betrayed the trust of family, teachers, school, and country. Then he told the children it was their duty to report anything they'd seen or heard. When no one responded, he added a touch of anger to his voice, told the kids no stone would go unturned, the truth would out; he vowed he'd find the culprit—it was only a question of time! When this brought no one forward, he pumped up the volume. His face turned red, the veins on his neck bulged, and he wagged a finger in the air and shouted, "I'm not through with this investigation, not by a long shot! And if any of you know anything, you better come tell me, privately, in private, because they're going to be in a lot of trouble, *a lot of trouble!*"   —SAM SWOPE, "The Case of the Missing Report Cards"

(4) Analyzing cause or consequence establishes why something happens or predicts results.

Writers who analyze cause or consequence raise the question *Why?* and must answer it to the satisfaction of their audience, differentiating the **primary cause** (the most important one) from **contributory causes** (which add to but do not directly cause a situation) or the **primary consequence** (the most important one) from **secondary consequences** (which occur because of an event but are less important than the primary consequence). Writers who analyze cause or consequence usually link events along a timeline, just as you would if you were describing a traffic accident to a police officer. Always keep in mind, though, that just because one event occurs before—or after—another event does not necessarily make it a cause—or a consequence—of that event. In paragraph 8, undergraduate Robyn Sylves analyzes some causes of credit card debt among college students.

Although companies market credit cards on many campuses, some students do not realize that a possible consequence of card use is debt.

8   Experts point to several factors for excessive credit card debt among college students. High on the list is students' lack of financial literacy. The credit card representatives on campus, the preapproved applications that arrive in the mail several times a week, and the incessant phone offers for credit cards tempt students into opening accounts

before they really can understand what they are getting themselves into. The people marketing these cards depend on the fact that many students don't know what an annual percentage rate is. Credit card companies count on applicants' failing to read the fine print, which tells them how after an "introductory" period, the interest rate on a given card can increase two to three times. The companies also don't want students to know that every year people send money (in the form of interest charges) to these companies that there is no need to send. That annual fee that credit card companies love to charge can be waived. I think that many people, students and nonstudents alike, might be surprised how often and easily it can disappear if people call the company to say they don't want to pay it.

—ROBYN SYLVES, "Credit Card Debt among College Students: Just What Does It Cost?"

Writers also catalogue consequences, as Jonathan Franzen does in paragraph 9, listing the effects of Alzheimer's disease on its victims.

9   For [award-winning science writer] David Shenk, one of the most illuminating aspects of Alzheimer's is its slowing down of death. Shenk likens the disease to a prism that refracts death into a spectrum of its otherwise tightly conjoined parts—death of autonomy, death of memory, death of self-consciousness, death of personality, death of body—and he subscribes to the most common trope of Alzheimer's: that its particular sadness and horror stem from the sufferer's loss of his or her "self" long before the body dies.

—JONATHAN FRANZEN, "My Father's Brain"

(5) Comparing or contrasting helps readers see similarities or differences.

A **comparison** points out similarities, and a **contrast** points out differences—to reveal information. When drafting, consider whether a comparison might help your readers see a relationship they might otherwise miss or whether a contrast might help them establish useful distinctions. In paragraph 10, Trudier Harris uses descriptive details in a revealing comparison of singing and performing.

10   I think of Zora Neale Hurston, folklorist and anthropologist, who complained about singer-actor Paul Robeson turning the spirituals into concerts. To her, he had taken the spirit out of the songs by performing them instead of singing them; he had transformed feeling that emerges from the heart, which cannot be duplicated, into feeling that can be constructed through art, which means that it can be duplicated on demand. One is genuine; the other is genuinely constructed. Hurston preferred the sounds emitted by the folks who couldn't compete and sing in the gospel choir or any other choir, but whose sincerity and relationship with God were apparent in their singing. These included those little old ladies who usually occupy what we

Kennedy: © Time-Life Pictures/Getty Images; King: © Flip Schulke

This magazine cover suggests a comparison of Martin Luther King, Jr., and Robert F. Kennedy as influential political leaders, while inviting a contrast of their individual backgrounds.

refer to as the "amen corners." They are better at lining-out hymns, using the "long meter" that folks untrained in music historically make when they sing their joyful noises in African American churches.

—TRUDIER HARRIS, "Make a Joyful Noise"

Two valuable kinds of comparisons are metaphors and analogies. A **metaphor** is a figure of speech that makes an indirect comparison of one thing to another, as in "He was a lion in uniform" (**35a**). An **analogy,** on the other hand, makes a direct comparison of the similarities between two things, as in "His hair was as thick and tawny as a lion's mane." Although analogies can invigorate your writing, you must remember that two things that are alike in some ways are rarely alike in all ways (**8i(7)**). In paragraph 11, Nelson Mandela uses a metaphor to compare leadership and gardening.

11   In some ways, I saw the garden as a metaphor for certain aspects of my life. A leader must also tend his garden; he, too, plants seed, and then watches, cultivates, and harvests the result. Like the gardener, a leader must take responsibility for what he cultivates; he must mind his work, try to repel enemies, preserve what can be preserved, and eliminate what cannot succeed.

—NELSON MANDELA, "Raising Tomatoes and Leading People"

(6) Classifying and dividing can give order to material.

To classify is to place things into groups based on shared characteristics. **Classification** is a way to understand or explain something by establishing how it fits within a category or group. For example, a book reviewer might classify a new novel as a mystery—leading readers to expect a plot based on suspense. **Division,** in contrast, separates an object or group into smaller parts and examines the relationships among them. A novel can also be discussed according to components such as plot, setting, and theme (chapter **12**).

Classification and division represent two different perspectives: ideas can be put into groups (classification) or split into subclasses (division). As a strategy for organizing (or developing) an idea, classification and

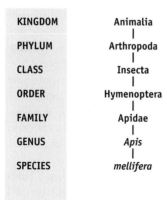

KINGDOM	Animalia
PHYLUM	Arthropoda
CLASS	Insecta
ORDER	Hymenoptera
FAMILY	Apidae
GENUS	*Apis*
SPECIES	*mellifera*

The scientific identification of the honeybee (*Apis mellifera*) requires a classification in the genus *Apis* and a division within that genus, the species *mellifera*.

division often work together. In paragraph 12, for example, classification and division work together to clarify the differences between the two versions of the cowboy icon. Like most paragraphs, this one mixes rhetorical methods; the writer uses description, comparison and contrast, and classification to make her point.

12   First, and perhaps most fundamentally, the cowboy icon has two basic incarnations: the cowboy hero and the cowboy villain. Cowboy heroes often appear in roles such as sheriff, leader of a cattle drive, or what I'll call a "wandering hero," such as the Lone Ranger, who appears much like a frontier Superman wherever and whenever help is needed. Writers and producers most commonly place cowboy heroes in conflict either with "Indians" or with the cowboy villain. In contrast to the other classic bad guys of the Western genre, cowboy villains pose a special challenge because they are essentially the alter ego of the cowboy hero; the cowboy villain shares the hero's skill with a gun, his horse-riding maneuvers, and his knowledge of the land. What distinguishes the two, of course, is character: the cowboy hero is essentially good, while the cowboy villain is essentially evil.

—JODY M. ROY, "The Case of the Cowboy"

(7) Defining an important concept or term clarifies meaning.
By defining a concept or a term, you efficiently clarify your meaning in your own mind and so develop your ideas. By defining a word for your readers, you immediately connect with them; they know what you are

and are not talking about. Definitions are usually constructed in a two-step process: the first step locates a term by placing it in a class; the second step differentiates this particular term from other terms in the same class. For instance, "A concerto [the term] is a symphonic piece [the class] consisting of three movements performed by one or more solo instruments accompanied at times by an orchestra [the difference]." A symphony belongs to the same basic class as a concerto; it too is a symphonic piece. However, a symphony is differentiated from a concerto in two specific ways: a symphony consists of four movements, and its performance involves the entire orchestra.

Paragraph 13 defines volcanos by putting them into a class ("landforms") and by distinguishing them ("built of molten material") from other members of that class. The definition is then clarified by examples.

13   Volcanos are landforms built of molten material that has spewed out onto the earth's surface. Such molten rock is called lava. Volcanos may be no larger than small hills, or thousands of feet high. All have a characteristic cone shape. Some well-known mountains are actually volcanos. Examples are Mt. Fuji (Japan), Mt. Lassen (California), Mt. Hood (Oregon), Mt. Etna and Mt. Vesuvius (Italy), and Paricutín (Mexico). The Hawaiian Islands are all immense volcanos whose summits rise above the ocean, and these volcanos are still quite active.   **—JOEL AREM, "Rocks and Minerals"**

Use the rhetorical methods just described to make your essay as a whole more understandable to your audience. Make sure, however, that you are using these methods to support your thesis and fulfill your overall purpose. If a paragraph developed with one of the methods is contributing to the main idea of your essay, then it is contributing to your purpose. If the development of a paragraph does not support the thesis, then you need to revise or delete that paragraph (4c and 4f).

4 Revising and Editing Essays

Revising, which literally means "seeing again," lies at the heart of all successful writing. When you see again, you see with a different set of eyes—those of the reader instead of the writer. **Revising** entails rethinking what you have already written in terms of your overall purpose: how successfully you have addressed your audience, how clearly you have stated your thesis, how effectively you have arranged your information, and how thoroughly you have developed your assertions. **Editing,** on the other hand, focuses on issues that are smaller in scale. When you are editing, you are polishing your writing: you choose words more precisely (chapter 35), shape prose more distinctly (chapter 36), and structure sentences more effectively (chapters 28–33). While you are editing, you are also **proofreading,** focusing even more sharply to eliminate surface errors in grammar, punctuation, and mechanics. Revising and editing often overlap (just as drafting and revising do), but they are distinct activities that concentrate on large-scale and small-scale issues, respectively. Usually revising occurs before editing, but not always. Edited passages may be redrafted, rearranged, and even cut as writers revise further.

As you revise and edit your essays, this chapter will help you

- consider your work as a whole (4a(1) and 4a(2)),
- evaluate your tone (4a(3)),
- compose an effective introduction and conclusion (4b),
- strengthen the unity and coherence of paragraphs (4c),
- improve transitions (4d),
- benefit from a reviewer's comments (4e),
- edit to improve style (4f),
- proofread to eliminate surface errors (4g), and
- submit a final draft (4h).

4a The essentials of revision

In truth, you are revising throughout the planning and drafting stages of the writing process, whether at the word, phrase, sentence, example, or paragraph level. But no matter how much you may have revised during those stages of the writing process, you will still do most of your revising after you have completed a draft. You may rewrite specific sentences and paragraphs as well as reconsider the draft as a whole. A few writers prefer to start revising immediately after drafting, while their minds are still fully engaged by their topic. But most writers like to let a draft "cool off," so that when they return to it, they can assess it more objectively, with fresh eyes. Even an overnight cooling-off period will give you more objectivity as a reader and will reveal more options to you as a writer the following morning.

TECH SAVVY
Most newer word-processing programs enable you to track your revisions easily, a feature that is especially useful if your instructor requires you to submit all drafts or if a peer group is reviewing your drafts. On the toolbar, click on Tools in order to see the pulldown menu. Track Changes will be listed on that menu. If your word-processing program does not have this feature, you can save each new version of your work in a separate file and date each one. By opening two or more of those files on your computer screen, you can easily compare the different versions.

(1) Anything and everything on the page can be revised.
As you reread your essay as a whole, you will want to recall your purpose, restate your thesis, and reconsider your audience. Does your main point come through clearly in every paragraph, or do some paragraphs digress, repeat information, or contradict what has come before (3c)?

In addition to sharpening your main idea, you will also want to revise in terms of audience expectations. Revising demands that you gauge what you have written to the audience you are addressing (1d). How will your audience respond to your thesis statement? Which of your assertions will your audience immediately understand or accept? Which examples or details will interest your audience? Which of your language choices are aimed expressly at this audience? In other words, revising successfully requires that you examine your work both as a writer and as a reader. As a writer, you must ask yourself whether your words accurately reflect your intention and meaning. As a reader, you must ask yourself whether what is clear and logical to you will also be clear to others.

(2) What is *not* on the page can be more important than what is on the page.

Writers are always aware of what they have put on the page—but they seldom spend enough time considering what they may have left out. In order to ensure that you have provided all the information necessary for your reader to understand your points, you will want to consider the following questions: What does your audience already know about your subject? What information might your audience be expecting? What information might strengthen your thesis? Your best ideas will not always surface in your first draft; you will sometimes come up with an important idea only after you have finished that draft, let it cool off, and then looked at it again. No matter how complete a draft seems, ask yourself whether some explanation, description, or example could be added that would enhance your message. You might use questioning strategies to discover whether anything is missing (3a(3)). Or you might share your draft with a classmate or colleague who is working on the same assignment, asking that person to mark confusing or unclear passages (4e).

(3) Your tone helps you fulfill your purpose.

Tone reflects a writer's attitude toward a subject, so you will want to make sure that your tone is appropriate to your purpose, audience, and context (1a). Decide what you intend your tone to be (how you want to "sound" to your intended audience in order to achieve your purpose), and then read your piece aloud to see if it sounds the way you want it to. Whether you are writing for school, work, or personal reasons, you will want to control the tone so that it reflects your confidence, your preparation, and your fair-mindedness. All of your words as well as your sentence structures should convey the tone you intend. If some passages sound defensive, self-centered, or apologetic, either to you or to your peer reviewer, revise those passages. Such attitudes rarely sustain a reader's interest, let alone goodwill. Your challenge is

The expressive tone of Dorothea Lange's photograph of a poor mother and children added depth and richness to a photodocumentary of the Great Depression.

to make sure that your tone contributes to eliciting from your readers the desired response—to you as well as to the information you are presenting.

Consider the tone in paragraph 1, which describes the wonders and terrors of growing up a poor young girl in South Carolina. (For ease of reference, each of the sample paragraphs in this chapter is numbered.)

1   Where I was born—Greenville, South Carolina—smelled like nowhere else I've ever been. Cut wet grass, split green apples, baby shit and beer bottles, cheap makeup and motor oil. Everything was ripe, everything was rotting. Hound dogs butted my calves. People shouted in the distance; crickets boomed in my ears. That country was beautiful, I swear to you, the most beautiful place I've ever been. Beautiful and terrible. It is the country of my dreams and the country of my nightmares: a pure pink and blue sky, red dirt, white clay, and all that endless green—willows and dogwood and firs going on for miles.

—**DOROTHY ALLISON**, *Two or Three Things I Know for Sure*

Exercise 1

Establishing your own tone, create a paragraph about the place where you were born (or grew up). Identify specific words and phrases from paragraph 1 that helped you with your version. Be prepared to read your paragraph aloud and share your list of words and phrases with the rest of the class.

When Richard Petraglia revised the first draft reprinted later in this chapter (pages 78–81), he decided to adjust his tone in response to a comment from his reader that his opening paragraph sounded too formal. Although Richard wanted to sound intelligent in his essay about taking foreign languages, he did not want to seem stuffy or imply that taking a foreign language should be easy. His aim was to strike the tone most appropriate for his rhetorical situation (**1a**).

TECH SAVVY
The thesaurus and grammar checker in your word-processing program may give you advice that can affect the tone of your writing. When you click on Tools on the toolbar, the pulldown menu will reveal the spelling and grammar checkers and usually a dictionary and a thesaurus as well. These tools are easy to find and use; however, only you can make the choices that will enhance the tone that is appropriate to your rhetorical situation. For example, a thesaurus may suggest a synonym for a word that you have been intentionally repeating in order to establish a rhythm. A grammar checker may flag a short fragment that you have deliberately inserted among some long sentences in order to highlight a point. If you are using these features of your word-processing program as you revise, give careful consideration to the suggestions they make, weighing those suggestions in terms of your rhetorical situation.

4b Guiding readers with your introduction and conclusion

Your introduction and conclusion play a special role in helping readers understand your essay as a whole. In fact, readers look for these parts of an essay and read them carefully, expecting guidance and clarification from them.

(1) An effective introduction arouses your reader's interest and establishes your topic and tone.

Experienced writers know that the opening paragraph is important; it is their best chance to arouse the reader's interest with provocative information, establish the topic and the writer as worthy of consideration, and set the tone. Effective introductions make readers want to read on. In paragraph 2, Nancy Mairs speaks directly to her readers—shocking them—in order to get their attention.

2   The other day I was thinking of writing an essay on being a cripple. I was thinking hard in one of the stalls of the women's room in my office building, as I was shoving my shirt into my jeans and tugging up my zipper.

Preoccupied, I flushed, picked up my book bag, took my cane down from the hook, and unlatched the door. So many movements unbalanced me, and as I pulled the door open I fell over backward, landing fully clothed on the toilet seat with my legs splayed in front [of] me: the old beetle-on-its-back routine. Saturday afternoon, the building deserted, I was free to laugh aloud as I wriggled back to my feet, my voice bouncing off the yellowish tiles from all directions. Had anyone been there with me, I'd have been still and faint and hot with chagrin. I decided that it was high time to write the essay.

—NANCY MAIRS, "On Being a Cripple"

Mairs's unsettling introduction takes her readers off guard: they are in the bathroom with a cripple—and a witty one at that. Her especially strong introduction orients readers to the direction her essay will take: she will candidly reveal her daily humanity in order to remind her readers that "cripples" are people, too.

Introductions have no set length; they can be as brief as a couple of sentences or as long as two or more paragraphs. Although introductions always appear first, they are often drafted and revised much later in the writing process—for introductions, as well as the thesis statements they often contain (3c), evolve naturally as writers revise their material, sharpening its focus and developing it to fulfill the overall purpose. You may wish to try several different introductions as you revise, to determine which is most effective.

You can arouse the interest of your audience by writing introductions in a number of ways.

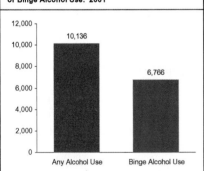

Figure 1. Estimated Numbers of Persons Aged 12 to 20 (in Thousands) Reporting Past Month Alcohol Use or Binge Alcohol Use: 2001

Opening with a thought-provoking statistic can be an effective introduction.

(a) Opening with an unusual fact or statistic

3   Americans aren't just reading fewer books, but are reading less and less of everything, in any medium. That's the doleful conclusion of "To Read or Not to Read," a report released last week by the National Endowment for the Arts.

—JENNIFER HOWARD, "Americans Are Closing the Book on Reading, Study Finds"

(b) Opening with an intriguing statement

4   I belong to a Clan of One-Breasted Women. My mother, my grandmothers, and six aunts have all had mastectomies. Seven are dead. The two who survive have just completed rounds of chemotheraphy and radiation.

                    —TERRY TEMPEST WILLIAMS, "The Clan of One-Breasted Women"

(c) Opening with an anecdote or example

5   When I used to ask my mother which we were, rich or poor, she refused to tell me. I was then nine years old and of course what I was dying to hear was that we were poor. I was reading a book called *Five Little Peppers* and my heart was set on baking a cake for my mother in a stove with a hole in it. Some version of rich, crusty old Mr. King—up till that time not living on our street—was sure to come down the hill in his wheelchair and rescue me if anything went wrong. But before I could start a cake at all I had to find out if we were rich or poor, and poor *enough*; and my mother wouldn't tell me, she said she was too busy. I couldn't wait too long; I had to go on reading and soon Polly Pepper got into more trouble, some that was a little harder on her and easier on me.   **—EUDORA WELTY, "A Sweet Devouring"**

(d) Opening with a question your essay will answer

6   Fellow-Citizens—pardon me, and allow me to ask, why am I called upon to speak here today? What have I, or those I represent, to do with your national independence? Are the great principles of political freedom and of natural justice, embodied in that Declaration of Independence, extended to us? and am I, therefore, called upon to bring our humble offering to the national alter, and to confess the benefits, and express devout gratitude for the blessings, resulting from your independence to us?

                    —FREDERICK DOUGLASS, "What to the Slave Is the Fourth of July?"

(e) Opening with an appropriate quotation

7   NO TRESSPASSING, it says. "*This railroad, all sidings, yards, buildings, and lands connected therewith, are the private property of Consolidated Rail Corporation. . . .*" Conrail. The company that took over the failing offspring of the Pennsylvania Railroad. Someone has scrawled [an expletive] across it. And someone, in neat, blue script, has written along the margin: *Gotta be prudent.* My mother and I used to stand on the landing of the fire escape behind my parents' restaurant, holding tight onto the iron grille, looking at the furious

vast expanse of shop yards below: the engines crisscrossing in slow force, the screech of metal on metal, the fire in the smoke. . . . Now I'm leaning into the fence and looking at suspension springs and running gear, rusted and covered with the delicate cream of Queen Anne's lace.

—MIKE ROSE, *The Mind at Work*

(f) Opening with general information or background about the topic

8   Scientists have long touted the benefits of the Mediterranean diet for heart health. But now researchers are finding more and more evidence that the diet can keep you healthy in other ways, too, including lowering the risk of certain cancers and easing the pain and stiffness of arthritis.

—MELISSA GOTTHARDT, "The Miracle Diet"

(g) Opening with a thesis, simply stated

9   My grandmother was American.   —ELENA PONIATOWSKA, "Yellow Magazine"

Whatever type of introduction you choose to write, use your opening paragraph to indicate your topic, engage your readers' attention, set your tone, and establish your credibility (8f(1)).

(2) An effective conclusion helps readers understand the most important points of your essay and why they are significant.

Just as a good introduction tantalizes readers, a good conclusion satisfies them. It helps readers recognize the important points of your essay and the significance of those points while, at the same time, wrapping up the essay in a meaningful, often thought-provoking way. As you draft and revise, you may want to keep a list of ideas for your conclusion, especially ones that go beyond a simple restatement of the thesis (3c). Some suggestions for writing effective conclusions follow, beginning with the technique of restating the thesis and main points.

(a) Rephrasing the thesis and summarizing the main points

10   The Endangered Species Act should not take into account economic considerations. Economics doesn't know how to value a species or a forest. Its logic drives people to exploit resources to the point of extinction. The Endangered Species Act tells us that extinction is morally unacceptable. It was enacted by a Congress and president in a wise mood, to express a higher value than a bottom line.

—DONELLA MEADOWS, "Not Seeing the Forest for the Dollar Bills"

(b) Calling attention to larger issues

11   Well, yes. But I'm imagining myself with five children under the age of 7, all alone after Dad goes off to work. And they're bouncing off the walls in that way little boys do, except for the baby, who needs to be fed. And fed. And fed again. And changed. The milk gets spilled. The phone rings. Mommy, can I have juice? Mommy, can I have lunch? Mommy, can I go out back? Mommy, can I come in? And I add to all that depression, mental illness, whatever was happening in that house. I'm not making excuses for Andrea Yates [who systematically drowned her five young children]. I love my children more than life itself. But just because you love people doesn't mean that taking care of them day in and day out isn't often hard, and sometimes even horrible. If God made mothers because he couldn't be everywhere, maybe he could have met us halfway and eradicated vomiting, and colic too, and the hideous sugarcoating of what we are and what we do that leads to false cheer, easy lies and maybe sometimes much, much worse, almost unimaginable.   —ANNA QUINDLEN, "Playing God on No Sleep"

(c) Calling for a change in action or attitude

12   As anyone who takes care of herself knows, the body is always trying to find and maintain a balance. Run on a treadmill and your body will sweat to bring your core temperature back to normal. Eat a meal and your insulin levels rise to metabolize the glucose produced. But often the balance is delicate, and losing it can have a domino effect on all kinds of other bodily processes. Sleep is one of those delicate functions—so vital that the body will actively force it on you if you fight it too long. Our message to you? Be as vigilant about sleep as you are about your time in the gym. It's just as important to your health.   —JORDANA BROWN, "The Science of Sleep"

(d) Concluding with a vivid image

13   At just past 10 a.m., farm workers and scrap-yard laborers in Somerset County looked up to see a large commercial airliner dipping and lunging as it swooped low over the hill country of southern Pennsylvania, near the town of Shanksville. A man driving a coal truck on Route 30 said he saw the jet tilt violently from side to side, then suddenly plummet "straight down." It hit nose first on the grassy face of a reclaimed strip mine at approximately 10:05 Eastern Daylight Time and exploded into a fireball, shattering windowpanes a half-mile away. The seventy-two-year-old man who was closest to the point of impact saw what looked to him like the yellow mushroom cloud of an atomic blast. Twenty-eight-year-old Eric Peterson was one of the first on the scene. He arrived to discover a flaming crater fifty feet deep.

Shredded clothing hung from the trees, and smoldering airplane parts littered the ground. It did not look much like the site of a great American victory, but it was.   —RANDALL SULLIVAN, "Flight 93"

(e) Connecting with the introduction

The introduction

14   Peterson Yazzie (Navajo) may be only 26, but this young contemporary painter from Greasewood Springs, Arizona has already garnered impressive accolades and is considered one of the rising stars of the Native art realm.

In the essay that follows this introduction, Debra Krol provides a brief biographical sketch of the artist's life and education, moving quickly to an enthusiastic assessment of his art.

The conclusion

15   Among other honors amassed over his meteoric career, Yazzie took home the best of class ribbon in painting from the Heard Museum Guild Indian Fair & Market in 2006, and looks forward to returning again this year as he continues to delve even further into expressing his worldview through art.

—DEBRA UTACIA KROL, "Peterson Yazzie"

Whatever technique you choose for your conclusion, provide readers with a sense of closure. Bear in mind that they may be wondering, "So what? Why have you told me all this?" Your conclusion gives you an opportunity to address that concern. If there is any chance that readers may not understand your purpose, use your conclusion to clarify why you have asked them to read what they have just read.

Exercise 2

Thumb through a magazine you enjoy, skimming the introductions of all the articles. Select two introductions that catch your attention. Copy them, word for word, and then consider the reasons *why* they interest you. What specific techniques for an introduction did the authors use? Next, look through the same or another magazine for two effective conclusions. Copy these, and analyze their effectiveness as well. Be prepared to share your findings with the rest of the class.

4c Revising for unified and coherent paragraphs

When revising the body of an essay, writers are likely to find opportunities for further development within each paragraph (3f and 3g) and to discover ways to make each paragraph more **unified** by relating every sentence within the paragraph to a single main idea (4c(2)), which might appear in a topic sentence. After weeding out unrelated sentences, writers concentrate on **coherence,** ordering the sentences so that ideas progress logically and smoothly from one sentence to the next. A successful paragraph is well developed, unified, and coherent.

(1) The topic sentence expresses the main idea.

Much like the thesis statement of an essay, a **topic sentence** states the main idea of a paragraph and comments on that main idea. Although the topic sentence is usually the first sentence in a paragraph, it can appear in any position within the paragraph. Sometimes, the topic sentence is implied by something in all of the sentences. If you need to work at improving the unity and coherence of your paragraphs, you might want to keep your topic sentences at the beginning. Not only will they serve to remind you of your focus, but they will also be obvious to your readers, who will grasp your main ideas immediately. More experienced writers may avoid repeating the same paragraph patterns by organizing their sentences differently within different paragraphs.

When you announce your general topic and then provide specific support for it, you are writing **deductively.** Your topic sentence appears first, like the one in italics in paragraph 16, which announces that the author will offer evidence as to why we are suspicious of rapid cognition.

16   *I think we are innately suspicious of . . . rapid cognition.* We live in a world that assumes that the quality of a decision is directly related to the time and effort that went into making it. When doctors are faced with a difficult diagnosis, they order more tests, and when we are uncertain about what we hear, we ask for a second opinion. And what do we tell our children? Haste makes waste. Look before you leap. Stop and *think.* Don't judge a book by its cover. We believe that we are always better off gathering as much information as possible and spending as much time as possible in deliberation. We really

only trust conscious decision making. But there are moments, particularly in times of stress, when haste does not make waste, when our snap judgments and first impressions can offer a much better means of making sense of the world.

—MALCOLM GLADWELL, *Blink*

If you want to emphasize the main idea of a paragraph or give its organization some extra support, you can begin and conclude the paragraph with two versions of the same idea. This strategy is particularly useful for long paragraphs because it gives readers whose attention may have wandered a second chance to grasp the main idea. In paragraph 17, both the first sentence and the last convey the idea that the English language has become a global language.

17 *English is the most widely spoken language in the history of our planet, used in some way by at least one out of every seven human beings around the globe.* Half of the world's books are written in English, and the majority of international telephone calls are made in English. English is the language of over sixty percent of the world's radio programs, many of them beamed, ironically, by the Russians, who know that to win friends and influence nations, they're best off using English. More than seventy percent of international mail is written and addressed in English, and eighty percent of all computer text is stored in English. *English has acquired the largest vocabulary of all the world's languages, perhaps as many as two million words, and has generated one of the noblest bodies of literature in the annals of the human race.*

—RICHARD LEDERER, "English Is a Crazy Language"

As you prepare to revise a draft, try underlining the topic sentences you can identify. If you cannot find a topic sentence, add a sentence stating the main idea of that paragraph. If you find that you open every paragraph with a topic sentence, you might try experimenting with another pattern, revising a paragraph so that the topic sentence appears at the end, as in paragraph 18.

18 The first time I visited Texas, I wore a beige polyester-blend lab coat with reinforced slits for pocket access and mechanical-pencil storage. I was attending a local booksellers' convention, having just co-written a pseudo-scientific book . . . , and my publicist suggested that the doctor getup would attract attention. It did. Everyone thought I was the janitor. Lesson No. 1: When in Texas, do not dress down. —PATRICIA MARX, "Dressin' Texan"

Placing the topic sentence toward or at the end of the paragraph works well when you are moving from specific supporting details to a generalization about those ideas—that is, when you are writing **inductively**. Effective writers try to meet the expectations of their readers, which often include the anticipation that the first sentence will be the topic sentence; however, writers and readers alike enjoy an occasional departure from the expected. And writers need to adjust their paragraph organization according to the rhetorical purpose of each paragraph.

(2) In a unified paragraph, every sentence relates to the main idea.

Paragraphs are **unified** when every sentence relates to the main idea; unity is violated when something unrelated to the rest of the material appears. Consider the obvious violation in paragraph 19.

19   The Marion, Ohio of my childhood offered activities to suit any child's taste. In the summer, I could walk to the library and spend the afternoon browsing or reading, either in the children's library in the dark cool basement or in the adult library, which was sunnier and warmer. On the way home, I could stop by Isaly's Dairy and buy a skyscraper ice cream cone for twenty-five cents. I could swim every afternoon in our neighborhood swimming pool, Fair Park pool, where kids played freely and safely, often without any parents around. If I wanted, I could make plans to meet up with my cousin Babs and walk downtown for a movie matinée or a grilled-cheese sandwich at Woolworth's lunch counter. *We used to be so close, but I haven't seen Babs since her mother's funeral five years ago.* If we didn't want to stay downtown, we could take a city bus out to the roller rink or, if something big was going on, out to the fairgrounds.

Easy to delete, the italicized sentence about not seeing Babs for five years violates the unity of a paragraph devoted to childhood activities in a small town. If the overall purpose of the essay includes a comparison of what the cousins did then and what they do now, the writer could simply develop the idea of what the cousins are doing now into a separate paragraph.

As you revise your paragraphs for unity, the following tips may help you.

TIPS FOR IMPROVING PARAGRAPH UNITY

Identify   Identify the topic sentence for each paragraph. Where is each located?

Relate   Read each sentence in a paragraph, and decide if and how it relates to the topic sentence.

Eliminate   Any sentence that violates the unity of a paragraph should be cut (or saved for use elsewhere).

Clarify   Any sentence that "almost" relates to the topic sentence should be revised until it does relate. You may need to clarify details or add information or a transitional word or phrase to make the relationship clear.

Rewrite   If more than one idea is being conveyed in a single paragraph, either rewrite the topic sentence so that it includes both ideas and establishes a relationship between them or split the paragraph into two.

---

(3) Clearly arranged ideas contribute to coherence.

Some paragraphs are unified (4c(2)) but not coherent. In a unified paragraph, every sentence relates to the main idea of the paragraph. In a **coherent** paragraph, the relationship among the ideas is clear and meaningful, and the progression from one sentence to the next is easy for readers to follow. Paragraph 20 has unity but lacks coherence.

Lacks coherence

20   The inside of the refrigerator was covered with black mold, and it smelled as if something had been rotting in there for years. I put new paper down on all the shelves, and my roommate took care of lining the drawers. The stove was as dirty as the refrigerator. *When we moved into our new apartment, we found that the kitchen was in horrible shape.* We had to scrub the walls with a brush and plenty of Lysol to get rid of the grease. The previous tenant had left behind lots of junk (from dented canisters and broken can openers to dirty dish towels and towel rack parts) that we had to get rid of. All the drawers and cabinets had to be washed.

Although every sentence in this paragraph concerns cleaning the kitchen after moving into an apartment, the sentences are not arranged coherently. This paragraph can easily be revised so that the italicized topic sentence controls the meaningful flow of ideas—from what the roommates saw to what they did.

Revised for coherence

21   *When we moved into our new apartment, we found that the kitchen was in horrible shape.* The previous tenant had left behind lots of junk that we had to get rid of, from dented canisters and broken can openers to dirty dish towels and towel rack parts. The inside of the refrigerator was covered with black mold, and it smelled as if something had been rotting in there for years. The stove was as dirty as the refrigerator. [New sentence:] So we set to work. All the drawers and cabinets had to be washed. I put new paper down on all the shelves, and my roommate took care of lining the drawers. We had to scrub the walls with a brush and plenty of Lysol to get rid of the grease.

Paragraph 21 is coherent as well as unified.

To achieve coherence and unity in your paragraphs, study the following patterns of organization (chronological, spatial, emphatic, and logical), and consider which ones you might use in your own writing.

(a) Using chronological order, according to time

When you use **chronological order**, you arrange ideas according to the order in which things happened. This organizational pattern is particularly useful in narrations.

22   When everyone was finished, we were given the signal to put our silverware on our plates. Each piece of silverware had its place—the knife at the top of the plate, sharp edge toward us; then the fork, perfectly lined up next to the knife; then the spoon—and any student who didn't put the silverware in the right place couldn't leave the table. Lastly, our napkins were refolded and put in their original spot. When we stood, we pushed our chair under the table and waited for the signal to turn right. Then we marched outside, single file, while the kitchen staff started to clean the dining room.

—**ANNE E. BOLANDER** AND **ADAIR N. RENNING,** *I Was #87*

(b) Using spatial order, according to the movement of the eyes

When you arrange ideas according to **spatial order,** you orient the reader's focus from right to left, near to far, top to bottom, and so on. This organizational pattern is particularly effective in descriptions. Often the organization is so obvious that the writer can forgo a topic sentence, as in paragraph 23.

23   The stores on Tremont Avenue seemed to be extensions of my domestic space. Each one had sensory memories that I associate with my mother. On

the corner was the delicatessen. From its counter, which was like a bar complete with a brass footrest, came the deeply dark smell of cured meats, the tang of frankfurters, with the steaming background scent of hot knishes on the griddle. —LENNARD J. DAVIS, *My Sense of Silence*

(c) Using emphatic order, according to importance

When you use **emphatic order,** you arrange information in order of importance, usually from least to most important. Emphatic order is especially useful in expository and persuasive writing, both of which involve helping readers understand logical relationships (such as what caused something to happen or what kinds of priorities should be established). In paragraph 24, the writer emphasizes the future as the most important arena for change.

24   Among the first things Goldsmith had taught the executive was to look only to the future, because, whatever he had done to make people angry, he couldn't fix it now. "Don't ask for feedback about the past," he says. Goldsmith has turned against the notion of feedback lately. He has written an article on a more positive methodology, which he calls "feedforward." "How many of us have wasted much of our lives impressing our spouse, partner, or significant other with our near-photographic memory of their previous sins, which we document and share to help them improve?" he says. "Dysfunctional! Say, 'I can't change the past—all I can say is I'm sorry for what I did wrong.' Ask for suggestions for the future. Don't promise to do everything they suggest— leadership is not a popularity contest. But follow up on a regular basis, and you know what's going to happen? You will get better."

—LARISSA MacFARQUHAR, "The Better Boss"

(d) Using logical order, moving from specific to general or from general to specific

Sometimes the movement within a paragraph follows a **logical order,** from specific to general or from general to specific. A paragraph may begin with a series of details and conclude with a summarizing statement, as paragraphs 18 and 25 do, or it may begin with a general statement or idea, which is then supported by particular details, as in paragraphs 21 and 26.

25   This winter, I took a vacation from our unfinished mess. Getting back to it was tough, and one morning, I found myself on my knees before the dishwasher, as if in prayer, though actually busting a water-pipe weld. To my

right were the unfinished cabinets, to my left the knobless backdoor, behind me a hole I'd torn in the wall. There in the kitchen, a realization hit me like a 2-by-4: for two years I'd been working on this house, and there was still no end in sight. It had become my Vietnam.

—ROBERT SULLIVAN, "Home Wrecked"

26   It was not the only disappointment my mother felt in me. In the years that followed, I failed her so many times, each time asserting my own will, my right to fall short of expectations. I didn't get straight As. I didn't become class president. I didn't get into Stanford. I dropped out of college.

—AMY TAN, "Two Kinds"

4d   Transitions within and between paragraphs

Even if the sentences are arranged in a seemingly clear sequence, a single paragraph may lack internal coherence and a series of paragraphs may lack overall coherence if transitions are abrupt or nonexistent. When revising your writing, you can improve the coherence by using pronouns, repetition, conjunctions, and transitional words or phrases (24c).

(1) Pronouns help establish links between sentences.

In paragraph 27, the writer enumerates the similarities of identical twins raised separately. She mentions their names only once, but uses the pronouns *both, their,* and *they* to keep the references to the twins always clear.

27   Jim Springer and Jim Lewis were adopted as infants into working-class Ohio families. **Both** liked math and did not like spelling in school. **Both** had law enforcement training and worked part-time as deputy sheriffs. **Both** vacationed in Florida, **both** drove Chevrolets. Much has been made of the fact that **their** lives are marked by a trail of similar names. **Both** married and divorced women named Linda and had second marriages with women named Betty. **They** named **their** sons James Allan and James Alan, respectively. **Both** like mechanical drawing and carpentry. **They** have almost identical drinking and smoking patterns. **Both** chew **their** fingernails down to the nubs. —CONSTANCE HOLDEN, "Identical Twins Reared Apart"

(2) Repetition of words, phrases, structures, or ideas can link a sentence to those that precede it.

In paragraph 28, the repetition of the key word *never* links sentences to preceding sentences and also provides emphasis (**32d**).

28   *Never* is the most powerful word in the English language, or perhaps any language. It's magic. Every time I have made an emphatic pronouncement invoking the word *never,* whatever follows that I don't want to happen happens. *Never* has made a fool of me many times. The first time I remember noticing the powerful effect of this word I was a student at Indian school. My best friend, Belinda Gonzalez, and I were filling out our schedules for spring semester. She was Blackfeet, a voice major from Yakima, Washington. I was a painting major and checking out times for painting and drawing courses. She suggested I sign up for drama class with her. I said, no I will *never* go on stage. Despite my initial protest I did sign up for drama and dance troupes in the country, and now I make my living performing. *Never* is that powerful.

—JOY HARJO, "The Power of Never"

In this case, the author wished to stress the expectations many people hold when they declare "never." By repeating the word five times in one paragraph, Harjo emphasizes its power.

Parallelism, another kind of repetition, is a key principle in writing coherent sentences and paragraphs (chapter **31**).

(3) Using conjunctions and other transitional words or phrases also contributes to coherence.

Conjunctions and other transitional words or phrases demonstrate the logical relationship between ideas. In the following sentences, in which two clauses are linked by different conjunctions, notice the subtle changes in the relationship between the two ideas:

The dog ran, **and** she threw the Frisbee.

The dog ran **while** she threw the Frisbee.

The dog ran **because** she threw the Frisbee.

The dog ran, **so** she threw the Frisbee.

The dog ran; **later** she threw the Frisbee.

The following list of frequently used transitional connections, arranged according to the kinds of relationships they establish, can help you with your critical reading as well as your writing.

TYPES OF TRANSITIONAL CONNECTIONS

Addition	and, and then, further, furthermore, also, too, again, in addition, besides
Alternative	or, nor, either, neither, on the other hand, conversely, otherwise
Comparison	similarly, likewise, in like manner
Concession	although this may be true, even so, still, nevertheless, at the same time, notwithstanding, nonetheless, in any event, that said
Contrast	but, yet, or, and yet, however, on the contrary, in contrast
Exemplification	for example, for instance, in the case of
Intensification	in fact, indeed, moreover, even more important, to be sure
Place	here, beyond, nearby, opposite to, adjacent to, on the opposite side
Purpose	to this end, for this purpose, with this objective, in order to, so that
Repetition	as I have said, in other words, that is, as has been noted, as previously stated
Result or cause	so, for, therefore, accordingly, consequently, thus, thereby, as a result, then, because, hence
Sequence	next, first, second, third, in the first place, in the second place, finally, last, then, afterward, later
Summary	to sum up, in brief, on the whole, in sum, in short
Time	meanwhile, soon, after a few days, in the meantime, now, in the past, while, during, since

The following checklist can guide you in revising your paragraphs.

CHECKLIST for Revising Paragraphs

- Does the paragraph have a clear (or clearly implied) topic sentence (4c(1))?
- Do all the ideas in the paragraph belong together? Do sentences link to previous and later ones? Are the sentences arranged in chronological, spatial, emphatic, or logical order, or are they arranged in some other pattern (4c(2))?
- How does the paragraph link to the preceding and following ones (4d)?
- Are sentences connected to each other with effective transitions (4d(2))?
- What evidence do you have that the paragraph is adequately developed (3f)? What idea or detail might be missing (4a(1))? What rhetorical methods have been used to develop each of the paragraphs (3g)?

When revising an essay, you must consider the effectiveness of the individual paragraphs at the same time as you consider how those paragraphs work (or do not work) together to achieve the overall purpose. Some writers like to revise at the paragraph level before addressing larger concerns; other writers cannot work on the individual paragraphs until they have grappled with larger issues related to the rhetorical situation (overall purpose, attention to audience, and context; 1c–e) or have finalized their thesis (3c). All experienced writers use a process to write, but they do not all use exactly the same process. Since there is no universal, predetermined order to the writing process, you can follow whichever steps work best for you each time you are revising. Be guided by the principles and strategies discussed in this chapter, but trust also in your own good sense.

4e   The benefits of peer review

Because writing is a form of communication, good writers check to see whether they are communicating their ideas effectively to their readers. Instructors are one set of readers, but they are often the last people to see your writing. Before you submit your work to an instructor, take advantage of other opportunities for getting responses to it. Consult with readers— at the writing center, in your dorm, in your classes, or from online writing groups—asking them for honest responses to your concerns.

(1) Clearly defined evaluation standards help both writers and reviewers. Although you will always write within a rhetorical situation (1a), you will often address that situation in terms of an assigned task. If you are fortunate, you will be responding to a clearly stated assignment as well as working with specific evaluation standards that your instructor has provided in class, on assignment sheets, or on separate handouts (5a(2)). If your instructor supplies you with such standards, use them as the starting point for discussion when working with your writing group, a classmate, or a writing center tutor. For example, if your instructor has told you that your essay will be evaluated primarily in terms of whether you have a clear thesis (3c) and adequate support for it (3f and 3g), then those features should be your primary focus. Your secondary concerns may be the overall effectiveness of your introduction (4b(1)) and sentence length and variety (chapter 33).

Evaluation guidelines do not guarantee useful feedback every time, but they help you focus on the advice you want to ask for in a writer's memo (4e(2)), and they help your reviewers focus on what kinds of specific advice to give as they read and reread your draft.

If a reviewer sees a problem that the writer did not identify, the reviewer should ask the writer if she or he wants to discuss it and should abide by the writer's decision. A reviewer's comments should point out what the writer has done well and suggest how to improve particular passages. For instance, the reviewer may frame recommendations in terms of personal engagement with the text (page 78): "This is an interesting point! However, it's not clear if this is your thesis." A reviewer can be honest and helpful simultaneously. Ultimately, however, the success of the essay is the responsibility of the writer, who will evaluate the reviewer's advice, rejecting any comments that would take the essay in a different direction and applying any suggestions that help fulfill the rhetorical purpose (1c).

If you are developing your own criteria for evaluation, the following checklist can help you get started. Based on the elements of the rhetorical situation, this checklist can be easily adjusted so that it meets your specific needs for a particular assignment.

CHECKLIST for Evaluating a Draft of an Essay

- Does the essay fulfill the assignment?
- Does the essay address a specific audience (1d)? Is that audience appropriate for the assignment?
- What is the tone of the essay (4a(3))? How does the tone align with the overall purpose, the intended audience, and the context for the writing (1c–e)?
- Is your topic sufficiently focused (3b)? What is the thesis statement (3c)?
- What assertions do you make to support the thesis statement? What specific evidence do you provide to support these assertions?
- Are paragraphs arranged in an effective sequence (3d and 4c(3))? What pattern of organization are you using? Is each paragraph thoroughly developed (3f and 3g)?
- Is the introduction effective (4b(1))? How do you engage the reader's attention?
- Is the conclusion appropriate for the essay's purpose (4b(2))? How exactly does it draw the essay together?

(2) You can help your reviewers by telling them about your purpose and your concerns.

When submitting a draft for review, you can increase your chances of getting the kind of help you want by introducing your work and indicating what your concerns are. You can provide such an orientation orally to a writing group, tutor, or peer reviewer in just a few minutes. Or, when doing so is not possible, perhaps because you are submitting a draft online, you can attach to your draft a cover letter consisting of a paragraph or two—sometimes called a **writer's memo.** In either case, adopting the following model can help ensure that reviewers will give you useful responses.

SUBMITTING A DRAFT FOR REVIEW

Topic and Purpose

State your topic and your exigence for writing (1b). Indicate your thesis (3c) and purpose (1c). Providing this information gives reviewers useful direction.

Strengths

Mark the passages of the draft you are confident about. Doing so directs attention away from areas you do not want to discuss and saves time for all concerned.

Concerns

Put question marks by the passages you find troublesome, and ask for specific advice wherever possible. For example, if you are worried about your conclusion, say so. Or if you suspect that one of your paragraphs may not fit the overall purpose, direct attention to that particular paragraph. You are most likely to get the kind of help you want and need when you ask for it specifically.

Richard Petraglia's writer's memo follows.

Topic and Purpose: I'm focusing on the way English speakers tend to believe that they don't need to learn a foreign language because many people already speak English abroad. I think that while it is true that English has become the language of international communication, there are many benefits to learning a foreign language that don't have to do with being able to communicate with people in a foreign country. My purpose is to explain what those benefits are and convince my readers that learning a foreign language is an important part of a person's overall education.

Concerns: I'm concerned about being able to show all the benefits of learning a foreign language in a clear and organized manner. There are many benefits to studying a foreign language, and I want to make sure that the order in which I talk about them makes sense to the reader.

Richard submitted the draft on pages 78–81 for peer review in a first-year writing course. He worked with a classmate, who was working on the same assignment, and gave this reviewer a set of criteria that he had prepared. Because the reviewer was learning how to conduct peer evaluations, her comments are representative of responses you might receive in a similar situation. As members of writing groups gain experience and learn to employ the strategies outlined in this section, their advice usually becomes more helpful.

TECH SAVVY

Some instructors may require students to do peer reviewing online, using e-mail or a computer network. You should always check with your instructor for specific peer-review guidelines and procedures, but here are some general suggestions for online reviewing.

- If you are responding to a classmate's draft via e-mail, reread your comments before sending them to be sure that your tone is appropriate and that you have avoided the kinds of misunderstandings that can occur with e-mail (6b and 6c).
- Always save a copy of your comments in case your e-mail message is lost or inadvertently deleted.
- If you are responding to a classmate's draft using an online course-management program, such as WebCT, ANGEL, or Blackboard, remember that your comments may be read by other classmates, too.
- Follow the advice in 4e(1), just as you would if you were commenting on a paper copy of your classmate's draft.

As you read the assignment and then Richard's draft, remember that it is only a first draft—not a model of perfect writing—and also that this is the first time the peer reviewer, Alyssa Gaebel, responded to it.

Richard sent his draft to Alyssa electronically, and she used the Track Changes function of her word-processing program to add suggested changes and comments throughout the essay.

> **The assignment** Draft a three- to four-page, double-spaced essay in which you analyze the causes or consequences of a choice you have had to make in the last year or two. Whatever choice you analyze, make sure that it concerns a topic you can develop with confidence and without violating your own sense of privacy. Moreover, consider the expectations of your audience and whether the topic you have chosen will help you communicate something meaningful to readers. As you draft, establish an audience for your essay, a group that might benefit from or be interested in any recommendation that grows out of your analysis.

First Draft

Why Take a Foreign Language?

Richard Petraglia

> Alyssa Gaebel 10/15/08 9:11 AM
> What a great topic! We're all wondering why we have to take a foreign language.

It is commonly acknowledged that as native English speakers we have an advantage when it comes to intercultural communication. Our language is, after all, the language of business, diplomacy, and global communication in general. It is therefore tempting to think that knowing English is enough because we are likely to find English speakers wherever we go and don't need to learn any other languages. Ironically, this potential advantage of ours then becomes a disadvantage, because it makes us less motivated to study other languages. We end up missing out on the other benefits—beyond communicating with others—that come with studying a language other than our own.

> Alyssa Gaebel 10/15/08 9:12 AM
> **Comment:** Yes, I agree--that's why we shouldn't have to take a foreign language. I like your opening.

> Alyssa Gaebel 10/15/08 9:12 AM
> **Comment:** I think your tone in the last two sentences sounds too formal. Maybe it would help to get rid of the "we" and talk about English speakers in general?

The primary reason we often give for studying a foreign language has to do with communication. The straight-forward, common sense answer you'll hear on the first day of elementary German when the instructor asks the students why they want to

> Alyssa Gaebel 10/15/08 9:13 AM
> **Comment:** This is an interesting point! However, it's not clear if this is your thesis.

learn German will inevitably be along the lines of "because I want to be able to communicate with people in their own language" or "because I want to learn more about German culture." And these are, of course, wonderful reasons for studying German or French or Spanish. Becoming familiar with other cultures is crucial to opening our minds and increasing our tolerance and understanding. Studying the language of a country you will visit will undoubtedly enrich your stay, and in my personal experience I've also found that we tend to overestimate how many people speak English abroad. Learning a foreign language for these reasons makes good sense.

> **Alyssa Gaebel 10/15/08 9:15 AM**
> **Comment:** Richard, you need a better transition between talking about communication and then culture. It might be worthwhile to consider putting these ideas into two separate paragraphs.

There is, however, another answer to that question, and one that I would argue is just as important, but that you'll probably never hear on that first day of German class. On that first day you won't hear a student saying that they want to learn German in order to learn more about English. And that, for me, has been the most rewarding part of studying foreign languages continuously since middle school. I think that we need to look beyond the idea that all we will learn is how to speak someone else's language. Learning another language has the fortunate side-effect of teaching us more about our own.

> **Alyssa Gaebel 10/15/08 9:34 AM**
> **Comment:** If this last sentence is your thesis statement (and I think it is), it needs to appear earlier in your essay.

There are statistics that show that students who pursue several years of foreign languages in high school tend to score higher on standardized tests. I am mostly interested in the reason for this, what produces these results. You could say that in general, more highly motivated students will be the ones who pursue an elective like Spanish or French all four years; that language study is just a characteristic of the more motivated students who will score higher on standardized tests any way. But it really has to do with the way

> **Alyssa Gaebel 10/15/08 9:34 AM**
> **Comment:** This change in topic from learning more about English to doing better on standardized tests sounds abrupt. Will you consider composing a sentence here that explains how learning more about English (and other languages) leads to better scores on standardized tests?

> **Alyssa Gaebel 10/15/08 9:34 AM**
> **Comment:** These two sentences seem repetitive. Maybe combine them?

studying a foreign language builds awareness of our own language. Studying a foreign language can improve reading comprehension because it gets students to think about how ideas are expressed, and therefore more easily get a better grasp of the idea a writer is trying to convey.

Learning languages also teaches us to learn in a combination of ways. First, learning a different language can be done intuitively, using the knowledge of your own language as a base and making educated guesses about the way the foreign language will work to express ideas. In conjunction with this method, foreign language learning develops the student's ability to follow complex rules. Expressing yourself in a different language is done differently than in English. Instead of being able to simply remember how ideas are expressed because you've been hearing it since you were a child, expressing yourself in the foreign language requires following complex rules of grammar that must be learned. Because learning a foreign language teaches us to learn in a combination of ways, it makes us better learners in general. A student can carry this knowledge of being able to apply complex rules as well as learn intuitively to any other discipline.

Learning German grammar improves writing in English because it improves knowledge of grammar. Confidence in grammar is the key to clear writing because knowing the structure of a language allows the student to express his or her ideas more clearly and precisely. There is an on-going debate about just how useful teaching grammar in our schools is in improving student writing. This is unclear. Because we intuitively know how to conjugate our verbs and generally make ourselves understood,

> Alyssa Gaebel 10/15/08 9:36 AM
> **Comment:** Do you mean teaching English grammar to English speakers? It's not clear what exactly you mean here.

it can seem pointless and frustrating to students to be taught the minute details of the language we already speak. The effects aren't immediately apparent or rewarding. But when learning about a foreign language, each time you learn to say something new, there is a sense of having produced a tangible result. As we learn how to express ourselves in a foreign language, we are also indirectly learning those things about our own language's structure.

> Alyssa Gaebel 10/15/08 9:38 AM
> **Comment:** I think you'll want to reorganize this paragraph so that it has a clear topic sentence in the beginning. Otherwise, a reader won't know where this paragraph is going and what point you want to make.

Moving beyond grammar, the way foreign languages express elements of time and patterns of description open up new ways of expressing ideas through language. Studying a foreign language also gives the student a basis for comparison because languages express the same ideas in different ways. This leads to a more creative use of our own language because the student is aware of the different ways the structures of language can be used to express ideas.

> Alyssa Gaebel 10/15/08 9:39 AM
> **Comment:** You're making some really good points. You will want those points to be clearer so that you can show how they relate to the rest of your essay. This paragraph needs to have those connections made clearer.

Overall, studying a foreign language has many benefits, but among the most rewarding is learning more about English and becoming a better writer. Learning a foreign language allows us to see English from a different perspective and enables us to understand the grammatical structures of language we take for granted. Gaining a better understanding of our own language through studying the language of another country helps us to understand the subtle changes of meaning that happen with changes of grammar, which allows for a more varied, precise, and effective use of our own language in both speaking and in writing.

Richard,

You make some really great points! However, I think you need to organize your essay, and especially your conclusion, to better reflect your thesis.

It seems like you're arguing that learning a foreign language makes you a better student, but the conclusion only talks about how it makes you a better writer. The point about becoming a better writer sounds like it belongs after the third paragraph, which ends with the sentence "Learning another language has the fortunate side effect of teaching us more about our own." I say that because your essay's argument focuses on more than just making the student a better writer. It makes more sense to have the paragraphs about doing better on standardized tests and learning in a combination of ways closer to the end of your essay.

Also, make sure your thesis clearly states your position in the argument. If your thesis is "We end up missing out on the other benefits—beyond communicating with others—that come with studying a language other than our own," your essay might have more focus if you can name some of those benefits in your thesis.

Great first draft! Thanks for letting me read it and respond.

Alyssa

Before revising, Richard considered the comments he received from Alyssa. Since he had asked her to respond to his introduction, conclusion, and organization, he had to weigh all of her comments—relevant and irrelevant—and use the ones that seemed to be most useful as he prepared his next draft.

Exercise 3

Reread the first draft of "Why Take a Foreign Language?" and the comments it received. Identify the comments you think are the most useful, and explain why. Which comments seem to be less useful? Explain why. What additional comments would you make if Richard had asked you to review his draft?

After Richard had time to reconsider his first draft and to think about the responses he received from readers (including the one from Alyssa), he made a number of large-scale changes, especially with regard to organization. He also strengthened his topic sentence. In addition, he dealt with sentence-level issues of repetition that Alyssa had pointed out. Richard used the Track Changes function of his word-processing program as he revised so that he could see his changes.

Second Draft

Why Take a Foreign Language?

Richard Petraglia

~~It is commonly acknowledged that as native~~ Native English speakers ~~we~~ have an advantage when it comes to intercultural communication. ~~Our language is, after all,~~ English is the language of business, diplomacy, and global communication in general. It is therefore tempting to think that as English speakers we don't need to learn a foreign language ~~knowing English is enough~~ because we are likely to find ~~English speakers wherever we go and don't need to learn any other languages~~someone who speaks English in any foreign country we visit. ~~Ironically, this~~This potential advantage of ~~ours then becomes~~already knowing the language of intercultural communication, however, can prove to be a disadvantage, because it makes ~~us~~ English speakers less motivated to study other languages. ~~We end up missing out on the other benefits--beyond communicating with others--that come with studing a language other than our own.~~ There are many benefits of studying a foreign language that have nothing to do with being able to communicate with people in foreign countries. Students who study a foreign language in school often have better writing skills, reading comprehension, and score higher on standardized tests.

~~The~~ Still, the primary reason ~~we~~ people often give for wanting to study~~ing~~ a foreign language has to do with ~~communication~~communicating with people in foreign countries. The straight-forward, common-sense answer you'll hear on the first day of elementary German when the instructor asks the students why they want to learn German will inevitably be along the lines of "because I want to be able to communicate with people in their own language" or "because I want to learn more about German culture." And these are, of course, wonderful reasons for studying German (or French or Spanish). Communicating with people in their own language and ~~Becoming~~becoming familiar with other cultures is crucial to opening our minds and increasing our tolerance and understanding. Studying the language of a country you will visit will undoubtedly enrich your stay~~, and in my personal experience I've~~ I have also found that ~~we~~ English speakers tend to overestimate how many people actually speak English abroad. ~~Learning a foreign language for these reasons makes good sense.~~

There is, however, another ~~answer to that question, and one~~reason for studying a foreign language that I would argue is just as important, but that you'll probably never hear about on that first day of German class. ~~On that first day you won't hear a student saying that they want to learn German in order to~~ And that is that learning German helps us learn more about English. ~~And that, for me,~~ For me, learning about English has been the most rewarding part of studying foreign languages continuously since middle school. I think that we need to look beyond the idea that all we will learn in a foreign language class is how to speak someone else's language~~. Learning~~, and realize that learning another language has the fortunate side- effect of teaching us more about our own.

For example, there is an ongoing debate about just how useful teaching grammar in our schools is in improving student writing. Because students intuitively know how to conjugate English verbs and generally make themselves understood, it can seem pointless and frustrating for them to be taught the minutiae of the language they already speak. The effects aren't immediately apparent or rewarding. But when learning about a foreign language, each time a student learns to say something new, there is a sense of having produced a tangible result. As students learn how to express themselves in a foreign language, they are also indirectly learning those things about their own language's structure. Therefore, learning German grammar improves writing as a side effect because it improves the student's knowledge of similar grammatical structures in English.

While studying a foreign language has many benefits, among the most fundamental is learning more about English and becoming a better writer. Learning a foreign language allows students to see English from a different perspective and enables them to understand the grammatical structures of their language that they often take for granted. Gaining a better understanding of their own language through studying the language of another country helps them to understand the subtle changes of meaning that happen with changes of grammar. This understanding of subtleties of grammar allows the student to have a more varied, precise, and effective use of his or her own language in both speaking and writing.

There are ~~also~~ statistics that show that students who pursue several years of foreign languages in high school tend to score higher on standardized tests. I ~~am mostly interested in the reason for this,~~ think it will be interesting to examine what produces these results. You could say that, in general, more highly motivated students will be the ones who pursue an elective like Spanish or French all four years~~;~~ and that language study is just a characteristic of the more motivated students who will score higher on standardized tests anyway. But it really has to do with the way studying a foreign language builds awareness of our own language. Studying a foreign language ~~can~~ improve~~s~~ reading comprehension because it gets students to think about how ideas are expressed through language and allows students to understand the complex use of language in any text more precisely. Once a student has more awareness of how ideas are expressed through language, he or she can ~~and therefore~~ more easily ~~get a better~~ grasp of the idea a writer is trying to convey.

~~Learning languages~~Studying a foreign language ~~also teaches us~~makes students better learners because it teaches them to learn in a combination of ways. First, ~~learning a different language can be done~~ students practice learning intuitively, using the knowledge of ~~your own language as a base and~~ their native language to ~~making~~ make educated guesses about the way the foreign language will work ~~to express ideas~~. In conjunction with this intuitive method, foreign language learning develops the student's ability to follow complex rules. ~~Expressing yourself in a~~ A different language often expresses ideas in a different way than in English, using unfamiliar grammatical rules and structures ~~is done differently than in English~~. The students are therefore forced to rely on their knowledge of complex grammatical rules to express ideas in a foreign language. ~~Instead of being able to simply remember how ideas are expressed because you'e been hearing it since you were a child, expressing yourself in the foreign language requires following complex rules of grammar that must be learned.~~ Because learning a foreign language teaches us to learn in a combination of ~~ways,~~ both the intuitive and rule-based methods, it makes us better learners in general. A student can carry this knowledge of being able to apply complex rules as well as learn intuitively to any other discipline.

~~Learning German grammar improves writing in English because it improves knowledge of grammar. Confidence in gramma is th ekey to clear writing because knowing the structure of a language allows the student to express his or her ideas more clearly and precisely. There is an on-going debate about just how useful teaching grammar in our schools is in improving student writing. This is unclear. Because we intuitively know how to conjugate our verbs and generally make ourselves understood, it can seem pointless and frustrating to students to be taught the minute details of the language we already speak. The effects aren't immediately apparent or rewarding. But when learning about a foreign language. each time you learn to say something new, there is a sinse of having produced a tangible result. As we learn how to express ourselves in a foreign language, we are also indirectly learning those things about our own language's structure.~~

~~Moving beyond grammar, the way foreign languages express elements~~
~~of time and patterns of description open up new ways of expressing ideas~~
~~through language. Studying a foreign language also gives the student a basis~~
~~for comparison because languages express the same ideas in different ways.~~
~~This leads to a more creative use of our own language because the student is~~
~~aware of the different ways th estructures of language can be used to express~~
~~ideas.~~

~~Overall, studying a foreign language has many benefits, but among~~
~~the most rewarding is learning more about English and becoming a better~~
~~writer. Learning a foreign language allows up to see English from a different~~
~~perspective and enables us to understand the grammatical structures of language~~
~~we take for granted. Gaining a better understanding of our own language~~
~~through studing the language of another country helps us to understand the~~
~~subtle changes of meaning that happen with changes of grammar, which allows~~
~~for a more varied, precise, and effective use of our own language in both~~
~~speaking and in writing.~~

After several more revisions, more peer review, and some careful editing and proofreading, Richard was ready to submit his essay to his instructor. His final draft is on pages 91–94.

4f Editing for clearer ideas, sentences, and paragraphs

If you are satisfied with the revised structure of your essay and the content of your paragraphs, you can begin editing individual sentences for clarity, effectiveness, and variety (chapters 28–36). The following checklist for editing contains cross-references to chapters or sections where you can find more specific information.

Just as photographic manipulation makes this image arresting, effective editing can make your writing more engaging.

CHECKLIST for Editing

1 Sentences

■ What is the unifying idea of each sentence (28)?

■ Are the sentences varied in length? How many words are in your longest sentence? Your shortest sentence?

■ How many of your sentences use subordination? Coordination? If you overuse any one sentence structure, revise for variation (33).

■ Which sentences have or should have parallel structure (31)?

■ Do any sentences contain misplaced or dangling modifiers (25)?

■ Do any of your sentences shift in verb tense or tone (27c)? Is the shift intentional?

■ Does each verb agree with its subject (27f)? Does every pronoun agree with its antecedent (26c)?

2 Diction

- Have you repeated any words? Is your repetition intentional?
- Are your word choices exact, or are some words vague or too general (35)?
- Is the vocabulary you have chosen appropriate for your audience, purpose, and context (1c, 1d, and 34)?
- Have you defined any technical or unfamiliar words for your audience (34c(4))?

4g Proofreading for an error-free essay

Once you have revised and edited your essay, it is your responsibility to format it properly (chapter 7) and proofread it. Proofreading means making a special search to ensure that the final product you submit is free from error, or nearly so. An error-free essay allows your reader to read for meaning, without encountering incorrect spelling or punctuation that can interfere with meaning. As you proofread, you may discover problems that call for further revision or editing, but proofreading is usually the last step in the writing process.

TECH SAVVY

With a computer, you can easily produce professional-looking documents. Showing that you care about presentation indicates respect for your audience (chapter 7). However, no matter how professional your paper looks when you print it, proofread it carefully. Mechanical mistakes can undermine your credibility.

Because the eye tends to see what it expects to see, many writers miss errors—especially minor ones, such as a missing comma or apostrophe—even when they think they have proofread carefully. To proofread well, then, you need to read your work more than once and read it aloud. Some people find it useful to read through a paper several times, checking for a different set of items on each pass. Other writers rely on peer editors to provide help with proofreading.

The proofreading checklist that follows refers to chapters and sections in this handbook where you will find detailed information to help you. Also, keep your dictionary (34e) at hand to look up any words whose meaning or spelling you aren't sure of.

CHECKLIST for Proofreading

1 Spelling (42)

- Have you double-checked the words you frequently misspell and any the spell checker may have missed (for example, misspellings that still form words, such as *form* for *from*)?
- If you used a spell checker, did it overlook homophones (such as *there/their, who's/whose,* and *it's/its*) (42c)?
- Have you double-checked the spelling of all foreign words and all proper names?

2 Punctuation (37–41) and Capitalization (43)

- Does each sentence have appropriate closing punctuation, and have you used only one space after each end punctuation mark (41)?
- Is all punctuation within sentences—commas (37), semicolons (38), apostrophes (39), hyphens (42f), and dashes (41e)—used appropriately and placed correctly?
- Are direct quotations carefully and correctly punctuated (40a)? Where have you placed end punctuation with a quotation (40d)? Are quotations capitalized properly (40a and 43c(1))?
- Are all proper names, people's titles, and titles of published works correctly capitalized (43a and 43b)?
- Are titles of works identified with quotation marks (40b), underlining (13b), or italics (44a)?

4h   The final draft

After producing the second draft reprinted on pages 83–87, Richard continued to edit and polish his essay. In the process, each draft was improved. The essay that Richard ultimately submitted to his teacher follows.

Richard Petraglia

Professor Glenn

English 15

October 20, 2009

Why Take a Foreign Language?

Native English speakers have an advantage when it comes to intercultural communication: English is the language of business, diplomacy, and global communication in general. It is therefore tempting to think that as English speakers we don't need to learn a foreign language because we are likely to find someone who speaks English in any foreign country we visit. This potential advantage of already knowing the language of intercultural communication, however, can prove to be a disadvantage because it makes English speakers less motivated to study other languages. There are many benefits of studying a foreign language that have nothing to do with being able to communicate with people in foreign countries. Students who study a foreign language in school often have better writing skills, reading comprehension, and scores on standardized tests.

Still, the primary reason people often give for wanting to study a foreign language has to do with communicating with people in foreign countries. The straightforward, commonsense answer you'll hear on the first day of elementary German when the instructor asks the students why they want to learn German will inevitably be along the lines of "because I want to be able to communicate with people in their own language" or "because I want to learn more about German culture." And these are, of course, wonderful reasons for studying German (or French or Spanish). Communicating with people in their own language and becoming familiar with other cultures is crucial to opening our minds and increasing our tolerance and understanding, and studying the language of a country

Petraglia 2

you visit will undoubtedly enrich your stay. I have also found that English speakers tend to overestimate how many people actually speak English abroad.

There is, however, another reason for studying a foreign language that I would argue is just as important, but that you'll probably never hear about on the first day of German class. And that is that learning German helps us learn more about English. For me, learning about English has been the most rewarding part of studying foreign languages continuously since middle school. I think that we need to look beyond the idea that all we will learn in a foreign language class is how to speak someone else's language and realize that learning another language has the fortunate side effect of teaching us more about our own.

For example, there is an ongoing debate about just how useful teaching grammar in our schools is in improving student writing. Because students intuitively know how to conjugate English verbs and generally make themselves understood, it can seem pointless and frustrating for them to be taught the minutiae of the language they already speak. The effects aren't immediately apparent or rewarding. But when learning about a foreign language, each time a student learns to say something new, there is a sense of having produced a tangible result. As students learn how to express themselves in a foreign language, they are also indirectly learning those things about their own language's structure. Therefore, learning German grammar improves writing as a side effect because it improves the student's knowledge of similar grammatical structures in English.

While studying a foreign language has many benefits, among the most fundamental is learning more about English and becoming a better writer. Learning a foreign language allows students to see English from a different perspective and enables them to understand the grammatical structures of their language that they often take for granted. Gaining a better understanding of their own language through studying the language of another country helps them to understand the subtle changes of meaning that happen with changes of grammar. This understanding of the subtleties of grammar allows the student to have a more varied, precise, and effective use of his or her own language in both speaking and writing.

There are also statistics that show that students who pursue several years of foreign languages in high school tend to score higher on standardized tests. I think it will be interesting to examine what produces these results. You could say that in general, more highly motivated students will be the ones who pursue an elective like Spanish or French all four years and that language study is just a characteristic of the more motivated students who will score higher on standardized tests anyway. But it really has to do with the way studying a foreign language builds awareness of our own language. Studying a foreign language improves reading comprehension because it gets students to think about how ideas are expressed through language and allows students to understand the complex use of language in any text more precisely. Once a student has more awareness of how ideas are expressed through language, he or she can more easily grasp the idea a writer is trying to convey.

Studying a foreign language also makes students better learners because it teaches them to learn in a combination of ways. First, students practice learning intuitively, using the knowledge of their native language to make educated guesses about the way the foreign language will work. In conjunction with this intuitive method, foreign language learning develops the students' ability to follow complex rules. A different language often expresses ideas in a different way than in English, using unfamiliar grammatical rules and structures. The students are therefore forced to rely on their knowledge of complex grammatical rules to express ideas in a foreign language. Because learning a foreign language teaches students to learn in a combination of both the intuitive and rule-based methods, it makes them better learners in general. A student can carry this knowledge of being able to apply complex rules as well as the ability to learn intuitively to any other discipline.

Exercise 4

Compare the three versions of "Why Take a Foreign Language?" reprinted in this chapter, and write a two-paragraph summary describing how Richard revised and edited his work. If he had shown his final draft to you, asking for your advice before submitting it for a grade, what would you have told him? Write a one-paragraph response to his draft.

5 Planning for Academic Success

You will not always have the luxury of planning, drafting, revising, getting feedback on, and editing a piece of writing over a stretch of days or weeks. Frequently, a college instructor or an employer will ask you to produce an essay or a report during a class period or within a day or two. Sometimes, the need for a timely response to current events or disasters can give rise to an unscheduled writing assignment (a quickly prepared report, proposal, or analysis).

No matter what their timeline, most writers feel some pressure. But when they are asked to write quickly or on demand, that pressure intensifies. The focus of this chapter is how to write well when faced with time constraints, especially when you feel as though you have only one shot at success. This chapter will help you

- ease the pressures of academic reading and writing (5a),
- take advantage of academic support services (5b),
- manage deadlines (5c),
- abbreviate the writing process (5d), and
- plan for essay examinations (5e).

The key to academic success is to use the available time as efficiently as possible.

5a   Easing the pressures of academic reading and writing

Successful college students develop an understanding of the rhetorical situation of every class by carefully reading every course syllabus and assignment sheet—written texts that establish student rights and responsibilities.

(1) The syllabus states course requirements and the plan for meeting them.

On the first day of class, an instructor usually passes out a **syllabus,** a concise description of the course, which includes the readings, due dates, and sometimes the assignment sheets. You will want to become familiar with the syllabus, reading it carefully as you prepare for each class meeting and every assignment.

CHECKLIST for Reading a Syllabus

- Note your instructor's name, office number, and office hours. See whether your instructor has included an e-mail address and indicated any preferred method for getting in touch with her or him outside of class.

- Note the texts required for the course. Editions of textbooks change often, so be sure you purchase the correct one.

- Look closely at what the syllabus says about assignments. How much reading and writing does the course require? When are assignments due? Are there penalties for turning in papers late? Are there opportunities for revision?

- When are exams scheduled (5e)? If there are quizzes, will they be announced in advance?

- Does the syllabus indicate that some assignments will be given more weight than others? If not, how will your final grade be determined?

- Does the syllabus indicate an attendance policy? Are there penalties for missing class or being late?

- Will there be a Web site or other online component (such as a course management system) for the course? If so, how will it be used, and how can you access it?

Many instructors post their syllabi on Web sites created for their courses. An electronic syllabus is easier for the instructor to modify once the course gains momentum. Be sure to review a course's electronic syllabus from time to time, or, if your instructor uses a print syllabus, keep track of any changes. Every course Web site is different, but there are basic guidelines to follow.

Coding for Corporate Survival
IST 301 & ENGL 202C

- -
Next Class Meeting: JanuaryEleven

CourseRoster - CodingSchedule - SyllaBus - DueDates - GroupFormations - WakkaFormatting - DiscussionPapers - SemesterLongProject - ProjectTopics - TwoExams - SoYouThinkYouCanWriteaFinalExam? - LogoContest -
- -

Web sites, such as this one constructed by instructor Jeff Pruchnic, have become a common source of course information—about everything from reading and writing assignments to recommendations for outside reading and study-group times.

CHECKLIST for Using a Course Web Site

- Access the course Web site immediately to find out which Web browser properly displays the site, including its specific links and other elements, and whether your Internet connection works quickly enough. See your instructor if you have any problems.

- Learn whether the course Web site contains information and resources that are not included on the syllabus. If an instructor briefly describes a writing assignment on the syllabus but includes extensive guide-lines and deadlines only on the course Web site, it is vital that you have easy access to and the ability to navigate that site.

- Check the links on the course Web site. There may be a link to a Web-based newsgroup for the course or to a required reading. It is essential that such links work properly on your browser.

(2) Reading assignments rhetorically is essential to academic success.

Instructors write out assignments so that they receive the kind of writing they want to read; therefore, you will want to respond to each assignment exactly as directed in terms of length, focus, format, and purpose. Do not risk misunderstanding an assignment because you read it too quickly. Rather, read every assignment carefully, and concentrate on doing what your instructor has asked you to do. Ask questions if you have any uncertainty about what is expected.

Whether you are asked to submit an essay, an argument, a research paper, or another form of writing, you have a better chance of completing your project successfully if you read the assignment sheet with the following concerns in mind.

Discussion Papers

The discussion paper should both prepare students for solving problems in class and lead to better problem results. To quickly apply knowledge from the readings while working on the problems in class, students need to have synthesized the material for it to serve as an effective resource.

Instructions

1. Read the assigned question.

2. Read each article with the question in mind, and prepare a summary of each (for yourself, not to hand in).

3. Compare the summaries and identify how each article relates to the question.

4. Develop a thesis that is related to the question (this will often narrow the scope of the question).

5. Write a 600-700 word (about one single spaced page) response and post it to the wiki. This response should explain your thesis (in three sentences or less) and support this thesis primarily with evidence from the readings as well as, if appropriate, personal experiences or knowledge gained from other classes.

Grading

Clear thesis statement (two points)
Effective application of assigned reading(s) (two points)
Organization and arrangement (two points)

Assignment sheets, such as this one created by Jeff Pruchnic, provide information that is crucial for successfully fulfilling instructors' requirements. Note that this sheet includes information on how the assignment will be evaluated.

CHECKLIST for Reading an Assignment Sheet

- What does this assignment require you to do? Does the assignment include any subject, formatting, or length restrictions? Are there guidelines for making choices?

- Have purpose, audience, context, and exigence been supplied for you, or will you choose these components of your assignment?

- What strengths can you bring to this assignment? What do you still need to learn if you are going to complete this assignment successfully?

- How much time should you devote to this assignment? When should you get started?

- How might a visit to the writing center help you (5b(2))?

- Are you expected to submit all of your process writing along with your final copy?

5b   Taking advantage of academic support opportunities

One of the biggest advantages of studying at a college or university is the availability of academic support services and trained personnel. All students inevitably need academic support at some point in their college careers. Too often, though, students do not get the help they need because they do not know what resources are available, where those resources are located, and—most important—how to use them for their own benefit. Successful students seek out the multiple means of support offered on their campus.

(1) Your instructor can clarify course assignments and requirements.
Your instructor should be able to help you with most of your course-related questions, whether they concern a reading assignment, the due date for an essay, or a concept essential to the subject matter. Although you can get answers or clarifications for most of your questions either in class or immediately afterward, you are likely to get more time and attention when you visit your instructor during office hours. The checklist that follows includes tips for making your office visit a productive one.

In addition to conferring with instructors in their offices, you may also be able to consult with them by e-mail or through a Web site created especially for a class. The course syllabus may include an e-mail (or other online) address as well as a policy about communicating online. If not, ask whether such communication is possible and under what circumstances it would be appropriate. Most instructors are happy to answer short questions online; however, questions needing longer answers probably merit an office visit.

CHECKLIST for Getting Help from Your Instructor

- Learn the instructor's office hours and the location of his or her office.
- Make an appointment during office hours, and then appear on time. Before the visit, write out your questions and concerns. What do you need to take away with you for the meeting to be productive?
- If you are planning to discuss a specific reading or writing assignment, bring a copy of it to the meeting.
- Tell your instructor what information or help you need.
- Once you have clearly stated your questions and concerns, pay close attention to the answers you receive, writing them down if necessary. Do not hesitate to return.

(2) Writing centers offer help from tutors.

Regardless of their major, many successful college writers benefit from visits to their school's writing center, where they can discuss their work in progress with fellow students who are trained to assist them with their writing. Because writing tutors usually represent many majors, they bring to their work a wide range of writing experiences from virtually all disciplines. Your school most likely has a writing center where this kind of student-to-student consultation regularly takes place. The writing center probably maintains a Web site where you can get information about services, hours of operation, and additional resources for writing. Students who visit a writing center are demonstrating their commitment to writing well and to reaching their own writing goals. They do not expect tutors to write or correct an essay for them.

TIPS FOR VISITING A WRITING CENTER

- Learn when the center is open, whether you can drop in or need to make an appointment, and how long tutoring sessions last.

- If you are working on a specific assignment, bring with you your assignment sheet and whatever you have already written, whether notes, an outline, or a draft.

- Be prepared to explain your understanding of the assignment to your tutor and to indicate the specific kind of help you need. If you bring along the instructor's comments or previously graded assignments, the tutor can use specific information from them to help you.

- Some students find that they benefit from a visit early in the writing process, after they have written a detailed outline or an initial draft. Others find that they benefit more toward the end of the process, during revision and before they are ready to edit and proofread.

- Recognize that tutors are ready to help you with your *writing;* rarely will they serve as proofreaders or editors. In fact, they may ask you to read aloud what you have written so that *you* can catch your own surface errors and organizational weaknesses. For this reason, you will want to visit the center at least a day or two before your assignment is actually due.

- If you have a good session with a tutor, learn his or her name so that you can develop a working relationship. Many writing centers encourage weekly meetings with the same tutor so that writer and tutor can develop a collaborative learning relationship.

- If you have a frustrating experience with a tutor, ask for someone else on your next visit. (Do not judge the entire staff by a single bad experience.)

5c Managing deadlines

You will almost always be working with deadlines—whether for essays, business plans, grant proposals, or other time-sensitive documents. Preparing ahead of time always helps. Even though an in-class essay exam may not be scheduled until midterm, start preparing on the first day of class. As you read your assignments and participate in class discussions, try

to determine what your instructor considers most important about the material you are learning. Whenever an instructor gives you instructions, ask questions until you know exactly what is expected of you.

The best preparation for a writing assignment with a longer deadline, such as a research paper, is to start early. If you are choosing your own topic, begin as soon as you can to narrow down your ideas (3b). The sooner you identify a subject, the sooner you can discuss it with your instructor. You can make deadlines work for you by establishing your own timeline. For an important project, you might even set yourself intermediate deadlines for writing an introduction with a thesis statement, composing a first draft, meeting with a classmate for review, revising your draft, and editing. If you carry a small notebook or handheld computer with you, you will always have a place to jot down notes and ideas.

5d   Abbreviating the writing process

Students and employees are often expected to write well with little notice. When faced with a short deadline, try to narrow the topic to a manageable scope or to relate the assignment to your academic or work experiences or personal knowledge. If you give your topic a sharp focus, you can write a thoughtful, in-depth analysis, rather than skimming the surface of a broader topic. Once you have a focused topic, organize your ideas. The following tips will help you abbreviate the writing process.

TIPS FOR ABBREVIATING THE WRITING PROCESS

- Generate ideas about the assignment or topic with a friend or colleague who is facing or has faced the same kind of deadline. That person can help you clarify your line of reasoning and develop counterarguments. Take notes.

- Draft an introductory paragraph that frames your position or approach and includes a clear thesis statement. E-mail your paragraph to your instructor, your supervisor, a classmate, or a colleague to make sure that you are on the right track.

- If your thesis statement and basic approach are on track, write down your main points; then flesh them out with examples and supporting text until you have a first draft.

- Read your draft aloud, slowly. Make sure that your topic sentences are clear. Reading aloud will help you locate passages that need transitional words or phrases to help your reader along.

- Write a conclusion that reiterates your main points and suggests their implications, the directions in which they point.

- Read over your text to make sure that it fulfills the assignment. Reread your introduction and conclusion to see whether they frame your piece. Examine your topic sentences and supporting paragraphs to make sure that they help you fulfill your purpose and are appropriate for your audience.

- Proofread one last time. Submit your work on time.

TECH SAVVY

You can use your computer to help you manage writing tasks efficiently.

- If you do not have much time for revising and editing, you can use the grammar checker and spell checker of your word-processing program to help you proofread, even while you are drafting.
- Many on-campus writing centers can receive drafts of student writing via e-mail or through a Web site, and writing tutors will often respond to a draft within twenty-four hours. If the writing center on your campus offers such a service, you can use it to get helpful advice on short notice when you have a tight deadline.

5e Taking essay examinations

If your instructor has posed a clear question and provided explicit instructions, you are (almost) home free. Write out your answer, framing it with a thesis statement, main points, and supporting arguments or examples. If a question does not make clear what is called for, ask your instructor for clarification. The steps described in the following sections will help you improve your ability to take essay examinations.

(1) Set up a time schedule.

If the exam has more than one question, figure out how much time to allot to each one. If you are faced with two questions that are worth the same number of points, give half the time to one and half to the other. When certain questions are weighted more heavily than others, however, you need to divide your time accordingly. However you allocate your time, allow ten minutes for final revising and proofreading.

Stick to your time allotment for each question. If you do not finish, leave room to complete your answer later and move on to the next question. Partial answers to *all* questions usually gain you more points than complete answers to only *some* questions. Besides, you can use the ten minutes you saved to put the finishing touches on any incomplete answers, even if you have to draw arrows to the margins or to the back of the page, or if you have to supply rough notes (5e(3)). Your instructor will probably appreciate the extra effort.

(2) Read instructions and questions carefully.

Students who take time to read instructions and questions carefully almost always do better than those who do not. Invest a few minutes in studying each question, putting that question in your own words, and then jotting down a few notes in the margin next to it. If you have been given a choice of questions to answer, choose those that best suit your knowledge yet do not overlap.

Most questions contain specific instructions about how, as well as what, to answer. Be alert for words such as *compare, define,* and *argue,* which identify the writing task and provide specific cues for organizing your response. Other words, such as *discuss* and *explain,* are less specific, so try to determine exactly what it is your instructor wants you to do. When these more general directions appear, be tuned in to such accompanying words as *similar* or *different* (which signal, respectively, a comparison or a contrast), *identify* (which signals a definition or description), and *why* (which signals the need to identify causes). You will also want to be clear about whether you are being asked to call up course-related information from memory or to respond with your own ideas. Words such as *think*, *defend*, and *opinion* signal that you are to frame a thesis and support it.

Most essay exam questions begin with or contain one of the words in the following list and end with a reference to the information you are to discuss. Understanding these terms and framing your answer in response to them will help you focus on what is being asked.

TERMS USED IN ESSAY EXAM QUESTIONS

Compare	Examine the points of similarity (compare) or difference (contrast) between two ideas or things (3g(5)).
Define	State the class to which the item to be defined belongs, and clarify what distinguishes it from the others of that class (3g(6)).
Describe	Use details in a clearly defined order to give the reader a clear mental picture of the item you are being asked to describe (3g(2)).
Discuss	Examine, analyze, evaluate, or state pros and cons. This word gives you wide latitude in addressing the topic and is thus more difficult to work with than some of the others in this set, since you must choose your own focus. It is also the one that, unfortunately, appears most frequently on exam questions.
Evaluate	Appraise the advantages and disadvantages of the idea or thing specified (chapter 8).
Explain	Clarify and interpret (3g(3)), reconcile differences, or state causes (3g(4)).
Illustrate	Offer concrete examples, or, if possible, create figures, charts, or tables that provide information about the item.
Summarize	State the main points in a condensed form; omit details, and curtail examples.
Trace	Narrate a sequence of events that show progress toward a goal or comprise a process (3g(1) and 3g(3)).

(3) Decide how to organize your response.

Even under time constraints, you should be able to draft a rough outline or jot down a few phrases for an informal list (3d). Identify your thesis. Then list the most important points you plan to cover. You might decide to rearrange ideas later, but the first step is to get some down on paper.

Before you begin to write the answer, quickly review the list, deleting any irrelevant or unimportant points and adding any better ones that come to you (keeping in mind how much time you have allotted to the specific question). Number the points in a logical sequence determined by chronology (reporting events in the order in which they occurred), by causation (showing how one event led to another), or by order of importance (moving from the most important point to the least important). Although arranging points in order of increasing importance is often effective, it can be risky in an exam situation because you might run out of time and not get to your most important point.

Following is a thesis statement and a list of supporting points that biology major Trish Parsons quickly composed and edited during the first few minutes of an essay exam. Trish was responding to the following question: "Discuss whether the term 'junk DNA' is an appropriate name for the nucleic DNA that does not code for proteins."

THESIS: The term "junk" applied to DNA with no apparent purpose is a misnomer; there are many possible purposes, both past and present, for the allegedly "junk" DNA.

1a.

1b. Though junk DNA sequences do not code for specific proteins, they may play an important role in DNA regulation. ⟶ go to point #5

2. Microbiology technology has had many amazing advances since the discovery of DNA. ~~Indeed,~~ DNA itself was not immediately recognized as the "plan for life." Further technological advances that are sure to come may find a definite purpose for "junk" DNA.

3. Junk DNA may have coded for proteins in our evolutionary past and a mechanism for disposing of it ~~never has~~ yet to evolve ~~evolved~~.

4. During DNA replication, the possibilities for mistakes are endless. The junk (filler) DNA decreases the chances of the more important, protein-coding DNA being mutated during this process.

5. Junk DNA may yet play an important role in the new field of eugenics, where it has been found that certain traits are heritable, but not directly coded for (possible relation to DNA regulation role in point # 1)

1a Many terms have been applied in genetics that end up creating confusion because scientists came to conclusions too quickly — e.g., dominant and recessive alleles are too simplistic. b/c genetics is a relatively new field we have only recently begun to understand. (BEGIN WITH THIS ONE)

Sometimes, the language of the question will tell you how you should organize your answer. Consider this example:

> Discuss how the two-party political system of the United States influenced the outcome of the last presidential election.

At first glance, this exam question might seem to state the topic without indicating how to organize a discussion of it. *To influence*, however, is to be responsible for certain consequences. In this case, the two-party political system is a cause, and you are being asked to identify its effects (3g(4)). Once you have recognized the meaning of *influence*, you might decide to discuss different effects in different paragraphs.

Here is another example:

> Consider Picasso's treatment of the human body early and late in his career. How did his concept of bodily form persist throughout his career? How did it change?

The reference to two different points in the artist's career, along with the words *persist* and *change*, indicates that your task is to compare and contrast. You could organize your response to this question by discussing Picasso's concept of the bodily form when his paintings were realistic and when they were cubist—preferably covering the same points in the same order in each part of the response. Or you could begin by establishing similarities and then move on to discuss differences. There is almost always more than one way to organize a thoughtful response. Devoting at least a few minutes to organizing your answer can help you better demonstrate what you know.

(4) State your main points clearly.

If you state your main points clearly, your instructor will see how well you have understood the course material. Make your main points stand out from the rest of the answer to an exam question by identifying them. For instance, you can make a main point be the first sentence of each paragraph. Or you can use transitional words such as *first, second,* and *third.* You might even create headings to separate your points. By the time you have outlined your essay exam answer, you should know which points you want to highlight, even if the points change slightly as you begin writing. Use your conclusion to summarize your main points. If you tend to make points that differ from those you had in mind when you started, try leaving space for an introduction at the beginning of the answer and then writing it after you have written the rest. Or simply draw a line pointing into the margin (or to the other side of the paper), and write the introduction there.

(5) Stick to the question.

Always answer each essay exam question as precisely and directly as you can, perhaps using some of the instructor's language in your thesis statement. If your thesis statement implies an organizational plan, follow that plan as closely as possible. If you move away from your original thesis because better ideas occur to you as you write, simply go back and revise your thesis statement (3c). If you find yourself drifting into irrelevance, stop and draw a line through that material.

If you find yourself facing a vague or truly confusing question, construct a clear(er) question and then answer it. Rewriting the instructor's question can seem like a risky thing to do, but figuring out a reasonable question that is related to what the instructor has written is actually a responsible move if you can answer the question you have posed.

(6) Revise and proofread each answer.

Save a few minutes to reread each answer. Make whatever deletions and corrections you think are necessary. If time allows, ask yourself if there is anything you have left out that you can still manage to include (even if you have to write in the margins or on the back of the page). Unless you are certain that your instructor values neatness more than knowledge, do not hesitate to make additions and corrections. Simply draw a caret ($\wedge$), marking the exact place in the text where you want an addition or correction to be placed. Making corrections will allow you to focus on improving what you have already written, whereas recopying your answer just to make it look neat is an inefficient use of time (and you may have recopied only half your essay when the time is up). Finally, check spelling, punctuation, and sentence structure.

6   Online Writing

Word-processing software makes it easy to capture and arrange ideas for writing, plan a writing task, compose, revise, edit, proofread, and produce professional-looking documents. In addition to word-processing capabilities, computers offer you the opportunity to communicate with a wider, often global, audience when you compose for Web sites and other online forums, such as chat rooms, listservs, and blogs.

Online writing is often **interactive** (that is, a writer is linked to other writers, and a document is linked to other documents), dramatically expanding your work's audience and context. Because composing in this medium differs somewhat from writing essays or research papers delivered in hard copy, it calls for different skills—many of which you already have. This chapter will help you

- assess the rhetorical situation for online writing (6a),
- participate in online discussions (6b),
- understand conventions for electronic communication (6c),
- compose effective Web documents (6d), and
- manage the visual elements of a Web site (6e).

6a   Assessing the online rhetorical situation

Whenever you compose material for a Web page, engage in an online discussion forum, or post updates on a blog, you are using rhetoric, or purposeful language, to influence the outcome of your interaction (1a). You are responding to a rhetorical situation, but your response can differ markedly from one you offer in a static, print medium.

Because the Web gives you access to so many different audiences, the unique nature of the online rhetorical situation becomes instantly evident when you begin composing for a Web site or a newsgroup posting. If you are constructing a Web page for a course assignment, your primary audience is probably your instructor and classmates. But as soon as you put your composition online, you open up your work to a variety of secondary audiences (1d(3)), whose responses you will also want to consider as you compose.

Keep in mind that primary or secondary audiences for online writing may be specialized, diverse, or multiple (1d). When writing an e-mail to an individual recipient, you have a very narrow audience. When writing a message for a listserv (an e-mail–based discussion forum organized around a particular subject), you are addressing a broader but specialized audience and can assume that its members share an interest in your topic. However, when creating a Web page about an important event or a current controversy, such as the devastation caused by the May 2008 earthquake in China or the debate over genetically modified food, you will write for a diverse audience, whose members have varying levels of knowledge, understanding of specialized terms, and interest in your subject matter.

In response to an online rhetorical situation, specify your purpose clearly, whether you wish to express your point of view, create a mood, or amuse or motivate your audience. For example, the purpose of a Web site such as the one developed by The Green Belt Movement (shown in fig. 6.4 on page 118) is to inform and then motivate the audience to become involved. Because readers may encounter your composition in a number of different ways—by having an e-mail message forwarded to them, by finding your Web page through a search engine, or by entering an online discussion forum—you need to take extra care to clarify your purpose and make it readily apparent.

Composing online also requires a greater responsiveness to context than you may be used to, given your experience with conventional academic writing projects (1e). Within the rhetorical situation of online composition, the boundary between writer and audience is often blurred, because participants are writing and responding simultaneously. In addition, the accessibility of online discussion communities (6b) encourages many people to add to or comment on compositions. This flow of new material contributes to an always evolving rhetorical situation, requiring you to be familiar with the preceding discussion and to understand the conventions of the forum in order to compose effectively.

In addition, many Internet users have come to expect online compositions to be especially timely, given the relative ease of updating an electronic document compared to a print-based publication. For example, a Web page about the effects of earthquakes produced just after the one in China in May 2008 would surely differ from one produced before that date. In order for such a document to be current, it would have to include continuous updates of the death count, the numbers of displaced people, and the effects of the aftershock, which included disastrous flooding.

6b   Participating in online discussion communities

Participating in online communities is a good way to learn more about topics that interest you, to network with friends and classmates, and to develop your writing skills. However, just as you evaluate information in print sources (chapter 10), you need to evaluate the information and advice you get from these online sources. There are two main types of online discussion groups: asynchronous forums and synchronous forums.

(1) Asynchronous forums allow easy access, regardless of time and place.

Some examples of asynchronous forums are blogs, listservs, and bulletin boards. A **blog** (from the phrase *Web log*) is a Web site that is part online journal and part discussion forum; a blog allows users to post their responses to its creator's opinions and usually maintains archives of past postings. Blogs cover a wide variety of topics: some serve as little more than personal journals, but others record responses to news, post advice, or collect information about a specific topic. Increasingly, print publications such as the *Columbia Journalism Review* are including blogs as part of their online presence, encouraging readers to respond to news via comments (fig. 6.1). A **listserv** is an e-mail–based discussion forum organized around a specific subject, such as short story writing, American history, or computer gaming, and distributed from a central e-mail address to everyone who has subscribed to the forum. Many listservs archive messages (as well as photographs, links, calendars, and membership lists), giving you the option of reading that information on a Web site rather than in your e-mail. A **bulletin board** (sometimes

Fig. 6.1. Some bloggers update their blogs daily, adding text and visuals.

called a **newsgroup**) keeps messages on a server, organized by topic (or **thread**) so that users can search for, read, and respond to messages concerning particular features of the subject covered by the group (fig. 6.2). Some universities use courseware (such as BlackBoard or WebCT) that includes separate bulletin boards for each class offered to students.

The delay between posting and viewing contributions to an asynchronous forum often leads to thoughtful discussions because it emphasizes the importance of *responding* to the existing rhetorical situation. Before joining a listserv or responding to a blog, you might want to **lurk,** that is, remain anonymous while you read previous and current postings to understand the various topics of discussion and the histories of the different "conversations." When you have a good sense of the rhetorical situation, you can add your own comments to an existing thread or start a new one—always keeping in mind the information and overall tone in the messages posted by other users.

(2) Synchronous forums allow discussion in real time.
Synchronous forums, provided by chat rooms, electronic meeting software, and instant-messaging programs, allow users to view text (and any

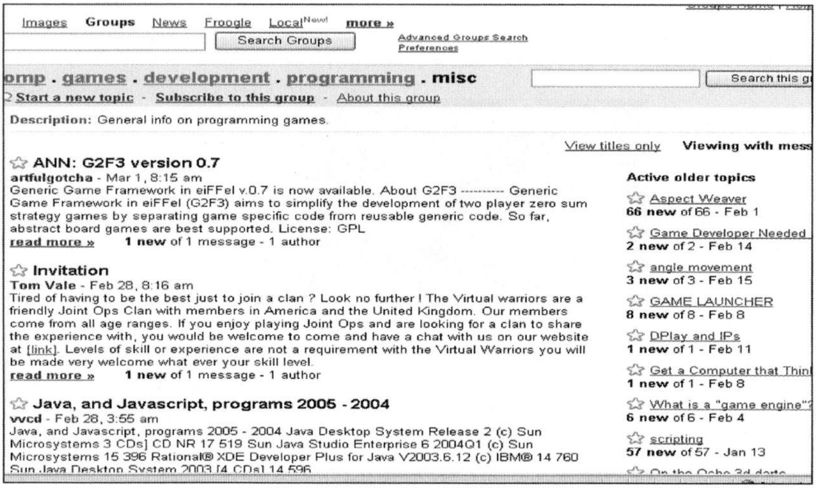

Fig. 6.2. A bulletin board allows participants to access and contribute to an online discussion at any time.

multimedia elements) in real time—that is, as it is being posted—and to respond immediately. Such discussions resemble face-to-face interactions. Their content may or may not be archived, depending on their formality and the technology used to communicate.

Synchronous discussion groups offer a convenient way for people who are in different physical locations to interact. In business, for example, a project team in New York City can "meet" with members of another team in Los Angeles by using a program such as NetMeeting. Academic courseware programs often host synchronous discussion forums that supplement class meetings or allow instructors to hold classes exclusively online. Offering not only a text-based environment but also voice and video capability, synchronous forums have the advantages of immediacy and a sense of physical presence.

Engaging in real-time online discussion can be disconcerting initially. Several different threads are usually being explored simultaneously, and it can take time to get used to having all the comments from current participants appear on your screen as though they were part of a single conversation (see fig. 6.3). Successful participation in a synchronous forum entails concentrating on who is participating and which thread

```
ses963psu (8:32:24 PM): 🖼
rhosarhetor (8:32:26 PM): ahem
rhosarhetor (8:32:38 PM): in any case, we have a list of several "issues" for
  sloop.
rhosarhetor (8:32:39 PM): mo?
raenalynn (8:32:40 PM): How does Signdefwegwqrhgwethwrty having problems with comptr
rhosarhetor (8:32:48 PM): i'd say
sallysarahfl (8:33:02 PM): these conversations move so quickly, quicker than i think!
rhosarhetor (8:33:06 PM): what an image i have in my mind: of both of you falling
  off your chairs!
ses963psu (8:33:09 PM): btw, i couldn't find the this american life show reference i heard! damn.
raenalynn (8:33:12 PM): yea for me too.
xkaren08 (8:33:20 PM): speaking of KB
rhosarhetor (8:33:29 PM): we can keep looking. in our spare time.
ses963psu (8:33:31 PM): they move fast and are fun...and fun and theory isn't bad
rhosarhetor (8:33:41 PM): fun isn't bad theory
xkaren08 (8:33:52 PM): what were you thinking we should focus on in RoM?
rhosarhetor (8:34:27 PM): the reason i thought of faigley earlier -- FRAGMENTS OF
  RATIONALITY -- is that he does a solid foucaudian and althusserian
  thing with this kind of mediated comm. it's vvvv early ... and kinda
  wrong. but it was powerful at the time
pplwhoh8snowcanstudyinfl (8:34:44 PM): The *speed* doesn't annoy me as much as the plurality of conversations--we can be
  discussing more than one thing at a time and I have to do investigative work to figure out which comments go with which
  conversations
```

Fig. 6.3. Comments from participants in an instant-messaging discussion appear in different colors, which helps to distinguish them.

each participant is pursuing at the point you enter the discussion. Given the speed of these discussions, convention dictates that comments be short and to the point, much more so than for newsgroups or listservs. Successful users join the discussions judiciously, taking care not to overwhelm other participants with too many messages or unannounced changes of the subject under discussion.

Both asynchronous and synchronous forums are used by a variety of online communities—social groups, scholarly or special-interest groups, and business groups. Both kinds of forums can also be used for course-related online discussions, as extensions of the classroom discourse. But remember that when you work, volunteer, or take classes with the other people in an online group, your rhetorical situation is somewhat different from that for online interactions with groups of strangers. You may want to lurk for a while so that you can learn the conventions of an unfamiliar online forum. Always remain aware that friends, teachers, and potential employers can easily access much of your online writing, even writing that appears on social sites such as Facebook and MySpace.

Exercise 1

Find an online discussion forum or a blog devoted to a subject you are currently interested in or researching. Lurk for a few days to a week. Then, introduce yourself to the members of the group, and ask a question or post a comment related to one of the topics they have been discussing. After reading responses to your posting, write a paragraph describing the experience.

6c Netiquette and online writing

Netiquette (from the phrase *Internet etiquette*) is a set of social practices that was developed by Internet users in order to regulate online language and manners. The most fundamental requirement of online etiquette is to convey respect.

TIPS FOR NETIQUETTE IN ONLINE DISCUSSION FORUMS

Audience

- Keep in mind the potential audience(s) for your message: those for whom it is intended and others who may read it.
- Make the subject line of your message as descriptive as possible so that your reader(s) will immediately recognize the topic.
- Keep your message focused and limit it to one screen, if possible. The reader's time and bandwidth may be limited, so delete anything that is not essential when posting or replying.
- Give people adequate time to respond.
- Consider the content of your posting, making sure that it pertains to the interests of a specific forum's audience.
- Respect copyright. Never post something written by someone else or pass it off as your own.

Style and Presentation

- Take care to establish a tone appropriate for your message and your audience.

- Be sure of your facts.
- Present ideas clearly and logically.
- Pay attention to spelling and grammar.
- Use emoticons (such as :>)) and abbreviations (such as IMHO for "in my humble opinion") only when you are sure your audience will understand them and find them appropriate.
- Use all capital letters only when you want to be perceived as SHOUTING.
- Abusive or profane language is never appropriate.

Context

- Observe what others say and how they say it before you engage in an online discussion; note what kind of information participants find appropriate to exchange.
- If someone is abusive, ignore that person or change the subject. Do not participate in **flaming** (online personal attacks).
- Understand that sarcasm and irony may appear to be personal attacks.
- Do not use your school's or employer's network for personal business.

Credibility

- Use either your real name or an appropriate online pseudonym to identify yourself to readers. Avoid suggestive or inflammatory pseudonyms.
- Be respectful of others even when you disagree, and be kind to new members of an online community.

6d Composing Web documents

The Web offers you the chance to communicate to many different audiences for a variety of purposes. More than an electronic library for information and research, the Web is also a kind of global marketplace, allowing people all over the world to exchange ideas. For example, the home page of The Green Belt Movement (fig. 6.4) presents to an international audience themes that are conveyed throughout the Web site, emphasizing the group's values and mission. The text on the page is designed to appeal to a diverse audience, from environmental activists to people interested in international development to conservationists

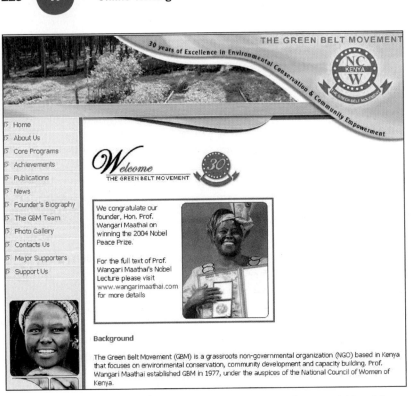

Fig. 6.4. The home page for The Green Belt Movement highlights the activities of the founder, Wangari Maathai, and emphasizes the group's values and focus: volunteerism, environmental conservation, accountability, and empowerment.

planning to start their own grass-roots organizations. Even though the group is based in Kenya, its Web site strives for international appeal by highlighting the founder's Nobel Peace Prize, offering multiple ways of contacting the organization, and providing the option of making an online donation in various currencies.

The home page of The Green Belt Movement introduces eleven main topics—from "About Us" to "Support Us"—each of which is the subject of a separate Web page. The **arrangement** (the pattern of organization of the ideas, text, and visual elements in a composition) of the site is clear. The site is thus easy to use: every page maintains the list of main topics in a navigation bar on the left. Arrangement also involves the balance of visual elements and text. The home page is unified by the use of several shades of green for the background, links, and headings, and the entire site is given coherence by the appearance of the organization's logo in the upper-right corner of every page. Finally, the trees shown in the bar that runs across the top of the home page create a visual link to one of The Green Belt Movement's key activities: planting trees as a means of fostering environmental consciousness and concern for the local environment. That visual link combines arrangement and **delivery** (the presentation and interaction of visual elements with content). Your intentions for your Web documents may well be more modest than those of The Green Belt Movement. Nevertheless, you will want to remember that Web sites (and other online compositions) are available to diverse audiences, and so their composition should be given as much forethought as possible in terms of context, purpose, and message (1a). Because of the flexible nature of electronic composition, you can have fun planning, drafting, and revising your Web documents.

(1) Effective Web documents take advantage of the unique features of electronic composition.

When you plan and compose a Web page or site, you will likely organize your material in a less linear arrangement than you use for print documents. However, you can create consistency, as well as help orient users, by placing design elements (such as logos and color) carefully and by including links to the home page on all other pages of the Web site.

The visual elements included on a Web page or site create important associations among the concepts and ideas that underlie your online composition. For instance, the central image on The Green Belt Movement's home page (fig. 6.4) is a photo of the organization's founder, which immediately creates an association for users who already know about Professor Maathai as well as connecting the organization to African women more generally.

A true electronic document contains **hypertext,** which includes links to other online text, graphics, and animations, as an integral part of its arrangement and content. That is, such a document is created and delivered with text, graphics, and animations integrated into its content. You are probably accustomed to navigating Web sites by clicking on hyperlinks, one of the distinguishing features of online documents. However, you may not have thought about how valuable hyperlinks can be as tools for Web site development. Of course, print documents converted for use on the Web often have hyperlinks (as well as text and images (7f–j)), but because they were not originally created with online capabilities in mind, these documents are not truly hypertextual.

Hypertext is rhetorically important because it allows users to customize their approach to a Web document. As you work to create an effective Web document, you need to consider the influences of hypertext on the use of that document. Basically, the inclusion of hyperlinks transfers control over the sequence of information from you (the writer) to your audience (the user). In other words, Web documents offer unlimited options for ordering the content, as users may click on links in any order they choose. Clearly, the individual interests and personalities of those who read your Web document will lead them to navigate it in different ways. Therefore, you will want to consider how users' different approaches may affect the intended purpose of your document and try to arrange your document accordingly.

Some basic principles can help you use hyperlinks effectively in your Web documents.

(a) Hyperlinks enhance the coherence of a Web document.

The choice and placement of hyperlinks should be a vital part of your organizational plan. Considering the ways in which users can exploit these links is an important part of your rhetorical strategy, leading you to use the links purposefully to connect related ideas and to provide additional information. A site map is essential for a large site and helpful for a compact one. Refer again to the home page for The Green Belt Movement (fig. 6.4). Notice that the main sections of the site are featured as a list of links in the navigation bar that appears along the left side of the home page. A link to a relevant external site—Wangari Maathai's professional Web site—appears within the text. Hyperlinks to the individual pages of a Web site provide transitions based on key words or ideas or logical divisions of the document. Because these links provide coherence and help users navigate your site, they are powerful rhetorical tools that aid you in creating an effective arrangement.

(b) Hyperlinks can be textual or graphical, linking to internal or external material.

You can use individual words, phrases, or even sentences as textual hyperlinks. Hyperlinks can also be icons or other graphical elements, such as pictures or logos. If you do use graphical links, be sure that their appearance is appropriate for the transitions you are indicating. In addition, you must get permission for text, graphics, or multimedia elements you draw from other sources. Even though such material is often free, its source must be acknowledged (11e).

Internal hyperlinks are those that take the user between pages or sections of the Web site in which they appear. When choosing hyperlinks that take the user to content *external* to your Web site (such as a hyperlink in a Web page about hurricanes that links to a meteorologist's Web site), be sure to select sites containing relevant, accurate, and well-presented information. You should also use any contact information provided on a site to request permission to link to it, and you should check your links periodically to be sure that they are still active.

(c) Hyperlinks have rhetorical impact.

Textual and graphical links establish persuasive rhetorical associations for the user. Compare the rhetorical impact of linking an image of the World Trade Center towers to a page about public memorials with that of linking the same image to a page about global terrorism. Because hyperlinks serve various rhetorical purposes, be sure to evaluate the impact of any you include on your Web document as you plan, compose, and revise it. You will also want to evaluate the rhetorical impact of the hyperlinks on Web documents you are reading or using.

TECH SAVVY

To create a Web page, you do not have to understand the computer code (HTML) that allows a browser to display text. Programs such as FrontPage and Netscape Composer, referred to generally as WYSIWYG (What You See Is What You Get) HTML editors, will do such coding for you automatically. But some writers find that knowledge of the basic HTML commands can be useful for troubleshooting and editing a Web page. A number of tutorials on the use of HTML are available on the Web.

(2) Planning a Web site involves working out an arrangement for presenting ideas.

As you develop a Web document, you need to keep all the elements of the rhetorical situation in mind. Depending on your audience and purpose, you must decide which ideas or information to emphasize and then work out how best to arrange your Web document to achieve that emphasis. While you are generating the textual content, you need to consider the supplementary links that will help you achieve your overall purpose. But you do not have to do everything at once; fine-tuning the visual design can wait until the content is in place.

When you are planning a Web site, you may find it helpful to create a storyboard or other visual representation of the site's organization. You can sketch a plan on a sheet of paper or in a word-processing file if your site is fairly simple, or you can use index cards tacked to a bulletin board if it is more complex. If you have some time to devote to the planning process, you may want to learn how to use software such as Web Studio or FrontPage to help you map out your site (such Web site design programs are often available on computers in school labs).

You can consider three basic arrangement patterns—linear, radial, and hierarchical—when planning your Web site. A linear site (fig. 6.5) is easy to set up. Hierarchical and radial arrangements are more complex to develop and may be better suited to group projects. The hierarchical arrangement (fig. 6.6) branches out at each level, and the radial arrangement (fig. 6.7), in which individual pages can be linked in a variety of sequences, allows the user to determine the sequence in which pages are viewed.

The possibilities for organizing a Web site are endless. The most important consideration is how the arrangement of your site will affect a user's experience in navigating it. However you decide to organize your site, be sure to represent each main element in your plan. A good plan will be invaluable to you as you draft text, incorporate visual and multimedia elements, and refine your arrangement.

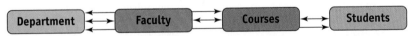

Fig. 6.5. Linear pattern for organizing a Web site.

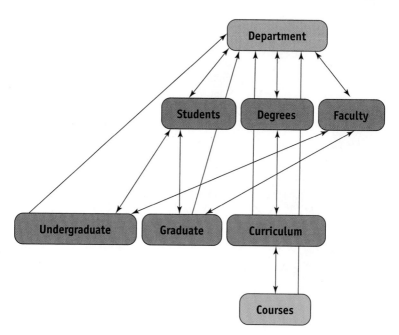

Fig. 6.6. Hierarchical pattern for organizing a Web site.

(3) Drafting Web documents can transform your composing process.

When drafting a Web document, you will undoubtedly consider various ways to organize your material. You may draft text for a linear arrangement and then later break the text into separate sections for different pages, which you link in sequence. At times, however, the arrangement and means of delivery required for an online document will force you to draft in unfamiliar ways. For example, you may find that you need to write the text for a Web site in chunks, drafting the text for a single page, including hyperlinks, and then moving on to the next page. Or you might wait until you revise your site to add hyperlinks or to replace some of your initial text links with graphical ones.

Once you have drafted and revised your site, get feedback from your classmates or colleagues, just as you would for an essay or a report. Since a Web site can include many pages with multiple links and images, you may want to ask for feedback not only about the content of your site but also about layout, graphics, and navigation (6e).

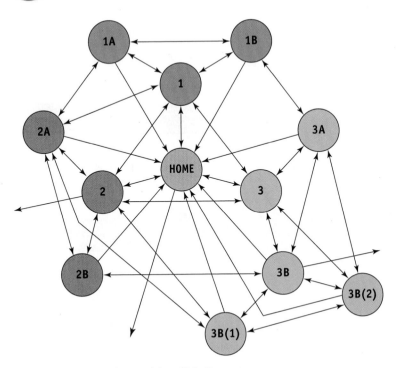

Fig. 6.7. Radial pattern for organizing a Web site.

Professional Web developers often put a site that is still in a draft stage on the Web and solicit reactions from users, a process called **usability testing**. The developers then use those reactions to refine the site. Because Web sites are more interactive than printed texts, it is a good idea to seek input from users during site development. To solicit feedback, specify on your home page how users can contact you. Be careful, though, to consider your own security—you may want to use a free e-mail account through Yahoo! or Hotmail or allow users to post comments directly on your site. Usability testing is particularly important given the wide variety of potential audiences for online documents. Be sure to make your Web document accessible to users who do not have a fast Internet connection or who have physical limitations affecting seeing, hearing, or keyboarding. Consider simplifying the design by using a restricted number of graphical elements, facilitating the downloading of materials by using low-resolution images (which have smaller file sizes), and avoiding animated graphics.

To accommodate users with physical disabilities or different means of accessing Web documents (for example, visually impaired users who employ talking computer programs that read Web pages), incorporate basic accessibility features such as **alt tags** (descriptive lines of text for each visual image that can be read by screen-reading software). Such accommodations will make your Web documents accessible to the greatest number of users.

The following checklist will help you plan a Web site and develop ideas for each page.

CHECKLIST for Planning and Developing a Web Site

- What information or ideas should a user take away from your site?

- How does the arrangement of your site reflect your purpose? How does it assist your intended users in understanding your purpose?

- How would you like a user to navigate your Web site? How might different users navigate within your site?

- Should you devote each page to a single main idea or combine several ideas on one page?

- How will you help users return to the home page and find key information quickly?

- What key connections between ideas or pieces of information might be emphasized through the use of hyperlinks?

- Will a user who follows external links be able to get back to your site?

- To ensure that your Web site has more impact than a paper document, have you used Web-specific resources—such as hyperlinks, sound and video clips, and animations—in creating it? How do those multimedia elements help you achieve your purpose?

- Do you need graphics—charts, photos, cartoons, clip art, logos, and so on—to enhance the site so that it will accomplish your purpose? Where should key visual elements be placed to be most effective?

- How often will you update your site?

- How will you solicit feedback for revisions to your site?

- Will your site be accessible to users with slow Internet access and those with physical limitations?

6e   Visual elements and rhetorical purpose

Visual design sends messages to users: an effective design not only invites them to explore a Web site but also conveys the designer's rhetorical purpose (chapter 7). All the design elements of an online document, like the tone and style of a printed one, are rhetorical tools that help you achieve your purpose and reach your intended audience. For instance, if a user has a negative reaction to a photograph of dead seals on a Web site devoted to protecting wildlife, that reaction is likely to affect the user's view of the site in general. When you choose visual elements such as photographs, try to anticipate how your audience may react.

(1) Adhering to basic design principles makes an online document visually pleasing and easy to navigate.

A number of basic principles apply to the visual design of writing presented on the Web.

- **Balance** involves the way in which design elements used in a document are spatially related to one another. Web pages with a symmetrical arrangement of elements convey a formal, static impression, whereas asymmetrical arrangements are informal and dynamic.
- **Proportion** has to do with the relative sizes of design elements. Large elements attract more attention than small ones and will be perceived as more important.
- **Movement** concerns the way in which our eyes scan a page for information. Most of us look at the upper-left corner of a page first and the lower-right corner last. Therefore, the most important information

on a Web page should appear in those locations. Vertical or horizontal arrangement of elements on a page implies stability; diagonal and zigzagging arrangements suggest movement.

- **Contrast** between elements can be achieved by varying their focus or size. For instance, a Web page about the Siberian Husky might show a photo of one of these dogs in sharp focus against a blurred background; the image of the dog might also be large relative to other elements on the page to enhance contrast. In text, you can emphasize an idea by presenting it in a contrasting font—for example, a playful display font such as Marker Felt Thin or an elegant script font such as Edwardian Script. (Remember, though, that older Web browsers may not display all fonts properly.) An easy-to-read font such as Arial or Helvetica, however, should be used for most of the text on a Web page.
- **Unity** refers to the way all the elements (and pages) of a site combine to give the impression that they are parts of a complete whole. For instance, choose a few colors and fonts to reflect the tone you want to convey, and use them consistently throughout your site. Creating a new design for each page of a Web site makes the site seem chaotic and thus is ineffective.

(2) Color and background play an important rhetorical role in online composition.

Like the other elements of a Web document, color and background are rhetorical tools that can be used to achieve various visual effects. Current Web standards allow the display of a wide array of colors for backgrounds, text, and frames. You can find thousands of background graphics on the Internet or create them with special software.

Designers recommend using no more than three main colors for a document, although you may use varying intensities, or shades, of a color (for example, light blue, dark blue, and medium blue) to connect related materials. Using more than three colors may create confusion on your Web pages. Besides helping to organize your site, color can have other specific effects. Bright colors, such as red and yellow, are more noticeable and can be used on a Web page to emphasize a point or idea. In addition, some colors have associations you may wish to consider. For instance, reds can indicate danger or an emergency, whereas brown shades such as beige and tan suggest a formal atmosphere. Textual hyperlinks usually appear in a color different from that of the surrounding text on a Web page so that they are more visible to users. Also, such links generally appear in one color before they are clicked and change to a different color when a user clicks on them. Select colors for textual hyperlinks that fit in with the overall color scheme of your document and help readers navigate between pages on your site.

Background, too, contributes to a successful Web site. Although a dark background can create a dramatic appearance, it often makes text difficult to read and hyperlinks difficult to see. A dark background can also cause a printout of a Web page to be blank or unreadable. If you do use a dark background, be sure that the color of the text is bright enough to be readable on screen and that you provide a version that will print clearly. Similarly, a background with a pattern can be dramatic but can obscure the content of a Web page or other online document. If you want to use a pattern for your background, check the readability of the text. You may need to change the color of the text or adjust the pattern of the background to make the page easier to read.

Use different background colors or patterns for different pages of your online document only if you have a good rhetorical reason for doing so (as you might, for instance, if you were using a different color for each of several related categories of information). When you do this, adhere closely to the other design principles in **6e(1)** so that your site appears coherent to your audience.

CHECKLIST for Designing an Online Document

- Have you chosen the background and text colors so that users can print copies of your pages if they wish?

- Have you used no more than three colors, but perhaps varied the intensity of one or more of them?

- Does a background pattern on your page make the text difficult or easy to read?

- Have you chosen a single, easy-to-read font such as Arial or Helvetica for most of your text? Are the type styles (bold, italic, and so on) used consistently throughout the document?

- Have you used visual elements sparingly? Are any image files larger than 500K, making it likely that they will take a long time to transfer? If so, can you shrink them by using a lower resolution or a smaller size?

- Have you indicated important points graphically by using bullets or numbers or visually by dividing the text into short blocks?

- Is any page or section crowded? Can users scan the information on a single screen quickly?
- Does each page include adequate white space for easy reading?
- Have you made sure that all links work?
- Have you identified yourself as the author and noted when the site was created or last revised?
- Have you run a spell checker and proofread the site yourself?

7 Composing with Visuals

Much of your education has focused on the production and interpretation of written or spoken words, whether they are words you use in writing or in giving oral presentations or words you interpret as you read or listen to others. In your daily experience, however, you interpret images at least as often as you do words. You decipher striking advertisements on posters and billboards, multicolored flyers papering bulletin boards, bold signs proclaiming campaign slogans, and the heavily illustrated chapters in your biology or psychology textbook.

All of us use visual elements to discern messages every day—even if we are not consciously aware of how we "read" these photos, graphics, and design features. Just as important as understanding how we make sense of visuals is understanding how to compose documents that use visuals in combination with words to communicate information to an intended audience.

In this chapter, you will learn the basic principles of interpreting and composing documents that include both text and images. In other words, you will learn the rhetorical principles of combining visual elements with text, the genres of visual documents, and the conventions of layout—all of which will help you achieve your purpose. More specifically, this chapter will help you

- understand visual documents in terms of the rhetorical situation (7a),
- employ the design principles of visual rhetoric (7b),
- effectively combine visual and verbal elements (7c), and
- identify the common genres and effective design features of visual documents (7d).

7a Visual documents and the rhetorical situation

Exigence, sender, audience, purpose, message, context—the rhetorical elements underlying the interpretation and composition of verbal texts—easily apply to visual documents as well. Therefore, any rhetorical analysis of a visual document (that is, a document that combines verbal and visual elements) takes into consideration the questions raised in chapter 1: To what exigence does the visual document respond? Who is the primary audience? Is there a secondary audience? What is the purpose of the document, and how is it linked to the intended audience? How does the context of this visual document influence the sender's meaning and the viewer's engagement with that meaning?

In this chapter, **visual documents** are documents that combine **visual elements,** such as images or graphics, with verbal text to express meaning or deliver a message to an intended audience. In addition to images and **graphics** (such as diagrams, tables, and photographs), visual elements also include the design and layout features of documents. Whether their purpose is expressive, expository, or argumentative (1c), visual documents represent various genres, ranging from advertisements that appear in glossy magazines to posters, billboards, brochures, newsletters, and Web sites.

Just like the rhetorical analyses you have performed on text documents, analyses of visual documents must always account for the relationship between purpose and audience. Consider, then, the advertisement in fig. 7.1 and the brochure in fig. 7.2, both of which address the topic of global warming. Despite their similar themes, each of these visual documents serves a distinct purpose—and thus employs rhetorical strategies that appeal to different audiences. The ad in fig. 7.1 addresses parents, adults with a wide range of interest in and expertise about the topic of global warming. Even parents who are not concerned about the future of the planet can be depended on to care about the future of their children. To connect with that concern, the ad's designer (the sender) chose a photo of an infant wrapped in a white blanket to make a powerful emotional appeal to an audience of parents, identifying the cause of the organization (reversing global warming) with the interests of the audience (parents). The text, which reads, "Start college fund. Revise will. Undo global warming," highlights the exigence for the ad and heightens the response of the audience. With this appeal to fear and call to action, the designer hopes to persuade potentially disinterested viewers and impel them to "undo global warming" for the sake of their children.

In contrast to the ad in fig. 7.1, the brochure in fig. 7.2 is aimed at readers with a vested interest in the topic—members of a specialized audience who are already predisposed to the message. This audience likely sought out the brochure and shares at least some of the sender's views and opinions about global warming. Therefore, the brochure need only respond to (rather than elicit) the audience's interest. With no need to argue the importance of paying attention to global

Fig. 7.1. The audience for this ad has a wide range of interest in and expertise regarding the topic.

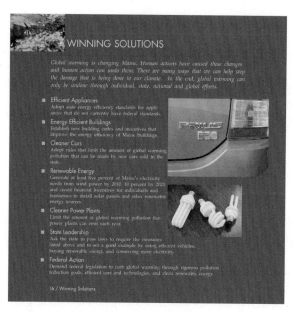

Fig. 7.2. This brochure effectively reaches a specialized audience.

warming, the brochure's designer can concentrate instead on outlining various strategies for slowing its progress. In other words, the purpose of the brochure is not to argue a point but to deliver new information to a specific audience. For both the ad and the brochure, the intended audience and the rhetorical purpose are linked.

As the preceding examples suggest, the rhetorical situation also influences the genre of visual document that is used to deliver a message. The global warming ad contains eight prominent words; the brochure contains several blocks of text. Most posters, billboards, and advertisements contain a small amount of text, allowing the audience to absorb the message visually, with only a brief glance. The ease of access helps these predominantly visual documents reach a large, diverse audience. By contrast, the designer of the global warming brochure has assumed that those in the intended audience will take the brochure with them, allowing them time to read the more extensive text. The greater volume of information in a brochure, as well as the specialized focus, makes this genre particularly appropriate for an educated, already interested audience.

Exercise 1

Select a visual document that has caught your attention. Write for five to ten minutes in response to that document. Then, analyze it in terms of its rhetorical situation and the relationship between words and images. Be prepared to share your document and analysis with the rest of the class.

7b The design principles of visual rhetoric

After considering the context of a visual document as a whole, you can analyze how the various elements work together to create a coherent message. Just as writers organize words into sentences and paragraphs, designers structure the visual elements of their documents in order to achieve coherence, develop ideas, and make a point. When reading verbal texts, for instance, you are accustomed to identifying the main points and supporting evidence in an argument. Furthermore, when asked to write a paper on a difficult academic subject, you likely use headings, sections, and paragraph breaks to give the reader clues to the broader structure of the paper.

Although you have developed skills for presenting academic material in written form, you may be asked to design a visual document as an academic assignment. Presenting complicated material in visual form requires a different set of strategies than those used in writing academic papers. Rather than relying on paragraph breaks and topic sentences, designers of visual documents call on four important principles to organize and develop ideas: alignment, proximity, contrast, and repetition. These four design principles will help you organize complex information, condensing it in a form that is both accessible to your audience and visually appealing. The poster in fig. 7.3, created by an undergraduate student and discussed throughout this section, illustrates how the four design principles can be used to organize detailed information visually.

The Shipwreck Austria:
by Faith Haney

An Historical and Archaeological Investigation on the Olympic Peninsula Pacific Coast

Introduction

The shipwreck Austria is a mid-nineteenth century wooden ship that foundered on Washington's outer coast during a blustery gale in January of 1887. Located on the tumultuous interidal zone of Cape Alava in the Olympic Coast National Marine Sanctuary (OCNMS) and on the Makah Reservation, wreckage remains lie scattered in tidepools and beach sand. Though a brief survey was conducted at the site area in 1997, new mapping techniques utilizing GPS technology will fill a data gap of the mapped locations of shipwreck remains in OCNMS and on the Makah Reservation.

The primary objectives of this study are to identify, map, and interpret the remains of the shipwreck *Austria*. Through a comparative analysis of current remains of the *Austria* to those recorded in an earlier study (Terrell, 2000), the aim is to determine the general degradation and movement of materials over time, as well as provide a GIS data layer to the National Oceanic Atmospheric Administration (NOAA) and the Makah Tribe for use in monitoring the shipwreck. Additionally, a field school is proposed at the site location to gather data, educate up-and-coming heritage resource managers, and compile the data for use in an interactive web-page and public presentation geared towards outreach and education. This inquiry will benefit the scientific community by addressing a research data gap of mapped shipwreck remains, contributing to an understanding of site dynamics, and providing a useful source of information for education and public outreach.

The primary objectives of this study are to identify, map, and interpret the remains of the shipwreck Austria.

Methods

The scope of this study includes three main components: 1) *mapping and documentation of shipwreck remains;* 2) *determination of debris movement over time;* and 3) *development of a webpage and presentation for public outreach and education.* These components share many methods, but also incorporate some unique approaches as well.

Mapping and Documentation
The survey area is approximately 360 meters north/south and 300 meters east/west. For the site recordation and mapping constituent, this study will integrate methods utilized by the National Park Service Submerged Resources Unit, which relies heavily on video to fill in details where mapping or illustration alone does not suffice (Lenihan, 1989), and both the National Marine Sanctuary's Maritime Heritage Program (NMSMHP) and Nautical Archaeological Society (NAS), both of which employ triangulation using a baseline grid (Thompson, n.d.). Since this is a foreshore archaeological site that is exposed at low tides, terrestrial site survey techniques will also be incorporated (Green, 2004). Terrestrial and foreshore survey and mapping techniques include:

1) pedestrian survey at five-meter intervals during low-tide
2) locating and flagging artifacts
3) setting up primary and secondary datums
4) using a GPS, compass, tapes, and rangefinder to record artifact, feature, and landmark locations
5) photographing and video-taping site overviews and artifacts

Determination of Debris Movement and Degradation Over Time
This study will also document the movement of shipwreck materials since the initial site survey in 1997 through comparing artifact locations as they were mapped during that study to the current locations of the artifacts, based on the previous datum (Terrell, 2000). Data from both surveys will be incorporated onto GIS data layers and then compared.

Public Outreach and Education
Video and photographic documentation of the site and associated artifacts will be incorporated into a webpage on the OCNMS website and a presentation will be offered to the public. The webpage is planned to be an interactive exploration of the shipwreck *Austria*, where the site visitor can click on various "hot spots" on a map of the wreck and see what the artifacts or features look like (either in a photographic image or small video clip) and view an historical account of the item. Field school participants will be responsible to perform research and documentation in order to contribute slides or video clips to a collaborative presentation.

Expected Results & Conclusion

Through this research, a useful GIS data layer illustrating the precise location of shipwreck remains in the intertidal zone at Cape Alava is expected to be acquired. This locational data combined with information from a previous study at the site will also contribute to an understanding of wreckage movement over space and time.

It is anticipated that many of the heavy metal artifacts will still remain, though locating them may prove difficult, as tidal and current action and human interference has likely caused significant movement. Additionally, the data acquired during the field school phase of the research project – including a site map, data on individual artifacts, and historical information – will be incorporated into an interactive web-page on the Olympic Coast National Marine Sanctuary website and a public presentation. By involving up-and-coming resource managers in site recordation, and including field school participants in the production of an interactive web-page and public presentation of the shipwreck *Austria*, both the academic and public realms will gain a greater understanding of the maritime heritage resources of Washington State and the nation.

References Cited

Green, J. (2004). *Maritime Archaeology: A Technical Handbook.* London, England: Elsevier Academic Press.

Lenihan, D. (ed.) (1989). *Submerged cultural resource study: USS Arizona Memorial and Pearl Harbor National Historic Landmark.* (Southwest Cultural Resources Center Professional Papers). Santa Fe, NM: Submerged Cultural Resources Unit, Dept. of the Interior.

Terrell, B. (2000). *Cultural Resource Survey Report: The Austria.* Port Angeles, WA: Olympic Coast National Marine Sanctuary.

Thompson, K. (n.d.). *Mash Shipwreck: An Exercise in Maritime Archaeology.* National Oceanic and Atmospheric Administration's National Marine Sanctuary Program. Retrieved February 20, 2007, from http://sanctuaries.noaa.gov/education/

Fig. 7.3. The material on this poster is organized according to the four principles of visual rhetoric.

(1) The principle of alignment involves an invisible grid system.

The principle of alignment involves the use of an invisible grid system to place elements on a page. These invisible lines run from top-to-bottom and/or from side to side on a page and help connect elements in different parts of the document. In visual documents, both visual and textual elements must be placed on the grid in an organized way. The more invisible lines a poster or brochure contains, the weaker or more scattered the document appears. The poster in fig. 7.3 has two primary lines: one down the left side of the page and one through the center. These lines define columns, which organize and unify the poster and give it a sharp, clean look. However, both the title and the statement of objectives in brown are not aligned with the main columns of text. This strategy gives more prominence to these two elements, clarifying the document's topic and purpose for the reader.

(2) The principle of proximity requires the grouping of related elements.

The principle of **proximity** requires the grouping of related visual or textual elements into clusters or chunks. Like elements of text are grouped together visually, whereas unlike elements are separated by significant **white space** (blank areas around blocks of text). In written documents, for example, headings typically appear closer to the section they relate to than to the previous section. Similarly, the audience will perceive each cluster or chunk of elements in a visual document as a single unit and interpret it as a whole before moving on to the next group. In other words, the chunks serve a function similar to sections in a written document, organizing the page and reducing clutter. In fig. 7.3, the proximity of the title and subtitle to each other links them and allows them to be read together, despite the fact that they appear in different colors and fonts. Moreover, white space and images distinguish sections and subsections, further clarifying the document's structure.

(3) The principle of contrast helps readers distinguish the most important elements.

The principle of **contrast** allows a reader to distinguish important elements from the rest of the document. The most salient visual or textual elements stand out from the rest of the page, while less important elements are not as noticeable. For example, academic and professional documents usually have headings in bold or italic type or capital letters to distinguish them from the rest of the text. Likewise, visual documents provide the viewer with clear clues as to the relative importance of various elements. Usually, the most significant elements of a document are contrasted with the surrounding elements by differences in size, color, or font. The poster in fig. 7.3 uses several strategies to heighten the contrast between its various components. Because they are so large, the title, images, and statement of objectives attract the most attention, and they convey a sense of the project's purpose. Moreover, lack of contrast also supplies important information about the document's organization. All headings are the same size and typeface, as are all subheadings. With a brief glance, the viewer can determine the hierarchy of information and the basic structure of the poster.

(4) The principle of repetition helps establish coherence.

The principle of **repetition** has to do with the replication of specific visual or textual elements throughout a document. For example, nearly all academic and professional papers use a consistent typeface for large blocks of text, which creates a unified look. Visual documents follow a similar strategy, rarely showing more than three typefaces in a single work. Moreover, other visual elements, such as bullets or colors, also enhance coherence when they are repeated in various parts of a document. In fig. 7.3, the title and statement of objectives appear in one font; the subtitle and the interior headings appear in another. The consistent use of the same two colors, blue and brown, reinforces the sense of unity. In addition, the pale blue waves repeating across the bottom not only give the poster a creative touch but also subtly unify all the elements. Particularly in the title and headings, repetition and contrast work hand in hand to structure the poster.

7c   Combining visual and verbal elements

Although words or images alone can have a tremendous impact on an audience, the combination of the two is often necessary, especially when neither verbal nor visual elements alone can successfully reach an audience and fulfill the sender's purpose. As you know, newspaper and magazine articles often include powerful images to heighten the emotional impact of a story. Diagrams that accompany a set of product-assembly instructions reinforce the process analysis and make assembly easier for the reader. When used together, words and images can supplement and reinforce to deliver a message—or even deliberately contradict each other to establish an ironic tone.

(1) Photos and text create the message in advertisements.

In fig. 7.4, the advertisement's words and image work together to argue that the viewer should consider buying a particular car. The image depicts a row of vehicles, two of which have been crushed by a falling tree. Considering the image alone, a viewer can see that the small vehicle is the focal point: prominently placed at the center of the frame, its unscathed body provides a strong contrast to the badly damaged vehicles on either side. The setting also contributes to the analysis, as the tall trees (one of which has fallen on the bigger, more rugged vehicles) convey an outdoorsy, back-to-nature mood. Ironically, the large vehicles are destroyed; the smaller vehicle remains intact. Along with the compelling image, the advertisement has three verbal elements. The first, printed on the license plate of the small car, is "ELECTRIC," a word that alerts the reader to the car's energy efficiency. Second, the sentence "HELLO, PARKING KARMA" appears below that car, the

Fig. 7.4. Both words and image are necessary to communicate the message of this ad.

only ecologically sensitive vehicle in the image. Finally, the small type at the bottom of the image reads, "With the right car, everything's better. Introducing the electric ZAP Worldcar L.U.V.," followed by the company's contact information and logo.

Without the accompanying text, the image in fig. 7.4 might convey the message that the central car was lucky to have been parked between two bigger vehicles. But combined with the three verbal elements, the image's message is clarified: the electric vehicle is environment-friendly, whereas the larger vehicles are gas hogs that burn fossil fuels and pollute the environment. The sentence about parking karma strongly suggests that the tree's falling was not accidental but was, in fact, an ethical consequence; that is, nature is punishing the gas hogs and sparing the electric vehicle. The argument of this advertisement is clear: pick the "right car," one that is compact and environmentally sound, and you will be rewarded.

(2) Graphics can clarify written material.

Many academic and professional documents that are primarily composed of text also include substantial visual displays, or **graphics,** to clarify written material. Graphics can be used to illustrate a concept, present data, provide visual relief, or simply attract readers' attention. Different types of graphics—tables, charts or graphs, and pictures—serve different purposes, and some may serve multiple purposes in a given document. Any of these types of graphics can enable readers to absorb a message more quickly than they would by reading long sections of text. However, if there is any chance that readers might not receive the intended message, it is a good idea to supplement graphics with text discussion.

(a) Tables organize data so that information can be easily accessed and compared.

Tables use a row-and-column arrangement to organize data (numbers or words) spatially; they are especially useful for presenting great amounts of numerical information in a small space, enabling the reader to draw direct comparisons among pieces of data or even to locate specific items. When you design a table, be sure to label all of the columns and rows accurately and to provide both a title and a number for the table. The table number and title traditionally appear above the table body, as table 7.1 demonstrates, and any notes or source information should be placed below it.

Most word-processing programs have settings that let you insert a table wherever you need one. You can determine how many rows and

TABLE 7.1
Modified Monthly Tornado Statistics

Month	2007 Final	2006 Final	2005 Final	2004 Final	4-Year Average
Jan	21	47	33	3	26
Feb	52	12	10	9	21
March	171	150	62	50	108
April	165	245	132	125	167
May	250	139	123	509	255
June	128	120	316	268	208
Jul	69	71	138	124	101
Aug	73	80	123	179	114
Sep	51	84	133	295	141
Oct	87	76	18	79	65
Nov	7	42	150	150	87
Dec	19	40	26	26	28
Total	1093	1106	1264	1817	1321

Source: National Weather Service.

columns the table will have, and you can also size each row and each column appropriately for the information it will hold.

(b) Charts and graphs provide visual representations of data.
Like tables, charts and graphs display relationships among statistical data in visual form; unlike tables, they do so using lines, bars, or other visual elements rather than just letters and numbers. Data can be displayed in several different graphic forms: pie charts, line graphs, and bar charts are the most common examples.

Pie charts are especially useful for showing the relationship of parts to a whole (see fig. 7.5), but they can only be used to display sets of data that add up to 100 percent (a whole).

Line graphs show the change in the relationship between one variable (indicated as a value on the vertical axis, or y axis) and another variable (indicated as a value on the horizontal axis, or x axis). The most common x-axis variable is time. Line graphs are very good at showing how a variable changes over time. A line graph might be used, for example, to illustrate the progression of sleep stages during one night (see fig. 7.6), increases or

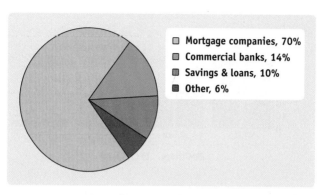

Fig. 7.5. Pie chart showing issuers of mortgage-based securities.

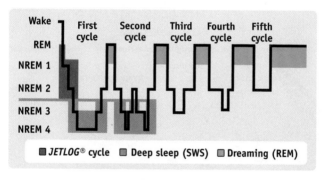

Fig. 7.6. Graph of nightly sleep stages.

decreases in student achievement from semester to semester, or trends in financial markets over a number of years.

Bar charts show correlations between two variables that do not involve smooth changes over time. For instance, a bar chart might illustrate gross national product for several nations, the relative speeds of various computer processors, or statistics about the composition of the U.S. military (see fig. 7.7).

In addition to charts, graphs, and tables, a variety of other graphics can be used to clarify complex ideas or to illustrate relationships among

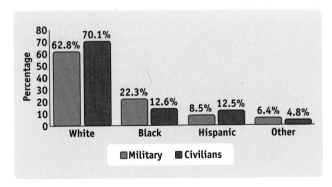

Fig. 7.7. Bar chart illustrating the composition of the U.S. military.

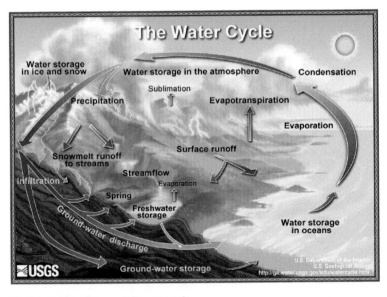

Fig. 7.8. Process diagram of the water cycle.

concepts. Figure 7.8 (a process diagram of the water cycle, or the movement of water in different forms through the environment) uses a simple graphical convention (superimposing arrows and labels on a semirealistic drawing) to present information that, in textual form, would require a great deal of space.

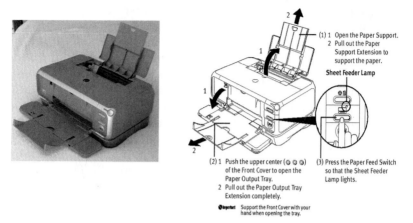

Fig. 7.9. A photo and a drawing of the same printer.

(c) Pictures illustrate the appearance of objects.

Pictures include photos, sketches, technical illustrations, paintings, icons, and other visual representations. Photographs are often used to reinforce textual descriptions or to show a reader exactly what something looks like. Readers of a used-car ad, for instance, will want to see exactly what the car looks like, not an artistic rendition of its appearance. Likewise, a Costa Rican travel brochure needs to contain lots of full-color photos of dazzling beaches, verdant forests, and azure water.

But photographs are not always the most informative type of picture. Compare the two images in fig. 7.9. Although the photograph is a more realistic image of the actual printer, the illustration more clearly shows the printer's important features: buttons, panels, and so forth. With its simple lines and clear labels, the illustration suits its purpose: to help the viewer set up and use the printer. Line drawings enable the designer of a document such as a user manual to highlight specific elements of an object while deemphasizing or eliminating unnecessary information. The addition of arrows, pointers, and labels adds useful detail to such an illustration.

(3) Visual and verbal elements can be effectively integrated.

To integrate visual elements into written text, you want to link them purposefully.

(a) Proximity is a paramount consideration for effective integration.
Proximity—placing an image as close as possibile to the text that refers to it—is one way of establishing a connection between text and a visual element. Wrapping the text around an image also serves to integrate words and visual; wrapping places a visual and its corresponding text in very close proximity, side by side. In addition, cropping unnecessary elements from an image strengthens connections between the visual and textual components of a document, highlighting what is most important while preserving what is authentic. When a visual element (a graph or table) is too large to fit on the same page as the related text, it is placed on a separate page or moved to an appendix. Thus, proximity must occasionally be forfeited for the sake of in-depth explanation or detailed support.

(b) Captions and labels also support visual and verbal integration.
Captions and labels also serve a crucial function in integrating the written and visual components of a document. In academic texts, figures and tables are labeled by being numbered consecutively and separately. Moreover, the main body of an academic text includes specific references to all images and graphics, in phrases such as "see fig. 5" and "as shown in table 2" (see the research paper in **18d**). Images and graphics in popular magazines and daily newspapers, though rarely labeled as figures or tables, enhance the verbal content and appeal to the reader. Effective magazine and newspaper articles integrate textual and visual elements through both captions and layout (see fig. 7.10). Although the conventions of academic and professional documents vary, no figure or table should be inserted into a text document without either a caption or a label (or both) to explain its relevance in the larger context of the work.

7d Common genres and effective features of visual documents

Although all visual documents adhere to the same rhetorical principles, each of the common genres is distinguished by its most effective features. Posters, flyers, brochures, and newsletters are among the most common genres of visual documents.

Red Sea, Israel

In diving circles, the Red Sea is famous for Egypt's Sinai Peninsula, a place known for spectacular reefs and occasionally suspect dive masters (in January 2007, three divers and a guide were lost in high seas). But right across the Israeli border to the north, there's an eight-mile stretch of Red Sea coast with hardly any current and some of the best shore-accessible dives in the world.

Dive this section of the Gulf of Aqaba, just south of Eilat's multistory hotels, and you'll explore the Satil missile boat, an Israeli military ship that was sunk specifically for divers in 1994 (three dives per day, $80; dolphinreef.co.il). Snorkelers can easily visit Moses and Joshua rocks, two shallow coral heads 300 yards from shore. At night go dancing on the beach at the waterfront Dolphin Reef bar. To experience Israel's best attempt at Vegas-style excess, visit the laser show at the Platinum disco, in Eilat.

STAY: The Dan Eilat Hotel in Eilat serves complimentary buffet breakfasts and a mega-resort-size Friday-night Shabbat dinner. Doubles, $298; danhotels.com

RED SEA FLIPPERS

A Land-Proof Dive Watch

Want to check your depth without feeling like you have to strap a saucer to your wrist? The new D4 dive watch from Suunto is tricked out for the depth set but sleek enough for the tiki bar. The D4 comes with standard dual-time and stopwatch functionality, calculates your depth three times per second, and logs your deepest and longest dives. $650; suunto.com —ANTHONY CERRETANI

Coral Sea, Australia

At the eastern edge of the Great Barrier Reef lies the Coral Sea, a two-million-square-mile submarine plateau. Visibility here can reach 200 feet, and Coral Sea divers have the increasingly rare opportunity to discover unexplored sites: Some of the coral heads were last mapped in the 1770s by Captain Cook. "Most of the dive sites don't have names yet," says Brad Doane, underwater cameraman for the BBC's *Blue Planet* series. "And everything is on steroids. The soft coral stalks are as big as a thigh."

GO WITH: There are only five live-aboard dive boats that cruise the Coral Sea; Cairns-based Mike Ball Dive Expeditions is the most reputable. Dive the remote Osprey and Cod Hole reefs, where eager 300-pound reef sharks show up if you smack a fist into your palm. Four-night trips from $1,400; mikeball.com

FIJI'S BEQA ISLAND

CORAL SEA LOW LIFE

Beqa Lagoon, Fiji

Surfers associate the southern coast of Viti Levu, Fiji's largest island, with Frigate Passage, one of the best left breaks in the South Pacific. But the coast is also home to the 150-square-mile Beqa Lagoon, one of the best "muck-diving" reefs in the world. Divers dig around the bottom of the 30-foot-deep soft-coral reef, searching for the harlequin ghost pipefish and juvenile sea horses that feed on the nutrient-rich silty runoff from the Navua River. For a laugh, head to Frigate Passage. "You can dive below the break and watch sharks watching the surfers," says Jayne Carlson, owner of the Lalati Resort and Spa, on Beqa Island.

STAY: Forty minutes from the mainland on Beqa Island, at the Lalati Resort and Spa, an eco-resort located between the rainforest and the beach. Guests stay in private, two-room beachfront villas; the owners are avid divers who lead free shore dives from the resort's pier. Villas, $310, including meals; boat dives, $110 per person for two dives, plus $25 gear rental; lalati-fiji.com

A Reef to Avoid

Covering 16 acres of seafloor, the Neptune Memorial Reef, three miles off the Miami coast, is boldly leading the ever-growing quest for new burial frontiers. An artificial reef that was modeled after a developer's vision of the lost city of Atlantis, Neptune houses an underwater graveyard exclusively for the cremated. The owners at the Neptune Reef Society hope that the reef, which opened for business in November, will soon become a sought-after diving destination. We're not holding our breath. $1,495 to have your ashes buried; nmreef.com —ABE STREEP

Fig. 7.10. This magazine page integrates visual and textual elements through both captions and layout.

(1) Posters and flyers quickly and easily reach a wide audience.

Posters and **flyers,** colorful sheets that paper walls, utility poles, and bulletin boards around most college campuses are used to advertise organizations, events, issues, and services. Although posters and flyers are often used to fulfill the same purpose, they are not always aimed at the same audiences. Therefore, their effectiveness depends on how and where they appear. Posters, for instance, usually appear on large walls and are seen from afar. For those reasons, a poster usually employs much more visual than verbal (or textual) information so that its audience can absorb the message at a glance. By contrast, the smaller, usually more text-heavy, single-sheet flyer is intended for mass distribution and is often handed out to passersby. Yet, despite these differences, both posters and flyers are meant to be seen by as many people as possible—with text and images that readily appeal to a target group (the intended audience).

Because the purpose of posters and flyers is to reach as many people as possible—and quickly—it is vitally important that the audience be able to locate the important information immediately. Both posters and flyers need a focal point that captures attention and highlights the basic information. Thus, artfully minimalistic posters and flyers will always be more effective than those that overwhelm viewers with too many images or fancy fonts.

The poster in fig. 7.11 relies heavily on the image to convey its message, allowing that message to be communicated to the audience almost instantly. This travel poster presents a solitary, jubilant figure in an outdoor setting. The subtitle, "She's a breath of fresh air," reinforces the sense of openness and freedom conveyed by the image. The poster is aimed at a young, active audience interested in nature and outdoor activites, and it invites a new generation of vacationers to visit the state of Virginia.

Fig. 7.11. This travel poster targets a specific audience and delivers its message almost instantly.

Fig. 7.12. The poster has a clear focal point to capture interest.

Fig. 7.13. Readers scan posters and flyers in a backward S pattern, as they read a page in book.

Keep in mind what you noticed in fig. 7.11 as you look at fig. 7.12. You can see that the monument and the central text are substantially larger than the other elements, providing a clear focal point in the center of the poster. Now consider the way you "read" the poster. Most people scan posters and flyers in a backward S pattern, beginning in the top-left corner and ending in the bottom right, as they read a page in a book (fig. 7.13). This poster was designed to take advantage of that typical strategy for scanning. While the central image and text generate immediate interest, the viewer will finish with the contact information on the bottom of the page and remember this important information.

Most importantly, the posters in figs. 7.11 and 7.12 have little text, rarely in full sentences, leaving ample white space for the image. The flyer in fig. 7.14, by contrast, requires ten lines of text to deliver the necessary information about the event and its sponsors. Ten lines might be too much text in another flyer, but this one is coherent and easy to read.

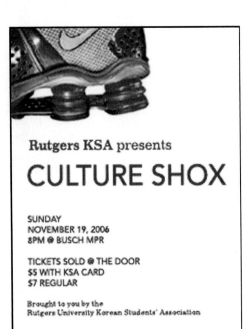

Fig. 7.14. This flyer uses a simple design and color scheme effectively.

The designer has used white space to group the lines of text into chunks and has employed only two fonts and a single color. The contrast between white and red makes a substantial visual impact without distracting the reader from the focal point. The result is an effective flyer.

TIPS FOR DESIGNING EFFECTIVE POSTERS AND FLYERS

- Identify your target audience.
- Determine your purpose.
- Consider where your poster will appear or how your flyer will be distributed.
- Provide a clear focal point.
- Aim for visual simplicity.
- Strive for coherence.
- Chunk information.
- Remember the backward S scanning pattern.

(2) Brochures and newsletters are strategically aimed at specialized audiences.

Like posters and flyers, **brochures** and **newsletters** rely on lively verbal text, visual elements, and effective design to appeal to their target audience. The audience has usually already indicated an interest in the topic by requesting the brochure or signing up for the newsletter. It is up to the designer of the newsletter or brochure to maintain that interest by effectively integrating visual and textual material. To that end, visual documents of these types often include striking photographs and bold colors that contrast with the black text.

Brochures are typically multipage, multicolored infomercials, printed on high-quality paper, to advertise or promote a particular organization, service, or issue and (unlike typical ads) are often requested by the reader rather than distributed indiscriminately. A brochure is not nearly as time sensitive as a newsletter, which is published regularly by an organization or group to update readers about activities and pertinent issues. A newsletter's periodic installments strive to sustain readers' interest in the organization or group while promoting its products or causes. Like all successful communicators, designers of brochures and newsletters are guided by several basic rhetorical principles.

Because many readers have voluntarily become part of the audience, designers of brochures and newsletters can assume the audience will read these documents, but not necessarily word for word. Therefore, they design the layout to allow for easy scanning. They know their readers want to locate relevant information quickly and easily. For these reasons, brochures and newsletters incorporate certain characteristics or design features that serve as signposts for readers, helping them navigate the document. Headings and subheadings allow a reader to gain an overview of the document's contents and pinpoint specific information. The principle of repetition emphasizes the overall structure. Often, each page of a brochure has the same basic layout, with variations in content and color. In other cases, a simple image or symbol appears throughout the document to unify it. In the brochure for cancer patients in fig. 7.15, each left-hand page contains an image of a survivor; the facing page has the same layout throughout the document, with variations in the content. The statement "I LIVE STRONG" is repeated beneath each picture. Moreover, many brochures, such as those in figs. 7.2 and 7.15, rely on bullets to organize information and make it more accessible.

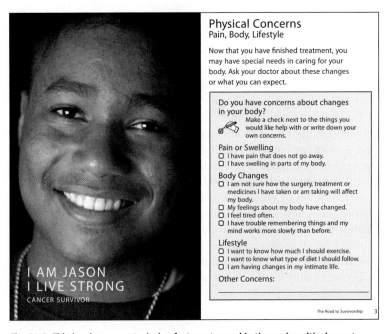

Fig. 7.15. This brochure repeats design features to provide the reader with signposts.

The bullets in fig. 7.2 allow the reader to quickly scan the entire list of global warming solutions, considering the efforts already underway, and then read closely those of most interest.

Both brochures and newsletters break text into blocks or chunks. In a typical brochure, the folds differentiate the blocks of text. The brochure in fig. 7.15 uses shading to distinguish the checklist from the introductory paragraph at the top of the page. Newsletter templates usually have a block for the title and date at the top of the page, as well as one to the side for a table of contents or calendar of upcoming events (fig. 7.16). And, like magazines and newspapers, most newsletters adopt a format with several columns, the shorter lines of text making for easy reading.

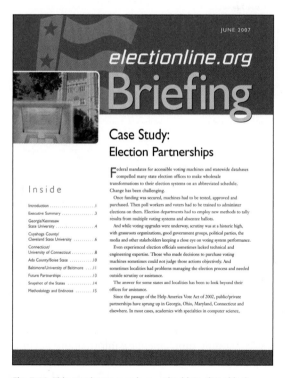

Fig. 7.16. This newsletter page is organized into three blocks of text.

security; inconsistencies between numbers of voters signing precinct registry and ballots cast; legal eligibility of certain employees for their job assignments; and election tabulation and related technical and security issues.[19]

The second report, detailing the election audit, was issued in April 2007. The Center coordinated the audit — which included representatives from both political parties — and offered methodological guidance and statistical analysis of the county's unofficial election results.

While stating the November election was an improvement over the May primary, Hoke said problems remained including continued issues with damaged or destroyed VVPATs.[21]

The audit report was released soon after Ohio Secretary of State Jennifer Brunner (D) asked for and eventually received the resignation of the four-member bipartisan Cuyahoga County board of elections in mid-March 2007. By early May of this year, four new members were appointed to the board which is now in the process of discussing the future role of the Center as public monitor.

Beyond its continued public monitor function, CEI also hopes in the future to partner with Brunner's office on implementing best practices in areas of election technology and security. One idea includes a pilot program that

"We needed to motivate and support election officials to seek the highest standards of performance, and to understand that they held a public trust of core value to our citizenry as well as our nation as a whole."

—Candice Hoke, Cleveland State University

would create temporary performance standards involving the accuracy, reliability and security of the state's elections.

Other potential projects include the establishment of academic programs within CSU's public administration program. Four counties have expressed interest in taking such courses about federal and Ohio election law specifically targeted at election officials.

It is this challenging role that Hoke sees as fundamental to the Center's mission — continuing education for election officials and creating a program for advanced coursework and degrees.

"For a number of years it has seemed that state and federal agencies had all but abandoned the tasks of providing to local election officials prompt, effective training, consultation, and guidance for problem-solving. But some Secretaries of State (including Ohio's) seem to be moving forward to redress this omission."[23]

Fig. 7.17. This page of a newsletter uses a pull quote and a simple graphic to draw the reader's attention.

In addition to applying the fundamental design principles just discussed, designers of successful brochures and newsletters often use other visual features to influence the reader's impression of the document. For instance, **pull quotes** (important phrases or sentences from the text reprinted in a way that contrasts with the body of text) and **sidebars** (shaded blocks of text containing supplementary information) are often employed to create visual interest for the reader (note the two cream-colored boxes in fig. 7.10). The newsletter page in fig. 7.17 uses both a pull quote and a simple graphic that lays behind the text to appeal visually to the reader.

TIPS FOR DESIGNING EFFECTIVE BROCHURES AND NEWSLETTERS

- Identify your target audience and the appropriate genre.

- Design each page of the brochure or newsletter for ease of scanning (remember the backward S).

- Provide verbal and visual signposts for your readers: headings, subheadings, shading, and bullets.

- Use blocks or chunks of text to emphasize main points and include pull quotes and sidebars.

- Employ striking photographs and bold colors to contrast with black type.

TECH SAVVY

Most features of a document—including typeface, font style and size, bullets, and line spacing—can be changed using the buttons on the standard word-processing toolbar. Other features—such as columns, borders, and page orientation—can be easily changed as well. Depending on the software you use, the relevant commands appear on the Page Layout tab or in the Formatting menu or palette.

Exercise 2

Locate a document containing one or more images that you composed for another class or for an extracurricular activity. Bring it (or a photocopy of it) to class. Be prepared to explain how you created the document and chose the image(s). If you cannot locate a copy of such a document, write for ten to fifteen minutes, reconstructing the process by which you created the document, including what you knew how to do before you started and what you learned as you progressed.

8 Writing Arguments

You write arguments on a regular basis. When you send your business partner a memo to tell her that a client needs to sign a contract, when you e-mail your parents to ask them for a loan, when you petition your academic advisor for a late drop, or when you demand that a mail-order company refund your money, you are writing an argument. You are expressing a point of view and then using logical reasoning to invite a specific audience to accept that point of view or adopt a course of action. *Argument* and *persuasion* are often used interchangeably, but they differ in two basic ways. Traditionally, **persuasion** has referred to winning or conquering with the use of emotional reasoning, whereas **argument** has been reserved for the use of logical reasoning to convince listeners or readers. But because writing often involves some measure of "winning" (even if it is only gaining the ear of a particular audience) and uses both emotion and reason, this book uses *argument* to cover the meanings of both terms.

Argumentation is about problem solving.

When writing arguments, you follow the same process as for all your writing: planning, drafting, and revising, as well as attending to audience and context (1d and 1e). Argumentative writing is distinct from other kinds of writing in its emphasis on the inseparability of audience and purpose. Recognizing and respecting the beliefs, values, and expertise of a specific audience is the only way to achieve the rhetorical purpose of an argument, which goes beyond victory over an opponent. Argument can be an important way to invite exchange, understanding, cooperation, consideration, joint decision making, agreement, or negotiation of differences. Thus, argument serves three basic and sometimes overlapping purposes: to analyze a complicated issue or question an established belief, to express or defend a point of view, and to invite or convince an audience to change a position or adopt a course of action.

This chapter will help you

- determine the purpose of an argument (8a),
- consider different viewpoints (8b),
- distinguish fact from opinion (8c),
- take a position or make a claim (8d),
- provide evidence to support a claim (8e),
- use the rhetorical appeals to ground an argument (8f),
- arrange ideas (8g),
- use logical reasoning (8h),
- avoid rhetorical fallacies (8i), and
- analyze an argument (8j).

As you proceed, you will understand the importance of determining your purpose, identifying your audience, marshaling your arguments, arguing ethically, and treating your audience with respect.

8a Determining the purpose of your argument

To what exigence are you responding? What is your topic? Why are you arguing about it? What is at stake? What is likely to happen as a result of making this argument? How important are those consequences? Who is in a position to act or react in response to your argument?

When writing an argument, you need to establish the relationships among your topic, purpose, and audience. The relationship between audience and purpose is particularly significant because the audience often shapes the purpose.

- If there is little likelihood that you can convince members of your audience to change a strongly held opinion, you might achieve a great deal by inviting them to understand your position.
- If the members of your audience are not firmly committed to a position, you might be able to convince them to agree with the opinion you are expressing or defending.
- If the members of your audience agree with you in principle, you might invite them to undertake a specific action—such as voting for the candidate you are supporting.

No matter how you imagine those in your audience responding to your argument, you must establish **common ground** with them, stating a goal toward which you both want to work or identifying a belief, assumption, or value that you both share. In other words, common ground is a necessary starting point, regardless of your ultimate purpose.

8b   Considering differing viewpoints

If everyone agreed on everything, there would be no need for argument, for taking a position or questioning a position held by someone else. But people do not always agree. For that reason, a good deal of the writing you will do in school or at work will require you to take an arguable position on a topic. The first step toward finding a topic for argumentation is to consider issues that inspire different opinions.

Behind any effective argument is a question that can generate more than one reasonable answer. If you ask "Is there racism in the United States?" almost anyone will agree that there is. But if you ask "Why is there still racism in the United States?" or "What can Americans do to eliminate racism?" you will hear different answers. Answers differ because people approach questions with various backgrounds, experiences, and assumptions. As a consequence, they are often tempted to use reasoning that supports what they already believe. As a writer, you will be tempted to employ such reasoning, and doing so is a good place to start. But as you expand and shape your argument, you will want to demonstrate not only that you are knowledgeable about your topic but also that you are aware of and have given fair consideration to other views about it. To be knowledgeable and yet respectful of others' views constitutes a worthy goal.

When you write an argument, you are trying to solve a problem or answer a question—with or for an audience. When you choose a topic for argumentation, you will want to take a stance that allows you to question, that provides you an exigence (or reason) for writing. First, you focus on a topic, on the part of some general subject that you will address in your essay (3b), and then you pose a question about it. As you craft your question, consider the following: (1) your own values and beliefs with respect to the question, (2) how your assumptions might differ from those of your intended audience, and (3) how you might establish common ground with members of your audience, while at the same time respecting any differences between your opinion and theirs. The question you raise will evolve into your **thesis,** an arguable statement.

The most important criterion for choosing an arguable statement for an essay is knowledge of the topic, so that you will be an informed writer, responsive to the expectations of your audience. When you are in a position to choose your own topic, you can draw on your knowledge of current events, politics, sports, fashion, or a specific academic subject. Topics may present themselves on television or the Web, as you find yourself agreeing or disagreeing with what you hear and read.

To determine whether a topic might be suitable, make a statement about the topic ("I believe strongly that . . . " or "My view is that . . . ") and then check to see if that statement can be argued. If you can answer all the questions in the following box to your satisfaction, you should feel confident about your topic.

TIPS FOR ASSESSING AN ARGUABLE STATEMENT ABOUT A TOPIC

- What reasons can you think of to support your belief about the topic? List those reasons.

- Who or what groups might disagree with your statement? Why? List those groups.

- Do you know enough about this topic to discuss other points of view? Can you find out what you need to know?

■ What are other viewpoints on the topic and reasons supporting those viewpoints? List them.

■ What is your purpose in writing about this topic?

■ What do you want your audience to do in response to your argument? In other words, what do you expect from your audience? Write out your expectation.

As you move further into the writing process, researching and exploring your topic in the library or on the Web (chapter 9), you may be able to clarify your purpose and improve your thesis statement.

8c   Distinguishing between fact and opinion

When you develop your thesis statement into an argument, you use both facts and opinions. It is important to distinguish between these two kinds of information so that you can use both to your advantage, especially in terms of establishing your credibility (8f(1)), an essential feature of successful argumentation. **Facts** are reliable pieces of information that can be verified through independent sources or procedures. **Opinions,** on the other hand, are assertions or inferences that may or may not be based on facts. Opinions that are widely accepted, however, may seem to be factual when they are not.

Just because facts are reliable does not mean that they speak for themselves. Facts are significant only when they are used responsibly to support a claim; otherwise, a thoughtful and well-informed opinion might have more impact. To determine whether a statement you have read is fact or opinion, ask yourself questions like these: Can it be proved? Can it be challenged? How often is the same result achieved? If a statement can consistently be proved true, then it is a fact. If it can be disputed, then it is an opinion.

Fact   Milk contains calcium.

Opinion   Americans should drink more milk.

To say that milk contains calcium is to state a well-established fact: it can be verified by consulting published studies or by conducting laboratory tests.

Whether or not this fact is significant depends on how a writer chooses to use it. As an isolated fact, it is unlikely to seem significant. But to say that Americans need to drink more milk is to express an opinion that may or may not be supported by facts. When considering the statement "Americans should drink more milk," a thoughtful reader might ask, "How much calcium does a human need? Why do humans need calcium? Is cow's milk good for humans? Might leafy green vegetables provide a richer source of calcium?" Anticipating questions such as these can help you develop an argument. These sorts of questions also help you recognize the evidence that will best support your argument, where you can obtain such evidence, and what to do if you discover conflicting evidence.

The line between fact and opinion is not always clear. Therefore, writers and readers of arguments should always be prepared to interpret and assess the reliability of the information before them, evaluating the beliefs supporting the argument's stance, the kinds of sources used, and the objections that could be made to the argument.

Exercise 1

Determine which of the following statements are fact and which are opinion. In each case, what kind of verification would you require in order to accept the statement as reliable?

1. Toni Morrison won the Nobel Prize in literature in 1993.
2. Women often earn less money than men who hold the same positions.
3. *Monsters, Inc.* is the most financially successful of all the Disney movies.
4. Writing well is a gift, like musical genius.
5. A college degree guarantees a good job.
6. Santa Fe is the oldest U.S. city that is a state capital.
7. Running is good for your health.
8. The United States won World War II.
9. In combination, ammonia and chlorine bleach result in a poisonous gas.
10. Researchers will find a cure for AIDS.

8d Taking a position or making a claim

When making an argument, a writer takes a position on a particular topic. Whether the argument analyzes, questions, expresses, defends, invites, or convinces, the writer needs to make clear his or her position. That position, which is called the **claim,** or **proposition,** clearly states what the writer wants the audience to do with the information being provided. The claim is the thesis of the argument and usually appears in the introduction and sometimes again in the conclusion.

(1) Effective writers claim no more than they can responsibly support.
Claims vary in extent; they can be absolute or moderate, large or limited. Absolute claims assert that something is always true or false, completely good or bad; moderate claims make less sweeping assertions.

Absolute claim	College athletes are never good students.
Moderate claim	Most colleges have low graduation rates for their athletes.
Absolute claim	Harry Truman was the best president we have ever had.
Moderate claim	Truman's domestic policies helped advance civil rights.

Moderate claims are not necessarily superior to absolute claims. After all, writers frequently need to take a strong position in favor of or against something. But the stronger the claim, the stronger the evidence needed to support it. Be sure to consider the quality and the significance of the evidence you use—not just its quantity.

(2) Types of claims vary in terms of how much they encompass.

(a) Substantiation claims assert that something exists or is evident.
Without making a value judgment, a **substantiation claim** makes a point that can be supported by evidence.

The job market for those who just received a PhD in English is limited.

The post office is raising rates again.

(b) Evaluation claims assert that something has a specific quality.
According to an **evaluation claim,** something is good or bad, effective or ineffective, attractive or unattractive, successful or unsuccessful.

> The graduation rate for athletes at Penn State is very high compared with that at the other Big Ten universities.
>
> The public transportation system in Washington DC is reliable and safe.

Sometimes, writers use evaluation claims as a way to invite their audience to consider an issue.

> It is important for us to consider the graduation rate of college athletes.

(c) Policy claims call for a specific action.
When making **policy claims,** writers call for something to be done.

> We must find the funds to hire better qualified high school teachers.
>
> We need to build a light-rail system linking downtown with the airport and the western suburbs.

Much writing involves substantiation, evaluation, and policy claims. When writing about the job market for engineers with newly minted degrees, you might tap your ability to substantiate a claim; when writing about literature (chapter 12), you might need to evaluate a character. Policy claims are commonly found in arguments about social issues such as health care, social security, and affirmative action. These claims often grow out of substantiation or evaluation claims: first, you demonstrate that a problem exists; then, you establish the best solution for that problem.

Policy claims, such as the one made by this famous Army recruiting poster, call for a specific action.

TIPS FOR MAKING A CLAIM ARGUABLE

- Write down your opinion.
- Describe the situation that produced your opinion.
- Decide who constitutes the audience for your opinion and what you want that audience to do about your opinion.
- Write down the verifiable and reliable facts that support your opinion.
- Using those facts, transform your initial opinion into a thoughtful claim that considers at least two sides to the issue under discussion.
- Ask yourself, "So what?" If the answer to this question shows that your claim leads nowhere, start over, beginning with the first tip.

As an example of transforming an opinion into an arguable claim, consider the following scenario. Helen thinks that air pollution is a problem. She describes the situation that has inspired her opinion: she was jogging on a busy street and had difficulty breathing because of the excessive car exhaust. Describing this situation helps Helen focus her opinion. She decides to narrow her topic to the need to reduce automobile emissions. Next, she imagines an audience for her topic, an audience who can do something about this issue. She decides to write to automobile manufacturers. Helen knows that she needs to do some research on this topic in order to write a convincing argument, so she researches the physics of automobile emissions and realizes that, with just a small amount of effort, car manufacturers could improve the efficiency of most automobile engines—and thereby reduce emissions. She also conducts a survey of fellow students and learns that most of them would prefer to buy cars with more efficient engines. Helen now has a specific audience, a specific claim for their consideration, and a specific reason for her audience to agree with her claim: automobile manufacturers should work to produce more efficient engines; if they do so, young adults will be more likely to purchase their automobiles.

Exercise 2

The following excerpt is from an argument analyzing racial strife in the United States, written by Cornel West, a scholar specializing in race relations. Evaluate the claims it presents. Are they absolute or moderate? Can you identify a substantiation or evaluation claim? What policy claim is implicit in this passage? (The sentences are numbered for ease of reference.)

[1]To engage in a serious discussion of race in America, we must begin not with the problems of black people but with the flaws of American society—flaws rooted in historic inequalities and longstanding cultural stereotypes. [2]How we set up the terms for discussing racial issues shapes our perception and response to these issues. [3]As long as black people are viewed as a "them," the burden falls on blacks to do all the "cultural" and "moral" work necessary for healthy race relations. [4]The implication is that only certain Americans can define what it means to be American—and the rest must simply "fit in."

—CORNEL WEST, *Race Matters*

8e | Providing evidence for an effective argument

Effective arguments are well developed and supported. You should explore your topic in enough depth to have the evidence to support your position intelligently and ethically, whether that evidence is based on personal experience or research (chapters 3 and 9). You will want to consider the reasons others might disagree with you and be prepared to respond to those reasons.

(1) An effective argument clearly establishes the thinking that leads to the claim.

If you want readers to take your ideas seriously, you must communicate the reasons that have led to your position as well as the values and assumptions that underlie your thinking. When you are exploring your topic, make a list of the reasons that have led to your belief (3d and 3f). For example, when Anna Seitz was working on her argumentative essay (at the end of this chapter; see pages 185–190), she listed the following reasons for her belief that universities should not allow individuals or corporations to buy naming rights to campus buildings:

1. By purchasing naming rights, donors gain influence over educational policy decisions, even though they are not qualified to make such decisions.
2. Significant donations can adversely affect overall university finances by replacing existing funding sources.
3. Donors who purchase naming rights are associated with the university, in spite of the fact that they or their corporations may subscribe to a different set of values.

Although it is possible to base an argument on one good reason (such as "The selling of naming rights distracts from the educational purposes of universities"), doing so can be risky. If your audience does not find this reason convincing, you have no other support for your position. When you show that you have more than one reason for believing as you do, you increase the likelihood that your audience will find merit in your argument. Sometimes, however, one reason is stronger—and more appropriate for your audience—than several others you could advance. To develop an argument for which you have only one good reason, explore the bases underlying your reason: the values and assumptions that led you to take your stand. By demonstrating the thinking behind the single reason on which you are building your case, you can create a well-developed argument.

Whether you have one reason or several, be sure to provide sufficient evidence from credible sources to support your claim:

- facts,
- statistics,
- examples, and
- testimony, from personal experience or professional expertise.

This evidence must be accurate, representative, and sufficient. Accurate information should be verifiable by others (8c). Recognize, however, that even if the information a writer provides is accurate, it may not be representative or sufficient if it was drawn from an exceptional case, a biased sample, or a one-time occurrence. If, for example, you are writing an argument about the advantages of using Standardized English but draw all of your supporting evidence from a proponent of the English-Only movement, your evidence represents only the views of that movement. If you draw all of your evidence from just one person (Bill Cosby, for instance, has strong views on the use of Standardized English, especially as a means to stamp out the Ebonics movement), your evidence is neither representative of all the support for the use of Standardized English nor sufficient to support a thoughtful argument. In order to better represent your viewpoint, you should gather supporting evidence from sociolinguists, speakers of other dialects and languages, education specialists, professors, and other experts. In other words, consult more than a single source (chapter 9).

When gathering evidence, be sure to think critically about the information you find. If you are using the results of polls or other statistics or statements by authorities, determine how recent and representative the information is and how it was gathered. Consider, too, whether the authority you plan to quote is qualified to address the topic under consideration and is likely to be respected by your readers.

Whatever form of evidence you use—facts, statistics, examples, or testimony—you need to make clear to your audience exactly *why* and *how* the evidence supports your claim. After all, facts do not really speak for themselves; even accurate information has to be interpreted by the writer and the reader. As soon as the relationship between your claim and your evidence is clear to you, make that connection explicit to your readers, helping them understand your thinking.

(2) Effective arguments respond to diverse views.

Issues are controversial because good arguments can be made on all sides. Therefore, effective arguments consider and respond to other points of view, fairly and respectfully. In order for your argument to be effective and convincing, your audience must realize that you are knowledgeable about points of view other than your own. The most common strategy for addressing opposing points of view is referred to as **refutation:** you introduce diverse views and then respectfully demonstrate why you disagree with each of them. As you consider opposing points of view, you are likely to discover some you cannot refute, perhaps because they are based in a belief system markedly different from your own. You are also likely to discover that some of the other views have real merit. If you understand the reasons behind opposing viewpoints but remain unconvinced, you will need to demonstrate why.

When you find yourself agreeing with a point that supports another side of the issue, you can benefit from offering a **concession.** By openly admitting that you agree with opponents on one or more specific points, you demonstrate that you are fair-minded and at the same time increase your credibility (8f(1)). Concessions also increase the likelihood that opponents will be inclined to find merit in your argument.

Whether you agree or disagree with other positions, work to recognize and assess them. It is hard to persuade people to agree with you if you insist that they are entirely wrong. If you admit that they are partially right, they are more likely to admit that you could be partially right as well. In this sense, then, argument involves working with an audience as much as getting them to work with you.

Exercise 3

The following paragraph is taken from an argument by Martin Luther King, Jr., in which he defends the struggle for civil rights against public criticism from a group of prominent clergymen. Write a short analysis of this paragraph in which you note (a) an opposing viewpoint to which he is responding, (b) a refutation he offers to this viewpoint, (c) a concession he makes, and (d) any questions this excerpt raises for you.

[1]You express a great deal of anxiety over our willingness to break laws. [2]This is certainly a legitimate concern. [3]Since we so diligently urge people to obey the Supreme Court's decision of 1954 outlawing segregation in the public schools, at first glance it may seem rather paradoxical for us consciously to break laws. [4]One may well ask: "How can you advocate breaking some laws and obeying others?" [5]The answer lies in the fact that there are two types of laws, just and unjust. [6]I would be the first to advocate obeying just laws. [7]One has not only a legal but a moral responsibility to obey just laws. [8]Conversely, one has a moral responsibility to disobey unjust laws. [9]I would agree with St. Augustine that "an unjust law is no law at all."   —MARTIN LUTHER KING, JR., "Letter from Birmingham Jail"

8f Using the rhetorical appeals to ground your argument

Effective arguments always incorporate several appeals to the audience simply because logical reasoning—providing good reasons—is rarely enough (8e and 8h). Human beings do not believe or act on the basis of facts or logic alone; if we did, we would all agree and act accordingly. In reality, we believe and act on the basis of our own concerns, experiences, and needs. When we do not listen to another point of view, we simply do not want to change our minds. An effective argument, then, is one that gets a fair hearing. If you want your views to be heard, understood, and maybe even acted on, you need to follow the necessary steps to gain a hearing.

(1) Three rhetorical appeals can shape any argument.

Aristotle, a Greek philosopher who lived over two thousand years ago, was the first to help speakers shape effective arguments through a combination of three persuasive strategies: the **rhetorical appeals** of ethos, logos, and pathos. **Ethos** (an ethical appeal) establishes the speaker's or writer's credibility and trustworthiness. An ethical appeal demonstrates goodwill toward the audience, good sense or knowledge of the subject at hand, and good character. Establishing common ground with the audience is another feature of ethos. But ethos alone rarely carries an argument; therefore, you also need to use **logos** (a logical appeal). Logos demonstrates an effective use of reason and judicious use of evidence, whether that evidence consists of facts, statistics, comparisons, anecdotes, expert opinions, personal experiences, or observations. You employ logos in the process of supporting claims, drawing reasonable conclusions, and avoiding rhetorical fallacies (8i). Aristotle also taught that persuasion comes about only when the audience feels emotionally stirred by the topic under discussion. Therefore, **pathos** (an emotional appeal) involves using language that will stir the feelings of the audience. If you misuse pathos in an attempt to manipulate your audience, your effort can backfire. But pathos can be used successfully when it establishes empathy and authentic understanding. Thus, the most effective arguments combine these three persuasive appeals responsibly and knowledgeably.

In the next three subsections, excerpts from Martin Luther King, Jr.'s "Letter from Birmingham Jail" illustrate how a writer can use all three of the classical rhetorical appeals.

(a) Ethical appeals establish a writer's credibility.

In his opening paragraph, King notes that his professional life is very demanding but that his critics' views are worthy of response. He thus demonstrates respect for his audience. He also indicates that he wishes to engage in "constructive work," thereby establishing common ground with his audience, whom he characterizes as being well-intentioned and sincere. He also establishes that he will argue in good faith.

As a writer and a speaker, Dr. Martin Luther King, Jr., successfully used the rhetorical appeals of ethos, logos, and pathos.

1   My Dear Fellow Clergymen:
     While confined here in the Birmingham city jail, I came across your recent statement calling my present activities "unwise and untimely." Seldom do I pause to answer criticism of my work and ideas. If I sought to answer all the criticisms that cross my desk, my secretaries would have little time for anything other than such correspondence in the course of the day, and I would have no time for constructive work. But since I feel that you are men of genuine good will and that your criticisms are sincerely set forth, I want to try to answer your statement in what I hope will be patient and reasonable terms.

(b) Logical appeals help an audience clearly understand the writer's ideas.

To help his audience understand why segregation is wrong, King defines key terms:

2   Let us consider a more concrete example of just and unjust laws. An unjust law is a code that a numerical or power majority group compels a minority group to obey but does not make binding on itself. This is difference made legal. By the same token, a just law is a code that a majority compels a minority to follow and that it is willing to follow itself. This is sameness made legal.

(c) Emotional appeals can move the audience to a new way of thinking or acting.

As he moves toward his conclusion, King evokes feelings of idealism as well as guilt:

3   I have travelled the length and breadth of Alabama, Mississippi, and all the other southern states. On sweltering summer days and crisp autumn mornings I have looked at the South's beautiful churches with their lofty spires pointing heavenward. I have beheld the impressive outlines of her massive religious-education buildings. Over and over I have found myself asking: "What kind of people worship here? Who is their God? . . . Where were their voices of support when bruised and weary Negro men and women decided to rise from the dark dungeons of complacency to the bright hills of creative protest?"   —MARTIN LUTHER KING, JR., "Letter from Birmingham Jail"

The full text of King's argument includes other examples of ethos, logos, and pathos.

Although ethos is often developed in the introduction, logos in the body, and pathos in the conclusion, these classical rhetorical appeals often overlap and appear throughout an argument.

(2) Rogerian appeals show other people that you understand them.

Rogerian argument derives from the work of Carl R. Rogers, a psychologist who believed that many problems are the result of a breakdown in communication. Rogers claimed that people often fail to understand each other because of a natural tendency to judge and evaluate, agree or disagree, without really listening to, let alone understanding, what is being said. His model calls for suspending judgment until you are able to restate fairly and accurately what others believe. When each person in a conflict demonstrates this ability, the likelihood of misunderstanding is significantly reduced.

Skills such as paraphrasing (11d(3)) and summarizing (11d(4)) are essential to the Rogerian approach. Although this model can be used to achieve a number of goals, it is especially useful for building consensus. To demonstrate that you have given fair consideration to the views of others, you begin a Rogerian argument by paraphrasing these views and demonstrating that you understand the thinking behind them. Then, you introduce your own position and explain why you believe it has merit. Because the Rogerian model is designed to build consensus, you conclude your argument by showing how everyone concerned about the issue could benefit from adopting your proposal. This emphasis on being fair-minded and nonconfrontational gives ethos (8f(1)) an essential place in a Rogerian argument.

The summary of benefits with which a Rogerian argument concludes gives you the opportunity to draw your threads together and appeal to your audience without simply restating what you have already said. In the following conclusion to an argument on public education, notice how the author cites benefits for students, teachers, and the public at large if her proposal is adopted:

4   Reducing the maximum class size in our secondary schools from thirty students to twenty-five will not solve all the problems in our system, but it will yield important benefits. Students will get more individualized instruction. Better able to give their full attention to the students who remain with them, teachers will gain greater job satisfaction. And in an era when events like the recent killings in Littleton, Colorado, raise legitimate concerns about the safety of public schools, an improved student-teacher ratio reduces the risk of a troubled student being overlooked—a comfort to parents as well as educators. Finally, even those citizens who do not have children will benefit, because in the long run everyone benefits from living in a community where people are well educated.   —LAURA BECHDEL, "Space to Learn"

8g   Purposefully arranging an effective argument

No single arrangement is right for every written argument. Unless your instructor asks you to demonstrate a particular type of arrangement, the decisions you make about arrangement should be based on several factors: your topic, your audience, and your purpose. You can develop a good plan by simply listing the major points you want to make (3d), deciding what order to put them in, and then determining where to include refutation or concession (8g(3)). You must also decide whether to place your thesis statement or claim at the beginning or the end of your argument. Once you sort out the reasons supporting your claim, you need to develop each reason with a separate paragraph (unless, of course, you are summarizing your reasons in the conclusion).

No matter which arrangement you use, your conclusion should move beyond a mere summary of what has already been stated and instead emphasize your emotional connection with your audience, a connection that reinforces your rhetorical purpose: getting readers to take a particular course of action, to further their understanding, or to accept the implications of your claim (8h). The student paper by Anna Seitz (pages 185–190) ends with a conclusion that not only reinforces her purpose but links it with the mission of universities.

In addition, there are a few basic principles that may be useful.

(1) Classical arrangement works well if your audience has not yet taken a position on your issue.

One way to organize your argument is to follow the plan recommended by classical rhetoric, which assumes that an audience is prepared to follow a well-reasoned argument.

FEATURES OF THE CLASSICAL ARRANGEMENT

Introduction	Introduce your issue, and capture the attention of your audience. Try using a short narrative or a strong example (3f(2) and 3g). Begin establishing your credibility (using ethos) and common ground.
Background information	Provide your audience with a history of the situation and state how things currently stand. Define any key terms. Even if you think the facts speak for themselves, draw the attention of your audience to those points that are especially important and explain why they are meaningful.
Proposition	Introduce the position you are taking: present the argument itself and provide the basic reasons for your belief. Frame your position as a thesis statement or a claim (3c and 8d).
Proof or confirmation	Discuss the reasons that have led you to take your position. Each reason must be clear, relevant, and representative. Provide facts, expert testimony, and any other evidence that supports your claim.
Refutation	Recognize and disprove the arguments of people who hold a different position and with whom you continue to disagree.

(Continued on page 172)

(Continued from page 171)

Concession	Concede any point with which you agree or that has merit; show why this concession does not damage your own case.
Conclusion	Summarize your most important points and appeal to your audience's feelings, making a personal connection. Describe the consequences of your argument in a final attempt to encourage your audience to consider (if not commit to) a particular course of action.

(2) Rogerian arrangement can help calm an audience strongly opposed to your position.

To write an argument informed by Rogerian appeals, use the following plan as your guide.

FEATURES OF THE ROGERIAN ARRANGEMENT

Introduction	Establish that you have paid attention to views different from your own. Build trust by stating these views clearly and fairly.
Concessions	Reassure the people you hope to persuade by showing that you agree with them to some extent and do not think that they are completely wrong.
Thesis	Having earned the confidence of your audience, state your claim, or proposition.
Support	Explain why you have taken this position and provide support for it.
Conclusion	Conclude by showing how your audience and other people could benefit from accepting your position. Indicate the extent to which this position will resolve the problem you are addressing. If you are offering a partial solution to a complex problem, concede that further work may be necessary.

(3) Refutation and concession are most effective when placed where readers will accept them.

Classical arrangement places refutation after the proof or confirmation of the argument, an arrangement that works well for an audience familiar with this organizational model. Sometimes, however, that refutation can come too late. Readers unfamiliar with classical arrangement may have decided that you are too one-sided—and may even have stopped reading. Therefore, when you are taking a highly controversial stand on an emotionally loaded subject, strive to establish common ground and then acknowledge opposing viewpoints and respond to them. This variation on classical arrangement assumes that readers will be unwilling to hear a new proposition unless they are first shown what is weak or incomplete about their current thinking.

In a Rogerian argument, a writer begins by reporting opposing views fairly and identifying what is valuable about them. The strategy here is not to refute the views in question but to concede that they have merit—thus putting the audience at ease before introducing a thesis or claim that might be rejected if stated prematurely.

However, sometimes readers may react negatively to a writer who responds to opposing views before offering any reasons to support his or her own view. These readers want to know from the start where an argument is headed. For this reason, writers often choose to state their position at the beginning of the argument and offer at least one strong reason to support it before turning to opposing views. They sometimes keep at least one other reason in reserve (often one responsibly laden with emotion, or pathos), so that they can present it after responding to opposing views, thereby ending with an emphasis on their confirmation.

Unless you are required to follow a specific arrangement, or organizational plan, you should respond to opposing views wherever your audience is most likely either to expect this discussion or to be willing to hear it. If your audience is receptive, you can place refutation and concession after your confirmation. If your audience adheres to a different position, you should respond to their views toward the beginning of your argument. You might also want to keep in mind that if you open a paragraph with an opposing view, you will want to move quickly to your response to that view so that your readers make only one shift between differing views. Your goal is to keep your readers focused on your line of thinking.

Exercise 4

Read the editorial pages of several consecutive issues of your community or college newspaper. Look for editorials that analyze or question an established belief, express or defend an opinion, invite consideration, or try to convince. Choose an editorial that strikes you as well argued, well developed, and well organized—even if it does not change your belief or action (it may only have changed your level of understanding). Bring several copies of the editorial to class, and be prepared to discuss its purpose, audience, use of appeals, and conclusion.

8h | Using logic to argue effectively and ethically

Because writers cannot argue on the basis of ethos alone, they need to understand the ways in which **logic**—the reasoning behind an argument—enhances or detracts from the argument. Logic is a means through which you can develop your ideas, realize new ones, and determine whether your thinking is clear enough to persuade readers to agree with you. By arguing logically, you increase the likelihood that your arguments will be taken seriously.

(1) Inductive reasoning is the process of using a number of specific facts or observations to draw a logical conclusion.

You use inductive reasoning every day. For example, if you get a stomachache within fifteen minutes of eating ice cream, you might conclude that there is a connection. Perhaps you are lactose intolerant. This use of evidence to form a generalization is called an **inductive leap,** and the leap should be in proportion to the amount of evidence gathered.

Inductive reasoning involves moving (or leaping) from discovering evidence to interpreting it, and it can help you arrive at probable, believable conclusions (but not absolute, enduring truth). Making a small leap from evidence (a stomachache) to a probable conclusion (lactose intolerance) is more effective and ethical than using the same evidence to make a sweeping claim that could easily be challenged (ice cream is bad for everyone) (8d(1)). Generally, the greater the weight of the evidence, the more reliable the conclusion.

When used in argument, inductive reasoning often employs facts (8c) and examples (3f(2) and 3g). When writers cannot cite all the information that supports their conclusions, they choose the evidence that is most reliable and most closely related to the point they are making.

(2) Deductive reasoning is the process of applying a generalization (or generalized belief) to a series of specific cases.

At the heart of a deductive argument is a **major premise** (a generalized belief that is assumed to be true), which the writer applies to a specific case (the **minor premise**), thereby yielding a conclusion, or claim. For example, if you know that all doctors must complete a residency and that Imogen is in medical school, then you can conclude that Imogen must complete a residency. This argument can be expressed in a three-part structure called a **syllogism.**

Major premise	All doctors must complete a residency. [generalized belief]
Minor premise	Imogen is studying to become a doctor. [specific case]
Conclusion	Imogen must complete a residency. [claim]

Sometimes premises are not stated, for the simple reason that the writer assumes a shared belief with the audience.

> Imogen has graduated from medical school, so she must complete a residency.

In this sentence, the unstated premise is that all doctors must complete a residency. A syllogism with an unstated premise—or even an unstated conclusion—is called an **enthymeme.** Frequently found in written arguments, enthymemes can be very effective because they presume shared beliefs or knowledge. For example, the argument "We need to build a new dormitory because the present overcrowded dorms are unsafe" contains the unstated premise that we should approve proposals that reduce unsafe overcrowding.

(3) The Toulmin model of reasoning provides an alternative to inductive and deductive reasoning.

To create a working system of logic suitable for the needs of all writers, philosopher Stephen Toulmin defined *argument* as a logical progression from the **data** (accepted evidence or reasons that support a claim) to the **claim** (a debatable or controversial statement), based on the **warrant** (the underlying assumption, like the major premise). If the warrant is controversial, it requires **backing** (independent support or justification). Writers who assume that they are drawing their evidence from reliable authorities should be able to cite the credentials of those authorities. And writers who base an argument on the law or another written code that has been widely agreed upon (a university's mission statement, for instance) should be able to cite the exact statute, precedent, or regulation in question or even include the law or code in the essay itself.

Like deductive reasoning, Toulmin's method establishes a reasonable relationship between the data and the claim. The following argument may help explain the progression:

> Universities should not sell naming rights to buildings because education, not pleasing corporate sponsors, should be the universities' primary goal.

Data	Selling naming rights to buildings forces universities to focus on pleasing the sponsors, rather than on education.
Claim	Universities should not sell naming rights to buildings.
Warrant	Education is the first priority of universities.

The warrant establishes a relationship with the data, providing a reasonable link with the claim that follows (fig. 8.1).

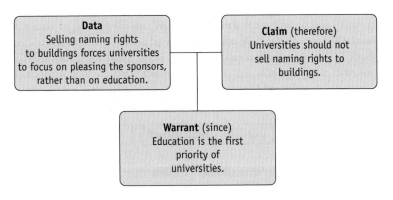

Fig. 8.1. A warrant linking data and a claim.

Of course, few arguments are as simple as this example. For instance, universities may view education as their first priority but see the sale of naming rights as a means of supporting that goal. In such cases, writers must make allowances for exceptions. Qualifiers such as *usually, probably, should,* and *possibly* show the degree of certainty of the conclusion, and rebuttal terms such as *unless* indicate exceptions.

> Because universities seek to promote education rather than business, they **should** avoid selling naming rights to buildings **unless** doing so supports the goal of educating students.

When using the Toulmin model to shape your arguments, you may be able to identify the claim, the data, and the qualifiers more easily than the warrant. Like the unstated premise in an enthymeme (8h(2)), the warrant is often assumed and backed up by something left unsaid. In the example above, the backing is the definition of a university—an institution established to provide higher education. To determine the backing for a warrant in an argument you are writing, trace your thinking back to the assumptions with which you began. As you do so, remember that backing can take different forms. It may be a law or regulation (such as a university regulation about student housing), a belief that the data came from a reliable source or that what is true of a sample is true of a larger group, or a moral, political, or economic value that is widely accepted in your culture.

8i Avoiding rhetorical fallacies

Logical reasoning not only enhances the overall effectiveness of an argument, it also enhances the ethos of the speaker or writer. Almost as important as constructing an argument effectively is avoiding errors in argument, or **rhetorical fallacies.** Rhetorical fallacies signal to your audience that your thinking is not entirely trustworthy and that your argument is not well reasoned.

Therefore, you need to recognize and avoid several kinds of fallacies. As you read the arguments of others (10a) and revise the arguments you draft (chapter 4), try to keep the following common rhetorical fallacies in mind.

(1) *Non sequitur,* **Latin for "it does not follow," means that just because the first part of a statement is true doesn't mean the second part will necessarily happen or become true.**

Non sequitur is the basis for most of the other rhetorical fallacies.

Faulty   Eddie is smart; therefore, he will do well in college.
[This assertion is based on the faulty premise that *all* smart people do well in college (**8h(2)**).]

(2) *Ad hominem* **refers to a personal attack on an opponent that draws attention away from the issues under consideration.**

Faulty   She is unfit to be a minister because she is divorced.
[The fact that a woman is divorced may reveal the condition of a previous marriage, but a divorce has little if anything to do with her spiritual beliefs and principles that could benefit a congregation.]

(3) *Appeal to tradition* **is an argument that says something should be done a certain way simply because it has been done that way in the past.**

Faulty   Because they are a memorable part of the pledge process, fraternity hazings should not be banned.
[Times change; what was considered good practice in the past is not necessarily considered acceptable now.]

(4) *Bandwagon* **is an argument saying, in effect, "Everyone's doing or saying or thinking this, so you should, too."**

Faulty   Everyone drives over the speed limit, so why shouldn't we raise the limit?
[The majority is not always right.]

(5) *Begging the question* **is an argument that assumes what in fact needs to be proved.**

Faulty   We need to fire corrupt officials in order to reduce the city's crime rate.
[If there are corrupt officials in city government, this point needs to be established.]

The CEO receives positive responses from all the board members, but they are thinking "No!" in different ways.

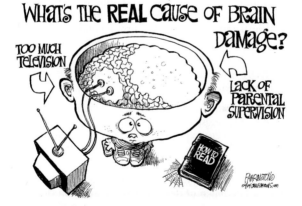

This cartoon begs the question "Are children brain damaged?" It also oversimplifies the potential causes of that damage.

(6) *Equivocation* **is an assertion that falsely relies on the use of a term in two different senses.**

Faulty   We know this is a natural law because it feels natural.
[In the first use, *natural* means "derived from nature or reason"; when used again, it means "easy or simple because of being in accord with one's own nature."]

Stealing in baseball is not the same as stealing in a store.

(7) *False analogy* **is the assumption that because two things are alike in some ways, they must be alike in others.**

Faulty   The United States lost credibility with other nations during the war in Vietnam, so we should not get involved in the Middle East, or we will lose credibility again.
[The differences between the war in Southeast Asia in the 1960s and 1970s and the current conflict in the Middle East may well be greater than their similarities.]

(8) *False authority* **is the assumption that an expert in one field can be credible in another.**

Faulty   We must stop sending military troops into Afghanistan, as Bruce Springsteen has argued.
[Springsteen's expertise in music does not automatically qualify him as an expert in foreign policy.]

(9) *False cause* **(sometimes called *post hoc, ergo propter hoc*, meaning "after this, so because of this") is the assumption that because one event follows another, the first is the cause of the second.**

Faulty   When Penn State football coach Joe Paterno turned 81, he was finally inducted into the College Football Hall of Fame.
[The assumption is that Paterno's age is solely responsible for his Hall of Fame honor.]

(10) *False dilemma* **(sometimes called the *either/or fallacy*) is a statement that only two alternatives exist, when in fact there are more than two.**

Faulty   We must either build more nuclear power plants or be completely dependent on foreign oil.
[Other possibilities exist.]

(11) *Guilt by association* **is an unfair attempt to make others responsible for a person's beliefs or actions.**

Faulty   Jon's father and grandfather were gamblers; therefore, Jon must be one, too.
[Several people can graduate from the same school, practice the same profession or religion, belong to the same family, or live in the same neighborhood without engaging in the same behavior.]

(12) *Hasty generalization* **is a conclusion based on too little evidence or on exceptional or biased evidence.**

Faulty   Ellen is a poor student because she failed her first history test.
[Her performance may improve in the weeks ahead or be good in all her other subjects.]

Without careful thinking, we often make hasty judgments about the people who are not like us.

(13) *Oversimplification* **is a statement or argument that leaves out relevant considerations in order to imply that there is a single cause or solution for a complex problem.**

Faulty   We can eliminate unwanted pregnancies by teaching birth control and abstinence.
[Teaching people about birth control and abstinence does not guarantee the elimination of unwanted pregnancies.]

(14) *Red herring* (sometimes called *ignoring the question*) means dodging the real issue by drawing attention to an irrelevant one.

Faulty   Why worry about violence in schools when we ought to be worrying about international terrorism?
[International terrorism has little if any direct relationship with school violence.]

(15) *Slippery slope* is the assumption that if one thing is allowed, it will be the first step in a downward spiral.

Faulty   Handgun control will lead to a police state.
[Handgun control has not led to a police state in England.]

"It started out with lactose, but now he's intolerant of everything."

Applying a slippery slope argument, this cartoon suggests that lactose intolerance leads to general intolerance.

Be alert for rhetorical fallacies in your writing. When you find such a fallacy, be sure to moderate your claim, clarify your thinking, or, if necessary, eliminate the fallacious statement. Even if your argument as a whole is convincing, rhetorical fallacies can damage your credibility (8d and 10a).

Exercise 5

For each of the following statements, write one or two sentences in which you identify and explain the faulty reasoning. Next, describe circumstances under which you might find these statements convincing. Finally, rewrite each statement so that it avoids rhetorical fallacies, regardless of the circumstances (if possible).

1. We must either build more dormitories or double up students in existing dormitories.

2. If we censor neo-Nazi demonstrations, we will ultimately lose freedom of speech.

3. If women dressed more conservatively, they would earn as much money as men.

4. We should cut social services because people on welfare are getting too many benefits.

5. Children would do a lot better at school if they didn't spend so much time watching television.

8j   Sample argument

The following paper was Anna Seitz's response to an assignment asking her to write an argumentative essay that identified a specific problem in her living quarters, on her campus, in her town, or in the world at large and then recommended a solution for that problem.

As you read Anna's essay, consider how she argued her case and whether she argued effectively. Note her use of classical rhetorical appeals (ethos, logos, and pathos) and arrangement and her inductive reasoning. Also, identify the kinds of evidence she uses (facts, examples, testimony, or authority).

Seitz 1

Anna Seitz

Professor Byerly

Library Science 313

November 30, 2007

Naming Opportunities: Opportunities for Whom?

> Chevy Chase Bank and the University of Maryland have
> expanded their long-term relationship in an agreeement that
> will mean the Terrapins' football and lacrosse teams will
> play on Chevy Chase Bank Field at Byrd Stadium. . . . The
> agreement will provide the university with $20 million. . . .
> ("Chevy Chase," pars. 1-2)

All over the nation, football stadiums, business schools, law schools, dining halls, and even coaching positions have become naming opportunities (also known as "naming rights" and "legacy opportunities"). Since the first college deal in 1979, when Syracuse University signed a deal with the Carrier Corporation for lifetime naming rights to their sports stadium--the Carrier Dome--naming has become a common practice with an alleged two-fold payoff: universities raise money and donors get their names writ large. Universities use the money from naming opportunities to hire more faculty, raise salaries, support faculty research, provide travel opportunities for students, and build stadium suites and boxes for game watching. Reser Stadium (Oregon State), The Donald Bren School of Law (University of California-Irvine), or the Malloy Paterno Head Football Coach Endowment (Penn State University)--all these naming opportunities seem like a good solution for raising money, especially at a time when state legislatures have cut

Introduction

Seitz 2

Introduction

back on university funding and when wealthy alumni are being besieged for donations from every college they have ever attended. Naming opportunities seem like a good solution for donors, too, because their donations will be broadly recognized. While naming opportunities may seem like a perfect solution for improving colleges and universities and simplifying funding, in reality they are not. In this paper, I argue against naming opportunities on college and university campuses because they create more problems than they solve.

The naming of sports stadiums is a familiar occurrence; after all, universities commonly highlight the sponsors of their athletic programs. But naming opportunities in other spheres of academic life are unfamiliar to most people, even though such naming is an established practice. A quick search of the Web pages of university libraries reveals that many of them, especially those in the midst of major development campaigns, have created a price list just for naming opportunities. Entire buildings are available, of course. For example, a $5 million donation earns the right to name the music library at Northwestern University (Northwestern). But parts of buildings are also available these days. North Carolina State University will name an atlas stand according to the donor's wishes for only $7,500 or put a specific name on a lectern for $3,500 (North Carolina).

Background information

Naming opportunities can clearly bring in a good deal of money. It has become commonplace for schools to offer naming opportunities on planned construction in exchange for 51 percent of the cost of the building! That's a big head start to a building project, and naming opportunities may be what allow some schools to provide their students with better facilities than their unnamed counterparts. In fact, donors are often recruited for the opportunity

Seitz 3

to pay for named faculty chairs, reading rooms, or major library or art
collections--all of which enhance student life.

Clearly the more opportunities and resources any university
can offer current and potential students and even alumni, the more that
university enhances its own growth and that of its faculty. Library
donors and recipients say that if it is possible for a library to pay for a
new computer lab just by adding a sign with someone's name over the
door, the advantages often seem to outweigh the disadvantages. Proponents
of naming opportunities point out that small donors are often hailed as
library supporters, even when big donors are maligned as corporate
flag-wavers.

Few would argue that these donations necessarily detract from the
educational mission of the institution. However, selling off parts of a
university library, for example, does not always please people, especially
those whose responsibility includes managing that donation. The curator of
rare books and manuscripts at a prominent state university told me that one
of the most frustrating parts of her job is dealing with "strings-attached"
gifts, which is what too many library donations turn out to be. Some
major donors like to make surprise visits, during which they monitor the
prominence of their "legacy opportunity." Others like to create rules which
limit the use of their funds to the purchase of certain collections or subjects;
still others just need constant personal maintenance, including lunches,
coffees, and regular invitations to events. But meddling in their donation
after the fact is just a minor inconvenience compared to some donors'
actions.

Background
information

Donors who fund an ongoing educational program and who give money on a regular basis often expect to have regular input. Because major donors want major prestige, they try to align themselves with successful programs. Doing that can result in damage to university budgets. First of all, high-profile programs can become increasingly well funded, while less prominent, less glamorous ones are continually ignored. Second, when corporate or private funds are regularly available, it can have the result of eroding existing funding sources. Simply put, if budgeted programs become funded by donation, those funds will, for better or worse, be redirected, and the next time the program needs funding, the department or unit will likely be told that finding a donor is their only option. Essentially, once donor-funded, always donor-funded.

Proposition

Additionally, many academics feel that selling off naming rights can create an image problem for a university. While buildings, schools, endowed chairs, even football stadiums were once named for past professors, university presidents, or others with strong ties to the university, those same facilities are now named for virtually anyone who can afford to donate, especially corporations. Regular input from a corporation creates the appearance of a conflict of interest in a university, which is exactly the reason such arrangements are so often vehemently opposed by the university community. Boise State University in Idaho received such negative press for negotiating a deal with labor-unfriendly Taco Bell that it was finally pressured to terminate the $4 million contract (Langrill 1).

Proof

Given these drawbacks, many universities are establishing guidelines for the selection of appropriate donors for named gifts. To that end,

Seitz 5

fundraising professional and managing director of Changing Our World, Inc. Robert Hoak suggests that naming opportunities should be mutually beneficial for the donor (whether a corporation or an individual) and the organization (university, for instance) and that these opportunities should be viewed as the start of a long-term relationship between the two, not the final gift (Hoak, para. 3). Additionally, he cautions that even if the donor seems the right fit for the organization, it is in the best interest of both parties to add an escape clause to the contract in order to protect either side from potential embarrassment or scandal. He provides the example of Seton Hall University, which regrettably had both an academic building and the library rotunda named for Tyco CEO Dennis Kozlowski. When Kozlowski was convicted of grand larceny, the university pulled the names (Hoak, para. 5).

Proof

Although many people prefer that naming be an honor given to recognize an accomplished faculty member or administrator, most realize that recruiting named gift donors is good business. Whether it is "good education" is another question. While signing contracts with donors has become a sales transaction, naming university property for major donors is not. New College in Cambridge, Massachussetts was just that--until local clergyman John Harvard died and left half his estate and his entire library to what would soon become Harvard College. Modern naming opportunities, however, are rarely so simple. They do not necessarily recognize and remember individuals who had significant influence on university life; rather, they create obligations for the university to operate in such a way as to please living donors or their descendents. Pleasing wealthy donors should not replace educating students as a university's primary goal.

Refutation

Works Cited

"Chevy Chase Bank Signs Naming Rights Agreement for Byrd Stadium
    Field." University of Maryland. 17 Sept. 2005 <http://www.umd.edu/
    umnews/chevy_chase_bank_field.html>.

Hoak, Robert. "Making the Most of Naming Opportunities." 28 March 2005.
    onPhilanthropy. 5 Nov. 2007 <http://www.onphilanthropy.com/site/
    News2?page= NewsArticle&id=6254>.

Langrill, Chereen. "BSU Faculty Says 'No Quiero' to Taco Bell." *Idaho
    Statesman* [Boise] 27 October 2004: 1+.

North Carolina State University Libraries. "NCSU Libraries East Wing
    Renovation: Naming Opportunities." 5 Nov. 2007 <http://
    www.lib.ncsu.edu/renovation/namingOp/>.

Northwestern University Library. "Making a Gift: Naming Opportunities."
    2007. *Naming Opportunities: Library Development Office*. 20
    Nov. 2007 <http://www.library.northwestern.edu/giving/gift/
    naming.html>.

Exercise 6

Reread Anna Seitz's essay and identify her claim and proof. What values
does Anna reveal as she argues against naming opportunities? What
personal experiences have shaped Anna's values?

R

RESEARCH

9 Finding Sources in Print, Online, and in the Field 193

10 Evaluating Print and Online Sources 216

11 Using Sources Effectively and Responsibly 229

The Internet gives students and scholars instant access to information from worldwide sources.

CHAPTER 9
Finding Sources in Print, Online, and in the Field 193

9a   Research and the rhetorical
     situation   193
9b   Finding books   198
9c   Finding articles   202
9d   Finding online sources   207
9e   Field research   211

CHAPTER 10
Evaluating Print and Online Sources 216

10a   Credibility of authors   216
10b   Credibility of publishers   221
10c   Online sources   223
10d   Relevance and timeliness   227

CHAPTER 11
Using Sources Effectively and Responsibly 229

11a   The rhetorical situation and the
      research paper   229
11b   Organizing notes   231
11c   Working bibliography and annotated
      bibliography   234
11d   Integrating sources   235
11e   Avoiding plagiarism   241
11f   Responding to sources   244

9 Finding Sources in Print, Online, and in the Field

Too often, the word *research* brings to mind laboratory experiments, archaeological digs, or hours spent in the library and not the ordinary research you yourself do every day as you decide which computer to buy (and then how to use that computer), how to prepare your taxes, which books to read for your courses, and even where to spend your vacation. Research is common to everyone's experience. To conduct useful research efficiently, you must first develop skills in accessing information. This chapter will help you

- use the rhetorical situation to frame your research (9a),
- find books (9b),
- find articles (9c),
- find Web-based sources (9d), and
- conduct field research (9e).

9a Research and the rhetorical situation

To make the most of the time you spend doing research, determine your rhetorical situation early in the research process. By understanding your exigence, audience, and purpose, you can gather relevant sources efficiently.

(1) Identifying an exigence can help you form a research question.

The starting point for any writing project is your exigence—the issue or problem that has prompted you to write (1b). For research assignments, the exigence also prompts you to find more information before you write. Once you are sure of the exigence, craft a question to guide your research. Your research will then become a quest to answer that question (in essence, to resolve your exigence).

Research questions often arise when you try to relate what you are studying for a course to your own experience. For instance, you may start wondering about voting regulations and procedures while reading about past elections for a history class and at the same time noticing the number of news stories about the role technology plays in elections or the unfair practices reported in some states. Such observations may prompt you to find more information. Each observation, however, may give rise to a different question. Focusing on the influence of technology may prompt you to ask, "What are the possible consequences of having electronic ballots only?" If you focus on unfair voting practices instead, you may ask, "How do voting procedures differ from state to state?" Because you can ask a variety of research questions about any topic, choose the one that interests you the most and that allows you to fulfill your assignment.

To generate research questions, you may find it helpful to ask yourself about causes, consequences, processes, definitions, or values, as in the following examples.

Questions about causes

What are the causes of low achievement in our schools?

What causes power outages in large areas of the country?

Questions about consequences

What are the consequences of taking antidepressants for a long period of time?

How might stronger gun control laws affect the frequency of public shootings?

Questions about processes

How can music lovers prevent corporations from controlling the development of new music?

How are presidential campaigns funded?

Questions about definitions

How do you know if you are addicted to something?

What is the opportunity gap in the American educational system?

Questions about values

Should the Makah tribe be allowed to hunt gray whales?

Would the construction of wind farms be detrimental to the environment?

If you have trouble coming up with a research question, you may need a jump start. The following tips can help you.

TIPS FOR FINDING A RESEARCH QUESTION

- Can you remember an experience that you did not understand fully or that made you feel uncertain? What was it that you did not understand? What were you unsure of?
- What have you observed recently (on television, in the newspaper, on campus, or online) that piqued your curiosity? What were you curious about?
- What widely discussed local or national problem would you like to help solve?
- Is there anything (lifestyles, political views, fashion preferences) that you find unusual or intriguing and would like to explore?

Research and writing require a commitment of time and effort, so you will find these tasks more pleasant, even easier, when you are interested in your research question. Other people can help you sharpen your question by telling you about their experiences and asking you about your own. To get a conversation about research started, have a friend or classmate ask you the following questions. Or use these questions to spark your focused freewriting.

- Why is it important for you to answer this research question? Why is it important for your audience to know the answer to the question?
- Why does the answer to your question require research? (There should not be a simple or obvious answer to the question.)
- What types of research might help you answer your question?
- Will you be able to carry out the necessary research in the amount of time allowed?

Exercise 1

Each of the following subjects would need to be narrowed down for a research paper. To experiment with framing a research question, compose two questions about each subject that could be answered in a ten-page paper (refer to the list on page 194 for examples of questions).

1. literacy
2. the job market
3. gender differences
4. globalization
5. No Child Left Behind Act
6. health care

(2) Research can help you address your audience and achieve a specific purpose.

Your audience and your purpose are interconnected. In general terms, your purpose is to have an impact on your audience; in more specific terms, your purpose may be to entertain your readers, to inform them, to explain something to them, or to persuade them to do something. Research can help you achieve any of these goals.

A research paper often has one of the following rhetorical purposes.

■ *To inform an audience.* The researcher reports current thinking on a specific topic, including opposing views, without analyzing them or siding with a particular position.

Example To inform an audience about current nutritional guidelines for children

■ *To analyze and synthesize information and then offer possible solutions.* The researcher analyzes a topic and synthesizes the available information about it, looking for points of agreement and disagreement and for gaps in coverage. Thus, part of the research consists of finding out what other researchers have written about the topic. After presenting the analysis and synthesis, the researcher sometimes offers possible ways to address any problems found.

Example To analyze and synthesize various national health care proposals

■ *To convince or issue an invitation to an audience.* The researcher states a position and backs it up with data, statistics, testimony, corroborating texts or events, or supporting arguments. The researcher's purpose is to persuade or invite readers to take the same position.

Example To persuade people to support a political candidate

A researcher presenting results from an original experiment or study must often achieve all of these purposes. In the introduction of a lab report, for example, the researcher analyzes and synthesizes previous work done on the same topic and locates a research niche—an area needing further study. The researcher then attempts to convince the readers that his or her current study will help address the need for more research. The body of the report is informative, describing the materials used, explaining the procedures followed, and presenting the results. In the conclusion, the researcher may try, based on the results of the experiment or study, to persuade the audience to take some action (for example, give up smoking, eat fewer carbohydrates, or fund future research).

(3) The sources you use may be primary, secondary, or both.

As you proceed with research, be aware of whether your sources are primary or secondary. **Primary sources** for researching topics in the humanities are generally documents such as archived letters, records, and papers, as well as literary, autobiographical, and philosophical texts. In the social sciences, primary sources can be field observations, case histories, and survey data. In the natural

Primary sources, such as a report from an archeological dig, are useful for many research projects.

sciences, primary sources are generally empirical, including field observations, measurements, or discoveries and experimental results.

Secondary sources are commentaries on primary sources. For example, a review of a new novel is a secondary source, as is a discussion of adolescence based on survey data. Experienced researchers usually consult both primary and secondary sources, read them critically, and draw on them carefully.

Like you, the authors of the sources you use have written in response to their rhetorical situations. They have specified a goal for their work, a group of readers who might be interested in their findings, and a document form that best expresses their ideas. Thinking about the rhetorical situations that underlie the sources you consider will help you locate those most useful to you, read them with a critical eye, and incorporate them into your paper appropriately.

9b   Finding books

Three types of books are commonly used in the research process. **Scholarly books** are written by experts to advance knowledge of a certain subject. Most include original research. Before being published, these books are reviewed by scholars in the same field as the author(s). **Trade books** may also be written by experts or scholars, though they may be authored by journalists or freelance writers instead. But the audience and purpose of trade books differ from those of scholarly books. Rather than addressing other scholars, authors of trade books write to inform a general audience of research that has been done by others. **Reference books** such as encyclopedias and dictionaries provide factual information. These secondary sources contain short articles or entries written and reviewed by experts in the field. Their audience includes both veteran scholars and those new to a field of study.

(1) An online catalog helps you locate books.

The easiest way to find books related to your research question is to consult your library's online catalog. When a research area is new to you, you can find many sources by doing either keyword searches or subject searches. To perform a **keyword search,** choose a word or phrase that you think might be found in the title of a book or in notes in the catalog's records. Some online catalogs allow users to be quite specific. The keyword search page in fig. 9.1 provides options for specifying a language, a location in the library, a type of book (or type of material other than a book, such as a brochure or government document), the way the results should be organized, the publisher, and the date of publication. The keyword search page in fig. 9.1 also provides some recommendations for entering words. By using a word or part of a word followed by asterisks, you can find all sources that include that root, even when suffixes have been added. For example, if you entered *environment**,* you would find not only sources with *environment* in the title, subject headings, and content notes, but also sources with *environments, environmental,* or *environmentalist* in those locations. This search technique is called **truncation.**

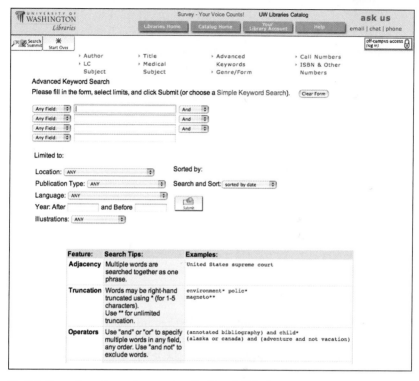

Fig. 9.1. Keyword search page from a university library's Web site.

You can also enter multiple keywords in search boxes by using **logical operators** such as *and, or, not,* and *near* (*and, or,* and *not* are sometimes called **Boolean operators**). These words narrow or broaden a search. They are used in electronic searches for books and for other documents such as articles and government brochures.

Although you will probably begin your research by using keyword searches, you may employ **subject searches** as well. To perform a successful subject search, you will have to enter words that correspond to the subject categories established by the Library of Congress. The best strategy for performing this type of search is to enter words familiar to you. If, for some reason, the search does not yield any results, ask a reference librarian for a subject-heading guide. Author searches and title searches can also be useful, though only when you already have a particular author or title in mind.

LOGICAL OPERATORS

The words *and, or, not,* and *near* are the most common logical operators. However, online catalogs and periodical databases have various instructions for using them. If you have trouble following the guidelines presented here, check the instructions for the particular search box you are using.

and   narrows a search (Entering "genetically modified **and** food" returns only those records that contain both keywords.)

or   broadens a search (Entering "genetically modified **or** food" finds all records that contain information about either keyword.)

not   excludes specific items (Entering "genetically modified **and** food **not** humans" excludes any records that mention genetic modification of human beings.)

near   finds records in which the two keywords occur in close proximity, within a preset number of words, and excludes those in which the keywords are widely separated (Entering "genetically modified **near** vegetables" lists only those records in which references to *genetically modified* and *vegetables* occur in close proximity.)

Once you find the online catalog record for a book you would like to use, write down its **call number.** This number appears on the book itself and indicates where the book is shelved. The online record will reveal the status of the book, letting you know whether it is currently checked out or has been moved to a special collection. To find the book, consult the key to your library's shelving system, usually posted throughout the library. Library staff can also help you find books.

(2) Specialized reference books are listed in your library's online catalog. A specialized encyclopedia or dictionary can often provide background information on people, events, and concepts related to the topic you are researching. To find such sources using an online search page, enter the type of reference book and one or two keywords identifying your topic. For example, entering "encyclopedia of alcoholism" resulted in the following list of titles:

Encyclopedia of Drugs, Alcohol, and Addictive Behavior
Encyclopedia of Drugs and Alcohol
The Encyclopedia of Alcoholism

USEFUL REFERENCE BOOKS

For a detailed list of reference books and a short description of each, consult *Guide to Reference Books* by Robert Balay and *American Reference Books Annual* (*ARBA*). A few widely used reference books are listed here.

Specialized Dictionaries and Encyclopedias

- *Dictionary of American History*
- *Dictionary of Art*
- *Encyclopedia of Bioethics*
- *Encyclopedia of Higher Education*
- *Encyclopedia of Psychology*

Collections of Biographies

- *American National Biography*
- *Dictionary of Scientific Biography*
- *Notable American Women*
- *Who's Who in America*

(3) You may need to consult books not listed in your library's online catalog.

If you cannot find a particular book in your library, you have several options. Frequently, libraries have links to the catalogs of other libraries. By using such links, you can determine whether another library has the book you want and then order it through your library's interlibrary loan service. In addition, your library may have the database WorldCat, which locates books as well as images, sound recordings, and other materials. You may also access reference, fiction, and nonfiction books at **www.Bartleby.com**.

Exercise 2

Choose a research question, perhaps one you composed in exercise 1. Find the titles of a scholarly book, a trade book, and a reference book related to your choice.

9c Finding articles

Articles can be found in various **periodicals** (publications that appear at regular intervals). Because they are published daily, weekly, or monthly, periodicals offer information that is often more recent than that found in books. **Scholarly journals** usually contain reports of original research written by experts for an academic audience. **Trade magazines** feature articles written by staff writers or industry specialists. Because they are written for members of a particular trade, these articles address on-the-job concerns. **Popular magazines** and **newspapers** are generally written by staff writers. These periodicals carry a combination of news stories that attempt to be objective and essays that reflect the opinions of editors or guest contributors. The following are examples of the various types of periodicals:

> **Scholarly journals:** *The Journal of Developmental Psychology, The Journal of Business Communication*
>
> **Trade magazines:** *Farm Journal, Automotive Weekly*
>
> **Magazines (news):** *Time, Newsweek*
>
> **Magazines (public affairs):** *The New Yorker, National Review*
>
> **Magazines (special interest):** *National Geographic, Discover*
>
> **Newspapers:** *The New York Times, The Washington Post*

(1) An electronic database can help you find articles.

Your library's online catalog lists the titles of periodicals; however, it does not provide the titles of individual articles within these periodicals. The best strategy for finding print articles is to use an **electronic database,** which is a collection of articles compiled by a company that indexes them according to author, title, date, keywords, and other features. The electronic databases available in libraries are sometimes called **database subscription services, licensed databases,** or **aggregated databases.** Similar to an online catalog, an electronic database allows you to search for sources by author, title, keyword, and so on. However, such databases focus on specific subject areas.

A database search will generally yield an **abstract,** a short summary of an article. By scanning the abstract, you can determine whether to locate the complete text of the article, which can often be downloaded and printed. You can access your library's databases by using its computers or, if you have a password, by using an Internet link from a remote computer. College libraries subscribe to a wide variety of database services, but the following are the most common:

ERIC: Articles related to education

JSTOR: Articles from journals in the arts, humanities, ecology, and social sciences

PsycINFO: Articles related to psychology

You may be able to access the search boxes for databases directly, or you may have to access databases through the search boxes of a vendor such as OCLC, InfoTrac, LexisNexis, or EBSCO. The Web site of the Penn State University Libraries, for instance, offers a lengthy list of databases accessible by name, by subject, and so on (see the Databases link near the top of the screen in fig. 9.2). To use the list, you can choose a database according to name, description, category, type, or database vendor (see the box at the left of the screen in fig. 9.2). You can also view an alphabetical listing of the various databases, beginning with 19th Century Newspapers British Library Collection and ABELL (Annual Bibliography of English Language and Literature) and ending with Zacks University Analysis Watch.

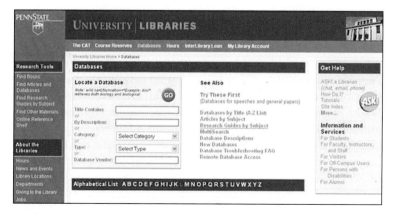

Fig. 9.2. Example of an online database access page from a university library.

If you were using this list of databases to research the relationship between alumni contributions and campus naming opportunities, as Anna Seitz did for her paper (8j), you could start with one of the following databases: ProQuest (Multiple Databases), Penn State University Web Site, or Standard & Poor's NetAdvantage. To research the status of genetically modified foods in the United States, as Marianna Suslin did for her paper (13c), you could select Agropedia (agriculture encyclopedias), Consumer Health, or Engineered Materials. To research tattooing trends, as Rachel L. Pinter and Sarah M. Cronin did for their paper (15c), you could select PsycARTICLES or Social Sciences Citation Index.

TIPS FOR CONDUCTING A SEARCH FOR PERIODICAL LITERATURE

- Identify keywords that clearly represent the topic.
- Determine the databases you want to search.
- Perform your search, using logical operators (9b(1)).
- Refine your search strategy if the first search returns too many or too few citations or (worse) irrelevant ones.
- Download and print the relevant articles.

(2) Print indexes provide essential information not found in electronic databases.

Before computers were widely used, researchers relied on **print indexes.** These bound volumes still provide essential backup when computers are out of service as well as access to older articles that may not be included in electronic databases. Some of the most useful print indexes, with their dates of beginning publication, are as follows:

Applied Science and Technology Index. 1958– .

Art Index. 1929– .

Biological and Agricultural Index. 1946– .

Business Periodicals Index. 1958– .

Cumulative Index to Nursing and Allied Health Literature (CINAHL).
1982– .

General Science Index. 1978– .

Humanities Index. 1974– .

Index to Legal Periodicals. 1908– .

Music Index. 1949– .

Philosopher's Index. 1967– .

Public Affairs Information Service (PAIS) Bulletin. 1915– .

Social Sciences Index. 1974– .

When they publish electronic versions of their indexes, some publishers change the title: *Current Index to Journals in Education* (*CIJE*) and *Resources in Education* (*RIE*) are the bound volumes for research in education, and ERIC is the electronic version. Consult the front of any bound volume for a key to the abbreviations used in individual entries.

(3) InfoTrac College Edition provides easy access to articles.
With InfoTrac College Edition and a passcode, you can conveniently search for articles with the Web browser on your own computer. You do not have to be networked to your library's Web site. InfoTrac College Edition indexes articles in over 3,800 journals and magazines and provides the full text of these articles. The InfoTrac screens in figs. 9.3 and 9.4 illustrate part of the research Marianna Suslin conducted for her paper (13c). Clicking in the box labeled "Mark" next to the article about labeling genetically modified foods, shown in fig. 9.3, and then clicking on "text and full content retrieval choices" (not shown in fig. 9.3) brought up the complete article, whose first page appears in fig. 9.4.

Exercise 3

Choose a research question, perhaps one from exercise 1. Find the titles of a scholarly article, a magazine article, and a newspaper article related to your choice.

INFOTRAC® COLLEGE EDITION
From Gale Group and Thomson Learning

Keyword search (in title, citation, abstract): genetically modified food

Citations 1 to 20 (of 284)

Genetically modified food products must be labeled.
The Times of India Nov 30, 2007 pNA (438 words)

Fourteen Global Experts Comment on the Safety and Use of Genetically Modified Food Crops; Online Video Captures Support for Contributions to the Environment and Third-World Farmers.
Internet Wire Nov 5, 2007 pNA (817 words)

Fourteen Global Experts Comment on the Safety and Use of Genetically Modified Food Crops.
PR Newswire Nov 5, 2007 pNA (827 words)

EU set to approve GM potato.(regulatory)(genetically modified food)(Brief article) Kara Sissell.
Chemical Week July 25, 2007 v169 i25 p35(1) (147 words)

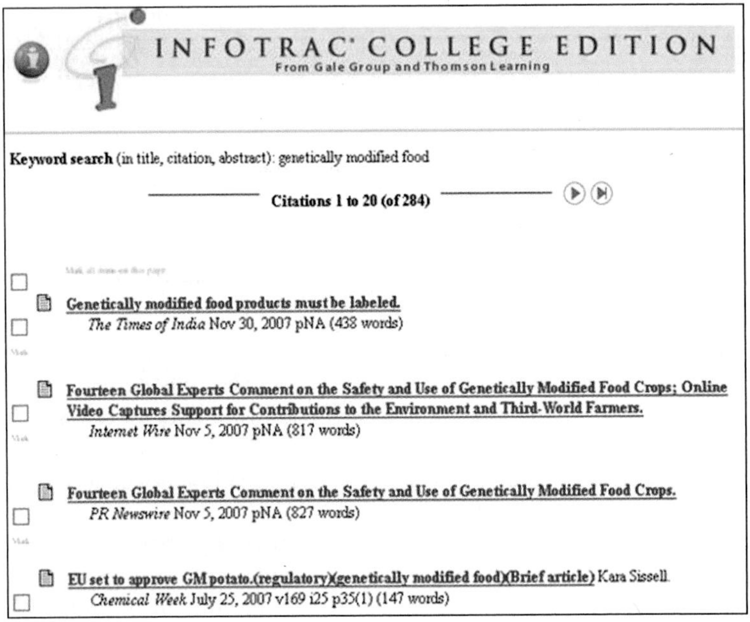

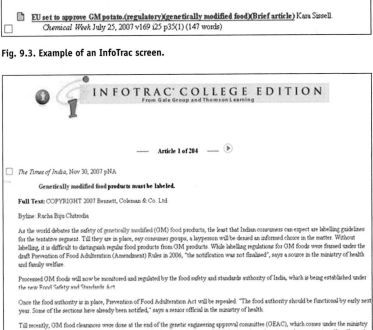

Fig. 9.3. Example of an InfoTrac screen.

INFOTRAC® COLLEGE EDITION
From Gale Group and Thomson Learning

Article 1 of 284

The Times of India, Nov 30, 2007 pNA

Genetically modified food products must be labeled.

Full Text: COPYRIGHT 2007 Bennett, Coleman & Co. Ltd.

Byline: Rucha Biju Chitrodia

As the world debates the safety of genetically modified (GM) food products, the least that Indian consumers can expect are labelling guidelines for the tentative segment. Till they are in place, say consumer groups, a layperson will be denied an informed choice in the matter. Without labelling, it is difficult to distinguish regular food products from GM products. While labelling regulations for GM foods were framed under the draft Prevention of Food Adulteration (Amendment) Rules in 2006, "the notification was not finalised", says a source in the ministry of health and family welfare.

Processed GM foods will now be monitored and regulated by the food safety and standards authority of India, which is being established under the new Food Safety and Standards Act.

Once the food authority is in place, Prevention of Food Adulteration Act will be repealed. "The food authority should be functional by early next year. Some of the sections have already been notified," says a senior official in the ministry of health.

Till recently, GM food clearances were done at the end of the genetic engineering approval committee (GEAC), which comes under the ministry of environment and forests. In September, however, GEAC exempted processed GM food products from its regulatory purview. "It will now be

Fig. 9.4. First page of an article found through InfoTrac.

9d Finding online sources

On the Internet, you can find not only text files but also audio and video files. Most researchers start their online research by using search engines, meta-search engines, or subject directories. **Search engines** are electronic indexes of words and terms from Web pages. To use them effectively, you should understand their features. Always consult the Help feature to learn how to perform an advanced search so that you will not waste time weeding out results that are not of interest to you. Advanced searches with a search engine are performed in much the same way as searches in online catalogs and databases. You can specify which words or phrases to use, how close words should be, which words should be excluded, and whether any word should be truncated (9b(1)). The following are the addresses for some commonly used search engines:

Google	**www.google.com**
Infoseek	**infoseek.go.com**
Lycos	**www.lycos.com**
MSN Search	**search.msn.com**
WebCrawler	**www.webcrawler.com**

If you are looking solely for news stories, consider using the following:

Google News	**www.google.com/news**
TotalNEWS	**www.totalnews.com**

Meta-search engines are also useful research tools. *Meta-* means "transcending" or "more comprehensive." Meta-search engines check a number of search engines, including those previously listed. Try the following for starters:

Dogpile	**www.dogpile.com**
MetaCrawler	**www.metacrawler.com**

Unlike search engines, **subject directories** are collections of Web sources arranged topically. Yahoo! (**www.yahoo.com**) offers a subject directory under Web Directory on its home page: it includes categories such as "Arts," "Health," and "Education." Some researchers find subject directories easier to use because most of the irrelevant Web sites have been weeded out. The following are some other useful subject directories for academic and professional research:

Academic Info	**www.academicinfo.net**
The Internet Public Library	**www.ipl.org/ref**
Librarians' Index to the Internet	**lii.org**
The WWW Virtual Library	**vlib.org**

Although searching the Web is a popular research technique, it is not the only technique you should use. Search engines cover only the portion of the Internet that allows free access. You will not find library books or database materials through a Web search because library and database services are available only to paid subscribers (students fall into this category). When you search the Web, remember that no single search engine covers the entire Web and that surprisingly little overlap occurs when different search engines are used to find information on the same topic. Thus, using more than one search engine is a good idea.

(1) Knowing your location on the Web will help you keep track of your sources.

It is easy to get lost on the Web as you click from link to link. You can keep track of your location by looking at the Web address, or **URL (uniform resource locator),** at the top of the screen. Web addresses generally include the following information: server name, domain name, directory (and perhaps subdirectory) name, file name, and file type.

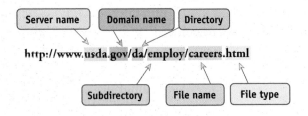

Sometimes when you click on a link, you will end up at a totally different Web site, so be sure to check the server and domain names when you are unsure of your location.

 CAUTION

If you find that a URL has changed, which is likely if a site is regularly updated, you may still be able to find the site you are looking for by dropping the last part of the address and trying again. You may need to do this several times. If this strategy does not work, you can also run a search or look at the links on related Web sites.

Because sites change and even disappear, scholarly organizations such as the Modern Language Association (chapter 13) require that bibliographic entries for Web sites include both the **access date** (the date on which the site was visited) and the **posting date** (the date when the site was last modified or updated). When you print out material from the Web, the access date usually appears at the top or bottom of the printout. The posting date generally appears on the site itself. Some sites do not show a posting date, however, and printouts sometimes will not have an access date. Keeping a separate record of this information can help you when you need to verify information on a site or list it in a bibliography. If a site does not have a posting date, note that it is undated; doing so will establish that you did not accidentally omit a piece of information.

TECH SAVVY

A convenient way to keep track of any useful Web site you visit is to create a **bookmark**—a record of a Web address you may want to return to in the future. The bookmarking function of a Web browser is usually labeled Bookmarks or Favorites.

Exercise 4

Perform a database search and a Web search using the same keywords for each. Print the first screen of the hits (results) you get for each type of search. Compare the two printouts, describing how the results of the two searches differ.

(2) The U.S. Government provides vast amounts of public information.
If you need information on particular federal laws, court cases, or population statistics, U.S. Government documents may be your best sources. You can find these documents by using online databases such as Congressional Universe, MARCIVE, LexisNexis Academic Universe, Census 2000, and STAT-USA. In addition, the following Web sites are helpful:

FirstGov	**www.firstgov.gov**
U.S. Government Printing Office	**www.gpoaccess.gov**
U.S. Courts	**www.uscourts.gov**
FedWorld	**www.fedworld.gov**

Fig. 9.5. Genetically modified foods look like naturally produced foods. (Photo courtesy of Alix/ Phanie/First Light, Canada.)

(3) Your rhetorical situation may call for the use of images.
If your rhetorical situation calls for the use of images, as did Marianna Suslin's (**13c**), the Internet offers you billions from which to choose. However, if an image you choose is copyrighted, you will need to contact the author, artist, or designer for permission to use it. Figure 9.5 is an example of an image with a caption and a credit line, which signifies that the image is used with permission. You do not need to obtain permission to use public domain images or those that are cleared for reuse.

Many search engines allow you to search for images. On the search pages for Google and AltaVista, you must first click on the Image button. For MetaCrawler, you must choose Images from the pull-down menu. Collections of specific images are available at the following Web sites:

Advertisements

Ad*Access	**scriptorium.lib.duke.edu/adaccess**
Adflip	**www.adflip.com**
Advertising World	**advertising.utexas.edu/world**

Art

The Artchive	**www.artchive.com**
The Web Gallery of Art	**www.wga.hu**

Clip art

The Icon Browser	**www.ibiblio.org/gio/iconbrowser**
Webclipz	**www.webclipz.com**

Photography

The New York Public Library Picture Collection Online	**digital.nypl.org/mmpco**
Smithsonian Images	**smithsonianimages.com**

9e Field research

Although much of your research will consist of reading, viewing, or listening to sources, you may also find it helpful to conduct **field research**—to gather information in a natural setting. Interviews, discussions, questionnaires, and observations are the most common methods for such research.

(1) Consider interviewing an expert.
After you have consulted some sources on your topic, you may find that you still have questions that might best be answered by someone who has firsthand experience in the area you are researching. Consider contacting a teacher, government official, business owner, or other

person with the relevant background to see whether it would be possible to schedule an interview. Most people welcome the opportunity to discuss their work, especially with a student who shows genuine interest. Because you will have done some reading on your topic before your meeting, you will be prepared to conduct a well-informed interview.

To arrange an interview, introduce yourself, briefly describe your project, and then explain your reasons for requesting the interview. Most people are busy, so try to accommodate the person you hope to interview by asking him or her to suggest an interview date. If you intend to tape your interview, ask for permission ahead of time.

Start preparing your list of questions before the day of the interview. Effective interviews usually contain a blend of open (or broad) questions and focused (or narrow) questions. Here are a few examples:

Open questions

What do you think about _____?

What are your views on _____?

Why do you believe _____?

Focused questions

How long have you worked as a/an _____?

When did you start _____?

What does _____ mean?

If you ask a question that elicits just "yes" or "no," reformulate the question so that it begins with *why, when, what, who, where,* or *how.* By doing so, you give your interviewee a chance to elaborate. If you know that the person you are interviewing has published articles or a book on your topic, ask questions that will advance your knowledge, rather than questions that the author has already answered in print.

Preparing a list of questions before an interview is essential, but do not just recite your questions during the meeting. An interview is a special kind of conversation. Although you will be guiding it, the person you are speaking with is likely to say something you did not expect but would like to know more about. Do not be afraid to ask questions that are not on your list but come to mind during the interview. Along with your list of questions, be sure to bring pen and paper so that you can take notes and a voice recorder if you will be recording the interview.

After the interview, take some time to review your notes. It will be hard to take down everything that is said during the interview, so expand on the notes you do have. If you recorded the interview, transcribe the relevant parts of the recording. The next step is to write extensively about the interview. Ask yourself what you found most important, most surprising, and most puzzling. You will find this writing especially worthwhile when you are able to use portions of it in your final paper.

(2) Consider participating in an online discussion group.
Less formal than an interview, a discussion with other people interested in your topic can also be useful. Online discussion groups, or forums (6b), allow you to read messages posted to all the members of a group interested in a specific topic and to post messages or questions yourself. For instance, a writing teacher may belong to a specialized e-mail list, or **listserv,** that is operated by the Alliance for Computers and Writing and called ACW-L. Participants in this online forum discuss issues related to using computers to teach writing. Someone on the ACW-L list can send an e-mail message to the **listserv address,** from which the message is redistributed to hundreds of other writing teachers around the world, and then receive replies from any of those teachers. You can find addresses of online discussion groups at **www.forumone.com** or **groups.google.com**. Your instructor may even have created a discussion forum especially for your class.

(3) Consider using a questionnaire to gather information from a large number of people.
Whereas an interview elicits information from one person whose name you know, a questionnaire provides information from a number of anonymous people. To be effective, a questionnaire should be short and focused. If the list of questions is too long, people may not be willing to take the time to answer them all. If the questions are not focused on your research topic, you will find it difficult to integrate the results into your paper.

Questionnaires elicit information in a variety of ways, through several types of questions. The types of questions you decide to use depend on the purpose of your survey. The first four types of questions in the following box are the easiest for respondents to answer. Open questions, which require much more time to answer, should be asked only when the other types of questions cannot elicit the information you want.

EXAMPLES OF TYPES OF SURVEY QUESTIONS

Questions that require a simple yes-or-no answer:

Do you commute to work in a car? (Circle one.)

Yes   No

Multiple-choice questions:

How many people do you commute with? (Circle one.)

0   1   2   3   4

Questions with answers on a checklist:

How long does it take you to commute to work? (Check one.)

___ 0–30 minutes   ___ 30–60 minutes   ___ 60–90 minutes
___ 90–120 minutes

Questions with a ranking scale:

If the car you drive or ride in is not working, which of the following types of transportation do you rely on? (Rank the choices from 1 for most frequently used to 4 for least frequently used.)

___ bus   ___ shuttle van   ___ subway   ___ taxi

Open questions:

What feature of commuting do you find most irritating?

Be sure to begin your questionnaire with an introduction stating what the purpose of the questionnaire is, how the results will be used, and how many questions it contains or approximately how long it should take to complete. In the introduction, you should also assure participants that their answers will remain confidential. To protect survey participants' privacy, colleges and universities have **institutional review boards (IRBs)** set up to review questionnaires. Before you distribute your questionnaire, check with the institutional review board on your campus to make certain that you have followed its guidelines.

Administering a questionnaire can sometimes be problematic. Many questionnaires sent through the mail are never returned. If you do decide to mail out a questionnaire, provide a self-addressed envelope and directions for returning it. It is a good idea to send out twice as many copies as you would like returned because the proportion of responses is generally low. Questionnaires can sometimes be distributed in college dormitories or in classes, but this procedure must be approved by school officials. Listservs (6b(1)) can also be used to conduct surveys. Just remember that a survey limited to people who have a strong interest in a topic will not yield results representative of other groups, such as the students at your school or the citizens of your state.

Once the questionnaires have been completed and returned, tally the results for all but the open questions on an unused copy. To find patterns in the responses to the open questions, first read through them all; you might find that you can create categories for the responses. For example, the open question "What feature of commuting do you find most irritating?" might elicit answers that fall into such categories as "length of time," "amount of traffic," or "bad weather conditions." By first creating categories, you will find it easier to tally the answers to the open questions.

CHECKLIST for Creating a Questionnaire

- Does each question relate directly to the purpose of the survey?
- Are the questions easy to understand?
- Are they designed to elicit short, specific responses?
- Are they designed to collect concrete data that can be analyzed easily?
- Have respondents been given enough space to write their answers to open questions?
- Do you have access to the group you want to survey?
- Have you asked a few classmates to "test-drive" your questionnaire?

10   Evaluating Print and Online Sources

As you find sources that seem to address your research question, you have to evaluate them to determine how, or even whether, you can use them in your paper. In short, you need to establish whether the information they contain is credible, relevant, and timely. This chapter will help you

- assess an author's credibility (10a),
- evaluate a publisher's credibility (10b),
- evaluate online sources (10c), and
- determine the relevance and timeliness of a source (10d).

10a   Credibility of authors

To be considered credible, authors must be trustworthy. They can attain such status by presenting information honestly, logically, fairly, and respectfully. That is, credible authors present facts accurately, support their opinions with evidence, connect their ideas reasonably, and demonstrate respect for any opposing views. To evaluate the credibility of the authors of your sources, find out what their credentials are, consider what world view informs their ideas, and note how other readers respond to their work.

(1) Credentials help establish an author's credibility.

When evaluating sources, consider whether the authors have credentials that are relevant to the topics they address. Although many works have only one author, some are composed collaboratively, so be sure to take into account the credentials of all of the authors responsible for the material in the sources you use.

Credentials take various forms, including academic or professional training, publications, and experience. A college biology professor who specializes in genetics is likely to be credible when writing about genes, for example, and a civil engineer who specializes in bridges should have credibility when writing about bridge strength and weakness. However, given their areas of specialization, the biologist would not necessarily be considered a credible source of information on the foraging habits of black bears, and the engineer would not have credibility concerning the design of hydroelectric power plants.

To find information about the credentials of an author whose work you want to use, look

- on the jacket of a book,
- on a separate page near the front or back of the book,
- in the preface of the book,
- in a note at the bottom of the first or last page of an article in print, or
- on a separate page of a periodical or a Web page devoted to providing background on contributors.

As you read about an author, ask yourself the following questions.

CHECKLIST for Assessing an Author's Credentials

- Does the author's education or profession relate to the subject of the work?
- With what institutions, organizations, or companies has the author been affiliated (10b)?
- What awards has the author won?
- What other works has the author produced?
- Do other experts speak of the author as an authority (10a(3))?

(2) An author's work reflects a specific world view.

An author's values and beliefs about the world constitute his or her **world view,** which underpins his or her research and publications. To determine what these values and beliefs are, consider the author's purpose and intended audience. For example, each of the following excerpts about malpractice lawsuits was written for a specific audience, with a specific purpose.

Published on a Web site for doctors, excerpt 1 focuses on the frivolous nature of some malpractice suits.

1   Just as quickly as medical knowledge and disease treatment options increase, so too do advances in the strategies lawyers use to bring medical malpractice suits.

Last year, an Ohio jury awarded $3.5 million to the family of a man who died of a heart attack.

His family claimed that the physician didn't do enough to help the man lose weight and stop smoking, given that physicians now know how smoking and excess weight contribute to heart disease and given the significant advances in treatment.   —TANYA ALBERT, "Lawyers Try New Tacks in Malpractice Suits"

Taken from an article in a university newspaper (in which no author was identified), excerpt 2 highlights the research of a professor at that university, whose findings downplay medical negligence and instead highlight poor doctor-patient rapport as the cause of malpractice suits.

2   A new study led by Wendy Levinson, Professor in Medicine, suggests that the most important reason a patient with a bad outcome decides to sue his or her doctor for malpractice is not medical negligence but how the doctor talks with the patient.   —"Bad Rapport with Patients to Blame for Most Malpractice Suits,"
University of Chicago Chronicle

In contrast to the first two excerpts, the next two are sympathetic toward patients. Appearing in a magazine for retired people, excerpt 3 stresses an action patients can take to protect themselves.

3   The more doctors you see, the more medical files you have. And the more scattered your medical records are, the higher your risk of drug errors, missed diagnoses, and other dangerous glitches.

The solution: Keep a set of your own records at home. It's easier than it sounds. And along with avoiding errors, you might even make yourself healthier.
—KRISTEN STEWART,
"The Paper Chase: Why You Need to Keep Your Own Medical Records"

In excerpt 4, taken from a news bulletin for retired people, the reporter questions whether doctors have the right to pass along the high costs of malpractice insurance to their patients.

4   A growing number of doctors fed up with skyrocketing malpractice insurance premiums are calling on their patients to bear part of the burden.

Some physicians are requiring patients to sign waivers promising not to sue for "frivolous" reasons or, in some cases, for any reason at all. Others are billing for telephone consultations, paperwork and other services that once were free.

Perhaps the most controversial—and possibly illegal—approach is charging user, or administrative, fees. Patients increasingly are protesting paying more—on top of their copayments, deductibles and premiums—for medical services already covered by their health plans.
—CAROLE FLECK, "Doctors' Fees Try Their Patients"

As you read and use sources, keep in mind that they reflect the world views of the authors and often of the audience for whom they were written. By identifying these various values and beliefs, you can responsibly represent and report the information in your sources. When you find yourself referring to information that reveals economic, political, religious, or social biases, you should feel free to question or argue with the author, as does Natalie Angier when she questions the views of Robert Wright and a few other evolutionary psychologists.

5 Now, it makes sense to be curious about the evolutionary roots of human behavior. It's reasonable to attempt to understand our impulses and actions by applying Darwinian logic to the problem. We're animals. We're not above the rude little prods and jests of natural selection. But evolutionary psychology as it has been disseminated across mainstream consciousness is a cranky and despotic Cyclops, its single eye glaring through an overwhelmingly masculinist lens. I say masculinist rather than male because the view of male behavior promulgated by hardcore evolutionary psychologists is as narrow and inflexible as their view of womanhood is.

—NATALIE ANGIER, *Woman: An Intimate Geography*

The following questions may help you determine the world view of an author whose work you hope to use.

CHECKLIST for Determining an Author's World View

- What is the author's educational and professional background?
- What are the author's and publisher's affiliations; that is, with what types of organizations do they align themselves?
- What is the editorial slant of the organization publishing the author's work? Where does it lie on the political spectrum from conservative to liberal?
- Can you detect any signs of bias on the part of the author or the publisher?
- Is the information purported to be factual? Objective? Personal?
- Who advertises in the source?
- To what types of Web sites do any links lead?
- How can you use the source? As fact? Opinion? Support? Authoritative testimony? Material to be refuted?

(3) Online sources, book reviews, and texts written by other authors can provide additional information about an author.

You can learn more about authors by searching the Internet for information about them. For example, the Web site of the Nobel Prize Organization provides background information about Nobel laureates (fig. 10.1). To locate information about authors on the Internet, use a general search engine such as Google or AltaVista or a specialized search engine such as the People search option offered by Lycos (**www.whowhere.lycos.com**). Either type of engine will locate sites containing background information on the author or bibliographical information about his or her other works.

Fig. 10.1. Background information about Nobel laureates may be found on the Web site of the Nobel Prize Organization.

Book reviews, both in print and online, often include information for determining whether an author is credible. Keep in mind, though, that being credible doesn't mean being perfect. A work by a credible author may get some negative responses, and one by an unreliable author may be referred to as "entertaining." For this reason, you must look for the main point of a review, and decide whether that main point amounts to a positive or negative response to the book as a whole. Dismiss from further consideration any writer whom more than one reviewer characterizes as ill-informed, careless with facts, biased, or dishonest in any way. Keep in mind, though, that few writers please all reviewers all the time, so you need to read reviews critically.

As you research a topic, you will find that writers often refer to the work of other writers. To gain insight into how an author influences the work of others, keep track of who is being discussed or cited by whom. If several well-known writers offer negative evaluations of an author's work or do not mention the work at all, that author's contribution is likely considered insignificant or unreliable. If, on the other hand, several writers praise or build on the work of the author you are evaluating, you can be confident in the credibility of your source.

Exercise 1

Choose a book you plan to use for your research paper. Locate at least two reviews of this book. Then, write a one-page report of what the reviews have in common and how they differ.

10b Credibility of publishers

Credible sources are published by reliable institutions, organizations, and companies. When you are doing research, consider not only the credibility of authors but also the credibility of the media through which their work is made available to you. Some publishers hold authors accountable to higher standards than others do.

(1) Book publishers are either commercial or academic.

When evaluating books, you can usually assume that publishers associated with universities demand a high standard of scholarship. Although some university presses have better reputations than others, the works such publishers produce are generally considered trustworthy—in great part because of the publishers' requirement that books be reviewed by experts before publication. Books published by commercial (or trade) presses, in contrast, typically do not undergo the same type of review.

Thus, to determine how a trade book has been received by others writing in the same area, you have to rely on book reviews (10a(3)).

(2) Periodicals are written for an academic audience or for the general public.

Periodicals are published daily, weekly, or monthly (9c). They include scholarly journals, magazines (trade, news, public affairs, and special interest), and newspapers. An article published in a scholarly journal is generally considered more credible than one published in a magazine because it has usually been both written and reviewed by an expert. Authors of these journal articles are expected to include both in-text citations and bibliographies so that other researchers can consult the sources used (chapters 13, 15, 17, and 19).

Articles that appear in magazines and newspapers may be reliable, but keep in mind that they are usually written quickly and chosen for publication by someone on the periodical's staff—not by an expert in the field. Because magazines and newspapers often report research results that were initially published elsewhere, you should try to find the original source to ensure the accuracy of their reports. Locating that source is not always an easy task, though, especially since in-text citations and bibliographies are rarely provided in these periodicals. Your best bet for finding the original source is to search online using a search engine.

When evaluating an article in a magazine or newspaper, also take into account the reputation of the publication itself. To gauge the credibility of magazines and newspapers, you can examine several issues and consider the space devoted to various stories, the tone of the commentary on the editorial pages, and the extent to which staff members (as opposed to wire services) are responsible for stories. Figure 10.2 shows examples of a byline for a staff writer and a byline for a wire service.

Forum defends right to know

By MIKE JOHNSTON
associate editor

Changes to the Clean Air Act
THE ASSOCIATED PRESS

Fig. 10.2. Examples of bylines for a staff writer of a local newspaper (left) and a wire service (right).

10c Online sources

If you are evaluating a periodical source that you obtained online, you can follow the guidelines for print-based sources (10a and 10b). But if you are evaluating a Web site, you also need to consider the nature of the site and its sponsor. Although many sites are created by individuals working on their own, many others are sponsored by colleges or universities, professional or nonprofit organizations, and commercial enterprises. The type of sponsor is typically indicated in the site's address, or URL, by a suffix that represents the domain. Colleges and universities are indicated by the suffix **.edu**, government departments and agencies by **.gov**, professional and nonprofit organizations by **.org**, network sites by **.net**, and businesses by **.com**. Depending on the nature of your research paper, you can access any or all of the various types of sites. But, as you evaluate their content, remember that every site is shaped to achieve a specific purpose and to address a target audience.

Suppose, for example, you wanted to write a paper about how a corporate bankruptcy revealed serious irregularities in the practices of a major communications company. An education site could provide a scholarly analysis of the practices in question; a government site could contain data compiled by the Securities and Exchange Commission (SEC); an organization site could give you the viewpoint of an association of accountants; and a business site could convey information from the communications company in question. Each of these sites would offer different content, which would be shaped by the rhetorical situation as envisioned by each site's sponsor. For example, when the World-Com bankruptcy shook the entire communications industry, various Web sites reported the news. When the British newspaper the *Guardian*, for instance, published an article on the sentencing of WorldCom's chief executive, the purpose was to demonstrate to online readers that the newspaper was critical and honest in its reporting (fig. 10.3). If you were to locate an account of the same incident on the SEC's Web site, you would read something entirely different. A federal agency that reports to the U.S. Congress (which, in turn, represents American citizens), the SEC provides oversight of business practices and reports cases like that of WorldCom to the public. WorldCom's commercial site, on the other hand, had a vested interest in making the company look good to current customers and potential clients.

Criteria for Evaluating Sources

TYPE OF SOURCE	PURPOSE	AUTHORS/PUBLISHERS
Scholarly books	To advance knowledge among experts	Experts/University presses
Trade (or commercial) books	To provide information of interest to the general public	Experts, journalists, professional writers/ Commercial presses
Reference books	To provide factual information	Experts/Commercial and university presses
Articles from scholarly journals	To advance knowledge among experts	Experts/Publishers associated with professions or universities
Articles from magazines or newspapers	To report current events or provide general information about current research	Journalists and professional writers (sometimes experts)/ Commercial presses
Editorials from newspapers	To state a position on an issue	Journalists/ Commercial presses
Sponsored Web sites	To report information	Often a group author
Interviews with experts	To report views of an expert	Professional or student writer reporting views of expert

SOURCES DOCUMENTED?	PRIMARY AUDIENCE	CHIEF ADVANTAGE
Yes	Other experts	Reliable because they are written and reviewed by experts
Sometimes	Educated public	Accessible because the language is not overly technical
Yes	Other experts and educated public	Reliable because the entries are written by experts
Yes	Other experts	Reliable because the entries are written and reviewed by experts
No	General public	Accessible because the language is not overly technical
No	General public	Current because they are published daily
No	General public	Accessible by computer
No	General public	Reliable because the interviewee is an expert

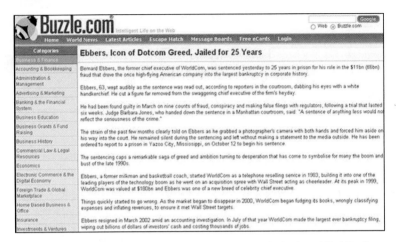

Fig. 10.3. The *Guardian*'s online article provides an unsympathetic view of WorldCom's collapse.

You can find out more about the sponsor of a Web site by using navigational buttons or links such as About Us or Our Vision. The following is an excerpt from a Web page for National Public Radio, found by clicking on About NPR on the organization's home page at **www.npr.org**:

What is NPR?

NPR is an internationally acclaimed producer and distributor of noncommercial news, talk, and entertainment programming. A privately supported, not-for-profit, membership organization, NPR serves more than 770 independently operated, noncommercial public radio stations. Each member station serves local listeners with a distinctive combination of national and local programming.

This passage provides information not only on NPR's radio programming but also on its status as a nonprofit organization.

For a summary of criteria you can use to evaluate both online and print sources, see pages 224 and 225.

Exercise 2

Exercise 2

Find Web sites that have three different kinds of sponsors but contain material relevant to a specific subject, such as global warming, saving energy, or disaster relief efforts. Explain the differences and similarities among the three sites you choose.

10d   Relevance and timeliness

A source is useful only when it is relevant to your research question. Given the ever-growing amount of information available on most topics, you should be prepared to put aside a source that will not help you answer your research question or achieve your rhetorical purpose. There are plenty of other sources, which you can locate by using the search strategies discussed in chapter 9. Some writers get off track when they cannot bring themselves to abandon a source they like, even if it is no longer relevant—as often happens when their focus has changed during the process of conducting research, drafting the paper, and revising it. It is better to abandon an irrelevant source than to write a poorly focused paper.

You may reject some sources altogether. You are also likely to use only parts of others. Seldom will an entire book, article, or Web site be useful for a specific research paper. A book may have just a chapter or a section or two on your topic. The table of contents can lead you to these relevant chapters or sections, and the index can lead you to relevant pages. Web sites have hyperlinks or buttons that you can click on to locate relevant information. Once you find potentially useful material, read it with your research question and rhetorical purpose in mind.

Useful sources are also timely. You should always seek up-to-date information. However, if you are writing about a specific era in the past, you should also consult sources written during that period, which are called **contemporary sources.** To determine when a source was published, look for the date of publication. In books, it appears with other copyright information on the page following the title page. (See the example on page 289.) Dates of periodicals appear on their covers and frequently on the top or bottom of pages throughout each issue (see page 294). The date on which a Web site was established or last updated frequently appears on the site, and the date on which you access it will usually appear on any hard copy you print out (see page 304). Do not confuse the access date with the posting date.

CHECKLIST for Establishing Relevancy and Timeliness

- Does the table of contents, index, or directory of the work include key words related to your research question?
- Does the abstract of a journal article contain information on your topic?
- If an abstract is not available, are any of the article's topic sentences relevant to your research question?
- Do the section heads of the source include words connected to your topic?
- On a Web site, are there hyperlinks or buttons that can lead you to relevant information?
- Is the work recent enough to provide up-to-date information?
- If you need a source from another time period, is the work from the right period?

11 Using Sources Effectively and Responsibly

To use sources effectively, you need to remember that you are a *writer*, not just a compiler of data. To use sources responsibly, you acknowledge others' ideas and words as you incorporate them into your paper. But even when you use sources responsibly, your voice remains the most important voice in the paper. This chapter will help you

- consider your rhetorical situation (11a),
- organize notes effectively (11b),
- compose a working bibliography or an annotated bibliography (11c),
- integrate sources (11d),
- avoid plagiarism (11e), and
- respond to sources (11f).

11a The rhetorical situation and the research paper

Like any other paper, a research paper should respond to an exigence with a purpose appropriate for a particular audience and context. It should not be a mere compilation of research findings or a list of works consulted. Rather, in a research paper, you discuss what others have discovered, creating a conversation in which you play an essential role: you orchestrate how your sources interact with one another and at the same time talk back to them.

By studying the following introductory paragraphs of a research article, you can see how the author, Timothy Quinn, chooses words, sentence types, organization strategies, and citation conventions according to his rhetorical situation. In the first paragraph, he alludes to his exigence: the increasing presence of coyotes in areas inhabited by people and the lack of a clear explanation for this presence. Because he states a problem with no easy solution, Quinn finds his own research niche. At the end of the second paragraph, Quinn states his purpose: to document coyotes' typical diet and assess changes in that diet caused by human population density and land use. Quinn shows his understanding of audience and context by citing other researchers' work according to the appropriate convention of providing the name(s) of author(s) and the year of publication.

> Coyotes (*Canis latrans*) are becoming increasingly common in human-modified habitats throughout North America (Atkinson and Shackleton 1991, MacCracken 1982). One possible explanation for this trend is that human-dominated areas produce abundant food sources for coyotes. Coyotes living in urban habitats have relatively small home ranges (Atkinson and Shackleton 1991, Shargo 1988), which may indicate abundant food resources. However, little is known about the diet of coyotes in these areas. MacCracken's (1982) description of the annual diet of coyotes in residential habitats was based on a small number of scats (n = 97) collected during a single month. Atkinson and Shackleton (1991) described the diet of coyotes in an area that was mostly ag-ricultural (>50% of the study area) and Shargo's (1988) description of urban coyote diet was based on 22 scats. Additionally, none of these studies looked at diet as a function of human density.
>
> Coyotes may play an important role in human-modified landscapes. Soulé et al. (1988) suggested that coyotes may reduce the abundance of house cats (*Felis catus*) and other small mammalian carnivores that prey on songbirds and thus indirectly contribute to the maintenance of native avifauna. My ob-jectives were to document the annual diet of coyotes in three types of urban habitat of western Washington and to qualitatively assess how coyote diets changed as a function of land use patterns and human density.
>
> —TIMOTHY QUINN, "Coyote (*Canis latrans*) Food Habits and Three Urban Habitat Types of Western Washington"

As you work toward providing an appropriate response to your rhe-torical situation, be sure to present yourself as thoughtful and informed. Whether your audience consists of a single instructor or some larger group, you must establish that you are a credible author (**10a**). By con-ducting research and citing sources, you demonstrate that you have

- educated yourself about your topic,
- drawn accurately on the work of others (including diverse points of view),
- understood what you have discovered,
- integrated research data into a paper that is clearly your own, and
- provided all the information readers will need to consult the sources you have used.

The rest of this chapter and chapters 13–19 will help you fulfill these responsibilities.

11b Organizing notes

Taking thorough and organized notes is critical when you are preparing to write a research paper in which you attribute specific words and ideas to others while taking credit for your own ideas. Some researchers are most comfortable taking notes in notebooks. Others like to write notes directly on pages they have photocopied or printed out from an online source. Still others write notes on index cards (also known as three-by-five cards) or type them into computer files—two methods that allow notes to be rearranged easily. Each method has advantages and disadvantages, and your choice should be guided by the requirements of your project and your own working style.

(1) Taking notes on photocopies and printouts

An easy way to take notes is to use photocopies of articles and excerpts from books or printouts of sources from the Web. On a printout or photocopy, you can mark quotable material while also jotting down your own ideas in the margins. The example in fig. 11.1 comes from the work Marianna Suslin did for her research paper on genetically modified foods (13c). This method reduces the risk of including inaccurate quotations in your paper, because you have eliminated the step of copying quotes exactly as they appear in the original source. Make sure to record the source on a photocopy if this information is not shown on the original page(s). Printouts from the Web almost always indicate the source and the date of access, but you should also note the date on which the site was posted or last updated (9d(1)).

(2) Organizing notes in computer files

You may find it efficient to use a computer for taking notes—recording them quickly and storing them safely. Then, later, you can easily copy and paste information into various files and ultimately into a draft of your paper. Given the ease of computer use, though, it is important to remember to identify which records are direct quotations (11d(2)), which are paraphrases (11d(3)), and which are your own thoughts. Always provide complete bibliographic information so

Genetic tinkering is the process of adding a gene or genes (the transgene) to plant or animal DNA (the recipient genome) to confer a desirable trait, for example, inserting the genes of an arctic flounder into a tomato to give antifreeze properties, or inserting human genes into fish to increase growth rates.

Author defines "genetic engineering"; his use of the word "tinkering" reveals how he feels about the technology.

But, as we are about to discover, this is a technology that no one wants, that no one asked for, and that no one but the biotech companies will benefit from. This is why the biotech lobby has such a vast, ruthless, and well-funded propaganda machine. If they can reinvent our food and slap a patent on it all, they have just created an unimaginably vast new market for themselves.

examples of genetic modification

Author believes no one but big corporations will benefit from this technology.

And to try to convince a suspicious public, they have given us dozens of laudable reasons why the world will benefit from this tinkering. The companies who so enthusiastically produce millions of tons of pesticides every year are now telling us that GMOs will help reduce pesticide use. The companies who have so expertly polluted the world with millions of tons of toxic chemicals are now telling us that GM will help the environment. The companies who have so nonchalantly used child labor in developing countries, and exported dangerous pesticides that are banned in the developed countries to the developing countries, are now telling us that they really do care about people and that we must have GM to feed the world.

Author seeks to discredit biotech companies.

Rees, Andy. *Genetically Modified Food: A Short Guide for the Confused.* Ann Arbor: Pluto, 2006. 8

Fig. 11.1. Photocopied source with notes.

that you will not have trouble finding the source later. The following tips can help you use your computer efficiently when taking and filing notes for a research paper.

TIPS ON USING A COMPUTER TO ORGANIZE NOTES

- Create a separate master folder (or directory) for the paper.
- Create folders within the master folder for your bibliography, notes, and portions of drafts.
- Keep all the notes for each source in a separate file.
- Use a distinctive font or a different color to distinguish your own thoughts from the ideas of others (fig. 11.2).
- Place direct quotations in quotation marks.
- When taking notes, record exactly where the information came from.
- When you discover new sources, add them to your working bibliography (11c).
- Consider using the Annotation or Comment feature of your word-processing program to make notes on documents you have downloaded.

Halweil, Brian
"Is Genetic Engineering Environmentally Sound?"

Patents are clearly an important ingredient in the industry's expansion. Global sales of transgenic crop products grew from $75 million in 1995 to $1.5 billion in 1998—a 20-fold increase. Sales are expected to hit $25 billion by 2010. And as the market has expanded, so has the scramble for patents. Recently, for example, the German agrochemical firm AgrEvo, the maker of "Liberty" herbicide, bought a Dutch biotech company called Plant Genetic Systems (PGS), which owned numerous wheat and corn patents. The patents were so highly valued that AgrEvo was willing to pay $730 million for the acquisition—$700 million more than PGS's annual sales.

It seems like genetic modification of crops has become a very lucrative industry. Big corporations seem most concerned with making a lot of money, and there is no mention of their trying to help farmers in developing countries. Maybe genetic modification is more about big business than helping poor countries become more economically competitive.

Fig. 11.2. The researcher used green to distinguish her response from a quotation taken from one of her sources.

(3) Arranging notes on note cards

Taking notes on index cards can be useful if you are working in a library without a laptop or if you prefer handwritten notes that you can rearrange as your research proceeds. Each index card should show the author's name (and a short title if the bibliography contains more than one work by that author), the exact page number(s) from which the information is drawn, and a brief comment on how you intend to use the information or a reflection on what you think about it. By putting a heading of two or three key words at the top of each card, you can easily arrange your cards as you prepare to draft your paper.

Whatever method you use to create your notes, consider the points in the following list.

TIPS FOR TAKING NOTES

■ Identify the source for every note.

■ Put the full bibliographic citation on the first page of every photocopy.

■ Copy verbatim any useful passage you think you may quote. Put quotation marks around quoted words. In computer files, you can also use different fonts or different colors to identify quoted text.

■ When a source has stimulated your thinking, identify both the source and your own idea based on that source.

11c   Working bibliography and annotated bibliography

A **working bibliography,** or preliminary bibliography, contains information (titles, authors' names, publication dates, and so on) about the materials you think you might use. Creating a working bibliography can help you evaluate the quality of your research. If you find that your most recent source is five years old, for example, or that you have relied exclusively on information from magazines or Web sites, you may need to find some other sources.

Some researchers find it convenient to put each bibliographic entry on a separate index card; this practice makes it easy to add or drop a card and to arrange the list alphabetically without recopying it. Others prefer to use a computer, which can sort and alphabetize automatically, making it easier to move material directly to the final draft.

It is also a good idea to follow the bibliographical format you have been instructed to use in your paper right from the start. This book covers the most common formats:

Modern Language Association (MLA), chapter **13**

American Psychological Association (APA), chapter **15**

The Chicago Manual of Style (CMS), chapter **17**

The Council of Science Editors (CSE), chapter **19**

The examples given in the rest of this chapter follow the MLA's bibliographical and documentation style.

If you are asked to prepare an **annotated bibliography,** you should list all your sources alphabetically according to the last name of the author. Then, at the end of each entry, summarize the content of the source in one or two sentences.

Zimmer, Carl. Soul Made Flesh: The Discovery of the Brain--and How It Changed the World. New York: Free, 2004. This book is a historical account of how knowledge of the brain developed and influenced ideas about the soul. It covers a span of time and place, beginning four thousand years ago in ancient Egypt and ending in Oxford, England, in the seventeenth century.

11d Integrating sources

You can integrate sources into your own writing in a number of ways: quoting exact words, paraphrasing sentences, and summarizing longer pieces of text or even entire texts. Whenever you borrow others' ideas in these ways, be careful to integrate the material—properly cited—into your own sentences and paragraphs. Once you have represented source material accurately and responsibly, you will be ready to respond to it.

(1) Writers introduce the sources they use.
When you borrow textual material, introduce it to readers by establishing the source, usually an author's name. You may also need to include

additional information about the author, especially if the author's name is unfamiliar to your audience. For example, in a paper on medications given to children, the following statement becomes more credible if the audience is given the added information about Jerome Groopman's background.

professor of medicine at Harvard University,

According to Jerome Groopman, "Pediatricians sometimes adopt extraordinary measures to insure that their patients are not harmed by treatments that have not been adequately studied in children" (33).

Phrases such as *According to Jerome Groopman* and *from the author's perspective* are called **attributive tags** because they attribute, or ascribe, information to a source. Most attributive tags in academic writing consist of the name of an author (or a related noun or pronoun) and a verb in order to report what that author has said, written, thought, or felt. Verbs commonly found in attributive tags are listed below. For a list of the types of complements that follow such verbs, see **27d(3)**.

VERBS USED IN ATTRIBUTIVE TAGS

admit	disagree	observe
advise	discuss	point out
argue	emphasize	reject
believe	explain	reply
claim	find	state
concede	imply	suggest
conclude	insist	think
deny	note	

When you integrate sources, be sure to find out whether it is appropriate to add evaluative remarks. If your assignment requires that you be objective, refrain from injecting your own opinions when introducing the ideas of another writer. You can convey your opinion of the material when responding to it (**11f**). If, on the other hand, your assignment allows you to voice your opinion when presenting ideas, you can easily add an adverb to the verb in an attributive tag to indicate your attitude toward the material: *persuasively* argue, *strongly* oppose, *inaccurately* represent.

If you decide to integrate graphics as source material, you must label them as figures and assign them arabic numbers. You can then refer to them within the text of your paper in a parenthetical comment, as

Fig. 11.3. Western coral snake.

in this example: "The red and black bands of the Western coral snake are bordered by narrower bands of yellow or white (fig. 11.3)." You may also want to include a title or caption with the figure number.

(2) Direct quotations draw attention to key passages.
Include a direct quotation in a paper only if

- you want to retain the beauty or clarity of someone's words,
- you need to reveal how the reasoning in a specific passage is flawed or insightful, or
- you plan to discuss the implications of the quoted material.

Keep quotations as short as possible, and make them an integral part of your text.

Quote *accurately.* Any quotation of another person's words should be placed in quotation marks or, if longer than four lines, set off as an indented block (13a(2)). If you need to clarify a quotation by changing it in any way, place square brackets around the added or changed words.

"In this role, he [Robin Williams] successfully conveys a diverse range of emotion."

If you want to omit part of a quotation, replace the deleted words with ellipsis points (39h).

"Overseas markets . . . are critical to the financial success of Hollywood films."

When modifying a quotation, be sure not to alter its essential meaning.

CHECKLIST for Using Direct Quotations

- Have you copied all the words and punctuation accurately?
- Have you attributed the quotation to a specific source?
- Have you used square brackets around anything you added to or changed in a direct quotation (39g)?
- Have you used ellipsis points to indicate anything you omitted (39h)?
- Have you used quotations sparingly? Rather than using too many quotations, consider paraphrasing or summarizing the information instead.

---

(3) Paraphrases convey another person's ideas in different words.

A **paraphrase** is a restatement of someone else's ideas in approximately the same number of words. Paraphrasing allows you to demonstrate that you have understood what you have read; it also enables you to help your audience understand it. Paraphrase when you want to

- clarify difficult material by using simpler language,
- use another writer's idea but not his or her exact words,
- create a consistent tone (4a(3)) for your paper as a whole, or
- interact with a point that your source has made.

Your paraphrase should be almost entirely in your own words and should accurately convey the content of the original passage.

(a) Use your own words and sentence structure when paraphrasing.

As you compare the source below with the paraphrases that follow, note the similarities and differences in both sentence structure and word choice.

Source

Zimmer, Carl. Soul Made Flesh: The Discovery of the Brain--and How It Changed the World. New York: Free, 2004. 7.

> The maps that neuroscientists make today are like the early charts of the New World with grotesque coastlines and blank interiors. And what little we do know about how the brain works raises disturbing questions about the nature of our selves.

Inadequate paraphrase

> The maps used by neuroscientists today resemble the rough maps of the New World. Because we know so little about how the brain works, we must ask questions about the nature of our selves (Zimmer 7).

If you simply change a few words in a passage, you have not adequately restated it. You may be committing plagiarism (**11e**) if the wording of your version follows the original too closely, even if you provide a page reference for the source.

Adequate paraphrase

> Carl Zimmer compares today's maps of the brain to the rough maps made of the New World. He believes that the lack of knowledge about the workings of the brain makes us ask serious questions about our nature (7).

In the second paraphrase, both vocabulary and sentence structure differ from those in the original. This paraphrase also includes an attributive tag ("Carl Zimmer compares").

(b) Maintain accuracy.

Any paraphrase must accurately maintain the sense of the original. If you unintentionally misrepresent the original because you did not understand it, you are being *inaccurate*. If you deliberately change the gist of what a source says, you are being *unethical*. Compare the original statement below with the paraphrases.

Source

Hanlon, Michael. "Apocalypse When?" <u>New Scientist</u> (17 Nov. 2007): 20.

> Disastrous images of climate change are everywhere. An alarming graphic recently appeared in the UK media showing the British Isles reduced to a scattered archipelago by a 60-metre rise in sea level. Evocative scenes of melting glaciers, all-at-sea polar bears and forest fires are routinely attributed to global warming. And of course Al Gore has just won a Nobel prize for his doomsday flick *An Inconvenient Truth,* starring hurricane Katrina.

. . . There is a big problem here, though it isn't with the science. The evidence that human activities are dramatically modifying the planet's climate is now overwhelming—even to a former paid-up sceptic like me. The consensus is established, the fear real and justified. The problem is that the effects of climate change mostly haven't happened yet, and for journalists and their editors that presents a dilemma. Talking about what the weather may be like in the 2100s, never mind the 3100s, doesn't sell.

Inaccurate or unethical paraphrase

Evocative scenes of melting glaciers, landless polar bears, and forest fires are attributed to global warming in Al Gore's *An Inconvenient Truth.* The trouble is that Gore cannot predict what will happen (Hanlon 20).

Accurate paraphrase

According to Michael Hanlon, the disastrous images of climate change that permeate the media are distorting our understanding of what is actually happening now globally and what might happen in the future (20).

Although both paraphrases include a reference to an author and a page number, the first focuses misleadingly on Al Gore, whereas the second paraphrase notes the much broader problem, which can be blamed on the media's focus on selling a story.

(4) Summaries convey ideas efficiently.

When you summarize, you condense the main point(s) of your source. Although a summary omits much of the detail used by the writer of the original source, it accurately reflects the essence of that work. In most cases, then, a **summary** reports a writer's main idea (3c) and the most important support given for it.

Whereas the length of a paraphrase (11d(3)) is usually close to that of the original material, a summary is shorter than the material it reports. When you paraphrase, you restate an author's ideas in order to present or examine them in detail. When you summarize, you present just the gist of the author's ideas, without including background information and details. Summaries can include short quotations of key words or phrases, but you must always enclose another writer's exact words in quotation marks when you blend them with your own.

Source

Marshall, Joseph M., III. "Tasunke Witko (His Crazy Horse)." <u>Native Peoples</u>
    (Jan./Feb. 2007): 76-79.

> The world knows him as Crazy Horse, which is not a precise translation of his name from Lakota to English. *Tasunke Witko* means "his crazy horse," or "his horse is crazy." This slight mistranslation of his name seems to reflect the fact that Crazy Horse the man is obscured by Crazy Horse the legendary warrior. He was both, but the fascination with the legendary warrior hides the reality of the man. And it was as the man, shaped by his family, community and culture—as well as the events in his life—that he became legend.

Summary

The Lakota warrior English speakers refer to as "Crazy Horse" was actually called "his crazy horse." That mistranslation may distort what Crazy Horse was like as a man.

This example reduces five sentences to two, retaining the key idea but eliminating the source author's analysis and speculation. A writer who believes that the audience needs to read such analysis might decide to paraphrase the passage instead.

Exercise 1

Find a well-developed paragraph in one of your recent reading assignments. Rewrite it in your own words, varying the sentence structure of the original. Make your paraphrase approximately the same length as the original. Next, write a one-sentence summary of the same paragraph.

11e   Avoiding plagiarism

To use the work of other writers responsibly, you need to ensure that your audience can distinguish between those writers' ideas and your own contributions and that you give credit for all information you gather through research. It is not necessary, however, to credit information that is **common knowledge,** which includes well-known facts such as the following: "The *Titanic* hit an iceberg and sank on its maiden voyage." This event has been the subject of many books and movies, so some information about it has become common knowledge.

If, however, you are writing a research paper about the *Titanic* and wish to include the ship's specifications, such as its overall length and gross tonnage, you will be providing *un*common knowledge, which must be documented. After you have read a good deal about a given subject, you will be able to distinguish between common knowledge and the distinctive ideas or interpretations of specific writers. If you have been scrupulous about recording your own thoughts as you took notes, you should have little difficulty distinguishing between what you knew to begin with and what you learned through your research.

Taking even part of someone else's work and presenting it as your own leaves you open to criminal charges. In the film, video, music, and software businesses, this sort of theft is called **piracy.** In publishing and education, it is called **plagiarism.** Whatever it is called, it is illegal, and penalties range from failing a paper or course to being expelled from school. Never compromise your integrity or risk your future by submitting someone else's work as your own.

TECH SAVVY

Although it is fairly easy to copy material from a Web site or even to purchase a paper on the Web, it is just as easy for a teacher or employer to locate that same material and determine that it has been plagiarized. Many teachers routinely use Internet search tools such as Google or special services such as Turnitin (available from Wadsworth, the publisher of this handbook) if they suspect that a student has submitted a paper that was plagiarized.

To review how to draw responsibly on the words and ideas of others, consider the following examples.

Source

McConnell, Patricia B. The Other End of the Leash. New York: Ballantine, 2002. 142.

Status in male chimpanzees is particularly interesting because it is based on the formation of coalitions, in which no single male can achieve and maintain power without a cadre of supporting males.

Paraphrase with documentation

Patricia B. McConnell, an authority on animal training, notes that by forming alliances with other male chimpanzees, a specific male can enjoy status and power (142).

This example includes not only the original author's name but also a parenthetical citation, which marks the end of the paraphrase and provides the page number where the source can be found.

Quotation with documentation

Patricia B. McConnell, an authority on animal training, argues that male chimpanzees achieve status "based on the formation of coalitions, in which no single male can achieve and maintain power without a cadre of supporting males" (142).

Quotation marks show where the copied words begin and end; the number in parentheses indicates the exact page on which those words appear. Again, the author is identified in the sentence, although her name could have been omitted at the beginning of the sentence and noted within the parenthetical reference instead:

An authority on animal training argues that male chimpanzees achieve status "based on the formation of coalitions, in which no single male can achieve and maintain power without a cadre of supporting males" (McConnell 142).

If, after referring to the following checklist, you cannot decide whether you need to cite a source, the safest policy is to cite it.

CHECKLIST of Sources That Should Be Cited

- Writings, both published and unpublished
- Opinions and judgments that are not your own
- Statistics and other facts that are not widely known
- Images and graphics, such as works of art, drawings, charts and graphs, tables, photographs, maps, and advertisements
- Personal communications, such as interviews, letters, and e-mail messages
- Public electronic communication, including television and radio broadcasts, motion pictures and videos, sound recordings, Web sites, and online discussion groups or forums

Exercise 2

After reading the source material, decide which of the quotations and paraphrases that follow it are written correctly and which would be considered problematic. Be prepared to explain your answers.

Source

Polsby, Daniel D. "Second Reading." Reason Mar. 1996: 33.

Generally speaking, though, it must be said that even among enthusiasts who think about the Second Amendment quite a lot, there has been little appreciation for the intricate and nuanced way in which constitutional analysis is practiced, and has to be practiced, by judges and lawyers.

1. People who care about the Second Amendment do not really understand how hard judges and lawyers have to work (Polsby 33).

2. Daniel Polsby has claimed that nobody understands the Second Amendment (33).

3. Daniel Polsby has claimed that public debate over the meaning of the Second Amendment seldom includes a deep understanding of the careful analysis judges and lawyers practice when interpreting the Constitution (33).

4. Those who tout the rights of the Second Amendment may not have a deep understanding of the careful analysis judges and lawyers practice when interpreting the Constitution (33).

5. According to Daniel Polsby, "there has been little appreciation for the intricate and nuanced way in which constitutional analysis is practiced, and has to be practiced, by judges and lawyers."

6. Few enthusiasts of the Second Amendment appreciate the nuanced ways in which constitutional analysis is practiced by judges and lawyers (33).

11f   Responding to sources

When incorporating sources, not only will you summarize, paraphrase, quote, and document them, you will often respond to them as well. To prepare for interacting with your sources, you may find it useful to make notes in the margins of whatever you are reading. Next to relevant passages, jot down your agreement, disagreement, surprise, questions, and so on (2d).

Readers of academic research papers or articles expect the authors of those works to be critical. They want to know whether facts are accurate or erroneous, whether logic is strong or weak, whether the organization is well planned or ill conceived, and whether conclusions are valid or doubtful. Researchers, therefore, critique the sources they use to ensure that their readers' concerns are being addressed. However, they also evaluate the strengths and weaknesses of sources in order to motivate a line of research. For example, they may try to show that previous research is insufficient in some way so that they can establish an exigence for their own research.

For your own paper, consider responding to your sources by examining their timeliness, coverage, reliability, and reasoning.

(1) Considering the currency of sources

Depending on the nature of your research, the currency of sources may be an important consideration. Using up-to-date sources is crucial when researching most topics. Historical research may also call for sources from a specific period in the past. When you consider the currency of a source, start by looking for the date of its publication. Then, examine any data reported. Even a source published in the same year that you are doing research may include data that are several years old and thus possibly irrelevant. In the following example, the writer questions the usefulness of an out-of-date statistic mentioned in a source:

> According to Jenkins, only 50% of all public schools have Web pages (23); however, this statistic is taken from a report published in 1997. A more recent count would likely yield a much higher percentage.

(2) Noting the thoroughness of research

Coverage refers to the comprehensiveness of research. The more comprehensive a study is, the more convincing are its findings. Similarly, the more examples an author provides, the more compelling are his or her conclusions. Claims that are based on only one instance are often criticized for being merely anecdotal or otherwise unsubstantiated. The writer of the following response suggests that the author of the source in question may have based his conclusion on too little information:

Johnson concludes that middle-school students are expected to complete an inordinate amount of homework given their age, but he bases his conclusion on research conducted in only three schools. To be more convincing, Johnson needs to conduct research in more schools, preferably located in different parts of the country.

(3) Checking the reliability of findings

Research, especially when derived from experiments or surveys, must be reliable (18b). Experimental results are considered **reliable** if they can be reproduced by researchers using a similar methodology. Results that cannot be replicated in this way are not reliable because they are supported by only one experiment.

Reliability is also a requirement for reported data. Researchers are expected to report their findings accurately and honestly, not distorting them to support their own beliefs or claiming others' ideas as their own. To ensure the reliability of their work, researchers must also report all relevant information, not intentionally excluding any that weakens their conclusions. When studies of the same phenomenon give rise to disputes, researchers should discuss conflicting results or interpretations. The writer of the following response focuses on the problematic nature of her source's methodology:

Jamieson concludes from her experiment that a low-carbohydrate diet can be dangerous for athletes, but her methodology suffers from lack of detail. No one would be able to confirm her experimental findings without knowing exactly what and how much the athletes consumed.

(4) Examining the author's reasoning

When a source is logical, its reasoning is sound. Lapses in logic may be the result of using evidence that does not directly support a claim, appealing to the reader's emotions, or encouraging belief in false authority. Faulty reasoning is often discussed in terms of rhetorical fallacies. A list of these fallacies, along with examples, can be found on pages 178–182.

D

DISCIPLINES AND DOCUMENTATION STYLES

Primary sources in the natural sciences include laboratory research.

12 Writing about Literature 249

13 MLA Documentation 273

14 Writing in the Social Sciences 329

15 APA Documentation 346

16 Writing in the Humanities 378

17 CMS Documentation 400

18 Writing in the Natural Sciences 430

19 CSE Documentation 450

20 Writing in Business 467

CHAPTER 12
Writing about Literature 249

12a Literature and its genres 249
12b Active reading and literary interpretation 251
12c Vocabulary for discussing literature 254
12d Approaches to interpreting literature 259
12e Conventions for writing about literature 263
12f Sample literary interpretation 266

CHAPTER 13
MLA Documentation 273

13a MLA-style in-text citations 273
13b MLA list of works cited 281
13c Sample MLA-style paper 315

CHAPTER 14
Writing in the Social Sciences 329

14a Audience, purpose, and the research
question 331
14b Evidence, sources, and reasoning 332
14c Conventions of language and organization 334
14d Samples of writing in the social
sciences 338

CHAPTER 15
APA Documentation 346

15a APA-style in-text citations 346
15b APA-style reference list 349
15c Sample APA-style paper 368

CHAPTER 16
Writing in the Humanities 378

16a Audience, purpose, and the research
question 380
16b Evidence, sources, and reasoning 382
16c Conventions of language and
organization 384
16d Samples of writing in the humanities 386

CHAPTER 17
CMS Documentation 400

17a CMS note and bibliographic forms 400
17b Sample CMS-style paper 415

CHAPTER 18
Writing in the Natural Sciences 430

18a Audience, purpose, and the research
question 431
18b Evidence, sources, and reasoning 434
18c Conventions of language and
organization 435
18d Samples of writing in the natural
sciences 437

CHAPTER 19
CSE Documentation 450

19a CSE citation-sequence, name-year, and
citation-name systems 450
19b Sample CSE-style paper 461

CHAPTER 20
Writing in Business 467

20a Conventions of language and
organization 467
20b Business letters 469
20c Business memos and e-mails 472
20d Résumés 475
20e Letters of application 480
20f Business plans 482
20g Oral presentations with PowerPoint 487
20h Business reports 491

12   Writing about Literature

You have been interpreting and writing about literature—talking about plot, characters, and setting—ever since you wrote your first book report. When you write about literature in college—whether the work is fiction, drama, poetry, an essay, or a memoir—you will still discuss plot, characters, and setting. But you will also apply many of the same strategies you use when writing about other topics: you will respond to an exigence, explore and focus your subject, formulate a thesis statement that can be supported by reference to the literary work itself, address an audience, and arrange your thoughts in the most effective way. In short, you will respond to the rhetorical situation.

Figure 12.1 shows how the elements of the rhetorical situation apply to a specific piece of writing about literature: a student essay on Alice Walker's short story "Everyday Use." In response to a disagreement among the characters in the story, Kaitlyn Andrews-Rice argues that embracing one's heritage every day is the best way to honor it.

This chapter will help you

- recognize the various genres of literature (12a),
- realize the value of a careful reading (12b),
- use the specialized vocabulary for discussing literature (12c),
- employ various critical approaches for interpreting literature (12d), and
- apply the special conventions for writing about literature (12e and 12f).

12a   Literature and its genres

Like all specialized fields, literature can be divided into categories, which are referred to as **genres.** A genre can be identified by its particular features or conventions. Some genres are timeless and universal (drama

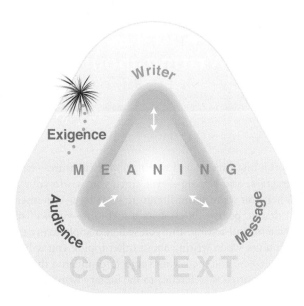

Exigence: Responding to the characters' disagreement about the best way to honor one's heritage

Writer: Kaitlyn Andrews-Rice

Audience: Kaitlyn's professor and her classmates

Message: Embracing one's heritage every day is the most authentic way to honor it.

Context: Classroom discussion about the disagreement among the characters in the story "Everyday Use" by Alice Walker

Fig. 12.1. Sample rhetorical situation for writing about literature.

and poetry, for instance); others are context-specific and develop within a specific culture (detective fiction is a recent Western cultural phenomenon).

Just as you can recognize film genres—action, suspense, horror, comedy, animated, Western, and science fiction—you can identify various literary genres: from poetry and drama to essays and narratives. Just as film genres sometimes overlap (for example, when an action film, such as *Beowulf*, is also animated), so do literary genres: some poems are referred to as prose poems, whereas some plays are written in verse. But even when genres overlap, the identifiable features of each genre are still evident.

Some of the most widely studied literary genres are fiction, drama, and poetry, though many forms of nonfiction (including personal essays and memoirs, literacy narratives, and manifestos) are being studied in college courses on literature. All imaginative literature can be characterized as fictional, but the term **fiction** is applied specifically to novels and short stories.

Drama differs from all other imaginative literature in one specific way: it is meant to be performed—whether on stage, on film, or on television—with the director and actors imprinting the lines with their own interpretations. In fact, the method of presentation distinguishes drama from fiction, even though the two genres share many of the same elements (setting, character, plot, and dialogue). In a novel, you often find extensive descriptions of characters and setting as well as passages revealing what characters are thinking. In a play, you learn what a character is thinking when he or she shares thoughts with another character in dialogue or presents a **dramatic soliloquy** (a speech delivered to the audience by an actor alone on the stage). And like fiction, nonfiction, and poetry, drama can be read—in which case you bring your interpretive abilities to the printed page rather than to a performance of the work.

Some poetry shares the components of fiction and drama. Dramatic monologues and narrative poems, for example, sometimes have a narrator with a point of view, a plot, a setting, and characters. But poetry is primarily characterized by its extensive use of connotative language, imagery, allusions, figures of speech, symbols, sound, meter, and rhythm.

12b Active reading and literary interpretation

The most successful writing about literature starts with active reading. Both understanding and interpretation of a literary work are fostered by active reading. Therefore, as you read, examine your own reactions. Were you amused, moved, or confused? Which characters interested you? Were you able to follow the plot? Did the work remind you of any experience of your own or other works you have read? Did it introduce you to a different historical or geographical setting, or did you encounter a familiar setting and cast of characters? These first impressions can provide the seeds from which strong essays will grow, especially when they are later modified as you consider the work further.

(1) You can understand your response by considering how it may be shaped by your identity.

When reflecting on your response to some element in a work of literature, consider how your reading might be shaped by the factors that define who you are. For example, if you find yourself responding positively or negatively to a character in a novel or play, you might ask yourself whether this response has anything to do with your

- psychological makeup,
- political beliefs,
- gender or sexual orientation,
- race,
- social class,
- religion, or
- geographic location.

Thinking about what you bring to a work of literature can help you decide how to focus your essay and prepare you for using one or more theoretical approaches as the basis for your interpretation (12d). Keep in mind, though, that your life experiences and world view might also limit your ability to understand a work. Such a limitation is another way that your identity can shape your response.

(2) After choosing a topic, develop it, using evidence in the text.

If you are choosing your own topic, your first step is to reflect on your personal response, focusing on that response as you formulate a tentative thesis statement. Next, consider what specific evidence from the text will best explain and support your interpretation and thesis statement.

Because most readers will be interested in what *you* think, you need to discover a way to demonstrate your originality by focusing on a topic you can develop adequately and applying one or more rhetorical methods (3g). You might define why you consider a character heroic, classify a play as a comedy of manners, or describe a setting that anchors a work's meaning. Perhaps you can compare and contrast two poems on a similar subject or explore cause-and-effect relationships in a novel. Why, for example, does an apparently intelligent character make a bad decision? Or you might show how the description of a family's house in a novel defines that family's values or reveals the effects of an underlying conflict.

(3) Research can reveal the ways other readers have responded to a literary work.

You will undoubtedly anchor your essay in your own interpretation. But if you read works of literary criticism, visit online discussion groups or forums (6b), participate in class discussions, or become active in a book club or reading group, you can engage in a dialogue that can enrich your own ideas. Many instructors want you to both advance your own ideas and use and give credit to outside sources. Although it is tempting to lean heavily on the interpretations of scholarly experts, remember that your readers are mainly interested in your interpretation and in your use of the sometimes conflicting interpretations of others (including the other members of your class) to support your own points.

To locate material on a specific writer or work, consult your library's catalog (see 9b and 9c) and *The MLA International Bibliography,* an index of books and articles about literature that is an essential resource for literary studies and is available in print and online.

In addition to having books and articles about specific writers, your library also possesses a number of reference books that provide basic information on writers, their works, and literary theory. Works such as *Contemporary Authors, The Oxford Companion to English Literature,* and *The New Princeton Handbook of Poetic Terms* can be useful when you are beginning your research or when you have encountered terms you need to clarify.

(4) Consider the types of literary interpretation you may be asked to write.

Writing a paper about a literary work usually requires you to focus on the work itself and to demonstrate that you have read it carefully—a process known as **close reading.** (Compare close reading with reading rhetorically, discussed in chapter 2.) Through close reading, you can offer an **interpretation,** an explanation of what you see in a work. An interpretation that attempts to explain the meaning of one feature of a literary work is called an **analysis.** To analyze a work of literature, a writer focuses on one of its elements, such as the setting or the main character, and determines how that one element contributes to the work's overall meaning. A common form of analysis is **character analysis,** in which a writer interprets one or more features of a single character. An analysis can also focus on a single scene, symbol, or theme.

An interpretation that attempts to explain every element in a literary work is called an **explication** and is usually used only with poetry. When explicating William Wordsworth's "A Slumber Did My Spirit Seal," a writer might note that the *s* sound reinforces the hushed feeling of sleep and death in the poem. But it would also be necessary to consider the meanings of *slumber, spirit,* and *seal.*

An **evaluation** of a work gauges how successful the author is in communicating meaning to readers. The most common types of evaluation are book, theater, and film reviews. A writer can also evaluate a work by focusing on how successfully one of its parts contributes to the meaning conveyed by the others. Like any other interpretation, an evaluation is a type of argument in which a writer cites evidence to persuade readers to accept a clearly formulated thesis. (See chapters 3 and 8.) An evaluation of a literary work should provide evidence from the text of its strengths as well as its weaknesses, if any.

Although summarizing a literary work can be a useful way to make sure you understand it, do not confuse a summary with an analysis, an explication, or an evaluation. Those who have read the work do not need to read a summary of it. Do not submit one unless your instructor has asked for it.

12c   Vocabulary for discussing literature

Like all specialized fields, literature has a unique vocabulary, which describes the various features of literary texts and concepts of literary analysis. As you learn this vocabulary, you will learn more than just a list of terms: you will learn how to understand, interpret, and write about literature.

(1) Characters carry the plot forward.

The **characters** are the humans or humanlike personalities (aliens, robots, animals, and other creatures) who carry the plot forward; they usually include a main character, called a **protagonist,** who is in external conflict with another character or an institution or in internal conflict with himself or herself. This conflict usually reveals the **theme,** or the central idea of the work (**12c**(7)).

Because writing about literature often requires character analysis, you need to understand the characters in any work you read. You can do so by paying close attention to their appearance, their language, and their actions. You also need to pay attention to what the narrator or other characters say about them. Whether you are writing about characters in a novel, in a play, or in a poem, you will want to concentrate on what those characters do and say—and why.

Understanding how a particular character moves the plot forward will help you interpret the work as a whole.

(2) Imagery is conveyed by descriptive language.

The imagery in a piece of literature is conveyed by **descriptive language,** or words that describe a sensory experience. Notice the images in "Portrait," a prose poem by Pinkie Gordon Lane that focuses on the death—and life—of a mother.

> My mother died walking along a dusty road on a Sunday morning in New Jersey. The road came up to meet her sinking body in one quick embrace. She spread out like an umbrella and dropped into oblivion before she hit the ground. In that one swift moment all light went out at the age of forty-nine. Her legacy: the blackened knees of the scrub-woman who ransomed her soul so that I might live, who bled like a tomato whenever she fought to survive, who laughed fully when amused—her laughter rising in one huge crescendo—and whose wings soared in dark despair. . . .
>
> —**PINKIE GORDON LANE,** *Girl at the Window*

The dusty road, the sinking body, the quick embrace—these images convey the loneliness and swiftness of death. The blackened knees, tomato-like bleeding, and rising laughter are, in contrast, images of a life's work, struggle, and joy.

(3) The narrator tells the story.

The **narrator** of a literary work tells the story, and this speaking voice can be that of a specific character (or of characters taking turns), can seem to be that of the work's author (referred to as the **persona,** which should not be confused with the author), or can be that of an all-knowing presence (referred to as an **omniscient narrator**) that transcends both characters and author. Whatever the type of voice, the narrator's tone reveals his or her attitude toward events and characters and even, in some circumstances, toward readers. By determining the tone and the impact it has on you as a reader, you can gain insight into the author's purpose (4a(3)).

(4) Plot is the sequence of events and more.

The plot is what happens in the story, the sequence of events (the narrative)—and more. The plot establishes how events are patterned or related in terms of conflict and resolution. Narrative answers "What comes next?" and plot answers "Why?" Consider this example:

Narrative The sister returned home to visit her family and left again.

Plot The city sister visited her country family, for whom she had no respect, and they were relieved when she left again.

Plot usually begins with a conflict, an unstable situation that sets events in motion (for instance, the state of tension or animosity between the city sister and her country family). In what is called the **exposition,** the author introduces the characters, setting, and background—the elements that not only constitute the unstable situation but also relate to the events that follow. The subsequent series of events leads to the **climax,** the most intense event in the narrative. The climax is also referred to as the **turning point** because what follows is **falling action** (or **dénouement**) that leads to a resolution of the conflict and a stable situation.

In Alice Walker's "Everyday Use," Dee and her boyfriend come to the country to visit her mother and sister.

(5) Setting involves place and time.

Setting involves place—not just the physical setting, but also the social setting (the morals, manners, and customs of the characters). Setting also involves time—not only historical time, but also the length of time covered by the narrative. Setting includes atmosphere, or the emotional response to the situation, often shared by the reader with the characters. For example, San Francisco in the nineteenth century is a markedly different setting from the same city in the twenty-first century. Not only has the physical appearance of the city changed, but so has the social setting and the atmosphere. Being aware of the features of the setting will help you better understand the story, whether it is written as fiction, drama, or poetry.

This nineteenth-century street scene, illustrating a time when both people and vehicles moved more slowly, suggests the spirit of early San Francisco.

(6) Symbols resonate with broader meaning.

Frequently used by writers of literature, a **symbol** is an object, usually concrete, that stands for something else, usually abstract. For example, at the beginning of *A Streetcar Named Desire,* a play by Tennessee Williams, one of the main characters buys a paper lantern to cover a naked light bulb. During the scenes that follow, she frequently talks about light, emphasizing her preference for soft lighting. At the end of the play, another character tears off the lantern, and a third character tries to return the ruined lantern to the main character as she is being taken away to a mental hospital. Anyone seeing this play performed or reading it carefully would note that the paper lantern is a symbol. It is an object that is part of the setting and the plot, but it also stands for something more—a character's avoidance of harsh truths.

When you write about a particular symbol, first note where it appears in the literary work. To determine what the symbol might mean, consider why it appears in those places and to what effect. Once you have an idea about the meaning, trace the incidents in the literary work that reinforce that interpretation.

(7) The theme is the main idea of a literary work.

The main idea of a literary work is its **theme.** Depending on how they interpret a work, different readers may identify different themes. To test whether the idea you have identified is central to the work in question, check to see if it is supported by the setting, plot, characters, and symbols. If you can relate these components to the idea you are considering, then that idea can be considered the work's theme. The most prominent literary themes arise out of conflict: person versus person, person versus self, person versus nature, or person versus society.

When you believe you have identified the theme, state it as a sentence—and be precise. A theme conveys a specific idea; it should not be confused with a topic.

Topic   family heritage

Vague theme   Alice Walker's "Everyday Use" is about family heritage.

Specific theme "Everyday Use" reveals a conflict between a sister who puts her heritage on display and a sister who puts her heritage to use, every day.

CHECKLIST for Interpreting a Literary Work

- From whose point of view is the story told?
- Who is the protagonist? How is his or her character developed?
- With whom or what is the protagonist in conflict?
- How are the other characters depicted and distinguished through dialogue?
- What symbols, images, or figures of speech does the author use? To what effect?
- What is the theme of the work? How does the author use setting, plot, characters, and symbols to establish that theme?

An interpretation of a literary work can be shaped by your personal response to what you have read, by the views of other readers, whom you wish to support or challenge, or by a specific type of literary theory.

Literary theory, the scholarly discussion of how the nature and function of literature can be determined, ranges from approaches that focus almost exclusively on the text itself (its language and structure) to approaches that show how the text relates to author, reader, language, society, culture, economics, or history. Familiarity with literary theory enriches your reading of literature as well as your understanding of the books and essays about literature that you will discover when you do research (chapter 9). Literary theory can also help you decide how you want to focus your writing about literature.

Although the most popular theoretical approaches to literature overlap somewhat, each has a different primary focus: the reader, some feature of the social or cultural context, the text itself, or the author or characters. Interpreting literature involves a responsible reliance on one or more of these approaches—*for whatever your interpretation, the text should support it.*

(1) Reader-response theory focuses on the reader.

According to **reader-response theory,** readers construct meaning as they read and interact with the elements within a text, with each reader bringing something different (intellectual values and life experiences) to the text on every reading. Thus, meaning is not fixed *on* the page but rather depends on what each reader brings *to* the page. Furthermore, the same reader can have different responses to the same literary work when rereading it after a number of years: a father of teenagers might find Gwendolyn Brooks's "we real cool" more disturbing than it had seemed when he first read it in high school. Although a reader-response approach to literature encourages diverse interpretations, you cannot simply say, "Well, that's what this work means to me" or "That's my interpretation." You must demonstrate to your audience how each element of the work supports your interpretation.

(2) Both feminist and gender-based literary theories focus on issues related to gender and sexuality.

The significance of sex, gender, or sexual orientation within a particular social context is the interpretive focus of **feminist** and **gender-based literary theories.** These theories enable a reader to analyze the ways in which a work (through its characters, theme, or plot) promotes or challenges the prevailing intellectual or cultural assumptions of its day regarding issues related to gender and sexuality, such as patriarchy and compulsory heterosexuality. For instance, Edith Wharton's *The Age of Innocence* compares two upper-class nineteenth-century women in terms of the specific social pressures that shaped and constricted their lives and loves. A feminist critic might emphasize the oppression of these women and the repression of their sexuality. Using a gender-based approach, another critic might read Henry James's *The Bostonians* and focus on the positive features of the domestic relationship between the financially independent Olive and Verena. That same critic might also try to explain why Jake Barnes in Ernest Hemingway's *The Sun Also Rises* bonds with some men and is contemptuous of others.

Like the early suffragists, many feminist literary critics focus on prevailing social and cultural constraints affecting women.

(3) Race-based literary theory focuses on issues related to race relations.

A useful form of race-based literary criticism, **critical race theory** focuses on the significance of race relations within a specific historical and social setting in order to explain the experience and literary production of any people whose history is characterized by political, social, and psychological oppression. Not only does this theoretical approach seek out previously neglected literary works, but it also illuminates the ways in which race, ethnicity, and the imbalance of power inform many works. Previously neglected works such as Zora Neale Hurston's *Their Eyes Were Watching God,* Rudolfo Anaya's *Bless Me, Ultima,* and Frederick Douglass's *Narrative,* which demonstrate how racism affects the characters' lives, have taken on considerable cultural value in the last twenty years. **African American literary criticism,** for example, has been particularly successful in invigorating the study of great African American writers, whose works can be more fully appreciated when readers consider how literary elements of some of these works have been informed by the social forces that helped produce them. Closely associated with critical race theory is **postcolonial theory,** which takes into account the relationship of the colonized with the colonizer and the challenge a text can direct at the dominant powers at a particular time and place, asserting a drive toward the liberation of oppressed social groups. Joseph Conrad's *Heart of Darkness,* Jean Rhys's *Wide Sargasso Sea,* Daniel Defoe's *Robinson Crusoe,* and E. M. Forster's *A Passage to India* can all be read productively through the lens of postcolonial theory.

Beloved, written by Nobel prize winner Toni Morrison, details the horrors of institutionalized racism, otherwise known as slavery.

(4) Class-based literary theory focuses on socioeconomic issues.

To explain the conflict between literary characters or between a character and a community or institution, **class-based literary theory** draws on the work of Karl Marx, Terry Eagleton, and others who have addressed the implications of social hierarchies and the accompanying economic tensions. These theorists argue that differences in socioeconomic class—in the material conditions of daily life—divide people in profoundly significant ways, more so than differences in race, ethnicity, culture, and gender. Thus, a class-based approach can be used to explain why Emma Bovary is unhappy, despite her "good" (that is, financially advantageous) marriage, in Gustave Flaubert's *Madame Bovary,* why Bigger Thomas gets thrown into such a confused mental state in Richard Wright's *Native Son,* or why a family loses its land in John Steinbeck's *The Grapes of Wrath.*

(5) Text-based literary theory focuses on the work itself.

Text-based literary theory demands concentration on the piece of literature itself; with this approach, only the use of concrete, specific examples from the text validates an interpretation. The reader must pay careful attention to the elements within the literary work—plot, characters, setting, tone, dialogue, imagery, and so on—to evaluate their interaction, overall effect, and meaning. According to this theory, nothing more than what is contained within the text itself—not information about the author's life or about his or her culture or society—is needed to understand and appreciate the text's unchanging meaning. Readers may change, but the meaning of the text does not. A close reading of the work is essential, then, in order to account for all of its particularities, including the ways in which the language and the structure fit within a specific literary genre.

(6) Context-based literary theory focuses on the time and place in which a work was created.

Context-based literary theory considers the historical period during which a work was written and the cultural and economic patterns that prevailed during that period. For example, recognizing that Willa Cather published *My Ántonia* during World War I can help account for the darker side of that novel about European immigrants' harsh life in the American West; similarly, understanding that Arthur Miller wrote *The Crucible* in response to the accusations of the House Un-American Activities Committee in the 1950s helps explain why that play generated so much excitement when it was first produced. Critics who use a context-based and class-based approach known as **cultural studies** consider how a literary work interacts with economic conditions, socioeconomic classes, and other cultural artifacts (such as songs or fashion) from the period in which it was written.

(7) Psychoanalytic theories focus on psychological factors affecting the writing and the reading of literature.

By focusing on the psychological states of the author and the characters as well as the reader, **psychoanalytic theories** seek to explain human experience and behavior in terms of sexual impulses and unconscious motivations (drives, desires, fears, needs, and conflicts). When applied to literature, these theories (based on the work of Nancy Chodorow, Hélène Cixous, Sigmund Freud, Melanie Klein, and Jacques Lacan, among others) help readers discern the motivations of characters, envision the psychological state of the author as implied by the text, and evaluate the psychological reasons for their own interpretations. Readers may apply the psychoanalytic approach to explain why Hamlet is deeply disturbed by his mother's remarriage, why Holden Caulfield rebels at school (in J. D. Salinger's *The Catcher in the Rye*), or why Rochester is blinded (in Charlotte Brontë's *Jane Eyre*).

Theorists who use the work of psychiatrist Carl Jung to explore **archetypes** (meaningful images that arise from the human unconscious and that appear as recurring figures or patterns in literature) are also using a psychoanalytic approach to interpret literature, whether the literary form is a fairy tale, fable, epic poem, Greek drama, postmodern novel, or movie script. Archetypal figures include the hero, the earth mother, the warrior, the outcast, and the cruel stepmother; archetypal patterns include the quest, the initiation, the test, and the return.

The powerful Hindu goddess Durga represents an archetype known as the warrior.

Exercise 1

Attend a film, a play, or a poetry reading at your school or in your community. Write a two- to three-page essay evaluating the work, using one of the theoretical approaches discussed in this chapter.

12e Conventions for writing about literature

Writing about literature involves adhering to several conventions.

(1) The first person is typically used.

When writing an analysis of a piece of literature, you usually use the first-person singular pronoun, *I*.

Although some critics believe Rudolfo Anaya's novel to be about witchcraft, I think it is about the power of belief.

By using *I,* you indicate that you are presenting your opinion about a work. To propose (or argue or offer) an opinion, belief, or interpretation, you must support it with specific evidence from the text itself.

(2) The present tense is used in discussions of literary works.
Use the present tense when discussing a literary work, since the author of the work is communicating to the reader at the present time (**27b(1)**).

> In "A Good Man Is Hard to Find," the grandmother reaches out to touch her killer just before he pulls the trigger.

Similarly, use the present tense when reporting how other writers have interpreted the work you are discussing.

> As Toni Morrison demonstrates in her analysis of the American literary tradition, black Americans continue to play a vital role.

(3) Documentation of sources follows certain formats.
When writing about a work assigned by your instructor, you may not need to give the source and publication information. However, if you are using an edition or translation that may be different from the one your audience will use, you should indicate this. You can cite the version of the work you are discussing by using the MLA format for listing works cited (**13b**), although your bibliography in this case will consist of only a single work. An alternative way of providing documentation for a single source is by acknowledging the first quotation from the work in an explanatory note on a separate page at the end of your paper and then giving parenthetical page numbers in the body of the paper for all subsequent references to the work.

> [1]Toni Morrison, *Playing in the Dark: Whiteness and the Literary Imagination* (New York: Vintage, 1992). All subsequent references to this work will be identified with page numbers within the text.

If you use this note form, you may not need to repeat the bibliographical information on a list of works cited, nor will you need to include the author's name in subsequent parenthetical references. Check with your instructor about the format he or she prefers.

When you use a bibliography to provide publication data, you must indicate specific references whenever you quote a line or passage. According to MLA style, such bibliographic information should be placed in the text in parentheses directly after the quotation, and a period, a semicolon, or a comma should follow the parentheses (13a(1) and 40d(1)). Quotations from short stories and novels are identified by the author's name and page number.

> "A man planning to spend money on me was an experience rare enough to feel odd"
> (Gordon 19).

Quotations from poems are referred to by line number.

> "O Rose, thou are sick!" (Blake 1).

And quotations from plays require act, scene, and line numbers.

> "How much better it is to weep at joy than to joy at weeping" (*Ado* 1.1.28).

This reference indicates that the line quoted is from act I, scene I, line 28 of Shakespeare's play *Much Ado about Nothing*.

(4) Quoting poetry involves several conventions.

For poems and verse plays, type quotations involving three or fewer lines in the text and insert a slash (see 41i) with a space on each side to separate the lines.

> "Does the road wind uphill all the way? / Yes, to the very end" (Rossetti 1–2). Chris-
> tina Rossetti opens her poem "Uphill" with this two-line question and answer.

Quotations of more than three lines should be indented one inch from the left-hand margin and double-spaced. Do not use slashes at the ends of lines, and make sure to follow the original text for line breaks, special indenting, or spacing. For this type of block quotation, place your citation outside the final punctuation mark.

(5) Authors' names are referred to in standard ways.

Use the full name of the author of a work in your first reference and only the last name in all subsequent references. For instance, refer to "Charles Dickens" or "Willa Cather" the first time, and after that, use "Dickens" or "Cather." Never refer to a female author differently than you do a male author. For example, use "Robert Browning and Elizabeth Barrett Browning" or "Browning and Barrett Browning" (not "Browning and Mrs. Browning" or "Browning and Elizabeth").

12f Sample literary interpretation

In the following essay, undergraduate English major Kaitlyn Andrews-Rice analyzes Alice Walker's short story "Everyday Use." In addition to reading the story, she watched a dramatization of it on DVD. Andrews-Rice had the opportunity to choose her own topic, and she focused (3b) on the ways two sisters use their heritage, showing that everyday use is the best way.

Kaitlyn Andrews-Rice

Dr. Glenn

English 100

March 7, 2005

Honoring Heritage with Everyday Use

"Everyday Use," one of the short stories in Alice Walker's In Love &
Trouble: Stories of Black Women, vividly demonstrates how three women,
Mrs. Johnson and her two daughters, regard their heritage.[1] Through the eyes
of Mrs. Johnson, the story unfolds when her older daughter returns to her
country home, mother, and sister. Throughout the story, Walker emphasizes
the shared heritage of these three women and the different ways they use it.
In "Everyday Use," an authentic appreciation of heritage does not come from
showcasing fashionable artifacts or practices; rather, it comes from embracing
that heritage every day.

Walker's physical description of the sisters illustrates the different ways
each puts her heritage to use. The beautiful, sophisticated Dee embraces her
heritage by showcasing the fashionable Afrocentric sentiment of the time. Her
mother describes her as wearing "a dress so loud it hurts my eyes. There are
yellows and oranges enough to throw back the light of the sun," and her hair
"stands straight up like the wool on a sheep" (52). But in addition to her African
style, Dee also has "neat-looking" feet, "as if God himself had shaped them with
a certain style" (52). That she's stylish comes as no surprise, for even before she
appears in the story, the reader is told that "at sixteen, she had a style of her own,
and knew what style was" (50). Dee is a book-smart city woman, who uses her
knowledge of fashion and style to enhance her physical attributes: she is "lighter
than [her sister] Maggie, with nicer hair and a fuller figure" (49). Maggie, on

the other hand, replicates her Southern black heritage every day, by helping her mother clean up the dirt yard (raking, lifting, sweeping), in preparation for Dee's homecoming. In addition, Maggie works hard churning butter, cooking over a wood-burning stove, and using the outhouse. She's darker skinned, "homely and ashamed of the burn scars down her arms and legs" (47), and her simple country clothes, "pink skirt and red blouse" (49), are in sharp contrast with Dee's fancy garb.

The filmed version of the story allows the viewer to see Dee arrive home with her boyfriend, Hakim-a-barber, both in their African clothes, exchanging glances of amusement as they take Polaroid snapshots of the unsophisticated mother and sister and their shabby house, as though Dee was completely separated from such living conditions, that heritage, her family (see fig. 1). Another way that Walker illustrates the divide between Dee's understanding of her heritage and her family's is through the use of names. When Dee arrives, she announces that she is "Not 'Dee,' Wangero Leewanika Kemanjo!" (53). According to the interview with Walker that accompanies the Wadsworth Original Film Series in Literature's filmed version of "Everyday Use," the changing of one's name to a more Afrocentric name was common during this time (Everyday Use). In Dee's mind, this fashionable African name is yet another way she is honoring her roots, embracing her heritage, and she tells her family that she "couldn't bear it any longer, being named after the people who oppress [her]" (53). Ironically, her given name carried with it a rich inheritance, that of a long line of Dees or Dicies. Yet Dee is the daughter who denies her Southern heritage and is embarrassed by her Southern family, especially by Maggie, who has taken no steps to "make something of [herself]" (59) other than a wife to local

John Thomas Dee. At this point in the story, though, Mrs. Johnson and Maggie agree to go along with Dee's ways and continue to try to please her, even if they do not understand her. It is not until later in Dee's visit that they come to realize the way Dee has embraced a heritage she does not fully understand or appreciate.

Fig. 1. Dee wants to capture the living conditions of her mother and sister. Photograph © Denna Bendell/Worn Path Productions.

To further emphasize the differences among the ways these women understand their heritage, Walker focuses on their educations. Mrs. Johnson describes the way Dee would read to them before she left for college: "She washed us in a river of make-believe, burned us with a lot of knowledge we didn't necessarily need to know" (50). Even though she's somewhat puzzled by Dee's knowledge, she maintains pride in her daughter, especially since Mrs. Johnson never had an education, and Maggie "knows she is not bright" and can read only by "stumbling along good-naturedly" (50). But when Dee accuses Maggie of being "backward," Mrs. Johnson realizes how little Dee's education has taught her about appreciating her heritage.

The focus on family-made quilts at the end of the story shines light on Walker's final take on how heritage is used differently by these women. Mrs. Johnson explains that Dee was offered these quilts before she left for college but refused them because they were "old-fashioned, out of style" (57). Now that the quilts are stylish, Dee wants them in her life. She wants to hang them on her walls, displaying them alongside the butter churn top that she plans to use as a "centerpiece on the alcove table" and dasher that she will do "something artistic" (56) with. For Dee, these artifacts should be on display, not used. But for Maggie and her mother, the quilts represent not only a direct link with their ancestors but a distinct form of African American expression. These particular quilts are made from scraps of Grandma Dee's dresses and from a scrap of fabric from Great Grandpa Ezra's uniform "that he wore in the Civil War" (56). The piecing together of these scraps to form a quilt is a testament to their importance in the heritage of this family. As Dee holds the quilts, she repeats "Imagine!" (57), as if it is so difficult to think of a time when all the stitching was done by hand, something that Maggie is capable of doing every day because "it was Grandma Dee and Big Dee who taught her how to quilt" (58). When Dee asks to take some quilts back to the city to hang on the wall, her mother resists, saying that Maggie planned to use them. Only then does Dee reveal her prejudices, accusing her sister of being "backward enough to put them [the quilts] to everyday use" (57), right before she storms out of the house.

At this point, when she's been denied the quilts, Dee accuses her family of not understanding their true heritage, saying "It's really a new day for us.

But from the way you and Mama still live you'd never know it" (59). She considers herself to be forward looking, because of her African style and name, her education, her cultural displays. In Dee's eyes, her "backward" family does not understand their heritage because they do not display the quilts or the butter churn, they *use* them every day. As Dee drives away, Maggie smiles, and it is "a real smile, not scared" (59), because she knows she embraces, lives, and understands her heritage in a very intimate way.

Notes

1. Alice Walker, "Everyday Use," In Love & Trouble: Stories of Black Women (New York: Harcourt, 1973) 47-59. All subsequent quotations from this work will be identified by page numbers.

Andrews-Rice 7

Works Cited

<u>Everyday Use</u>. Dir. Bruce Schwartz. Perf. Karen ffolkes, Rachel Luttrell, and

   Lyne Odums. 2003. DVD. Thomson Wadsworth, 2005.

Walker, Alice. <u>In Love & Trouble: Stories of Black Women</u>. New York:

   Harcourt, 1973. 47-59.

Exercise 2

Based on your reading of Kaitlyn Andrews-Rice's paper on "Everyday Use," what personal or political values do you think she brought to her interpretation of that text? Which of the theoretical approaches to literature did she use as the basis for her interpretation (**12d**)? Write a one- to two-page paper analyzing her interpretation of the story.

13 MLA Documentation

The Modern Language Association (MLA) provides guidelines for documenting research in literature, languages, linguistics, and composition studies. The *MLA Handbook for Writers of Research Papers* is published specifically for undergraduates. Updates to the handbook's content can be found at **www.mla.org**. This chapter includes

- guidelines for citing sources within the text of a paper (13a),
- guidelines for documenting sources in the works-cited list (13b), and
- a sample student paper (13c).

13a MLA-style in-text citations

(1) In-text citations indicate that a writer has drawn material from other sources.

The citations you use within the text of a research paper refer your readers to the list of works cited at the end of the paper, tell them where to find the borrowed material in the original source, and indicate the boundaries between your ideas and those you have borrowed. In the following example, the parenthetical citation guides the reader to page 88 of the book by Pollan in the works-cited list.

In-text citation

Since the 1980s virtually all the sodas and most of the fruit drinks sold in the supermarkets have been sweetened with high-fructose corn syrup (HFCS)--after water, corn sweetener is their principal ingredient (Pollan 88).

Works-cited entry

Pollan, Michael. The Omnivore's Dilemma: A Natural History of Four Meals. New York: Penguin, 2006.

The MLA suggests reserving numbered notes for supplementary comments—for example, when you wish to explain a point further but the subject matter is tangential to your topic. When numbered notes are used, superscript numbers are inserted in the appropriate places in the text, and the notes are gathered at the end of the paper on a separate page titled "Notes." Each note begins with an indent. You can create a superscript number in Microsoft Word by typing the number, highlighting it, pulling down the menu for Format, clicking on Font, and then clicking in the box next to Superscript. Other word-processing programs have similar procedures for creating superscript numbers.

In-text note number

Most food found in American supermarkets is ultimately derived from corn.[1]

Notes entry

[1]Nearly all farm animals--from cows and chickens to various kinds of farmed fish-- are fed a diet of corn.

An in-text citation usually provides two pieces of information about borrowed material: (1) information that directs the reader to the relevant source on the works-cited list, and (2) information that directs the reader to a specific page or section within that source. An author's last name and a page number generally suffice. To create an in-text citation, either place both the author's last name and the page number in parentheses or introduce the author's name in the sentence and supply just the page number in parentheses.

A "remarkably narrow biological foundation" supports the variety of America's supermarkets (Pollan 18).

Pollan explains the way corn products "feed" the familiar meats, beverages, and dairy products that we find on our supermarket shelves (18).

When referring to information from a range of pages, separate the first and last pages with a hyphen: (34-42). If the page numbers have the same hundreds or thousands digit, do not repeat it when listing the final page in the range: (234-42) or (1350 55) but (290-301) or (1395-1402). If you refer to an entire work, no page numbers are necessary.

The following examples are representative of the types of in-text citations you might be expected to use. For more details on the placement and punctuation of citations, including those following long quotations, see pages 279–281.

Directory of MLA Parenthetical Citations

1. Work by one author   275
2. More than one work by the same author(s)   275
3. Work by two or three authors   275
4. Work by more than three authors   276
5. Works by different authors with the same last name   276
6. Work by a corporate author   276
7. Two or more works in the same citation   276
8. Multivolume work   277
9. Anonymous work   277
10. Indirect source   277
11. Poetry, drama, and sacred texts   277
12. Constitution   278
13. Works with numbered paragraphs or screens   278

1. Work by one author

Set on the frontier and focused on characters who use language sparingly, Westerns often reveal a "pattern of linguistic regression" (Rosowski 170).

OR

Susan J. Rosowski argues that Westerns often reveal a "pattern of linguistic regression" (170).

2. More than one work by the same author(s)

When your works-cited list includes more than one work by the same author(s), provide a shortened title in your in-text citation that identifies the relevant work. Use a comma to separate the name (or names) from the shortened title when both are in parentheses. For example, if you listed two works by Antonio Damasio on your works-cited page, then you would cite one of those within your text as follows:

According to one neurological hypothesis, "feelings are the expression of human flourishing or human distress" (Damasio, Looking for Spinoza 6).

OR

Antonio Damasio believes that "feelings are the expression of human flourishing or human distress" (Looking for Spinoza 6).

3. Work by two or three authors

Some environmentalists seek to protect wilderness areas from further development so that they can both preserve the past and learn from it (Katcher and Wilkins 174).

Use commas to separate the names of three authors: (Bellamy, O'Brien, and Nichols 59).

4. Work by more than three authors

Use either the first author's last name followed by the abbreviation *et al.* (from the Latin *et alii,* meaning "and others") or all the last names. (Do not italicize or underline the abbreviated Latin phrase, which ends with a period.)

In one important study, women graduates complained more frequently about "excessive control than about lack of structure" (Belenky et al. 205).

OR

In one important study, women graduates complained more frequently about "excessive control than about lack of structure" (Belenky, Clinchy, Goldberger, and Tarule 205).

5. Works by different authors with the same last name

When your works-cited list includes works by different authors with the same last name, provide a first initial, along with the last name, in parenthetical citations, or use the author's first and last name in the text. For example, if your works-cited list included entries for works by both Richard Enos and Theresa Enos, you would cite the work of Theresa Enos as follows.

Pre-Aristotelian rhetoric still has an impact today (T. Enos 331-43).

OR

Theresa Enos mentions the considerable contemporary reliance on pre-Aristotelian rhetoric (331-43).

If two authors have the same last name and first initial, spell out each author's first name in a parenthetical citation.

6. Work by a corporate author

A work has a corporate author when individual members of the group that created it are not identified. If the corporate author's name is long, you may use common abbreviations for parts of it—for example, *Assn.* for "Association" and *Natl.* for "National."

Strawbale constructions are now popular across the nation (Natl. Ecobuilders Group 2).

7. Two or more works in the same citation

When two sources provide similar information or when you combine information from two sources in the same sentence, cite both sources, separating them with a semicolon.

Agricultural scientists believe that crop productivity will be adversely affected by solar dimming (Beck and Watts 90; Harris-Green 153-54).

8. Multivolume work

When you cite material from more than one volume of a multivolume work, include the volume number (followed by a colon and a space) before the page number.

Katherine Raine claims that "true poetry begins where human personality ends" (2: 247).

You do not need to include the volume number in a parenthetical citation if your list of works cited includes only one volume of a multivolume work.

9. Anonymous work

The Tehuelche people left their handprints on the walls of a cave, now called Cave of the Hands ("Hands of Time" 124).

Use the title of an anonymous work in place of an author's name. If the title is long, provide a shortened version. For example, the shortened title for "Chasing Down the Phrasal Verb in the Discourse of Adolescents" is "Chasing Down."

10. Indirect source

If you need to include material that one of your sources quoted from another work because you cannot obtain the original source, use the following format (*qtd.* is the abbreviation for "quoted").

The critic Susan Hardy Aikens has argued on behalf of what she calls "canonical multiplicity" (qtd. in Mayers 677).

A reader turning to the list of works cited should find a bibliographic entry for Mayers, the source consulted, but not for Aikens.

11. Poetry, drama, and sacred texts

When you refer to poetry, drama, or sacred texts, you should give the numbers of lines, acts and scenes, or chapters and verses, rather than page numbers. This practice enables readers to consult an edition other than the one you have used. Act, scene, and line numbers (all arabic numerals) are separated by periods with no space before or after them. The MLA suggests that biblical chapters and verses be treated similarly, although some writers prefer to use colons instead of periods in such citations. In all cases, the progression is from larger to smaller units.

The following example illustrates a citation referring to lines of poetry.

Emily Dickinson alludes to her dislike of public appearance in "I'm Nobody! Who Are
You?" (5-8).

The following citation shows that the famous "To be, or not to be" soliloquy appears in act 3, scene 1, lines 56-89 of *Hamlet.*

In <u>Hamlet,</u> Shakespeare presents the most famous soliloquy in the history of the English
theater: "To be, or not to be . . ." (3.1.56-89).

Citations of biblical material identify the book of the Bible, the chapter, and the pertinent verses. In the following example, the writer refers to the creation story in Genesis, which begins in chapter 1 with verse 1 and ends in chapter 2 with verse 22.

The Old Testament creation story, told with remarkable economy, culminates in the arrival
of Eve (<u>New American Standard Bible,</u> Gen. 1.1-2.22).

Mention in your first citation which version of the Bible you are using; list only book, chapter, and verse in subsequent citations. Note that the names of biblical books are neither underlined nor enclosed in quotation marks.

The MLA provides standard abbreviations for the parts of the Bible, as well as for the works of Shakespeare and Chaucer and certain other literary works.

12. Constitution

When referring to the U.S. Constitution, use in-text citations only. You do not need to include a works-cited entry. The following are common abbreviations for in-text citations:

United States Constitution	US Const.
article	art.
section	sec.

The testimony of two witnesses is needed to convict someone of treason (US Const.,
art. 3, sec. 3).

13. Works with numbered paragraphs or screens

If an electronic source does not have page numbers, provide paragraph or screen numbers instead. If paragraphs are numbered, cite the number(s) of the paragraph(s) after the abbreviation *par.* (for one paragraph) or *pars.* (for more than one). If a screen number is provided, cite that number after the word *screen* (or *screens* for more than one).

Alston describes three types of rubrics for evaluating customer service (pars. 2-15).

Hilton and Merrill provide examples of effective hyperlinks (screen 1).

If an electronic source includes no numbers distinguishing one part from another, you should cite the entire source. In this case, to establish that you have not accidentally omitted a number, avoid using a parenthetical citation by providing what information you have within the sentence that introduces the material.

Raymond Lucero's <u>Shopping Online</u> offers useful advice for consumers who are concerned about transmitting credit card information over the Internet.

(2) The MLA offers guidelines for placing and punctuating in-text citations and quotations.

(a) Placement of in-text citations

When you acknowledge your use of a source by placing the author's name and a relevant page number in parentheses, insert this parenthetical citation directly after the information you used, generally at the end of a sentence but *before* the final punctuation mark (a period, question mark, or exclamation point).

Oceans store almost half the carbon dioxide released by humans into the atmosphere (Wall 28).

However, you may need to place a parenthetical citation earlier in a sentence to indicate that only the first part of the sentence contains borrowed material. Place the citation after the clause containing the material but before a punctuation mark (a comma, semicolon, or colon).

Oceans store almost half the carbon dioxide released by humans into the atmosphere (Wall 28), a fact that provides hope for scientists studying global warming but alarms scientists studying organisms living in the oceans.

(b) Lengthy quotations

When a quotation is more than four lines long, set it off from the surrounding text by indenting all lines one inch (or ten spaces) from the left margin. The first line should not be indented further than the others. The right margin should remain the same. Double-space the entire quotation.

In <u>Nickel and Dimed</u>, Barbara Ehrenreich describes the dire living conditions of the working poor:

> The lunch that consists of Doritos or hot dog rolls, leading to faintness before the end of the shift. The "home" that is also a car or a van. The illness or injury that must be "worked through," with gritted teeth, because there's no sick pay or health insurance and the loss of one day's pay will mean no groceries for the next. These experiences are not part of a sustainable lifestyle, even a lifestyle of chronic deprivation and relentless low-level punishment. They are, by almost any standard of subsistence, emergency situations. And that is how we should see the poverty of millions of low-wage Americans--as a state of emergency. (214)

A problem of this magnitude cannot be fixed simply by raising the minimum wage.

Note that the period precedes the parenthetical citation at the end of an indented (block) quotation. Note, too, how the writer introduces and then comments on the block quotation from Ehrenreich, explaining the signficance of the quotation to the larger essay.

Rarely will you need to quote more than a paragraph, but if you do, indent the first line of each paragraph an extra quarter of an inch (or three spaces).

(c) Punctuation within citations and quotations

Punctuation marks clarify meaning in quotations and citations. The following list summarizes their common uses.

- A colon separates volume numbers from page numbers in a parenthetical citation.

  (Raine 2: 247)

- A comma separates the author's name from the title when it is necessary to list both in a parenthetical citation.

  (Kingsolver, <u>Animal Dreams</u>)

  A comma also indicates that page or line numbers are not sequential.

  (44, 47)

- Ellipsis points indicate an omission within a quotation.

  "They lived in an age of increasing complexity and great hope; we in an age of . . . growing despair" (Krutch 2).

- A hyphen indicates a continuous sequence of pages or lines.

  (44-47)

■ A period separates acts, scenes, and lines of dramatic works.

(3.1.56)

A period also distinguishes chapters from verses in biblical citations.

(Gen. 1.1)

■ A question mark placed inside the final quotation marks indicates that the quotation is a question. Notice that the period after the parenthetical citation marks the end of the sentence.

Peter Elbow asks, "What could be more wonderful than the pleasure of creating or appreciating forms that are different, amazing, outlandish, useless--the opposite of ordinary, everyday, pragmatic?" (542).

When placed outside the final quotation marks, a question mark indicates that the quotation is part of a question posed by the writer of the paper.

What does Kabat-Zinn mean when he advises people to practice mindfulness "as if their lives depended on it" (305)?

■ Square brackets enclose words that have been added to the quotation as clarification and are not part of the original material.

"The publication of this novel [Beloved] establishes Morrison as one of the most important writers of our time" (Boyle 17).

13b MLA list of works cited

All of the works you cite should be listed at the end of your paper, beginning on a separate page with the heading "Works Cited." Use the following tips as you prepare your list.

TIPS FOR PREPARING A LIST OF WORKS CITED

- Center the heading "Works Cited" (not underlined or enclosed in quotation marks) one inch from the top of the page.

- Arrange the list of works alphabetically by the author's last name.

- If a source has more than one author, alphabetize the entry according to the last name of the first author.

- If you use more than one work by the same author, alphabetize the works by the first major word in each title. For the first entry, provide the author's

(Continued on page 282)

(Continued from page 281)

complete name (last name given first), but substitute three hyphens (---) for the author's name in subsequent entries.

■ For a work without an author or editor, alphabetize the entry according to the first important word in the title.

■ Type the first line of each entry flush with the left margin and indent subsequent lines one-half inch or five spaces (a hanging indent).

■ Double-space equally throughout—between lines of an entry and between entries.

CAUTION

Automatic bibliography composers found online and included in some software packages often make mistakes. They may fail to include all elements of a bibliographic entry or may order elements incorrectly. If you decide to use an automatic composer, be sure to check the results against the model entries provided in this chapter.

Directory of MLA-Style Entries for a Works-Cited List

BOOKS

1. Book by one author 290
2. Book by two authors 290
3. Book by three authors 290
4. Book by more than three authors 290
5. Book by a corporate author 290
6. Book by an anonymous author 290
7. Book with an author and an editor 290
8. Book with an editor instead of an author 291
9. Edition after the first 291
10. Introduction, preface, foreword, or afterword to a book 291
11. Anthology 291
12. A work originally published in an anthology 291
13. A work from a journal reprinted in a textbook or an anthology 292

14. A work from an edited collection reprinted in a textbook or an anthology 292
15. Translated book 292
16. Republished book 292
17. Multivolume work 292
18. Article in a multivolume work 293
19. Book in a series 293

ARTICLES

20. Article in a journal with continuous pagination 296
21. Article in a journal with each issue paginated separately 296
22. Article in a monthly magazine 296
23. Article in a weekly magazine or newspaper 296
24. Article in a daily newspaper 296
25. Unsigned article or wire service article 296
26. Editorial in a newspaper or magazine 297
27. Book or film review in a magazine 297
28. Book or film review in a journal 297

OTHER PRINT SOURCES

29. Encyclopedia entry 297
30. Dictionary entry 297
31. Sacred text 298
32. Government publication 298
33. Law case 298
34. Public law 298
35. Pamphlet or bulletin 298
36. Published dissertation 299
37. Published letter 299

LIVE PERFORMANCES AND DIGITAL RECORDINGS

38. Play performance 299
39. Lecture or presentation 299
40. Interview 299
41. Film 300
42. Radio or television program 300
43. DVD 300
44. Multidisc DVD 301
45. Sound recording on CD 301

IMAGES

46. Work of art 301
47. Cartoon or comic strip 302
48. Map or chart 302
49. Advertisement 302

ONLINE BOOKS, ARTICLES, AND DOCUMENTS

50. Online book 305
51. Online book with separate date of print publication 306
52. Part of an online book 306
53. Online encyclopedia entry 306
54. Encyclopedia entry from a library subscription service 306
55. Online journal article 306
56. Article from a scholarly archival database 307
57. Online abstract 307
58. Online magazine article 307
59. Online newspaper article 307
60. Review in an online newspaper 307
61. Article from a library subscription database or subscription service 307
    a. ERIC 308
    b. EBSCO 309
    c. LexisNexis 309
    d. ProQuest 309
    e. InfoTrac 309
62. Online congressional document 309
63. Online document from a government office 310
64. Online law case 310
65. Online public law 310
66. Online sacred text 310

ONLINE RECORDINGS AND IMAGES

67. Online music 310
68. Online speech 311
69. Online video 311
70. Online television or radio program 311
71. Online interview 311
72. Online work of art 311
73. Online photograph 311
74. Online map or chart 312

75. Online advertisement 312
76. Online cartoon or comic strip 312

WEB SITES

77. Web site 312
78. Web site with incomplete information 312
79. Section of a Web site 313
80. Personal home page 313

ONLINE COMMUNICATIONS

81. E-mail 313
82. Discussion group or forum 313
83. Newsgroup 314
84. Web log (blog) 314

OTHER SOURCES ACCESSED BY COMPUTER

85. CD-ROM 314
86. Work from a periodically published database on CD-ROM 314
87. DVD-ROM 314
88. Multidisc publication 314

When writing down source information for your bibliography, be sure to copy the information directly from the source (e.g., the title page of a book). (See fig. 13.1, on page 289.)

General Documentation Guidelines for Print-Based Sources

Author, Artist, or Editor

One author or artist. Place the last name before the first, separating them with a comma. Add any middle name or initial after the first name. Use another comma before any abbreviation or number that follows the first name. Indicate the end of this unit of the entry with a period.

Halberstam, David.

Johnston, Mary K.

King, Martin Luther, Jr.

(Continued on page 286)

Author, Artist, or Editor *(Continued from page 285)*

Two or three authors or artists.
List names in the same order used on the title page of the book. The first person's name is inverted (that is, the last name appears first); the others are not. Separate all names with commas, placing the word *and* before the final name.

West, Nigel, and Oleg Tsarev.

Green, Bill, Maria Lopez, and Jenny T. Graf.

Four or more authors or artists.
List the names of all the authors or artists, or provide just the first person's name (inverted) and the abbreviation *et al.* (for *et alii,* meaning "and others").

Quirk, Randolph, Sidney Greenbaum, Geoffrey Leech, and Jan Svartvik.

OR
Quirk, Randolph, et al.

Corporate or group author. Omit any initial article (*a, an,* or *the*) from the name.

Institute of Medicine.

Department of Natural Resources.

Editor. If an editor or editors are listed instead of an author or authors, include the abbreviation *ed.* for "editor" or *eds.* for "editors."

Espinoza, Toni, ed.

Gibb, Susan, and Karen Enochs, eds.

Title

Underlined titles. Underline the titles of books, magazines, journals, newspapers, plays, films, and Web sites. Capitalize all major words (nouns, pronouns, verbs, adjectives, adverbs, and subordinating conjunctions). Make the underlining continuous, not separate under each word. Do not use a period after the title of a periodical or underline the period that follows the title of a book, play, film, or Web site.

<u>Newsweek</u>

<u>Hamlet</u>.

<u>Weird English</u>.

<u>The Aviator</u>.

Titles in quotation marks. Use quotation marks to enclose the titles of short works such as journal or magazine articles, short stories, poems, and songs (40b).	"Three Days to See." "Selling the Super Bowl." "Generations."
Subtitles. Always include a subtitle if the work has one. Use a colon to separate a main title and a subtitle.	<u>Lost in Translation: Life in a New Language</u>. "Silence: Learning to Listen."
Titles within titles. When an underlined title includes the title of another work normally underlined, do not underline the embedded title.	<u>Essays on</u> Death of a Salesman. BUT <u>Death of a Salesman</u>.
If the embedded title normally requires quotation marks, it should be underlined as well as enclosed in quotation marks.	<u>Understanding "The Philosophy of Composition" and the Aesthetic of Edgar Allan Poe</u>. BUT "The Philosophy of Composition."
When a title in quotation marks includes the title of another work normally underlined, retain the underlining.	"A Salesman's Reading of <u>Death of a Salesman</u>."
If the embedded title is normally enclosed in quotation marks, use single quotation marks.	"The European Roots of 'The Philosophy of Composition.'"

Publication Data

City of publication. If more than one city is listed on the title page, mention only the first. Place a colon after the name of the city.	Boston: New York:

(Continued on page 288)

If the work was published *outside* the United States and the city of publication may be unfamiliar to readers, add an abbreviation for the country or for the province if the city is in Canada.	Norwich, Eng.: Prince George, BC:
Publisher's name. Provide a shortened form of the publisher's name, and place a comma after it. To shorten the name of the publisher, use the principal name. For books published by university presses, abbreviate *University* and *Press* without periods or italics.	Knopf (for Alfred A. Knopf) Random (for Random House) Harvard UP (for Harvard University Press)
If two publishers are listed, provide the city of publication and the name of the publisher for each. Use a semicolon to separate the two.	Manchester, Eng.: Manchester UP; New York: St. Martin's
Publisher's imprint. You will sometimes need to list both a publisher's name and an imprint. The imprint is usually listed above the publisher's name on the title page. In a works-cited entry, use a hyphen to separate the two names: imprint-publisher.	Quill-HarperCollins Vintage-Random
Copyright date. Although the copyright date may be found on the title page, it is usually found on the next page—the copyright page (see fig. 13.2). Place a period after the date.	

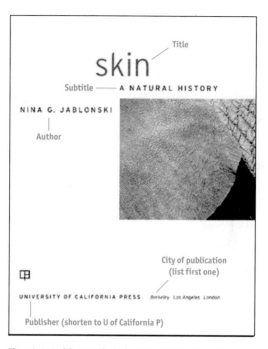

Fig. 13.1. A title page includes most, if not all, of the information needed for a bibliographic entry. In this case, the title page omits the publication date.

University of California Press, one of the most distinguished university presses in the United States, enriches lives around the world by advancing scholarship in the humanities, social sciences, and natural sciences. Its activities are supported by the UC Press Foundation and by philanthropic contributions from individuals and institutions. For more information, visit www.ucpress.edu.

University of California Press
Berkeley and Los Angeles, California

University of California Press, Ltd.
London, England

─────────────── Copyright year

©2006 by Nina G. Jablonksi

Fig. 13.2. If the title page does not give the book's date of publication, turn to the copyright page, which is usually the page following the title page.

BOOKS

1. Book by one author

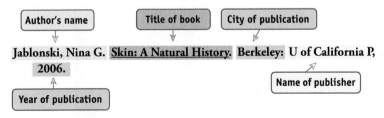

Jablonski, Nina G. Skin: A Natural History. Berkeley: U of California P, 2006.

2. Book by two authors

West, Nigel, and Oleg Tsarev. The Crown Jewels: The British Secrets at the Heart of the KGB Archives. New Haven: Yale UP, 1999.

3. Book by three authors

Spinosa, Charles, Ferdinand Flores, and Hubert L. Dreyfus. Disclosing New Worlds: Entrepreneurship, Democratic Action, and the Cultivation of Solidarity. Cambridge: MIT P, 1997.

4. Book by more than three authors

Bullock, Jane A., George D. Haddow, Damon Cappola, Erdem Ergin, Lissa Westerman, and Sarp Yeletaysi. Introduction to Homeland Security. Boston: Elsevier, 2005.
OR
Bullock, Jane A., et al. Introduction to Homeland Security. Boston: Elsevier, 2005.

5. Book by a corporate author

Institute of Medicine. Blood Banking and Regulation: Procedures, Problems, and Alternatives. Washington: Natl. Acad., 1996.

6. Book by an anonymous author

Primary Colors: A Novel of Politics. New York: Warner, 1996.

Begin the entry with the title. Do not use *Anonymous* or *Anon.*

7. Book with an author and an editor

Stoker, Bram. Dracula. Ed. Glennis Byron. Peterborough, ON: Broadview, 1998.

Include both the name of the author and the name of the editor (preceded by *Ed.*). Note that this book was published in Ontario, Canada, so the abbreviation for the province is included (see page 288).

8. Book with an editor instead of an author

Kachuba, John B., ed. <u>How to Write Funny</u>. Cincinnati: Writer's Digest, 2000.

9. Edition after the first

Murray, Donald. <u>The Craft of Revision</u>. 4th ed. Boston: Heinle, 2001.

10. Introduction, preface, foreword, or afterword to a book

Olnos, Edward James. Foreword. <u>Vietnam Veteranos: Chicanos Recall the War</u>. By Lea

Ybarra. Austin: U of Texas P, 2004. ix-x.

The name that begins the entry is that of the author of the section of the book, not of the entire book. That person's name is followed by the title of the section (Introduction, Preface, Foreword, of Afterword).

11. Anthology (a collection of works by different authors)

Buranen, Lisa, and Alice M. Roy, eds. <u>Perspectives on Plagiarism and Intellectual</u>

<u>Property in a Postmodern World</u>. New York: State U of New York P, 1999.

Include the name(s) of the editor(s), followed by the abbreviation *ed.* (or *eds*). For individual works within an anthology, consult the following two models.

12. A work originally published in an anthology

Rowe, David. "No Gain, No Game? Media and Sport." <u>Mass Media and Society</u>. 3rd ed.

Ed. James Curran and Michael Gurevitch. New York: Oxford UP, 2000. 346-61.

Use this form for an article, essay, story, poem, or play that was published for the first time in the anthology you are using. Place the title of the anthology after the title of the individual work, noting the edition if it is not the first. Provide the name(s) of the editor(s) after the abbreviation *Ed.* for "edited by." List the publication data for the anthology and the range of pages on which the work appears. (See pages 274 and 295 for information on noting inclusive page numbers.)

If you cite more than one work from an anthology, provide only the name(s) of the author(s), the title of the work, the name(s) of the editor(s), and the inclusive page numbers in an entry for each work.

Then, also provide an entry for the entire anthology, in which you include the relevant publication data (see the sample entry for an anthology in item 11).

Clark, Irene L. "Writing Centers and Plagiarism." Buranen and Roy 155-67.

Howard, Rebecca Moore. "The New Abolitionism Comes to Plagiarism." Buranen and Roy 87-95.

13. A work from a journal reprinted in a textbook or an anthology

Selfe, Cynthia L. "Technology and Literacy: A Story about the Perils of Not Paying Attention." College Composition and Communication 50.3 (1999): 411-37. Rpt. in Views from the Center: The CCCC Chairs' Addresses 1977-2005. Ed. Duane Roen. Boston: Bedford; Urbana: NCTE, 2006. 323-51.

Use the abbreviation *Rpt.* (not italicized) for "Reprinted."

14. A work from an edited collection reprinted in a textbook or an anthology

Brownmiller, Susan. "Let's Put Pornography Back in the Closet." Take Back the Night: Women on Pornography. Ed. Laura Lederer. New York: Morrow, 1980. 252-55. Rpt. in Conversations: Readings for Writing. 4th ed. By Jack Selzer. New York: Allyn, 2000. 578-81.

See item 12 for information on citing more than one work from the same anthology.

15. Translated book

Garrigues, Eduardo. West of Babylon. Trans. Nasario Garcia. Albuquerque: U of New Mexico P, 2002.

Place the abbreviation *Trans.* (not italicized) for "Translated by" before the translator's name.

16. Republished book

Alcott, Louisa May. Work: A Story of Experience. 1873. Harmondsworth, Eng.: Penguin, 1995.

After the title of the book, provide the original publication date, followed by a period.

17. Multivolume work

Young, Ralph F., ed. Dissent in America. 2 vols. New York: Longman-Pearson, 2005.

Cite the total number of volumes in a work when you have used material from more than one volume. Include the year the volumes were published. If the volumes were published over a span of time, provide inclusive dates: (1997-99) or (1998-2004).

If you have used only one volume, include that volume's number (preceded by the abbreviation *Vol.*) in place of the total number of volumes.

Young, Ralph F., ed. <u>Dissent in America</u>. Vol. 1. New York: Longman-Pearson, 2005.

Note that the publisher's name in this entry is hyphenated: the first name is the imprint; the second is the publisher.

18. Article in a multivolume work

To indicate a specific article in a multivolume work, provide the author's name and the title of the article in quotation marks. Note the page numbers for the article after the date of publication.

Baxby, Derrick. "Edward Jenner." <u>Oxford Dictionary of National Biography</u>. Ed. H. C. G.

Matthew and Brian Harrison. Vol. 30. Oxford: Oxford UP, 2004. 4-8.

If required by your instructor, include the number of volumes and the inclusive publication dates after the page numbers: 382-89. 23 vols. 1962-97.

19. Book in a series

Sumner, Colin, ed. <u>Blackwell Companion to Criminology</u>. Blackwell Companions to

Sociology 8. Malden: Blackwell, 2004.

When citing a book that is part of a series, provide the name of the series and, if one is listed, the number designating the work's place in it. The series name is not underlined. Abbreviate words in the series name according to the MLA guidelines; for example, the word *Series* is abbreviated *Ser.*

ARTICLES

A **journal** is a publication written for a specific discipline or profession. **Magazines** and **newspapers** are written for the general public. You can find most of the information required for a works-cited entry for a journal article on the first page of the journal (fig. 13.3) or at the bottom of the first page of the article you are citing.

Title of article and name of periodical

Put the article title in quotation marks with a period inside the closing quotation marks. Underline the name of the periodical, but do

Date of publication
Volume number
Issue number

Spring / Summer 2008
Volume 20
Number 1–2

American Literary History — Name of journal

Twenty Years of American Literary History: The Anniversary Volume

Title of article
Author

What Good Can Literary History Do? **1** —— Initial page number
Jonathan Arac

A Response to Jonathan Arac **12**
Jonathan Elmer

Antipodean American Literature: Franklin, Twain, and the Sphere of Subalternity **22**
Paul Giles

Can the Antipodean Speak? A Response to Paul Giles **51**
Lauren M. E. Goodlad

Women, Blood, and Contract **57**
Shirley Samuels

Blood, Republicanism, and the Return of George Washington: A Response to Shirley Samuels **76**
Andy Doolen

The Rise of the New Atlantic Studies Matrix **83**
William Boelhower

Oceanic, Traumatic, Post-Paradigmatic: A Response to William Boelhower **102**
Jed Esty

National Treasure, Global Value, and American Literary Studies **108**
Eric Lott

Blood and Treasure: A Response to Eric Lott **124**
Susan M. Ryan

The Unkillable Dream of the Great American Novel: *Moby-Dick* as Test Case **132**
Lawrence Buell

A Response to Lawrence Buell **156**
Robert Milder

Border Literary Histories, Globalization, and Critical Regionalism **160**
José E. Limón

Glocal Matters: A Response to José E. Limón **183**
Richard T. Rodríguez

Fig. 13.3. First page of a journal.

not add any punctuation following the name. Capitalize all major words (nouns, pronouns, verbs, adjectives, adverbs, and subordinating conjunctions). Omit the word *A*, *An*, or *The* from the beginning of the name of a periodical.

"Into the Void." New Scientist

Volume and issue numbers
In an entry for an article from a journal, provide the volume number. For a journal with continuous pagination, include only the volume number after the name of the journal. For a journal whose issues are paginated separately, put a period after the volume number and add the issue number.

Contemporary Review 194   Studies in the Literary Imagination 26.3

A journal paginated *continuously* uses the number 1 to identify only the first page of the first issue in a volume. The first page of a subsequent issue in that volume is numbered to follow the last page of the first volume, and so on. In contrast, a journal paginated *separately* uses the number 1 to identify the first page of each issue in a volume.

Date
For journals, place the year of publication in parentheses after the volume or issue number. For magazines and newspapers, provide the date of issue after the name of the periodical. Note the day first (if provided), followed by the month (abbreviated except for May, June, and July) and year.

Journal   Journal of Marriage and Family 65 (2003)

Magazine   Economist 13 Aug. 2005

Newspaper   Chicago Tribune 24 July 2002

Page numbers
Use a colon to separate the date from the page number(s). Note all the pages on which the article appears, separating the first and last page with a hyphen: 21-39. If the page numbers have the same hundreds or thousands digit, do not repeat it when listing the final page in the range: 131-42 or 1680-99. Magazine and newspaper articles are often interrupted by advertisements or other articles. If the first part of an article appears on pages 45 through 47 and the rest on pages 92 through 94, give only the first page number followed by a plus sign: 45+.

20. Article in a journal with continuous pagination

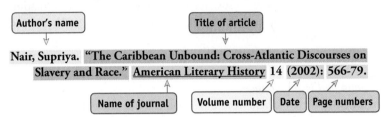

Author's name		Title of article

Nair, Supriya. "The Caribbean Unbound: Cross-Atlantic Discourses on Slavery and Race." American Literary History 14 (2002): 566-79.

Name of journal	Volume number	Date	Page numbers

21. Article in a journal with each issue paginated separately

Andrews, William L. "Postmodern Southern Literature: Confessions of a Norton

Anthologist." Studies in the Literary Imagination 35.1 (2002): 105-12.

When you use an article from a journal paginated separately, include the issue number as well as the volume number. In this example, 35 is the volume number, and 1 is the issue number.

22. Article in a monthly magazine

Keizer, Garret. "How the Devil Falls in Love." Harper's Aug. 2002: 43-51.

23. Article in a weekly magazine or newspaper

Chown, Marcus. "Into the Void." New Scientist 24 Nov. 2007: 34-37.

24. Article in a daily newspaper

Moberg, David. "The Accidental Environmentalist." Chicago Tribune 24 Sept. 2002, final

ed., sec. 2: 1+.

When not part of the newspaper's name, the name of the city where the newspaper is published should be given in brackets after the title: Star Telegram [Fort Worth]. If a specific edition is not identifed on the masthead, put a colon after the date and then provide the page reference. Specify the section by inserting the section letter as it appears in the newspaper (A7 or 7A, for example).

25. Unsigned article or wire service article

"View from the Top." National Geographic July 2001: 140.

26. Editorial in a newspaper or magazine

Beefs, Anne. "Ending Bias in the Human Rights System." Editorial. <u>New York Times</u> 22
    May 2002, natl. ed.: A27.

27. Book or film review in a magazine

Denby, David. "Horse Power." Rev. of <u>Seabiscuit</u>, dir. Gary Ross. <u>New Yorker</u> 4 Aug.
    2003: 84-85.

Include the name of the reviewer, the title of the review (if any), the
phrase *Rev. of* (for "Review of"), the title of the work being reviewed,
and the name of the editor, author, or director.

28. Book or film review in a journal

Graham, Catherine. Rev. of <u>Questionable Activities: The Best</u>, ed. Judith Rudakoff.
    <u>Canadian Theatre Review</u> 113 (2003): 74-76.

OTHER PRINT SOURCES

29. Encyclopedia entry

Robertson, James I., Jr. "Thomas Jonathan Jackson." <u>Encyclopedia of the American Civil</u>
    <u>War: A Political, Social, and Military History</u>. Ed. David S. Heidler and Jeanne T.
    Heidler. 5 vols. Santa Barbara: ABC-CLIO, 2000.

When the author of an encyclopedia article is indicated only by initials,
check the table of contents for a list of contributors. If an article is
anonymous, begin the entry with the article title.

Full publication information is not necessary for a well-known reference work that is organized alphabetically. Along with the author's
name, the title of the article, and the name of the encyclopedia, list the
edition and year of publication in one of two ways: 5th ed. 2004 or
2002 ed.

Petersen, William J. "Riverboats and Rivermen." <u>The Encyclopedia Americana</u>. 1999 ed.

30. Dictionary entry

When citing a specific dictionary definition for a word, use the abbreviation *Def.* (for "Definition"), and indicate which one you used if the
entry has two or more.

"Reactive." Def. 2a. <u>Merriam-Webster's Collegiate Dictionary</u>. 10th ed. 2001.

31. Sacred text

Begin your works-cited entry for a sacred text with the title of the work, rather than information about editors or translators.

New American Standard Bible. Anaheim: Foundation, 1997.

The Qur'an. Trans. Muhammad A. S. Abdel Haleem. Oxford: Oxford UP, 2004.

32. Government publication

United States. Office of Management and Budget. A Citizen's Guide to the Federal
    Budget. Washington: GPO, 1999.

When citing a government publication, list the name of the government (e.g., United States or Minnesota) and the agency that issued the work. Underline the title of a book or pamphlet. Indicate the city of publication. Federal publications are usually printed by the Government Printing Office (GPO) in Washington, DC, but be alert for exceptions.

When the name of an author or an editor appears on a government publication, insert that name after the title and introduce it with the word *By* or the abbreviation *Ed.* to indicate the person's contribution.

33. Law case

Chavez v. Martinez. No. 01-1444. Supreme Ct. of the US. 27 May 2003.

Include the last name of the first plaintiff, the abbreviation *v.* for "versus," the last name of the first defendant, the case number preceded by the abbreviation *No.,* the name of the deciding court, and the date of the decision. Although law cases are underlined in the text of a paper, they are *not* underlined in works-cited entries.

34. Public law

No Child Left Behind Act of 2001. Pub. L. 107-110. 8 Jan. 2002. Stat. 115.1425.

Include the name of the act, its public law number, the date it was enacted, and its Statutes at Large cataloging number. Notice the use of abbreviations in the example.

Although no works-cited entry is needed for familiar sources such as the U.S. Constitution, an in-text citation should still be included (see page 278).

35. Pamphlet or bulletin

Stucco in Residential Construction. St. Paul: Lath & Plaster Bureau, 2000.

If the pamphlet has an author, begin with the author's name, as you would for a book.

36. Published dissertation

Fukuda, Kay Louise. <u>Differing Perceptions and Constructions of the Meaning of</u>

<u>Assessment in Education</u>. Diss. Ohio State U, 2001. Ann Arbor: UMI, 2002.

After the title of the dissertation, include the abbreviation *Diss.,* the name of the university granting the degree, the date of completion, and the publication information. In the example, *UMI* stands for "University Microfilms International," which publishes many dissertations.

37. Published letter

In general, treat a published letter like a work in an anthology, adding the date of the letter and the number (if the editor assigned one).

Helen Hunt Jackson. "To Thomas Bailey Aldrich." 4 May 1883. <u>The Indian Reform</u>

<u>Letters of Helen Hunt Jackson, 1879-1885</u>. Ed. Valerie Sherer Mathes. Norman:

U of Oklahoma P, 1998. 258-59.

LIVE PERFORMANCES AND DIGITAL RECORDINGS

38. Play performance

<u>Proof</u>. By David Auburn. Dir. Daniel Sullivan. Walter Kerr Theater, New York. 8 Oct. 2002.

Cite the date of the performance you attended.

39. Lecture or presentation

Guinier, Lani. Address. Barbara Jordan Lecture Series. Schwab Auditorium. Pennsylvania

State U., University Park. 4 Oct. 2004.

Scharnhorst, Gary. Class lecture. English 296.003. Dane Smith Hall, U of New Mexico,

Albuquerque. 30 Apr. 2008.

Identify the site and the date of the lecture or presentation. Use the title if available; otherwise, provide a descriptive label.

40. Interview

Furstenheim, Ursula. Personal interview. 16 Jan. 2003.

Sugo, Misuzu. Telephone interview. 20 Feb. 2003.

For an interview you conducted, give only the name of the person you interviewed and the date of the interview. If the interview was conducted by someone else, add the name of the interviewer, a title or a descriptive label, and the name of the source.

Harryhausen, Ray. Interview with Terry Gross. <u>Fresh Air</u>. Natl. Public Radio. WHYY,

Philadelphia. 6 Jan. 2003.

41. Film

<u>My Big Fat Greek Wedding</u>. Dir. Joel Zwick. IFC, 2002.

The name of the company that produced or distributed the film (IFC, in this case) appears before the year of release. It is not necessary to cite the city in which the production or distribution company is based.

When you want to highlight the contribution of a specific person, list the contributor's name first. Other supplementary information may be included after the title.

Gomez, Ian, perf. <u>My Big Fat Greek Wedding</u>. Screenplay by Nia Vardalos. Dir. Joel

Zwick. IFC, 2002.

42. Radio or television program

When referring to a specific episode, place quotation marks around its title. Underline the title of the program.

"'Barbarian' Forces." <u>Ancient Warriors</u>. Narr. Colgate Salsbury. Dir. Phil Grabsky.

Learning Channel. 1 Jan. 1996.

To highlight a specific contributor, begin the entry with that person's name.

Finch, Nigel, dir. "The Lost Language of Cranes." By David Leavitt. Prod. Ruth Caleb.

Great Performances. PBS. WNET, New York. 24 June 1992.

43. DVD

<u>A River Runs through It</u>. Dir. Robert Redford. Screenplay by Richard Friedenberg. 1992.

DVD. Columbia, 1999.

Cite relevant information about the title and director as you would for a film. Note the original release date of the film, the medium (i.e., DVD), and the release date for the DVD. If the original company producing the film did not release the DVD, list the company that released the DVD instead.

44. Multidisc DVD

<u>More Treasures from American Film Archives, 1894-1931: 50 Films</u>. Prod. Natl. Film

   Preservation Foundation. DVD. 3 discs. Image Entertainment, 2004.

List the number of discs after noting the medium. For a particular segment from a multidisc DVD, indicate the title of the work, relevant information about the author or director, and the date the work was initially released. In place of the number of discs, indicate the number of the disc used.

<u>A Bronx Morning</u>. By Jay Leyda. 1931. <u>More Treasures from American Film Archives,</u>

   <u>1894-1931: 50 Films</u>. Prod. Natl. Film Preservation Foundation. DVD. Disc 2.

   Image Entertainment, 2004.

45. Sound recording on CD

Franklin, Aretha. <u>Amazing Grace: The Complete Recordings</u>. Atlantic, 1999.

For a sound recording on another medium, identify the type (*Audiocassette* or *LP*).

Raitt, Bonnie. <u>Nick of Time</u>. Audiocassette. Capitol, 1989.

When citing a recording of a specific song, begin with the name of the performer, and place the song title in quotation marks. Identify the author(s) after the song title. If the performance is a reissue from an earlier recording, provide the original date of recording (preceded by *Rec.* for "Recorded").

Horne, Lena. "The Man I Love." By George Gershwin and Ira Gershwin. Rec. 15 Dec.

   1941. <u>Stormy Weather</u>. BMG, 1990.

IMAGES

46. Work of art

Gauguin, Paul. <u>Ancestors of Tehamana</u>. 1893. Art Institute of Chicago, Chicago.

Identify the artist's name, the title of the work (underlined), the organization or individual holding the work, and the city in which the work is located. The date of creation is optional but, if included, should follow the work's title. For a photograph of a work of art, provide publication information for its source after the name of the city in which the original is located.

47. Cartoon or comic strip

Cheney, Tom. Cartoon. <u>New Yorker</u> 9 June 2003: 93.

Trudeau, Garry. "Doonesbury." Comic strip. <u>Daily Record</u> [Ellensburg] 21 April 2005: A4.

After the creator's name, place the title of the work (if given) in quotation marks and include the descriptor *Cartoon* or *Comic strip*.

48. Map or chart

<u>Cincinnati and Vicinity</u>. Map. Chicago: Rand, 2008.

Include the title and the appropriate descriptor, *Map* or *Chart*.

49. Advertisement

Nu by Yves Saint Laurent. Advertisement. <u>Allure</u> June 2003: 40.

The name of the product and/or that of the company being advertised is followed by the designation *Advertisement*.

ONLINE BOOKS, ARTICLES, AND DOCUMENTS

Many of the guidelines for documenting online sources are similar to those for print sources. In fact, if a document exists in print as well as online, you must provide the information required for that type of print-based source before providing information about the document's online publication and access. For a source found only in electronic form, provide just the information about its online publication and access.

Electronic publication information
Indicate the title of an Internet site, the date of publication (or of the most recent update), and the site's sponsoring organization, usually found at the bottom of the site's home page (see fig. 13.4).

Access information
State the date of access and the URL (Internet address) for a Web site. You can find this information by printing out a page you are using. The

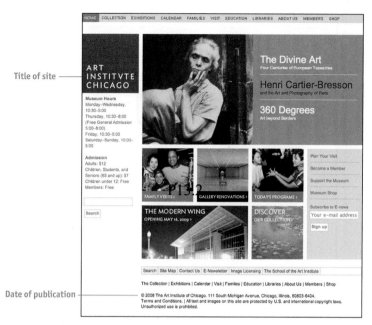

Title of site

Date of publication

Fig. 13.4. The home page for the Art Institute of Chicago indicates the title of the site (which is also the name of the sponsoring organization) and the date of publication.

date you accessed the site and the URL can be found at the top or the bottom of the printed page (see fig. 13.5).

By providing your readers with a complete URL, including the protocol (http, ftp, telnet, news), all punctuation marks, and both path and file names, you tell them how to locate the source.

<http://stanfordmag.org.marapril99/>

<ftp://beowulf.engl.uky.edu/pub/beowulf>

Place the address within angle brackets, <>, so that it is clearly separated from any other punctuation in your citation. Divide the address after a slash when it does not fit on a single line. Make sure that the address is accurate; Web browsers (such as Mozilla Firefox) distinguish between uppercase and lowercase letters in a URL, and they will not be able to find a site if marks such as hyphens and underscores are missing. If the URL for the specific page you want to cite is extremely long, you may use the

Fig. 13.5. When you print a page from a Web site, the URL and the date of access usually appear at the top or bottom of the page.

URL for the site's search page instead. If there is no search page, cite the site's home page, followed by the word *Path,* a colon, and the sequence of links you used. Separate the links with semicolons.

<http://www.essentialsofmusic.com>. Path: Eras; Classical; Composer; Mozart.

Also keep in mind that Internet addresses often change, so double-check the URLs you list before submitting your work. Because sites may disappear, it is wise to print a hard copy of any online material you use as a source.

THE COLUMBIA GUIDE TO ONLINE STYLE

Recognizing that increasing numbers of writers conduct most of their research online, Columbia University Press published *The Columbia Guide to Online Style* (COS), which offers formatting guidelines, sample in-text citations, and sample bibliographic entries.

50. Online book

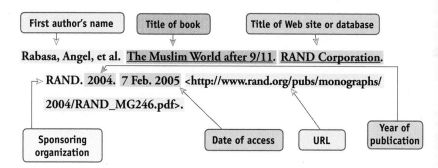

Because there are more than three authors, the abbreviation *et al.* has been used in the example, but listing all names is also acceptable: Rabasa, Angel, Cheryl Benard, Peter Chalk, C. Christine Fair, Theodore W. Karasik, Rollie Lal, Ian O. Lesser, and David E. Thaler. Note that in this example the name of the sponsoring organization is in the title of the Web site.

When the book has an editor or a translator, list that name after the title. The name of a site editor follows the title of the site.

Flaubert, Gustave. <u>Madame Bovary</u>. Trans. Eleanor Marx Aveling. New York: Modern

　　Library, 1918. <u>Electronic Text Center</u>. Ed. David Seaman. 2001. Alderman Lib.,

　　U of Virginia. 7 Jan. 2005 <http://etext.lib.virgina.edu/toc/modeng/public/

　　FlaBova.html>.

51. Online book with separate date of print publication

Rohrbough, Malcolm J. <u>Days of Gold: The California Gold Rush and the American</u>
<u>Nation</u>. Berkeley: U of California P, 1997. <u>History E-book Project</u>. American
Council of Learned Societies. 2005. Scholarly Publication Office, U of Michigan
Lib. 17 Feb. 2005 <http://name.umdl.umich.edu/HEB00571>.

52. Part of an online book

Strunk, William, Jr. "Elementary Rules of Usage." <u>The Elements of Style</u>. Ithaca:
Humphrey, 1918. <u>Bartleby.com: Great Books Online</u>. Ed. Steven van Leeuwen.
1999. 6 June 2003 <http://www.bartleby.com/141/strunk.html>.

53. Online encyclopedia entry

"Iran." <u>Encyclopaedia Britannica Online</u>. 2002. Encyclopaedia Britannica. 6 Mar. 2004
<http://search.eb.com/>.

54. Encyclopedia entry from a library subscription service

Turk, Austin T. "Terrorism." <u>Encyclopedia of Crime and Justice</u>. 2nd ed. Ed. Joshua
Dressler. 4 vols. New York: Macmillan Reference USA, 2002. <u>Gale Virtual</u>
<u>Reference Library</u>. Thomson Gale. Pennsylvania State U, Pattee Lib., University
Park. 7 Feb. 2005 <http://find.galegroup.com/gvrl/>.

Include the name of the database (Gale Virtual Reference Library), the
name of the subscription service (Thomson Gale), the name of the subscriber (Pennsylvania State U, Pattee Lib.), and the subscriber's location
(include a state abbreviation if the state is not part of the subscriber's
name). The name of the database is underlined; the name of the service
is not.

55. Online journal article

Harnack, Andrew, and Gene Kleppinger. "Beyond the MLA Handbook: Documenting
Sources on the Internet." <u>Kairos</u> 1.2 (1996). 14 Aug. 1997 <http://www.english.ttu/
acw/kairos/index.html>.

Page numbers may not be provided for online journals; include them
after the year if they are given.

56. Article from a scholarly archival database

Ganter, Granville. "Red Jacket and the Decolonization of Republican Virtue." <u>American
   Indian Quarterly</u> 31.4 (2007): 559-81. <u>Project Muse</u>. 29 Apr. 2008
   <http://muse.uq.edu.au/journals/american_indian_quarterly/v031/31.4ganter.pdf>.

Include the name of the database (underlined) following all the information about the article. JSTOR and Project Muse are frequently used databases.

57. Online abstract

Landers, Susan J. "FDA Panel Findings Intensify Struggles with Prescribing of
   Antidepressants." <u>American Medical News</u> 47.37 (2004): 1-2. Abstract. ProQuest
   Direct. Washington State U Lib., Pullman. 7 Feb. 2005 <http://proquest.umi.com/>.

Add the word *Abstract* after the page numbers.

58. Online magazine article

Plotz, David. "The Cure for Sinophobia." <u>Slate</u> 4 June 1999. 15 June 1999
   <http://www.slate.com/StrangeBedfellow/99-06-04/StrangeBedfellow.asp>.

The first date is the publication date; the second is the date of access.

59. Online newspaper article

"Tornadoes Touch Down in S. Illinois." <u>New York Times on the Web</u> 16 Apr. 1998.
   20 May 1998 <http://www.nytimes.com/aponline/a/AP-Illinois-Storms.html>.

When no author is identified, begin with the title of the article. If the article is an editorial, include *Editorial* after the title: "America's Promises." Editorial.

60. Review in an online newspaper

Parent, Marc. "A Father, a Son and an Ideal That's Painfully Tested." Rev. of <u>Scout's
   Honor</u>, by Peter Applebome. <u>New York Times on the Web</u> 6 June 2003. 12 June 2003
   <http://www.nytimes.com/2003/06/06/books/06BOOK.html>.

61. Article from a library subscription database or subscription service

You can find most of the information you need for a works-cited entry on the abstract page of the article you select (see fig. 13.6). Subscription services provide access to various databases. The name of a data-

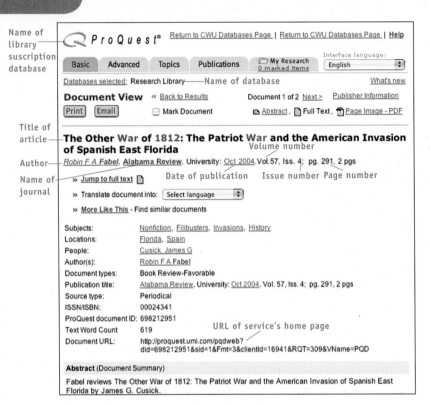

Name of library suscription database

Name of database

Title of article

Author

Name of journal

Volume number

Date of publication   Issue number   Page number

URL of service's home page

Fig. 13.6. Abstract page from a subscription service.

base (such as JSTOR, Project Muse, ERIC, or Acadamic Universe) is underlined; the name of a service (such as LexisNexis, ProQuest, Info-Trac, or EBSCO) is not. The service is the interface through which the database is offered. (Sometimes the database and the service have the same name.)

a. ERIC

Holmes, Julie A. "The Least Restrictive Environment: Is Inclusion Best for All Special

     Needs Students?" (1999): 1-12. ERIC. Inst. of Education Sciences, Dept. of

     Education, Washington. ED437760. 6 Nov. 2004 <http://www.eric.ed.gov/>.

Be sure to include the ERIC database number.

b. EBSCO

Folks, Jeffrey J. "Crowd and Self: William Faulkner's Sources of Agency in The Sound
and the Fury." Southern Literary Journal 34.2 (2002): 30- . Academic Search
Premier. EBSCO. Wright State U, Dunbar Lib., Dayton, OH. 6 June 2003
<http://www.epnet.com/>.

For sources that list only the page number on which a work begins,
include that number and a hyphen. Leave a space before the period.

c. LexisNexis

Suggs, Welch. "A Hard Year in College Sports." The Chronicle of Higher Education
19 Dec. 2003: 37. Academic Universe: News. LexisNexis. U of Texas at Austin,
U Texas Lib., Austin. 17 July 2004 <http://www.lexis-nexis.com/>.

Provide the name of the LexisNexis-accessed database (e.g., Academic
Universe or State Capitol) in which you found the article. Add a colon,
and then indicate the path you followed for your search (e.g., News,
Business, or Legal). Underline both name and path.

d. ProQuest

Fabel, Robin F. A. "The Other War of 1812: The Patriot War and the American
Invasion of Spanish Florida." Alabama Review. AMA Titles. ProQuest. Central
Washington U, Brooks Memorial Lib., Ellensburg. 8 Mar. 2005 <http://
proquest.umi.com/>.

e. InfoTrac

Priest, Ann-Marie. "Between Being and Nothingness: The 'Astonishing Precipice' of
Virginia Woolf's Night and Day." Journal of Modern Literature 26.2 (2002-03):
66-80. InfoTrac College Edition. Gale. Alabama Virtual Library. 12 Jan. 2004
<http://www.galegroup.com/>.

62. Online congressional document

United States. Cong. Senate. Special Committee on Aging. Global Aging: Opportunity or
Threat for the U.S. Economy? 108th Cong., 1st sess. S. Hrg. 108-30. Washington:
GPO, 2003. 7 Jan. 2005 <http://frwebgate.access.gpo.gov/cgibin/
getdoc.cgi?dbname=108_senate_hearings&docid=f:86497.wais.pdf>.

Provide the number and session of Congress and the type and number of publication. (*S* stands for "Senate"; *H* or *HR* stands for "House of Representatives.")

Bills	S 41, HR 82
Reports	S. Rept. 14, H. Rept. 18
Hearings	S. Hrg. 23, H. Hrg. 25
Resolutions	S. Res. 32, H. Res. 52
Documents	S. Doc. 213, H. Doc. 123

63. Online document from a government office

United States. Dept. of State. Bur. of Democracy, Human Rights, and Labor. Guatemala
Country Report on Human Rights Practices for 1998. Feb. 1999. 1 May 1999
<http://www.state.gov/www/global/human_rights/1998_hrp_report/guatemal.html>.

Begin with the name of the country, state, or city whose government is responsible for the document and the department or agency that issued it. If a subdivision of the larger organization is responsible, name the subdivision. If an author is identified, provide the name, preceded by the word *By*, between the title and the date of issue of the document.

64. Online law case

Tennessee v. Lane. No. 02-1667. Supreme Ct. of the US. 17 May 2004. 28 Jan. 2005
<http://www.usdoj.gov/osg/briefs/2003/3mer/2mer/2002-1667.mer.aa.pdf>.

65. Online public law

Individuals with Disabilities Education Act. Pub. L. 105-17. 4 June 1997. Stat. 104.587-698.
29 Jan. 2005 <http://www.ed.gov/policy/spece/leg/idea/idea.pdf>.

66. Online sacred text

Sama Veda. Trans. Ralph T. H. Griffith. 1895. Sacred-Texts.com. Ed. John B. Hare. 2 Feb.
2005. 6 Mar. 2005 <http://www.sacred-texts.com>.

ONLINE RECORDINGS AND IMAGES

67. Online music

Moran, Jason. "Jump Up." Same Mother. Blue Note, 2005. 7 Mar. 2005
<http://www.bluenote.com/detail.asp?SelectionID=10376>.

68. Online speech

Malcolm X. "The Ballot or the Bullet." Detroit, 12 Apr. 1964. <u>American Rhetoric: Top One Hundred Speeches</u>. Ed. Michael E. Eidenmuller. 2005. 14 Jan. 2005 <http://www.americanrhetoric.com/speeches/malcomxballot.htm>.

"12 Apr. 1964" is the date the speech was delivered, "2005" is the year of the speech's electronic publication, and "14 Jan. 2005" is the date of access.

69. Online video

Riefenstahl, Leni, dir. <u>Triumph of the Will</u>. 1935. <u>Movieflix.com</u>. 2005. 17 Feb. 2005 <http://www.movieflix.com/movie_info.mfx?movie_id=404>.

"1935" is the year in which the movie was originally released, "2005" is the year in which it was made available online, and "17 Feb. 2005" is the date of access.

70. Online television or radio program

"Religion and the American Election." Narr. Tony Hassan. <u>The Religion Report</u>. Radio National. 3 Nov. 2004. Transcript. 18 Feb. 2005 <http://www.abc.net.au/rn/talks/8.30/relrpt/stories/s1243269.htm>.

If the source is a transcript rather than the visual or audio broadcast, include the word *Transcript* between the date the program aired and the date of access.

71. Online interview

McLaughlin, John. Interview with Wolf Blitzer. <u>CNN</u>. 14 July 2004. 21 Dec. 2004 <http://www.cnn.com/2004/US/07/14/transcript.mclaughlin/index.html>.

72. Online work of art

Vermeer, Johannes. <u>Young Woman with a Water Pitcher</u>. c. 1660. Metropolitan Museum of Art, New York. 2 Oct. 2002 <http://www.metmuseum.org/collection/view1.asp?dep_11&item_89%2E15%2E21>.

73. Online photograph

Lange, Dorothea. <u>Migrant Mother</u>. 1936. Prints and Photographs Division, Lib. of Congress, Washington. Digital id. fsa 8b29516. 9 Feb. 2005 <http://www.loc.gov/rr/print/list/128_migm.html>.

The identification number for a photograph (such as "Digital id. fsa 8b29516" in the preceding example) is included if it is available.

74. Online map or chart

"Virginia 1624." Map. Map Collections 1544-1996. Library of Congress. 26 Apr. 1999
    <http://memory.loc.gov/cgibin/map_mp/_ammmem_8kk3::&title_Virginia++>.

"Daily Cigarette Smoking among High School Seniors." Chart. National Center for
    Health Statistics. 27 Jan. 2005. Centers for Disease Control and Prevention, US
    Dept. of Health and Human Services. 25 Feb. 2005 <http://www.cdc.gov/nchs/
    images/hp2000/hdspr/hdslide13.gif>.

75. Online advertisement

Milk Processor Education Program. "Got Milk?" Advertisement. 16 Feb. 2005
    <http://www.milkpep.org/programs/lebron.cfm>.

76. Online cartoon or comic strip

Cagle, Daryl. "Social Security Pays 3 to 2." Cartoon. Slate.com. 4 Feb. 2005. 5 Feb. 2005
    <http://cagle.slate.msn.com/politicalcartoons/>.

WEB SITES

77. Web site

The Rossetti Archive. Ed. Jerome McGann. 2002. Institute for Advanced Technology in
    the Humanities, U of Virginia. 4 June 2003 <http://www.iath.virginia.edu/rossetti/
    index.html>.

Include the title of the site (underlined), the name of the editor or editors (if listed), the version number (if given), the date of publication or of the last update, the name of the sponsoring organization or institution, and the URL. (See pages 302–304.)

78. Web site with incomplete information

Breastcancer.org. 2 Feb. 2005. 5 Feb. 2005 <http://www.breastcancer.org/>.

If a Web site does not provide all the information usually included in a works-cited entry, list as much as is available.

79. Section of a Web site

Altman, Andrew. "Civil Rights." 3 Feb. 2003. <u>Stanford Encyclopedia of Philosophy</u>. Ed.

Edward N. Zalta. Spring 2003 ed. Center for the Study of Lang. and Information,

Stanford U. 12 June 2003 <http://plato.stanford.edu/archives/spr2003/entries/

civilrights/>.

Mozart, Wolfgang Amadeus. Concerto No. 3 for Horn, K. 447. <u>Essentials of Music</u>. 2001.

Norton and Sony. 18 Feb. 2005 <http://www.essentialsofmusic.com>. Path: Eras;

Classical; Composer; Mozart.

If the URL does not vary for different pages of a site, indicate how you accessed your source by listing the sequence of links after the word *Path* and a colon.

80. Personal home page

Gladwell, Malcolm. Home page. 8 Mar. 2005 <www.gladwell.com>.

After the name of the site's creator, provide the title or include the words *Home page*.

ONLINE COMMUNICATIONS

81. E-mail

Peters, Barbara. "Scholarships for Women." E-mail to Rita Martinez. 10 Mar. 2003.

The entry begins with the name of the person who created the e-mail. Put the subject line of the e-mail message in quotation marks. The recipient of the message is identified after the words *E-mail to*. If the message was sent to you, use *the author* rather than your name.

82. Discussion group or forum

Schipper, William. "Re: Quirk and Wrenn Grammar." Online posting. 5 Jan. 1995.

Ansaxnet. 12 Sept. 1996 <http://www.mun.ca/Ansaxdat/>.

Provide the name of the forum (in this case, Ansaxnet) between the date of posting and the date of access.

83. Newsgroup

May, Michaela. "Questions about RYAs." Online posting. 19 June 1996. 29 June 1996

    <news:alt.soc.generation-x>.

The name of a newsgroup (in angle brackets) begins with the prefix *news* followed by a colon.

84. Web log (blog)

Cuthbertson, Peter. "Are Left and Right Still Alright?" <u>Conservative Commentary</u>.

    7 Feb. 2005. 18 Feb. 2005 <http://concom.blogspot.com/2005/02/

    are-left-and-right-still-alright.html>.

OTHER SOURCES ACCESSED BY COMPUTER

85. CD-ROM

"About <u>Richard III</u>." <u>Cinemania 96</u>. CD-ROM. Redmond: Microsoft, 1996.

Indicate which part of the CD-ROM you are using, and then provide the title of the CD. Begin the entry with the name of the author if one has been provided.

Jordan, June. "Moving Towards Home." <u>Database of Twentieth-Century African American</u>

    <u>Poetry on CD-ROM</u>. CD-ROM. Alexandria: Chadwyck-Healey, 1999.

86. Work from a periodically published database on CD-ROM

Parachini, John V. "Combating Terrorism: The 9/11 Commission Recommendations and

    the National Strategies." <u>RAND Electronically Distributed Documents</u>. CT-231-1.

    CD-ROM. Disc 8. RAND. 2004.

87. DVD-ROM

Klein, Norman M. <u>Bleeding Through: Layers of Los Angeles, 1920-1986</u>. DVD-ROM.

    Karlsruhe, Ger.: ZKM Center for Art and Media, 2003.

88. Multidisc publication

<u>CDA: The Contextual Data Archive</u>. 2nd ed. CD-ROM. 7 discs. Los Altos: Sociometrics,

    2000.

13c Sample MLA-style paper

(1) Submit a title page if your instructor requires one.

The MLA recommends omitting a title page and instead providing the identification on the first page of the paper (see page 317). Some instructors require a final outline with a paper; this serves as a table of contents. If you are asked to include an outline, prepare a title page as well. A title page usually provides the title of the paper, the author's name, the instructor's name, the name of the course with its section number, and the date—all centered on the page. A sample title page is shown in fig. 13.7. (If your instructor requires a title page, you may omit the heading on the first page of your paper.)

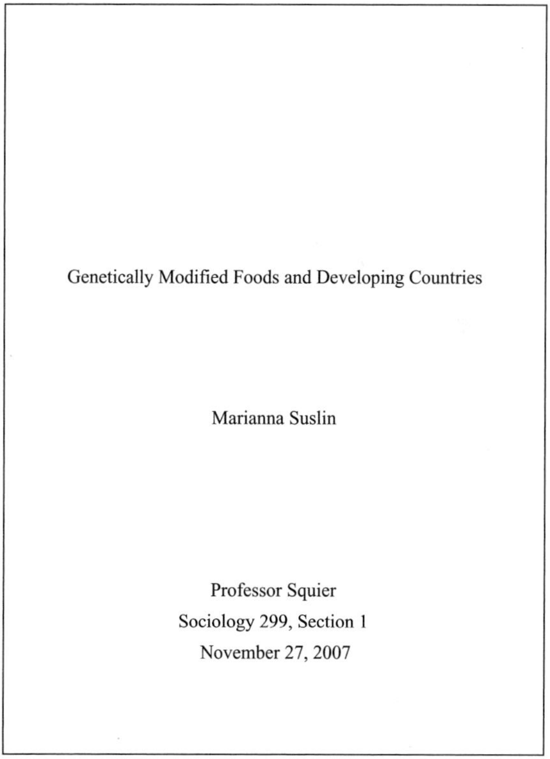

Genetically Modified Foods and Developing Countries

Marianna Suslin

Professor Squier
Sociology 299, Section 1
November 27, 2007

Fig. 13.7. Sample title page for an MLA-style paper.

(2) Studying a sample MLA-style paper prepares you to write your own.
Interested in the controversy surrounding genetically modified foods,
Marianna Suslin explores both sides of the debate as she comes to her
conclusion. As you study her paper, notice how she develops her thesis
statement, considers more than one point of view, and observes the
conventions for an MLA-style paper.

TIPS FOR PREPARING AN MLA-STYLE PAPER

- Number all pages (including the first one) with an arabic numeral in the upper-right corner, one-half inch from the top. Put your last name before the page number.
- On the left side of the first page, one inch from the top, type a heading that includes your name, the name of your professor, the course number, and the date of submission.
- Double-space between the heading and the title of your paper, which should be centered on the page. If your title consists of two or more lines, double-space them and center each.
- Double-space between your title and the first line of text.
- Indent the first paragraph, and every subsequent paragraph, one-half inch (or five spaces).
- Double-space throughout.

Suslin 1

The writer's last name and the page number

Marianna Suslin

Professor Squier

Sociology 299, Section 1

November 27, 2007

Heading

Genetically Modified Foods and Developing Countries

Center the title.

Genetic engineering first appeared in the 1960s. Since then, thousands

of genetically modified plants, also referred to as "genetically modified

organisms" (GMOs) and "transgenic crops," have been introduced to global

markets. Those who argue for continued support of genetic modification

claim that the crops have higher yield, grow in harsher conditions, and

benefit the ecology. Some experts even argue that genetic engineering holds

great potential for benefiting poor farmers in developing countries, given

that genetically modified plants increase the production of food, thereby

alleviating world hunger. Despite these claims, the practice of genetic

engineering--of inserting genetic material into the DNA of a plant--continues

to be controversial, with no clear answers as to whether genetically engineered

foods can be the answer for developing countries, as proponents insist.

Double-space throughout.

Use one-inch margins on both sides of the page.

Thesis

One of the most important potential benefits of the technology to both

proponents and opponents of genetic engineering is its potential to improve

the economies of developing countries. According to Sakiko Fukuda-Parr,

"Investing in agricultural technology increasingly turns up these days on the

lists of the top ten practical actions the rich world could take to contribute

to reducing global poverty" (3). Agriculture is the source of income for the

world's poorest--70 percent of those living on less than a dollar a day support

themselves through agriculture (Fukuda-Parr 3). These farmers could benefit

Background information

Suslin 2

greatly from higher yield crops that could grow in nutrient poor soil. Genetic

modification "has shown how high-yielding varieties developed at international

centers can be adapted to local conditions, dramatically increasing yields and

farm incomes" (Fukuda-Parr 3).

Indent each paragraph five spaces.

Theoretically, genetic engineering can bring about an increase in farm

productivity that would give people in developing countries the chance to enter

the global market on better terms. Developing countries are often resource

poor and thus have little more than labor to contribute to world economy.

Farming tends to be subsistence level as farmers can grow only enough on the

The writer describes some advantages of growing genetically modified crops.

land--which tends to be nutrient poor--to feed themselves. But the higher yield

of genetically modified crops along with the resistance to pests and ability

to thrive in nutrient poor soil can enable the farmers to produce more crops,

improve the economy, and give their countries something more to contribute

globally by exporting extra crops not needed for subsistence (Fukuda-Parr 1).

Genetic modification can also help poor farmers by using genetics to delay the

ripening process. If fruits and vegetables don't ripen as quickly, the farmer is

able to store the crops longer and thus have more time in which to sell the crops

without fear of spoilage. Small-scale farmers often "suffer heavy loses because

Citation of a work by an organization

of uncontrolled ripening and spoiling of fruits and vegetables" (Royal Society et

al. 238).

Today, eighteen percent of people living in developing countries do not

have enough food to meet their needs (Royal Society et al. 235). "Malnutrition

plays a significant role in half of the nearly 12 million deaths each year of

children under five in developing countries" (UNICEF, qtd. in Royal Society

et al. 235). Genetically modified foods that produce large yields even in nutrient poor soils could potentially help to feed the world's increasing population. Moreover, scientists are working on ways to make the genetically modified foods more nutritious than unmodified crops, which would not only feed large numbers of people, but help to combat malnutrition. The modification of the composition of food crops has already been achieved in some species to increase the amount of protein, starch, fats, or vitamins. Genetically modified rice, for example, has already been created that "exhibits an increased production of beta-carotene," which is a precursor to vitamin A (Royal Society et al. 240). Because vitamin A deficiencies are common in developing countries and contribute to half a million children becoming partially or totally blind each year, advances in genetic engineering offer hope for millions of people who live with nutrient deficiencies (Royal Society et al. 239).

Proponents of genetic engineering have also argued that genetically modified crops have the potential to decrease the amount of damage modern farming technologies have on ecology, thereby improving the economy of developing countries without the ecological damage many developed countries have suffered. For example, genetically modified plants with resistance to certain insects would decrease the amount of pesticides that farmers have to use. Genes for insect resistance have already been introduced into cotton, making possible a huge decrease in insecticide use (Royal Society et al. 238). A decrease in the amount of pesticides used is good from an ecological perspective.[1] Pesticides not only can be washed into streams and be harmful to wildlife but have also been known to appear in groundwater, thus potentially causing harm to humans.

A superscript number indicates an endnote.

Suslin 4

Scientists have argued that genetic engineering is only the latest step in the human involvement in plant modification that has been going on for thousands of years.[2] Since the dawn of the agricultural revolution, people have been breeding plants for desirable traits and thus altering the genetic makeup of plant populations. The key advantage of genetic engineering over traditional plant breeding is that genetic engineering produces plants with the desirable trait much faster (Fukuda-Parr 5).

While there are many potential benefits that can come from genetic engineering for farmers in developing countries and even in the United States, many people remain skeptical about this new technology. Research shows that many Americans are uneasy about consuming foods that have been genetically enhanced. That same research points out potential risks of consuming GMOs, which some believe outweigh the benefits of this new technology (Brossard, Shanahan, and Nesbitt 10). Considering the risks of genetically modified foods, people in developing countries are likely to feel the same way: that the risks outweigh the benefits. No matter how many potential benefits genetically modified crops may bring, if they are not safe for consumption, they will not help but hurt the economies of developing countries.

In "Genetically Modified Food Threatens Human Health," Jeffrey Smith argues that inserting foreign genetic material into food is extremely dangerous because it may create unknown toxins or allergens. Smith argues that soy allergies increased significantly after genetically modified soybean plants were introduced in the United Kingdom (103). Smith also points to the fact that gene insertion could damage a plant's DNA in unpredictable ways. For example, when scientists were working with the soybean plant, the

The writer describes disadvantages of eating genetically modified foods.

Suslin 5

process of inserting the foreign gene damaged a section of the plant's own DNA, "scrambling its genetic code" (Smith 105). The sequence of the gene that was inserted had inexplicably rearranged itself over time. The protein the gene creates as a result of this rearrangement is likely to be different, and since this new protein has not been evaluated for safety, it could be harmful or toxic (Smith 105).

Direct quotation of a phrase from a cited work

In <u>Genetically Modified Food: A Short Guide for the Confused</u>, Andy Rees argues a similar point: genetically modified foods carry unpredictable health risks. As an example, he cites the 1989 incident in which bacteria genetically modified to produce large amounts of the food supplement L-tryptophan "yielded impressively toxic contaminants that killed 37 people, partially paralyzed 1,500 and temporarily disabled 5,000 in the US" (Rees 75). Rees also argues that genetically modified foods can have possible carcinogenic effects. He states that "given the huge complexity of genetic coding, even in very simple organisms such as bacteria, no one can possibly predict the overall, long-term effects of GM [genetically modified] foods on the health of those who eat them" (Rees 78). Rees cites the 1999 study on male rats fed genetically modified potatoes to illustrate the possible carcinogenic effect. The study found that the genetically modified potatoes had "a powerful effect on the lining of the gut (stomach, small bowel, and colon)" leading to a proliferation of cells. According to histopathologist Stanley Ewen, this proliferation of cells caused by genetically modified foods is then likely to "act on any polyp present in the colon . . . and drastically accelerate the development of cancer in susceptible persons" (Rees 78).

Three ellipsis points mark an omission in quoted material.

Suslin 6

In addition to the health risks involved in consuming genetically modified foods, some experts also argue that such foods will not benefit farmers in developing countries but will aid big corporations here in the United States. Brian Halweil, author of "The Emperor's New Crops," brings up the fact that global sales for genetically modified crops grew from seventy-five million dollars in 1995 to one and a half billion dollars in 1998, which is a twenty-fold increase. Genetically modified crops are obviously lucrative for large companies. In addition, of the fifty-six transgenic products approved for commercial planting in 1998, thirty-three belonged to just four corporations (Halweil 256).

The writer focuses on social disadvantages of genetically modified foods.

The spread of genetic engineering can change power relations between nations (Cook 3). The big American corporations that sell genetically modified seeds can hold power over the governments of developing countries, hindering their further economic development. For example, all transgenic seeds are patented. Because the seeds are patented, it is illegal for farmers to practice "seed saving"--reserving a certain amount of seeds from the harvest to plant in the next growing season. Farmers thus have to depend entirely on the big corporations for their seeds. Since these corporations have a monopoly on genetically modified seeds, the prices for these seeds are likely to remain high, and poor farmers are unlikely to be able to afford them. Genetically altered seeds can then become just one more way that rich countries and their corporations exploit the people of developing countries. Genetic engineering could then become one more way of hindering the development of poor countries, and not the opportunity for economic improvement and increased social equality that its proponents claim it is. For example, unscrupulous companies can use the economic vulnerability of developing countries to develop and test genetically modified products that have been rejected in the United States or Europe (Newell 68). People in developing countries would be the ones to suffer if the genetically modified products turned out to be hazardous.

With many concerned about the health risks associated with GMOs, there has been a push to institute the practice of labeling genetically modified foods. International organizations such as Greenpeace and Friends of the Earth have advocated food labeling for GMOs because they believe that consumers should have the right to choose whether or not to buy genetically modified foods and expose themselves to the risks associated with consuming GMOs (Huffman 3). The FDA, however, contends that scientific studies "detect no substantial difference between food from traditional crops and GM crops" (Federal Register 22991) and regards genetic modification as not altering the product enough to require labeling (see fig. 1). Interestingly, one of the reasons for not labeling genetically modified food is the concern that consumers will shun the products with the GMO label, and thus the industry producing genetic modifications will suffer (Weirich 17). The interests of corporate giants, therefore, appear to be able to influence decision making in the United States, where the government and economy are comparatively strong. The impact of corporations on the governments of poorer countries, then, is likely to be much more pronounced, and poorer countries are likely to be victimized by big corporations.

Moreover, there is some evidence that genetically modified foods do not live up to their promise and, therefore, lack the benefits that could

The writer continues to explore both sides of the controversy.

Suslin 8

Fig. 1. Not all genetically modified foods are labeled.

help farmers in poor countries. For example, Rees argues against the assertion

that genetically modified crops will be able to ameliorate world hunger. Rather,

he believes that more than enough food is produced to feed everyone in the

world without these crops and that people go hungry because they cannot afford

to buy from the plenty around them for socioeconomic reasons (49). Rees also

argues that genetically modified crops have not increased farmers' incomes,

regardless of what proponents of genetic engineering may claim. He points to a

2003 study by Professor Caroline Saunders at Lincoln University, New Zealand,

which found that "GM food releases have not benefited producers anywhere in

the world" and that "the soil association's 2002 'Seeds of Doubt' report, created

with feedback from farmers and data from six years of commercial farming in

Suslin 9

North America, shows that GM soy and maize crops deliver less income to farmers (on average) than non-GM crops" (Rees 50-51). The potential benefit of genetically modified crops thus remains uncertain.

While proponents of genetic engineering insist that genetically modified crops can increase yield and help feed the hungry, opponents point to health risks and challenge the research that appears to prove that genetically modified foods are beneficial. However, even if genetically modified crops do prove to be as beneficial as proponents claim, there is nothing to ensure that this technology would benefit poor farmers in developing countries. Since large corporations hold patents on all genetically modified seeds, there is nothing to guarantee that poor farmers would have access to these seeds, no matter how advanced or beneficial the technology turns out to be. As of now, developing countries continue to be at a disadvantage despite the creation and wide distribution of genetically modified crops. Therefore, it is far from certain whether this new technology will benefit developing nations in the dramatic way that proponents of genetic engineering assert.

The writer's conclusion is drawn from research reported on the previous pages.

1 inch

Notes

[1]There is some concern, however, about the long-term effects of crops genetically engineered for pest resistance. Since these plants are engineered to continually produce a form of the pesticide used to combat the pest problem, insects are constantly exposed to the chemical used to kill them. This increases the likelihood that the insects will develop a tolerance for this chemical, making the pesticide ineffective.

[2]The main difference between genetic engineering and the breeding of plants for desired traits that people have practiced for thousands of years is that genetic engineering actually alters the DNA of a particular plant. Traditional breeding cannot alter the DNA of an individual plant but instead seeks to increase the number of plants that have a trait that occurs naturally. While the end product of both genetic engineering and selective breeding is similar in that both produce plants with desirable traits, the actual processes are radically different.

Suslin 11

Works Cited

Brossard, Dominique, James Shanahan, and T. Clint Nesbitt, eds. <u>The Public,</u>
    <u>the Media, and Agricultural Biotechnology</u>. Cambridge: CABI, 2007.

Cook, Guy. <u>Genetically Modified Language: The Discourse of Arguments</u>
    <u>for GM Crops and Food</u>. New York: Routledge, 2005.

Easton, Thomas A., ed. <u>Taking Sides: Clashing Views on Controversial</u>
    <u>Environmental Issues</u>. 11th ed. Dubuque: McGraw, 2005.

Federal Register 54.104 (1992): 22991.

Fukuda-Parr, Sakiko, ed. <u>The Gene Revolution: GM Crops and Unequal</u>
    <u>Development</u>. Sterling: Earthscan, 2007.

Gerdes, Louise I., ed. <u>Humanity's Future</u>. Detroit: Gale, 2006.

Halweil, Brian. "The Emperor's New Crops." Easton 249-59.

Huffman, W. E. "Production, Identity Preservation, and Labeling in a Marketplace
    with Genetically Modified and Non-Genetically Modified Foods." <u>Plant</u>
    <u>Physiology</u> 134 (2004): 3-10. American Society of Plant Biologists. 5
    December 2007 <http://www.plantphysiol.org/cgi/content/full/134/1/3>.

Newell, Peter. "Corporate Power and 'Bounded Autonomy' in the Global
    Politics of Biotechnology." <u>The International Politics of Genetically</u>
    <u>Modified Food: Diplomacy, Trade, and Law</u>. Ed. Robert Falkner.
    Hampshire, Eng.: Palgrave, 2007. 67-84.

Rees, Andy. <u>Genetically Modified Food: A Short Guide for the Confused</u>. Ann
    Arbor: Pluto, 2006.

Royal Society et al. "Transgenic Plants and World Agriculture." Easton 234-45.

Smith, Jeffrey M. "Genetically Modified Food Threatens Human Health."
    Gerdes 103-8.

Center the heading.

Alphabetize the entries according to the authors' last names.

Indent second and subsequent lines of each entry one-half inch or five spaces.

Place a URL within angle brackets.

Weirich, Paul, ed. <u>Labeling Genetically Modified Food: The Philosophical and Legal Debate</u>. New York: Oxford UP, 2007.

14 Writing in the Social Sciences

The **social sciences** include such disciplines as psychology, anthropology, sociology, political science, and economics. Researchers in these disciplines study how humans behave as members of groups—families, peer groups, ethnic communities, political parties, and many others. The goal of research in the social sciences is to examine and explain behavior occurring under a particular set of circumstances. Some social scientists study the behavior of animals other than humans. For example, Jason Wallin, the student whose work is featured later in this chapter (14d(4)), wrote about the behavior of captive chimpanzees.

Typical assignments in the social sciences include reflection papers, library research papers, case studies, and laboratory or field reports. Because such assignments differ in significant ways, take the time to analyze the rhetorical situation of any assignment you receive. Figure 14.1 illustrates how the elements of the rhetorical situation underpin "The Evolution and Functions of Laughter and Humor," one of the sources Jason Wallin used in his paper on chimpanzee behavior. In this article, researchers Matthew Gervais and David Sloan Wilson propose a framework for understanding the development of laughter and humor. The exigence and the context for their work are evident in the first two sentences of the abstract to the article (see fig. 14.2). According to Gervais and Wilson, current research does not sufficiently explain the origin of laughter and humor. The authors' purpose is thus to provide a better explanation. The audience for their article can be easily inferred. The use of technical language and the allusions to previous research suggest that Gervais and Wilson are writing for scholars rather than for the general public. (For an excerpt from Gervais and Wilson's introduction, see 14d(2).)

Exigence: Insufficiency of previous explanations for the development of laughter and humor

Writers: Matthew Gervais and David Sloan Wilson, researchers at Binghamton University

Audience: Scholars interested in the evolution of humor

Message: The researchers propose a new framework for understanding the development of laughter and humor

Context: Competing hypotheses on the evolution of humor

Fig. 14.1. Sample rhetorical situation for writing in the social sciences.

ABSTRACT

A number of recent hypotheses have attempted to explain the ultimate evolutionary origins of laughter and humor. However, most of these have lacked breadth in their evolutionary frameworks while neglecting the empirical existence of two distinct types of laughter—Duchenne and non-Duchenne—and the implications of this distinction for the evolution of laughter as a signal. . . .

Fig. 14.2. An excerpt from an abstract in the social sciences.

This chapter will help you

- determine the audience, purpose, and research question for a paper in the social sciences (**14a**),
- decide which types of evidence, sources, and reasoning to use in such a paper (**14b**),
- use appropriate language, style, and formatting when writing the paper (**14c**), and
- understand the types of assignments you might receive (**14d**).

14a   Audience, purpose, and the research question

The first step to take in completing a writing assignment for a course in the social sciences is to determine your audience and purpose. Your audience will always include your instructor, but it could include students in your class as well. You may also be writing for others outside your class. For example, you may have the opportunity to present your work at a student research conference. Identifying your audience will help you decide how much background information to present, how much technical language to include, and what types of reasoning and sources to use.

Most researchers in the social sciences write either to inform or to persuade. If they are simply reporting the results of a study, their purpose is informative. However, if they urge their audience to take some action, their purpose is persuasive. Once you know what your purpose is and to whom you are writing, you can craft a research question that will help you find sources, evaluate them, and use them responsibly (chapters 9–11). Here are some examples of different types of research questions that could be posed about the topic of community service performed by students:

Questions about causes or purposes

Why do students perform community service?

Questions about consequences

What do students believe they have learned through their community service?

Questions about process

How do college instructors help students get involved in community service?

Questions about definitions or categories

What does community service entail?

Questions about values

What values do instructors hope to cultivate by encouraging students to perform community service?

All of the writers of the student papers in this book responded to a research question. For example, Rachel Pinter and Sarah Cronin, whose paper appears at the end of chapter 15 (see pages 370–377), asked a question about process:

How have trends in tattooing changed over the years?

14b Evidence, sources, and reasoning

Researchers in the social sciences commit themselves to observing closely the activities of humans and other animals. To make accurate observations, these researchers either design controlled laboratory experiments or conduct field research. Interviews and surveys are the two most common techniques for gathering data in the field, although observations are also widely used. Both laboratory experiments and field research yield data that social science researchers can use as evidence to make statements (or claims) about the behavior of humans and other animals.

Researchers in the social sciences distinguish between quantitative studies and qualitative studies. **Quantitative studies,** such as laboratory experiments and surveys, yield data that can be presented in numerical form, as statistics. Using statistical data and formulas, researchers show how likely it is for a behavior to occur or to have certain consequences. If you decide to undertake a quantitative study, you should turn your research question into a **hypothesis,** a prediction of what the results of your experiment or survey will be. The study you design will be based on this hypothesis, which should be as objective as possible. Obviously, you cannot entirely eliminate the influence of your own preconceptions, but you can strive to be impartial by avoiding any value judgments. The results of your study will either prove or disprove your hypothesis. Be prepared to provide possible explanations for either result.

Hypotheses are best formed after a sustained period of observation and preliminary research. When presenting his hypotheses about the play of chimpanzees, Jason Wallin states his predictions in the context of existing research.

Research in the social sciences may involve observing and recording a subject's reactions to stimuli. The scientist in this photograph is observing a chimp's reaction to a stuffed toy.

Object play. Mendoza-Granados and Sommer (1975) observed a 2:1 ratio of play *without* objects to play *with* objects among captive chimpanzees. If this is a typical pattern of captive chimpanzee groups, object play in this family of chimpanzees should be considerably less common than play without objects.

Sex differences in play. Male chimpanzees play more often than females (Hayaki, 1985; King, Steves, & Mellen, 1980). In this family of chimpanzees, the males, Loulis and Dar, should play more often than do the females, Washoe, Moja, and Tatu.

Researchers who perform **qualitative studies,** such as observations and interviews, are interested in interpreting behavior by first watching, listening to, or interacting with individuals or a group. If you decide to conduct a qualitative study, you will not reason *from* a hypothesis; you will reason *to* a hypothesis. You will observe a phenomenon and note what you see or hear. Then, instead of reporting numbers as evidence, you will provide detailed descriptions and discuss their significance. Although you may not be able to demonstrate the degree of impartiality prescribed for quantitative research, you should still strive to maintain an objective stance.

Researchers in the social sciences recognize that some studies, such as Jason's research, will contain both quantitative and qualitative features. They also expect to use both primary and secondary sources (see **9a(3)**) in many of their research projects. Primary sources comprise data derived from experiments, observations, surveys, or interviews. Secondary sources are articles or case studies written about a research topic. Be sure to cite any sources you use and to provide a corresponding bibliographic entry on the reference list at the end of your paper.

14c   Conventions of language and organization

(1) Writers in the social sciences follow the style of their discipline.
The words and grammatical structures you use will depend on the style manual prescribed by the discipline in which you are writing. Most of the social sciences follow the guidelines presented in the *Publication Manual of the American Psychological Association* (APA; see chapter **15**). The APA manual stresses the importance of writing prose that is clear, concise, unbiased, and well organized. The following specific tips can help you write in the style recommended by the manual.

TIPS FOR PREPARING A PAPER IN THE SOCIAL SCIENCES

- Use the active voice as often as possible, although the passive voice may be acceptable for describing methodology. (See page 629.)

- Choose verb tenses carefully. Use the present tense to discuss results and report conclusions (as in "The findings suggest . . ."). Reserve the past tense for referring to specific events in the past and for describing your procedures (as in "Each participant signed a consent form . . .").

- Use a first-person pronoun rather than referring to yourself or to any coauthor(s) and yourself in the third person.

  I
  ∧~~The experimenter~~ described the procedure to each participant.

  We
  ∧~~The experimenters~~ retested each participant after a rest period.

- Clarify noun strings by placing the main noun first.

  the method for testing literacy   NOT   the literacy testing method

(2) Information is organized according to specific conventions.

Assignments in the social sciences will generally require you to (1) state a research question, thesis, or hypothesis, (2) discuss research that has already been published about your topic, (3) describe your methodology, and (4) present your conclusions or results. Specific formats are discussed in 14d.

To keep information organized, writers in the social sciences use headings, which are designed to signal levels of importance. The American Psychological Association describes five levels of headings.

LEVEL 5 IS CENTERED WITH EACH LETTER CAPITALIZED
Level 1 Is Centered With Each Major Word Capitalized
Level 2 Is Centered and Italicized With Each Major Word Capitalized
Level 3 Begins at the Left Margin and Is Italicized With Each Major Word Capitalized
Level 4 is italicized and indented, with only the first word capitalized and a period at the end.

Most papers that students write have two or three levels of headings. For a paper with two levels, use levels 1 and 3. For a paper with three levels, use levels 1, 3, and 4. For examples of headings from Jason Wallin's method section, see page 343.

In addition to inserting headings, social scientists use tables and graphs to organize information. Jason includes a table to show how frequently chimpanzees participated in various types of play (see fig. 14.3). If you decide to use a table in your paper, be sure to introduce it in the paragraph preceding the table. Without an explanation, your readers may have difficulty understanding the information you are providing. Here is how Jason introduces his table: "Table 1 shows the participation of each individual chimpanzee, as well as males and females together, in pretend play, locomotor play, social play, contact play, object play, and unknown play, as well as in play overall." Jason also aids his readers' understanding by explaining the data in the table: "The two males, Loulis and Dar, appeared in 255 descriptions of play bouts, a mean of 127.5 play bouts per male. The three females, Washoe, Moja, and Tatu, appeared in 197 descriptions of play, a mean of 65.7 per female." Notice that Jason places the title of the table above the table and the notes about the data below the table.

Table 1

Individual Participation in Play Types, Grouped by Sex of Individual

Individual	Play Type						
	Pretend	Locomotor	Social	Contact	Object	Unknown	Total
(Females)[a]	(1)	(3)	(11)	(67)	(85)	(30)	(197)
Washoe	1	2	5	42	41	18	109
Moja	0	1	2	7	23	7	40
Tatu	0	0	4	18	21	5	48
(Males)	(3)	(9)	(28)	(67)	(95)	(53)	(255)
Dar	1	6	12	23	40	19	101
Loulis	2	3	16	44	55	34	154
Total[b]	4	12	19	61	115	34	252

[a] Numbers in parentheses are subtotals for females and males, in the first and fifth rows, respectively. The totals of these rows, in the rightmost column, reflect the total number of play bouts for females and males, respectively. [b] The total row reflects the number of vignettes in the data for each play type. This is usually different from the sum of that column, as more than one individual can participate in a single play bout. This total is the sum of the pretend play column and of the locomotor play column, as all the examples of these play types consisted of one chimpanzee playing alone.

Fig. 14.3. A table from a student paper in the social sciences.

TECH SAVVY
To insert a table into your document, choose Table on the menu bar and click on Insert, then on Table in the pulldown menu. You will see a dialogue box that allows you to choose the number of rows and columns for your table.

Graphs provide a visual representation of data. Jason uses a bar graph to highlight his comparison of the play behaviors of male and female chimpanzees. Note that graphs are labeled as numbered figures. The number of the figure and a descriptive caption are placed below the graph. Figures should also be introduced and discussed in the text. Jason's introduction begins this way: "Figure 2 illustrates how

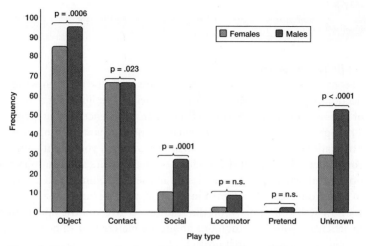

Figure 2. The frequency of males and females in descriptions of play.

Fig. 14.4. A bar graph from a student paper in the social sciences.

frequently males and females are mentioned in descriptions of differ-ent play types." Jason also explains the statistics his graph represents.

TECH SAVVY
To insert a graph into your document, choose Insert on the menu bar and click on Object in the pulldown menu. You will see a dialogue box in which you can click on the type of chart or graph you would like to create. Follow the directions specified.

(3) A reference list provides detailed information about the sources used.
At the end of any paper you write for a course in the social sciences, you should include a list of all the sources you used. By doing so, you provide your readers with the details they need to consult these sources on their own. You can find guidelines for creating a reference list in **15b** and a sample list of references on page 377.

14d   Samples of writing in the social sciences

(1) Reflection paper

In some of your social science courses, you might be asked to write reflection papers. These short, informal papers are assigned for a number of reasons. If you are asked to reflect on an experience such as a visit to a first-grade classroom, your instructor may want you to compare your expectations with your observations. For example, you might compare your expectations about the teaching of mathematics and your observations of an actual mathematics lesson in the classroom. If you are asked to reflect on a reading assigned in a course, your instructor may want to see how well you understood the reading, to give you the opportunity to articulate your own thoughts about the material, or to help you get started on a larger research project.

To complete these types of assignments, be sure to summarize your experience or the assigned reading before you write your reflection. Although those in your audience may be familiar with the experience or the reading, do not assume that they have it as clearly in mind as you do. In fact, it is often helpful to write as if the audience includes people you have never met. That way, you will provide all necessary details. In addition, read your instructor's assignment carefully. Your instructor's directions will help you develop the purpose for your paper. In the following excerpt, Jeff Hayes responds to an assignment that requires the comparison of two articles about online communities. Jeff's purpose, then, is to summarize both articles, discuss the authors' views on these communities, and present his own perspective on the issues discussed in the articles.

In "Mind the Gap: The Digital Divide as the Civil Rights Issue of the New Millennium," Andy Carvin discusses the problems created by the gap between those who have access to information technology and those who do not. Carvin claims that to ensure access, we must help everyone obtain hardware and software, but we must also address other issues as well. For example, he proposes that we promote literacy so that more people will be able to understand information available on the Internet. He also believes that teachers need to be trained to use the Internet to its fullest potential.

Along with encouraging literacy and effective pedagogy, Carvin emphasizes that more opportunities should be created for new users of the Internet to find content and communities relevant to their interests. Although I agree with Carvin's encouragement of literacy, pedagogy, and relevant content, I question his emphasis on community. Participating in an online community might not always be beneficial.

Rebecca Mead, in "You've Got Blog: How to Put Your Business, Your Boyfriend, and Your Life Online," gives a different perspective on community. She describes the life of Meg Hourihan, whom she has not met but knows personally from reading Hourihan's Web site. Mead is able to provide intimate details about Hourihan—that she writes short stories, that she does not have a boyfriend, that she has a good relationship with her mother—even when she hasn't talked with Hourihan. Mead follows the events listed on Hourihan's Web site enough to learn about Hourihan's blogging community—a community that values publication of one's inner life. The bloggers in Hourihan's community seem to spend hours at the computer. I wonder, however, whether by spending hours with their online communities, bloggers are neglecting the communities they actually live in. I believe that endless chats on the computer can result in damage to one's face-to-face relationships.

(2) Library research report

Library research reports are written by both students and professionals. The purpose of such reports is to bring together several related sources on a specific topic in order to examine that topic closely and comprehensively. Writing such a report will require you to read a number of sources and then summarize, critique, and synthesize these sources (see chapter 11). Library research reports generally include the following elements:

- Statement of the research question or thesis
- Presentation of background information, using sources
- Discussion of major findings presented in the sources
- Application of those findings to the specific research question
- Conclusions
- References

An excerpt from a library research report is shown in fig. 14.5. In the report's introduction, authors Matthew Gervais and David Sloan

INTRODUCTION

LAUGHTER AND HUMOR were accorded high evolutionary significance by Darwin (1872) and have received increasing attention from biologists and psychologists during the last 30 years. This attention has resulted in myriad empirical advances and has left laughter and humor well characterized on multiple proximate levels (see Provine 2000; Vaid 2002; Bachorowski and Owren 2003; van Hooff and Preuschoft 2003; Wild, Rodden et al. 2003). Laudably, this research has spawned a number of hypotheses attempting to explain the ultimate evolutionary origins of laughter and humor (e.g., Eibl-Eibesfeldt 1989; Weisfeld 1994; Pinker 1997; Ramachandran 1998; Harris 1999; Miller 2000; Provine 2000; Owren and Bachorowski 2001; Caron 2002; Howe 2002; Jung 2003; Storey 2003). Nevertheless, the scientific study of laughter and humor is still in its infancy relative to other comparable subjects in emotions and communication research.

Many empirical questions about laughter and humor remain unanswered or neglected. For example, most researchers (e.g., Provine 2000; Owren and Bachorowski 2003; Vettin and Todt 2004) have failed to make the important distinction between Duchenne (stimulus-driven and emotionally valenced) and non-Duchenne (self-generated and emotionless) laughter (Keltner and Bonanno 1997; see also Wild, Rodden et al. 2003). While laughter has recently been found to occur most frequently during casual conversation and not following deliberate humor (Provine 1993; LaGreca et al. 1996; Vettin and Todt 2004), researchers have yet to question whether such conversational laughter is different in kind from that following humor. This oversight might well be the root cause of the widespread confusion concerning the diversity of forms and functions that characterizes laughter today (Keltner and Bonanno 1997).

As regards theory, the results of empirical findings of laughter and humor research remain disjointed and only partially accounted for by any one framework. In most cases, such hypotheses are not mutually exclusive but potentially complementary, yet a synthesis remains unrealized. As a result, theoretical limitations abound.

Fig. 14.5. An excerpt from the introduction of a library research report.

Wilson, whose abstract appears in fig. 14.2, present background information for their study. Notice that the authors maintain a neutral stance that conveys an impression of impartiality, although they clearly and strongly state their point of view. Another example of a library research report is Rachel Pinter and Sarah Cronin's paper on tattooing (see 15c).

(3) Case study

A case study is a qualitative project that requires a researcher to describe a particular participant or group of participants. The researcher refrains from making generalizations about the participant(s) in the study and instead focuses on the behavior of the participant(s). After describing the behavior, the researcher may suggest a solution to any problem encountered by the participant(s). Most case studies include the following information:

- An introduction to the participant(s)
- A description of the problem
- A description of observations
- A presentation of strategies to solve the problem

Figure 14.6 is an excerpt from a case study, one of many that can be found at the Web site Improving Provision for Disabled Psychology Students. The excerpt includes an introduction to the participant, Bill, and describes his academic difficulties.

Bill is a . . . psychology student with dyslexia. In addition to difficulties with arithmetic and organisational skills, he has particular problems with short-term memory. . . .

He has always found psychology a fascinating subject. Though he doesn't feel that his impairment directed his decision to study psychology, he suggests that it may be one reason why he was interested in "how the mind works."

Bill finds that he has to work harder than most people to achieve the same level of performance. Since reading takes him a long time, he has found it difficult to keep up with all the allocated work necessary for the degree, and feels overwhelmed by the sheer volume and rate of work he has to get through. The biggest barrier he has to overcome is only having a period of one week to submit some of his laboratory reports: "I can't even get the reading for lab reports done in the week we have to complete reports, never mind getting the actual report written up!"

In terms of more positive experiences, he has found it particularly beneficial when lecturers put their lecture slides on the web before classes, giving him adequate time to print them out and thus enabling him to make notes on the printed-out slide during the lecture. This saves him from having to take so many notes, and allows him time to take in the material that is being taught.

Fig. 14.6. An excerpt from a case study posted online.

(4) Laboratory or field (observation) report

Social science students and professionals often conduct research in a laboratory or in the field (that is, in a natural setting). Reports based on this type of research contain standard sections: introduction, method, results, and discussion. Each of these sections is illustrated in the following excerpts from Jason Wallin's report on his research on chimpanzees.

3

Play, Laughter, and Humor in Captive Chimpanzees (*Pan troglodytes*)

Studies of play, laughter, and humor are at least as old as the Greeks. Plato, in a late Socratic dialogue, *Philebus*, and Aristotle, in *Poetics*, both advance theories of humor based on two of the themes that persist in modern theories: superiority and incongruity. Despite at least 2,500 years of waxing and waning interest in human play, laughter, and humor as subjects of serious consideration, little consensus exists as to their natures or purposes (Bekoff & Byers, 1998; Burghardt, 2005; McGhee, 1979; Provine, 2000). Investigation into the play, laughter, and humor of nonhuman animals is a relatively recent affair, and appears even less settled and more contentious than the research on humans (Gamble, 2001; McGhee, 1979; Palagi, Cordoni, & Borgognini Tarli, 2004; Provine, 2000).

The writer establishes the need for the current study.

5

Method

Participants

The 5 chimpanzees included 2 adult females, Washoe and Moja; a late adolescent/early adult female, Tatu; and 2 late juvenile/early adolescent males, Dar and Loulis. . . .

Procedure

From July 30, 1986, until February 2, 1995, chimpanzee caregivers at Central Washington University wrote reports at the end of every shift with the chimpanzees. . . .

Data collectors read through each page in the archived shift reports, selecting any instances of play, laughter, and humor. . . .

Definitions of play, laugher, and humor. Data collectors coded as play any direct references to chimpanzee play in the shift reports (e.g., "Dar was playing with Loulis."). . . .

Coding the data. The basic unit of data was the vignette, that portion of a shift report that contained description of play, laughter, or humor (or any combination of the three). . . .

The writer describes how the study was performed (so that other researchers can replicate it). This section may include subsections that describe the participants, the materials used, and the procedure.

7

Results

The writer
presents
findings,
often using
tables or
graphs (see
pages 335–
337).

The shift reports included descriptions of all five types of play—social play, contact play, object play, pretend play, and locomotor play. Table 4 details the frequency and percentage for each of the play types, including unknown play, along with an example of each. The nature of the play is quite varied, even within a given category, so the examples should be seen as but a taste of the content of the category, not as illustrative of all or even a majority of the play observed.

9

Discussion

This study examined the play and laughter of chimpanzees, only when they were playing or laughing with one another. However, data were collected on the many occasions when the chimpanzees were playing and laughing with their human caregivers. Preliminary analysis shows some interesting effects of the presence of humans. For example, Loulis and Dar both laugh and play very regularly with human caregivers, while Tatu plays and laughs very infrequently with humans. Future research should address the differences and similarities between chimpanzee-only play and chimpanzee-human play. Such research could inform recommendations for human-chimpanzee interactions in captive settings.

The writer discusses the significance of the findings, relating them to the original hypothesis and to other research done on the topic.

15   APA Documentation

The American Psychological Association (APA) publishes a style guide entitled *Publication Manual of the American Psychological Association*. Its documentation system (called an *author-date system*) is used for work in psychology and many other disciplines, including education, economics, and sociology. Updates to the style guide are provided at **www.apastyle.org**. This chapter includes

- guidelines for citing sources within the text of a paper (15a),
- guidelines for documenting sources in a reference list (15b), and
- a sample student paper (15c).

15a   APA-style in-text citations

APA-style in-text citations usually include just the last name(s) of the author(s) of the work and the year of publication. However, be sure to specify the page number(s) for any quotations you use in your paper. The abbreviation *p.* (for "page") or *pp.* (for "pages") should precede the number(s). If you do not know the author's name, use a shortened version of the source's title instead. If your readers want to find more information about your source, they will look for the author's name, or in its absence, the title of the work, in the bibliography at the end of your paper.

You will likely consult a variety of sources for your research paper. The following examples are representative of the types of in-text citations you can expect to use.

> **Directory of APA-Style Parenthetical Citations**

1. Work by one author 347
2. Work by two authors 347
3. Work by more than two authors 348
4. Anonymous work 348
5. Two or more works by different authors in the same parenthetical citation 348
6. Two or more works by the same author in the same parenthetical citation 348
7. Personal communication 349
8. Indirect source 349

1. Work by one author

Yang (2006) admits that speech, when examined closely, is a "remarkably messy means of communication" (p. 13).

OR

When examined closely, speech is "a remarkably messy means of communication (Yang, 2006, p. 13).

Use commas within a parenthetical citation to separate the author's name from the date and the date from the page number. Include a page number or numbers only when you are quoting directly from the source.

2. Work by two authors

Darvas and Walsh (2002) claim that, regardless of whether children spend time in day care, their development in early childhood is determined primarily by the nature of the care they receive from parents.

OR

Regardless of whether children spend time in day care, their development in early childhood is determined primarily by the nature of the care they receive from parents (Darvas & Walsh, 2002).

When the authors' names are in parentheses, use an ampersand (&) to separate them.

3. Work by more than two authors

The speech of Pittsburgh, Pennsylvania, is called *Pittsburghese* (Johnstone, Bhasin, & Wittkofski, 2002).

For works with three to five authors, cite all the authors the first time the work is referred to, but in subsequent references give only the last name of the first author followed by *et al.* (meaning "and others").

According to Johnstone et al. (2002), newspapers and magazines published in Pittsburgh frequently use nonstandard spelling to represent the pronunciation of /aw/.

For works with six or more authors, provide only the last name of the first author followed by *et al.* in both the first and subsequent citations.

4. Anonymous work

Use a shortened version of the title to identify an anonymous work.

Chronic insomnia often requires medical intervention ("Sleep," 2009).

This citation refers to an article identified in the bibliography as "Sleep disorders: Standard methods of treatment."

If the word *Anonymous* is used in the source itself to designate the author, it appears in place of an author's name.

The documents could damage the governor's reputation (Anonymous, 2009).

5. Two or more works by different authors in the same parenthetical citation

Smokers frequently underestimate the long-term effects of smoking. (O'Conner, 2005; Polson & Truss, 2007).

Arrange the citations in alphabetical order, using a semicolon to separate them.

6. Two or more works by the same author in the same parenthetical citation

The amygdala is active when a person experiences fear or anger (Carey, 2001, 2002).

Jameson (2007a, 2007b) has proposed an anxiety index for use by counselors.

Order the publication dates of works by the same author from earliest to most recent; however, if the works have the same publication date, distinguish the dates with lowercase letters (a, b, c, and so on) assigned according to the order in which the entries for the works are listed in your bibliography (see page 350).

7. Personal communication

State educational outcomes are often interpreted differently by teachers in the same school (J. K. Jurgensen, personal communication, May 4, 2009).

Personal communications include letters, memos, e-mail messages, interviews, and telephone conversations. These sources are cited in the text only; they do not appear in the reference list.

8. Indirect source

Korovessis (2002, p. 63) points out Toqueville's description of the "strange melancholy" exhibited by citizens living amid abundance.

Toqueville (as cited in Korovessis, 2002, p. 63) observed the "strange melancholy" exhibited by citizens living amid abundance.

In the reference list, include a bibliographic entry for the source read, not for the original source. Use an indirect source only when you are unable to obtain the original.

15b   APA-style reference list

All of the works you cite should be listed at the end of your paper, beginning on a separate page with the heading "References." The following tips will help you prepare your list.

TIPS FOR PREPARING A REFERENCE LIST

- Center the heading "References" one inch from the top of the page.
- Include in your reference list only those sources you explicitly cited in your paper. Do not, however, include entries for personal communications or for original works cited in indirect sources.

- Arrange the list of works alphabetically by the author's last name. If a source has more than one author, alphabetize by the last name of the first author.

- If you use more than one work by the same author(s), arrange the entries according to the date of publication, placing the entry with the earliest date first. If two or more works by the same author(s) have the same publication date, the entries are arranged so that the titles of the works are in alphabetical order, according to the first important word in each title; lowercase letters are then added to the date (e.g., 2008a, 2008b) to distinguish the works.

- When an author's name appears both in a single-author entry and as the first name in a multiple-author entry, place the single-author entry first.

- For a work without an author, alphabetize the entry according to the first important word in the title.

- Type the first line of each entry flush with the left margin and indent subsequent lines one-half inch or five spaces (a hanging indent).

- Double-space throughout—between lines of each entry and between entries.

Whether you are submitting an APA-style paper in a college course or preparing a manuscript for publication, you can be guided by the format of the following sample entries.

 CAUTION

Automatic bibliography composers found online and included in some software packages often make mistakes. They may fail to include all elements of a bibliographic entry or may order elements incorrectly. If you decide to use an automatic composer, be sure to check the results against the model entries provided in this chapter.

Directory of APA-Style Entries for the Reference List

BOOKS

1. Book by one author 356
2. Book by two or more authors 357
3. Book with editor(s) 357
4. Book with a corporate or group author 358
5. Edition after the first 359
6. Translation 359
7. Multivolume work 359
8. Government report 359
9. Selection from an edited book 359
10. Selection from a reference book 360

ARTICLES IN PRINT

11. Article with one author in a journal with continuous pagination 360
12. Article with two authors in a journal with each issue paginated separately 360
13. Article with three to six authors 360
14. Article with more than six authors 360
15. Article in a monthly, biweekly, or weekly magazine 360
16. Article in a newspaper 362
17. Letter to the editor 362
18. Book review 362

SOURCES PRODUCED FOR ACCESS BY COMPUTER

19. Online journal article with a Digital Object Identifier (DOI) 364
20. Online journal article without a DOI 364
21. Online magazine article based on a print source 364
22. Online magazine article not found in print 364
23. Article in an online newspaper 364
24. Online book 364
25. Online book chapter 365
26. Message posted to a newsgroup, forum, or discussion group 365
27. Weblog posting 365
28. Lecture notes posted online 365
29. Authored document from a Web site 365
30. Online document with no identified author 366

31. Personal communication 366
32. Online encyclopedia 366
33. Online dictionary 366
34. Online consumer brochure 367
35. Online white paper 368

OTHER SOURCES

36. Motion picture 368
37. Television program 368

The following guidelines are for books, articles, and most electronic sources. For additional guidelines for documenting electronic sources, see pages 362–368.

When preparing entries for your reference list, be sure to copy the bibliographic information directly from the sources (e.g., the title page of a book). (See fig. 15.1, on page 357.)

General Documentation Guidelines for Print-Based Sources

Author or Editor

One author. Use the author's first initial and middle initial (if given) and his or her last name. Invert the initials and the last name; place a comma after the name. Include a space between the first and middle initials. Any abbreviation or number that is part of a name, such as *Jr.* or *II*, is placed after a comma following the initials. Indicate the end of this information unit with a single period.

Walters, D. M.

Thayer-Smith, M. S.

Villa, R. P., Jr.

Two to six authors. Invert the last names and initials of all authors. Use a comma to separate names from initials and use an ampersand (&) (in

Vifian, I. R., & Kikuchi, K.

Kempf, A. R., Cusack, R., & Evans, T. G.

addition to the comma) before the
last name of the last author.

Seven or more authors. List the
names of the first six authors, but
substitute *et al.* for the remaining
names.

Bauer, S. E., Berry, L., Hacket, N. P.,
Bach, R., Price, T. M., Brown, J. B.,
et al.

Corporate or group author. Provide
the author's full name.

Hutton Arts Foundation.

Center for Neuroscience.

Editor. If a work has an editor or
editors instead of an author or authors, include the abbreviation *Ed.*
for "editor" or *Eds.* for "editors" in
parentheses after the name(s).

Harris, B. E. (Ed.).

Stroud, D. F., & Holst, L. F. (Eds.).

Publication Date

Books and journals. Provide the year
of publication in parentheses, placing
a period after the closing parenthesis.
For books, this date can be found on
the copyright page, which is the page
following the title page (see fig. 15.2,
on page 358). The publication date of
a journal article can be found at the
bottom of the first page of the article
(see fig. 15.3, on page 361). For a
work that has been accepted for publication but has not yet been published,
place *in press* in parentheses. For a
work without a date of publication,
use *n.d.* in parentheses.

(2008).

(in press).

(n.d.).

Magazines and newspapers. For
monthly publications, provide both
the year and the month, separated
by a comma. For daily publications,
provide the year, month, and day.
Use a comma between the year and
the month.

(2007, January).

(2008, June 22).

(Continued on page 354)

Publication Date *(Continued from page 353)*

Conferences and meetings. If a paper presented at a conference, symposium, or professional meeting is published, the publication date is given as the year only, in parentheses. For unpublished papers, provide the year and the month in which the gathering occurred, separated by a comma.	(2008). (2009, September).

Title

Books. Capitalize only the first word and any proper nouns in a book title. Italicize the entire title and place a period at the end of this information unit.	*Language and the mind.* *Avoiding work-related stress.*
Journals, magazines, or newspapers. In the name of a journal, magazine, or newspaper, capitalize all major words, as well as any other words consisting of four or more letters. Italicize the entire name and place a comma after it.	*Journal of Child Psychology,* *Psychology Today,* *Los Angeles Times,*
Articles and chapters. Do not italicize the titles of short works such as journal articles or book chapters. In a bibliographic entry, titles of articles and chapters appear before book titles and the names of journals, magazines, or newspapers. Capitalize only the first word of the title and any proper nouns.	Treating posttraumatic stress disorder.
Subtitles. Always include any subtitle provided for a source. Use a colon to separate a main title and a subtitle. Capitalize only the first word of the subtitle and any proper nouns.	*Reading images: The grammar of visual design.* Living in Baghdad: Realities and restrictions.

Volume, Issue, Chapter, and Page Numbers

Journal volume and issue numbers. A journal paginated *continuously* designates only the first page of the first issue in a volume as page 1. The first page of a subsequent issue in the same volume is given the page number that follows the last page number of the previous issue. In contrast, each issue of a journal paginated *separately* begins with page 1. When you use an article from a journal paginated continuously, provide only the volume number (italicized). When you use an article from a journal paginated separately, provide the issue number (placed in parentheses) directly after the volume number. Do not insert a space between the volume and issue numbers. Italicize only the volume number. Place a comma after this unit of information.

Journal of Applied Social Psychology, *32,*

Behavior Therapy, 33(2),

Book chapters. Provide the numbers of the first and last pages of the relevant chapter preceded by the abbreviation *pp.* (for "pages"). Place this information in parentheses. Use an en dash (a short dash; see **42f**) between the page numbers.

New communitarian thinking (pp. 126–140).

Articles. List the page numbers after the comma that follows the volume or issue number.

TESOL Quarterly, 34(2), 213–238.

Publication Data

City and state. Identify the city in which the publisher of the work is located. If two or more cities are given on the title page, use the first one listed.

Boston:

(Continued on page 356)

Publication Data *(Continued from page 355)*

Add the two-letter U.S. Postal Service abbreviation for the state unless the city is one of the following: Baltimore, Boston, Chicago, Los Angeles, New York, Philadelphia, or San Francisco. If the publisher is a university press whose name mentions a state, do not include the state abbreviation. When a work has been published in a city outside the United States, add the name of the country unless the city is Amsterdam, Jerusalem, London, Milan, Moscow, Paris, Rome, Stockholm, Tokyo, or Vienna—in these cases, the name of the city alone is sufficient.

Lancaster, PA:

University Park: Pennsylvania State University Press.

Oxford, England:

Publisher's name. Provide only enough of the publisher's name so that it can be identified clearly. Omit words such as *Publishers* and abbreviations such as *Inc.* However, include *Books* and *Press* when they are part of the publisher's name. The publisher's name follows the city and state or country, after a colon. A period ends this unit of information.

New Haven, CT: Yale University Press.

New York: Harcourt.

Cambridge, England: Cambridge University Press.

BOOKS

1. Book by one author

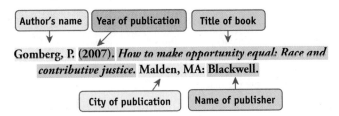

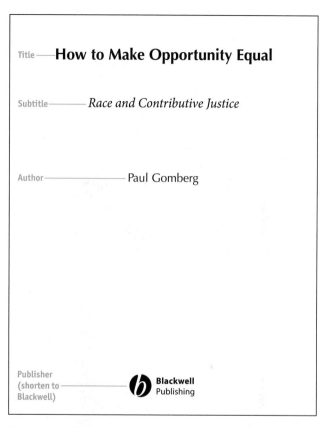

Title ——**How to Make Opportunity Equal**

Subtitle ——— *Race and Contributive Justice*

Author ——————— Paul Gomberg

Publisher
(shorten to ———
Blackwell)

Blackwell Publishing

Fig. 15.1. The title page of a book provides most of the information necessary for creating a bibliographic entry for a research paper.

2. Book by two or more authors

Thomas, D., & Woods, H. (2003). *Working with people with disabilities: Theory and practice*. London: Jessica Kingsley.

If there are more than six authors, list the first six names and use the abbreviation *et al.* in place of the remaining names (see page 353).

3. Book with editor(s)

Wolfe, D. A., & Mash, E. J. (Eds.). (2005). *Behavioral and emotional disorders in adolescents: Nature, assessment, and treatment*. New York: Guilford Press.

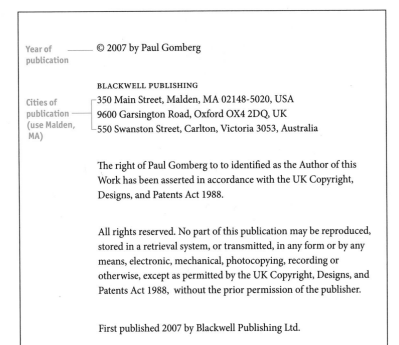

Year of publication —— © 2007 by Paul Gomberg

BLACKWELL PUBLISHING

Cities of publication (use Malden, MA)
- 350 Main Street, Malden, MA 02148-5020, USA
- 9600 Garsington Road, Oxford OX4 2DQ, UK
- 550 Swanston Street, Carlton, Victoria 3053, Australia

The right of Paul Gomberg to to identified as the Author of this Work has been asserted in accordance with the UK Copyright, Designs, and Patents Act 1988.

All rights reserved. No part of this publication may be reproduced, stored in a retrieval system, or transmitted, in any form or by any means, electronic, mechanical, photocopying, recording or otherwise, except as permitted by the UK Copyright, Designs, and Patents Act 1988, without the prior permission of the publisher.

First published 2007 by Blackwell Publishing Ltd.

Fig. 15.2. The year in which a book was published and the city where it was published can be found on the copyright page, which follows the title page.

4. Book with a corporate or group author

U.S. War Department. (2003). *Official military atlas of the Civil War*. New York: Barnes & Noble.

When the author and the publisher of a book are the same, use the publisher's name at the beginning of the entry and *Author* at the end.

American Psychiatric Association. (1995). *American Psychiatric Association capitation handbook*. Washington, DC: Author.

5. Edition after the first

Lycan, W., & Prinz, J. (Eds.). (2008). *Mind and cognition* (3rd ed.). Malden, MA: Blackwell.

Identify the edition in parentheses immediately after the title. Use abbreviations: *2nd, 3rd,* and so on for the edition number and *ed.* for "edition."

6. Translation

Rank, O. (2002). *Psychology and the soul: A study of the origin, conceptual evolution, and nature of the soul* (G. C. Richter & E. J. Lieberman, Trans.). Baltimore: Johns Hopkins University Press. (Original work published 1930)

A period follows the name of the publisher but not the parenthetical note about the original publication date.

7. Multivolume work

Doyle, A. C. (2003). *The complete Sherlock Holmes* (Vols. 1–2). New York: Barnes & Noble.

If the multivolume work was published over a period of more than one year, use the range of years for the publication date.

Hawthorne, Nathaniel. (1962–1997). *The centenary edition of the works of Nathaniel Hawthorne* (Vols. 1–23). Columbus: Ohio University Press.

8. Government report

Executive Office of the President. (2003). *Economic report of the President, 2003* (GPO Publication No. 040-000-0760-1). Washington, DC: U.S. Government Printing Office.

9. Selection from an edited book

Empson, R. (2007). Enlivened memories: Recalling absence and loss in Mongolia. In J. Carsten (Ed.), *Ghosts of memory: Essays on remembrance and relatedness* (pp. 58–82). Malden, MA: Blackwell.

Italicize the book title but not the title of the selection.

10. Selection from a reference book

Wickens, D. (2001). Classical conditioning. In *The Corsini encyclopedia of psychology and behavioral science* (Vol. 1, pp. 293–298). New York: John Wiley.

ARTICLES IN PRINT

11. Article with one author in a journal with continuous pagination

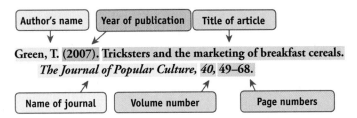

12. Article with two authors in a journal with each issue paginated separately

Rudisill, J. R., & Edwards, J. M. (2002). Coping with job transitions. *Consulting Psychology Journal, 54*(1), 55–62.

13. Article with three to six authors

Frost, R. O., Steketee, G., & Williams, L. (2002). Compulsive buying, compulsive hoarding, and obsessive-compulsive disorder. *Behavior Therapy, 33*(2), 201–213.

14. Article with more than six authors

Reddy, S. K., Arora, M., Perry, C. L., Nair, B., Kohli, A., Lytle, L. A., et al. (2002). Tobacco and alcohol use outcomes of a school-based intervention in New Delhi. *American Journal of Health Behavior, 26,* 173–181.

15. Article in a monthly, biweekly, or weekly magazine

Winson, J. (2002, June). The meaning of dreams. *Scientific American, 12,* 54–61.

Figure 15.3 shows where the information for this type of entry is found on the first page of an article.

Title —— Tricksters and the Marketing of
Breakfast Cereals

Author —— THOMAS GREEN

B REAKFAST CEREALS ARE SOLD BY TRICKSTERS. FROM LUCKY THE
Leprechaun to the Cookie Crook to the mischievous live-action
squirrels who vend General Mills Honey Nut Clusters, an astounding number of Saturday morning television commercials feature 30-second
dramatizations of trickster tales that are designed to promote breakfast
cereals. True, breakfast cereals are not the only products sold by tricksters,
and not all cereals are sold by tricksters—especially in the last decade. But
the association is common enough to persist as an unexamined assumption
that seems obvious to most Americans once it is pointed out. Naturally,
breakfast cereals are often sold by animated tricksterish mascot characters,
and naturally such commercials feature motifs and narrative patterns that
are common in trickster tales. But the perception of an inherent internal
logic in this scheme overlooks a couple of key questions. Why, for example,
are tricksters considered a particularly appropriate or effective means of
marketing breakfast cereals? And why breakfast cereals in particular (and a
few other breakfast products), almost to the exclusion of tricksters in other
types of marketing campaigns? The answers to these questions, it turns out,
may lie back in the semi-mystical, pseudoreligious origins of prepared
breakfast foods and the mating of the mythology of those foods with the
imperatives of the competitive, prepared-foods marketplace.

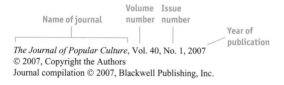

                      Volume Issue
      Name of journal   number number
                  | | | Year of
                                  publication

The Journal of Popular Culture, Vol. 40, No. 1, 2007
© 2007, Copyright the Authors
Journal compilation © 2007, Blackwell Publishing, Inc.

**Fig. 15.3. The first page of a journal article provides the information needed to complete
a bibliographic entry for that source.**

For magazines published weekly or biweekly, add the day of the issue: (2003, May 8).

16. Article in a newspaper

Simon, S. (2007, October 14). Winning hearts, minds, homes. *Los Angeles Times,* p. A1.

Include the letter indicating the section with the page number.

17. Letter to the editor

Mancall, M. (2002, June 17). Answer to cynicism [Letter to the editor]. *The New York Times,* p. A20.

After the title, indicate within brackets that the work is a letter to the editor.

18. Book review

Orford, J. (2007). Drug addiction and families [Review of the book *Drug addiction and families*]. *Addiction, 102,* 1841–1842.

If the review has its own title, use that instead of the title of the book. Retain the bracketed information.

SOURCES PRODUCED FOR ACCESS BY COMPUTER

The APA guidelines for electronic sources are similar to those for print sources. Exceptions are explained after the sample entries that follow. Information about when and/or how a source was retrieved appears at the end of the entry. The period that normally ends an entry is omitted after a URL because it could cause difficulty in retrieving a file. If a URL has to continue on a new line, break it before a punctuation mark or other special character. Note that many scholarly journals now use a Digital Object Identifier (DOI) to simplify searching for an article. Whenever possible, use a DOI (without a period following it) instead of a URL at the end of a reference list entry. The DOI will be listed on the first page of the article, which usually contains the abstract. Figure 15.4 shows the location of a DOI and other pertinent bibliographic information on the first page of an online journal article.

Journal of Experimental Psychology: Applied — Name of journal
2001, Vol. 7, No. 1, 27–50

Volume and issue number — Page numbers

Year of publication

Copyright 2001 by the American Psychological Association, Inc.
I076-898X/01/S5.00 DOI: 10.1037//1076-898X.7.1.27

DOI

Children's Eyewitness Reports After Exposure
to Misinformation From Parents — Title of article

Debra Ann Poole — Authors of article
Central Michigan University

D. Stephen Lindsay
University of Victoria

This study examined how misleading suggestions from parents influenced children's eyewitness reports. Children (3 to 8 years old) participated in science demonstrations, listened to their parents read a story that described experienced and nonexperienced events, and subsequently discussed the science experience in two follow-up interviews. Many children described fictitious events in response to open-ended prompts, and there were no age differences in suggestibility during this phase of the interview. Accuracy declined markedly in response to direct questions, especially for the younger children. Although the older children retracted many of their false reports after receiving source-monitoring instructions, the younger children did not. Path analyses indicated that acquiescence, free recall, and source monitoring all contribute to mediating patterns of suggestibility across age. Results indicate that judgments about the accuracy of children's testimony must consider the possibility of exposure to misinformation prior to formal interviews.

During the past decade, there has been keen interest in young children's performance when interviewed about autobiographical events. This interest was sharpened by broad social changes that led the public to be more concerned about crimes to which child victims are often the sole witnesses (e.g., child sexual abuse), but it also reflected a movement in psychology away from relatively artificial research paradigms (e.g., studies of memory for word lists) and toward more naturalistic and multifaceted approaches to research. Although the field of eyewitness testimony receives considerable attention for its forensic implications, researchers increasingly view eyewitness paradigms as tools for studying basic issues in memory and cognition.

There have been several recent reviews of the literature on interviewing children for forensic purposes

Debra Ann Poole, Department of Psychology, Central Michigan University; D. Stephen Lindsay, Department of Psychology, University of Victoria.

This material is based on work supported by National Science Foundation Grant SBR-9409231. Any opinions, findings, and conclusions or recommendations expressed in this material are those of the authors and do not necessarily reflect the views of the National Science Foundation. We thank the members of our research team for assistance in data collection and coding (Sonya Lucke, Scott Kuligoski, Lisa Wolf, Carolyn Miska, Chad Stabler, Rachel Johnson, Erin Henderson, Doug Haseley, Rachel Franceschina, Laura Whitlock, and Susan Williams), and Dan and Linda King (National Center for PTSD, Boston VA Medical Center) for consultations regarding data analyses. We also extend special thanks to the parents and children in Michigan who have volunteered their time to support our work.

Correspondence concerning this article should be addressed to Debra Ann Poole, Department of Psychology, 231 Sloan Hall, Central Michigan University, Mt. Pleasant, Michigan 48859.

(e.g., Ceci & Bruck, 1995; Poole & Lamb, 1998), and we do not offer an exhaustive recapitulation here. In its broadest outlines, the literature can be crudely summarized by saying that even very young children (i.e., 3- to 4-year-olds) can provide quite detailed and accurate accounts of past autobiographical events under some conditions but that even older children and adults often provide impoverished and inaccurate accounts under others. The aim of the current research was to provide additional insight into factors that compromise or enhance the amount and accuracy of the information interviewers gain from young children. Borrowing terms from Wells's (1993) analysis of eyewitness suspect identification, our research examined both "system variables" (i.e., factors that are under the control of investigators in forensic cases, such as the way questions are phrased) and "estimator variables" (i.e., factors that may affect the amount or accuracy of information children report but that cannot be controlled by investigators, such as the age of the child or the nature of the alleged event).

Numerous studies have documented that the accuracy of children's testimonies can be degraded when interviewers ask misleading questions or provide social feedback that favors particular answers (Ceci & Bruck, 1995). Rather than emphasizing suggestive interviewing techniques, the central focus of the current study was on the effects of misleading information presented to young children by their parents prior to and outside of an interviewing situation. It is likely that many children who are involved in forensic investigations were exposed to information from trusted adults, ranging from overheard conversations to deliberate coaching before participating in a formal forensic interview. This raises the worrisome possibility that false reports based on prior exposure to suggestions may intrude into forensic interview responses even when those interviews are conducted in an optimally nonsuggestive manner.

Fig. 15.4. First page of an online journal article.

19. Online journal article with a Digital Object Identifier (DOI)

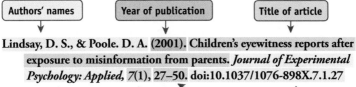

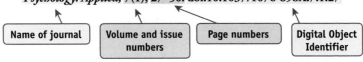

Lindsay, D. S., & Poole. D. A. (2001). Children's eyewitness reports after
exposure to misinformation from parents. *Journal of Experimental
Psychology: Applied, 7*(1), 27–50. doi:10.1037/1076-898X.7.1.27

20. Online journal article without a DOI

Tuladhar-Douglas, W. (2007). Leaf blowers and antibiotics: A Buddhist stance for science
and technology. *Journal of Buddhist Ethics, 14,* 200–238. Retrieved from
http://www.buddhistethics.org/14/tuladhar-article.html

If the article is available only by subscription, use the URL for the
journal's home page instead of the URL for the article.

21. Online magazine article based on a print source

Acocella, J. (2008, May 26). A few too many. *The New Yorker, 84*(15), 32–37.
Retrieved from http://www.newyorker.com/reporting/2008/05/26/080526fa
_fact_acocella?currentPage=1

22. Online magazine article not found in print

Saletan, W. (2008, August 27). Unfinished race: Race, genes, and the future of medicine.
Slate. Retrieved August 29, 2008, from http://www.slate.com/id/2198731/

23. Article in an online newspaper

McGrath, C. (2002, June 15). Father time. *The New York Times.* Retrieved from
http://nytimes.com/pages/science/index.html

24. Online book

Stevens, K. (n.d.). *The dreamer and the beast.* Available from http://www.onlineoriginals
.com/showitem.asp?itemID=321&action=setvar&vartype=history&varname
=bookmark&v1=1&v2=46&v3=1

If access to the book is not free, use "Available from" instead of "Retrieved from."

25. Online book chapter

Wallner, F., & Durnwalder, K. (n.d.). Sciences, psychology, and realism. In V. Shen, R.

Knowles, & T. Doan (Eds.), *Psychology, phenomenology and Chinese philosophy:*

Vol. 6. Chinese philosophical studies (n.p.). Retrieved from http://www.crvp.org

/book/Series03/III-6/chapter_i__science.htm#N_1_

If page numbers are not provided, use the abbreviation *n.p.*

26. Message posted to a newsgroup, forum, or discussion group

Vellenzer, G. (2004, January 24). Synonyms of entreaty [Msg 2]. Message posted to

http://groups.google.com/groups?selm=MPG.1a7cacccd54e9c27989b95%40news

.CIS.DFN.DE&output=gplain

If the message has been archived at another address, a comma should be placed after the first URL, followed by "archived at" and the URL for the archived version.

27. Weblog posting

Chatham, C. (2008, August 29). Action without intention: Parietal damage alters attention

awareness. Message posted to http://scienceblogs.com/developingintelligence

/2008/08/action_without_intention_parie.php

28. Lecture notes posted online

Wolfe, J. (2004). *Lecture 18: Freud and fairy tales.* Retrieved from Massachusetts

Institute of Technology OpenCourseWare Web site: http://ocw.mit.edu

/OcwWeb/Brain-and-Cognitive-Sciences/9-00Fall-2004/LectureNotes

/index.htm

29. Authored document from a Web site

Ennis, R. H. (2002, July 20). *An outline of goals for a critical thinking curriculum and*

its assessment. Retrieved August 6, 2007, from http://faculty.ed.uiuc.edu/rhennis

/outlinegoalsctcurassess3.html

When the document is from a large Web site, such as one sponsored by a university or government body, provide the name of the host organization before the URL.

Darling, C. (2002). *Guide to grammar and writing.* Retrieved September 12, 2003, from Capital Community College Web site: http://cctc2.commnet.edu/grammar /modifiers.htm

30. Online document with no identified author

American School Counselor Association. (2006). *Position statement: Equity for all students.* Retrieved October 17, 2007, from http://asca2.timberlakepublishing .com/content.asp?contentid=503

Use the name of the organization hosting the Web site as the author of the document. In fig. 15.5, the name of the organization appears in the upper-left corner. If a date for the document is provided (as on the printout in fig. 15.5, under the title), place it in parentheses. If no date is listed, use the abbreviation *n.d.* The date of retrieval and the URL are located at either the top or the bottom of a printout. In fig. 15.5, the date of retrieval is at the top of the printout; the URL is at the bottom.

31. Personal communication

Personal communications such as e-mail messages, letters, interviews, and telephone conversations are not included in the reference list but should be cited in the text as follows: (S. L. Johnson, personal communication, September 3, 2003).

32. Online encyclopedia

Dowe, P. (2007). Causal processes. In E. N. Zalta (Ed.), *The Stanford encyclopedia of philosophy.* Retrieved August 29, 2008, from http://plato.stanford.edu/archives /sum2007/entries/cognitive-science/

33. Online dictionary

Paranormal. (2000). In *The American Heritage dictionary of the English language: Fourth edition.* Retrieved September 2, 2008, from http://www.bartleby.com /61/35/P0063500.html

34. Online consumer brochure

American Psychological Association. (2008). Elder abuse and neglect: In search of
solutions [Brochure]. Retrieved from http://www.apa.org/pi/aging/eldabuse.html

Fig. 15.5. Computer printout of a Web document with no identified author.

35. Online white paper

Yones, M. (n.d.). Psychology of happiness and unhappiness [White paper]. Retrieved

    from International Institute of Management: http://www.iim-edu.org

    /executivejournal/index.htm

OTHER SOURCES

36. Motion picture

Smith, M. (Producer/Writer), & Gaviria, M. (Producer/Director). (2001). *Medicating kids*

    [Motion picture]. (Available from the Public Broadcasting Service, 1320 Braddock

    Place, Alexandria, VA 22314)

Begin with the primary contributor(s), identifying the nature of the contribution. Then provide the release date, the title, and the descriptive label in square brackets. For a film with limited distribution, provide, within parentheses, information about how it can be obtained. For a widely distributed film, indicate the country where it was produced and the name of the studio, after the descriptive label: [Motion picture]. United States: Paramount Pictures.

37. Television program

Holt, S. (Producer). (2002, October 1). *The mysterious lives of caves* [Television

    broadcast]. Alexandria, VA: Public Broadcasting Service.

Give the title of the program in italics. If citing an entire series (e.g., *Nova* or *The West Wing*), cite the producer for the series as a whole. Use the descriptive label *Television series* in the square brackets.

15c   Sample APA-style paper

The APA recognizes that a paper may have to be modified so that it adheres to an instructor's requirements. The following boxes offer tips for preparing a title page, an abstract page, and the body of a typical student paper. For tips on preparing a reference list, see 15b.

TIPS FOR PREPARING THE TITLE PAGE OF AN APA-STYLE PAPER

- Place the number 1 (to indicate that this is the first page) an inch from the right side of the paper and a half inch from the top.

- Place a **manuscript page header** (the first two or three words of the title) in the upper-right corner, five spaces before the page number. The manuscript page header should appear on all subsequent pages along with the appropriate page number.

- Below the page header but on the left side of the page, list the **running head**, a shortened version of the title (no more than fifty characters). Use *all* uppercase letters for the running head.

- Place the title in the center of the page, with your name below it. You may include your affiliation and a course name or number if your instructor requests one. Double-space these lines.

TIPS FOR PREPARING THE ABSTRACT AND THE BODY OF AN APA-STYLE PAPER

- Place the number 2 an inch from the right side of the paper and a half inch from the top on the abstract page.

- Place a manuscript page header five spaces to the left of the page number.

- Center the word *Abstract* (neither italicized nor underlined) one inch from the top of the paper.

- Be sure that the abstract (a short summary) is no more than 120 words. For advice on summarizing, see 11d(4).

- Double-space throughout the body of the abstract. Do not indent the first line of the abstract.

- Place the number 3 on the first page of the body of the paper, along with the manuscript page header.

- Center the title of the paper one inch from the top of the page.

- Use one-inch margins on both the left and right sides of your paper.

- Double-space throughout the body of the paper, indenting each paragraph one-half inch or five to seven spaces.

1/2 inch

The Science Behind   1

1 inch

Running Head: THE SCIENCE BEHIND AN ART

Place the page header in the top right corner, five spaces to the left of the page number.

The running head should consist of no more than 50 characters.

Use 1-inch margins on both sides of the page.

If required by the instructor, the course name and number replace the affiliation.

The Science Behind an Art: Historical and Current Trends in Tattooing

Rachel L. Pinter and Sarah M. Cronin

Central Washington University

1 inch

1/2 inch

The Science Behind   2

Abstract

Center the heading.

Current research demonstrates that the social practice of tattooing

has changed greatly over the years. Not only have the images chosen for

The maximum length for an abstract is 120 words.

tattoos and the demographic of people getting tattoos changed, but the

ideology behind tattooing itself has evolved. This paper first briefly

describes the cross-cultural history of the practice. It then examines

current social trends in the United States and related ideological issues.

1 inch

Center the title.

The Science Behind an Art: Historical and Current Trends in Tattooing

Tattoos, defined as marks made by inserting pigment into the skin, have existed throughout history in countless cultures. Currently, tattoos are considered popular art forms. They can be seen on men and women from all walks of life in the United States, ranging from a trainer at the local gym to a character on a television show or even a sociology professor. Due to an increase in the popularity of tattooing, studies of tattooing behavior have proliferated as researchers attempt to identify trends. This paper seeks to explore both the history of tattooing and its current practice in the United States.

Use 1-inch margins on both sides of the page.

The writers' thesis statement forecasts the content of the essay.

Tattooing can be found in the histories of people worldwide, though its origin is currently unknown. Krcmarik (2003) provides a helpful geographical overview. In Asia, tattooing has existed for thousands of years in Chinese, Japanese, Middle Eastern, and Indian cultures. Evidence of its existence can be seen on artifacts such as 7,000-year-old engravings. In Europe, tattooing flourished during the 19th century, most notably in England. Many of the sailors traveling with Captain James Cook returned with tales of exotic tattooing practices and sometimes with tattoos themselves. The Samoans in the South Pacific are famous for their centuries old tattooing practice, known as *tatau*—the word from which *tattoo* is said to have originated. The Maori of New Zealand are also well known for their hand-carved facial tattoos, known as *Moko* (see Figure 1).

The writers provide historical and cultural information about tattooing.

In Africa, tattoos can be found on Egyptian and Nubian mummies, which date back to approximately 2000 BCE. The tattooing history of South America is noted in the written accounts of Spanish explorers' encounters with tattooed Mayans. Finally, in North America, tattooing became popular during the 1900s and has experienced advances and retreats in social acceptance since then.

The Science Behind   4

Starting in the 1960s, its popularity rose dramatically and continues to rise.

Clearly, the history of tattooing spans generations and cultures. The practice has gained and lost popularity, often as a result of rather extreme changes in the ideologies supporting or discouraging it. This rollercoaster pattern of acceptance is well demonstrated in the United States. Since the 19th century, the wearing of

Figure 1. A Maori man with a facial tattoo.

tattoos has allowed for subculture identification by such persons as sailors, bikers, circus "freak" performers, and prison inmates (DeMello, 1995). As a collective group behavior indicating deviant subculture membership, tattooing flourished during this time but remained plagued by negative stereotypes and associations. In the last 10 years, however, the practice has represented a more individualistic yet mainstream means of body adornment, gaining popularity in unprecedented numbers. Now, as Figure 2 illustrates, tattooing can be seen among both teenagers and older adults, men and women, urbanites and suburbanites, the college-educated and the uneducated, and the rich as well as the poor (Kosut, 2006).

The writers discuss changing perspectives on the appropriateness of tattoos.

The trend toward acceptance of tattoos may be a result of how American society views the people who wear them. Earlier, tattoos were depicted in mainstream print and visual media as worn by people with low socioeconomic or marginal status; now, they are considered to be an artful

Citation of a work by one author

expression among celebrities as well as educated middle and upper classes (Kosut, 2006). This shift in the symbolic status of tattoos—self-expression among the social elite rather than deviant expression among the working class—has allowed tattoos to be obtained in greater numbers, owing in great part to the importance placed on self-expression in the United States. Even in the workplace, where employees were often forbidden to display tattoos, employers now "take advantage of the open-mindedness and innovation that younger [tattooed] employees bring into the workplace" (Org, 2003, p. D.1).

> To clarify a direct quotation from a source, the writers insert a word in square brackets.

As the popularity and acceptability of tattoos have increased, tattooing has become part of the greater consumer culture and has thus undergone the process of commercialization that frequently occurs in American society. Tattoos are now acquired as embodied status symbols and are used to sell tattoo maintenance products, clothing lines, skateboards, décor, and other fashion items (Kosut, 2006). This introduction into the consumer culture allows tattoos to gain even more popularity; they are now intertwined with mainstream enterprises.

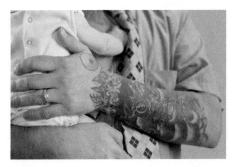

Figure 2. Tattoos are becoming more common among middle-class professionals.

The Science Behind 6

Researchers have been tracking the popularity of tattoos, though no one seems able to agree on a number (Libbon, 2000). In 2000, MSNBC aired a documentary called "Skin Deep," which cited the tattooing rate at 20% of the population (Rosenbaum, 2000). In 2003, citing a lower number, Harris Interactive reported that 16% of all adults in the United States have at least one tattoo (Sever, 2003). The actual number of individuals with tattoos is unknown, but most researchers believe the trend has been consistently gaining ground since the 1960s. Within the context of the larger population, statistics on the frequency of tattooing among specific age groups show a similar increase (Armstrong, Owen, Roberts, & Koch, 2002; Mayers, Judelson, Moriarty, & Rundell, 2002). However, due to the limitations of the various research designs, more research on a national level is needed to obtain truly representative figures.

Significantly, the increase in acquisition of tattoos has resulted in trends concerning the images and locations of tattoos, which appear to be divided down lines of gender. Many of the tattoo images commonly found on men include, but are not limited to, death themes, various wildlife, military insignia, tribal armbands, and family crests or last names. During the 1980s, cartoon images such as Bugs Bunny and the Tasmanian Devil were also popular for males. Males choose various locations for tattoos, but the most popular male sites are the upper back, back of the calves, and the upper arm, according to tattoo artist Ben Reames (personal communication, July 12, 2007). Conversely, females often obtain tattoos that symbolize traditional femininity, such as flowers, stars, hearts, and butterflies. A noticeable trend for females in the 1980s was the rose tattoo, which was often located on the breast or ankle. Stars and butterflies now rival the rose in popularity. The

The writers list statistics to support a claim.

Two citations of articles, both written by four authors, are separated by a semicolon.

Citation of an interview with a tattoo artist

The Science Behind　7

The writers include a photograph to support a point.

Figure 3. Many females who get a tattoo choose to have it on the foot.

ankle continues to be a popular location for females today. Other popular spots for tattoos include the hip, the foot (see Figure 3), and the lower back. In fact, the lower back experienced a huge surge in popularity during the 1990s (B. Reames, personal communication, July 12, 2007).

The art of tattooing has existed in many culturally determined forms throughout human history, and its current manifestations are as varied as the cultures themselves. However, based on the current literature, the social behavior of tattooing is experiencing unparalled growth in the United States. In fact, Kosut (2000) argues, "New generations of American children are growing up in a cultural landscape that is more tattoo-friendly and tattoo-flooded than any other time in history" (p. 1037). Because today's children see tattoos and tattoo-related products everywhere, usually in neutral or positive situations, they will likely be more accepting of tattoos than earlier generations were. Certainly, the tattooing trend shows no signs of leveling off.

Conclusion

References

Armstrong, M. L., Owen, D. C., Roberts, A. E., & Koch, J. R. (2002). College students and tattoos: Influence of image, identity, and family. *Journal of Psychosocial Nursing, 40*(10), 20–30.

DeMello, M. (1995). Not just for bikers anymore: Popular representations of American tattooing. *Journal of Popular Culture, 29*(3), 37–53.

Kosut, M. (2006). An ironic fad: The commodification and consumption of tattoos. *Journal of Popular Culture, 39*(6), 1035–1049.

Krcmarik, K. L. (2003). *History of tattooing*. Retrieved April 7, 2007, from Michigan State University: http://www.msu.edu/~krcmri1/individual /history.html

Libbon, R. P. (2000). Dear data dog: Why do so many kids sport tattoos? *American Demographics, 22*(9), 26. Retrieved from http://amiga.adage.com/de

Mayers, L. B., Judelson, D. A., Moriarity, B. W., & Rundell, K. W. (2002). Prevalence of body art (body piercing and tattooing) in university undergraduates and incidence of medical complications. *Mayo Clinic Proceedings, 77,* 29–34.

Org, M. (2003, August 28). The tattooed executive. *The Wall Street Journal.* Retrieved from http://online.wsj.com/public/us

Rosenbuam, S. (Executive Producer). (2000, August 20). *MSNBC investigates: Tattoos—skin deep* [Television broadcast]. New York and Englewood Cliffs, NJ: MSNBC.

Sever, J. (2003, October 8). *A third of Americans with tattoos say they make them feel more sexy*. Retrieved July 20, 2007, from http://www .harrisinteractive.com/harris_poll/index.asp?PID=868

Center the heading.

Alphabetize the entries according to the first or only author's last name.

Indent second and subsequent lines of each entry one-half inch or five spaces.

Identification of the type of medium is placed in square brackets.

No period follows a URL at the end of an entry.

16 Writing in the Humanities

The humanities include disciplines such as philosophy, art history, history, foreign languages, religion, comparative literature, cultural studies, women's and gender studies, and English. (For more detail on writing about literature, see chapter 12.) Scholars in the humanities study the artifacts of human culture (artwork, novels, plays, architecture, musical compositions and forms, philosophical treatises, and handicrafts, as well as popular media). The humanities distinguish themselves from the creative arts (such as painting, music, and drama) in their focus on *analyzing* cultural artifacts rather than *creating* them. Many students as well as professional researchers study cultural artifacts in order to better understand the wide variety of human experience in both past and present societies and to help explain why people think and feel as they do. Common writing assignments in the humanities include informal reflection papers (also called journal responses or response papers), historical research papers, position papers, critical reviews, and critical analyses.

As a writer in the humanities, you will write in a variety of ways and for various purposes; it is therefore important to analyze your rhetorical situation before you begin drafting. For example, fig. 16.1 illustrates the rhetorical situation for art historian Amalia Amaki's profile of twentieth-century African American artist Romare Bearden. In her article, "Romare Bearden and the Fine Art of Activism," Amaki explains how Bearden drew his artistic inspiration from themes of African American experience and describes his lifelong support for serious study of African American art. In the second paragraph of her introduction (see fig. 16.2), Amaki reveals the exigence for her profile: a new exhibit of Bearden's work (the largest to date) is opening shortly at the Smithsonian National Gallery of Art. Thus, Amaki's purpose is to help potential viewers better appreciate this artist.

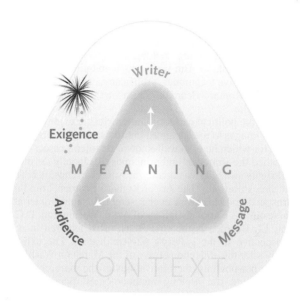

Exigence: The opening of a new exhibit of Romare Bearden's work

Writers: Amalia Amaki, assistant professor of Black American studies and curator of the Paul R. Jones Collection of African American art at the University of Delaware

Audience: Since *The Crisis*, the journal in which the article appears, is sponsored by the NAACP, the primary audience is likely African Americans and others interested in African American art as well as art historians who study twentieth-century American art.

Message: A brief profile of Romare Bearden that describes both his personal history and his artistic motivations

Context: Growing interest in the works of African-American artists, including Bearden, who have been largely overlooked in art history circles until recently

Fig. 16.1. Sample rhetorical situation for writing in the humanities.

This chapter will help you

- determine the audience, purpose, and research question for a paper in the humanities (**16a**),
- decide which types of evidence, sources, and reasoning to use in such a paper (**16b**),

Romare Bearden walked the walk and talked the talk that led to his renown long before making the conscious decision to become an artist. . . . But while much attention is given to his amazing creative techniques, prolificacy and popularity, the art and life of Romare Bearden are, in fact, profoundly political and symbolic.

From the political cartoons and satirical drawings that were his first images to the advanced improvisational, collage-based works for which he is so well-known, Bearden's career and life embodied the strategies and principles that largely defined the civil rights struggle for equality in America. Thus, it is fitting that the exhibition, "The Art of Romare Bearden," the largest retrospective of his work ever assembled, should open at the Smithsonian's National Gallery of Art in Washington, D.C., on Sept. 14. Bearden is the first Black artist featured in a solo retrospective in the gallery's 62-year history. The exhibit is shortly after the 40th anniversary of the March on Washington. Though not obvious, the motivations of the march organizers are linked to the lifelong methodologies, persistence, and personal objectives of Bearden. . . .

Fig. 16.2. An excerpt from the introduction to a profile in the humanities.

- follow appropriate style, formatting, and documentation conventions when writing the paper (16c), and
- understand the types of writing assignments you may receive in humanities courses (16d).

16a Audience, purpose, and the research question

Before writing a paper for a humanities course, you will want to determine your exigence (1b), your audience (1d), your purpose in writing (1c), and the research question you would like to answer. Thinking about your exigence (what you are writing in response to, and why) will help you identify your audience and narrow your purpose. Your instructor will always be part of your audience, of course, but your audience may also include other readers as well, such as other students in your class. In some cases, your professor might stipulate a particular audience as part of the assignment. For example, if you are writing a review for your school paper of a play staged by the drama department, your audience might include other students on your campus as well as interested alumni. Knowing who comprises your audience helps you to determine how much background information on your topic to provide, how technical your language should be, and what kinds of evidence will be most persuasive.

Romare Bearden's paintings, such as *The Dove* (1964), often emphasize themes of African American identity. *Source:* Bearden, Romare (1814–1999) © VAGA, NY. THE DOVE, 1964. Cut-and-pasted photoreproductions and papers gouache, pencil and colored pencil on cardboard, 13 3/8 x 18. Blanchette Rockefeller Fund (377.1971) Digital image © The Museum of Modern Art/Licensed by SCALA/Art Resource, NY. Art © Romare Bearden Foundation/Licensed by VAGA, New York, NY VAGA, NY.

Most researchers in the humanities write to convey a particular interpretation of a cultural artifact to a specific audience or to inform readers about the history of a particular event, individual, artifact, or social movement. Writers in the humanities may also write to evaluate a work of art or a performance. Once you have determined your purpose for writing, you can develop a research question that will help you focus your research, find and evaluate sources, and use those sources responsibly (see chapters 9–11). Research questions in the humanities often focus on texts or cultural products that help the researcher understand a given issue. The following are some potential questions that scholars in the humanities might ask about the experience of African Americans during the civil rights movement:

Questions about causes or purposes

What events stimulated the Montgomery bus boycott during the civil rights movement?

Questions about consequences

How did Romare Bearden's paintings contribute to the assertion of African American identity during the civil rights movement?

Questions about process

What did civil rights workers do to achieve a platform for their grievances?

Questions about definitions or categories

What kinds of protest tactics did different African American leaders, such as Martin Luther King and Malcolm X, advocate during the civil rights movement?

Questions about values

What does the struggle for equal rights for African Americans reveal about the values of white Americans during the 1960s?

16b   Evidence, sources, and reasoning

Because writers in the humanities aim to understand the human experience through the observation and interpretation of cultural artifacts, most claims in the humanities are not put forth as statements of absolute fact. Instead, researchers in the humanities often seek to demonstrate to others the validity of their interpretations through detailed analyses of texts or artifacts. Scholars in the humanities thus rely on textual evidence, logical reasoning, and the work of other scholars in the particular field to present a compelling argument for an interpretation. After considering the available evidence, researchers in the humanities advance a claim, or **thesis,** that expresses their interpretation of the artwork, performance, text, theory, or historical event (3c).

(1) Using primary sources

Most researchers in the humanities begin their studies by working directly with an artifact or text, that is, a **primary source.** For art historians, this primary source might be a drawing, a painting, or a sculpture. Art historians evaluate their primary sources by paying attention to the formal qualities of the work (line, color, shape, texture, composition, and so forth) and to images or themes that might have symbolic importance; they then write an explanation of how these features work together to create meaning in the work. For instance, in a classic analysis of Jan van Eyck's *Arnolfini Portrait*, art historian Erwin Panofsky argues that the elaborate details of the scene, such as the dog (representing fidelity), the two additional figures reflected in a mirror on the wall who may have served as witnesses, and van Eyck's signature on the wall, indicate that the scene documents a wedding. More recently, art historians have challenged this interpretation: Margaret Carroll has argued that this scene is not a wedding, but an important document that gives the wife power of attorney; Margaret Koster suggests instead that the painting is a memorial for Arnolfini's wife, painted after her death. Each of these different interpretations draws on formal and stylistic evidence from the painting itself as well as on knowledge of the cultural context in which it was created.

Jan van Eyck's *Arnolfini Portrait* (1434) has been the subject of many analyses by art historians.
Source: *Amolfini Portrait,* Jan van Eyck (1430–1441/Flemish). Oil on wood panel, National Gallery, London, England/© SuperStock, Inc.

For historians, primary sources include letters, government documents, newspapers, pamphlets, and other materials produced during a particular time period about some person, group, or event. For example, in her biography of Sarah Winnemucca, a nineteenth-century Paiute activist, historian Sally Zanjani uses letters written by Winnemucca, transcriptions of her public speeches, newspaper accounts of her activities, photographs, diaries, and other first-hand accounts to reconstruct Winnemucca's personal life and motivations. Like other historians, Zanjani analyzes these sources by comparing what they say, evaluating the reliability of their creators, and then generating her own interpretation of Winnemucca's life.

(2) Using secondary sources

Researchers in the humanities also use **secondary sources,** or works written by other scholars on their topic, to understand what these scholars think about the topic and to help establish the social and historical context for the topic. For instance, Zanjani refers to earlier biographies of Winnemucca to demonstrate how her work offers new evidence about Winnemucca's life. Zanjani also relies on other historians for historical context that is not part of her direct research, such as information about nineteenth-century Indian reservations, government military policies regarding Native Americans, and so forth.

(3) Using logic and observation

In addition to using primary and secondary sources, some researchers in the humanities, such as philosophers and other theorists, rely on evidence that is grounded in the rules of formal logic and individual observation. A theory or interpretation is considered valid if it adequately explains a particular phenomenon of human experience and if the reasons used to support the conclusion are logically sound (**8h**). Consider, for example, the following passage:

> Free will in the sense that matters, in the sense that makes you responsible for your actions and that gives meaning to both your strivings and your regrets, is determined by *how* your brain deals with the reasons it finds for acting. Philosophers have established that you can still have free will and moral responsibility when the decisions your brain arrives at are *your* decisions, based on your very own reasoning and experience, not on any brainwashing or manipulation by others. If your brain is normal, it enables you to consider and reconsider your options and values indefinitely, and to reflect on what kind of a person you want to be, and since these reflections can lead to decisions and the decisions can lead to actions, you can be the author of your deeds and hence have free will in a very important sense.
>
> —DANIEL C. DENNETT, "Some Observations on the Psychology of Thinking about Free Will"

Here, Dennett concludes that humans with normally functioning brains have free will, based on the following logical premises:

The ability to act consciously constitutes free will. [major premise]

A normally functioning brain allows humans to act consciously. [minor premise]

Humans with normally functioning brains have free will. [conclusion]

16c   Conventions of language and organization

(1) Writers in the humanities follow the style of their discipline.

As a writer in the humanities, you will use language and apply formatting as prescribed by the style manual of your discipline. Some writers in the humanities, particularly those writing about languages and literature, use MLA style (chapter 13). Other writers in the humanities, including historians and art historians, follow conventions outlined in *The Chicago Manual of Style* (CMS) or in Kate Turabian's *A Manual for Writers of Papers, Theses, and Dissertations*, which is based on CMS style (chapter 17).

Unlike writers in the sciences, who strive for objectivity in their writing, most writers in the humanities recognize that an interpretation is typically colored by the perspective of the person expressing it. Thus, writers in the humanities often acknowledge their own position on a topic, especially if it has a clear effect on their interpretation (12c). In particular, many writers in the humanities use the first-person pronoun *I* when describing the results of their research. Writers in the humanities also use the active voice, which focuses readers' attention on the agent performing the action (27d).

(2) Information is organized according to specific conventions.

Research papers in the humanities often have a less formal structure than those in the sciences, but nearly all papers in the humanities include a thesis statement that indicates the author's position on the topic (3c), evidence that supports the thesis statement, and a conclusion that restates the major claim and explains why the topic is important. (Specific formats for organizing papers in the humanities are discussed in 16d.)

Headings can help you organize your writing. Most short humanities papers do not require headings, but for longer papers, the style manual by Kate L. Turabian suggests the following heading levels:

The First Level Is Centered, Bold or Italicized, with Major Words Capitalized

The Second Level Is Centered, Regular Type, with Major Words Capitalized

The Third Level Begins at the Left Margin, Bold or Italicized, with Major Words Capitalized

(3) A bibliography provides detailed information about the sources used.

Include any sources you have used for your paper in a bibliography at the end of the paper. A bibliography not only demonstrates that you have done sufficient research but also allows your readers to follow up on any sources they may be interested in. You can find information on putting together a bibliography according to CMS style in 17a and a sample bibliography in 17b.

16d   Samples of writing in the humanities

(1) Reflection paper

Many of your professors in humanities courses may require you to write **reflection papers** (also known as journal responses): short, informal pieces that express your thoughts on something related to the course content. In some cases, you may be asked to write about your response to an exhibit or a performance. Your professor may be interested in knowing what you thought about the subject of the exhibit or the theme of the performance prior to your experience and how your experience changed your thinking. In other cases, you will be asked to respond to a reading or a work of art studied in the course. In this case, your professor may want to know how well you understood the reading or the artwork and what you thought of the ideas it presented. Sometimes, informal reflection papers are assigned to encourage you to start thinking about a topic for a research paper and to help you identify an exigence for the paper. If so, your professor may be able to provide you with early feedback that will help you start writing the research paper.

When writing a reflection paper, start by summarizing your understanding of the event or work. Even if your professor (and others in the class) have seen the same exhibit, performance, or artwork or have read the same text, they may have understood it differently. Next, go on to explain what you think about the topic (2d). Consider also how this event or work relates to other material you have read or discussed as a class—often, professors want to see evidence that you are making connections between different class topics. As you write, make sure that you refer to specific elements of the exhibit, performance, artwork, or text to support your thinking. Finally, if your professor has given you specific instructions for your reflection paper (for example, posing one or more questions to be answered or requiring a particular organizational pattern), make sure that your response fits the requirements.

In the following excerpt from a reflection paper, student Matthew Marusak makes a connection between his response to a film about sexual harassment and an article on the role of silence in sexual harassment that was a reading for his class. He begins by summarizing his understanding of the film and the reading and then explains his own reaction to the topic.

In "Witnessing Silence," Cheryl Glenn discusses the critical role silence plays in cases of sexual harassment, specifically in Anita Hill's famous testimony against Clarence Thomas. Glenn places particular emphasis on the double bind in which Hill found herself: she could continue to remain silent about the incident, or she could speak up and face public humiliation, with the added risk that no one would take her seriously. I would like to discuss the elements of Hill's initial decision to remain silent in connection with the 2005 film *North Country*, a fictionalized account of the first landmark sexual harassment class action lawsuit. The film stars Charlize Theron as Josey Aimes, a single mother who takes a job in an iron mine in Minnesota, despite protests from her father, who insists the mine is no place for a woman. Unfortunately, Josey's male coworkers feel the same, and she and her few female coworkers are harassed daily. Josey, however, is the only one to speak out; the other women, fearing for their jobs, remain silent and turn on Josey, demanding that she keep silent. Ultimately, Josey quits and brings a lawsuit against the company. Like Anita Hill, the character of Josey Aimes is met with scorn and public humiliation for speaking out against male tyranny. She feels the same emotions Hill experienced, including disbelief and a loss of self-worth. Yet where Hill and Josey differ is in their class positions, and Glenn suggests that working-class and professional women often put up with sexual harassment for the very same reason: they need their job.

I can imagine I would go through a similar response to sexual harassment: trying to cope with the loss of my own worth as a respectable human being, while deciding if I am willing to put my job on the line. It's a difficult call in any case, though I think it's not always as easy to spot sexual harassment as it is in these cases. Sexual harassment can be someone purposefully making you uncomfortable solely on the basis of your sex; the harassment needn't be lewd remarks made to or about you. The decision to remain silent can be devastating, but I think I would have greater trouble living with never saying anything at all than with facing what may come through speaking up. Both the Anita Hill case and *North Country* have the same message: you must stand up for your beliefs, even if you stand alone.

(2) Historical research paper

Historical research papers are written to reconstruct a past event or era or to profile an individual. Most historians use a combination of primary sources (newspapers, diaries, cookbooks, medical guides, and so forth, published at the time of the event or during the lifetime of the person) and secondary sources (writings by later historians about the event or person or about the primary sources) to understand some aspect of the past. When your professor assigns you a historical research paper, he or she wants to see that you understand how to compare different primary sources to reconstruct what might have happened during a particular time or to a specific person. A historical research paper also allows you to place your interpretation in the context of others that have been offered, using some sources to support your interpretation and other sources to refute the alternative interpretations.

The introduction to a historical research paper illustrates the importance of the topic and provides the thesis. In her paper about race in the U.S. Army (17b), Nicole Hester begins by explaining that many people do not understand how President Harry Truman's executive order for integration of the military influenced the civil rights movement. She concludes her introduction with her thesis: "Thus, Truman's executive order in 1948 became an important step in the long-term struggle for civil rights" (page 416).

Following the introduction and thesis, the body of a historical research paper provides evidence from both primary and secondary sources to support the thesis. In Hester's paper, the first part of the body explains the historical context of Truman's act, including the existing military policy regarding Blacks and some of the effects of segregation. The remainder of the paper provides evidence for Hester's claim that Truman's executive order was an important step in the struggle for civil rights: she describes the strong popular and military opposition to Truman's action and explains how the Fahy committee helped convince army officials that integration was necessary. Hester's evidence comes from primary sources such as the Supreme Court ruling in *Plessy v. Ferguson* and President Truman's public papers as well as from secondary sources such as biographies about Truman and histories of the civil rights movement.

Finally, the conclusion to a historical research paper should review the major claim of the paper and explain the significance of the topic. Hester concludes by reminding readers why Truman's executive order was an important show of support for civil rights, particularly since he had little to gain politically from this act.

(3) Position paper

Some humanities courses, particularly those in philosophy, may require you to write a position paper. The purpose of a position paper is to think critically and carefully about a specific topic, such as the nature of reality, ethical practices in science and medicine, the existence of free will, the purpose of human life, and so on. In a position paper, you state what you believe about the topic and provide reasons to support your claim. You may be asked to take a side in an existing philosophical debate or to express your own thoughts on the topic. In either case, you need to consider both what you agree with and what you disagree with.

A position paper is likely to be organized using a variation of classical argument (8g(1)). The paper begins with a brief introduction to the topic and its importance and includes a statement of the **claim.** For instance, if you are asked to write about the existence of free will, you might claim that people have some agency to choose their own actions but that most actions are based on what society expects, rather than on independent judgments. Following the statement of the claim, you provide an **explication,** which explains the basis for your belief. In this section, you define any terms that are important to your topic (*free will,* for instance) and provide any necessary background information. The next section in a position paper discusses any possible **counterarguments** to your position. Here, you summarize some of the most prominent scholarly positions on the topic, particularly those positions that are opposed to yours. This section will likely require some research. Because you are trying to demonstrate your ability to think critically and rationally, you want to present these other beliefs in as fair and unbiased a manner as possible. Following the discussion of counterarguments, you need to provide a **resolution.** After restating your own position, explain why the counterarguments are convincing or not. You refute or concede each counterargument based on its logic or on specific information it includes. Then, provide reasons that support your argument. In the conclusion, briefly restate the purpose for your paper, your major claim, and the primary reasons supporting your claim.

As you write your position paper, try not to prove too much. Choose a feature of the topic that you can reasonably defend in three to five pages. Your professor will be more impressed with a concise, well-reasoned paper on a narrow topic than a longer paper that offers only shallow proof for its points. As you frame your argument, be sure to avoid the logical fallacies that could weaken it (8i).

The following excerpt from student Kaycee Hulet's position paper on the existence of numbers illustrates an introduction and a claim.

> The metaphysical question of whether or not numbers exist is one that has been debated for hundreds of years. There are two basic positions that have historically been held on the matter: that numbers do exist and are therefore not invented but discovered, or conversely that numbers are a human invention that do not exist, but yet have a usefulness in describing objects or explaining the relationship of objects in the natural world. I posit that numbers do not exist in the real world, but have a value entirely dependent on their relation to objects in the real world. Brief consideration is given to the existence of numbers in the currently dominant schools of thought regarding mathematics: formalism, neo-platonism, and constructivism.

Following her claim that numbers are a human invention, Kaycee gives a definition of numbers (her explication) and describes formalist, neo-platonist, and constructivist positions regarding the existence of numbers (potential counterarguments). She then provides a resolution by suggesting that there is no evidence that numbers exist, but that this fact does not diminish their usefulness as symbols.

(4) Critical review

Students in humanities courses, as well as professional writers, are often asked to write reviews of various creative works, including films, literary works, exhibits of artwork, musical performances, theatrical performances, and dance performances. The purpose of a critical review is to evaluate the quality of the work for interested audiences. Audiences for reviews want to know what the work is about as well as whether it would be worthwhile to experience the work for themselves. Accordingly, when you write a critical review, begin with a brief introduction to the work (the title and the artist, composer, or director as well as the location where the work can be seen or heard) and some kind of evaluative statement, or thesis, that gives readers your general opinion of the work. Following this introduction, you may provide a brief description of the work that helps readers unfamiliar with it to understand the review. As you evaluate the strengths and weaknesses of the work, be sure to provide examples from it to support your evaluation. Finally, most reviews conclude with a summary statement that drives home the final evaluation of the work.

In the following theatrical review, student Matthew Marusak makes an argument for his negative review of a production of Tennessee Williams's play *Suddenly Last Summer*.

1

NOT SO *SUDDENLY LAST SUMMER*

BY

MATTHEW MARUSAK

THEATRE 464

PROFESSOR HEADRICK

MARCH 15, 2008

I began to nod off halfway through Carla Gugino's ardent, over-the-top, twenty-minute monologue at the end of Tennessee Williams's *Suddenly Last Summer* (Roundabout at Laura Pels Theatre, Harold and Miriam Steinberg Center for Theatre; 4 November 2006). It's not that there is anything inherently wrong with the material: Williams's stark, deeply ambiguous play about the dangers of sexual repression, denial, and deception remains as potent as ever. Rather, Roundabout's production turns an urgent and emotionally explosive work into an uncomfortably dull, embarrassingly archaic exercise in trying an audience's patience.

The writer introduces the performance and gives a brief evaluation of the production.

In theory, any revival of this play should be utterly and wholly riveting. In its production at the Laura Pels theatre, however, something has gone inexplicably awry. Violet Venable (an imposing Blythe Danner) is a wealthy widow—mannered and shrouded in a contradictory haze of unrelenting misery and dreamy-eyed idealism—suffering from the great loss of her son, Sebastian (discussed but never seen), who perished under a veil of mystery the previous summer. As her story unfolds, Mrs. Venable does her best to cloud Sebastian's implicit homosexuality and the events surrounding his death

This section describes the basic plot of the play for readers.

2

by praising him as a great artist—the way she wants him to be remembered. Mrs. Venable sends the sophisticated yet suspicious Dr. Cukrowicz (a debonair Gale Harold) to evaluate her niece, Catharine Holly (a woefully miscast Carla Gugino), who, having allegedly witnessed Sebastian's death, was sent away to a psychiatric hospital because of her allegations. The decision is made that a lobotomy is to be performed on the young woman, naturally against her will and at the wishes of her clandestinely cruel, manipulative aunt. Only under the influence of a powerful truth serum does Catharine finally reveal the shocking circumstances of her cousin's death.

Gale Harold and Carla Gugino perform in Tennessee Williams's play *Suddenly Last Summer.*

The writer provides both positive and negative evidence for his review.

Suddenly Last Summer is a staggering achievement of drama; but this revival, directed with a heavy hand by Mark Brokaw, has no life. Immediately noteworthy, though, is Santo Loquasto's dazzling set design. He translates Sebastian's magical greenhouse garden onto the stage better than I could have imagined it, while scenes in the interior of the house are simple yet elegant.

3

Loquasto's costume design is also impressive, while Peter Golub's original score is by turns lovely and haunting. Perhaps the most baffling technical aspect, however, is David Weiner's lighting design, which seems both inappropriate from scene to scene and peculiarly inconsistent.

Unfortunately, there are problems with the cast as well. Blythe Danner, while giving a respectable performance, is nowhere near as good as she could have been. She speaks in a distracting, maddeningly uneven dialect and gives the character far more nervous tics than are necessary. Lost is the nuance of the character, as is her caustic wit (as seen in Katharine Hepburn's superior portrayal in the 1959 film version). Danner's polished poise works for the character in many ways, but too often she seems overly rehearsed. Moreover, Carla Gugino should never have been cast as Catharine. She has neither the presence nor the charm to pull off the role convincingly, and Catharine's fiery passion is lost in what seems to be little more than a bid for a Tony nomination in the monologue. Rounding out the leads is Gale Harold, who does his best with the play's most underwritten role, making Dr. Cukrowicz at once both charismatic and calculating.

Roundabout's revival of *Suddenly Last Summer,* while technically robust, leaves its audience exhausted and bored, suspended in a time capsule of clashing theatrical ideologies. Everyone involved tries too hard to make an impression, instead of allowing genuine talent and Williams's wonderful material to speak for themselves. I cannot rightfully recommend this production, though it might be worth seeing for Gale Harold alone. He's an underrated, underutilized actor, and his authenticity is an unadulterated pleasure to watch.

The conclusion summarizes the major strengths and weaknesses of the production and indicates why the weaknesses outweigh the strengths.

(5) Critical analysis

Many researchers in the humanities write critical analyses—of visual arts, musical and theatrical performances, literary works, and other works—in which they argue for a specific interpretation of the work in question and aim at deepening audiences' understanding of and appreciation for that work. If your assignment is to write a critical analysis, your professor is likely interested in assessing both your understanding of the work and your ability to think critically about it. Critical analyses usually focus on formal, stylistic, and/or symbolic features of a work and explain how these elements work together to create meaning. (See **16b** for more information on evidence in critical analyses.) Such analyses sometimes explore the ways class, gender, or racial relationships are expressed in a work (**12c**).

Most critical analyses include the following sections:

- **Introduction.** The introduction provides a brief historical context for the work. It may also explain why the work ought to be reexamined— perhaps scholars have overlooked the work's significance or have not considered other possible meanings of the work. At the end of the introduction, the **thesis,** a clearly focused claim, states the writer's interpretation of the work.
- **Body.** The body of the paper provides the evidence—the formal, stylistic, symbolic, or contextual details that support the writer's interpretation. Many analyses also address differing interpretations of the work, explaining why the writer's interpretation is more convincing. This section can be organized in any of a number of ways, including comparison and contrast of data or artifacts and chronological, thematic, or emphatic (from less to more familiar or from less to more contestable) arrangement.
- **Conclusion.** The conclusion should review the thesis as well as the most important evidence supporting the writer's interpretation. Frequently, the conclusion also addresses implications—in other words, the writer explains to readers why his or her interpretation is so important, what effect the work may have had on other works or the cultural context, and/or what the writer's interpretation may mean to readers today.

In the following critical analysis, student Carla Spohn analyzes two early Italian Renaissance paintings by comparing and contrasting stylistic elements of the two works.

1

TWO ANNUNCIATIONS

BY

CARLA SPOHN

THEATER 464

PROFESSOR HEADRICK

MARCH 15, 2008

 The Annunciation of Christ's birth to the Virgin Mary by the Angel
Gabriel is a sacred scene that is revered and portrayed by many artists throughout
the Middle Ages and the Renaissance. Fra Angelico and Leonardo da Vinci,
both transitional artists, painted two different Annunciation paintings that reflect
the changing artistic styles and techniques of the fifteenth century. However,
while Fra Angelico's *Altarpiece of the Annunciation* is still in some ways
reminiscent of medieval conventions, Leonardo's *The Annunciation* depicts a
complete embracing of Renaissance ideals. While both artists render a scene of
otherworldliness, their different approaches to color, to setting, and to portrayal
of the figures parallel their use of or departure from Renaissance characteristics
and evoke two images of Mary: one of ethereal piety and the other of naturalistic
regality.

 The most obvious difference between the two Annunciations can be
seen through their varied use of color. The medieval influence employed in Fra
Angelico's is shown through the bright blue which contrasts with the lighter
primary colors. While this contrast creates bold visual interest, it underscores
the reality of the image. Leonardo, however, uses shading to blend the colors,

The
introduction
provides
a brief
historical
context for
the paper and
concludes
with a thesis.

This section
provides
evidence for
the different
styles of Fra
Angelico and
Leonardo da
Vinci in the
same order as
the features
are presented
in the thesis
statement.

2

Fra Angelico's *Altarpiece of the Annunciation* (c. 1430–1432). (Source: © Prado, Madrid, Spain, Giraudon/The Bridgeman Art Library.)

Leonardo da Vinci's *The Annunciation* (c. 1472–1475). (Source: © Galleria degli Uffizi, Florence, Italy/The Bridgeman Art Library.)

creating subtle hues which provide variation and a much more naturalistic effect than the stark use of dark and light by Fra Angelico. The color used is

3

also affected by the artists' depiction of light. While Fra Angelico's scene is one of bright sunlight that bathes the figures in vibrant luminosity, the solid beam of light upon the Virgin indicates again a lack of reality with little depth. In contrast, Leonardo creates reality through his use of natural light and atmospheric effects, which allows for greater solidity and substance lacking in Fra Angelico's depiction.

The setting in which the two scenes are placed also contributes to the paintings' differences. While both use the Annunciation convention of enclosing the figures, Fra Angelico's is much more apparent with a Roman-style portico; Leonardo's is simply implied by the stone wall whose cornerstones form a frame around Mary. Both also convey Renaissance characteristics through classical details, such as the Corinthian columns and round arches in Fra Angelico's and the stone table carved with Roman-like designs in Leonardo's. In contrast to these Renaissance attributes, Fra Angelico exercises the medieval tradition of depicting more than one story in a single scene, which in this instance are separated by the Roman architecture; the figures of Adam and Eve being expelled from the Garden combined with the Annunciation of Christ's birth link salvation to the Fall.

Also contributing to the overall setting of each scene is the use of perspective. Both artists use linear perspective, creating a vanishing point in which all orthogonal lines converge. However, although Fra Angelico uses architecture to create spatial depth and three-dimensionality, he only employs linear perspective. Leonardo, on the other hand, uses both linear and aerial perspective, which allows him to employ his characteristic *sfumato*—a smoky haze. Sfumato also contributes to another characteristic of his paintings—a

4

mysterious and somewhat magical landscape in the background. While the background in Leonardo's scene may seem dreamlike and unreal, his use of both linear and aerial perspective depicts a scene significantly more realistic than that of Fra Angelico's.

The last feature reflecting the artists' use of or departure from Renaissance conventions is their portrayal of the figures. Both Fra Angelico and Leonardo portray naturalistic figures that demonstrate a sculptural quality in themselves and their draperies. Fra Angelico depicts the angel and Mary as devout figures in profile. Their serene religious attitude is conveyed by the soft curve in their bow of reverence towards each other. While the emotions evoked are those of ethereal spirituality and piety, their faces and gestures capture humanity. Mary is depicted as humble and human, and yet still celestial as she receives a vision from a ray of light.

Leonardo's figure suggests a slightly more regal Mary; while the angel bows and greets her, Mary remains upright and only raises her left hand in greeting. The Virgin is also turned more, for a frontal view rather than a profile view. This view somewhat recalls the Byzantine and medieval depiction of Mary enthroned as the central figure, so as to completely convey her majesty to the viewer. Leonardo's Mary is the Queen of Heaven, but depicted as beautifully human and realistic, embodying the Renaissance humanistic belief that humanity is God's greatest creation.

Both Fra Angelico's and Leonardo's Annunciations capture the reverential nature of the subject, despite their many differences in relation to color, setting, and portrayal of the figures. Fra Angelico's painting is truly

5

a transitional piece, combining medieval and Renaissance artistic elements. Leonardo, however, demonstrates that he is a true Renaissance man by illustrating his skillful mastery of the newly emerging techniques. Their diverse treatments of the Annunciation reveal two separate ideals concerning religion. Fra Angelico's Mary reflects the medieval notion of humanity's ultimate submission to God, as shown through the Virgin's humble and pious aura. The emphasis on the idea of the Annunciation rather than realistic details of the scene places religion above this world and humanity's comprehension. Leonardo's Mary exemplifies the Renaissance belief in human greatness, as shown by her realistic and glorious humanity, which is placed in a natural setting; this Mary depicts a divinity that is still above humanity, but one to whom we can relate.

The conclusion reasserts the main argument for the artists' stylistic differences and explains the implications of this argument.

17 CMS Documentation

The Chicago Manual of Style (CMS), published by the University of Chicago Press, provides guidelines for writers in history and other subject areas in the humanities. The manual recommends documenting sources by using either footnotes or endnotes and, for most assignments, a bibliography. Updates to the manual can be found at **www.press .uchicago.edu**. For college-level papers, Kate L. Turabian's *Manual for Writers of Term Papers, Theses, and Dissertations* gives formatting and style guidelines based on CMS.

This chapter includes

- guidelines for citing sources within a CMS-style research paper and documenting sources in a bibliography (**17a**) and
- a sample student paper (**17b**).

17a CMS note and bibliographic forms

According to CMS style, in-text citations take the form of sequential numbers that refer to **footnotes** (notes at the bottom of each page) or **endnotes** (notes at the end of the paper). The information in these notes is condensed if a bibliography lists all the sources used in the paper. The condensed, or short, form for a note includes only the author's last name, the title (shortened if longer than four words), and the relevant page number(s): Eggers, *Court Reporters,* 312–15.

When no bibliography is provided for a paper, the full note form is used. For either footnotes or endnotes, a superscript number is placed in the text wherever documentation of a source is necessary. The number should be as close as possible to whatever it refers to, following the punctuation that appears at the end of the direct quotation or paraphrase.

TIPS FOR PREPARING FOOTNOTES

- Most word-processing programs will footnote your paper automatically. In Microsoft Word, pull down the Insert menu and choose Footnote. A superscript number will appear in the cursor's position. A box will also appear at the bottom of your page, in which you can insert the requisite information.

- Each note begins with a full-size number followed by a period and a space.

- Indent the first line of a note five spaces.

- Single-space lines within a footnote.

- Double-space between footnotes when more than one appears on a page.

- Use the abbreviation *Ibid.* (not italicized) to indicate that the source cited in an entry is identical to the one in the preceding entry. Include page numbers if they differ from those in the preceding entry: Ibid., 331–32.

- No bibliography is necessary when the footnotes provide complete bibliographic information for all sources.

TIPS FOR PREPARING ENDNOTES

- Place endnotes on a separate page, following the last page of the body of the paper and preceding the bibliography (if one is included).

- Center the word *Notes* (not italicized) at the top of the page.

- Use the abbreviation *Ibid.* (not italicized) to indicate that a source cited in an entry is identical to the one in the preceding entry. Include page numbers if they differ from those in the preceding entry: Ibid., 331–32.

- Indent the first line of a note five spaces.

- Single-space between lines of an endnote and leave one blank line between endnotes.

- No bibliography is necessary when the endnotes provide complete bibliographic information for all sources used in the paper.

TIPS FOR PREPARING A BIBLIOGRAPHY

- Start the bibliography on a separate page, following the last page of the body of the paper if footnotes are used or following the last page of endnotes.
- Center the word *Bibliography* (not italicized) at the top of your paper. (Some instructors may prefer that you use *Works Cited*.)
- Alphabetize entries in the bibliography according to the author's last name.
- If a source has more than one author, alphabetize by the last name of the first author.
- For a work without an author, alphabetize the entry according to the first important word in the title.
- To indicate that a source has the same author(s) as in the preceding entry, begin an entry with a three-em dash (———) instead of the name(s) of the author(s). (If you do not know how to create this mark, search for *em dash*, using the Help function of your word processor.)
- Indent the second and subsequent lines of an entry five spaces.
- Single-space between lines of an entry and leave one blank line between entries.

 CAUTION

Automatic bibliography composers found online and included in some software packages often make mistakes. They may fail to include all elements of a bibliographic entry or may order elements incorrectly. If you decide to use an automatic composer, be sure to check the results against the model entries provided in this chapter.

Directory of CMS Note and Bibliographic Forms

BOOKS

1. Book with one author 407
2. Book with two authors 408
3. Book with three authors 408
4. Book with more than three authors 408

5. Book with an editor 409
6. Book with an author and an editor 409
7. Translated book 409
8. Edition after the first 410
9. One volume in a multivolume work 410
10. Government document 410
11. Selection from an anthology 410
12. Published letter 411
13. Indirect source 411

ARTICLES

14. Article in a journal 411
15. Article in a popular (general-circulation) magazine 412
16. Article from an online journal 412
17. Article from a journal database 413
18. Article from an online magazine 413
19. Newspaper article 413

OTHER SOURCES

20. Interview 414
21. Videocassette or DVD 414

The following guidelines are for books and articles. Both full note forms and bibliographic forms are provided. Remember that a short note form consists of just the author's last name, the title (shortened if longer than four words), and relevant page numbers.

General Documentation Guidelines for Print-Based Sources

Author or Editor

One author—note form. Provide the author's full name, beginning with the first name and following the last name with a comma. For the short note form, use only the last name(s) of author(s) or editor(s).

Full note form
1. Jamie Desler,

(Continued on page 404)

Author or Editor *(Continued from page 403)*

One author—bibliographic form. Invert the author's name so that the last name appears first. Place a period after the first name.	*Bibliographic form* Desler, Jamie.
Two authors—note form. Use the word *and* between the names.	*Full note form* 2. Pauline Diaz and Edward Allan,
Two authors—bibliographic form. Invert the first author's name only. Place a comma and the word *and* after the first author's name. A period follows the second author's name.	*Bibliographic form* Diaz, Pauline, and Edward Allan.
Three authors—note form. Use commas after the names of the first and subsequent authors. Include *and* before the final author's name.	*Full note form* 3. Joyce Freeland, John Bach, and Derik Flynn,
Three authors—bibliographic form. Invert the order of the first author's name only. Place a comma after this name and after the second author's name. Use *and* before the final author's name.	*Bibliographic form* Freeland, Joyce, John Bach, and Derik Flynn.
Corporate or group author—note and bibliographic forms. Provide the full name of the group in all forms—full note, short note, and bibliographic.	*Note form* 4. Smithsonian Institution, *Bibliographic form* Smithsonian Institution.
Editor—note and bibliographic forms. Place the abbreviation *ed.* after the editor's name.	*Full note form* 5. Peggy Irmen, ed., *Bibliographic form* Irmen, Peggy, ed.

Titles

Italicized titles. Italicize the titles of books, magazines, journals, newspapers, and films. Capitalize all major words (nouns, pronouns, verbs, adjectives, adverbs, and subordinating conjunctions). A book title is followed by a comma in the short note form and by a period in the bibliographic form. In the short note form, a title longer than four words is shortened by omitting any article at its beginning and using only important words from the rest of the title.

Full note form
The Great Design of Henry IV from the Memoirs of the Duke of Sully

Short note form
Great Design of Henry IV,

Bibliographic form
The Great Design of Henry IV from the Memoirs of the Duke of Sully.

Titles in quotation marks. Use quotation marks to enclose the titles of journal or magazine articles, selections from anthologies, and other short works (38b). In the note form, a title of a short work is followed by a comma. In the bibliographic form, it is followed by a period.

Full note form
"The Humor of New England,"

Bibliographic form
"The Humor of New England."

Subtitles. Include subtitles in the full note and bibliographic forms but not in the short note form.

Full note form
Appreciations: Painting, Poetry, and Prose

Bibliographic form
Appreciations: Painting, Poetry, and Prose.

Journal volume and issue numbers. Whenever possible, include both the volume number and the issue number for any journal article you use. The volume number should appear after the title, and the issue number should appear after the volume number (preceded by the abbreviation no.). Use a comma to separate the two numbers.

American Naturalist 154, no. 2

(Continued on page 406)

Publication Data

List the city of publication, publisher's name, and date. A colon follows the city of publication, and a comma follows the publisher's name. In the full note form, this information should be placed within parentheses. No parentheses are needed for the bibliographic form. The short note form does not include publication data.

Full note form
(New York: Alfred A. Knopf, 2005),

Bibliographic form
New York: Alfred A. Knopf, 2005.

For a journal, place the year of publication in parentheses after the volume or issue number. For a magazine, provide the full date of publication.

International Social Work 47 (2004)

Journal of Democracy 14, no. 1 (2003)

Time, January 24, 2005

City and state. Identify the city of publication. If the city is not widely known, add a two-letter state abbreviation (or, for a city outside the United States, a province or country abbreviation). If the city of publication is Washington, include the abbreviation for the District of Columbia, *DC.* When two cities are listed on the title page, use only the first in the bibliographic entry unless both are located in the same state.

Baltimore

Carbondale, IL

Waterloo, ON

Harmondsworth, UK

Carbondale and Edwardsville: Southern Illinois University Press

Publisher's name. Provide either the full name of each publisher, as given on the title page, or an abbreviated version. The style chosen must be consistent throughout the notes and bibliography. Even when the full name is provided, some words may be omitted: an initial *The* and words such as *Company* or *Corporation* or abbreviations such as *Co.* or *Inc.* The word *University* may be abbreviated to *Univ.*

Univ. of Chicago Press

Penguin Books

HarperCollins

Page Numbers

If you are citing information from a specific page or pages of a book or article, place the page number(s) at the end of the footnote or endnote. If you are citing more than one page, separate the first and last page with an en dash (or short dash): 35–38. If the page numbers have the same hundreds or thousands digit, do not repeat it when listing the final page in the range: 123–48. Page numbers are not included in a bibliographic entry for an entire book. A bibliographic entry for an article ends with the range of pages on which the article appears.

The following list contains entries for the full note form and the bibliographic form. The short note form is provided only for a source that has previously been cited in full. For more examples of short forms, see the endnotes of the sample student paper (pages 426–427).

BOOKS

1. Book with one author

Full note form

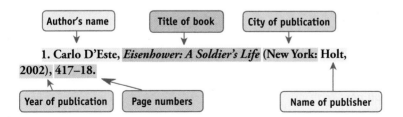

Author's name → Title of book → City of publication

1. Carlo D'Este, *Eisenhower: A Soldier's Life* (New York: Holt, 2002), 417–18.

Year of publication ← Page numbers — Name of publisher

Short note form

1. D'Este, *Eisenhower*, 417–18.

Bibliographic form

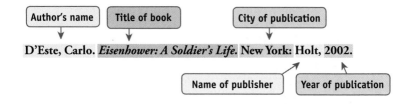

D'Este, Carlo. *Eisenhower: A Soldier's Life.* New York: Holt, 2002.

2. Book with two authors

Full note form

2. Cathy Scott-Clark and Adrian Levy, *The Stone of Heaven* (Boston: Little, Brown, 2001), 28.

Bibliographic form

Scott-Clark, Cathy, and Adrian Levy. *The Stone of Heaven.* Boston: Little, Brown, 2001.

3. Book with three authors

Full note form

3. Karen A. Foss, Sonja K. Foss, and Cindy L. Griffin, *Feminist Rhetorical Theories* (Thousand Oaks, CA: Sage, 1999).

Bibliographic form

Foss, Karen A., Sonja K. Foss, and Cindy L. Griffin. *Feminist Rhetorical Theories.* Thousand Oaks, CA: Sage, 1999.

4. Book with more than three authors

Full note form

4. Mike Palmquist and others, *Transitions: Teaching Writing in Computer-Supported and Traditional Classrooms* (Greenwich, CT: Ablex, 1998), 153.

In the note form, just the first person's name is used, followed by the phrase *and others*, which is not italicized. The bibliographic form should include all the authors' names.

Bibliographic form

Palmquist, Mike, Kate Kiefer, James Hartvigsen, and Barbara Goodlew. *Transitions: Teaching Writing in Computer-Supported and Traditional Classrooms.* Greenwich, CT: Ablex, 1998.

5. Book with an editor

Full note form

5. Hanna Schissler, ed., *The Miracle Years* (Princeton, NJ: Princeton Univ. Press, 2001).

Bibliographic form

Schissler, Hanna, ed. *The Miracle Years.* Princeton, NJ: Princeton Univ. Press, 2001.

6. Book with an author and an editor

Full note form

6. Ayn Rand, *The Art of Fiction,* ed. Tore Boeckmann (New York: Plume, 2000).

Use the abbreviation *ed.* for "edited by."

Bibliographic form

Rand, Ayn. *The Art of Fiction.* Edited by Tore Boeckmann. New York: Plume, 2000.

Write out the words *Edited by.*

7. Translated book

Full note form

7. Murasaki Shikibu, *The Tale of Genji,* trans. Royall Tyler (New York: Viking, 2001).

Use the abbreviation *trans.* for "translated by."

Bibliographic form

Shikibu, Murasaki. *The Tale of Genji.* Translated by Royall Tyler. New York: Viking, 2001.

Write out the words *Translated by.*

8. Edition after the first

Full note form

8. Edward O. Wilson, *On Human Nature,* 14th ed. (Cambridge: Harvard Univ. Press, 2001).

Bibliographic form

Wilson, Edward O. *On Human Nature.* 14th ed. Cambridge: Harvard Univ. Press, 2001.

9. One volume in a multivolume work

Full note form

9. Thomas Cleary, *Classics of Buddhism and Zen,* vol. 3 (Boston: Shambhala Publications, 2001), 116.

Bibliographic form

Cleary, Thomas. *Classics of Buddhism and Zen.* Vol. 3. Boston: Shambhala Publications, 2001.

10. Government document

Full note form

10. U.S. Bureau of the Census, *Statistical Abstract of the United States,* 120th ed. (Washington, DC, 2001), 16.

Bibliographic form

U.S. Bureau of the Census. *Statistical Abstract of the United States.* 120th ed. Washington, DC, 2001.

11. Selection from an anthology

Full note form

11. Elizabeth Spencer, "The Everlasting Light," in *The Cry of an Occasion,* ed. Richard Bausch (Baton Rouge: Louisiana State Univ. Press, 2001), 171–82.

Bibliographic form

Spencer, Elizabeth. "The Everlasting Light." In *The Cry of an Occasion,* edited by
Richard Bausch, 171–82. Baton Rouge: Louisiana State Univ. Press, 2001.

When only one selection from an anthology is used, inclusive page
numbers precede the publication data in the bibliographic entry.

12. Published letter

Full note form

12. Lincoln to George McClellan, Washington, DC, 13 October 1862, in *This Fiery
Trial: The Speeches and Writings of Abraham Lincoln,* ed. William E. Gienapp (New
York: Oxford Univ. Press, 2002), 178.

Bibliographic form

Lincoln, Abraham. Abraham Lincoln to George McClellan, Washington DC, 13 October
1862. In *This Fiery Trial: The Speeches and Writings of Abraham Lincoln,* ed.
William E. Gienapp, 178. New York: Oxford Univ. Press, 2002.

13. Indirect source

Full note form

13. Toni Morrison, *Playing in the Dark* (New York: Vintage, 1992), 26, quoted in
Jonathan Goldberg, *Willa Cather and Others* (Durham, NC: Duke Univ. Press, 2001), 37.

Bibliographic form

Morrison, Toni. *Playing in the Dark.* New York: Vintage, 1992, 26. Quoted in Jonathan
Goldberg, *Willa Cather and Others*, 37. Durham, NC: Duke Univ. Press, 2001.

Cite both the original work and the secondary source in which you
found it quoted. Begin with the name of the author you have quoted,
and provide information about the work (which should be available in
the notes or bibliography of the indirect source you used). Then provide
information about the secondary source.

ARTICLES

14. Article in a journal

Full note form

14. A. Schedler, "The Menu of Manipulation," *Journal of Democracy* 13, no. 2
(2002): 48.

Use initials for an author's first and middle names only when they are used in the original publication.

Bibliographic form

Schedler, A. "The Menu of Manipulation." *Journal of Democracy* 13, no. 2 (2002): 36–50.

15. Article in a popular (general-circulation) magazine

Full note form

15. John O'Sullivan, "The Overskeptics," *National Review,* June 17, 2002, 23.

Bibliographic form

O'Sullivan, John. "The Overskeptics." *National Review,* June 17, 2002, 22–26.

For a magazine published monthly, include only the month and the year, with no comma inserted between them.

16. Article from an online journal

Full note form

16. Lars Wik and others, "Quality of Cardiopulmonary Resuscitation during Out-of-Hospital Cardiac Arrest," *Journal of the American Medical Association* 293, no. 3 (2005), http://jama.ama-assn.org/cgi/content/full/293/3/299 (accessed January 28, 2005).

Place the URL along with the date of access (in parentheses) after the date of publication.

Bibliographic form

Wik, Lars, Jo Kramer-Johansen, Helge Myklebust, Hallstein Sorebo, Leif Svensson, Bob Fellows, and Petter Andreas Steen. "Quality of Cardiopulmonary Resuscitation during Out-of-Hospital Cardiac Arrest." *Journal of the American Medical Association* 293, no. 3 (January 19, 2005). http://jama.ama-assn.org/cgi/content/full/293/3/299 (accessed January 28, 2005).

Include the full date of publication as well as the date of access.

17. Article from a journal database

Full note form

17. Samuel Guy Inman, "The Monroe Doctrine and Hispanic America," *Hispanic America Historical Review* 4, no. 4 (1921): 635, http://links.jstor.org/sici?sici=0018 -2168(192111)4%3A4%3C635%3ATMDAHA%3E2.0.CO%3B2-8.

A URL that runs onto a second line may be broken *after* a single or double slash or *before* a comma, a period, a hyphen, a question mark, a percent symbol, a number sign (#), a tilde (~), or an underscore (_). It can be broken either before or after an ampersand (&) or an equals sign. Include an access date in parentheses between the URL and the final period if the material you are using is time-sensitive or if an access date is required by your discipline.

Bibliographic form

Inman, Samuel Guy. "The Monroe Doctrine and Hispanic America." *Hispanic America Historical Review* 4, no. 4 (1921): 635–76. http://links.jstor.org/sici?sici=0018 -2168(192111)4%3A4%3C635%3ATMDAHA%3E2.0.CO%3B2-8.

18. Article from an online magazine

Full note form

18. Mark Frank, "Judge for Themselves: Why a Supreme Court Ruling on Sentencing Guidelines Puts More Power Back on the Bench," *Time*, January 24, 2005, http://www.time.com/time/magazine/printout/0,8816,1018063,00.html.

Bibliographic form

Frank, Mark. "Judge for Themselves: Why a Supreme Court Ruling on Sentencing Guidelines Puts More Power Back on the Bench." *Time*, January 24, 2005. http://www.time.com/time/magazine/printout/0,8816,1018063,00.html.

19. Newspaper article

Full note form

19. Rick Bragg, "An Oyster and a Way of Life, Both at Risk," *New York Times*, June 15, 2002, national edition, sec. A.

If the city of publication is not part of the newspaper's name, it should be added at the beginning and italicized as if part of the name: *St. Paul Pioneer Press.* If the city is not well known or could be confused with another city with the same name, add the state name or abbreviation within parentheses after the city's name. If the paper is a well-known national one, such as the *Wall Street Journal,* it is not necessary to add the city of publication.

Bibliographic form

Bragg, Rick. "An Oyster and a Way of Life, Both at Risk." *New York Times.* June 15,

2002, national edition, sec. A.

If the name of the newspaper and the date of publication are mentioned in the text of the paper, no bibliographic entry is needed.

OTHER SOURCES

20. Interview

Full note form

20. Yoko Ono, "Multimedia Player: An Interview with Yoko Ono," interview by Carolyn Burriss-Krimsky, *Ruminator Review,* no. 10 (Summer 2002): 28.

Bibliographic form

Ono, Yoko. "Multimedia Player: An Interview with Yoko Ono." By Carolyn Burriss-

Krimsky. *Ruminator Review,* no. 10 (Summer 2002): 26–29.

If you are required to list interviews, each entry should include the name of the person being interviewed, the title of the interview, the name of the person who conducted it, and any available publication data.

21. Videocassette or DVD

Full note form

21. *Araby,* VHS, produced and directed by Dennis J. Courtney (Los Angeles: American Street Productions, 1999).

Bibliographic form

Araby. VHS. Produced and directed by Dennis J. Courtney. Los Angeles: American Street

Productions, 1999.

Place *VHS* (for videocassette) or *DVD* after the title.

17b Sample CMS-style paper

The following student paper addresses an important development in the civil rights movement. Because it includes a full bibliography, the endnotes are written in short form (see page 400). Although CMS does not provide guidelines for a title page for a student paper, one is shown in fig. 17.1 as a sample.

RACE IN THE U.S. ARMY:

AN EXECUTIVE ORDER FOR HOPE

BY

NICOLE HESTER

AMERICAN HISTORY 257

DR. MELISSA HILL

DECEMBER 6, 2002

Fig. 17.1 Sample title page for a CMS-style paper.

1

RACE IN THE U.S. ARMY: AN EXECUTIVE ORDER FOR HOPE

While students of the Civil Rights movement are often familiar with the Supreme Court decision *Brown v. The Board of Education,* which acknowledged the inherent inequality in separate but equal practices, that decision would not happen until 1955, nearly eight years after President Harry S. Truman issued an executive order to integrate the federal government and, in particular, the United States military. Although the earlier Thirteenth (1865), Fourteenth (1868), and Fifteenth (1870) Amendments redefined freedom, citizenship, and voting, these amendments were diluted by Supreme Court decisions in the nineteenth and early twentieth centuries. In cases like *Plessy v. Ferguson,* the court established the precedent of "separate but equal," which legally allowed the separation of races in public facilities.[1] Thus, Truman's executive order in 1948 became an important step in the long-term struggle for civil rights.

Like American schools, the United States Army was segregated, and this segregation remained in place until after the Second World War (1941–1945). In July of 1948, by executive order, President Truman demanded equal treatment and equal opportunity in the armed forces, setting into motion a series of events that would force change, however slow it might be:

> It is hereby declared to be the policy of the President that there
> shall be equality of treatment and opportunity for all persons
> in the armed services without regard to race, color, religion or
> national origin. This policy shall be put into effect as rapidly as
> possible, having due regard to the time required to effectuate any
> necessary changes without impairing efficiency or morale.[2]

2

President Truman reviews Black troops. (Source: © Bettmann/Corbis.)

With such language as "all persons" and "as rapidly as possible,"
Truman showed that his statement was more than a publicity stunt. While
understanding the scale of the change he was demanding, Truman was also
aware of the sentiment of the American people and numerous government
officials. Examining the desegregation of the Army from the viewpoints
of those who sought to keep the races segregated and those who wanted
integration leads to understanding how the law can begin to secure the
pathways to justice and freedom.[3] Truman's executive order in 1948 illustrates
how the government can be a vehicle for social change.

Historically, approximately 200,000 Blacks enlisted to fight in the
Civil War, but their involvement was strongly influenced by the need for
manpower.[4] After the Civil War, the Army maintained only four Black

3

regiments. Although there were 380,000 Blacks in the Army during the First World War, no more than 42,000 actually served in combat units; most Blacks served as laborers.[5] The end of the First World War ushered in a time of analysis and redefinition of the roles of Blacks in the armed forces. The Selective Service Act of 1940 would forbid discrimination because of race with regard to enlisting and being inducted into the armed forces.[6] However, in October 1940, Robert P. Patterson, the Secretary of War, stated that the Selective Service Act would not eliminate segregation within the armed forces; instead, it would allow Blacks to serve in segregated units:[7]

> The policy of the War Department is not to intermingle colored
> and white enlisted personnel in the same regimental organizations.
> This policy has been proven satisfactory over a long period of
> years and to make changes would produce situations destructive to
> morale and detrimental to the preparations for national defense.[8]

Patterson's statement followed the idea of "separate but equal" and ultimately undercut any effect the Selective Service Act could have had on integration. The enlistment of Blacks was increasing, but their advancement was not, no doubt because they were restricted to separate units. The existence of segregation, stemming from earlier war practices and later defined by War Department policy, would become the norm in the Second World War. From the perspective of those in the War Department, the policy was working effectively, and to "experiment" with its segregated structure would be detrimental to all within military ranks.[9]

These beliefs were reinforced by unreliable data. Supporting the policy outlined by the War Department, results from the U.S. Army General Classification Tests (AGCT), which tested general learning ability, showed

4

45 percent of Blacks and only 5 percent of Whites in the lowest class of exam scores. However, the War Department did not assess any reasons *why* the test results showed the deficit. Because of the "differences in opportunity and background," Blacks generally did not receive the same level of educational opportunity as Whites, so a difference in overall level of performance in standardized testing was bound to exist.[10] Although the Army was correct in its statement about the difference in test results, it ignored the direct effect that segregation and social constraints were having on the academic performance of Black Americans.

The testing issue, however, was only an excuse for preventing integration. For those who believed that segregation was *right*, allowing Blacks equal opportunities in the armed services would enable them to "achieve equality in America by force."[11] Simply put, separatists were afraid that the growing political power of Blacks would lead to a revolt, bringing about the end of segregation, which threatened what separatists thought was right. More importantly, the Army did not believe the government should intervene, forcing desegregation within an otherwise segregated nation. In January 1948, nearly seven months before Truman's executive order, a Gallup poll showed that 81 percent of Southerners had heard of Truman's civil rights plan, and 58 percent felt that it should *not* be passed in Congress, compared to the 14 percent in the New England and Middle Atlantic region who felt that Truman's civil rights initiative should not be passed. In the same survey, Southern Whites responded 5-to-1 in an overwhelming show of support for segregation.[12] In a memorandum from December 1941, when the United States entered the Second World War, Chief of Staff General George C. Marshall reflected the sentiment that existed in

5

the country and explained the Army's resistance to promote social change. In his words, integrating the U.S. Army

> would be tantamount to solving a social problem which has perplexed the American people throughout the history of this nation. The army cannot accomplish such a solution, and should not be charged with the undertaking. The settlement of vexing racial problems cannot be permitted to complicate the tremendous task of the War Department and thereby jeopardize discipline and morale.[13]

When Truman asked for the equal treatment of soldiers regardless of "race, color, religion, or national origin,"[14] he was essentially asking the government to ignore the widespread sentiment of White Americans. Undoubtedly, there were significant numbers of Blacks, Whites, and others craving freedom, but the nation as a whole was not ready for what Truman demanded. After so many years of segregation and prejudice, Truman was fighting a widely supported status quo.

Knowing the greatness of the change he had demanded, Truman established a committee that would be known as the Fahy Committee. Named after its chairman, Charles H. Fahy, the multiracial committee consisted of seven men, including Black leader Lester Granger and the executive secretary of the Urban League, John H. Sengstacke, who were responsible for examining the existing procedures and practices of the armed forces to devise a way to carry out the president's new policy.[15] The Fahy Committee set out to show the ways in which segregation was hurting the "effectiveness" of the armed forces and to establish the positive results that would follow from integrating the armed forces, particularly the Army.[16]

The Fahy Committee wrestled tirelessly with the Army to put an end to the quota system, which limited the number of Black enlistees to 10 percent, as well as the segregation that prevented the advancement of Blacks within the Army.[17] Essentially the Army needed to use every individual within its ranks as effectively as possible, regardless of race, but the quota system and segregation made this impossible.[18] Because the skills of Black soldiers could be used only in Black units, White units sometimes had to leave essential positions unfilled.

When the Army could no longer deny the statistical and practical truth that segregation was inefficient and ineffective, Adjutant General of the Army Edward F. Witsell finally announced on March 27, 1950, that *all* appointments would be open to *all* applicants without regard to race or color.[19] As Mershon and Schlossman discuss in *Foxholes and Color Lines*, by assessing the integration of the armed forces, the Fahy Committee helped Truman to fight segregation and essentially prepare Americans for change.[20] Having the law on their side, Blacks were encouraged in their pursuit of equal opportunity. They began to hope that the equality being fostered in the federal government would eventually affect state practices and that prejudice and bigotry would soon fade.

However, changing the minds of individuals is an entirely different task from changing the laws. Lee reports the statement of an unnamed White officer requesting relief in 1945 from the Ninety-Second Division, an engineer battalion where Black troops worked with Whites:

> Although I can still find such interest in a few specific
> individuals, for the rank and file I can feel only disgust for their
> inherent slovenliness, and their extreme indolence, indifference
> and frequent insolence. . . . I am likewise convinced that with few

> exceptions colored officers with whom I have come into contact
> are thoroughly incompetent, and for the most part are to be
> viewed in a light little different from enlisted men.[21]

This statement shows that while the law can create an environment in which
freedom can exist, the law cannot change racist minds.

Knowing that legal equality was far off and that a deeply changed
society was a hope for the distant future, Blacks in the military were then faced
with daunting questions about their dual role as Blacks and as Americans.
From their perspective, they enlisted to defend a country that would not defend
them. For what reason should Blacks then enlist? What were they fighting
for? Who were they really fighting against? The simplified answer to these
questions came for Blacks in what would become known as the Double V
Campaign: victory abroad and victory at home. In early 1942, this campaign
was explained in the *Courier*, a Black newspaper, as a "struggle to remove the
contradiction between the claims of American democratic ideology and the
racial inequalities evident in American life."[22] Blacks were fighting for what
they knew America was capable of, and ultimately created for, even while
being bound by the racial policies of the Army; they still had a larger vision of
what America could truly be. Fighting on the battlefields of foreign countries
for a nation that rejected them in so many ways, the pursuit of freedom
and equality came at a high emotional cost for Blacks in the Army. Hubert
Humphrey used a quotation by James Baldwin, who served in the Second
World War, to exemplify the Black experience and struggle:

> You must put yourself in the skin of a man who is wearing a uniform
> of his country, is a candidate for death in its defense, and who is

8

called a "nigger" by his comrades-in-arms and his officers . . . and
who watches German prisoners of war being treated by Americans
with more human dignity than he has ever received at their hands.
And who, at the same time, as a human being, is far freer in a
strange land than he has even been at home. HOME! The very word
begins to have a despairing and diabolical ring. You must consider
what happens to this citizen, after all he has endured, when he
returns—home; search, in his shoes, for a job, for a place to live;
ride, in his skin, on segregated buses; see, with his eyes, the signs
saying "White" and "Colored," and especially the signs that say
"White Ladies" and "Colored Women" . . . imagine yourself being
told to "Wait." And all of this happening in the richest and freest
country in the world, and in the middle of the twentieth century.[23]

Between fighting for the freedom of others in the war and hoping justice
would permeate the policies and social hierarchies in America, Black soldiers
had an immense struggle that would not end after the war.

However, Blacks were not alone, there were others fighting along with
them, and President Truman was certainly one of them. By issuing executive
order 9981 in 1948, Truman clearly established his position concerning
racial bias within the government by "tak[ing] significant unilateral action
to alter the stance of the federal government toward minority groups . . .
demonstrat[ing] dedication to the legal equality for racial minorities without
waiting for congressional approval."[24] In short, Truman's order required action
within the armed forces to end racial bias and to do so within a reasonable
amount of time.[25] Sidestepping a conservative Congress and the prejudice of

many Americans, Truman supported Blacks in their struggle for advancement and equality in the armed forces, even though he moved the law to a place where the American people were not necessarily ready to follow.

Understanding Truman's order concerning segregation, we are left to wonder why he would take such a political risk. Why should Truman be any different from other government officials or separatists who surrounded him? What could Truman gain from alienating himself from the legislative branch? Of course, Truman undoubtedly gained the support of Black voters because of his bold stance concerning race, but could that be the entirety of his motivations? What Truman *really* thought or felt is something we can never know, but in October 1948 in an address in Harlem, New York, where he would receive the Franklin Roosevelt Award, Truman had this to say:

> It was the authors of the Declaration of Independence who stated the principle that all men are created equal in their rights, and that it is to secure these rights that governments are instituted among men. It was the authors of the Constitution who made it clear that, under our form of government, all citizens are equal before the law, and that the Federal Government has a duty to guarantee to every citizen equal protection of the laws.[26]

In his own words, Truman stated what the founding documents of this nation intended, and he was determined to see those principles put into action. Truman's biographer David McCullough describes Truman as "the kind of president the founding fathers had in mind for this country."[27] Yet Truman himself reveals that growing international concerns such as the Cold War were also influencing him:

10

Today the democratic way of life is being challenged all over the world. Democracy's answer to the challenge of totalitarianism is its promise of equal rights and equal opportunities for all mankind.

The fulfillment of this promise is among the highest purposes of government.

Our determination to attain the goal of equal rights and equal opportunity must be resolute and unwavering.

For my part, I intend to keep moving toward this goal with every ounce of strength and determination that I have.[28]

Simply, Truman effected the change in government because he was compelled by the same truth that compelled individuals in the Civil Rights movement and that compels individuals today to stand against injustice and discrimination.

Despite politics and despite the prevailing attitudes of many Americans, Truman initiated change. Beginning a process that would affect the Civil Rights movement, Truman established the grounds by which the government could step beyond the stance of most White Americans. Truman's executive order in 1948 showed how the action of one president can work against injustice and encourage those in the midst of a growing struggle for freedom. Legally free to advance in all branches of the armed forces, Blacks were able to prove the truth that they had been proclaiming for so long—that equality in humanity transcends racial differences.

11

Notes

1. *Plessy v. Ferguson,* 163 U.S. 537 (1896).

2. Merrill, *Documentary History,* 11:741.

3. It is beyond the scope of my paper to discuss all the non-Whites who were affected by Truman's order. In this essay, I focus on the effect of Truman's order on people whom I refer to as Black.

4. Lee, *Employment of Negro Troops,* 4.

5. Ibid., 73–74.

6. Mershon and Schlossman, *Foxholes and Color Lines,* 44–45.

7. Ibid., 73–77.

8. Nalty and MacGregor, *Blacks in the Military,* 108.

9. Ibid.

10. Lee, *Employment of Negro Troops,* 141.

11. Reddick, "Negro Policy," 12.

12. Gallup, *Public Opinion 1935–1971,* 2:782–83.

13. Nalty and MacGregor, *Blacks in the Military,* 114–15.

14. Merrill, *Documentary History,* 11:741.

15. Gardner, *Truman and Civil Rights,* 114.

16. Billington, "Freedom to Serve," 273.

17. Mershon and Schlossman, *Foxholes and Color Lines,* 209.

18. Nalty and MacGregor, *Blacks in the Military,* 289.

19. Ibid., 269.

20. Mershon and Schlossman, *Foxholes and Color Lines,* 217.

21. Lee, *Employment of Negro Troops,* 187.

22. Osur, *Blacks in the Army Air Forces,* 11–12.

12

23. Quoted in Hubert H. Humphrey, *Beyond Civil Rights*, 19. Humphrey provides no indication of the source of Baldwin's statement, and I have been unable to track it down.

24. Mershon and Schlossman, *Foxholes and Color Lines,* 167–68.

25. Mayer, *Stroke of a Pen*, 4.

26. Truman, *Public Papers*, 923–25.

27. McCullough, *Truman*, 991.

28. Truman, *Public Papers,* 923–25.

13

Bibliography

Billington, Monroe. "Freedom to Serve: The President's Committee on Equality of Treatment and Opportunity in the Armed Forces, 1949–1950." *Journal of Negro History* (1966): 262–74. http://links.jstor.org/sici?sici=0022-2992(196610)51%3A4%3C262%3AFTSTPC%3E2.0.CO%3B2-B.

Gallup, George H. *The Gallup Poll: Public Opinion 1935–1971.* Vol. 2. New York: Random House, 1972.

Gardner, Michael R. *Harry Truman and Civil Rights: Moral Courage and Political Risks.* Carbondale and Edwardsville: Southern Illinois Univ. Press, 2002.

Humphrey, Hubert H. *Beyond Civil Rights: A New Day of Equality.* New York: Random House, 1968.

Lee, Ulysses. *The Employment of Negro Troops.* Washington, DC: Center of Military History, 1963.

Mayer, Kenneth. *With the Stroke of a Pen: Executive Orders and Presidential Power.* Princeton: Princeton Univ. Press, 2001.

McCullough, David. *Truman.* New York: Simon & Schuster, 1992.

Merrill, Dennis, ed. *Documentary History of the Truman Presidency.* Vol. 11. Bethesda, MD: University Publishers of America, 1996.

Mershon, Sherie, and Steven Schlossman. *Foxholes and Color Lines.* Baltimore: Johns Hopkins Univ. Press, 1998.

Nalty, Bernard C., and Morris J. MacGregor. *Blacks in the Military.* Wilmington, DE: Scholarly Resources, 1981.

14

Osur, Alan M. *Blacks in the Army Air Forces During World War II.*
    Washington, DC: Office of Air Force History, 1941.

Plessy v. Ferguson, 163 U.S. 537 (1896).

Reddick, L. D. "The Negro Policy of the United States Army, 1775–1945."
    Journal of Negro History 34, no. 1 (1949): 9–29. http://www.jstor.org/
    sici?sici=0022-2992(194901)34%3A1%3C9%3ATNPOTU3E2.0.CO
    %3B2-M.

Truman, Harry. *Public Papers of the Presidents of the United States: Harry
    S. Truman, 1945–53.* Vol. 4. Washington, DC: GPO, 1964.

18 Writing in the Natural Sciences

The **natural sciences** include mathematics, the biological sciences (botany and zoology), the physical sciences (chemistry and physics), and the earth sciences (geology and astronomy). The natural sciences also include **applied sciences** such as medicine and allied health studies, engineering, and computer science. The natural sciences are problem-solving disciplines that report or analyze results derived from meticulous observation and experimentation. For example, Heather Jensen, whose paper appears at the end of this chapter, examined onion root tip cells during five stages of mitosis (cell division). Based on her results, she was able to describe how this cell division occurs.

Scientific writing appears in many forms, ranging from technical reports that scientists write for an audience of other scientists to newspaper articles directed at a general audience. Figure 18.1 illustrates how Gina Kolata, a reporter for the *New York Times,* addressed the elements of the rhetorical situation in producing a newspaper article. In her article, "Scientists Bypass Need for Embryo to Get Stem Cells," Kolata reports on a development in stem-cell research. (See fig. 18.2 for an excerpt from the article.) Her opening sentence reveals the exigence and context for this news story: researchers have created a new way of producing stem cells, thereby avoiding the ethical issues raised about research that used human embryos. Kolata's purpose is to update her audience, the general public, on a controversial topic.

Writing assignments you can expect to receive in science courses include literature reviews, field reports, technical background reports, and laboratory reports.

This chapter will help you

- determine the audience, purpose, and research question for a paper in the natural sciences (**18a**),
- decide which types of evidence, sources, and reasoning to use in such a paper (**18b**),

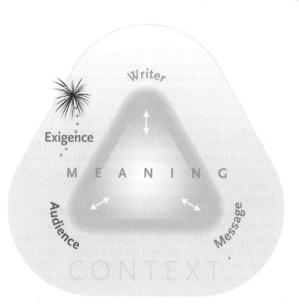

Exigence: New developments in stem-cell research

Writer: Gina Kolata, a reporter for the *New York Times*

Audience: Readers interested in the controversial topic of stem-cell research

Message: The author describes a recent development in stem-cell research that may silence debate.

Context: Past debate over using human embryos to produce stem cells

Fig. 18.1. Sample rhetorical situation for writing in the natural sciences.

- use appropriate language, style, and formatting when writing the paper (**18c**), and
- understand typical assignments in the social sciences (**18d**).

18a Audience, purpose, and the research question

Before you start working on a writing assignment for a course in the natural sciences, be sure to consult with your instructor as you determine your audience and your purpose. Your instructor will always be one of your

Two teams of scientists reported yesterday that they had turned human skin cells into what appear to be embryonic stem cells without having to make or destroy an embryo – a feat that could quell the ethical debate troubling the field.

All they had to do, the scientists said, was add four genes. The genes reprogrammed the chromosomes of the skin cells, making the cells into blank slates that should be able to turn into any of the 220 cell types of the human body, be it heart, brain, blood, or bone. Until now, the only way to get such human universal cells was to pluck them from a human embryo several days after fertilization, destroying the embryo in the process.

The need to destroy embryos has made stem cell research one of the most divisive issues in American politics, pitting President Bush against prominent Republicans like Nancy Reagan, and patient advocates who hoped that stem cells could cure diseases like Alzheimer's. The new studies could defuse the issue as a presidential election nears.

The reprogrammed skin cells may yet prove to have subtle differences from embryonic stem cells that come directly from human embryos, and the new method includes potentially risky steps, like introducing a cancer gene. But stem cell researchers say they are confident that it will not take long to perfect the method and that today's drawbacks will prove to be temporary.

Researchers and ethicists not involved in the findings say the work, conducted by independent teams from Japan and Wisconsin, should reshape the stem cell field. At some time in the near future, they said, today's debate over whether it is morally acceptable to create and destroy human embryos to obtain stem cells should be moot.

Fig. 18.2. An excerpt from a newspaper article on stem-cell research.

readers, but he or she may plan to ask you to share your work with other readers as well. If you are enrolled in an advanced class, you may be expected to present your work at a local, regional, or national conference. By knowing who constitutes your audience(s), you will be able to gauge how much background information is adequate, how much technical language is appropriate, and what types of evidence and reasoning are necessary.

Researchers in the sciences generally write to inform their readers, either by discussing studies pertaining to a specific topic or by reporting the results of an experiment. However, their purpose may be evaluative if they are critiquing a journal article or argumentative if they are encouraging readers to take a specific action. After you have determined your purpose and audience, craft a research question that will guide you to sources and help you to use them responsibly (chapters 9–11). The following examples of research questions focus on global warming:

Questions about cause

What causes global warming?

Questions about consequences

What are the effects of global warming?

Questions about process

How can global warming be stopped?

Questions about definitions or categories

What types of greenhouse gases are responsible for global warming?

Questions about values

What are a scientist's responsibilities to the public in the face of global warming?

Research questions in the sciences are often narrowed to enable precise measurements:

Questions about length, distance, frequency, and so on

How far has Mendenhall Glacier receded each year for the past decade, and do the values show any trend?

Questions about comparisons and correlations

How are emission intensities related to the total amount of emissions?

The question Heather Jensen responds to in her laboratory report focuses on a process:

What happens to onion root tip cells during mitosis?

Michelle Tebbe, whose paper appears at the end of chapter 19 (pages 462–466), also asks a question about process:

How does agate form?

18b Evidence, sources, and reasoning

Researchers in the natural sciences attempt to quantify phenomena in the world around them. They look for **empirical evidence**—facts that can be measured or tested—to support their claims. Most of their investigations, then, are set up as experiments. If you conduct an experiment for a course in the natural sciences, you will be expected to start with a **hypothesis,** a prediction that serves as a basis for experimentation. To test the hypothesis, you will follow a procedure—one designed by yourself, established in another study, or specified by your instructor. The results of your experiment will either validate your hypothesis or show it to be in error. This systematic way of proceeding from a hypothesis to verifiable results is called the **scientific method.** Consisting of six steps, this method helps ensure the objectivity and accuracy of experimental findings.

THE SCIENTIFIC METHOD

1. *State a problem*: When you recognize and then state the problem, you establish the exigence (the reason for your writing).

2. *Collect evidence*: Close observation is the most important skill for collecting evidence. Be sure to record all details as accurately as you can. Alternatively, you may read the reports of other researchers who have addressed a problem similar to yours. If you draw on observations and experiments, you are using primary sources; if you use scientific articles and statistical charts, you are using secondary sources.

3. *Form a hypothesis*: A hypothesis is a tentative claim, or prediction, about the phenomenon you are studying.

4. *Test the hypothesis*: Although you have conducted some research before formulating the hypothesis, you now continue that research through additional observation or experimentation.

5. *Analyze the results*: Look at your results in light of your hypothesis. Attempt to find patterns, categories, or other relationships.

6. *State the conclusion*: If you have validated your hypothesis, explain why it accounts for *all* of your data. If your hypothesis is disproved, suggest revisions to it or offer a new one.

Reports based on the six steps of the scientific method are **quantitative studies,** because their results are presented as numerical data (**14b**). Heather Jensen's mitosis lab report is a quantitative study. Another type of study performed by scientists, especially those working in the field, is the **qualitative study.** The data in qualitative studies are produced through observation and analysis of natural phenomena. It is not uncommon, however, for studies to include both quantitative and qualitative features, as does Michelle Tebbe's study of agate formation (**19b**).

Regardless of the type of study they perform, scientists depend on previous research to place their work in context. They draw from both primary sources (experiments, observations, surveys, and so on) and secondary sources (books and articles already published on a topic). Any sources used are cited in the body of the paper and documented on a reference list. (See chapter **19**.)

18c Conventions of language and organization

(1) Writers in the natural sciences follow the style of their discipline.
The conventions that most writers in the sciences follow are presented in a manual titled *Scientific Style and Format,* compiled by the Council of Science Editors (CSE). However, you may sometimes be asked to use one of the following manuals.

American Chemical Society. *The ACS Style Guide: Effective Communication of Scientific Information.* 3rd ed. Washington, DC: American Chemical Society, 2006.

American Institute of Physics. *AIP Style Manual.* 4th ed. New York: American Institute of Physics, 1990.

American Mathematical Society. *A Manual for Authors of Mathematical Papers.* Rev. ed. Providence, RI: American Mathematical Society, 1990.

American Medical Association. *AMA Manual of Style: A Guide for Authors and Editors.* 10th ed. Oxford: Oxford Univ. Press, 2007.

United States Geological Society. *Suggestions to Authors of the Reports of the United States Geological Survey.* 7th ed. Washington, DC: Government Printing Office, 1991.

Before starting any writing project, check with your instructor to see which style manual you should use.

CSE guidelines encourage prose that is "accurate, clear, economical, fluent, and graceful." The following tips can help you write in the style recommended by the CSE manual.

TIPS FOR PREPARING A PAPER IN THE NATURAL SCIENCES

- Select words that convey meaning precisely (**35a**).
- Avoid gender bias (**25c(2)**).
- If two possible wordings are possible, choose the more succinct (**34a**).
- Clarify noun strings by placing modifiers after the main noun.

  the system for measuring frequency   NOT the frequency measuring system

- When using an introductory participial phrase, be sure that it modifies the subject of the sentence (**24d**). Participial phrases that begin with *based on* are particulary troublesome, so doublecheck to make sure they modify the subject.

  Based on the promising results, the decision to approve the new medication seemed reasonable.

  NOT Based on the promising results, the new medication was approved.

---

(2) Information is organized according to specific conventions.

The most frequent writing assignments in the natural sciences are various types of reports—literature reviews, field reports, technical background reports, and laboratory reports. The specific formats for these reports are presented in **18d**.

All scientific reports include headings and often subheadings to help readers find and understand information. The headings and subheadings indicate how the various sections of a report are related. CSE recognizes four levels of headings.

The First Level Uses Boldfaced Uppercase and Lowercase Letters
The Second Level Uses Uppercase and Lowercase Letters
THE THIRD LEVEL USES SMALL UPPERCASE LETTERS
The Fourth Level Uses Italicized Uppercase and Lowercase Letters

Two or three levels of subheadings should suffice for most college-level assignments. Heather Jensen uses three levels in her lab report at the end of this chapter. Some instructors may expect you to center some headings or subheadings, so be aware of your instructor's preferences.

Writers in the natural sciences also use tables and figures (such as graphs, drawings, and photographs) to organize their material. Essential for presenting numerical data, tables should be numbered and titled. Heather includes two tables in her lab report: one to show the number and percentage of cells in each phase of mitosis and one to show the percentages of cells (18d(4)). Heather also uses six figures in her report. The first five are drawings that illustrate the five phases of cell division. The sixth is a graph that indicates how much time the onion root tip cells she examined spent in each phase. Like tables, figures should be numbered and titled. For instructions on how to create tables and bar graphs electronically, see 14c(2). For an example of a photograph used as a figure, see Michelle Tebbe's introduction to her study of agate formation (19b).

If you use a table or figure in your paper, introducing it in the paragraph that precedes it will help readers understand its purpose. Heather presented her first table this way: "Table 1 shows the number of cells found in each phase of mitosis."

(3) A reference list provides detailed information about the sources used.

CSE provides three options for citing sources and listing them at the end of a paper: the citation-sequence system, the citation-name system, and the name-year system. You can find specific guidelines for creating a reference list in chapter 19.

18d Samples of writing in the natural sciences

(1) Literature review

A **literature review** is essentially an evaluative overview of research directly related to a specific topic. It focuses on both strengths and weaknesses of previous research—in methodology or interpretation—with the goal of establishing what steps need to be taken to advance research on the topic. A literature review may be assigned as part of a longer paper, in which case the information it contains appears in the introductory section of the paper. Michelle Tebbe's paper on agate formation includes a literature review that is a historical account of research on her topic.

Scientific interest in agate dates back at least to the 18th century when Collini (1776) contemplated the source of silica for agate formation and suggested a mechanism for producing repetitive banding. In the mid-19th century, Noeggerath (1849) hypothesized that the repetitive banding of agate is indicative of natural, external (to the agate-bearing cavity), rhythmic processes such as bedrock leaching of silica by a fluid that enters into cavities via infiltration canals, forming agate after many separate infiltrations. Other processes such as variation in water-table height (Bauer 1904) and alternating wet-dry seasons (Linck and Heinz 1930) have been credited as responsible for rhythmic infilling of cavities by silica-rich solutions.

These now traditional ideas on agate formation imply fluid-rock interaction at low temperatures (<250 °C). Empirical support for low formation temperatures comes from several published studies. Based on hydrogen and oxygen isotope data, Fallick et al. (1985) estimated the temperature of formation of Devonian and Tertiary basalt-hosted Scottish agate to be approximately 50 °C. Using the same methods, Harris (1989) inferred the temperature of formation for basalt-hosted agate from Namibia to be approximately 120 °C. Lueth and Goodell (2005) performed fluid-inclusion analyses for agate from the Paraná Basalts, Rio do Sul, Brazil, and inferred the temperature of formation to be <50 °C for darker-colored samples and 140–180 °C for lighter-colored samples.

(2) Field report

Field work is research done in a natural environment rather than in a laboratory. Examples of field work range from recording beach erosion to studying avalanche patterns. To record their observations and analyses, researchers working in the field write **field reports**. These reports consist mainly of two elements: description and analysis. The researchers may choose to present these elements together or in separate sections. Field reports sometimes include a reference list of sources mentioned in the text. The following excerpt is from a field report on the behavior of ducks written by Mike Demmon for a course in avian ecology. It contains a description of a brief field study and a sample of the data recorded.

Procedures

During the class field trip to Eagle Lake, I participated in a quantitative evaluation of several diving duck species. My classmates and I monitored several different
variables to see whether feeding practices were staggered between species, whether
frequencies of dives were different between species, and whether any of the species
interacted with each other. The three species we studied were Ruddy Duck (*Oxyura
jamaicensis*), Redhead (*Aytheya americana*), and Bufflehead (*Bucephala albeola*).

Data

Time	Species	Sex	Number of Dives	Dive Time (seconds, respectively)	Other Activities
8:30–8:40	Bufflehead	Male	0	N/A	Preening & sleeping
8:45–8:55	Bufflehead	Female	1	Lost after 4 minutes	Preening & followed by 2 males
9:00–9:10	Ruddy	Female	4	21, 27, 33, 19, lost after 5 minutes	Paired with 2 females, ran males off, preening

Mike's report also contains analysis. In the following excerpt, he
attempts to interpret the tabulated data.

Discussion

As the data indicate, there is no evidence of variation in diving time or frequency of
dives among the species observed. Neither was there evidence that any of the species
directly and intentionally interact. Surprisingly, the data do seem to show that activities do not begin until mid-morning. When we arrived, about 8 AM, a large percentage
of the birds were still sleeping. Once the birds awaken, it appears that they ritually
preen themselves before feeding. The data also show that the majority of the birds
following birds of the same species but of opposite sex were Buffleheads. The Buffleheads also appeared to be courting at times.

(3) Technical background report

A **technical background report** provides information to an audience that needs it to make a decision. (This type of report is sometimes called a **white paper** when it is issued by a government agency.) Generally, the report acknowledges a problem, such as a specific type of pollution, and provides information to help decision makers try to solve the problem. The content of technical background reports varies according to the problem, the information available, and the decision-making body's needs. If you are assigned a technical background report, use the following checklist when deciding what types of information to include.

> **CHECKLIST** for Information in a Technical Background Report
>
> - Do any terms need to be defined?
> - What were the events or conditions leading to the problem?
> - What research related to solving the problem has already been done?
> - What are the possible solutions to the problem?
> - What are the economic, social, political, legal, or ethical implications of the problem or of the proposed solution?

The sections of a technical background report depend on the information gathered for the report. The excerpts in fig. 18.3 are from a white paper on mercury in the environment produced by the United States Environmental Protection Agency (EPA).

(4) Laboratory report

The most common writing assignment in the natural sciences is the **laboratory report**. The purpose of a lab report is to describe an experiment, including the results obtained, so that other researchers understand the procedure used and the conclusions drawn. When writing a lab report, you should explain the purpose of your research, recount the procedure you followed, and discuss your results. The format of this type of report follows the steps of the scientific method by starting with a problem and a hypothesis and concluding with a statement proving, modifying, or disproving the hypothesis.

MERCURY WHITE PAPER

The Utility Hazardous Air Pollutants Regulatory Determination
To reduce the risk mercury poses to people's health, EPA Administrator
Carol M. Browner announced that the Environmental Protection Agency will
regulate emissions of mercury and other air toxics from coal- and oil-fired
electric utility steam generating units (power plants). EPA plans to propose a
regulation to control air toxics emissions, including mercury, from coal- and
oil-fired power plants by the end of 2003. This regulation will be one more
important piece of an Agency-wide effort to protect people and wildlife from
exposure to the toxic pollutant mercury.

Sources and Fate of Mercury in the Environment
Like all elements, the same amount of mercury has existed on the planet since
the Earth was formed. However, the amount of mercury mobilized and released
into the environment has increased since the beginning of the industrial age.
Mercury moves through the environment as a result of both natural and human
activities. The human activities that are most responsible for causing mercury
to enter the environment are burning materials (such as batteries), fuels (such
as coal) that contain mercury, and certain industrial processes. These activities
produce air pollution containing mercury. . . .

Health Effects and Exposure
For the general U.S. population, exposure to mercury occurs primarily through
eating contaminated fish. Women of childbearing age, and people who
regularly and frequently eat highly contaminated fish (or large amounts of
moderately contaminated fish), are the most likely to be at risk from mercury
exposure. Those groups include subsistence fishermen (people who fish for
their food) and some Native American populations. . . .

Recent Actions to Reduce Mercury Pollution
EPA has taken a number of actions to reduce mercury pollution, including
issuing stringent regulations for industries that significantly contribute to
mercury pollution. Once fully implemented, these actions will reduce U.S.
mercury emissions caused by human activities by nearly 50 percent from 1990
levels. . . .

Planned Actions to Reduce Mercury Pollution
In addition to developing regulations to limit mercury emissions from utilities,
EPA has developed an action plan to address other sources of mercury
pollution. Already there are a number of planned activities under way:
> EPA is developing a revised human health-based mercury standard for
> water quality and has identified the need to develop a standard that will
> protect wildlife from mercury's effects. . . .

Fig. 18.3. Excerpts from an EPA white paper.

- The **abstract** states the problem and summarizes the results. (You may not have to include an abstract if your report is short or if your instructor does not require it.)

- The **introduction** states the research question or hypothesis clearly and concisely, explains the scientific basis for the study, and provides brief background material on the subject of the study and the techniques to be used. The introduction usually includes citations referring to relevant sources.

- The **methods and materials** section is a narrative that describes how the experiment was conducted. It lists the materials that were used, identifies where the experiment was conducted, and describes the procedures that were followed. (Your lab notes should help you remember what you did.) Anyone who wants to repeat your work should be able to do so by following the steps described in this section.

- **Results** are reported by describing (but not interpreting) major findings and supporting them with properly labeled tables or graphs showing the empirical data.

- The **discussion** section includes an analysis of the results and an explanation of their relevance to the goals of the study. This section also reports any problems encountered and offers suggestions for further testing of the results.

- **References** are listed at the end of the paper. The list includes only works that are referred to in the report. The comprehensiveness and the accuracy of this list allow readers to evaluate the quality of the report and put it into a relevant context.

Heather Jensen's paper is representative of a report based on an experiment outlined in a lab manual for a first-year biology course. It includes section headings and graphics—drawings of the various stages of mitosis and a graph showing the results. The report ends with a reference list formatted according to CSE's citation-sequence system.

1

Observations and Calculations of Onion Root Tip Cells

Heather Jensen

Biology 101

June 7, 2002

Abstract

This laboratory experiment examined *Allium* (onion) root tip cells in the
five stages of mitosis. The five stages of mitotic division were identified and
recorded, and a 50-cell sample was chosen for closer examination. Of those 50
cells, 64% were found to be in interphase, 20% in prophase, 6% in metaphase,
6% in anaphase, and only 4% in telophase. The results showed that onion root
tip cells spend the majority of their life cycle in a rest period (interphase).
Prophase was calculated to be the longest phase of active division, while
telophase was the shortest. These results were consistent with the experiments
completed by other students and scientists.

Summary
of the
experiment

Introduction

This lab report outlines a laboratory experiment on mitosis, the
division of the nucleus of a cell to form two new cells with the same number
of chromosomes as the parent cell. Mitotic cell division consists of five
visually identifiable stages: interphase, prophase, metaphase, anaphase, and
telophase. The purpose of this laboratory experiment was to identify and
observe cells in each phase of mitosis, as well as to calculate an estimation of
the real time involved in each stage of mitosis in an onion root tip cell. The
onion root tip was chosen for this experiment because of easy availability and

Introduction
describing the
purpose of the
experiment

rapid growth. Rapid root growth resulted in an easy opportunity to observe

multiple cells in the phases of mitosis in a small sample, on one or two slides.

Superscript
number
referring to
the first
source

Onion root cells complete the entire cycle of division in 80 minutes,[1] and

it was expected that larger numbers of cells would be found in interphase,

because the majority of a life cycle is spent performing normal cell functions.

Materials and Methods

List of
materials and
description of
methodology

    The materials required for this experiment include a compound microscope

and prepared slides of a longitudinal section of *Allium* (onion) root tip.

First, the slides were placed on a compound microscope under low power, a

40x magnification level. The end of the root tip was located; then the cells

immediately behind the root cap were examined. These cells appeared as a

darker area under low power. This area of cells was identified as the apical

meristem,[1] an area of rapid growth and division in the onion root tip. This area

of cells was examined while keeping the microscope on low power, to find and

Superscript
number
referring to
the second
source

identify cells in interphase, prophase, metaphase, anaphase, and telophase.[2]

Then high power, a 400x magnification, was used to further examine and

record the appearance of these cells.

    After the multiple phases of mitosis were observed, a large area of 50 cells

in mitosis was selected for further examination. This area was located under

low power in order to assess rows of cells in an easily countable space. Then

the number of cells in each stage of mitosis was counted. These numbers were

divided by the total number of cells examined, or 50 cells, and multiplied by

100 in order to calculate the percentage of cells in each phase of mitosis.

For example, if 10 cells were observed in interphase, then $10/50 = 0.20$ and

$0.20 \cdot 100 = 20\%$ of cells were in interphase. The actual time of each phase

3

of mitosis in this sample of cells was calculated by multiplying the percentage
by the total time of the division cycle, 80 minutes for the onion root tip cell.[1]
For example, if 20% of the cells were observed in interphase, then 20%
$(20/100) \cdot 80$ minutes = 16 minutes total time were spent in interphase.

Results

Drawings and Observations

INTERPHASE

This phase lasts from the completion of a division cycle to the beginning
of the next cycle. All regular cell functions occur in this phase (except
reproduction).[3]

Figure 1   Two cells observed in interphase

PROPHASE

Technically the first phase of mitosis, this stage is marked by the thickening and
shortening of chromosomes, which makes them appear visible under a compound
microscope. The nucleus appears grainy at first and then the chromosomes
appear more clearly defined as prophase progresses.

Figure 2   Two cells observed in prophase

Description
of phases
with labeled
drawings as
support

Superscript
number
referring to
the third
source

4

METAPHASE

This phase is identified by the lining up of double chromosomes along the center line, the equator, of the cell.

Figure 3   Two cells observed in metaphase

ANAPHASE

This phase is classified by the separation of the double chromosomes. They will begin to pull apart to opposite poles of the cell.

Figure 4   Two cells observed in anaphase

TELOPHASE

In telophase, the chromosomes have reached the opposite poles of the cell, and the connection between the chromosomes begins to break down as the nuclear membrane begins to form around each chromosomal clump. At the end of telophase, cytokinesis, or the division of the cytoplasm, takes place. In plant cells, a cell plate begins to form in the center of the cell and then grows outward

5

to form a new cell wall, completely dividing the old cell into two new cells, both with a complete set of chromosomes.

Figure 5   Two cells observed in telophase

Table 1 shows the number of cells found in each phase of mitosis.

Table 1   Number of cells in each phase

Interphase	Prophase	Metaphase	Anaphase	Telophase
32 cells	10 cells	3 cells	3 cells	2 cells

Table summarizing findings

Table 2 shows the calculated percentage of cells in each phase of mitosis.

Table 2   Percentage of cells in each phase

Interphase	Prophase	Metaphase	Anaphase	Telophase
64% of cells	20% of cells	6% of cells	6% of cells	4% of cells

Figure 6 shows the actual time cells spent in each phase of mitosis.

Graph of data

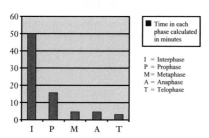

Figure 6   Time spent in each phase of mitosis

6

Discussion

This laboratory experiment provided firsthand experience with the phases of cell division. The five phases became more easily recognizable as each cell was examined and classified. Cells often looked like they could be classified in interphase or prophase or like they were between phases. Observation led to the confirmation that mitosis is a fluid process and not just a series of distinct phases. During the experiment, difficulties with overdyed and gray areas caused uncertainty because visual indications of phase were impossible to detect. This problem was lessened through the careful selection of clear patches of cells for observation. The expectation that a large number of cells would be found in interphase was confirmed by the numbers of cells counted in the cell sample of the onion root tip. Online comparison of the results of this experiment to those of other similar experiments confirmed the results found here as typical of an onion (*Allium*) root tip.[4] This indicated that the careful selection of clear patches of cells for sampling proved an effective method for eliminating error that might have been caused by the incorrect labeling of cells or the poor visibility of cells in overdyed or gray areas. Further studies might include larger samples of cells. Experiments with larger numbers of cells would offer additional evidence to confirm the results found in this experiment.

Explanation of how the results of the experiment fulfilled its purpose

Description of a problem that was encountered

Superscript number referring to the fourth source

7

References

1. Schraer WD, Stoltze H. Biology: the study of life. 4th ed. Needham (MA): Prentice Hall; 1991. Mitosis and asexual reproduction; p. 397–415.

2. Smith DW, Maier CGA. Plant biology lab manual. Dubuque (IA): Kendall/ Hunt; 1995. Topic 5, The plant cell; p. 52–66.

3. Alexander GM, Goodson P, Hanneman PJ, Melear, CT. Scott, Foresman biology. Glenview (IL): Scott, Foresman; 1985. Information storage and transfer in cells; p. 117–143.

4. Yesnik A, Jaster K. The bio 1 super virtual lab book [Internet]. Washington (DC): Sidwell Friends School; 1998 [modified 2002; cited 2002 Jun 7]. Mitosis lab. Available from: http://www.sidwell.edu/us/science/vlb/mitosis/

List of references in citation-sequence format

19 CSE Documentation

The Council of Science Editors (CSE) has established guidelines for writers in the life and physical sciences: *Scientific Style and Format: The CSE Manual for Authors, Editors, and Publishers*, seventh edition, covers both general style conventions for spelling, punctuation, capitalization, and so forth, as well as specific scientific conventions for such items as chemical names and formulas. In addition, the manual presents three systems for citing and documenting research sources: the citation-sequence system, the name-year system, and the citation-name system. This chapter includes

- guidelines for citing sources within a CSE-style research paper and documenting sources on the reference list (**19a**) and
- excerpts from a sample student paper (**19b**).

19a CSE citation-sequence, name-year, and citation-name systems

As you prepare to write your paper, be sure to find out which system your instructor prefers—the citation-sequence system, the name-year system, or the citation-name system. Because these systems differ significantly, it is important to know which you will be expected to use before you get started. Once you know your instructor's preference, follow the guidelines in one of the following boxes as you prepare your in-text references and end references (the list of bibliographic entries at the end of your paper).

TIPS FOR PREPARING CITATION-SEQUENCE IN-TEXT REFERENCES

- Place a superscript number after each mention of a source or each use of material from it. This number corresponds to the number assigned to an end reference.

- Be sure to place the number immediately after the material used or the word or phrase indicating the source: Herbert's original method[1] was used.

- Use the same number each time you use material from or refer to the source.

- Order the numbers according to the sequence in which sources are introduced: Both Li[1] and Holst[2] have shown. . . .

- When referring to more than one source, use commas to separate the numbers corresponding to the sources; note that there is no space after each comma. Use an en dash between two numbers to indicate a sequence of sources: The early studies[1,2,4–7]. . . .

TIPS FOR PREPARING NAME-YEAR IN-TEXT REFERENCES

- Place the author's last name and the year of publication in parentheses after the mention of a source: In a more recent study (Karr 2009), these findings were not replicated. Using the author's last name, the reader will be able to find the corresponding entry in the reference list, which is arranged alphabetically.

- Omit the author's name from the parenthetical citation if it appears in the text preceding it: In Karr's study (2009), these findings were not replicated.

- If the source has two authors, use both of their last names: (Phill and Richardson 2009). If there are three or more authors, use the first author's last name and the abbreviation *et al.*: (Drake et al. 2008).

- Use semicolons to separate multiple citations within a set of parentheses. Order these citations chronologically when the years differ but alphabetically when the years are the same: (Li 2008; Holst 2009) but (Lamont 2008; Li 2008).

TIPS FOR PREPARING CITATION-NAME IN-TEXT REFERENCES

- Arrange your end references alphabetically. Then assign each reference a number. Use the superscript form of this number in the text immediately after the material used or the word or phrase indicating the source: Stress-related illnesses are common among college students.[1]

- Use the same number each time you use material from or refer to the source.

- When referring to more than one source, use commas to separate the numbers corresponding to the sources; note that there is no space after each comma. Use an en dash between two numbers to indicate a sequence of sources: Recent studies of posttraumatic stress disorder[1,2,4–7]. . . .

TIPS FOR PREPARING END REFERENCES

- Place the heading "References" or "Cited References" next to the left margin.

- If you are using the citation-sequence system, list the sources in the order in which they were introduced in the text. If your paper employs the citation-name system, your end references should be ordered alphabetically according to the first author's last name and then numbered.

- If your paper employs the name-year system, your end references should be ordered alphabetically. See pages 465–466 for an example of end references in alphabetical order.

- Entries on citation-sequence and citation-name reference lists differ only in overall organization: citation-sequence references are listed according to the order of occurrence within the text; citation-name references are listed alphabetically. The name-year system differs from both the citation-sequence and citation-name systems only in the placement of the date of publication: the name-year system calls for the date to be placed after the author's name; the citation-sequence and the citation-name systems call for the date to be placed after the publisher's name in entries for books and after the name of the periodical in entries for articles.

 CAUTION

Automatic bibliography composers found online and included in some software packages often make mistakes. They may fail to include all elements of a bibliographic entry or may order elements incorrectly. If you decide to use an automatic composer, be sure to check the results against the model entries provided in this chapter.

Use the following directory to find sample end references for the citation-sequence or citation-name system.

Directory of CSE Citation-Sequence or Citation-Name Bibliographic Entries

BOOKS

1. Book with one author 457
2. Book with two or more authors 458
3. Book with an organization (or organizations) listed as author 458
4. Book with editor(s) 458
5. Chapter or part of an edited book 458

ARTICLES

6. Article in a scholarly journal 458
7. Article in a popular (general-circulation) magazine 458
8. Article in a newspaper 459

ELECTRONIC SOURCES

9. Online book 459
10. Article in an online journal 459
11. Article in an online magazine 459
12. Article in an online newspaper 459
13. Web site 459
14. Database 459

The following guidelines are for both books and articles.

General Documentation Guidelines

Author or Editor

One author. Begin the entry with the author's last name and the initials for the first name and the middle name (if one is given). Notice that there is no comma after the last name and no period or space between initials.	Klemin TK. Laigo MS.
Two or more authors. Invert the names and initials of all authors, using commas to separate the authors' names.	Stearns BL, Sowards JP. Collum AS, Dahl PJ, Steele TP.
Organization as author. Whenever possible, use an abbreviation or acronym for the name of the organization.	AMA. UNICEF. CDC.
Editor. Add the word *editor* or *editors* after the last name.	Walter PA, editor. Mednick VB, Henry JP, editors.

Titles

Books. Use the title given on the book's title page. Titles are neither underlined nor italicized. Capitalize only the first word of the title and any proper nouns or adjectives. Subtitles are not capitalized.	The magpies: the ecology and behaviour of black-billed and yellow-billed magpies.
If the book is a second or subsequent edition, follow the title with a period and then the number of the edition: 3rd ed.	Genetics. 5th ed.

Journals, magazines, and newspapers. For the names of journals and magazines that are longer than one word, use standard abbreviations (for example, *Sci Am* for *Scientific American*). Rules for abbreviating journal titles are given in Appendix 29.1 of *Scientific Style and Format* and can also be found using a search engine (enter "CSE abbreviations"). Use full names of newspapers, omitting any initial *The*.

J Mamm. (for *Journal of Mammology*)

New York Times.

Publication Data

Books. Include the place of publication, the publisher's name, and the year of publication. The place of publication can usually be found on the title page. If more than one city is mentioned, use the first one listed. If the city is not well known, clarify the location by including an abbreviation for the state, province, or country in parentheses after the name of the city. The publisher's name should be listed next, separated from the place of publication by a colon and one space. (Standard abbreviations for publishing companies may be used.) If you are using the citation-sequence or citation-name system, list the year of publication after the publisher's name; separate the year from the publisher's name, using a semicolon and one space.

London: Chatto & Windus; 2008.

Orlando (FL): Harcourt; 2009.

Journals and magazines. Use one space after the name of the journal or magazine; then indicate the year of publication, the volume number, and

Nature. 2009;420(6911)

Natl Geogr Mag. 2009;211(3)

(Continued on page 456)

Publication Data *(Continued from page 455)*

the issue number. Place a semicolon between the year of publication and the volume number. Put the issue number in parentheses. Note that there are no spaces separating the year, the volume number, and the issue number.

Newspapers. Place the year, month, and day of publication (if any) after the name of the newspaper.

New York Times. 2009 Aug 1

Page Numbers

Books. Page numbers are not always required, so ask your instructor for guidance. If page numbers are required, provide the total number of pages, excluding preliminary pages with roman numerals, when you are citing an entire book. Use the abbreviation *p* for *pages*: 431 p. If you have used only part of a book, list just the pages used: p. 136–154.

Journals and magazines. Page numbers should be expressed as a range: 237–245 or 430–434.

Newspapers. Include the section letter, the page number, and the column number: Sect. A:2 (col. 1).

Electronic Sources

Entries for electronic sources are similar to those for books and articles; however, they include three additional pieces of information:

1. The word *Internet* is placed in square brackets after the title of the book or the name of the journal to indicate that the work is an online source. If you are not using an Internet-based electronic source, indicate the medium of the source: [CD-ROM] or [disk].

2. The date of access, preceded by the word *cited*, is given in square brackets after the date of publication.

3. The Internet address (URL) is included at the end of the entry. If the Internet address is excessively long, provide the URL for a main page, such as a table of contents, and instruct the reader to click on a link. (See example 11 on page 459.)

Ollerton J, Johnson SD, Cranmer L, Kellie S. The pollination ecology of an assemblage of grassland asclepiads in South Africa. Ann Bot [Internet]. 2003 [cited 2005 May 13]; 92(6): 807–834. Available from: http://aob.oupjournals.org/cgi/content/full/92/6/807

See page 459 for other examples.

BOOKS

1. Book with one author

Citation-sequence or citation-name system

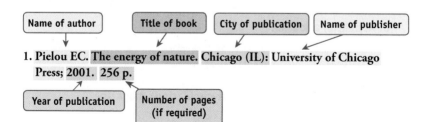

| Name of author | Title of book | City of publication | Name of publisher |

1. Pielou EC. The energy of nature. Chicago (IL): University of Chicago Press; 2001. 256 p.

| Year of publication | Number of pages (if required) |

Name-year system

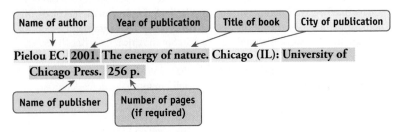

Pielou EC. 2001. The energy of nature. Chicago (IL): University of Chicago Press. 256 p.

2. Book with two or more authors

2. McPherson GR, DeStefano S. Applied ecology and natural resource management. Cambridge (GB): Cambridge University Press; 2002.

3. Book with an organization (or organizations) listed as author

3. Seattle Times. Natural wonders: the flora, fauna & formations of Washington. Seattle (WA): Seattle Times; 2003.

4. Book with editor(s)

4. Lund B, Hunter P, editors. The microbiological safety of food in healthcare settings. Malden (MA): Blackwell; 2007.

5. Chapter or part of an edited book

5. Martin DJ. Social data. In: Wilson J, Fotheringham AS, editors. The handbook of geographic information science. Malden (MA): Blackwell; 2008. p. 35–48.

ARTICLES

6. Article in a journal

6. Milad MR, Quirk GJ. Neurons in medial prefrontal cortex signal memory for fear extinction. Nature. 2002;420(6911):70–73.

7. Article in a popular (general-circulation) magazine

7. McKibben B. Carbon's new math. Natl Geogr Mag. 2007;212(4):33–37.

8. Article in a newspaper

8. O'Connor A. Heart attack risk linked to time spent in traffic. New York Times. 2004 Oct 26;Sect. F:9 (col. 4).

ELECTRONIC SOURCES

9. Online book

9. Committee on Planetary and Lunar Exploration. National Research Council. The quarantine and certification of Martian samples [Internet]. Washington (DC): National Academy Press; 2002 [cited 2007 Oct 31]. Available from: http://www.nap.edu/openbook.php?isbn=0309075718

10. Article in an online journal

10. Miller MR, White A, Boots M. Host life span and the evolution of resistance characteristics. Evol [Internet]. 2007 [cited 2007 Oct 31]; 61(1):2–14. Available from: http://www.blackwell-synergy.com/doi/full/10.1111/j.1558–5646.2007.00001.x

11. Article in an online magazine

11. Shermer M. Weirdonomics and quirkology: how the curious science of the oddities of everyday life yields new insights. Sci Am [Internet]. 2007 [cited 2007 Nov 1]; 1297(5):45. Available from: http://www.sciam.com/issue.cfm after clicking on the article link.

12. Article in an online newspaper

12. Forero J. As Andean glaciers shrink, water worries grow. New York Times on the Web [Internet]. 2002 Nov 23 [cited 2002 Dec 7]; [2 p.]. Available from: http://www.nytimes.com/2002/11/24/international/americas/24BOLI.html?pagewanted51

13. Web site

13. Corvus corax [Internet]. Bay Shore (NY): Long Island Ravens MC; c2000–2002 [updated 2001 Dec 3; cited 2003 Jan 3]. Available from: http://www.liravensmc.org/About/about_ravens.htm

14. Database

14. Honey Bee Genome Project [Internet]. Houston (TX): Baylor College of Medicine. [date unknown] -   [updated 2005 Jan 27; cited 2007 Nov 1]. Available from: http://www.hgsc.bcm.tmc.edu/projects/honeybee/

If you do not know the date of publication, place the words *date unknown* (not italicized) in square brackets; then add a space, a hyphen, and three more spaces.

Name-year system

The following sample entries for a reference list in the name-year format correspond to those listed in the section on the citation-sequence or citation-name system. The individual entries for books and articles differ from those in the citation-sequence and citation-name formats only in the placement of the date. In the name-year system, the date follows the author's name. Because the CSE manual provides only one format for online sources, the entries for these sources are not repeated in this list. For more samples of end references, see pages 465–466.

References

Lund B, Hunter P, editors. 2007. The microbiological safety of food in healthcare settings. Malden (MA): Blackwell.

Martin DJ. 2008. Social data. In: Wilson J, Fotheringham AS, editors. The handbook of geographic information science. Malden (MA): Blackwell. p. 35–48.

McKibben B. 2007. Carbon's new math. Natl Geogr Mag. 212(4):33–37.

McPherson GR, DeStefano S. 2002. Applied ecology and natural resource management. Cambridge (GB): Cambridge University Press.

Milad MR, Quirk GJ. 2002. Neurons in medial prefrontal cortex signal memory for fear extinction. Nature. 420(6911):70–73.

O'Connor A. 2004 Oct 26. Heart attack risk linked to time spent in traffic. New York Times. Sect. F:9 (col. 4).

Pielou EC. 2001. The energy of nature. Chicago (IL): University of Chicago Press.

Seattle Times. 2003. Natural wonders: the flora, fauna & formations of Washington. Seattle (WA): Seattle Times.

19b Sample CSE-style paper

Papers written for courses in the natural sciences often report the results of a study. They are generally divided into six main sections: **abstract, introduction, methods and materials, results, discussion,** and **references.** Heather Jensen's lab report, "Observations and Calculations of Onion Root Tip Cells," follows this organization (see **18d**), as does Michelle Tebbe's report for a geology course. The following excerpts from Michelle's report, "Trace Element Distribution in Agate: Open Versus Closed System Formation," will help you understand how to format an abstract, an introduction, and a bibliography. Heather used the citation-sequence system for her paper (see pages 443–449). Michelle used the name-year system for hers. Because the CSE guidelines were not intended to be applied to undergraduate papers, you should follow your instructor's directions for formatting a title page similar to the one shown here.

Trace Element Distribution in Agate: Open Versus Closed Systems Formation

Michelle Tebbe

Geology 481: Advanced Mineralogy

January 14, 2008

1

Abstract

Agate is a silica-rich rock that preserves a record of ancient hydrology and water/rock interaction. However, there is little consensus on how agate forms. Two end-member formation models exist for agate hosted by basalt and are tested here by trace element investigation of agate samples from Brazil, Germany, and Washington, US.

[The abstract continues.]

2

Introduction

Agate is a semiprecious gemstone prized for millennia for its colors and complex patterns (Figure 1). The mining of agate has historically been a thriving industry in countries such as Germany and Scotland and continues to be so today in Brazil and Mexico, where agate is fashioned into objects of art and jewelry (Figure 2). Agate is also of interest to the geologist because it preserves a record of rock formation and may be one of the most striking examples of self-organization in geology.

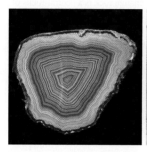

Fig. 1. Agate from Scurdie Ness, Scotland, illustrating the typical concentrically banded texture of most agate worldwide. Width of sample is 8 cm. Photo by Brian Jackson, Natural History Museum, Edinburgh.

Fig. 2. Agate forms part of the decorative base of these candlesticks by Julian Cross. The 46-cm-high candlesticks are displayed in the Small Dining Room at 10 Downing Street, London, the residence of the Prime Minister of Great Britain. Photo from the Silver Trust.

Agate is found in a large variety of rock types (Moxon and Reed 2006). In igneous rocks it is commonly found in joints and void space in both felsic and mafic volcanic rocks, as well as lavas and pyroclastic rocks of a large range in age. Agate is of use to the geologist because it records a wealth of

3

information on how minerals grow from solution, where crustal fluids come from, and how these fluids interact with rocks. Agate, like freshwater chert, may be an indicator of ancient climate and hydrologic conditions (Abruzzese et al. 2005). Agate also records information on how natural systems self-organize to generate periodic and ordered structures and textures (Ortoleva et al. 1987; Merino et al. 1995). Agate is of scientific interest not only because of self-organization but because of, more generally, its preservation of a historical record of the rock in which it is found. Understanding the processes that form and change rock is a central focus of the discipline of geology.

[The introduction continues and is followed by the remainder of the paper.]

9

References

Abruzzese MJ, Waldbauer JR, Chamberlain, CP. 2005. Oxygen and hydrogen isotope ratios in freshwater chert as indicators of ancient climate and hydrologic regime. Geochim Cosmochim. 69(6):1377–1390.

Bryxina NA, Halden NM, Ripinen OI. 2002. Oscillatory zoning in an agate from Kazakhstan: autocorrelation function and fractal statistics of trace element distributions. Math Geol. 34(8):915–927.

Friedman I, O'Neil JR. 1977. Compilation of stable isotope fractionation factors of geochemical interest. In: Fleischer M, editor. Data of geochemistry. 6th ed. Reston (VA): United States Geological Survey.

Gilg HA, Morteani G, Kostitsyn Y, Preinfalk C, Gatter I, Strieder AJ. 2003. Genesis of amethyst geodes in basaltic rocks of the Serra Geral Formation (Ametista do Sul, Rio Grande do Sul, Brazil): a fluid inclusion, REE, oxygen, carbon, and Sr isotope study on basalt, quartz, and calcite. Miner Deposita. 38(8):1009–1025.

Götze J, Tichomirowa M, Fuchs H, Pilot J, Sharp, ZD. 2001. Geochemistry of agates: a trace element and stable isotope study. Chem Geol. 175(3–4):523–541.

Hamilton A. 2002. Relative ages and timing of deformation of the Manastash and Taneum formations in Kittitas County, Central Washington [senior thesis]. [Ellensburg (WA)]: Central Washington University.

Merino E, Wang Y. 2001. Geochemical self-organization in rocks: occurrences, observations, modeling, testing—with emphasis on agate genesis. In: Krug HJ, Kruhl, JH, editors. Nonequilibrium processes and dissipative structures in geoscience. Berlin (GR): Drucker & Humboldt. p. 13–45.

10

Merino E, Wang Y, Deloule E. 1995. Genesis of agates in flood basalts: twisting of chalcedony fibers and trace element geochemistry. Am J Sci. 295(9):1156–1176.

Moxon, T, Reed, SJB. 2006. Agate and chalcedony from igneous and sedimentary hosts aged from 13 to 3480 Ma: a cathodoluminescence study. Mineral Mag. 70(5):485–498.

Moxon, T, Ríos, S. 2004. Moganite and water content as a function of age in agate: an XRD and thermogravimetric study. Eur J Mineral. 16(2): 269–278.

[The reference list continues.]

20 Writing in Business

Writing in business requires the same attention to audience, purpose, and context as writing in any other situation or discipline. However, the nature of authorship differs: although you are the writer, you must project both your own image and that of your employer as credible and reliable. To do so, you need to follow the conventions and formats expected by the business community.

If you take business courses, you will receive a variety of writing assignments: letters, memos and e-mails, business plans, PowerPoint presentations, oral reports, and business reports are some of the more common. To complete such assignments successfully, you must start by analyzing the rhetorical situation. Figure 20.1 illustrates the elements of the rhetorical situation for "The Day the E-mail Dies," one of the articles used by the student preparing the business report discussed later in this chapter. This chapter will help you

- recognize the stylistic conventions of standard business writing (20a),
- draft a business letter (20b),
- produce business memos and e-mails (20c),
- compose a résumé (20d) and a letter of application (20e),
- develop a business plan (20f),
- prepare an oral report including a PowerPoint presentation (20g), and
- research and write a formal business report (20h).

20a Conventions of language and organization

Whether you are writing on a screen or on paper, preparing a memo or a business plan, you will need to meet deadlines—both anticipated and unexpected ones. The strategies presented in the following box will

Exigence: Uncertainty about how best to make use of new media for communicating in business environments

Writer: Marlon A. Walker, staff reporter at the *Wall Street Journal*

Audience: Business professionals interested in improving their own or their companies' communication practices

Message: E-mail is not always the most effective medium and is generally overused.

Context: Changing attitudes and understandings of the benefits and drawbacks of e-mail

Fig. 20.1. Sample rhetorical situation for business writing.

help you produce comprehensive, concise, and well-organized documents on time, by introducing you to some of the stylistic characteristics of effective business communication.

STRATEGIES FOR EFFECTIVE BUSINESS COMMUNICATION

Be direct.

- Know who your audience is and consider their needs.
- State the purpose of your document in your opening sentence or paragraph.

- Write straightforward sentences, beginning with a subject and an active verb (27d(2)).
- Use technical language sparingly, unless the document is intended for a specialized audience (34c(4)).

Be concise.

- Compose direct sentences that are neither too long nor too complicated.
- Include only necessary details.
- Use numbers, bullets, or descriptive headings that help readers locate information easily.
- Use graphs, tables, and other visual elements that convey information succinctly.

Use conventional formatting.

- Follow the standard formats developed for your type of business or company, or use those outlined in this chapter (20b–f).
- Avoid using informal language, unless you know that a casual tone is acceptable.
- Edit carefully for errors; typos, grammatical mistakes, sentence fragments, and missing words detract significantly from your ethos as a businessperson and as a representative of your employer.

20b Business letters

Business letters serve a variety of purposes—to inquire, to inform, to complain, to respond. (For letters of application, see 20e.) Regardless of its purpose, a business letter usually fits on a single sheet of paper, single-spaced. It also follows a standard block format: each element is typed flush with the left margin, with double spacing between paragraphs.

ELEMENTS OF A STANDARD BUSINESS LETTER

- **Return address.** Your employer may require you to use letterhead stationery. If not, type your mailing address one inch from the top of the paper, flush left on a one-inch margin, and single-spaced.

■ **Date.** Type the date beneath your return address. If you are using letter-head stationery, type the date one or two lines below the letterhead's last line.

■ **Recipient's name and address.** Provide the full name and address of the recipient. Single-space these lines, and allow an extra line space above them. If you do not know the person's name, try to find it by checking the company's Web site or phoning the company. If you cannot find the recipient's name, use an appropriate title such as *Personnel Director* or *Customer Service Manager* (not italicized).

■ **Greeting.** Type your greeting two lines below the last line of the recipient's address. The conventional greeting is *Dear* _____ (not italicized) followed by a colon. If you and the recipient use first names to address each other, use the person's first name. Otherwise, use *Mr., Ms., Mrs.,* or *Miss* and the last name. (Choose *Ms.* when you do not know a woman's preference.) Avoid the sexist *Dear Sir, Gentlemen,* or *Dear Madam* and the stilted *To Whom It May Concern* or *Dear Sir or Madam*.

■ **Body of the letter.** Begin the first paragraph two lines below the greeting. Single-space lines within a paragraph; double-space between paragraphs. If your letter must continue on a second page, include the recipient's last name, the date, and the page number in three single-spaced lines at the top left on the second page.

■ **Closing.** Close your letter two lines after the end of the body with an expression such as *Sincerely* or *Cordially* (not italicized) followed by a comma.

■ **Signature.** Type your full name four lines below the closing. Then, in the space above your typed name, sign your full name, using blue or black ink. If you have addressed the recipient by his or her first name, sign just your first name.

■ **Additional information.** If you are enclosing extra material such as a résumé, type the word *Enclosure* or the abbreviation *Encl.* (not italicized) two lines below your name. You may also note the number of enclosures or the identity of the document(s): for example, *Enclosures (3)* or *Encl.: 2002 Annual Year-End Report*. If you would like the recipient to know the names of people receiving copies of the letter, use the abbreviation *cc* (for "carbon copy") and a colon followed by the other recipients' names. Place this element on the line directly below the enclosure line or, if there is no enclosure, two lines below your name.

The sample **letter of inquiry** (a letter intended to elicit information) on the next page illustrates the parts of a typical business letter.

Letter of inquiry

550 First Avenue
Ellensburg, WA 98926
February 4, 2004

Mr. Mark Russell
Bilingual Publications
5400 Sage Avenue
Yakima, WA 98907

Dear Mr. Russell:

I am a junior in the Bilingual Education Program at Central Washington
University. For my coursework, I am investigating positions in publishing that
include the use of two languages. Your name and address were given to me by
my instructor, Marta Cole, who worked for you from 1999 through 2004.

I have learned something about your publications on your Web site. I am
most interested in dual documents—one in English and one in Spanish.
Could you please send me samples of such documents so that I can have a
better idea of the types of publications you produce?

I am also interested in finding out what qualifications I would need to
work for a business like yours. I am fluent in both Spanish and English and
have taken a course in translation. If possible, I would like to ask you a few
questions about your training and experience. Would you have time for an
interview some day next week?

Sincerely,

Chris Humphrey

Chris Humphrey

*Return address
and date*

*Name and
address of
recipient*

Greeting

Body of letter

Closing

Signature

20c Business memos and e-mails

A **memo** (short for *memorandum*) is a brief document sent within a business to announce a meeting, set a schedule, or request information or action. E-mail is also used for these purposes as well as for external communication with clients, prospective employees, or other companies. The basic guidelines for writing memos also apply to e-mail messages.

Because it is circulated internally, a memo or e-mail is usually less formal than a letter, but it should still be direct and concise—a memo should be no longer than a page, and an e-mail no longer than a screen. The following guidelines for formatting these kinds of documents are fairly standard, but note that a particular company or organization may establish its own format.

ELEMENTS OF A STANDARD BUSINESS MEMO OR E-MAIL

- **Heading.** On four consecutive lines, type *To* (not italicized) followed by a colon and the name(s) of the recipient(s), *From* followed by a colon and your name and title (if appropriate), *Date* followed by a colon and the date, and *Subject* followed by a colon and a few words identifying the memo's subject. (The abbreviation *Re*, for "regarding," is sometimes used instead of *Subject*.) This information should be single-spaced. If you are sending copies to individuals whose names are not included in the *To* line, place those names on a new line beginning with *cc* ("carbon copy") and a colon. Most e-mail software supplies these header lines on any new message.

- **Body.** Use the block format (**20b**), single-spacing lines within each paragraph and double-spacing between paragraphs. Double-space between the heading and the body of the memo.

Business memo

To: Intellectual Properties Committee
From: Leo Renfrow, Chair of Intellectual Properties Committee
Date: March 15, 2007
Subject: Review of Policy Statement

Heading

At the end of our last meeting, we decided to have our policy statement reviewed by someone outside our university. Clark Beech, chair of the Intellectual Properties Committee at Lincoln College, agreed to help us. Overall, as his review shows, the format of our policy statement is sound. Dr. Beech believes that some of the content should be further developed, however. It appears that we have used some ambiguous terms and included some conditions that would not hold up in court.

Body of memo

Early next week, my assistant will deliver a copy of Dr. Beech's review to each of you. Please look it over by our next meeting, on March 29. If you have any questions or comments before then, please call me at ext. 1540.

The effectiveness of memos and e-mails depends on several characteristics, especially tone, length, and directness.

Although ease and speed are hallmarks of e-mailing, these same features can compromise a sender's ability to establish a fitting tone, an essential element of effective communication. A conversational tone may be acceptable for a message to a co-worker asking about a deadline, but a professional tone is required for a memo or an e-mail to a supervisor or a group. To enhance your ethos as a professional, create a signature line for your e-mails that identifies yourself and your institution or company. Consider the content of a message, especially anything that the sender might prefer to keep private, before forwarding it to others. When in doubt, seek the sender's permission before forwarding a message. Also keep in mind that anything you send in an e-mail can easily be forwarded. (For information on writing to multiple audiences, see **1d**). Finally, unless you are sure that recipients will welcome chain letters, petitions, and jokes, do not send them.

Lengthiness can detract from the effectiveness of your memos and e-mails. Keep such messages to one rhetorical unit: one page for a memo, one screen (or twenty lines) for an e-mail. Because people tend to read only one rhetorical unit, you will want to compose a message that fits on a single screen or page yet has the white space necessary for easy reading.

Because most regular users of e-mail receive a large volume of messages, they have become used to scanning the messages and quickly responding to or deleting them. Announcing your topic in the subject line and then arranging and presenting it in concise, readable chunks help ensure that recipients do not overlook important information. Short paragraphs also provide more white space, which helps readers to maintain attention and absorb the key points.

 CAUTION

E-mail that you send from or receive at your workplace is not necessarily private or secure. Employers have been vindicated in cases where they were charged with privacy violations for reading employees' e-mail. Be sure to check your employer's policy with regard to the use of e-mail. Avoid using your work e-mail for personal communications.

TIPS FOR SENDING ATTACHMENTS WITH E-MAIL MESSAGES

■ Before you send any attachment, consider the size of the file—many in-boxes have limited space and cannot accept or store large files that contain streaming video, photographs, or sound clips. If you want to send a file larger than 1000K or multiple files whose combined size is larger than that, call or e-mail your recipient first to ask permission. A large file could crash the recipient's e-mail program.

■ If you do not know the type of operating system or software installed on your recipient's computer, send text-only documents in rich text format (**.rtf**), which preserves most formatting and is recognized by many word-processing programs.

■ Because attachments are notorious for transmitting computer viruses, never open an attachment sent by someone you do not know. Before opening an attachment, make sure that you are working on a computer with antivirus software that scans all incoming files for viruses. Check Web sites such as www.symantec.com for updates on viruses. You can also get virus-related updates and alerts on the Web site of the manufacturer of your computer or software.

20d Résumés

A **résumé** is essentially an argument (chapter 8) designed to emphasize a person's job qualifications by highlighting his or her experience and abilities. Along with its accompanying letter of application (20e), a résumé should command attention and establish a positive first impression. If you create and save your résumé as a word-processing file, you can easily tailor it for each position you seek.

Writing a strong résumé requires smart choices about what to include, what to exclude, and what to emphasize. The first step in writing a résumé is listing your current and past employment as well as your relevant educational background and extracurricular activities. You will want to emphasize the latter if you have little actual work experience. If you have sufficient relevant work experience, information about extracurricular activities is generally considered superfluous. Be sure to include dates, job titles, and responsibilities. Once you have listed potentially relevant information, decide what to exclude, include, and emphasize by reviewing what the job advertisement says about desired experience and traits. To familiarize yourself with a company's goals and philosophy, check its Web site.

The next step is to decide how to organize your résumé. A **chronological résumé** lists positions and activities in *reverse* chronological order; that is, your most recent experience comes first. This format works well if you have a steady job history and want to emphasize your most recent experience because it is closely related to the position for which you are applying. An alternative way to organize a résumé is to list experience in terms of job skills rather than jobs held. This format, called a **functional résumé,** is especially useful when you have the required skills but your work history in the particular field is modest or you are just starting your career.

TECH SAVVY

When you are ready to create your résumé, you may find it helpful to use a software program (such as Resume Wizard from Microsoft) that allows you to select the kind of résumé you need and then prompts you to complete the various sections. Such software also allows you to view your completed document in its entirety and redesign any or all of it. Some job applicants create **online résumés**, Web-based versions that may include links to documents representative of the applicants' work. In addition, they create non-Web versions that can be downloaded and printed out or scanned into a résumé database. If a job advertisement instructs you to e-mail your résumé directly, you will want to send both a Web-based résumé and the non-Web version (in case the recipient wants to print it out for any reason).

Regardless of the format you choose, remember that your résumé is, in effect, going to someone's office for a job interview. Make sure that it is dressed for success. Whenever possible, design the résumé to fit on a single page. Use good-quality paper (preferably white or off-white) and a laser printer. Choose a format and make sure to apply it consistently throughout. Use boldface or italic type for headings. Remember that your choices regarding indentations, spacing, fonts, and margins help to shape the overall readability and effectiveness of your résumé. Resist the impulse to make the design unnecessarily complicated, however. When in doubt, opt for simplicity.

Joe Delaney's résumé incorporates features of both the chronological and the functional formats. He starts with his education, then proceeds to a description of his computer skills, clubs, and activities because those skills and experiences relate directly to the position he is applying for, much more so than his library job, which he lists later.

Sample résumé

Joseph F. Delaney III

138 Main Street, Apt 10D

Cityville, PA 16800

(555) 544-9988

JoeDel4@psu.edu

Objective   To obtain a position specializing in project and risk management

Education

Pennsylvania State University, University Park, PA, 2003–2007

Majors: IST B.S. (Information Context Option),

   Psychology B.S. (Quantitative Option)

Dean's List: Summer 2006, Fall 2006, and Spring 2007

Cumulative G.P.A.: 3.60

Relevant Classes:

- Project Management in Technology — dealt with the application of basic concepts, methodologies, and tools of project management in the field of information sciences and technology

- Database Management — managed a project team that applied MySql, PHP, and HTML in completing Rabble Mosaic Creator, which is described at www.schoolproject.psu.edu/~100

Computer and Technical Skills

- MySql, PHP, GD Library, C++ (2 years experience), Java (1 year experience)

- TCP/IP, network security, LANs and WANs
- HTML, XML, and project and risk management

Clubs/Activities

IST Student Government:

- Active and voting member of my college's student government
- Regular participation in the student government's Academic Committee
- Student resource for the IST Student Executive Board

IST Academic Committee:

- Participated in regularly scheduled meetings with the dean, Henry C. Foley, and the professor in charge, John Yen
- Worked with the administration to address students' problems

Work Experience

Penn State Pollock Library, University Park, PA, May–July 2006

- Assisted patrons of the library in using computers, printers, and the Internet via a wireless network using VPN
- Coordinated computers in my designated area and assisted with defragmenting, rebooting, reformatting, charging, and normal maintenance of laptops

Honors

- 2005 scholarship student in the College of IST; recipient of the Cingular Wireless Trustee Scholarship
- Pollock Library 2004 student employee of the year

TIPS FOR RÉSUMÉ WRITING

- Include your name, address, telephone number, and an e-mail address or fax number, if available.

- Identify your career or job objective simply, without elaborating on future goals. If you do not feel that you have such an objective, do not mention one in the résumé. Communicating a career objective in a compelling way is a challenge, and a résumé can be effective without one. You can provide details about your future plans when you are asked about them during an interview.

- Whenever possible, establish a clear relationship between jobs you have had and the job you are seeking. Offer detailed explanations of the tasks and responsibilities in each of your jobs that most closely correspond with the position you seek.

- List your college or university degree and any pertinent areas in which you have had special training. Decide what details about your education best show your qualifications for the job at hand. Consider including your GPA (your overall GPA or your GPA in your major, whichever is more impressive), particular coursework (list specific classes or note areas of specialization, such as twenty hours of coursework in accounting), and relevant class projects.

- Do not include personal data such as age, marital status, race, religion, or ethnicity.

- Even if an advertisement or posting asks you to state a salary requirement, any mention of salary is usually deferred until an interview.

- The names and addresses of **references** (people who have agreed to speak or write on your behalf) are not usually listed on a résumé, though you may want to mention that references are available on request. Instead, job candidates are advised to take a list of references to interviews. Make sure that the individuals on your list understand the nature of the position you are seeking. The list should include their names and addresses as well as their telephone numbers and/or e-mail addresses.

- To show that you are well organized and thoughtful, use a clean, clear format (see pages 477–478).

- Meticulously proofread your résumé before sending it and have others read it carefully as well. Errors in business writing always detract from your credibility, but errors in a résumé or letter of application (20e) can ruin your chances of getting an interview.

20e Letters of application

Writing a letter of application, or cover letter, is an essential step in applying for a job. Because this letter usually accompanies a résumé (**20d**), it is crucial that it do more than simply repeat information that can be found in the résumé. Otherwise, you risk boring or irritating your reader. Your letter of application provides you with the chance to sound articulate, interesting, and professional, and to put a personal face on the factual content of the résumé—in other words, to make a good first impression.

In your opening paragraph, identify the position you are applying for, explain how you learned about it, and—in a single sentence—state why you believe you are qualified to fill it. This statement serves as the thesis for the rest of the letter. In the paragraphs that follow, describe the experience and abilities that qualify you for the job. Generally, two body paragraphs follow the introductory paragraph: one describing relevant education, the other relevant work experience. (Many applicants find that their education and their work experience are not equally pertinent to the job at hand. In that case, you might use these two paragraphs to describe two particular course projects or two particular jobs.) In your closing paragraph, offer any additional useful information and make a direct request for an interview.

Letters of application follow the general format of all business letters (**20b**).

Model letter of application

Joseph F. Delaney III
138 Main Street, Apt 10D
Cityville, PA 16800
June 4, 2007

Return address and date

Mr. Jim Konigs, Human Resource Director
E. G. Hickey Technical Enterprise
333 Cumberville State Road, Suite 110
West Cumberville, PA 19428-2949

Name and address of recipient

Dear Mr. Konigs:

Greeting

I am applying for the position of project manager advertised on Monster.com. I graduated on May 15 with a B.S. degree in information sciences and technology from Pennsylvania State University. I believe that my in-depth research and education in information technology make me an ideal candidate for this position.

Body of letter

I have completed the required coursework and an internship in information technology, consulting, and security, working under such distinguished professors as James Wendle and David Markison. I am currently a teaching instructor with Dr. Markison, responsible for student evaluation and advising. I have served as a project team leader in database management; my team created Rabble Mosaic Creator, a Web site that allows users to create mosaics out of images.

In addition to my studies, I have applicable experience as a member of the student government's Academic Committee, which manages students' problems through policy and hands-on work before presenting the issues to the dean and professor in charge. I have also worked in the Penn State libraries.

I would appreciate the opportunity to talk with you about the position and my interest in risk and project management. I am available for an interview and can be reached at the phone number or e-mail address at the top of my résumé.

Sincerely,

Closing

Joseph F. Delaney

Signature

Joseph F. Delaney III

Encl.: résumé

Enclosure line

TIPS FOR WRITING LETTERS OF APPLICATION

- Address your letter to a specific person. If you are responding to an ad that mentions a department without giving a name, call the company and find out who will be doing the screening. If you cannot obtain a specific name, use an appropriate title such as *Human Resource Director* (not italicized).

- Be brief. You can assume that the recipient will be screening many applications, so keep your letter to one page.

- Mention that you are enclosing a résumé or refer to it, but do not summarize it. Keep in mind that your goal is to get a busy person (who will not want to read the same information twice) to look at your résumé.

- Indicate why you are interested in working for the company or organization to which you are applying. Demonstrating that you already know something about the company and the position will show that you are a serious and motivated candidate. Extensive information on most companies is available in their annual reports. You can also find information by searching the Web (**9d**).

- In your closing, be sure to specify how and where you can be reached and emphasize your general availability for an interview.

20f   Business plans

Business plans have three main purposes: (1) to ensure that the writer of the plan has considered all the potential risks as well as benefits of the business venture, (2) to persuade lenders and potential investors that their money will be safely invested because the writer has planned realistically and has sufficient expertise, and (3) to help the new business stay on track during its early development. To fulfill these purposes adequately, a business plan should be well researched, clearly written, and complete—that is, it should provide all the information a loan officer or investor might need.

ELEMENTS OF A BUSINESS PLAN

- **Cover page.** Include the name and address of the business.
- **Table of contents.**

- **Executive summary.** State briefly the objectives of the business and describe the business. Indicate who will own the business and under what form of ownership (partnership, corporation, or sole proprietorship). Finally, explain why the business will be successful. Write the summary *after* you have completed the following sections.

- **Business overview.** Identify the kind of business you are planning to start up (service or retail), explain why the business is distinctive, and briefly describe its market.

- **Market.** Characterize the market—its size and potential for growth and the typical customers. Describe how the business will attract customers—through advertising, pricing, product quality, and/or services.

- **Business location.** Discuss lease or sale terms, the need for and costs of renovation, and features of the neighborhood.

- **Licenses and permits.** Explain what kinds of licenses and permits must be obtained and whether the business name is registered.

- **Management.** Include information about managers' experience and education, the organizational structure, proposed salaries and wages, and any other pertinent management resources (accountant, attorney, and so on).

- **Personnel.** List the personnel needed—full-time or part-time, skilled or un-skilled—and explain whether training will be required and how it will be provided.

- **Insurance.** Describe insurance needs and potential risks.

- **Competition.** Analyze competitors, and describe how the business addresses a market need.

- **Financial data.** Include a current balance sheet and income statement and projected (or actual) income statements by month and quarter for two years as well as cash flow and balance sheet projections.

- **Supporting documents.** Include résumés, financial statements, and letters of reference for the owner(s) as well as letters of intent from suppliers, leases, contracts, deeds, and other legal documents.

For an assignment requiring them to design and start their own business, Emily Cohen and her group started a business called Posters Ink, through which college students in the Boston area could create their own posters from a collage of existing pictures and documents. Three brief excerpts from the group's business plan follow, providing examples of a market analysis, description of management responsibilitites, and projected financial plan for the first six weeks.

5

III. Market

The introduction to the Market section of the Posters Ink business plan

In the company's short selling period, the target market must be made aware of the product and the promotions that Posters Ink will offer. Posters Ink's target market consists mainly of college students who attend Babson College, Boston University, Boston College, Northeastern University, and Wellesley College. Posters Ink will attempt to reach friends and family members of these college students as well as Wellesley high school students. This provides the company with a target market of about 64,000. The plan is to reach 1 percent of this target market.

There is no direct competition that offers the same one-of-a-kind collage option that Posters Ink offers its customers. Similar products can be produced by several online photo programs such as Webshots, PhotoMix, and 111 Print. They offer options such as enlarging pictures, lining the pictures up on a poster, and online scrapbooking, all of which are different from Posters Ink's main collage option. Our product is also convenient because people with enough computer skills to create their own digital picture collage will no longer need to lay out their own photos or take them to a print shop.

7

VI. Management

Company Job Descriptions for Posters Ink

Division/Department: CEO

Reports to: Board of Directors

Summary: As the leader of the business, the CEO will coordinate and motivate staff, manage the business, and troubleshoot.

Primary Responsibilities:

1. Ensure that the needs of employees are in accord with the needs of the organization as a whole
2. Act as a spokesperson to inform others of the progress of the business
3. Find both problems and opportunities and come up with the ways to deal with them
4. Approve all major actions of the business
5. Oversee the day-to-day functions of the business
6. Develop an interpersonal relationship with employees through motivation and definition of achievable goals
7. Preside at board meetings
8. Sign all contracts relating to the business
9. Be available to important clients
10. Be present at any negotiations involving an agreement or contract with another organization
11. Report to the Board of Directors regularly
12. Receive reports from the business managers
13. Analyze reports and provide feedback
14. Schedule and oversee staff meetings as well as managers' meetings

The first portion of the Management section of the Posters Ink business plan

Posters Ink Cash Budget (Weeks 1–6)

Outline for the first six weeks' income and expenses, from the Finances section of the business plan

	Week 1 1/29/2007	Week 2 2/5/2007	Week 3 2/12/2007	Week 4 2/19/2007	Week 5 2/26/2007	Week 6 3/5/2007
Beginning Cash Balance	193.75	0.00	361.87	530.21	499.17	348.33
Receipts						
Sales— Small Posters	494.09	411.75	219.60	137.25	109.80	164.70
Sales— Large Posters	469.39	391.16	208.62	130.39	104.31	156.46
Sales— Foam Posters	271.75	226.46	120.78	75.49	60.39	90.58
Total Receipts	$1235.24	$1029.36	$548.99	$343.12	$274.50	$411.75
Cash Available	1428.99	1029.36	910.87	873.33	773.66	760.8
Disbursements						
Inventory Purchases						
Small Purchases	313.71	261.43	139.43	87.14	69.71	104.57
Large Purchases	223.52	186.27	99.34	62.09	49.67	74.51
Foam Purchases	161.76	134.80	71.89	44.93	35.95	53.92
Rent Expense	0.00	0.00	0.00	0.00	100.00	0.00
Website Expense	380.00	30.00	15.00	15.00	15.00	15.00
Advertising Expense	125.00	30.00	30.00	30.00	30.00	30.00
Phone Expense	0.00	0.00	0.00	10.00	0.00	0.00
Supplies Expense	200.00	0.00	0.00	100.00	0.00	0.00
Entertainment Expense	0.00	0.00	0.00	0.00	100.00	0.00
Sales Tax	0.00	0.00	0.00	0.00	0.00	0.00
Miscellaneous Expense	25.00	25.00	25.00	25.00	25.00	25.00
Total Disbursed	$1428.99	$667.49	$380.66	$374.16	$425.33	$303.00

20g Oral presentations with PowerPoint

Oral reports accompanied by PowerPoint presentations are common-place in business. Such reports can be either internal (for supervisors and colleagues) or external (for clients or investors). They may take the form of project status reports, demonstrations of new equipment or software, research reports, or recommendations.

ELEMENTS OF A STANDARD ORAL PRESENTATION

- **Introduction.** Taking no more than one-tenth of your overall presentation time (for example, one minute of a ten-minute presentation), your introduction should indicate who you are, your qualifications, your topic, and the relevance of that topic to your audience. The introduction provides an outline of your main points so that listeners can easily follow your presentation.

- **Body.** Make sure the organization of your presentation is clear through your use of transitions. You can number each point (first, second, third, and so on) and use cause-and-consequence transitions (*therefore, since, due to*) and chronological transitions (*before, following, next, then*). Provide internal summaries to remind your listeners where you have been and where you are going as well as comments to help your audience sense the weight of various points (for example, "Not many people realize that . . ." or "The most important thing I have to share is . . . ").

- **Conclusion.** Anyone can simply restate the main ideas in the conclusion to an oral presentation; you will want to consider ways to make your conclusion memorable. To do so, you may want to end with a proposal for action, a final statistic, recommendations, or a description of the benefits of a certain course of action. In general, conclusions should be even shorter than introductions.

Keep in mind the following guidelines as you create PowerPoint slides to accompany an oral report.

TIPS FOR INCORPORATING POWERPOINT INTO AN ORAL PRESENTATION

- Design your slides for your audience, not for yourself. If you need speaking notes for your talk, write them on notecards or type them into the notes section provided below each slide in the PowerPoint program.

- Use text and visuals on the PowerPoint slides that complement the oral part of your presentation not repeat what you have said. If your listeners realize that everything you are saying is on the slide, they will skim each slide and then become bored listening to you catch up.

- Be aware of the limitations of PowerPoint. For example, PowerPoint slides do not accommodate large amounts of text. In general, use no more than five lines of text per slide. The text font should be sized at 14 to 16 points minimum. Because PowerPoint tends to encourage oversimplification of information, be sure to tell your audience whenever you had to simplify the information presented on a slide (for example, in order to fit time constraints) and let them know where they can find more details.

- In general, keep text and visuals separate. Alternating predominantly visual slides with slides of text will keep your audience's attention. Let visuals (charts, pictures, or graphs) stand alone with just a heading or a title. Use text slides to define terms, to present block quotes that might be difficult to follow orally, and to list the main points you will be making.

- Time your speaking with your presentation of the slides so that the two components are synchronized. Make sure to give your audience enough time to absorb complex visuals.

For their Posters Ink business plan, Emily Cohen and her group members created PowerPoint slides to accompany an oral presentation requesting funding. Figures 20.2 through 20.5 show a few of those slides.

MISSION STATEMENT

• Provide Boston area college students a home-like
  dorm atmosphere

• Offer students the opportunity to design posters

• Supply all 30 student workers with a structured
  business setting and entrepreneurial experience

Fig. 20.2. This mission statement uses the maximum amount of text recommended for a PowerPoint slide, but the bulleted list effectively presents the main goals of the company.

Fig. 20.3. This slide uses visuals to complement the spoken part of the presentation.

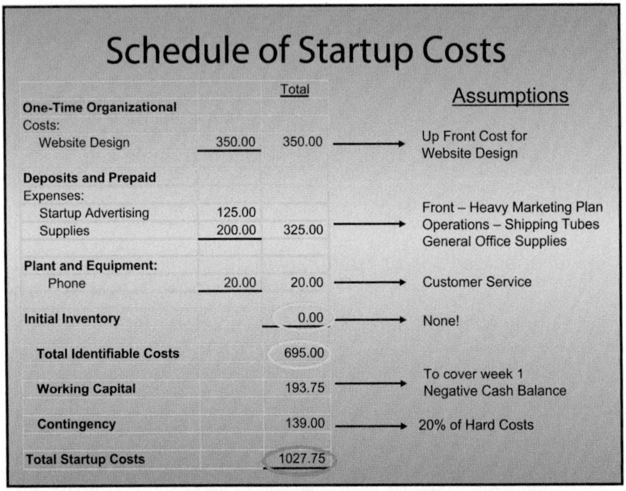

Fig. 20.4. This slide illustrates the versatility of PowerPoint, which allows a user to display a chart and add highlighting and comments on key parts.

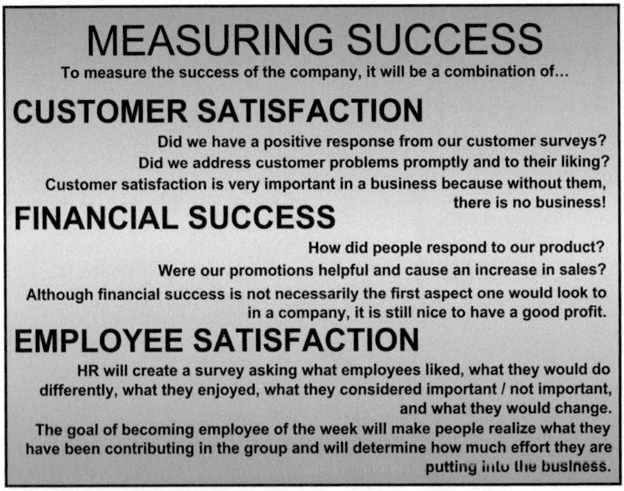

Fig. 20.5. This slide uses too much text and does not incorporate bullets or numbers to organize the text.

20h Business reports

Business reports take many forms: periodic reports, sales reports, progress reports, incident reports, and longer reports that assess relocation plans, new lines of equipment or products, marketing schemes, and so on. A sample business report, in which a student makes recommendations for changes in a business communication curriculum based on research into day-to-day business practices, follows the box describing elements of such reports.

ELEMENTS OF A STANDARD BUSINESS REPORT

- **Front matter.** Depending on the audience, purpose, and length of a given report, the front matter materials may include a letter of transmittal (explaining the relevance of the report), a title page, a table of contents, a list of illustrations, and/or an abstract.

- **Introduction.** This section should include background information, identification of the problem addressed by the report (the exigence), a purpose statement, and a description of the scope of the report (a list of the limits that framed the investigation). In a long report, each of these elements may be several paragraphs long, and some may have their own subheadings. An introduction should not take up more than ten to fifteen percent of a report.

- **Body or discussion.** This, the longest section of the report, presents the research findings. It often incorporates charts and graphs to help make the data user-friendly. This section should be subdivided into clear subsections by subheadings or, for a shorter report, paragraph breaks.

- **Conclusion(s).** This section summarizes any conclusions and generalizations deduced from the data presented in the body of the report.

- **Recommendation(s).** While not always necessary, a section that outlines for readers what should be done about the findings is included in many business reports.

- **Back matter.** Like the front matter, the back matter of a report depends on the audience, purpose, and length of the report. Back matter may include a glossary, references cited, and/or one or more appendixes.

Changing Forms of Business Communication:

Implications for Business Communication Curricula

Joseph F. Delaney III

Penn State University

June 11, 2007

2

Table of Contents

ABSTRACT 3

INTRODUCTION 3

Background 3

Problem 4

Purpose 5

Scope 5

DISCUSSION 5

Successful Business Communication 5

E-mail Overuse 8

Implementation of Communication Strategies 9

Personal Relationships 10

CONCLUSION 11

RECOMMENDATION 11

Overview of the Problem 11

Possible Solutions 11

Benefits 12

REFERENCES 13

Abstract

American businesses gain a competitive advantage in today's global economy by properly and effectively using various means of business communication. The use of different communication strategies in the workplace is essential to the success of businesses ranging from large corporations to on-campus student technology centers. Thus, any successful business education program must also prepare students to use and choose between the diverse media used for business communication today. This report discusses the strengths and weaknesses of different communication modes such as telephone, e-mail, and face-to-face communication, relying largely on an in-depth study of the Computer Store at Penn State University. Based on research and observations of staff, managers, and executives of the organization, the research team developed some strategies for successful business communication, in particular a critique of the overuse of e-mail in business settings. Finally, this report proposes changes to the business communication curriculum at Penn State University, in light of the team's research into real-world business communication practices.

Introduction

Background

Business communication is constantly evolving as technology provides new and better methods for communication. In the past two decades, e-mail, instant messaging, video conferencing, and cell phone technology have allowed business colleagues to cooperate with unparalleled efficiency. The number of e-mails sent daily in 2006 is estimated at around 62 billion. The International Data Corporation also reports 600 billion minutes of usage by mobile phone

4

users (Berkeley School of Information Management and Systems, 2003, p. 10).
However, these new methods have not replaced more traditional forms of
communication. The average office worker uses about 12,000 sheets of paper
per year. With so many options available, it is sometimes difficult to choose
the best option for the situation at hand. Furthermore, the range of options
for business communication necessitates changes to business communication
curricula.

Problem

In the world of modern business, it can be difficult to choose between
memos, telephone calls, voice mails, e-mails, meetings, and other modes of
communication. All too often employees choose a form of communication that
may not be properly suited to their purpose. More specifically, e-mail is easy to
use, but at the same time it leads to impersonal interactions between the sender
and the receiver. Many employees use e-mail when contacting individuals they are
not closely acquainted with, such as new clients. The problem with this strategy is
that, in business, building relationships and networking are valuable activities and
can increase productivity and quality throughout an organization.

Jeremy Burton, Vice-President of VERITAS Software Corporation
in Silicon Valley, like many other executives, has taken this issue to heart.
Burton banned e-mails on Fridays, imposing a small fine for each e-mail
sent. Though his 240 employees initially resisted the change, they began to
think more critically about their communication with others, and productivity
increased (Walker, 2004). The real problem, however, is that this kind of critical
thinking should be encouraged before employees reach the workforce. Business
communication skills like those that innovative employers like Burton are

5

teaching their employees should be addressed in college coursework, not just on the job. The research team believes that the Penn State College of Business is not currently addressing this need.

Purpose

The object of this report is to encourage the College of Business at Penn State to consider changes to the business communication curriculum. Specifically, this report examines a few major forms of communication, evaluates their strengths and weaknesses, and gives suggestions for when and how to use them effectively. This analysis shows that such topics need to be more thoroughly addressed in business classes at Penn State. The analysis is followed by a set of recommendations for the college.

Scope

This report includes a general analysis of various types of communication and their uses. A case study of communication practices at Penn State's Computer Store examines, in particular, e-mail overuse and some factors that may contribute to it. The report shows the value of employees who can properly identify appropriate communication strategies and media. The recommendations suggest the relevance and consequences of the findings for the business curriculum at Penn State.

Discussion

Successful Business Communication

Like those at many other contemporary businesses, the employees of the Computer Store at Penn State University use many forms of communication. As Robin Becker, the Director of Sales and Marketing, said, "There is no one ideal form of communication" (personal communication,

6

June 15, 2007). The Computer Store uses three effective forms of communication for communicating with clients, besides e-mail. During in-house technical consulting, employees assist students and parents in person as they purchase and learn to use a laptop. Second, consultants use telephones to advise individuals about purchasing laptops and accessories. The last medium, which has taken off recently, is the store's Web site. The Computer Store Web site has become a very useful tool for assisting people in their decision making and preparing them for computer ownership, and it complements the first two methods for communicating with clients. The site helps the meeting with a consultant run more smoothly, whether it takes place face to face or over the phone.

As for communication between the workers at the Computer Store, no one form is ideal. Figure 1 shows the different modes of communication and ranks them on their appropriateness for different day-to-day events. Generally, e-mail is used for follow-ups or quick notes. For other tasks, such as negotiating an agreement with a corporation to make its software available to all Penn State students, a face-to-face conference or a conference call is preferred. For passing quick notes and bits of information through the office in the Computer Store, Becker explains, e-mail or instant messaging works best (personal communication, June 15, 2007). James Murphy, the team leader for consultants, advised, "Use a mix [of communication], try not to limit yourself to one style, and try to cater to other people. If I need to get a lot of information across, I'll write a memo and send it via e-mail, but if I just need to get across one thing to one person, I will walk over there and tell that person face to face" (personal communication, June 15, 2007).

7

How Well Medium Is Suited to:	Hard Copy	Phone Call	Voice Mail	E-mail	Meeting	Web Site
Assessing commitment	3	2	3	3	1	3
Building consensus	3	2	3	3	1	3
Mediating a conflict	3	2	3	3	1	3
Resolving a misunderstanding	3	1	3	3	2	3
Addressing negative behavior	3	2	3	2	1	3
Expressing support/ appreciation	1	2	2	1	2	3
Encouraging creative thinking	2	3	3	1	3	3
Making an ironic statement	3	2	2	3	1	3
Conveying a reference document	1	3	3	3	3	2
Reinforcing one's authority	1	2	3	3	1	1
Providing a permanent record	1	3	3	1	3	3
Maintaining confidentiality	2	1	2	3	1	3
Conveying simple information	3	1	1	1	2	3
Asking an informational question	3	1	1	1	3	3
Making a simple request	3	1	1	1	3	3
Giving complex instructions	3	3	2	2	1	2
Addressing many people	2	2	2	2	3	1
Key: 1 = Excellent 2 = Adequate 3 = Inappropriate						

Figure 1. **Effective business communication.**

Note. From *Email Composition and Communication (EmC2)* by T. Galati.

Practical Communications, Inc. (www.praccom.com), 2001.

8

Research into business communication confirms the necessity of the Computer Store's reliance on modes of communication other than e-mail. When working with a large number of people, businesses need to be able to get a message across accurately and in a timely manner. If a message is misinterpreted by just one individual, a large-scale problem might result. When an e-mail message requires immediate attention, some businesses, like the Computer Store at Penn State, address the problem of delayed response by using instant messaging.

Though instant messenging may alleviate in-house communication lapses, other forms of media, like Web sites, are more suited to growing foreign audiences. Foreign investment by U.S. companies was approximately 9 trillion dollars in 1966 but had grown to 300 trillion dollars in 2002 (Blalock, 2007). This rising foreign investment by U.S. companies has increased the need for better communication among companies that are now communicating globally. Though the Penn State Computer Store is, for the most part, not communicating on a global scale, its practices demonstrate the same sense of a need for a variety of communication media, without an uncritical overreliance on e-mail.

E-mail Overuse

Many factors go into choosing the proper medium for a given rhetorical situation, such as privacy concerns, the size of the group, the type of information, and the desired level of immediacy. People tend to overuse e-mail because it is an easy, inexpensive way to send information to several people. When asked why sending an e-mail to a team of 100 people is not as effective as sending to a team of five, Carol Hildenbrand, a CIO, answered:

9

As a group increases in size, you have a whole slew of management challenges. Communicating badly exponentially increases the possibility of making fatal mistakes. A large-scale project has a lot of moving parts, which makes it that much easier to break down. Communication is the oil that keeps everything working properly. It's much easier to address an atmosphere of distrust among a group of five team members than it is with a team of 500 members. (Schwalbe, 2006, p. 399)

Information distribution, therefore, involves more than creating and sending status reports, and different media are suited to different contexts, purposes, and audiences. Figure 1 shows some findings about the suitability of forms of communication to particular business goals, but each situation should be assessed individually.

Implementation of Communication Strategies

One of the most important functions of business communication is to transfer information from one level in a hierarchy to another: from employee to manager, for example, or vice versa. After examining the functioning of the Penn State Computer Store, the research team found that it had a very effective communication structure. Employees shared their insights as to how different kinds of information are conveyed through different media. Ideas, proposals, and other important information are generally communicated in person or over the phone. E-mail is relied on for notifications and follow-ups, but not for complex tasks where interactivity and collaboration are desired.

10

Personal Relationships

It is vital for a business to network and build successful relationships that might prove beneficial in the future. Yet in today's workplace, it is becoming harder to develop relationships because of the overuse of e-mail. The Penn State Computer Store avoids this problem by having employees within the office interact face to face. The store also maintains good relationships with customers at other campuses by sending out consultants to meet clients. Face-to-face communication creates a perceived added value to the services and products the store offers. When a consumer buys a product or a warranty from the Computer Store on campus, he or she reaps the benefits of a strong network of co-workers who have good communication skills that they use among themselves as well as with clients.

Conclusion

Over the past few decades, modes of communication have changed rapidly. When we have something to say, we have the option of sending an instant message or an e-mail, making a phone call, sending a text message, posting information on a Web site or blog, or even creating a podcast. The rise of these new methods of communication has posed some problems for businesses that are not operating with a high level of efficiency. Without employees who can both use the technologies and, more importantly, choose the most fitting technology for a given situation, businesses will not be able to communicate efficiently either internally or externally, with clients and other businesses.

11

Research at the Penn State Computer Store showed that each form of communication has its own benefits and drawbacks. If an important message needs to be conveyed, a face-to-face meeting is recommended. However, if an employee wants to check with a supervisor before leaving the office for an hour, an instant message is sufficient. However, there is an overuse of e-mail, which has become a mode used between people who are unfamiliar with each other and are likely, if using this medium, to remain that way. This impersonality may hurt businesses because networking and building relationships are crucial to business success.

Recommendation

Overview of the Problem

Business curricula are not spending enough time teaching potential new employees strategies and procedures for communicating properly through different media. This issue needs to be addressed immediately by the College of Business at Penn State.

Possible Solutions

The way to correct this problem is to increase the amount of business communication courses offered in the College of Business. The inclusion of more communication-oriented material will increase graduates' abilities to begin and maintain careers in the business world. The curriculum should cover facets of contact such as the use and misuse of e-mail and the advantages and disadvantages thereof. Courses should cover networking within businesses and explore how this networking can create successful relationships among employees. The curriculum should also present students with multiple opportunities to work in groups using various media as well as

12

the opportunity to develop these skills before entering the business community.

Benefits

Implementation of this new curriculum will put Penn State business students in an enviable position for future employment with successful companies. Businesses need employees well versed in communication techniques crucial to a global market. Penn State students will be well placed with these revisions to the business communication curriculum. Ultimately, as Penn State students achieve more success in business, the prestige and reputation of the College of Business will continue to grow.

13

References

Berkeley School of Information Management and Systems. (2003). *Executive summary: How much information?* Retrieved June 11, 2007, from http://www2.sims.berkeley.edu/research/projects/how-much-info-2003/execsum.htm

Blalock, M. (2005, December 23). *Why good communication is good business.* Retrieved June 5, 2007, from http://www.bus.wisc.edu/update/winter05/business_communication.asp

Schwalbe, K. (2006). *Information techonology project management* (4th ed.). Waterloo, Ontario, Canada: Thomson Course Technology.

Walker, M. (2004, August 26). The day the e-mail dies. *The Wall Street Journal Online.* Retrieved June 4, 2007, from http://www.lucid-minds.com/public/p66.htm

G

GRAMMAR

"Sorry, but I'm going to have to issue you a summons for
reckless grammar and driving without an apostrophe."

21 Sentence
Essentials 508

22 Phrases and Clauses in
Sentences 528

23 Sentence
Fragments 553

24 Comma Splices and
Fused Sentences 562

25 Modifiers 572

26 Pronouns 588

27 Verbs 607

CHAPTER 21
Sentence Essentials   508

21a Parts of speech   508
21b Subjects and predicates   517
21c Complements   521
21d Basic sentence patterns   523

CHAPTER 22
Phrases and Clauses in Sentences   528

22a Phrases   528
22b Clauses   538
22c Conjunctions and conjunctive adverbs   543
22d Sentence forms   547
22e Sentence functions   550

CHAPTER 23
Sentence Fragments   553

23a Recognizing sentence fragments   553
23b Phrases as sentence fragments   556
23c Dependent clauses as sentence fragments   558

CHAPTER 24
Comma Splices and Fused Sentences   562

24a Punctuating independent clauses   563
24b Recognizing comma splices and fused sentences   565
24c Revising comma splices and fused sentences   567
24d Divided quotations   570

CHAPTER 25
Modifiers   572

25a Recognizing modifiers   572
25b Comparatives and superlatives   577
25c Placement of modifiers   580
25d Double negatives   585

CHAPTER 26
Pronouns   588

26a Recognizing pronouns   588
26b Pronoun case   593
26c Pronoun-antecedent agreement   599
26d Clear pronoun reference   603

CHAPTER 27
Verbs   607

27a Verb forms   607
27b Verb tenses   616
27c Verb tense consistency   627
27d Voice   628
27e Mood   631
27f Subject-verb agreement   634

TECH SAVVY

Using a Grammar Checker

Most word-processing programs have grammar checkers, which can help you identify grammar errors as well as problems with usage and style, but these grammar checkers have significant limitations. A grammar checker will usually identify

- fused sentences, sometimes called run-on sentences (chapter 24),
- some misused prepositions (35c),
- wordy or overly long sentences (chapters 30 and 36), and
- missing apostrophes in contractions (39b).

However, a grammar checker can easily miss

- sentence fragments (chapter 23),
- problems with adverbs or adjectives (25a),
- dangling or misplaced modifiers (25c and 25d),
- problems with pronoun-antecedent agreement (26c),
- errors in subject-verb agreement (27f), and
- misused or missing commas (chapter 37).

Because these omissions can weaken your credibility as a writer, you should never rely solely on a grammar checker to find them. Furthermore, grammar checkers can mark as wrong words or phrases that are actually correct. Some of these "errors" may be choices you have made deliberately to suit your rhetorical situation (chapter 1).

Used carefully, a grammar checker can be a helpful tool, but keep the following advice in mind:

- Use a grammar checker only in addition to your own editing and proofreading. When in doubt, consult the appropriate chapters in this handbook.
- Always evaluate any sentences flagged by a grammar checker to determine whether there is, in fact, a problem.
- Adjust the settings on your grammar checker to look for specific types of errors. If you are using Microsoft Word, select Tools; then select either Spelling and Grammar or Options to customize your settings.
- Carefully review the revisions proposed by a grammar checker before accepting them. Sometimes the proposed revisions create new errors.

21 Sentence Essentials

When you think of the word *grammar*, you might also think of the word *rule*—a regulation that you must obey. But *rule* has another meaning: "a description of what is true in most cases." A grammar rule, then, describes how language is commonly or conventionally used. However, what is appropriate in one rhetorical situation (chapter 1) may not be appropriate in another. Thus, to know which rules to follow, you must first determine your intended audience, overall purpose, and specific context. Once you establish your rhetorical situation, you will be ready to consider the options the English language provides—an extensive selection of words and word arrangements will be at your disposal. By also learning basic grammar terms and concepts, you will better understand how to choose among the options available to you.

This chapter will help you

- identify the parts of speech (**21a**),
- recognize the essential parts of a sentence (**21b**),
- identify complements (**21c**), and
- recognize basic sentence patterns (**21d**).

21a Parts of speech

When you look up a word in the dictionary, you will often find it followed by one or more of these labels: *adj., adv., conj., interj., n., prep., pron.,* and *v* (or *vb.*). These are the abbreviations for the traditional eight parts of speech: *adjective, adverb, conjunction, interjection, noun, preposition, pronoun,* and *verb.* The definition of a word depends on which of these labels it has. When labeled as a noun, the word *turn* has several meanings, one of which is "curve" (*We were surprised by the turn in the road*). When *turn* is labeled as a verb, one of its possible meanings is "to change color" (*The leaves have turned*). By learning the parts of speech, not only will you be able to use a dictionary effectively, you will also be able to understand advice on punctuation and writing style.

(1) Verbs usually express action or being.

Thousands of verbs are **action verbs.** Just think of everything you do in one day: wake, eat, drink, wash, walk, drive, study, work, laugh, smile, talk, and so on. In contrast, only a few verbs express being or experiencing. These verbs are called **linking verbs** and include *be, seem,* and *become* and the sensory verbs *look, taste, smell, feel,* and *sound.* Both action verbs and linking verbs are frequently accompanied by other verbs that add shades of meaning, such as information about time (*will* study this afternoon), ability (*can* study), or obligation (*must* study). These verbs are called **auxiliary verbs** or **helping verbs.** See chapter 27 for more details about verbs.

The dictionary (base) form of most action verbs fits into this frame sentence:

We should ＿＿＿＿＿＿ (it). [With some verbs, *it* is not used.]

The dictionary (base) form of most linking verbs fits into this frame sentence:

It should ＿＿＿＿＿＿ good (terrible, fine).

THINKING RHETORICALLY

 VERBS

Decide which of the following sentences evokes a clearer image.

The team captain **was** absolutely ecstatic.
Grinning broadly, the team captain **shot** both her arms into the air.

You probably chose the sentence with the action verb *shot* rather than the sentence with *was.* Most writers avoid using the verb *be* in any of its forms (*am, is, are, was, were,* or *been*) when their rhetorical situation calls for vibrant imagery. Instead, they use vivid action verbs.

(2) Nouns usually name people, places, things, and ideas.

Nouns fall into two main categories. **Proper nouns** are specific names. You can identify them easily because they are capitalized: *Bill Gates, Redmond,*

Relax and watch the beautiful sunset at the infamous "My Bar"

Put on a "Mask and Fins" and see the island's Real Treasures

Nestle yourself in cozy, spacious Oceanview Rooms

Savor the spice of East & West Indian flavors at the SeaHarvest Restaurant

www.sunsethouse.com

(800) 854-4767

Writers of travel brochures often choose action verbs to create images of fun-filled vacations. (Courtesy of Sunset House.)

Microsoft Corporation. **Common nouns** refer to any member of a class or category: *person, city, company.* There are three types of common nouns.

- **Count nouns** refer to people, places, things, and ideas that can be counted. They have singular and plural forms: *boy, boys; park, parks; car, cars; concept, concepts.*
- **Noncount nouns** refer to things or ideas that cannot be counted: *furniture, information.*
- **Collective nouns** are nouns that can be either singular or plural, depending on the context: *The **committee** published its report* [singular]. *The **committee** disagree about their duties* [plural]. (See 27f(7).)

> Most nouns fit into this frame sentence:
> (The) _____ is (are) important
> (unimportant, interesting, uninteresting).

(3) Pronouns function as nouns.

Most pronouns (*it, he, she, they,* and many others) replace nouns that have already been mentioned. These nouns are called **antecedents** (26c). Sometimes an antecedent is a single noun.

THINKING RHETORICALLY

✳ NOUNS

Nouns like *entertainment* and *nutrition* refer to concepts. They are called **abstract nouns.** In contrast, nouns like *guitar* and *apple* refer to things perceivable by the senses. They are called **concrete nouns.** When your rhetorical situation calls for the use of abstractions, balance them with tangible details conveyed through concrete nouns. For example, if you use the abstract nouns *impressionism* and *cubism* in an art history paper, also include concrete nouns that will enable readers to see the colors, shapes, and brushstrokes of the paintings you are discussing.

Dan thinks **he** will have the report done by Friday.

An antecedent may also be a noun and the words modifying it.

My parents bought the cheap, decrepit house because they thought **it** had charm.

A pronoun and its antecedent may be found either in the same sentence or in separate, though usually adjacent, sentences.

The students collaborated on a research project last year. **They** even presented their findings at a national conference.

The pronouns in the preceding examples are called **personal pronouns.** However, there are other types of pronouns as well: indefinite, possessive, relative, interrogative, reflexive/intensive. For a detailed discussion of pronouns, see chapter 26.

THINKING RHETORICALLY

✳ PRONOUNS

Why is the following passage somewhat unclear?

> The study found that students succeed when they have clear directions, consistent and focused feedback, and access to help. This led administrators to create a tutoring center at our university.

The problem is that the pronoun *This* at the beginning of the second sentence could refer to all of the information provided by the study or just to the single finding that students need access to help. If you discover that one of your pronouns lacks a clear antecedent, replace the pronoun with more specific words.

> **The results of this study** led administrators to create a tutoring center at our university.

(4) Adjectives modify nouns or pronouns.

Adjectives most commonly modify nouns: *spicy* food, *cold* day, *special* price. Sometimes they modify pronouns: *blue* ones, anyone *thin*. Adjectives usually answer one of these questions: Which one? What kind of . . . ? How many? What color or size or shape (and so on)? Although adjectives usually precede the nouns they modify, they occasionally follow them: *enough* time, time *enough*. Adjectives may also follow linking verbs such as *be, seem,* and *become*:

The <u>moon</u> is **full** tonight.   <u>He</u> seems **shy.**

When an adjective follows a linking verb, it modifies the subject of the sentence (**21b(3)**).

Nouns sometimes function as adjectives; these nouns modify other nouns.

The **weather** turned cold unexpectedly. [*Weather* is a noun.]

We listened to the **weather** forecast. [*Weather* is a noun functioning as a modifier.]

> Most adjectives fit into one of these frame sentences:
>
> He told us about a/an _____ idea (person, place).
>
> The idea (person, place) is very _____.

Articles are a subclass of adjectives because, like adjectives, they are used before nouns. There are three articles: *a, an,* and *the.* The article *a* is used before a consonant sound (**a** yard, **a** university, **a** VIP); *an* is used before a vowel sound (**an** apple, **an** hour, **an** NFL team).

MULTILINGUAL WRITERS

ARTICLE USAGE

English has two types of articles: indefinite and definite. The **indefinite articles** *a* and *an* indicate that a singular noun is used in a general way. For example, *a planet* refers to any planet, not to a specific planet. Indefinite articles are often used in the following contexts:

- Upon first mention of a noun. Use an indefinite article when you introduce a singular noun for the first time.

  Pluto is **a** dwarf <u>planet</u>.

- After the introductory word *there*. Use an indefinite article when you introduce a topic that includes a singular noun.

  There has been **a** <u>controversy</u> over the classification of Pluto.

- In definitions. When you are defining a word, use an indefinite article.

  A <u>planet</u> is a celestial body orbiting a star such as our sun.

- If a noun is plural or if it does not have a plural form, then no article is needed.

  Planets orbit a star.   **Astrology** is the study of celestial bodies.

The **definite article,** *the,* is used before a noun that has already been introduced or when a reference is obvious. *The* often appears in the following contexts:

- For subsequent mention of a noun. Once a noun has been introduced, use the definite article to refer to it a second time.

  Scientists distinguish between planets and <u>dwarf planets</u>. Three of **the** <u>dwarf planets</u> in our solar system are Ceres, Pluto, and Eris.

- Subsequent mention does not always include exact repetition of a noun. However, the noun chosen must be close in meaning to a word already introduced.

  Scientists were not sure how to <u>classify</u> celestial bodies. **The** <u>classification</u> of Pluto proved to be particularly controversial.

- When indicating something unique. A noun may be considered unique if everyone in the audience will know what it refers to. Common examples are *moon, universe, solar system, sun, earth,* and *sky.*

  The <u>moon</u> is full tonight.

- Less common examples, such as *observatory,* may be preceded by *the* only when all members of the audience will think of the same observatory.

  We all met at **the** <u>observatory</u>.

MULTILINGUAL WRITERS

ABSTRACT NOUNS AND ARTICLES

In English, the articles, *a, an,* and *the,* are not used before abstract nouns that refer to general qualities or ideas (see 21a(2)).

> Patience is a virtue.   Liberty ensures justice.

In other languages, such as Italian, an article does precede abstract nouns.

> *La pazienza è una virtù.* [The definite article *la* precedes the noun *pazienza*.]

Be sure to omit articles before abstract nouns used in a general way. However, if the abstract noun is used in a specific way, include an article.

> The patience they have for sifting through old documents is remarkable. [A type of patience is specified.]

(5) Adverbs modify verbs, adjectives, and other adverbs.

Adverbs most frequently modify verbs. They provide information about time, manner, place, and frequency, thus answering one of these questions: When? How? Where? How often?

The conference <u>starts</u> **tomorrow.** [time]

I **rapidly** <u>calculated</u> the cost. [manner]

We <u>met</u> **here.** [place]

They **often** <u>work</u> late on Thursdays. [frequency]

Adverbs that modify verbs can often move from one position in a sentence to another.

> **Yesterday** the team traveled to St. Louis.
>
> The team traveled to St. Louis **yesterday.**

He **carefully** removed the radio collar.

He removed the radio collar **carefully.**

Most adverbs that modify verbs fit into this frame sentence:

They _____ moved (danced, walked) across the room.

Adverbs also modify adjectives and other adverbs by intensifying or otherwise qualifying the meanings of those words.

I was **extremely** <u>curious</u>. [modifying an adjective]

He was **unusually** <u>generous</u>. [modifying an adjective]

The changes occurred **quite** <u>rapidly</u>. [modifying an adverb]

The team played **surprisingly** <u>well</u>. [modifying an adverb]

For more information on adverbs, see 25a.

THINKING RHETORICALLY

✳ ADVERBS

What do the adverbs add to the following sentences?

The scientist **delicately** places the slide under the microscope.

"You're late," he whispered **vehemently.**

She is **wistfully** hopeful.

Adverbs can help you portray an action, indicate how someone is speaking, and add detail to a description.

(6) Prepositions set up relationships between words.

A **preposition** is a word that combines with a noun and any of its modifiers to provide additional detail—often answering one of these questions: Where? When?

We walked **through** <u>our old neighborhood</u>. [answers the question *Where?*]

We left **in** <u>the early afternoon</u>. [answers the question *When?*]

A preposition may also combine with a pronoun.

We walked **through** it.

Common one-word prepositions are *on, in, at, to, for, over,* and *under.* Common **phrasal prepositions** (prepositions consisting of more than one word) are *except for, because of, instead of,* and *according to.* For a list of prepositions and information on prepositional phrases, see **22a(4)**.

(7) Conjunctions are connectors.

Conjunctions fall into three categories: coordinating, correlative, and subordinating. A **coordinating conjunction** connects similar words or groups of words; that is, it generally links a noun to a noun, an adjective to an adjective, a phrase to a phrase, and so on.

He played <u>football</u> **and** <u>basketball</u>. [connecting nouns]

The game was <u>dangerous</u> **yet** <u>appealing</u>. [connecting adjectives]

There are seven coordinating conjunctions. Use the made-up word *fanboys* to help you remember them.

F	A	N	B	O	Y	S
for	and	nor	but	or	yet	so

A **correlative conjunction** (or **correlative**) consists of two parts. The most common correlatives are *both . . . and, either . . . or, neither . . . nor,* and *not only . . . but also.*

The defeat left me feeling **both** <u>sad</u> **and** <u>angry</u>. [connecting adjectives]

Either <u>Pedro</u> **or** <u>Sue</u> will introduce the speaker. [connecting nouns]

For more information on coordinating and correlative conjunctions, see **22c(1)** and **22c(2)**.

A **subordinating conjunction** introduces a dependent clause (**22b(2)**) and indicates its relation to an independent clause (**22b(1)**).

The river rises **when** the snow melts.

Common subordinating conjunctions are *because, although, when,* and *if.* For a longer list of subordinating conjunctions, see **22c(3)**.

(8) Interjections are expressions of emotion.

Interjections most commonly indicate surprise, dread, resignation or some other emotion. They may also be expressions used to get someone's attention. Interjections that come before a sentence end in a period or an exclamation point.

Oh. Now I understand.

Wow! Your design is astounding.

Interjections that begin or interrupt a sentence are set off by commas.

Hey, what are you doing?

The solution, **alas,** was not as simple as I had hoped it would be.

Exercise 1

Identify the part of speech for each word in the sentences below.

1. Lee and I hiked to Lake Ann.
2. The hike to the lake was short but quite challenging.
3. Oh, were we hot and dirty!
4. We found the perfect campsite near a spring.
5. After we unpacked, we swam slowly across the lake.

21b **Subjects and predicates**

A sentence consists of two parts:

SUBJECT + PREDICATE

The **subject** is generally someone or something that either performs an action or is described. The **predicate** expresses the action initiated by the subject or gives information about the subject.

The <u>landlord</u> + <u>renovated</u> the apartment.
[The subject performs an action; the predicate expresses the action.]
<u>They</u> + <u>had sounded</u> reasonable.
[The subject is described; the predicate gives information about the subject.]

The central components of the subject and the predicate are often called the **simple subject** (the main noun or pronoun) and the **simple predicate** (the main verb and any auxiliary verbs). They are underlined in the examples above.

Compound subjects and **compound predicates** include a connecting word (conjunction) such as *and, or,* or *but.*

<u>The Republicans</u> **and** <u>the Democrats</u> are debating this issue. [compound subject]
The candidate <u>stated his views on abortion</u> **but** <u>did not discuss stem-cell research</u>. [compound predicate]

THINKING RHETORICALLY

 ## SUBJECT AND PREDICATES

Generally, sentences have the pattern subject + predicate. However, writers often vary this pattern to provide cohesion, emphasis, or both.

He + elbowed his way into the lobby and paused. [subject + predicate]
From a far corner of the lobby came + shrieks of laughter. [predicate + subject]

These two sentences are cohesive because the information in the predicate that begins the second sentence is linked to information in the first sentence. The reversed pattern in the second sentence, predicate + subject, also places emphasis on the subject (*shrieks of laughter*).

(1) Subjects are usually pronouns, nouns, or nouns with modifiers.
Notice that a pronoun, a noun, or a noun with modifiers can serve as the subject of the following sentence:

He
Lucas   ⎤— organized the film festival.
My best friend ⎦

To identify the subject of a sentence, find the verb and then use it in a question beginning with *who* or *what,* as shown in the following examples.

Jennifer works at a clinic.	Meat contains cholesterol.
Verb: **works**	Verb: **contains**
Who works? **Jennifer** (not the clinic) **works.**	*What* contains? **Meat** (not cholesterol) **contains.**
Subject: **Jennifer**	Subject: **Meat**

Some sentences begin with an **expletive**—*there* or *it.* Such a word occurs in the subject position, forcing the true subject to follow the verb.

There were **no exercise machines**.

A subject following the expletive *it* is often an entire clause. You will learn more about clauses in chapter **22**.

It is essential **that children learn about nutrition at an early age**.

MULTILINGUAL WRITERS

Beginning a Sentence with *There*

In sentences beginning with the expletive *there,* the verb comes before the subject. The verb *are* is often hard to hear, so be careful that you do not omit it.

There ˄ many good books on nutrition.
    are

(2) The key word in the predicate is always a verb.
A verb may be a single word, or it may consist of a main verb accompanied by one or more auxiliary verbs. The most common auxiliaries are

be (am, is, are, was, were, been), have (has, had), and *do (does, did).* Others, including *can, may,* and *might,* are called **modal auxiliaries.**

They **work** as volunteers. [single-word verb]
They **have been working** as volunteers. [verb with two auxiliaries]
They **might work** as volunteers. [verb with modal auxiliary]

Occasionally an adverb intervenes between the auxiliary and the main verb.

They **have** <u>always</u> **worked** as volunteers.

Exercise 2

Identify the subject and the predicate in each sentence, noting any compound subjects or compound predicates.

1. Magicians are in our oceans.
2. They are octopuses.
3. Octopuses can become invisible.
4. They just change color.
5. They can also change their shape.
6. These shape-changers look frightening.
7. Octopuses can release poisons and produce spectacles of color.
8. The blue-ringed octopus can give an unsuspecting diver an unpleasant surprise.
9. Researchers consider the poison of the blue-ringed octopus one of the deadliest in the world.
10. Octopuses and their relatives have been living on Earth for millions of years.

Exercise 3

In the sentences in exercise 2, identify all main verbs and auxiliary verbs.

21c Complements

Complements are parts of the predicate required by the verb to make a sentence complete. For example, the sentence *The chair of the committee presented* is incomplete without the complement *his plans*. There are four different complements: direct objects, indirect objects, subject complements, and object complements. A complement is generally a pronoun, a noun, or a noun with modifiers.

The chair of the committee introduced

- **her.** [pronoun]
- **Sylvia Holbrook.** [noun]
- **the new <u>member</u>.** [noun with modifiers]

(1) A direct object follows an action verb.

The **direct object** either receives the action of the verb or shows the result of the action.

I. M. Pei designed **the East Building of the National Gallery.**

Steve McQueen invented **the bucket seat** in 1960.

Compound direct objects include a connecting word, usually *and*.

Thomas Edison patented **the phonograph <u>and</u> the microphone.**

To identify a direct object, first find the subject and the verb; then use them in a question ending with *what* or *whom*.

Marie Curie discovered radium.	They hired a new engineer.
Subject and verb:	Subject and verb:
Marie Curie discovered	**They hired**
Marie Curie discovered *what?*	They hired *whom?*
radium	**a new engineer**
Direct object: **radium**	Direct object: **a new engineer**

A direct object may be a clause (22b).

Researchers found **that patients responded favorably to the new medication.**

(2) Indirect objects usually identify to whom or for whom an action is performed.

Indirect objects typically name the person(s) receiving or benefiting from the action indicated by the verb. Verbs that often take indirect objects include *bring, buy, give, lend, offer, sell, send,* and *write.*

The supervisor gave **the new employees** <u>computers.</u>

[*To whom* were the computers given?]

She wrote **them** <u>recommendation letters.</u>

[*For whom* were the recommendation letters written?]

Like subjects and direct objects, indirect objects can be compound.

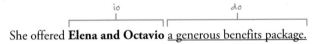

She offered **Elena and Octavio** <u>a generous benefits package.</u>

(3) A subject complement renames, classifies, or describes the subject.

The **subject complement** follows a linking verb (**21a(1)**). The most common linking verb is *be* (*am, is, are, was, were, been*). Other linking verbs are *become, seem,* and *appear* and the sensory verbs *feel, look, smell, sound,* and *taste.* A subject complement can be a pronoun, a noun, or a noun with modifiers; however, it can also be an adjective (**21a(4)**). The adjective may be accompanied by a word that softens or intensifies its meaning (such *as somewhat, very,* or *quite*).

The winner was —

you. [pronoun]

Harry Solano. [noun]

the person with the highest score. [noun with modifiers]

ecstatic. [adjective]

(4) An object complement renames, classifies, or describes the direct object.

The object complement helps complete the meaning of a verb such as *call, elect, make, name,* or *paint.* Like the subject complement, the object complement can be either a noun or an adjective, along with any modifiers.

> Reporters called the rookie **the best <u>player</u>.** [noun with modifiers]
>
> The strike left the fans **somewhat <u>disappointed</u>.** [adjective with modifiers]

Exercise 4

In the sentences in exercise 2, identify all direct objects, indirect objects, subject complements, and object complements.

21d   Basic sentence patterns

The six basic sentence patterns presented in the following box are based on three verb types: intransitive, transitive, and linking. Notice that *trans* in the words *transitive* and *intransitive* means "over or across." Thus, the action of a **transitive verb** carries across to an object, but the action of an **intransitive verb** does not. An intransitive verb has no complement, although it is often followed by an adverb (pattern 1). A transitive verb is followed by a direct object (pattern 2), by both a direct and an indirect object (pattern 3), or by a direct object and an object complement (pattern 4). A linking verb (such as *be, seem, sound,* and *taste*) is followed by a subject complement (pattern 5) or a phrase that includes a preposition (pattern 6).

BASIC SENTENCE PATTERNS

Pattern 1 SUBJECT + INTRANSITIVE VERB

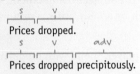

Prices dropped.

Prices dropped precipitously.

Pattern 2 SUBJECT + TRANSITIVE VERB + DIRECT OBJECT

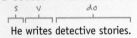

He writes detective stories.

Pattern 3 SUBJECT + TRANSITIVE VERB + INDIRECT OBJECT + DIRECT OBJECT

My father sent me a care package.

Pattern 4 SUBJECT + TRANSITIVE VERB + DIRECT OBJECT + OBJECT COMPLEMENT

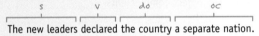

The new leaders declared the country a separate nation.

Pattern 5 SUBJECT + LINKING VERB + SUBJECT COMPLEMENT

Dr. Vargas is the discussion leader.

Pattern 6 SUBJECT + LINKING VERB + PREPOSITIONAL PHRASE

They are in the library.

MULTILINGUAL WRITERS

WORD ORDER

Some languages, such as French and Cantonese, have sentence patterns similar to English sentence patterns. These languages are called **SVO (subject-verb-object) languages**, even though not all sentences have objects. The patterns for other languages vary. **SOV (subject-object-verb) languages** and **VSO (verb-subject-object) languages** are also common. Keep the SVO pattern in mind to help you write English sentences.

When declarative sentences, or statements, are turned into questions, the subject and the auxiliary verb are usually inverted; that is, the auxiliary verb is moved to the beginning of the sentence, before the subject.

Statement: A Chinese skater (has) won a gold medal.

Question: Has a Chinese skater won a gold medal?

Often, a question word such as *what* or *why* opens an interrogative sentence. As long as the question word is *not* the subject of the sentence, the auxiliary verb precedes the subject.

Question: What has a Chinese skater won? [*What* is the object of *has won*.]

COMPARE: Who has won a gold medal? [*Who* is the subject of the sentence.]

If a statement does not include an auxiliary verb or a form of the linking verb *be,* then a form of *do* is added to form the corresponding question. Once again, the auxiliary verb is placed in front of the subject.

Statement: A Chinese skater won a gold medal.

Question: Did a Chinese skater win a gold medal?

As you study sentences more closely, you will find patterns other than the six presented in this section. For example, another pattern requires mention of a destination or location. The sentence *I put the documents* is incomplete without a phrase such as *on your desk.* Other sentences have phrases that are not essential but do add pertinent information. These phrases can sometimes be moved. For example, the phrase *on Friday* can be placed either at the beginning or at the end of the following sentence.

I finished my assignment **on Friday.**

On Friday, I finished my assignment.

To learn how to write effective sentences by varying their structure, see chapter 33.

MULTILINGUAL WRITERS

INVERTING THE SUBJECT AND THE VERB IN QUESTIONS

English is one of a few languages in which the subject and the verb are inverted in questions. Most languages rely on intonation to indicate that a question is being asked, without a change in word order. (English speakers occasionally use uninverted questions to ask for clarification or to indicate surprise.) In languages other than English, a frequently occurring option for making a statement into a question is to add a particle, such as the Japanese *ka.*

THINKING RHETORICALLY

SENTENCE PATTERNS

If you want to emphasize a contrast or intensify a feeling, alter the sentence pattern by placing the direct object at the beginning of the sentence.

I acquired English at home. I learned **French** on the street.

I acquired English at home. **French** I learned on the street.

A comma is sometimes used after the direct object in such sentences.

They loved the queen. They despised **the king.**

They loved the queen. **The king,** they despised.

Exercise 5

1. Identify the basic pattern of each sentence in exercise 2.
2. Write a question corresponding to each of the sentences. Put a check mark next to those questions in which the subject and the verb are inverted.

Exercise 6

Shift the emphasis in the underlined sentences by moving the direct objects to the beginning of the sentence.

1. Leah considers her medical studies her priority. <u>She calls her rock band a hobby</u>.
2. He learned to play the clarinet when he was eight. <u>He mastered the saxophone later on</u>.
3. They renovated the state house. <u>They condemned the old hotel</u>.
4. We played volleyball in the fall. <u>We played basketball in the winter</u>.
5. They named their first child Theodore. <u>They named their second child Franklin</u>.

22 Phrases and Clauses in Sentences

Within a sentence, groups of words form phrases and clauses. Like single words, these larger units function as specific parts of speech. By understanding how word groups can serve as nouns, verbs, adjectives, or adverbs, you will be able to make your sentences clear, concise, and complete.

This chapter will help you

- recognize phrases (**22a**),
- recognize clauses (**22b**),
- recognize words that connect words, phrases, and clauses (**22c**), and
- identify sentence forms and functions (**22d** and **22e**).

22a Phrases

A **phrase** is a sequence of grammatically related words without a subject, a predicate, or both. A phrase is categorized according to the most important word in it. This section introduces noun phrases, verb phrases, verbal phrases, and prepositional phrases as well as appositives and absolute constructions.

(1) A noun phrase consists of a main noun and its modifiers.

Noun phrases serve as subjects (**21b**) and complements (**21c**). They can also be objects of prepositions such as *in, of, on, at,* and *to.* (See **22a(4)** for a longer list of prepositions.)

The heavy frost killed **many fruit trees.** [subject and direct object]

My cousin is **an organic farmer.** [subject and subject complement]

His farm is in **eastern Oregon.** [subject and object of the preposition *in*]

THINKING RHETORICALLY

NOUN PHRASES

In the preceding example sentences, the adjectives *heavy, organic,* and *eastern* add specificity. For example, the noun phrase *an organic farmer* tells the reader more than *farmer* alone would. By composing noun phrases carefully, you will make your sentences more precise.

Much of Greenland lies within the Arctic Circle. ~~The area~~ This large island is owned by Denmark. Its name is Kaballit Nunaat. native

[*The area* could refer to either Greenland or the area within the Arctic Circle. *This large island* clearly refers to Greenland. *Its native name* is more precise than just *Its name.*]

MULTILINGUAL WRITERS

NUMBER AGREEMENT IN NOUN PHRASES

Some words must agree in number with the nouns they precede. The words *a, an, this,* and *that* are used before singular nouns; *some, few, these, those,* and *many* are used before plural nouns:

an/that opportunity [singular noun]

some/few/those opportunities [plural noun]

The words *less* and *much* precede nouns representing abstract concepts or masses that cannot be counted (noncount nouns) (**21a(2)**):

less freedom, **much** water [noncount nouns]

(2) A verb phrase includes a main verb and its auxiliary verbs.
A verb is essential to the predicate of a sentence (**21b**). It generally expresses action or a state of being. Besides a main verb, a verb phrase

includes one or more **auxiliary verbs**, sometimes called *helping verbs,* such as *be, have, do, will,* and *should.*

> The flight **arrived.** [main verb]

> The passengers **have deplaned.** [auxiliary verb + main verb]

> The flight **will be departing** at 7:00 p.m. [two auxiliary verbs + main verb]

For a comprehensive discussion of verbs, see chapter 27.

(3) Verbal phrases are used as nouns or modifiers.

A **verbal phrase** differs from a verb phrase (22a(2)) in that the verb form in a verbal phrase serves as a noun or a modifier rather than as a verb.

> He <u>was</u> **<u>reading</u>** the story aloud. [*Reading* is part of the verb phrase *was reading.*]

> **Reading** is fundamental to academic success. [*Reading* serves as a noun. COMPARE: **It** is fundamental to academic success.]

> The student **reading** aloud is an education major. [*Reading aloud* modifies *the student.*]

Because of their origin as verbs, verbals in phrases often have their own objects (21c) and modifiers (chapter 25).

> He decided **<u>to read</u> the story aloud.** [The object of the verbal *to read* is *the story. Aloud* is a modifier.]

Verbal phrases are divided into three types: gerund phrases, participial phrases, and infinitive phrases.

Central to a **gerund phrase** is the *-ing* verb form (see 27a(1)). A gerund phrase serves as a noun, usually functioning as the subject (21b) or object (21c) in a sentence.

> **<u>Writing</u> a bestseller** was her only goal. [subject]

> My neighbor enjoys **<u>writing</u> about distant places.** [object]

Because gerund phrases act as nouns, pronouns can replace them.

> **That** was her only goal.

> My neighbor enjoys **it.**

THINKING RHETORICALLY

GERUNDS

What is the difference between the following sentences?

> They bundle products together, which often results in higher consumer costs.
>
> Bundling products together often results in higher consumer costs.

In the first sentence, the actor, *they,* is the focus. In the second sentence, the action of the gerund phrase, *bundling products together,* is the focus. As you revise, ask yourself whether you want to emphasize actors or actions.

Participial phrases include either a present participle (*-ing* form) or a past participle (*-ed* form for regular verbs or another form for irregular verbs). (See 27a for more information on verb forms.)

> <u>**Planning**</u> **her questions carefully,** she was able to hold fast-paced and engaging interviews. [present participle]

> <u>**Known**</u> **for her interviewing skills,** she was asked to host her own radio program. [past participle]

Participial phrases function as modifiers (25a(2)). They may appear at the beginning, middle, or end of a sentence.

> <u>**Fearing**</u> **a drought,** all the farmers in the area used less irrigation water.

> All the farmers in the area, <u>**recognizing**</u> **the signs of drought,** used less irrigation water.

> Farmers used less irrigation water, <u>**hoping**</u> **to save water for later in the season.**

The commas setting off the participial phrases in the preceding examples signal that the phrases are not essential for readers to understand who is using less irrigation water. Instead, the phrases add descriptive details or reasons to the sentence. Sometimes, however, a participial phrase provides necessary information that specifies who or what is being discussed. This type of participial phrase, an **essential phrase**, is *not* set off by commas.

> The reporter **providing the most accurate account of the war** was once a soldier.
> [The participial phrase distinguishes this reporter from others.]

For more advice on using punctuation with phrases containing verbals, see **37b(2)** and **37d(1)**.

A present participle (*-ing* form) cannot function alone as the main verb in a sentence. It must be accompanied by a form of *be* (*am, is, are, was, were,* or *been*).

> They _∧ *are* **thinking** about the future.

THINKING RHETORICALLY

✳ PARTICIPIAL PHRASES

If some of your sentences sound monotonous or choppy, try combining them by using participial phrases.

> The ecstatic fans crowded along the city streets. They were celebrating their team's first state championship.

REVISED

> **Crowded along the city streets,** the ecstatic fans celebrated their team's first state championship.

OR

> **Celebrating their team's first state championship,** the ecstatic fans crowded along the city streets.

Infinitive phrases serve as nouns (**21a(2)**) or as modifiers (chapter **25**). The form of the infinitive is distinct—the infinitive marker *to* followed by the base form of the verb.

> The company intends **to hire** twenty new employees. [noun]

We discussed his plan **to use** **a new packing process.** [modifier of the noun *plan*]

To attract **customers,** the company changed its advertising strategy. [modifier of the verb *changed*]

BEYOND THE RULE

SPLIT INFINITIVES

Some instructors advise against putting words between the infinitive marker *to* and the base form of the verb.

Be sure to carefully consider the evidence. *(carefully)*

This is good advice to remember if the intervening words create a cumbersome sentence.

The jury was unable to, under the circumstances, convict the defendant. *(Under the circumstances, the)*

However, most writers today recognize that a single word splitting an infinitive can provide emphasis.

He did not expect to actually publish his work.

MULTILINGUAL WRITERS

VERBS FOLLOWED BY GERUNDS AND/OR INFINITIVES

Some verbs in English can be followed by a gerund, some can be followed by an infinitive, and some can be followed by either.

Verbs Followed by a Gerund

admit   avoid   consider   deny   dislike   enjoy   finish   suggest

Example: She **enjoys playing** the piano.

(Continued on page 534)

(Continued from page 533)

Verbs Followed by an Infinitive

> agree   decide   deserve   hope   need   plan   promise   seem

> Example: She **promised to play** the piano for us.

Verbs Followed by a Pronoun, Noun, or Noun Phrase and an Infinitive

> advise   encourage   invite   order   persuade   require   teach

> Example: Her father **taught** her **to play** the piano.

When an infinitive follows the verb *make* or *have* and a pronoun, noun, or noun phrase, the marker *to* is omitted.

> Example: The teacher **had** the student **repeat** the song.

The marker *to* is optional when it follows the verb *help* and a pronoun, noun, or noun phrase.

> Example: He **helped** her (**to**) **learn** the song.

Verbs Followed by Either a Gerund or an Infinitive

> begin   continue   like   prefer   remember   stop   try

> Examples: She **likes to play** the piano. She **likes playing** the piano.

Although either a gerund phrase or an infinitive phrase can follow these verbs, the resulting sentences may differ in meaning.

> We **stopped discussing** the plan. [The discussion has ended.]

> We **stopped to discuss** the plan. [The discussion has not yet started.]

Specialized dictionaries provide information on the use of gerunds and infinitives with verbs (see **34e(1)** for a list of recommendations).

(4) Prepositional phrases are used as modifiers.

Prepositional phrases provide information about time, place, cause, manner, and so on. They can also answer one of these questions: Which one? What kind of . . . ?

With great feeling, Martin Luther King expressed his dream **of freedom.**
[*With great feeling* describes the way the speech was delivered, and *of freedom* specifies the kind of dream.]

King delivered his most famous speech at a **demonstration in Washington, DC.**
[Both *at a demonstration* and *in Washington, DC* provide information about place.]

A **prepositional phrase** consists of a **preposition** (a word such as *at, of,* or *in*) and a pronoun, noun, or noun phrase (called the **object of the preposition**). A prepositional phrase modifies another element in the sentence.

Everyone **in class** went to the play. [modifier of the pronoun *everyone*]

The actors **in it** [the play] were all students. [modifier of the noun *actors*]

Some students met the professor **after the play.** [modifier of the verb *met*]

A prepositional phrase sometimes consists of a preposition and an entire clause (**22b**).

They will give the award **to whoever produces the best design.**

BEYOND THE RULE

ENDING A SENTENCE WITH A PREPOSITION

A grammar rule that has caused much controversy over the years is the one that advises against ending a sentence with a preposition. Most professional writers now follow this rule only when they adopt a formal tone. If their rhetorical situation calls for an informal tone, they will not hesitate to place a preposition at the end of a sentence.

He found friends **on** whom he could depend. [formal]
He found friends he could depend **on.** [informal]

SOME COMMON PREPOSITIONS

about	behind	except	of	through
above	beside	for	on	to
after	between	from	out	toward
around	by	in	over	under
as	despite	into	past	until
at	down	like	regarding	up
before	during	near	since	with

Phrasal prepositions consist of more than one word.

Except for the last day, it was a wonderful trip.

The postponement was **due to** inclement weather.

PHRASAL PREPOSITIONS

according to	due to	in spite of
apart from	except for	instead of
as for	in addition to	out of
because of	in case of	with regard to
by means of	in front of	with respect to

MULTILINGUAL WRITERS

PREPOSITIONS IN IDIOMATIC COMBINATIONS

Some verbs, adjectives, and nouns combine with prepositions to form idiomatic combinations (35c).

Verb + Preposition	Adjective + Preposition	Noun + Preposition
apply to	fond of	interest in
rely on	similar to	dependence on
trust in	different from	fondness for

(5) An appositive can expand the meaning of a noun or a noun phrase.

An **appositive** is most often a noun or a noun phrase that refers to the same person, place, thing, or idea as a preceding noun or noun phrase but in different words. The alternate wording provides extra details that make the reference clear. By using an occasional appositive, you can add both clarity and variety to your writing.

When an appositive provides essential information, no commas are used.

> Cormac McCarthy's novel *The Road* won a Pulitzer Prize.
> [The appositive specifies which of McCarthy's novels won the award.]

When an appositive phrase provides details that are not essential, commas set it off.

> *The Road*, **a novel by Cormac McCarthy,** won a Pulitzer Prize.
> [The appositive provides extra details about the book.]

For more information on punctuating nonessential appositives, see 37d(2).

(6) Absolute phrases provide descriptive details or express causes or conditions.

An **absolute phrase** is usually a noun phrase modified by a participial phrase (22a(3)) or a prepositional phrase (22a(4)).

> She left town at dawn, **all her belongings packed into a Volkswagen Beetle.**

> **Her guitar in the front seat,** she pulled away from the curb.

The preceding absolute phrases provide details; the following absolute phrase expresses cause.

> **More vaccine having arrived,** the staff scheduled its distribution.

Be sure to use commas to set off absolute phrases.

Exercise 1

Label the underlined phrases in the following sentences as noun phrases, verb phrases, prepositional phrases, or verbal phrases. For verbal phrases, specify the type: gerund, participial, or infinitive. When a long phrase includes a short phrase, identify just the long phrase. Finally, identify any appositive phrases or absolute phrases in the sentences.

1. The Smithsonian is the largest museum complex in the world.
2. Dedicated to the collection and diffusion of knowledge, the Smithsonian comprises over a dozen museums.
3. People come from every state to visit the museums.
4. Scientists and scholars visiting a Smithsonian museum can use its outstanding facilities.
5. Receiving a Smithsonian fellowship is the dream of many students.
6. The Smithsonian owes its existence to James Smithson, a scientist from Great Britain.
7. Without ever having visited the United States, Smithson included this country in his last will and testament.
8. His bequest firmly rooted in the Enlightenment ideals of democracy and education, James Smithson left the citizens of the United States an unsurpassable legacy.

22b   Clauses

(1) An independent clause can stand alone as a complete sentence.

A **clause** is a group of related words that contains a subject and a predicate. An **independent clause,** sometimes called a *main clause,* has the same grammatical structure as a simple sentence: both contain a subject and a predicate (see **21b**).

The students earned high grades.

Other clauses can be added to independent clauses to form longer, more detailed sentences.

(2) A dependent clause is connected to an independent clause.
A **dependent clause** also has a subject and a predicate (**21b**). However, it cannot stand alone as a complete sentence because of the word introducing it—usually a relative pronoun or a subordinating conjunction.

The athlete **who placed first** grew up in Argentina. [relative pronoun]

She received the gold medal **because she performed flawlessly.** [subordinating conjunction]

If it is not connected to an independent clause, a dependent clause is considered a sentence fragment (**23c**).

(a) Dependent clauses can be used as subjects or objects.
Dependent clauses that serve as subjects (**21b**) or objects (**21c**) are called **noun clauses** (or **nominal clauses**). They are introduced by *if, that,* or a *wh-* word such as *why, what,* or *when.* Notice the similarity in usage between noun phrases and noun clauses.

Noun phrases	Noun clauses
The testimony may not be true. [subject]	**What the witness said** may not be true. [subject]
We do not understand **their motives.** [direct object]	We do not understand **why they did it.** [direct object]
Send the money to **a charity.** [object of the preposition *to*]	Send the money to **whoever needs it most.** [object of the preposition *to* (**22a(4)**)]

When no misunderstanding would result, the word *that* can be omitted from the beginning of a clause.

The scientist said **she was moving to Australia.** [*that* omitted]

However, *that* should always be retained when there are two noun clauses.

> The scientist said **that she was moving to Australia** and **that her research team was planning to accompany her.** [*that* retained in both noun clauses]

(b) Dependent clauses can be used as modifiers.

Two types of dependent clauses—adjectival (relative) clauses and adverbial clauses—serve as modifiers. An **adjectival clause,** or **relative clause,** follows a pronoun, noun, or noun phrase and answers one of these questions: Which one? What kind of . . . ? Such clauses, which nearly always follow the words they modify, usually begin with a **relative pronoun** (*who, whom, that, which,* or *whose*) but sometimes start with a **relative adverb** (*when, where,* or *why*). Notice the similarity in usage between adjectives and adjectival clauses.

Adjectives	Adjectival clauses
Nobody likes **malicious** gossip. [answers the question *What kind of gossip?*]	Nobody likes news reports **that pry into someone's private life.** [answers the question *What kind of news reports?*]
Some **diligent** students begin their research early. [answers the question *Which students?*]	Students **who have good study habits** begin their research early. [answers the question *Which students?*]
The **public** remarks were troubling. [answers the question *Which remarks?*]	The remarks **that were made public** were troubling. [answers the question *Which remarks?*]

An **essential (restrictive) adjectival clause** contains information necessary to specify a noun reference. Such a clause is *not* set off by commas. The essential adjectival clause in the following sentence is needed for the reader to know which state carries a great deal of influence in a presidential election.

> The state **that casts the most electoral votes** greatly influences the outcome of a presidential election.

A **nonessential (nonrestrictive) adjectival clause** provides extra details that, even though they may be interesting, are not needed for the purpose of identifying the preceding noun. An adjectival clause following a proper noun (21a(2)) is almost always nonessential. A nonessential adjectival clause should be set off by commas.

> California, **which has fifty-five electoral votes,** greatly influences the outcome of any presidential election.

Many writers use *that* to begin essential clauses and *which* to begin nonessential clauses. You should follow this convention if you are required to use APA, CMS, or MLA guidelines (although MLA accepts *which* instead of *that* in essential clauses).

THINKING RHETORICALLY

 ADJECTIVAL CLAUSES

If you find that your sentences tend to be short, try using adjectival clauses to combine them into longer sentences.

> *Dub* is a car magazine. It appeals to drivers with hip-hop attitudes.
>
> *Dub* is a car magazine **that appeals to drivers with hip-hop attitudes.**

> A Hovercraft can go where many vehicles cannot. It is practically amphibious.
>
> A Hovercraft, **which can go where many vehicles cannot,** is practically amphibious.

A relative pronoun can be omitted as long as the meaning of the sentence is still clear.

> Mother Teresa was someone **the whole world admired.**
> [*Whom,* the direct object of the clause, has been omitted: the whole world admired *whom.*]

> She was someone **who cared more about serving than being served.**
> [*Who* cannot be omitted because it is the subject of the clause.]

The relative pronoun is not omitted when the clause is set off by commas (that is, when it is a nonessential clause).

Mother Teresa, **whom the whole world admired,** cared more about serving than being served.

An **adverbial clause** usually answers one of the following questions: Where? When? How? Why? How? How frequently? In what manner? Adverbial clauses are introduced by subordinating conjunctions such as *because, although,* and *when.* (For a list of subordinating conjunctions, see page 545.) Notice the similarity in usage between adverbs and adverbial clauses.

Adverbs	Adverbial clauses
Occasionally, the company hires new writers. [answers the question *How frequently does the company hire new writers?*]	**When the need arises,** the company hires new writers. [answers the question *How frequently does the company hire new writers?*]
She acted **selfishly.** [answers the question *How did she act?*]	She acted **as though she cared only about herself.** [answers the question *How did she act?*]

Adverbial clauses can appear at various points in a sentence. Use commas to set off an adverbial clause placed at the beginning or in the middle of a sentence.

Because they disagreed, the researchers made little progress.

The researchers, **because they disagreed,** made little progress.

If you place an adverbial clause at the end of a sentence, you will usually not need a comma.

The researchers made little progress **because they disagreed.**

If, however, an adverbial clause at the end of a sentence contains an extra detail—the type of clause you would want a reader to pause before if he or she were reading it aloud—use a comma to set it off.

I slept soundly that night, **even though a storm raged outside.**

THINKING RHETORICALLY

ADVERBIAL CLAUSES

In an adverbial clause that refers to time or establishes a fact, both the subject and any form of the verb *be* can be omitted. Using such **elliptical clauses** will make your writing more concise.

> **While fishing,** he saw a rare owl.
> [COMPARE: **While he was fishing,** he saw a rare owl.]

> **Though tired,** they continued to study for the exam.
> [COMPARE: **Though they were tired,** they continued to study for the exam.]

Be sure that the omitted subject of an elliptical clause is the same as the subject of the independent clause. Otherwise, revise either the adverbial clause or the main clause.

> While ^(I was) reviewing your report, a few questions occurred to me.

OR

> While reviewing your report, ^(I thought of) a few questions ~~occurred to me~~.

For more information on the use of elliptical constructions, see **36c**.

22c Conjunctions and conjunctive adverbs

(1) Coordinating conjunctions join words, phrases, or clauses.

In the following examples, note that coordinating conjunctions (**21a(7)**) link grammatical elements that are alike. Each conjunction, though, has a specific meaning.

> tired **yet** excited [*Yet* joins two words and signals contrast.]

> in the boat **or** on the pier [*Or* joins two phrases and marks them as alternatives.]

> We did not share a language, **but** somehow we communicated. [*But* joins two independent clauses and signals contrast.]

When a coordinating conjunction joins two independent clauses, as in the last example, it should be preceded by a comma. A coordinating conjunction may also link independent clauses that stand alone as sentences.

> The momentum in the direction of globalization seems too powerful to buck, the economic logic unmatchable. **But** in a region where jobs are draining away, and where an ethic of self-reliance remains a dim, vestigial, but honored memory, it seems at least an outside possibility.
>
> —BILL McKIBBEN, "Small World"

(2) Correlative conjunctions are two-part conjunctions.

Correlative conjunctions (21a(7)) join words, phrases, or clauses. However, they do not join sentences.

either you **or** I [*Either . . . or* joins two words and marks them as alternatives.]

neither on Friday **nor** on Saturday [*Neither . . . nor* joins two phrases and marks them both as false or impossible.]

Not only did they run ten miles, **but** they **also** swam twenty laps. [*Not only . . . but also* joins two independent clauses and signals addition.]

Generally, a correlative conjunction links similar structures. The following sentence has been revised because the correlative conjunction was linking a phrase to a clause.

                   did he save
Not only ~~saving~~ the lives of the accident victims, **but** he **also** prevented many spinal injuries.

(3) Subordinating conjunctions introduce dependent clauses.

A subordinating conjunction introduces a dependent clause (22b(2)). It also carries a specific meaning; for example, it may indicate cause, concession, condition, or purpose.

She studied Spanish **because** she wanted to work in Costa Rica. [*Because* signals a cause.]

Unless the project receives more funding, the research will stop. [*Unless* signals a condition.]

SUBORDINATING CONJUNCTIONS

after	how	than
although	if	though
as if	in case	unless
as though	in that	until
because	insofar as	when, whenever
before	once	where, wherever
even if	since	whether
even though	so that	while

The word *that* can be omitted from the subordinating conjunction *so that* if the meaning remains clear.

I left ten minutes early **so** I would not be late. [*That* has been omitted.]

However, when *that* is omitted, the remaining *so* can be easily confused with the coordinating conjunction *so*.

I had some extra time, **so** I went to the music store.

Because sentences with subordinating conjunctions are punctuated differently from sentences with coordinating conjunctions (21a(7)), be careful to distinguish between them. If *so* stands for "so that," it is a subordinating conjunction. If *so* means "thus," it is a coordinating conjunction.

(4) Conjunctive adverbs link independent clauses.

Conjunctive adverbs—such as *however, nevertheless, then,* and *therefore*—link independent clauses (22b(1)). These adverbs, sometimes called **adverbial conjunctions,** signal relationships such as cause, condition, and contrast.

CONJUNCTIVE ADVERBS

also	however	moreover	still
consequently	indeed	nevertheless	then
finally	instead	next	therefore
furthermore	likewise	nonetheless	thus
hence	meanwhile	otherwise	

Any conjunctive adverb can be used at the beginning of an independent clause. Some may also appear in the middle or at the end of a clause. *However* indicates contrast in the following sentences:

My mother and father hold many of the same values; **however,** they favor opposing political candidates.

My mother and father seldom argue about politics in front of their children; in front of a televised football game, **however,** they bicker incessantly.

My mother and father have differing political views; they rarely argue, **however.**

Because an independent clause can stand alone as a sentence, the clause after the semicolon in each of the previous sentences can also be written as a separate sentence.

My mother and father hold many of the same values. However, they favor opposing political candidates.

My mother and father seldom argue about politics in front of their children. In front of a televised football game, however, they bicker incessantly.

My mother and father have differing political views. They rarely argue, however.

For more information on the use of conjunctive adverbs and related transtion words, see **24c(5)**. For guidelines on punctuating linked independent clauses, see **37a** and **38a**.

Exercise 2

1. Identify the dependent clauses in the following paragraph.
2. Identify the underlined words as coordinating conjunctions, correlative conjunctions, subordinating conjunctions, or conjunctive adverbs.

   [1]<u>If</u> you live by the sword, you might die by the sword. [2]<u>However,</u> <u>if</u> you make your living by swallowing swords, you will not necessarily die by swallowing swords. [3]At least, this is the conclusion Brian Witcombe

and Dan Meyer reached <u>after</u> they surveyed forty-six professional sword swallowers. ⁴(Brian Witcombe is a radiologist, <u>and</u> Dan Meyer is a famous sword swallower.) ⁵Some of those surveyed mentioned <u>that</u> they had experienced <u>either</u> "sword throats" <u>or</u> chest pains, <u>and</u> others who let their swords drop to their stomachs described perforation of their innards, <u>but</u> the researchers could find no listing of a sword-swallowing mortality in the medical studies they reviewed. ⁶The researchers did not inquire into the reasons for swallowing swords in the first place.

22d Sentence forms

You can identify the form of a sentence by noting the number of clauses it contains and the type of each clause.

(1) A simple sentence consists of a single independent clause.

ONE INDEPENDENT CLAUSE

A **simple sentence** is equivalent to one independent clause; thus, it must have a subject and a predicate.

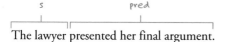

The lawyer presented her final argument.

However, you can expand a simple sentence by adding one or more verbal phrases (22a(3)) or prepositional phrases (22a(4)).

Encouraged by the apparent sympathy of the jury, the lawyer presented her final argument. [The verbal phrase adds detail.]

The lawyer presented her final argument **in less than an hour.** [The prepositional phrase adds information about time.]

(2) A compound sentence consists of at least two independent clauses but no dependent clauses.

> INDEPENDENT CLAUSE + INDEPENDENT CLAUSE

The independent clauses of a compound sentence are most commonly linked by a coordinating conjunction. However, punctuation may sometimes serve the same purpose (38a).

The Democrats proposed a new budget, but the Republicans opposed it. [The coordinating conjunction *but* links two independent clauses and signals contrast.]

The Democrats proposed a new budget; the Republicans opposed it. [The semicolon serves the same purpose as the coordinating conjunction.]

(3) A complex sentence consists of one independent clause and at least one dependent clause.

> INDEPENDENT CLAUSE + DEPENDENT CLAUSE

A dependent clause in a complex sentence can be a noun clause, an adjectival clause, or an adverbial clause (22b(2)).

Because he was known for architectural ornamentation, no one predicted **that the house <u>he designed for himself</u> would be so plain.** [This sentence has three dependent clauses. *Because he was known for architectural ornamentation* is an adverbial clause. *That the house he designed for himself would be so plain* is a noun clause, and *he designed for himself* is an adjectival clause within the noun clause. The relative pronoun *that* has been omitted from the beginning of the embedded adjectival clause.]

(4) A compound-complex sentence consists of at least two independent clauses and at least one dependent clause.

> INDEPENDENT CLAUSE + INDEPENDENT CLAUSE +
> DEPENDENT CLAUSE

The combination of a compound sentence and a complex sentence is called a **compound-complex sentence.**

Conflict is essential to good storytelling, **so** fiction writers often create a character **who faces a major challenge.**
[The coordinating conjunction *so* joins the two independent clauses; the relative pronoun *who* introduces the dependent clause.]

THINKING RHETORICALLY

 ## SENTENCE FORMS

If one of your paragraphs has as many simple sentences as the one below, try combining some of your ideas into compound, complex, or compound-complex sentences. As you do, you might need to add extra detail as well.

> I rode the school bus every day. I didn't like to, though. The bus smelled bad. And it was always packed. The worst part was the bumpy ride. Riding the bus was like riding in a worn-out sneaker.

REVISED

> As a kid, I rode the school bus every day, but I didn't like to. I hated the smell, the crowd, and the bumpy ride itself. Every seat was filled, and many of the kids took their shoes off for the long ride home on roads so bumpy you couldn't even read a comic book. Riding that bus was like riding inside a worn-out sneaker.

Exercise 3

Identify each sentence in the paragraph in exercise 2 as simple, compound, complex, or compound-complex.

Exercise 4

Vary the sentence forms in the following paragraph. Add details as needed.

> We arrived at the afternoon concert late. We couldn't find any seats. It was hot, so we stood in the shade. We finally found seats under an umbrella. The shade didn't help, though. We could feel our brains melting. The music was cool, but we weren't.

22e   Sentence functions

Sentences serve a number of functions. Writers commonly state facts or report information with **declarative sentences**. They give instructions with **imperative sentences**. They use questions, or **interrogative sentences**, to elicit information or to introduce topics. And they express emotion with **exclamatory sentences**.

Declarative	The runners from Kenya won the race.
Imperative	Compare their times with the record.
Interrogative	What were their times?
Exclamatory	The runners from Kenya won the race! Check their times! What an incredible race that was!

Expect great things.

Now more daily nonstops to China from the U.S. than any other airline.

Discover endless opportunities when you go great lengths. United can take you there with daily nonstop service to Beijing from Chicago, San Francisco and Washington, D.C. You can also travel nonstop to Shanghai from Chicago and San Francisco. In fact, United offers more transpacific flights than any other airline. To book, visit **united.com** today.

UNITED
It's time to fly.

Advertisers often use imperatives to attract the reader's attention. (Courtesy of United Airlines.)

Taking note of end punctuation can help you identify the function of a sentence. Generally, a period indicates the end of a declarative sentence or an imperative sentence, and a question mark ends an interrogative sentence. An exclamation point indicates that a sentence is exclamatory. To distinguish between an imperative sentence and a declarative sentence, look for a subject (21b). If you cannot find one, the sentence is imperative. Because an imperative is directed to another person or persons, the subject *you* is implied:

Look over there.
[COMPARE: You look over there.]

BEYOND THE RULE

SENTENCE FUNCTIONS

Declarative, imperative, interrogative, and exclamatory sentences can be used for a variety of purposes. For example, imperative sentences are used not only to give directions but also to make suggestions (*Try using a different screwdriver*), to issue invitations (*Come in*), to extend wishes (*Have a good time*), and to warn others (*Stop there*). Furthermore, a particular purpose, such as getting someone to do something, can be accomplished in more than one way.

Imperative	Close the window, please.
Declarative	We should close the window.
Interrogative	Would you please close the window?

THINKING RHETORICALLY

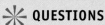 ### QUESTIONS

One type of interrogative sentence, the **rhetorical question**, is not a true question, because an answer is not expected. Instead, like a declarative sentence, it is used to state an opinion. However, a positive rhetorical question can correspond to a negative assertion, and vice versa.

Rhetorical questions	**Equivalent statements**
Should we allow our rights to be taken away?	We should not allow our rights to be taken away.
Isn't it time to make a difference?	It's time to make a difference.

Because they are more emphatic than declarative sentences, rhetorical questions focus the reader's attention on major points.

Exercise 5

Identify each sentence type.

1. I did not look at the weather forecast.
2. Did you see me slosh through the puddles?
3. Next time remind me to bring an umbrella.
4. What a terrible day that was!

23 Sentence Fragments

As its name suggests, a **sentence fragment** is only a piece of a sentence; it is not complete. This chapter can help you

- recognize sentence fragments (**23a**) and
- revise fragments resulting from incorrectly punctuated phrases and dependent clauses (**23b** and **23c**).

23a Recognizing sentence fragments

A complete sentence consists of a subject and a predicate (**21b**), but a fragment is missing one or both of these parts. Sentence fragments are easy to recognize when they are not surrounded by other sentences.

The placement of a patient into a sleeplike state.

This fragment makes the reader wonder what *the placement of a patient into a sleeplike state* does or is. In other words, this fragment lacks a verb—the essential part of a predicate. When placed next to another sentence, however, this fragment is more difficult to recognize.

Alternative medical treatment may include hypnosis. **The placement of a patient into a sleeplike state.**

A fragment such as this one can often simply be attached to the sentence preceding it by adding appropriate punctuation.

Alternative medical treatment may include hypnosis—**the placement of a patient into a sleeplike state.**

Another type of fragment has the essential components of a sentence but begins with a word that marks it as a dependent clause (22b(2)). Compare the complete sentence with the fragment.

The depth of the trance for each person varies. [complete sentence]
Although the depth of the trance for each person varies. [fragment]

The fragment makes more sense when attached to an independent clause (22b(1)).

Most people can be hypnotized easily, **although the depth of the trance for each person varies.**

Note that imperative sentences (22e) are not considered fragments. In these sentences, the subject, *you,* is not stated explicitly. Rather, it is implied.

Find out as much as you can about alternative treatments.
[COMPARE: You find out as much as you can about alternative treatments.]

MULTILINGUAL WRITERS

SUBJECT PRONOUNS

In some languages, subject pronouns are dropped when there is no risk of misunderstanding. In Japanese, a sentence such as *Sushi o tabemasu* ("Eat sushi") is permissible when the subject pronoun can be determined from the context. In Spanish, a verb form reveals information about the subject; unless needed for clarity or emphasis, a subject pronoun can thus be omitted, as in *Trabajo en un banco* ("I work in a bank"). In English, however, subject pronouns must be included in all except imperative sentences.

FOUR METHODS FOR IDENTIFYING FRAGMENTS

If you have trouble recognizing fragments, try one or more of these methods:

1. Read each paragraph backwards, sentence by sentence. When you read your sentences out of order, you may more readily note the incompleteness of a fragment.

2. Locate the essential parts of each sentence. First, find the main verb and any accompanying auxiliary verbs. Remember that verbals cannot function as main verbs (27a). After you find the main verb, identify the subject (21b). Finally, check to see that the sentence does not begin with a relative pronoun (22b(2)) or a subordinating conjunction (22c(3)).

Test sentence 1: The inventor of the Frisbee.

Test: Main verb? *None.*
[Because there is no verb, this test sentence is a fragment.]

Test sentence 2: Walter Frederick Morrison invented the Frisbee.

Test: Main verb? *Invented.*

Subject? *Walter Frederick Morrison.*

Relative pronoun or subordinating conjunction? *None.*

[The test sentence is complete: it contains a subject and a verb and does not begin with a relative pronoun or a subordinating conjunction.]

3. Put any sentence you think might be a fragment into this frame sentence:

They do not understand the idea that _____ .

Only a full sentence will make sense in this frame sentence. If a test sentence, other than an imperative, does not fit into the frame sentence, it is a fragment.

Test sentence 3: Because it can be played almost anywhere.

Test: They do not understand the idea that *because it can be played almost anywhere.*

[The frame sentence does not make sense, so the test sentence is a fragment.]

Test sentence 4: Ultimate Frisbee is a popular sport because it can be played almost anywhere.

Test: They do not understand the idea that *Ultimate Frisbee is a popular sport because it can be played almost anywhere.*

[The frame sentence makes sense, so the test sentence is complete.]

4. Rewrite any sentence you think might be a fragment as a question that can be answered with *yes* or *no*. Only complete sentences can be rewritten this way.

(Continued on page 556)

(Continued from page 555)

Test sentence 5: That combines aspects of soccer, football, and basketball.

Test: *Is that combines aspects of soccer, football, and basketball?*
[The question does not make sense, so the test sentence is a fragment.]

Test sentence 6: Ultimate Frisbee is a game that combines aspects of soccer, football, and basketball.

Test: *Is Ultimate Frisbee a game that combines aspects of soccer, football, and basketball?*
[The question makes sense, so the test sentence is complete.]

Exercise 1

Identify the sentence fragments in the following paragraph. Be prepared to explain how you identified each fragment. Revise the fragments by attaching them to related sentences or by recasting them as complete sentences.

¹The name *Calder* often brings to mind huge mobiles. ²Hanging from the ceilings of art museums. ³Well known for these playfully balanced arrangements of abstract or organic forms, Alexander Calder (1898–1976) was actually a versatile sculptor. ⁴His work ranging from jewelry to outdoor sculptures. ⁵Yet Calder did not begin his career as an artist. ⁶Instead, he studied mechanical engineering. ⁷Even though he came from a family of sculptors. ⁸Four years after he earned his degree, he enrolled in an art school. ⁹Moving to Paris shortly thereafter. ¹⁰Calder first earned worldwide recognition for wire sculptures. ¹¹In the 1930s, he started to experiment with motion. ¹²Eventually developing the mobiles he is best known for today.

23b Phrases as sentence fragments

A phrase (22a) may be mistakenly written as a sentence fragment. You can revise such a fragment by attaching it to a related sentence, usually the one preceding it. If you are unsure of the correct punctuation to use with phrases, see 37b and 37d.

Verbal phrase as a fragment

Early humans valued color. *, creating* ~~Creating~~ permanent colors with natural pigments.

Prepositional phrase as a fragment

For years, the Scottish have dyed sweaters with soot. *, originally* ~~Originally~~ from the chimneys of peat-burning stoves.

Compound predicate as a fragment

Arctic foxes turn white when it snows. *and* ~~And~~ thus conceal themselves from prey.

Appositive phrase as a fragment

During the Renaissance, one of the most highly valued pigments was ultramarine. *—an* ~~An~~ extract from lapis lazuli.

Appositive list as a fragment

To derive dyes, we have always experimented with what we find in nature. *: shells,* ~~Shells,~~ roots, insects, flowers.

Absolute phrase as a fragment

The deciduous trees of New England are known for their brilliant autumn color. *, sugar* ~~Sugar~~ maples dazzling tourists with their orange and red leaves.

Instead of attaching a fragment to the preceding sentence, you can recast the fragment as a complete sentence. This method of revision elevates the importance of the information conveyed in the fragment.

Fragment	Humans painted themselves for a variety of purposes. **To attract a mate, to hide themselves from game or predators, or to signal aggression.**

Revision   Humans used color for a variety of purposes. For example, they painted themselves to attract a mate, to hide themselves from game or predators, or to signal aggression.

Exercise 2

Revise each fragment by attaching it to a related sentence or by recasting it as a complete sentence.

1. A brilliant twenty-three-year-old Englishman. Isaac Newton was the first person to study color.
2. By passing a beam of sunlight through a prism. Newton showed that white light comprised all the visible colors of the spectrum.
3. White light passed through the prism. And separated into the colors of the rainbow.
4. Rainbows are arcs of color. Caused by water droplets in the air.
5. Sometimes rainbows contain all the spectrum colors. Red, orange, yellow, green, blue, indigo, and violet.
6. Particles of spray in waterfalls can act as prisms. Producing a variety of colors.
7. Our brains easily fooled. We sometimes see more colors than are actually present.

23c   Dependent clauses as sentence fragments

A dependent clause punctuated as a complete sentence is a fragment. To revise such a fragment, attach it to a related sentence, usually the sentence preceding it.

The iceberg was no surprise. ~~Because~~ the *Titanic*'s wireless operators had received reports of ice in the area.
(because)

More than two thousand people were aboard the *Titanic.* ~~Which~~ was , which
the largest ocean liner in 1912.

Two other methods can be used to revise these types of fragments.
You can recast the fragment as a complete sentence by removing the
subordinating conjunction or relative pronoun and supplying any
missing elements. This method of revision draws attention to the information originally conveyed in the fragment. Compare the following
revisions with the ones above:

> The iceberg was no surprise. The *Titanic*'s wireless operators had
> received reports of ice in the area.

> More than two thousand people were aboard the *Titanic*. In 1912, this
> ocean liner was the world's largest.

You can also reduce a clausal fragment to a phrase (**22a**) and then
attach it to a related sentence.

> More than two thousand people were aboard the *Titanic*, the largest
> ocean liner in 1912. [fragment reduced to an appositive phrase]

If you are unsure of the punctuation to use with phrases or dependent
clauses, see chapter **37**.

THINKING RHETORICALLY

FRAGMENTS

When used judiciously, fragments—like short sentences—emphasize ideas,
add surprise, or enhance the rhythm of a paragraph. Fragments are not appropriate for all types of writing, however. They are generally permitted only
when the rhetorical situation allows the use of a casual tone.

> **May. When the earth's Northern Hemisphere awakens from winter's sleep
> and all of nature bristles with the energies of new life.** My work has kept
> me indoors for months now. I'm not sure I'll ever get used to it.
> —KEN CAREY, *Flat Rock Journal: A Day in the Ozark Mountains*

BEYOND THE RULE

ABBREVIATED SENTENCES

You encounter sentence fragments every day—in conversations, in e-mail messages, and even in some instructional materials. In conversation, someone might ask you, "Going anywhere tonight?" And you might respond, "Maybe." To end an e-mail message, you might write, "See you later." When preparing a meal, you have probably read instructions similar to these: "Just heat and serve." "Cook to golden brown." The writers of such instructions expect you to know what is to be heated or browned. These kinds of fragments, in which words that can be understood from the context are omitted, are called **abbreviated sentences.**

Package directions often include abbreviated sentences.

Exercise 3

Revise each fragment by attaching it to a related sentence or by recasting it as a full sentence.

1. The ship was christened *Titanic*. Which means "of great size."
2. The shipbuilders thought the *Titanic* was unsinkable. Because it had sixteen watertight compartments.
3. The ship sank in less than three hours. Even though the damage caused by the iceberg was not massive.
4. The extent of the damage to the ship's hull was unknown. Until researchers started examining the wreckage in the late 1990s.
5. In 1987, a controversial French expedition recovered dishes, jewelry, and other artifacts from the *Titanic*. Which were later displayed in France and Germany.

Exercise 4

Follow the guidelines in this chapter to locate and revise the fragments in the following paragraph. If you find it necessary, make other improvements as well. Be prepared to explain your revisions.

¹Folklore from around the world contains references to wild men in the woods. ²Such as the Greek saytrs, the Russian *leshiy*, and the Yetis of the Himalayas. ³In North America, many people, including normally skeptical citizens and scientists, are fascinated by stories of Sasquatch. ⁴A name originating in the Salish word *saskehavas*. ⁵Another name commonly used is Big Foot. ⁶An allusion to the size of the footprints reportedly belonging to a giant apelike creature. ⁷That smells bad. ⁸Most sightings of Sasquatch occur in the Pacific Northwest. ⁹From northern California to central Alaska. ¹⁰Although reports have come from almost every state. ¹¹During the settlement of the United States, stories of hairy ape-men were told by Native Americans. ¹²And later on by trappers. ¹³Teddy Roosevelt recorded one such story.

24 Comma Splices and Fused Sentences

Comma splices and fused sentences are sentence-level mistakes resulting from incorrect or missing punctuation. Both are punctuated as one sentence when they should be punctuated as two sentences (or two independent clauses). By revising comma splices and fused sentences, you indicate sentence boundaries and thus make your writing easier to read. This chapter will help you

- review the rules for punctuating independent clauses (24a),
- recognize comma splices and fused sentences (24b), and
- learn ways to revise them (24c and 24d).

A **comma splice,** or **comma fault,** refers to the incorrect use of a comma between two independent clauses (38a).

                                            but
Most stockholders favored the merger,ₐthe management did not.

Because a comma is a weak mark of punctuation, it is not conventionally used to join independent clauses. For this purpose, you should use a connecting word, a stronger mark of punctuation, or both.

A **fused sentence** consists of two independent clauses run together without any punctuation at all. This type of sentence is sometimes called a **run-on sentence.**

                                            ; however,
The first section of the proposal was approvedₐthe budget will have to be resubmitted.

To revise a fused sentence, include appropriate punctuation and any necessary connecting words.

24a **Punctuating independent clauses**

In case you are unfamiliar with or unsure about the conventions for punctuating independent clauses, here is a short review.

A comma and a coordinating conjunction can join two independent clauses (37a). The coordinating conjunction indicates the relationship between the two clauses. For example, *and* signals addition, whereas *but* and *yet* signal contrast. The comma precedes the conjunction.

> INDEPENDENT CLAUSE, **and** INDEPENDENT CLAUSE.

The new store opened this morning, **and** the owners greeted everyone at the door.

A semicolon can join two independent clauses that are closely related. A semicolon generally signals addition or contrast.

> INDEPENDENT CLAUSE; INDEPENDENT CLAUSE.

One of the owners comes from this area; the other grew up in Cuba.

A semicolon may also precede an independent clause that begins with a conjunctive adverb such as *however* or *nevertheless*. Notice that a comma follows this type of connecting word.

The store will be open late on Fridays and Saturdays; **however,** it will be closed all day on Sundays.

BEYOND THE RULE

PUNCTUATION IN SENTENCES CONTAINING CONJUNCTIVE ADVERBS

A comma used to set off a conjunctive adverb is sometimes omitted when there is no risk of misreading.

The sea was unusually hot; **thus** the coral turned white.
[No misreading is possible, so the comma can be omitted.]

He was so nervous that his stomach was churning; **however,** he answered the question calmly and accurately.
[The comma is needed. Without it, *however* might be interpreted as meaning "in whatever way" rather than "in contrast." COMPARE: However he answered the question, he would offend someone.]

A colon can join two independent clauses. The second clause usually explains or elaborates the first.

> INDEPENDENT CLAUSE: INDEPENDENT CLAUSE.

The owners have extended a special offer: anyone who makes a purchase during the opening will receive a 10 percent discount.

If you are following MLA guidelines, capitalize the first word of a clause following a colon when the clause expresses a rule or principle (41d).

A period separates clauses into distinct sentences.

> INDEPENDENT CLAUSE. INDEPENDENT CLAUSE.

The store is located on the corner of Pine Street and First Avenue. It was formerly an insurance office.

Occasionally, commas are used between independent clauses, but only when the clauses are short, parallel in form, and unified in meaning.

They came, they shopped, they left.

For more information on punctuating sentences, see chapters 37, 38, and 41.

24b Recognizing comma splices and fused sentences

If you have trouble recognizing comma splices or fused sentences, try one of the following methods.

TWO METHODS FOR IDENTIFYING COMMA SPLICES AND FUSED SENTENCES

1. Locate a sentence that may be problematic. Put it into this frame sentence:

They do not understand the idea that _____.

Only complete sentences make sense when placed in the frame sentence. If just part of a test sentence fits, you have probably located a comma splice or a fused sentence.

Test sentence 1: Plasma is the fourth state of matter.

Test: They do not understand the idea that *plasma is the fourth state of matter.*
[The test sentence makes sense in the frame sentence. No revision is necessary.]

Test sentence 2: Plasma is the fourth state of matter, some scientists believe that 99 percent of the universe is made of it.

Test: They do not understand the idea that *plasma is the fourth state of matter, some scientists believe that 99 percent of the universe is made of it.*
[The frame sentence does not make sense because there are two sentences completing it, rather than one. The test sentence contains a comma splice and thus should be revised.]

Revision: Plasma is the fourth state of matter. Some scientists believe that 99 percent of the universe is made of it.

2. Try to rewrite a possibly incorrect sentence as a question that can be answered with *yes* or *no*. If just part of the sentence makes sense, you have likely found a comma splice or a fused sentence.

Test sentence 3: Plasma is used for a number of purposes.

Test: *Is plasma used for a number of purposes?*
[The question makes sense. No revision is necessary.]

Test sentence 4: Plasma is used for a number of purposes it may even power rockets someday.

(Continued on page 566)

(Continued from page 565)

Test: *Is plasma used for a number of purposes it may even power rockets someday?*
[The question does not make sense because only one part of the test sentence has been made into a question. The test sentence is a fused sentence and thus should be revised.]

Revision: Plasma is used for a number of purposes. It may even power rockets someday.

You can also find comma splices and fused sentences by remembering that they commonly occur in certain circumstances.

▪ With transitional words and phrases such as *however, therefore,* and *for example* (see also **24c(5)**)

Comma splice: The director is not able to meet with you this week; however, next week she will have time on Monday and Tuesday.

[Notice that a semicolon replaces the comma.]

▪ When an explanation or an example is given in the second sentence

Fused sentence: The cultural center has a new collection of spear points. Many of them were donated by a retired anthropologist.

▪ When a positive clause follows a negative clause, or vice versa

Comma splice: A World Cup victory is not just an everyday sporting event. It is a national celebration.

▪ When the subject of the second clause is a pronoun whose antecedent is in the preceding clause

Fused sentence: Lake Baikal is located in southern Russia. It is 394 miles long.

24c Revising comma splices and fused sentences

If you find comma splices or fused sentences in your writing, try one of the following methods to revise them.

(1) Use a comma and a coordinating conjunction to link clauses.

By linking clauses with a comma and a coordinating conjunction (such as *and* or *but*), you signal the relationship between the clauses (addition or contrast, for example).

Fused sentence: Joseph completed the first experiment, and he will complete the other by Friday.

Comma splice: Some diplomats applauded the treaty, but others opposed it vehemently.

(2) Use a semicolon or a colon to link clauses or a period to separate them.

When you link independent clauses with a semicolon, you signal their connection indirectly. There are no explicit conjunctions to use as cues. The semicolon usually indicates addition or contrast. When you link clauses with a colon, the second clause serves as an explanation or an elaboration of the first. A period indicates that each clause is a complete sentence, distinct from surrounding sentences.

Comma splice: Our division's reports are posted on our Web page, hard copies are available by request.

Revision 1: Our division's reports are posted on our Web page; hard copies are available by request.

Revision 2: Our division's reports are posted on our Web page. Hard copies are available by request.

Fused sentence: His choice was difficult: he would either lose his job or betray his ethical principles.

(3) Rewrite one clause as a phrase or as a dependent clause.

A dependent clause (22b(2)) includes a subordinating conjunction such as *although* or *because,* which indicates how the dependent and independent clauses are related (in a cause-and-effect relationship, for example). A prepositional phrase (22a(4)) includes a preposition such as *in, on, because of,* or *in spite of* that may also signal relationships directly. Verbal, appositive, and absolute phrases (**22a(3)**, **22a(5)**, and **22a(6)**) suggest relationships less directly because they do not include connecting words.

Comma splice: The wind had blown down trees and power lines, the whole city was without electricity for several hours.

Revision 1: Because the wind had blown down power lines, the whole city was without electricity for several hours. [dependent clause]

Revision 2: Because of the downed power lines, the whole city was without electricity for several hours. [prepositional phrase]

Revision 3: The wind having blown down power lines, the whole city was without electricity for several hours. [absolute phrase]

(4) Integrate one clause into the other.
When you integrate clauses, you will generally retain the important details but omit or change some words.

Fused sentence: The proposal covers all but one point it does not describe how the project will be assessed.

Revision: The proposal covers all the points except assessment procedures.

Exercise 1

Connect each pair of sentences in two of the following ways: (a) join them with a semicolon or colon, (b) join them with a coordinating conjunction, (c) reduce one sentence to a phrase or a dependent clause (see **22c(3)** for a list of subordinating conjunctions), or (d) integrate one clause into the other.

1. Our national parks offer a variety of settings. They attract millions of visitors every year.
2. The Grand Teton National Park includes a sixteen-peak mountain range. It offers extensive hiking trails and wildlife-viewing opportunities.
3. Yellowstone National Park is generally full of tourists. The geysers and cliffs are worth the visit.
4. Hikers especially enjoy their vacations at Yellowstone National Park. The park consists of two million acres of backcountry perfect for hiking.
5. Vacationers enchanted by cascading water should visit Yosemite National Park. The waterfalls at Yosemite reach heights of more than two thousand feet.

(5) Use transitional words or phrases to link independent clauses.
Another way to revise comma splices and fused sentences is to use transitional words and phrases such as *however, on the contrary,* and *in the meantime.* (For examples, see the list on page 73.) You can use these words and phrases to begin new sentences.

> **Fused sentence:** Sexual harassment is not just an issue for
>
> women‸men can be sexually harassed too.
>   . After all,

You can also use them to join two clauses into one sentence.

> **Comma splice:** The word *status* refers to relative position within
>
> a group‸ it is often used to indicate only positions of prestige.
>   ; however,

If you have questions about punctuating sentences with transitional words and phrases, see **22c(4)** and **38a.**

As you edit fused sentences and comma splices, you will refine the connections between your sentences and thereby help your readers follow your train of thought. The following checklist will help you find and fix comma splices and fused sentences.

CHECKLIST for Comma Splices and Fused Sentences

1. Common Sites for Comma Splices or Fused Sentences

- With transitional words such as *however* and *therefore*
- When an explanation or an example occurs in the second clause
- When a positive clause follows a negative clause, or vice versa
- When the subject of the second clause is a pronoun whose antecedent is in the first clause

2. How to Fix Comma Splices and Fused Sentences

- Link the clauses with a comma and a coordinating conjunction.
- Link the clauses, using a semicolon or a colon.
- Separate the clauses by punctuating each as a sentence.
- Make one clause dependent.
- Reduce one clause to a phrase.
- Rewrite the sentence, integrating one clause into the other.

Exercise 2

Connect each pair of sentences by including a transitional word or phrase and any necessary punctuation.

1. The average human brain weighs about three pounds. The average brain of a sperm whale weighs seventeen pounds.

2. The body of a brain cell can move. Most brain cells stay put, extending axons outward.

3. The brain needs water to function properly. Dehydration commonly leads to lethargy and hinders learning.

4. Researchers studying brain hemispheres have found that many professional musicians process music in their left hemisphere. The notion that musicians and artists depend on the right side of their brain is considered outmoded.

5. Discoveries in neuroscience have yielded many benefits. Researchers have developed medication for schizophrenia and Tourette's syndrome.

24d   Divided quotations

When you divide quotations with attributive tags such as *he said* or *she asked* (11d and chapter 40), be sure to use a period between independent clauses.

Comma splice: "Beauty brings copies of itself into being," states Elaine
Scarry, "it makes us draw it, take photographs of it, or describe it to
other people."

[Both parts of the quotation are complete sentences, so the attributive tag is attached to the first, and the sentence is punctuated with a period. The second sentence stands by itself.]

A comma separates two parts of a single quoted sentence.

"Musing takes place in a kind of meadowlands of the imagination," writes Rebecca Solnit, "a part of the imagination that has not yet been plowed, developed, or put to any immediately practical use." [Because the quotation is a single sentence, a comma is used.]

Exercise 3

Revise each comma splice or fused sentence in the following paragraph. Some sentences may not need revision.

¹In the introduction to his book of true stories, *I Thought My Father Was God,* Paul Auster describes how he was able to collect these accounts of real and sometimes raw experience. ²In October 1999, Auster, in collaboration with National Public Radio, began the *National Story Project,* during an interview on the radio program *Weekend All Things Considered,* he invited listeners to send in their stories about unusual events—"true stories that sounded like fiction." ³In just one year, over four thousand stories were submitted Auster read every one of them. ⁴"Of the four thousand stories I have read, most have been compelling enough to hold me until the last word," Auster affirms, "most have been written with simple, straightforward conviction, and most have done honor to the people who sent them in." ⁵Some of the stories Auster collected can now be read in his anthology choosing stories for the collection was difficult, though. ⁶"For every story about a dream or an animal or a missing object," explains Auster, "there were dozens of others that were submitted, dozens of others that could have been chosen."

25 Modifiers

Modifiers are words, phrases, or clauses that modify; that is, they qualify or limit the meaning of other words. For example, if you were to describe a sandwich as "humdrum," as "lacking sufficient mustard," or as something "that might have tasted good two days ago," you would be using a word, a phrase, or a clause to modify *sandwich*. When used effectively, modifiers enliven writing with details and enhance its coherence.

This chapter will help you

- recognize modifiers (25a),
- use conventional comparative and superlative forms (25b),
- place modifiers effectively (25c), and
- revise double negatives (25d).

25a Recognizing modifiers

The most common modifiers are adjectives and adverbs. **Adjectives** modify nouns and pronouns (21a(4)); **adverbs** modify verbs, adjectives, and other adverbs (21a(5)). You can distinguish an adjective from an adverb, then, by determining what type of word is modified.

Adjectives	**Adverbs**
She looked **curious.** [modifies pronoun]	She looked at me **curiously**. [modifies verb]
productive meeting [modifies noun]	**highly** productive meeting [modifies adjective]
a **quick** lunch [modifies noun]	**very** quickly [modifies adverb]

In addition, consider the form of the modifier. Many adjectives end with one of these suffixes: *able, -al, -ful, -ic, ish, -less,* or *-y.*

accept**able** rent**al** event**ful** angel**ic** sheep**ish** effort**less** sleep**y**

MULTILINGUAL WRITERS

ADJECTIVE SUFFIXES IN OTHER LANGUAGES

In some languages, adjectives and nouns agree in number. In Spanish, for example, when a noun is plural, the adjective is plural as well: *vistas claras.* In English, however, adjectives do not have a plural form: *clear views.*

Present and past participles (27a(5)) can also be used as adjectives.

a **determining** factor a **determined** effort
[present participle] [past participle]

Be sure to include the complete *-ed* ending of a past participle.

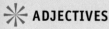

Please see the ~~enclose~~ documents for more details.

THINKING RHETORICALLY

✳ ADJECTIVES

When your rhetorical situation calls for vivid images or emotional intensity, choose appropriate adjectives to convey these qualities. That is, instead of describing a movie you did not like with the overused adjective *boring*, you could say that it was *tedious* or *mind-numbing*. When you sense that you might be using a lackluster adjective, search for an alternative in a thesaurus. If any of the words listed there are unfamiliar, be sure to look them up in a dictionary so that you use them correctly.

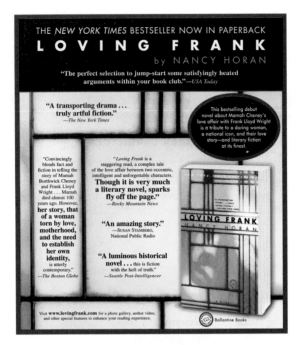

Book ads often include descriptive adjectives.

MULTILINGUAL WRITERS

USING PARTICIPLES AS ADJECTIVES

Both present participles and past participles are used as adjectives; however, they cannot be used interchangeably. For example, when you want to indicate an emotion, use a present participle with a noun referring to someone or something that is the cause of the emotion. In the phrase *the exciting tennis match,* the tennis match is the cause of the excitement. Use the past participle with a noun referring to someone who experiences an emotion. In the phrase *the excited crowd,* the crowd is experiencing the excitement.

Here is a list of commonly confused participles:

annoying, annoyed	frustrating, frustrated
boring, bored	interesting, interested
confusing, confused	surprising, surprised
embarrassing, embarrassed	tiring, tired

The easiest type of adverb to identify is the adverb of manner (21a(5)). It is formed by adding -*ly* to an adjective.

carefu**lly**   unpleasant**ly**   silent**ly**

If the adjective ends in -*y*, the -*y* is changed to -*i* before -*ly* is added.

eas**y** [adjective]   eas**ily** [adverb]

If the adjective ends in -*le*, the -*e* is dropped and just *y* is added.

simp**le** [adjective]   simp**ly** [adverb]

However, not all words ending in -*ly* are adverbs. Certain adjectives related to nouns also end in -*ly* (*friend, friendly; hour, hourly*). In addition, not all adverbs end in -*ly*. Adverbs that indicate time or place (*today, tomorrow, here,* and *there*) do not have the -*ly* ending. Neither does the negator *not*. A few words—for example, *fast* and *well*—can function as either adjectives or adverbs.

They like **fast** cars. [adjective]

They ran **fast** enough to catch the bus. [adverb]

(1) Nouns can be modifiers.

Adjectives and adverbs are the most common modifiers, but nouns (21a(2)) can also be modifiers (***movie** critic, **reference** manual*).

MULTILINGUAL WRITERS

NOUN MODIFIERS

In noun combinations, the first noun is the modifier. Different orders produce different meanings.

A *company phone* is a phone that belongs to a company.

A *phone company* is a company that sells phones or provides phone service.

(2) Phrases and clauses can be modifiers.

Participial phrases, prepositional phrases, and some infinitive phrases are modifiers (**22a(3)** and **22a(4)**).

> **Growing in popularity every year,** mountain bikes now dominate the market. [participial phrase]
>
> Mountain bikes first became popular **in the 1980s.** [prepositional phrase]
>
> Some people use mountain bikes **to commute to work.** [infinitive phrase]

Adjectival (relative) clauses and adverbial clauses are both modifiers (see **22b(2)**).

> BMX bicycles have frames **that are relatively small.** [adjectival clause]
>
> **Although mountain bikes are designed for off-road use,** many people use them on city streets. [adverbial clause]

Exercise 1

Underline the modifiers in the following paragraph.

> ¹Although it seems unbelievable, there once was a race of little people. ²The first skeleton of *Homo floresiensis* was found in September 2003 on an island near Bali. ³Archaeologists working in the area excavated the skeleton from a limestone cave. ⁴Some believe that this species of human is a version of *Homo erectus,* who arrived on the island and became small to adapt to its conditions.

---

(3) Adjectives and adverbs are sometimes confused.

An adjective used after a sensory linking verb (*look, smell, taste, sound,* or *feel*) modifies the subject of the sentence (**21b**). A common error is to use an adverb after this type of linking verb.

>   bad
> I felt ~~badly~~ about missing the rally. [The adjective *bad* modifies *I.*]

However, when *look, smell, taste, sound,* or *feel* is used as an action verb (**21a(1)**), it can be modified by an adverb.

She looked **angrily** at the referree. [The adverb *angrily* modifies *looked*.]

BUT She looked **angry**. [The adjective *angry* modifies *she*.]

The words *good* and *well* are easy to confuse. In academic rhetorical situations, *good* is considered an adjective and so is not used with action verbs.

The whole team played ~~good~~ well.

Another frequent error is the dropping of *-ly* endings from adverbs. Although you may not hear the ending when you speak, be sure to include it when you write.

They bought only ~~local~~ locally grown vegetables.

Exercise 2

Revise the following sentences to use adjectives and adverbs considered conventional in academic writing.

1. My brother said he was real nervous.
2. He did not think he could drive good enough to pass the driver's test.
3. I told him that to pass he would have to drive just reasonable well.
4. He looked calmly as he got into the tester's car.
5. As I knew he would, my brother passed his test easy.

25b Comparatives and superlatives

Many adjectives and adverbs change form to show degrees of quality, quantity, time, distance, manner, and so on. The **positive form** of an adjective or adverb is the word you would look for in a dictionary: *hard, urgent, deserving*. The **comparative form**, which either ends in *-er* or is preceded by *more* or *less*, compares two elements: *I worked **harder** than I ever had before.* The **superlative form**, which either ends in *-est* or is preceded by *most* or *least*, compares three or more elements: *Jeff is the **hardest** worker I have ever met.*

Positive	Comparative	Superlative
hard	harder	hardest
urgent	more/less urgent	most/least urgent
deserving	more/less deserving	most/least deserving

The following guidelines can help you decide when to add the suffix *-er* or *-est* and when to use *more/less* or *most/least*.

GUIDELINES FOR FORMING COMPARATIVES AND SUPERLATIVES

- One syllable words generally take the ending *-er* or *-est*: *fast, faster, fastest*.
- Two-syllable words ending in a consonant and *-y* also generally take the ending *-er* or *-est*, with the *y* changed to an *i*: *noisy, noisier, noisiest*.
- Two-syllable adjectives ending in *-ct*, *-nt*, or *-st* are preceded by *more/less* or *most/least*: *less exact, least exact; more recent, most recent; more honest, most honest*. Two-syllable adjectives with suffixes such as *-ous*, *-ish*, *-ful*, *-ing*, and *-ed* are also preceded by *more/less* or *most/least*: *more/most famous; more/most squeamish; less/least careful; more/most lasting, less/ least depressed*.
- Two-syllable adjectives ending in *-er*, *-ow*, or *-some* take either *-er/-est* or a preceding qualifier: *narrower, more narrow, less narrow, narrowest, most narrow, least narrow*.
- Words of three or more syllables are preceded by *more/less* or *most/least*: *less/least fortunate; more/most elegantly*.
- Some modifiers have irregular comparative and superlative forms:

  little, less, least

  good/well, better, best

  bad/badly, worse, worst

  far, further/farther, furthest/farthest

(See the Glossary of Usage.)

---

(1) Effective comparisons are complete and logical.

When you use the comparative form of an adjective or an adverb, be sure to indicate what two elements you are comparing. The revision of the following sentence makes it clear that a diesel engine and a gas engine are being compared.

A diesel engine is **heavier**. *~~than a gas engine~~*

Occasionally, the second element in a comparison is implied. The word *paper* does not have to be included after *second* in the sentence below. The reader can infer that the grade on the second paper was better than the grade on the first paper.

She wrote **two** papers; the instructor gave her a **better** grade on the second.

A comparison should also be logical. The following example illogically compares *population* and *Wabasha*.

The **population** of Winona is larger than **Wabasha**.

You can revise this type of faulty comparison in three ways:

- Repeat the word that refers to what is being compared.

    The **population** of Winona is larger than the **population** of Wabasha.

- Use a pronoun that corresponds to the first element in the comparison.

    The **population** of Winona is larger than **that** of Wabasha.

- Use possessive forms.

    Winona's population is larger than **Wabasha's**.

(2) A double comparative or superlative is redundant.
Use either an ending (*-er* or *-est*) or a preceding qualifier (*more* or *most*), not both, to form a comparative or superlative.

The first bridge is **more ~~narrower~~** than the second.

The **~~most~~ narrowest** bridge is in the northern part of the state.

Comparative and superlative forms of adjectives or adverbs that generally have absolute meanings, as in *a more perfect society, the most unique campus* (see the Glossary of Usage), and *less completely exhausted,* are rarely used in academic writing.

Exercise 3

Provide the correct comparative or superlative form of each modifier within parentheses.

1. Amphibians can be divided into three groups. Frogs and toads are in the (common) group.
2. Because they do not have to maintain a specific body temperature, amphibians eat (frequently) than mammals do.
3. Reptiles may look like amphibians, but their skin is (dry).
4. During the Devonian period, the (close) ancestors of amphibians were fish with fins that looked like legs.
5. In general, amphibians have (few) bones in their skeletons than other animals with backbones have.
6. Color markings on amphibians vary, though the back of an amphibian is usually (dark) than its belly.

25c　Placement of modifiers

Effective placement of modifiers will improve the clarity and coherence of your sentences. A **misplaced modifier** obscures the meaning of a sentence.

(1) Keep related words together.
Place the modifiers *almost, even, hardly, just,* and *only* before the words or word groups they modify. Altering placement can alter meaning.

The committee can **only** nominate two members for the position. [The committee cannot *appoint* the two members to the position.]

The committee can nominate **only** two members for the position. [The committee cannot nominate more than two members.]

Only the committee can nominate two members for the position. [No person or group other than the committee can nominate members.]

(2) Place phrases and clauses as close as possible to the words or word groups they modify.

Readers expect phrases and clauses to modify the nearest grammatical element. The revision of the following sentence clarifies that the prosecutor, not the witness, was skillful.

With great skill, the

~~The~~ prosecutor cross-examined the witness ~~with great skill~~.

The following revision makes it clear that the phrase *crouched and ugly* describes the phantom, not the boy.

The   *crouched and ugly*

~~Crouched and ugly, the~~ young boy gasped at the phantom moving across the stage.

The next sentence is fine as long as Jesse wrote the proposal, not the review. If he wrote the review, the sentence should be recast.

I have not read the review of the proposal Jesse wrote.

Jesse's

I have not read the review of the proposal ~~Jesse wrote~~.

MULTILINGUAL WRITERS

ORDERING ADJECTIVES THAT MODIFY THE SAME NOUN

In English, two or three adjectives modifying the same noun are used in a particular order based on their meanings. (The use of more than two consecutive adjectives is rare.) The following list shows the usual order of adjectives and gives examples.

Size	*large, long, small, short*
Evaluator	*fascinating, painful, content*
Shape	*square, round, triangular*
Age	*young, old, aged, newborn, antique*
Color	*black, white, green, brown*
Origin	*Arabian, Cuban, Peruvian, Slavic*
Material	*silk, paper, pine, rubber*

We visited a **fascinating Italian** village. [evaluator, origin]

An **old black** dog stared at us. [age, color]

MULTILINGUAL WRITERS

ADVERBS OF FREQUENCY

Adverbs of frequency (such as *always, never, sometimes,* and *often*) appear before one-word verbs.

He **rarely** <u>goes</u> to horror movies.

However, these adverbs appear after a form of *be* when it is the main verb.

Novels written by Stephen King <u>are</u> **always** popular.

When a sentence contains more than one verb in a verb phrase, the adverb of frequency is placed after the first auxiliary verb.

My friends <u>have</u> **never** <u>read</u> *The Shining.*

(3) Revise squinting modifiers so that they modify only one element.
A **squinting modifier** can be interpreted as modifying either what precedes it or what follows it. To avoid such lack of clarity, you can reposition the modifier and/or add word(s) or punctuation.

Even though Erikson lists some advantages **overall** his vision of a successful business is faulty.

Revisions

Even though Erikson lists some **overall** advantages, his vision of a successful business is faulty. [modifer repositioned; punctuation added]

Erikson lists some advantages**; however, overall,** his vision of a successful business is faulty. [word and punctuation added]

Exercise 4

Improve the clarity of the following sentences by moving the modifiers. Not all sentences require editing.

1. Alfred Joseph Hitchcock was born the son of a poultry dealer in London.
2. Hitchcock was only identified with thrillers after making his third movie, *The Lodger.*
3. Hitchcock moved to the United States in 1939 and eventually became a naturalized citizen.
4. Hitchcock's most famous movies revolved around psychological improbabilities that are still discussed by movie critics today.
5. Although his movies are known for suspense sometimes moviegoers also remember Hitchcock's droll sense of humor.
6. Hitchcock just did not direct movie thrillers; he also produced two television series.
7. Originally a British citizen, Queen Elizabeth knighted Alfred Hitchcock in 1980.

(4) Revise dangling modifiers.

Dangling modifiers are phrases (22a) or elliptical clauses (22b(2)) that lack an appropriate word to modify. To avoid including dangling modifiers in your essays, first look carefully at any sentence that begins with a phrase or an elliptical clause. If the phrase or clause suggests an action, be sure that what follows the modifier (the subject of the sentence) names the actor. If there is no actor performing the action indicated in the phrase, the modifier is dangling. To revise this type of dangling modifier, name an actor—either in the modifier or in the main clause.

Lying on the beach, time became irrelevant. [Time cannot lie on a beach.]

Revisions

While **we** were lying on the beach, time became irrelevant. [actor in the modifier]

Lying on the beach, **we** found that time became irrelevant. [actor in the main clause]

While eating lunch, the phone rang. [A phone cannot eat lunch.]

Revisions

While **we** were eating lunch, the phone rang. [actor in the modifier]

While eating lunch, **we** heard the phone ring. [actor in the main clause]

The following sentences illustrate revisions of other common types of dangling modifiers:

To avoid getting sunburn, ∧you should apply sunscreen ~~should be applied~~ before going outside.

[Sunscreen cannot avoid getting sunburn.]

∧Because they were in ~~In~~ a rush to finish their work, an accident occurred.

[An accident cannot be in a rush.]

Although you will most frequently find a dangling modifier at the beginning of a sentence, you may sometimes find one at the end of a sentence.

Adequate lighting is important ∧for anyone ~~when~~ studying.

[Lighting cannot study.]

Sentence modifiers and absolute phrases are not considered to be dangling.

The fog finally lifting, planes were able to depart.

Marcus played well in the final game, **on the whole.**

Exercise 5

Revise the following sentences to eliminate misplaced and dangling modifiers. Some sentences may not require editing.

1. Climbing a mountain, fitness becomes all-important.
2. To make the climb a true adventure, climbers must doubt whether they will reach the summit.
3. Having set their goals, the mountain must challenge the climbers.
4. In determining an appropriate challenge, considering safety precautions is necessary.
5. Taking care to stay roped together, accidents are less likely to occur.
6. Even when expecting sunny weather, rain gear should be packed.
7. Knowing how to rappel is necessary before descending a cliff.
8. Although adding extra weight, climbers should not leave home without a first-aid kit.
9. Climbers should not let themselves become frustrated if they are not immediately successful.
10. By taking pains at the beginning of a trip, agony can be averted at the end of a trip.

(5) Use noun modifiers sparingly.

A string of noun modifiers can be cumbersome. The following example shows how a sentence with too many noun modifiers can be revised.

The ~~Friday afternoon~~ Student Affairs Committee meeting has been postponed. *scheduled for Friday afternoon*

25d Double negatives

The term **double negative** refers to the use of two negative words—often modifiers—to express a single negation. Unless you are portraying dialogue, revise any double negatives you find in your writing.

He did**n't** keep any ~~no~~ records. *(any)*

OR

He ~~didn't keep~~ **no** records. *(kept)*

Because *hardly, barely,* and *scarcely* denote severely limited or negative conditions, using *not* or *nothing* with any of these modifiers creates a double negative. The following examples show how sentences containing such double negatives can be revised:

I could**n't** **hardly** quit in the middle of the job.

OR

I could**n't** ~~hardly~~ quit in the middle of the job.

The motion passed with ~~not~~ **scarcely** a protest.

OR

The motion passed with ~~not scarcely~~ a protest. *(little)*

Occasionally, emphasis in a sentence requires the use of two negatives. Such a construction is not considered a double negative.

It would**n't** be safe **not** to install smoke detectors. [This construction is permissible when *not* is being emphasized. Otherwise, the sentence should be revised. COMPARE: It would be dangerous not to install smoke detectors.]

MULTILINGUAL WRITERS

NEGATION IN OTHER LANGUAGES

The use of two negative words in one sentence is common in languages such as Spanish:

*Yo **no** compré **nada**.* ["I didn't buy anything."]

If your native language allows this type of negation, be especially careful to check for and revise any double negatives you find in your English essays.

Exercise 6

Using what you have learned in this chapter, revise the following sentences to remove modifier errors.

1. As a woman of both the nineteenth and twentieth centuries, the life of Gertrude Bell was unusual.

2. Young, wealthy, and intelligent, many people were impressed by the red-headed Bell.

3. Among the first women to graduate from Oxford, she couldn't hardly be satisfied with domestic life.

4. Instead, Bell traveled to what were considered the most remotest countries in the world, saw the wonders of the Ottoman Empire, and explored the desert of Iraq.

5. Several of the Arab sheiks who knew Bell thought that she acted bold.

6. The war in Iraq did not give Bell no time to pursue her research.

7. She became an Arab rebellion supporter.

8. While traveling in Iraq, meetings with important politicians took place.

9. In 1921, Winston Churchill invited Bell to a conference in the Middle East because the other Great Britain conference participants knew little about Iraq.

10. When the photo of the conference participants was taken, Bell looked elegantly in her feathered hat and silk dress among the thirty-six black-suited males.

26 Pronouns

When you use pronouns effectively, you add clarity and coherence to your writing. However, if you do not provide the words, phrases, or clauses that make the pronoun reference clear, you might unintentionally cause confusion. This chapter will help you

- recognize various types of pronouns (**26a**),
- use appropriate pronouns (**26b**),
- make sure that pronouns agree with their antecedents (**26c**), and
- provide clear pronoun references (**26d**).

26a Recognizing pronouns

A **pronoun** is commonly defined as a word used in place of a noun that has already been mentioned.

John said **he** would guide the trip.

A pronoun may also substitute for a group of words acting as a noun (see **22b(2)**).

The participant with the most experience said **he** would guide the trip.

Most pronouns refer to nouns, but some modify nouns.

This man is our guide.

The following sections introduce several types of pronouns: personal pronouns, reflexive/intensive pronouns, relative pronouns, interrogative pronouns, demonstrative pronouns, and indefinite pronouns.

(1) Personal pronouns are identified according to person, number, and case.

To understand the uses of personal pronouns, you must first be able to recognize person, number, and case. **Person** indicates whether a pronoun refers to the writer (**first person**), to the reader (**second person**), or to another person, place, thing, or idea (**third person**). **Number** reveals whether a pronoun is singular or plural. **Case** refers to the form a pronoun takes depending on its function in a sentence. Pronouns can be subjects, objects, or possessives. When they function as subjects (**21b(1)**) they are in the subjective case; when they function as objects (**21b(2)**), they are in the objective case; and when they are possessives, they are in the possessive case (see **26b** for more information on case). Possessives can be divided into two groups based on whether they are followed by nouns. *My, your, his, her, its, our,* and *their* are all followed by nouns; *mine, yours, his, hers, ours,* and *theirs* are not.

> **Their** budget is higher than **ours.**
> [*Their* is followed by a noun; *ours* is not.]

CASE:	Subjective		Objective		Possessive	
NUMBER:	**Singular**	**Plural**	**Singular**	**Plural**	**Singular**	**Plural**
First person	I	we	me	us	my mine	our ours
Second person	you	you	you	you	your yours	your yours
Third person	he, she, it	they	him, her, it	them	his, her, hers, its	their theirs

THINKING RHETORICALLY

☀ PRONOUNS

As you write, choose pronouns appropriate for your rhetorical situation. In some situations, you will be expected to use *I*; in others, you will not. In some situations, you will address the reader as *you* (as is done in this handbook), but in others, you will avoid addressing the reader directly. Whatever pronouns you decide to use, be sure to use them consistently.

> you
> First, ~~one~~ must determine **your** priorities.

OR

> First, **one** must determine **one's** priorities.

---

(2) Reflexive pronouns direct the action back to the subject; intensive pronouns are used for emphasis.

Myself, yourself, himself, herself, itself, ourselves, yourselves, and *themselves* are used as either **reflexive pronouns** or **intensive pronouns.** Both types of pronouns are objects and must be accompanied by subjects. Reflexive pronouns are used when the actor and the recipient of the action are the same. Intensive pronouns are used to provide emphasis.

Reflexive pronoun	**He** was always talking to **himself.**
Intensive pronoun	**I, myself,** delivered the letter.

Avoid using a reflexive pronoun as a subject. A common error is using *myself* in a compound subject.

> I
> Ms. Palmquist and ~~myself~~ discussed our concern with the senator.

Hisself, themself, and *theirselves* are inappropriate in college or professional writing. Instead, use *himself* and *themselves.*

> themselves
> The young researchers worked by ~~theirselves~~.

(3) A relative pronoun introduces a dependent clause functioning as an adjective.

An adjectival clause (or relative clause) ordinarily begins with a relative pronoun: *who, whom, which, that,* or *whose.* To provide a link between this type of dependent clause and the main clause, the relative pronoun corresponds to a word or words in the main clause called the **antecedent.**

The students talked to **a reporter who** had just returned from overseas.

Notice that if you rewrite the dependent clause as a separate independent clause, you use the antecedent in place of the relative pronoun.

A reporter had just returned from overseas.

Who, whose, and *whom* ordinarily refer to people; *which* refers to things; *that* refers to things and, in some contexts, people. The possessive *whose* (used in place of the awkward *of which*) usually refers to people but sometimes refers to things.

The poem, **whose** author is unknown, has recently been set to music.

	Refers to people	Refers to things	Refers to either
Subjective	who	which	that
Objective	whom	which	that
Possessive			whose

Knowing the difference between an essential clause and a nonessential clause will help you decide whether to use *which* or *that.* A clause that a reader needs in order to identify the antecedent correctly is an **essential clause.**

The person who presented the award was last year's winner.

If the essential clause were omitted from this sentence, the reader would not know which person was last year's winner.

A **nonessential clause** is *not* needed for correct identification of the antecedent and is thus set off by commas. A nonessential clause often follows a proper noun (a specific name).

   ant   noness cl

Andrea Bowen, who presented the award, was last year's winner.

Notice that if the nonessential clause were removed from this sentence, the reader would still know the identity of last year's winner.

According to a traditional grammar rule, *that* is used in essential adjectival clauses, and *which* is used in nonessential adjectival clauses.

I need a job **that** pays well.

I took a job, **which** pays well enough.

However, some professional writers do not follow both parts of this rule. Although they will not use *that* in nonessential clauses, they will use *which* in essential clauses. Nonetheless, if you are following MLA, APA, or CMS guidelines, use *which* only in nonessential clauses.

(4) Interrogative pronouns introduce questions.
The **interrogative pronouns** *what, which, who, whom,* and *whose* are question words. Be careful not to confuse *who* and *whom* (see **26b(5)**). *Who* functions as a subject; *whom* functions as an object.

Who won the award? [COMPARE: **He** won the award.]
Whom did you see? [COMPARE: I saw **him**.]

(5) Demonstrative pronouns provide information about distance in time, space, or thought.
The **demonstrative pronouns,** *this* and *these,* indicate that someone or something is close by in time, space, or thought. *That* and *those* signal remoteness.

These are important documents; **those** can be thrown away.

Demonstrative pronouns sometimes modify nouns.

These documents should be filed.

(6) Indefinite pronouns are generally nonspecific.

Indefinite pronouns usually do not refer to specific persons, objects, ideas, or events.

anyone	anybody	anything
everyone	everybody	everything
someone	somebody	something
no one	nobody	nothing
each	either	neither

Many indefinite pronouns differ from personal pronouns in that they do not refer to an antecedent. In fact, some indefinite pronouns *serve* as antecedents (see **26c(1)**).

Someone forgot **her** purse.

Exercise 1

Identify the following pronouns. Some pronouns can be identified in more than one way.

EXAMPLE   we   subjective, first-person, plural

1. I	6. theirs	11. this
2. you	7. myself	12. these
3. he, she	8. who	13. everyone
4. they	9. whose	14. anyone
5. their	10. me	

26b Pronoun case

The term *case* refers to the form a pronoun takes to indicate its relationship to other words in a sentence. There are three cases: subjective, objective, and possessive. The following sentence includes all three.

He [subjective] wants **his** [possessive] legislators to help **him** [objective].

(1) Pronouns in the subject or subject complement position are in the subjective case.

A pronoun that is the subject of a sentence, even when it is part of a compound subject (21b), is in the subjective case. To determine which pronoun form is correct in a compound subject, say the sentence using the pronoun alone, omitting the noun. For the following sentence, notice that "*Me* solved the problem" sounds strange, but "*I* solved the problem" sounds fine.

~~Me and~~ Marisa ∧ *and I* solved the problem.

In addition, remember that when you use the pronoun *I* in a compound subject, you should place it last in the sequence. If the compound subject contains two pronouns, test each one by itself to ensure that you are using the appropriate case.

∧ *He* ~~Him~~ and I joined the club in July.

A subject complement renames the subject (see 21c). Pronouns functioning as subject complements should also be in the subjective case.

The first to arrive were Kevin and ∧ ~~me~~ *I*.

MULTILINGUAL WRITERS

NOUN OR PRONOUN AS SUBJECT

In some languages, a noun in the subject position may be followed by a pronoun. In Standardized English, though, such a pronoun should be omitted.

My roommate ~~he~~ works in the library for three hours a week.

(2) Pronouns functioning as objects are in the objective case.

Whenever a pronoun is an object—a direct object (21c(1)), an indirect object (21c(2)), or the object of a preposition (22a(4))—it takes the **objective case**.

Direct object	The whole staff admired **him**.
Indirect object	The staff sent **him** a card.
Object of a preposition	The staff depended on **him**.

Pronouns in compound objects are also in the objective case.

They will appoint you or ~~I~~ me. [direct object]

They lent Tom and ~~I~~ me money for tuition. [indirect object]

He gets nowhere by scolding Jane or ~~I~~ me. [direct object of the gerund]

Dad wanted Sheila and ~~I~~ me to keep the old car. [direct object of the sentence]

Janice sat between my brother and ~~I~~ me. [object of the preposition]

To determine whether to use the subjective or objective case, remember to say the sentence with just the pronoun. Notice that "Dad wanted *I* to keep the old car" does not sound right. Another test is to substitute *we* and *us*. If *we* sounds natural, use the subjective case. If *us* sounds better, use the objective case, as in "Dad wanted *us* to keep the old car."

(3) Possessive forms are easily confused with contractions.
Its, their, and *whose* are possessive forms. Be sure not to confuse them with common contractions: *it's* (*it is*), *they're* (*they are*), and *who's* (*who is*).

(4) Appositive pronouns are in the same case as the nouns they rename.
If the noun that an appositive pronoun renames is in the subjective case, the appositive pronoun should be in the subjective case (**26a(1)**).

The red team—Rebecca, Leroy, and ~~me~~ I —won by only one point.

Likewise, if the noun is in the objective case, the appositive pronoun should be in the objective case.

A trophy was presented to the red team—Rebecca, Leroy, and ~~I~~ me.

When the order is reversed and a pronoun is followed by a noun, the pronoun must still be in the same case as the noun.

We
~~Us~~ students need this policy.

us
The director told ~~we~~ extras to go home.

To test the case of a pronoun that is followed by an appositive, remove the appositive.

We need this policy.

The director told **us** to go home.

Exercise 2

Revise the following paragraph, using appropriate pronouns. Some sentences may not require editing.

[1]When I was twelve, my family lived in Guatemala for a year. [2]My parents taught English at a university; me and my younger brother went to a local school. [3]Although the Spanish language was new to both Sam and I, we learned to speak it quickly. [4]At first, we couldn't understand much at all, but with the help of a tutor, who we met every day after school, we started learning "survival" Spanish. [5]Sam had better pronunciation than me, but I learned vocabulary and grammar faster than him. [6]After we learned to ask and answer some basic questions, we started making friends, whom eventually introduced us to they're own version of Spanish. [7]They taught us slang words that our tutor didn't even know. [8]However, though Sam and me benefited from all our Spanish lessons, we learned the language so quickly because, unless we were with our parents or by ourself, we listened to it, read it, wrote it, and spoke it all day long.

(5) Who/whoever and whom/whomever are often misused.

To choose between *who* and *whom* or between *whoever* and *whomever,* you must first determine whether the word is functioning as a subject

(21b) or an object (21c). A pronoun functioning as the subject takes the subjective case.

Who won the award? [COMPARE: **She** won the award.]

The teachers know **who** won the award.

The student **who** won the award was quite surprised.

Whoever won the award deserves it.

When the pronoun is an object, use *whom* or *whomever*.

Whom did they hire? [COMPARE: They hired **him**.]

I do not know **whom** they hired.

The student **whom** they hired graduated in May.

Whomever they hired will have to work hard this year.

Whom may be omitted in sentences when no misunderstanding would result.

The friend he relied on moved away.
[*Whom* has been omitted after *friend*.]

BEYOND THE RULE

WHO/WHOEVER OR WHOM/WHOMEVER

Although many writers still prefer *whom* or *whomever* as object pronouns, dictionaries also allow the use of *who* or *whoever* in informal contexts.

I wonder **who** she voted for.

Give the campaign literature to **whoever** you see.

Who do you plan to vote for?

In college writing, though, it is better to use *whom* or *whomever* as the object pronoun.

Whom will they elect president?

Following the guidelines for college and professional writing, choose the pronouns that appropriately complete the following sentences.

1. Separate the white chess pieces from the black pieces and decide (who/whom) will play with the white pieces.
2. The opening move is made by (whoever/whomever) has received the white game pieces.
3. (Whoever/Whomever) the black pieces were given to makes the next move.
4. The player (who/whom) can put the other player's king in check is close to becoming the winner.
5. (Whoever/Whomever) is unable to free his or her king must concede the game.

(6) Object pronouns precede and follow infinitives; possessive pronouns precede gerunds.

A pronoun grouped with an infinitive, either as its subject or as its object, takes the objective case.

> The director wanted **me** to help **him**. [*Me* is the subject of the infinitive; *him* is the object.]

A gerund (*-ing* verb form functioning as a noun) is preceded by a possessive pronoun.

> I appreciated **his** helping Denise. [COMPARE: I appreciated **Tom's** helping Denise.]

Notice that a possessive pronoun is used before a gerund but not before a present participle (*-ing* verb form functioning as an adjective). (See also 37a(6).)

> I saw **him** helping Luke.

(7) The case of a pronoun in an elliptical construction depends on what has been omitted.

The words *as* and *than* frequently introduce **elliptical constructions**—clauses in which the writer has intentionally omitted words. To check whether you have used the correct case in an elliptical construction, read the written sentence aloud, inserting any words that have been omitted from it.

> She admires Clarice as much as **I**. [subjective case]
>
> Read aloud: She admires Clarice as much as *I do.*
>
> She admires Clarice more than **I**. [subjective case]
>
> Read aloud: She admires Clarice more than *I do.*
>
> She admires Clarice more than **me**. [objective case]
>
> Read aloud: She admires Clarice more than *she admires me.*

Exercise 4

Correct the pronoun errors in the following sentences. Some sentences may not require editing.

1. The board of directors has asked you and I to conduct a customer survey.
2. They also recommended us hiring someone with extensive experience in statistical analysis.
3. You understand statistics better than me.
4. Although the board asked me to be in charge, I would like you to recruit and interview candidates.
5. The directors recognize your expertise and will surely approve of you taking the lead.

26c Pronoun-antecedent agreement

A pronoun and its antecedent (the word or word group to which it refers) agree in number (both are singular or both are plural).

The **supervisor** said **he** would help.
[Both antecedent and pronoun are singular.]

My **colleagues** said **they** would help.
[Both antecedent and pronoun are plural.]

A pronoun also agrees with its antecedent in gender (masculine, feminine, or neuter).

Joseph claims **he** can meet the deadline. [masculine antecedent]

Anna claims **she** can meet the deadline. [feminine antecedent]

The **committee** claims **it** can meet the deadline. [neuter antecedent]

MULTILINGUAL WRITERS

POSSESSIVE PRONOUNS

A possessive pronoun (*his, her, its, their, my, our,* or *your*), also called a **possessive determiner,** agrees with its antecedent, not with the noun it precedes.

Ken Carlson brought ~~her~~ his young daughter to the office today.

[The possessive pronoun *his* agrees with the antecedent, *Ken Carlson*, not with the following noun, *daughter*.]

(1) Indefinite pronouns can serve as antecedents.

Although most antecedents for pronouns are nouns, they can be indefinite pronouns (26a(6)). Notice that an indefinite pronoun such as *everyone, someone,* and *anybody* takes a singular verb form.

Everyone **has** [not *have*] the right to an opinion.

Difficulties arise, however, because words like *everyone* and *everybody* seem to refer to more than one person even though they take a singular verb. Thus, the definition of grammatical number and our everyday notion of number conflict. In conversation and informal writing, a plural pronoun is often used with the singular *everyone*. Nonetheless, when you write for an audience that expects you to follow traditional grammar rules, make sure to use a third-person singular pronoun.

Each of these companies had ~~their~~ its books audited.

Everyone has the combination to ~~their~~ his or her private locker.

You can avoid the awkwardness of using *his or her* by using an article instead, making both the antecedent and the possessive pronoun plural, or rewriting the sentence using the passive voice (27d).

Everyone has the combination to **a** private locker. [article]

Students have combinations to **their** private lockers. [plural antecedent and plural possessive pronoun]

The combination to a private locker **is issued** to everyone. [passive voice]

(2) An antecedent sometimes refers to both genders.

When an antecedent can refer to people of either gender, rewrite the sentence to make the antecedent plural or, if not too cumbersome, use *he or she* or *his or her*.

~~A lawyer~~ Lawyers represent ~~his~~ their clients. [plural pronoun and plural antecedent]

A lawyer represents the clients **he or she** has accepted.

A lawyer represents **his or her** clients.

(See 34d for more information on using inclusive language.)

> ⚠ **CAUTION**
>
> Be careful not to introduce errors into your writing when you are trying to avoid sexist language (34d(1)).
>
>   ~~drivers let~~   licenses
> Whenever ˄a ~~driver lets~~ their ˄~~license~~ expire, they have to take a driving test.

(3) The pronoun agrees with the nearer of two antecedents joined by *or* or *nor*.

If a singular and a plural antecedent are joined by *or* or *nor,* place the plural antecedent second and use a plural pronoun.

> Either Jennifer **or** her <u>roommates</u> will explain how <u>they</u> chose their majors.
>
> Neither the president **nor** the <u>senators</u> stated that <u>they</u> would support the proposal.

(4) When a collective noun is the antecedent, the number of the pronoun depends on the meaning of the noun.

When an antecedent is a collective noun such as *team, faculty,* or *committee* (21a(2)), determine whether you intend the noun to be understood as singular or plural. Then, make sure that the pronoun agrees in number with the noun.

>   it
> The choir decided that ˄~~they~~ would tour during the winter.
> [Because the choir decided as a group, *choir* should be considered singular. The singular form, *it,* replaces the plural, *they.*]
>
>   they
> The committee may disagree on methods, but ˄~~it~~ must agree on basic aims.
> [Because the committee members are behaving as individuals, *committee* is regarded as plural. The plural form, *they,* replaces the singular, *it.*]

Exercise 5

Revise the following sentences so that pronouns and antecedents agree.

1. A researcher relies on a number of principles to help him make ethical decisions.
2. Everyone should have the right to participate in a study only if they feel comfortable doing so.
3. A team of researchers should provide its volunteers with consent forms, in which they describe to the volunteers the procedures and risks involved in participation.
4. Every participant should be guaranteed that the information they provide will remain confidential.
5. Institutions of higher education require that a researcher address ethical issues in their proposal.

26d Clear pronoun reference

The meaning of each pronoun in a sentence should be immediately obvious. In the following sentence, the pronouns *them* and *itself* clearly refer to their antecedents, *shells* and *carrier shell,* respectively.

The **carrier shell** gathers small empty **shells** and attaches **them** to **itself.**

A pronoun may refer to two or more antecedents.

Jack and I have collected shells since **we** were eight years old.

Sometimes an antecedent follows a pronoun.

Because of **their** beauty and rarity, **shells** attract collectors worldwide.

(1) Ambiguous or unclear pronoun references can confuse readers.
When a pronoun can refer to either of two antecedents, the ambiguity may confuse readers. To make the antecedent clear, replace the pronoun

with a noun or rewrite the sentence. The following revised sentences clarify that Mr. Eggers, not Mr. Anderson, will be in charge of the project.

Mr. Anderson told Mr. Eggers that ~~he~~ Mr. Eggers would be in charge of the project.

OR

Mr. Anderson put Mr. Eggers in charge of the project.

(2) Remote or awkward references can cause readers to misunderstand.

To help readers understand your meaning, place pronouns as close to their antecedents as possible. The following sentence needs to be revised so that the relative pronoun *that* is close to its antecedent, *poem*. Otherwise, the reader would wonder how a new book could be written in 1945.

The **poem** that was originally written in 1945 has been published in a new book ~~that was originally written in 1945~~.

Notice, however, that a relative pronoun does not always have to follow its antecedent directly. In the following example, there is no risk of misunderstanding.

We slowly began to notice **changes** in our lives **that** we had never expected.

(3) Broad or implied references can make writing vague.

Pronouns such as *it, this, that,* and *which* may refer to a specific word or phrase or to the sense of a whole clause, sentence, or paragraph.

The weight of the pack was manageable, once I became used to **it**.
[*It* refers specifically to *weight.*]

Large corporations may seem stronger than individuals, but **that** is not true.
[*That* refers to the sense of the whole first clause.]

Unless the meaning is clear, avoid reference to the general idea of a preceding clause or sentence. Instead, state clearly what *this* or *that* refers to.

When class attendance is compulsory, some students feel that

education is being forced on them. This~perception~is unwarranted.

[In the original sentence, *this* had no clear antecedent.]

In addition, remember to express an idea explicitly rather than merely implying it.

My father is a music teacher. ~Teaching music~ ~~It~~ is a profession that requires much

patience.

[In the original sentence, *it* had no expressed antecedent.]

Be especially careful to provide clear antecedents when you are referring to the work or possessions of others. The following sentence requires revision because *she* can refer to someone other than Jen Norton.

In ~her~ ~~Jen Norton's~~ new book, ~Jen Norton~ ~~she~~ argues for election reform.

(4) The use of the expletive *it* can result in wordiness or ambiguity.
The expletive *it* does not have a specific antecedent (see **21b(1)**). Instead, it is used to postpone, and thus give emphasis to, the subject of a sentence. A sentence that begins with this expletive can sometimes be wordy or awkward. Revise such a sentence by replacing *it* with the postponed subject.

~Trying to repair the car~ ~useless~ ~~It was~~ ~~no use trying to repair the car.~~

Avoid placing one *it* near another *it* with a different meaning.

~Staying in the old apartment~ ~~It~~ would be simpler ~~to stay in the old apartment~~, but it is too far from

my job.

[The first *it* is an expletive; the second *it* refers to *apartment*.]

Exercise 6

Edit the following sentences to make all references clear. Some sentences may not require editing.

1. It is remarkable to read about Lance Armstrong's victories.

2. A champion cyclist, a cancer survivor, and a humanitarian, it is no wonder that Lance Armstrong is one of the most highly celebrated athletes in the world.

3. Armstrong's mother encouraged his athleticism, which led to his becoming a professional triathlete by age sixteen.

4. Though you might not believe it, Armstrong was only a senior in high school when he started training for the Olympic developmental team.

5. By the time he was twenty-five, Armstrong was ranked as the top cyclist in the world.

6. Not long afterward, because of intense pain, he sought medical attention, and they told him he had testicular cancer.

7. The cancer had spread to his lungs and brain; thus, they said his chances for recovery were slim.

8. Armstrong underwent dramatic surgery and aggressive chemotherapy; this eventually helped him recover.

9. Armstrong started training five months after their diagnosis and went on to win major championships, including the Tour de France.

10. For Lance Armstrong, it hasn't been only about racing bikes; he has become a humanitarian as well, creating the Lance Armstrong Foundation to help cancer patients and to fund cancer research around the world.

27 Verbs

Choosing verbs to convey your message precisely is the first step toward writing clear sentences. The next step is to ensure that the verbs you choose conform to the conventions your audience expects you to follow.

This chapter will help you

- identify conventional verb forms (27a),
- use verb tenses to provide information about time (27b),
- use verb tenses consistently within sentences (27c),
- distinguish between the active voice and the passive voice (27d),
- use verbs to signal the factuality or likelihood of an action or event (27e), and
- ensure that subjects and verbs agree in number and person (27f).

27a Verb forms

Most English verbs have four forms, following the model for *walk.*

walk, walks, walking, walked

However, English also includes irregular verbs, which may have as few as three forms or as many as eight:

let, lets, letting   be, am, is, are, was, were, being, been

(1) Regular verbs have four forms.

A regular verb has a **base form.** This is the form you find in a dictionary. *Talk, act, change,* and *serve* are all base forms.

The second form of a regular verb is the **-s form.** To derive this form, add to the base form either -s (*talks, acts, changes, serves*) or, in some cases, -es (*marries, carries, tries*). See 42d for information on changing *y* to *i* before adding -es.

The third form of a regular verb is the **-*ing* form,** also called the **present participle.** It consists of the base form and the ending *-ing* (*talking, acting*). Depending on the verb, a spelling change may occur (*changing, chatting*) (42d).

The fourth form of a regular verb consists of the base form and the ending *-ed* (*talked, acted*). Again, spelling may vary when the suffix is added (*changed, chatted*) (42d). The *-ed* form has two names. When it is used without the auxiliary verb *have* or *be*, it is called the **past form:** We *talked* about the new plan. In contrast, when the *-ed* form is used with one of these auxiliary verbs, it is called the **past participle:** We *have talked* about it several times. A committee *was formed* to investigate the matter.

Verb Forms of Regular Verbs

Base Form	-s Form (Present Tense, Third Person, Singular)	-ing Form (Present Participle)	-ed Form (Past Form or Past Participle)
work	works	working	worked
watch	watches	watching	watched
apply	applies	applying	applied
stop	stops	stopping	stopped

⚠ CAUTION

When verbs are followed by words with similar sounds, you may find their endings (-s or -ed) difficult to hear. In addition, these verb endings may seem unfamiliar because your dialect does not have them. Nonetheless, you should use -s and -ed when you write for an audience that expects you to include these endings.

She seem satisfied with the report.
(seems — insertion above "seem")

We were suppose to receive the results yesterday.
(supposed — insertion above "suppose")

(2) Irregular verbs have from three to eight forms.

Most irregular verbs, such as *write,* have forms similar to some of those for regular verbs: base form (*write*), -*s* form (*writes*), and -*ing* form (*writing*). However, the past form (*wrote*) and the past participle (*written*) vary from the regular forms. In fact, some irregular verbs have two acceptable past forms and/or past participles (see *awake, dive, dream* and *get* in the following chart). Other irregular verbs have only three forms because the same form serves as the base form, the past form, and the past participle (see *set* in the chart). If you are unsure about verb forms not included in the chart, consult a dictionary.

<table>
<tr><td colspan="5" align="center">**Verb Forms of Irregular Verbs**</td></tr>
<tr>
<td>**Base Form**</td>
<td>**-*s* Form (Present Tense, Third Person, Singular)**</td>
<td>**-*ing* Form (Present Participle)**</td>
<td>**Past Form**</td>
<td>**Past Participle**</td>
</tr>
<tr><td>arise</td><td>arises</td><td>arising</td><td>arose</td><td>arisen</td></tr>
<tr><td>awake</td><td>awakes</td><td>awaking</td><td>awaked, awoke</td><td>awaked, awoken</td></tr>
<tr><td>begin</td><td>begins</td><td>beginning</td><td>began</td><td>begun</td></tr>
<tr><td>break</td><td>breaks</td><td>breaking</td><td>broke</td><td>broken</td></tr>
<tr><td>bring</td><td>brings</td><td>bringing</td><td>brought</td><td>brought</td></tr>
<tr><td>buy</td><td>buys</td><td>buying</td><td>bought</td><td>bought</td></tr>
<tr><td>choose</td><td>chooses</td><td>choosing</td><td>chose</td><td>chosen</td></tr>
<tr><td>come</td><td>comes</td><td>coming</td><td>came</td><td>come</td></tr>
<tr><td>dive</td><td>dives</td><td>diving</td><td>dived, dove</td><td>dived</td></tr>
<tr><td>do</td><td>does</td><td>doing</td><td>did</td><td>done</td></tr>
<tr><td>dream</td><td>dreams</td><td>dreaming</td><td>dreamed, dreamt</td><td>dreamed, dreamt</td></tr>
<tr><td>drink</td><td>drinks</td><td>drinking</td><td>drank</td><td>drunk</td></tr>
<tr><td>drive</td><td>drives</td><td>driving</td><td>drove</td><td>driven</td></tr>
</table>

(Continued on page 610)

(Continued from page 609)

Base Form	-s Form (Present Tense, Third Person, Singular)	-ing Form (Present Participle)	Past Form	Past Participle
eat	eats	eating	ate	eaten
forget	forgets	forgetting	forgot	forgotten
forgive	forgives	forgiving	forgave	forgiven
get	gets	getting	got	gotten, got
give	gives	giving	gave	given
go	goes	going	went	gone
hang (suspend)	hangs	hanging	hung	hung
hang (execute)	hangs	hanging	hanged	hanged
keep	keeps	keeping	kept	kept
know	knows	knowing	knew	known
lay (see the Glossary of Usage)	lays	laying	laid	laid
lead	leads	leading	led	led
lie (see the Glossary of Usage)	lies	lying	lay	lain
lose	loses	losing	lost	lost
pay	pays	paying	paid	paid
rise (see the Glossary of Usage)	rises	rising	rose	risen
say	says	saying	said	said

Base Form	-s Form (Present Tense, Third Person, Singular)	-ing Form (Present Participle)	Past Form	Past Participle
see	sees	seeing	saw	seen
set (see the Glossary of Usage)	sets	setting	set	set
sink	sinks	sinking	sank	sunk
sit (see the Glossary of Usage)	sits	sitting	sat	sat
speak	speaks	speaking	spoke	spoken
stand	stands	standing	stood	stood
steal	steals	stealing	stole	stolen
swim	swims	swimming	swam	swum
take	takes	taking	took	taken
tell	tells	telling	told	told
throw	throws	throwing	threw	thrown
wear	wears	wearing	wore	worn
write	writes	writing	wrote	written

The verb *be* has eight forms:

be	**Be** on time!
am	I **am** going to arrive early tomorrow.
is	Time **is** of the essence.
are	They **are** always punctual.
was	The meeting **was** scheduled for 10 a.m.

were	We **were** only five minutes late.
being	He is **being** delayed by traffic.
been	How long have we **been** here?

MULTILINGUAL WRITERS

OMISSION OF FORMS OF *BE* IN OTHER LANGUAGES

Forms of the verb *be* can be omitted in some languages. In English, however, they are necessary.

Sentence without an auxiliary verb: The population˄growing.

Sentence without a linking verb: It˄quite large.

(3) A phrasal verb consists of a main verb and a particle.

A **phrasal verb** is a combination of a verb and a particle such as *up, out,* or *on.* A **particle** resembles an adverb or a preposition, but it is so closely associated with a verb that together they form a unit of meaning. In fact, a verb + particle unit is often idiomatic, conveying a meaning that differs from the common meanings of the individual words. For example, the definitions that first come to mind for the words *blow* and *up* are not likely to help you understand the phrasal verb *blow up* when it means "to enlarge": She *blew up* the photograph so that she could see the faces better. However, the meanings of other phrasal verbs are similar to common definitions of the verbs themselves; the particles just add a sense of completion or emphasis: They *wrote up* the report by six o'clock. The particle *up* in *wrote up* does not refer to a direction; instead, it emphasizes the completion of the report. Still other phrasal verbs retain the common meanings of the verb and the particle: The protesters *hung up* a banner.

The verb and particle in most phrasal verbs may be separated by a short noun phrase (22a(1)) or by a pronoun (21a(3)).

She **called** the meeting **off.**

The student **turned** it **in** yesterday.

Some phrasal verbs are not separable, however.

The group **went over** the proposal.

I **came across** an interesting fact.

Particles that add little meaning are often deleted, especially if they seem redundant.

I **sent** ~~out~~ the invitations.

MULTILINGUAL WRITERS

PHRASAL VERBS

If you cannot find phrasal verbs in a conventional dictionary, use a specialized dictionary that provides both definitions and information about the separability of these verbs. (See **34e** for a list of dictionaries.)

(4) Auxiliary verbs combine with main verbs.

The auxiliary verbs *be, do,* and *have* combine with main verbs, both regular and irregular.

be	*am, is, are, was, were surprised*
	am, is, are, was, were writing
do	*does, do, did call*
	doesn't, don't, didn't spend
have	*has, have, had prepared*
	has, have, had read

When you combine auxiliary verbs with main verbs, you alter the meanings of the main verbs in subtle ways. The resulting verb combinations may provide information about time, emphasis, or action in progress.

Be, do, and *have* are not just auxiliary verbs, though. They may be used as main verbs as well.

be	I **am** from Texas.
do	He **does** his homework early in the morning.
have	They **have** an apartment near a park.

A sentence may even include one of these verbs as both an auxiliary and a main verb.

They **are being** careful.

Did you **do** your taxes by yourself?

She **has** not **had** any free time this week.

Another type of auxiliary verb is called a **modal auxiliary.** There are nine modal auxiliaries: *can, could, may, might, must, shall, should, will,* and *would.* By combining a modal auxiliary such as *will, should,* or *could* with the base form of a main verb, you can make a request (*Could* you help?), give an instruction (You *should* attend), or express certainty (We *shall* overcome), necessity (She *must* sleep), possibility (You *can* dream), or probability (It *could* happen).

MULTILINGUAL WRITERS

MODAL AUXILIARIES AND MAIN VERBS

Although English verbs are often followed by the infinitive marker *to* (as in *want to go* and *plan to leave*), modal auxiliaries do not follow this pattern.

We **should ~~to~~** finish our report by Friday.

Each modal auxiliary has more than one meaning. For example, *may* can indicate permission or probability.

The instructor said we **may** have an extension. [permission]

The weather **may** improve by tomorrow. [probability]

The following box provides examples of common meanings conveyed by modal auxiliaries.

COMMON MEANINGS OF MODAL AUXILIARIES

Meaning	Modal Auxiliary +	Main Verb	Example
Ability	can, could	afford	They *can afford* to buy a small house.
Certainty	will	leave	We *will leave* tomorrow.
Obligation	must	return	You *must return* your books soon.
Advice	should	talk	He *should talk* with his counselor.
Permission	may	use	You *may use* the computers in the library.

⚠ CAUTION

When a modal auxiliary occurs with the auxiliary *have* (*must have forgotten, should have known*), *have* frequently sounds like the word *of*. When you proofread, be sure that modal auxiliaries are not followed by *of*.

They **could ~~of~~ taken** another route. *(have)*

Writers generally do not combine modal auxiliaries unless they want to portray a regional dialect.

We **might ~~could~~** plan the meeting for after the holidays. *(be able to)*

MULTILINGUAL WRITERS

PHRASAL MODALS

English also has **phrasal modals**, or modal auxiliaries, consisting of more than one word. They have meanings similar to those of one-word modals.

be able to (ability): We **were able to** find the original document.

have to (obligation): You **have to** report your test results.

Other common phrasal modals are *be going to, be supposed to, had better, used to,* and *ought to.* Most phrasal modals have more than one form (*am able to, is able to, were able to*). Only *had better, ought to,* and *used to* have a single form.

(5) Participles are accompanied by auxiliary verbs.

Present participles (*-ing* verb forms) are used with the auxiliary verb *be*: We *were waiting* for the next flight. Depending on the intended meaning, past participles can be used with either *be* or *have*: The first flight *was canceled.* We *have waited* for an hour. If a sentence contains only a participle, it is probably a fragment (**23b**).

I sit on the same bench every day, dreaming of far-off places.

When a participle is part of a verbal phrase, it often appears without an auxiliary verb (**27a(4)**).

Swatting at mosquitoes and **cursing** softly, we packed our gear.
[COMPARE: We **were swatting** at mosquitoes and **cursing** softly as we packed our gear.]

Exercise 1

Revise the following sentences. Explain any changes you make.

1. Any expedition into the wilderness suffer its share of mishaps.
2. The Lewis and Clark Expedition began in May 1804 and end in September 1806.
3. Fate must of smiled on Meriwether Lewis and William Clark, for there were no fatalities under their leadership.
4. Lewis and Clark lead the expedition from St. Louis to the Pacific Ocean and back.
5. President Thomas Jefferson commission the expedition in 1803 in part because he was interest in finding the Northwest Passage— a hypothetical waterway connecting the Atlantic and Pacific Oceans.
6. By 1805, the Corps of Discovery, as the expedition was call, included thirty-three members.
7. The Corps might of lost all maps and specimens had Sacajawea, a Native American woman, not fish them from the Missouri River.
8. Sacajawea could of went off with her own people in Idaho, but she accompany Lewis and Clark to the Pacific.
9. When the Mandans had finish inspecting York, William Clark's African American servant, they assume he was the expedition's leader.
10. The success of the expedition depend on its members' willingness to help one another.

27b   Verb tenses

Verb tenses provide information about time. For example, the tense of a verb may indicate that an action took place in the past or that an action is ongoing. Verb tenses are labeled as present, past, or future; they are also labeled as simple, progressive, perfect, or perfect progressive. The chart shows how these labels apply to the tenses of *walk*.

Verb Tenses

	Present	Past	Future
Simple	walk, walks	walked	will walk
Progressive	am, is, are walking	was, were walking	will be walking
Perfect	has, have walked	had walked	will have walked
Perfect progressive	has, have been walking	had been walking	will have been walking

Some of the tenses have more than one form because they depend on the person and number of the subject. **Person** refers to the role of the subject. First person (*I, we*) indicates that the subject of the verb is the writer or writers. Second person (*you*) indicates that the subject is the audience. Third person (*he, she, it, they*) indicates that the subject is someone or something other than the writer or audience. **Number** indicates whether the subject is one or more than one (*I/we, building/buildings*). In the following subsections, conjugation tables show how person and number influence the forms of the regular verb *work*.

(1) Simple tenses have many uses, not all related to specific points in time.

The conjugation for the simple present tense includes two forms of the verb: the base form and the *-s* form. Notice that the third-person singular form is the only form with the *-s* ending.

Simple Present Tense

	Singular	Plural
First person	I **work**	We **work**
Second person	You **work**	You **work**
Third person	He, she, it **works**	They **work**

Tense is not the same as time. Although the words *present, past,* and *future* may lead you to think that these tenses refer to actions happening now, in the past, and in the future, this strict separation does not always hold. For example, the simple present tense is used to indicate a current state, a habitual action, or a general truth.

We **are** ready. [current state]

Dana **uses** common sense. [habitual action]

The sun **rises** in the east. [general truth]

The simple present tense is also commonly used to add a sense of immediacy to historical actions and to discuss literary and artistic works (see fig. 27.1).

Fig. 27.1. In his painting *Sun Rising through Vapor,* J. M. W. Turner divides the canvas into areas of light and dark. (Notice the use of the simple present tense—"divides"—to describe an artistic work.) © National Gallery Collection. By kind permission of the Trustees of the National Gallery, London/Corbis.

In 1939, Hitler's armies **attack** Poland. [historical present]

Joseph Conrad **writes** about what he sees in the human heart. [literary present]

On occasion, the simple present tense is used to refer to future time.

The festival **begins** next month.

The simple past tense of regular verbs has only one form: the base form with the *-ed* ending. The past tense for irregular verbs varies (27a(2)).

Simple Past Tense
I, you, he, she, it, we, they **worked**

The simple past tense is used to refer to completed past actions or events.

He **traveled** to the Philippines. [past action]

The accident **occurred** several weeks ago. [past event]

The simple future tense also has only one form: the base form accompanied by the auxiliary *will.*

Simple Future Tense
I, you, he, she, it, we, they **will work**

The simple future tense refers to future actions or states.

I **will call** you after work today. [future action]

The video **will** be ready by Friday. [future state]

MULTILINGUAL WRITERS

SIGNALING THE FUTURE WITH *BE GOING TO*

The phrasal modal *be going to* indicates future actions, events, or states.

I **am going to** study in Russia next year.

Be going to is considered less formal than *will.*

(2) Progressive tenses indicate that events have begun but have not been completed.

The present progressive tense of a verb consists of a form of the auxiliary verb *be* and the present participle (*-ing* form) of the main verb.

Present Progressive Tense

	Singular	Plural
First person	I **am working**	We **are working**
Second person	You **are working**	You **are working**
Third person	He, she, it **is working**	They **are working**

Notice that the present participle remains the same regardless of person and number, but the auxiliary *be* appears in three forms: *am* for first-person singular, *is* for third-person singular, and *are* for the other person-number combinations.

The present progressive tense signals an activity in progress or a temporary situation.

> The doctor **is attending** a conference in Nebraska. [activity in progress]

> We **are living** in a yurt right now. [temporary situation]

The present progressive tense can refer to a future event when it occurs with an expression indicating time.

> They **are leaving** for Alaska next week. [*Next week* indicates a time in the future.]

Like the present progressive, the past progressive tense is a combination of the auxiliary verb *be* and the present participle (*-ing* form) of the main verb. However, the auxiliary verb is in the past tense, rather than in the present tense.

Past Progressive Tense

	Singular	Plural
First person	I **was working**	We **were working**
Second person	You **were working**	You **were working**
Third person	He, she, it **was working**	They **were working**

The past progressive tense signals an action or event that occurred in the past and was repeated or ongoing.

The new member **was** constantly **interrupting** the discussion. [repeated past action]

We **were eating** dinner when we heard the news. [ongoing past action]

The future progressive tense has only one form. Two auxiliaries, *will* and *be,* are used along with the *-ing* form of the main verb.

Future Progressive Tense

I, you, he, she, it, we, they **will be working**

The future progressive tense refers to actions that will occur over some period of time in the future.

She **will be giving** her report at the end of the meeting. [future action]

MULTILINGUAL WRITERS

VERBS NOT USED IN THE PROGRESSIVE FORM

Some verbs that do not express actions but rather mental states, emotions, conditions, or relationships are not used in the progressive form. These verbs include *believe, belong, contain, cost, know, own, prefer,* and *want.*

     contains
The book is containing many Central American folktales.

  knows
He is knowing many old myths.

(3) Perfect tenses indicate action performed prior to a particular time.
The present perfect tense is formed by combining the auxiliary *have* with the past participle of the main verb.

Present Perfect Tense		
	Singular	**Plural**
First person	I **have worked**	We **have worked**
Second person	You **have worked**	You **have worked**
Third person	He, she, it **has worked**	They **have worked**

The participle remains the same regardless of person and number; however, the auxiliary has two forms: *has* for third-person singular and *have* for the other person-number combinations. The present perfect tense signals a time prior to the present. It can refer to a situation originating in the past but continuing into the present. It can also refer to a past action that has current relevance.

> They **have lived** in New Zealand for twenty years. [situation originating in the past and still continuing]

> I **have read** that book already, but I could certainly read it again. [past action that is completed but currently relevant]

The past perfect tense is also formed by combining the auxiliary *have* with the past participle. However, the auxiliary is in the past tense. There is only one form of the past perfect.

Past Perfect Tense
I, you, he, she, it, we, they **had worked**

The past perfect tense refers to an action completed at a time in the past prior to another past time or past action.

> Before 1990, he **had worked** in a shoe factory. [past action prior to a given time in the past]

> I **had studied** geology before I transferred to this school. [past action prior to another past action]

The future perfect tense consists of two auxiliaries, *will* and *have,* along with the past participle of the main verb. There is only one form of the future perfect tense.

Future Perfect Tense
I, you, he, she, it, we, they **will have worked**

The future perfect tense refers to an action that is to be completed prior to a future time.

By this time next year, I **will have finished** medical school.

(4) Perfect progressive tenses combine the forms and meanings of the progressive and the perfect tenses.

The present perfect progressive tense consists of two auxiliaries, *have* and *be,* plus the present participle (*-ing* form) of the main verb.

Present Perfect Progressive Tense		
	Singular	Plural
First person	I **have been working**	We **have been working**
Second person	You **have been working**	You **have been working**
Third person	He, she, it **has been working**	They **have been working**

The form of the auxiliary *have* varies with person and number. The auxiliary *be* appears as the past participle, *been.* The present perfect progressive signals that an action, state, or event originating in the past is ongoing or incomplete.

I **have been feeling** tired for a week. [ongoing state]

We **have been organizing** the conference since April. [incomplete action]

The past perfect progressive tense follows the pattern *had* + *been* + present participle (*-ing* form) of the main verb. The auxiliary *have* is in the past tense.

Past Perfect Progressive Tense

I, you, he, she, it, we, they **had been working**

The past perfect progressive tense refers to a situation or an action occurring over a period of time in the past and prior to another past action or time.

> She **had been living** so frugally all year that she saved enough money for a new car. [past situation prior to another action in the past]

The future perfect progressive tense follows the pattern *will* + *have* + *been* + present participle (*-ing* form) of the main verb.

Future Perfect Progressive Tense

I, you, he, she, it, we, they **will have been working**

The future perfect progressive tense refers to an action that is occurring in the present and will continue to occur for a specific amount of time.

> In one more month, I **will have been working** on this project for five years.

(5) The auxiliary verb *do* is used for questioning, negating, or emphasizing.

Unlike *be* and *have*, the auxiliary verb *do* does not occur with other verbs to indicate tense. Instead, it is used in questions, negations, and emphatic sentences.

> **Do** you have any questions? [question]
>
> I **do** not have any questions. [negation]
>
> I **do** have a few questions. [emphatic sentence]

The auxiliary *do* is used only in the simple present (*do, does*) and the simple past (*did*).

Exercise 2

Explain how the meaning of each sentence changes when the verb tense changes.

1. In "Fiji's Rainbow Reef," Les Kaufman (describes/described) the coral reefs of Fiji and (discusses/discussed) the factors affecting their health.
2. Rising water temperatures (damaged/have damaged/did damage) the reefs.
3. The algae that (provide/provided) color (do not survive/did not survive) in the warmer water.
4. The lack of algae (has left/had left) the coral "bleached."
5. Strangely, though, new life (is flourishing/was flourishing/has been flourishing) in some of these areas.
6. Scientists (study/will study) this area to understand its resilience.

(6) Verb tenses help convey the duration or time sequence of actions and events.

When you use more than one tense in a single sentence, you give readers information about how actions or events are related in time and duration.

> Whenever he **calls** on me, I **stutter** nervously. [Both present tense verbs indicate habitual actions.]

> When the speaker **had finished,** everyone **applauded.** [The past perfect tense *had finished* indicates a time before the action expressed by *applauded*.]

Infinitives and participles can be used to express time relations within a sentence. The present infinitive (*to* + base form) of a verb expresses action occurring later than the action expressed by the main verb.

> They **want to design** a new museum. [The action of designing will take place in the future.]

The perfect infinitive (*to* + *have* + past participle) signals that an action, state, or event is potential or hypothetical or that it did not occur.

> She **hopes to have earned** her degree by the end of next year.

The governor **would like to have postponed** the vote. [The postponement did not occur.]

The present participle (*-ing* form) indicates simultaneous or previous action.

Laughing loudly, the old friends **left** the restaurant arm in arm. [The friends were laughing as they were leaving.]

Hearing that she was ill, I **rushed** right over. [The action of hearing occurred first.]

The perfect participle (*having* + past participle) expresses action completed before the action conveyed by the main verb.

Having learned Spanish at an early age, she **spoke** to the Mexican diplomats in their native language.

The past participle can be used to express either simultaneous action or previous action.

Led by a former Peace Corps worker, the volunteers **provided** medical assistance. [Both actions occur simultaneously.]

Encouraged by job prospects, he **moved** to Atlanta. [The encouragement preceded the move.]

Exercise 3

Revise the following sentences so that all verbs express logical time sequences.

1. We expected the storm to have bypassed our town, but it didn't.
2. We would like to have prior notice; however, even the police officers were taken by surprise.
3. Not having known much about flooding, the emergency crew was at a disadvantage.
4. Having thrown sandbags all day, the volunteers had been exhausted by 5 p.m.
5. They went home, succeeding in preventing a major disaster.

27c   Verb tense consistency

By using verb tenses consistently within your sentences, you will help your readers understand when the actions or events you are describing took place.

Whenever we **are** at my grandmother's house, we ~~helped~~ her clean.
                                                                 help

If you are writing in the historical or literary present (27b(1)), you might encounter some difficulties maintaining consistency because you are using the present tense to discuss the past.

The governess in "The Turn of the Screw" **finds** her new position

pleasant at first but soon ~~witnessed~~ apparitions.
                            witnesses

Because it is easy to shift verb tense inadvertently, check all your verbs when you edit your paper to make sure your choice of tense is consistent. For information on the consistent use of verb tenses within a paragraph, see 29a.

Exercise 4

Edit the following sentences so that each one uses tense consistently.

1. Solomon reveals little about his past, but he had much to say about the other characters' histories.

2. He blames his sisters for his bankruptcy; he never even considered their circumstances.

3. Genny and Lena, though, refused to accept the blame, but they are afraid to refute his claims in person.

4. When Solomon's daughter returns from college, she noted her father's depression.

5. She knew the others are depending on her for help.

27d   Voice

Voice indicates the relationship between a verb and its subject. When a verb is in the **active voice,** the subject is generally a person or thing performing an action. When a verb is in the **passive voice,** the subject is usually the *receiver* of the action.

> Jen Wilson **wrote** the essay. [active voice]

> The essay **was written** by Jen Wilson. [passive voice]

Notice that the actor, Jen Wilson, appears in a prepositional phrase beginning with *by* in the passive sentence. Some sentences, however, do not include a *by* phrase because the actor is unknown or unimportant.

> Jen Wilson's essay **was published** in the student newspaper.

In the sentence above it is not important to know who accepted Jen's essay for publication, only that it was published. The best way to decide whether a sentence is in the passive voice is to examine its verb phrase.

(1) Sentences in the passive voice include a form of the auxiliary verb *be* and a past participle.

The verb phrase in a sentence written in the passive voice consists of a form of the auxiliary verb *be* (*am, is, are, was, were, been*) and a past participle (27a(1)). Depending on the verb tense, other auxiliaries such as *have* and *will* may appear as well. The following sentences include common forms of *call* in the passive voice:

Simple present	The meeting *is called* to order.
Simple past	The recruits *were called* to duty.
Present progressive	The council *is being called* to act on the proposal.
Past perfect	Ms. Jones *had been called* to jury twice last year, but she was glad to serve again.

If a verb phrase does not include both a form of the auxiliary verb *be* and a past participle, it is in the active voice.

(2) Sentences in the active voice and the passive voice differ in emphasis.

Sentences in the active voice are generally clearer and more vigorous than their passive counterparts. To use the active voice for emphasizing an actor and an action, first make the actor the subject of the sentence; then choose verbs that will help your readers see what the actor is doing. Notice how the sentence in the active voice emphasizes the role of the students.

Active voice	A group of students planned the graduation ceremony. They invited a well-known columnist to give the graduation address.
Passive voice	The graduation ceremony was planned by a group of students. A well-known columnist was invited to give the graduation address.

For more information on using the active voice to write forceful sentences, see **32e**.

Use the passive voice when you want to stress the recipient of the action, rather than the actor, or when the actor's identity is unimportant or unknown. For example, you may want to emphasize the topic of a discussion.

Tuition increases **will be discussed** at the next board meeting.

Or you may be unable to identify the actor who performed some action.

The lights **were left** on in the building last night.

Writers of scientific prose often use the passive voice to highlight the experiment rather than the experimenter. The following is an excerpt from student Heather Jensen's lab report (see **18d(4)** for the full paper):

First, the slides **were placed** on a compound microscope under low power, a 40× magnification level. The end of the root tip **was located**; then the cells immediately behind the root cap **were examined**. These cells appeared as a darker area under low power. This area of cells **was identified** as the apical meristem, an area of rapid growth and division in the onion root tip.

TECH SAVVY

Grammar checkers cannot distinguish between a true passive construction, such as *have been seen*, and a form of *be* followed by an adjective, such as *have been healthy*. Thus, they incorrectly flag the latter as a passive construction. In addition, they cannot tell when passive constructions are appropriate and so generally advise writers to "correct" them.

Exercise 5

Identify the voice in each sentence as active or passive.

1. In a *National Geographic* report, Tom O'Neill describes the discovery of ancient art in Guatemala.
2. Archaeologist William Saturno recently discovered the oldest known Maya mural.
3. The mural was found in a tunnel used by looters.
4. The tunnel was actually a small room attached to a pyramid.
5. The small room was covered with debris; its exact dimensions were hard to gauge.
6. The archaeologist found the mural by accident.
7. The mural was dated to about 150 years before the beginning of the Maya Classic period.

Exercise 6

Rewrite the sentences in exercise 5, making active verbs passive and passive verbs active. Add or delete actors when necessary. If one version of a sentence is better than the other, explain why.

27e Mood

The **mood** of a verb expresses the writer's attitude toward the factuality of what is being expressed. The **indicative mood** is used for statements and questions regarding fact or opinion. The **imperative mood** is used to give commands or directions. The **subjunctive mood** is used to state requirements, make requests, and express wishes.

Indicative	We will be on time.
Imperative	Be on time!
Subjunctive	The director insists that we be on time.

The subjunctive mood is also used to signal hypothetical situations (for example, *If I were president, . . .*). By using moods correctly, you can show your readers how you feel about the content of your sentences—certain, confident, doubtful, hesitant, ambivalent, and so on. Verb forms in the indicative mood are presented in 27b. The form for the imperative mood is simply the base form of the verb. Verb forms used for the subjunctive mood are described in the following subsection.

(1) Verb forms in the subjunctive mood serve a variety of functions.

A verb in the subjunctive mood can be present subjunctive, past subjunctive, or perfect subjunctive. The **present subjunctive** is the base form of the verb. It is used to express necessity.

The doctor recommended that he **go** on a diet.

The curator requested that I **be** at the museum by five o'clock.

In the passive voice, the present subjunctive form consists of *be* and the past participle of the main verb.

We demanded that you **be reimbursed.**

The **past subjunctive** has the same form as the simple past (for example, *had, offered, found,* or *wrote*). However, the past subjunctive form of *be* is *were*, regardless of person or number. This form is used to present hypothetical situations (situations that are not real or not currently true).

If they **offered** me the job, I would take it.

She acts as if she **were** the employer rather than the employee.

The past subjunctive form in the passive voice consists of *were* and the past participle.

Even if he **were promoted,** he would not change his mind.

Although it is called "past," the past subjunctive refers to the present or the future.

The **perfect subjunctive** verb has the same form as the past perfect tense: *had* + past participle. The perfect subjunctive signals that a statement is not factual.

I wish I **had known** about the scholarship competition.

To use a perfect subjunctive form in the passive voice, add the past participle of the main verb to the auxiliaries *had been.*

If she **had been awarded** the scholarship, she would have quit her part-time job.

(2) The subjunctive is mainly used in dependent clauses.

Although you might not use the subjunctive when speaking with your friends, using it in your writing shows readers who may not know you how you feel about your claims. In addition, your audience may expect you to adhere to the conventions for formal writing. The following guidelines should help you avoid pitfalls when using the subjunctive.

TIPS FOR USING THE SUBJUNCTIVE

- In clauses beginning with *as if* and *as though*, use the past subjunctive or the perfect subjunctive:

  He acts as if he ~~was~~ *were* the owner.

  She looked at me as though she ~~heard~~ *had* heard this story before.

- In nonfactual dependent clauses beginning with *if*, use the past subjunctive or the perfect subjunctive. Avoid using *would have* in the *if* clause.

  If I ~~was~~ *were* rich, I would buy a yacht.

  If the driver ~~would have~~ *had* **checked** his rearview mirror, the accident would not have happened.

Note that *if* does not always mark a clause as nonfactual.

If it is sunny tomorrow, I'm going fishing. [indicative mood]

■ In dependent clauses following verbs that express wishes, requirements, or requests, use the past subjunctive or the perfect subjunctive.

I wish I ^were^ ~~was~~ taller.

My brother wishes he ^had^ **studied** harder years ago.

BEYOND THE RULE

DECLINE OF THE SUBJUNCTIVE

Some linguists believe that certain subjunctive forms are disappearing from the English language. It is not unusual to find such clauses as *I wish I was* . . . (instead of *I wish I were* . . .) in the essays of many well-known writers. Nonetheless, the subjunctive is still expected in most academic rhetorical situations.

Exercise 7

Use subjunctive verb forms to revise the following sentences.

1. The planners of Apollo 13 acted as if the number 13 was a lucky number.
2. Superstitious people think that if NASA changed the number of the mission, the astronauts would have had a safer journey.
3. They also believe that if the lunar landing would have been scheduled for a day other than Friday the Thirteenth, the crew would not have encountered any problems.
4. The crew used the lunar module as though it was a lifeboat.
5. If NASA ever plans a space mission on Friday the Thirteenth again, the public would object.

27f   Subject-verb agreement

A verb agrees with its subject in number. That is, when a subject is plural, the verb takes a plural form; when the subject is singular, the verb takes a singular form. The subject and verb also agree in person (**26a(1)**). First-person subjects require first-person verb forms, second-person subjects require second-person verb forms, and third-person subjects require third-person verb forms. Notice in the following examples that the singular third-person subject takes a singular verb (*-s* form) and that the plural third-person subject takes a plural verb (base form). (If you cannot easily recognize verbs and their subjects, see **21b**.)

Singular   The **car** in the lot **looks** new. [*Car* and *looks* are both singular.]

Plural   The **cars** in the lot **look** new. [*Cars* and *look* are both plural.]

You can refer to the following subsections for guidance on ensuring subject-verb agreement in particular situations:

- when words come between the subject and the verb (**27f(1)**),
- when two or more subjects are joined by conjunctions (**27f(2)** and **27f(3)**),
- when word order is inverted (**27f(4)**),
- when the subject is a relative pronoun (**27f(5)**), an indefinite pronoun (**27f(6)**), or a collective noun or measurement word (**27f(7)**),
- when the subject is a noun that is plural in form but singular in meaning (**27e(8)**),
- when the subject and its complement differ in number (**27e(9)**), and
- when the subject is a noun clause beginning with *what* (**27e(10)**).

MULTILINGUAL WRITERS

ADDING -S TO NOUNS AND VERBS

Standardized English requires the addition of -s to mark most nouns as plural but most verbs as third-person singular. (Modal auxiliaries are the exception.) Be careful not to confuse the verb ending and the noun ending.

The **students** need attention. [noun + -s]

The student **needs** attention. [verb + -s]

Except for the verb *be,* verbs have different forms to distinguish the third-person singular only in the simple present tense.

Simple present tense of *be*: I **am,** he/she/it **is,** you, we, they **are**

Simple past tense of *be*: I, he/she/it **was,** you, we, they **were**

Simple present tense of other verbs: I, you, we, they **read,** he/she/it **reads**
I, you, we **push,** he/she/it **pushes**

Most problems with subject-verb agreement occur when the present tense is used. As you edit your writing, watch for the common problems described in the following subsections.

(1) Agreement errors are likely when other words come between the subject and the verb.

The **rhythm** of the pounding waves **is** calming.

[*Waves* is not the subject; it is the object of the preposition *of.*]

Certain phrases commonly occur between the subject and the verb; however, they do not affect the number of the subject or the form of the verb:

accompanied by	as well as	not to mention	including
along with	in addition to	no less than	together with

Her **salary,** together with tips, **is** just enough to live on.

Tips, together with her salary, **are** just enough to live on.

(2) Subjects joined by *and* usually take a plural verb.

> **Writing on a legal pad** and **writing with a computer are** not the same at all.

A compound subject that refers to a single person or thing takes a singular verb.

> The **founder <u>and</u> president** of the art association **was** elected to the board of the museum.
>
> **Red beans <u>and</u> rice is** the specialty of the house.

(3) Agreement errors are common when subjects are joined by *or* or *nor*.
When singular subjects are linked by *or, either . . . or,* or *neither . . . nor,* the verb is singular as well.

> The **provost <u>or</u>** the **dean** usually **presides** at the meeting.
>
> <u>**Either**</u> his **accountant <u>or</u>** his **lawyer has** the will.
>
> <u>**Neither**</u> the **car <u>nor</u>** the **motorcycle is** for sale.

If one subject is singular and one is plural, the verb agrees in number with the subject closer to the verb.

> Neither the basket nor the **apples were** expensive. [plural]
>
> Neither the apples nor the **basket was** expensive. [singular]

The verb also agrees in person with the nearer subject.

> Either Frank or **you were** going to make the announcement. [second person]
>
> Either you or **Frank was** going to make the announcement. [third person]

(4) Inverted word order may lead to agreement errors.
In most sentences, the subject precedes the verb.

> The large **cities** of the Northeast **were** the hardest hit by the winter storms.

The subject and verb can sometimes be inverted for emphasis; however, they must still agree.

> The hardest hit by the winter storms **were** the large **cities** of the Northeast.

When the expletive *there* begins a sentence, the subject and verb are always inverted (21b(1)); the verb still agrees with the subject, which follows it.

There **are** several **cities** in need of federal aid.

(5) Clauses with relative pronouns are common sites for agreement errors.

In an adjectival (relative) clause (22b(2)), the subject is generally a relative pronoun (*that, who,* or *which*). To determine whether the relative pronoun is singular or plural, you must find its antecedent (the word or words it refers to). When the antecedent is singular, the relative pronoun is singular; when the antecedent is plural, the relative pronoun is plural. In essence, the verb in the adjectival clause agrees with the antecedent.

sing ant *sing v*

The person who reviews proposals is out of town this week.

pl ant *pl v*

The director met with the **students who are** studying abroad next quarter.

pl ant *pl v*

The Starion is one of the new **models that include** a DVD player as standard equipment.

BEYOND THE RULE

ONE AS A POSSIBLE ANTECEDENT

According to traditional grammar, in sentences containing the pattern *one* + *of* + plural noun + adjectival clause (such as the sentence just before this box), the antecedent for the relative pronoun (*that,* in this case) is the plural noun (*models*). The verb in the adjectival clause is thus plural as well. However, professional writers often consider *one,* instead of the plural noun, to be the antecedent of the relative pronoun and thus make the verb singular:

The Starion is **one** of the new models **that includes** a DVD player as standard equipment.

(6) Agreement errors frequently occur with indefinite pronouns.

The indefinite pronouns *each, either, everybody, everyone,* and *anyone* are considered singular and so require singular verb forms (26c(1)).

> <u>**Each**</u> **has bought** a first-class ticket.
>
> <u>**Either**</u> of them **is willing** to lead the discussion.
>
> <u>**Everybody**</u> in our apartment building **has** a parking place.

Other indefinite pronouns, such as *all, any, some, none, half,* and *most,* can be either singular or plural, depending on whether they refer to a unit or quantity (singular) or to individuals (plural).

My sister collects comic **books;** <u>**some**</u> **are** quite valuable.

My sister collects antique **jewelry;** <u>**some**</u> of it **is** quite valuable.

Singular subjects that are preceded by *every* or *each* and joined by *and* require a singular verb.

> **Every** cat **and** dog in the county **has** to be vaccinated.
>
> **Each** fork **and** spoon **has** to be polished.

However, placing *each* after a plural compound subject does not affect the verb form. The verb should agree with the plural subject.

> Colleges and vocational schools **each have** their advantages.

When an indefinite pronoun is followed by a prepositional phrase beginning with the preposition *of,* the verb agrees in number with the object of the preposition.

<u>**None**</u> of **those are** spoiled.

<u>**None**</u> of the **food is** spoiled.

More than <u>**half**</u> of the **population** in West Texas **is** Hispanic.

More than <u>**half**</u> of the **people** in West Texas **are** Hispanic.

BEYOND THE RULE

AGREEMENT WITH *NONE*

Some grammarians reason that *none*, like *no one*, is singular and thus should be followed by a singular verb:

None of the grant requests **has** been rejected.

Nonetheless, many reputable writers have used *none* with plural verbs, leading to the widespread acceptance of this usage:

None of the grant requests **have** been rejected.

(7) Collective nouns and measurement words often cause agreement difficulties.

Collective nouns (21a(2)) and measurement words require singular verbs when they refer to groups or units. They require plural verbs when they refer to individuals or parts.

Singular (regarded as a group or unit)	Plural (regarded as individuals or parts)
The **majority rules.**	The **majority** of us **are** in favor.
Ten million gallons of oil **is** more than enough.	**Ten million gallons** of oil **were spilled.**
The **number is** insignificant.	A **number** of workers **were** absent.

Although using the nouns *data* and *media* as singular has gained currency, treat *data* and *media* as plural in most academic writing. (See the Glossary of Usage.)

The data **are** in the appendix.

The media **have** shaped public opinion.

(8) Words ending in -s are sometimes singular.

Titles of works that are plural in form (for example, *Star Wars* and *Dombey and Son*) are treated as singular because they refer to a single book, movie, recording, or other work.

Mr. and Mrs. Smith **is** one of the films she discussed in her paper.

A reference to a word is also considered singular.

Beans **is** slang for "a small amount": I don't know beans about football.

Some nouns ending in *-s* are actually singular: *linguistics, news,* and *Niagara Falls.*

The **news is** encouraging.

Nouns such as *athletics, politics,* and *electronics* can be either singular or plural, depending on their meanings.

Singular	Plural
Statistics is an interesting subject.	**Statistics are** often misleading.

(9) Verbs agree with subjects, not with subject complements.
Some sentences may have a singular subject (**21b**) and a plural subject complement (**21c**), or vice versa. In either case, the verb agrees with the subject.

Her primary **concern is** rising health-care **costs.**

Croissants are the bakery's **specialty.**

THINKING RHETORICALLY

 AGREEMENT OF RELATED SINGULAR AND PLURAL NOUNS

When a sentence has two or more nouns that are related, use either the singular form or the plural form consistently.

The **student** raised her **hand.**

The **students** raised their **hands.**

Occasionally, you may have to use a singular noun to retain an idiomatic expression or to avoid ambiguity.

They kept their **word.**

The **participants** were asked to name their favorite **movie.**

(10) An agreement error may occur when the subject of a sentence is a noun clause beginning with *what*.

In noun clauses (22b(2)), *what* may be understood as either "the thing that" or "the things that." If it is understood as "the thing that," the verb in the main clause is singular.

> What we need **is** a new policy. [*The thing that* we need is a new policy.]

If *what* is understood as plural (the things that), the verb in the main clause is plural.

> What we need **are** new guidelines. [*The things that* we need are new guidelines.]

Note that the main noun following the verb in these examples (*policy*, *guidelines*) also agrees with the verb: *policy* and *is* are singular; *guidelines* and *are* are plural.

BEYOND THE RULE

WHAT IN NOUN CLAUSES

According to a traditional grammar rule, a singular verb should be used in both the noun clause beginning with *what* and the main clause.

> What **is** needed **is** new guidelines.

However, many current writers and editors consider this rule outmoded.

Exercise 8

In each sentence, choose the correct form of the verb in parentheses. Make sure that the verb agrees with its subject according to the conventions for academic and professional writing.

1. There (is/are) at least two good reasons for changing motor oil: risk of contamination and danger of additive depletion.
2. Reasons for not changing the oil (include/includes) the cost to the driver and the inconvenience of the chore.
3. What I want to know (is/are) the number of miles I can drive before changing my oil.
4. My best friend and mechanic (says/say) three thousand miles.
5. But my brother says three thousand miles (is/are) not long enough.
6. Each of the car manuals I consulted (recommends/recommend) five-thousand-mile intervals.
7. Neither the automakers nor the oil station attendants (know/knows) how I drive, however.

Exercise 9

Complete the following sentences, making sure that subjects and verbs agree.

1. Applying for college and enrolling in courses . . .
2. Erik is one of the students who . . .
3. Either of them . . .
4. The list of volunteers . . .
5. Hidden beneath the stairs . . .
6. The teacher, along with her students, . . .
7. What we requested . . .

S

EFFECTIVE
SENTENCES

28 Sentence
Unity   646

29 Consistency   655

30 Subordination and
Coordination   662

31 Parallelism   668

32 Emphasis   674

33 Variety   682

Let there be justice for all.
Let there be peace for all.
Let there be work, bread, water and salt for all.
         —Nelson Mandela, Inaugural Address

At his inauguration in 1994, President Mandela
effectively used repetition and parallelism in his
call for an end to discrimination in South Africa.

CHAPTER 28
Sentence Unity 646

28a Choosing and arranging details 646
28b Including necessary words 648
28c Revising mixed metaphors 649
28d Relating sentence parts 650
28e Completing comparisons 653
28f Completing intensifiers 654

CHAPTER 29
Consistency 655

29a Verb tense 655
29b Point of view 658
29c Tone 659

CHAPTER 30
Subordination and Coordination 662

30a Using subordination effectively 662
30b Using coordination effectively 664
30c Avoiding faulty or excessive subordination
and coordination 666

CHAPTER 31
Parallelism 668

31a Recognizing parallel elements 668
31b Repeating words and grammatical forms 669
31c Linking two or more sentences 670
31d Correlative conjunctions 671
31e Emphasizing key ideas in introductions
and conclusions 672

CHAPTER 32
Emphasis 674

32a Placing words for emphasis 674
32b Using cumulative and periodic
sentences 676
32c Ordering ideas from least to most
important 676
32d Repeating important words 677
32e Choosing between the active voice and the
passive voice 677
32f Inverting word order 679
32g Using an occasional short sentence 680

CHAPTER 33
Variety 682

33a Revising sentence length and form 683
33b Varying sentence openings 687
33c Using questions, exclamations, and
commands 689

THINKING RHETORICALLY

✳ SENTENCE STYLE

Most professional writers and readers use the following words to describe effective sentences.

- *Exact.* Precise words and word combinations ensure exactness and enable readers to come as close as they can to a full understanding of the writer's message.
- *Conventional.* Sentences are conventional when they conform to the usage expectations of a particular community. For most academic assignments, you will be expected to use Standardized English.
- *Consistent.* A consistent writing style is characterized by the use of the same types of words and grammatical structures throughout a piece of writing. A style that is inconsistent jars the reader's expectations.
- *Parallel.* Related to consistency, parallelism refers to the placement of similar ideas into similar grammatical structures.
- *Concise.* Concise prose is free of redundancies.
- *Coherent.* Coherence refers to clear connections between adjacent sentences and paragraphs.
- *Varied.* To write appealing paragraphs, a writer uses both short and long sentences. When sentences vary in length, they usually also vary in structure, rhythm, and emphasis.

In the following chapters, you will learn to identify the rhetorical options considered effective by most academic and professional writers. Remember, though, that appropriateness varies across rhetorical situations. You may find that it does not make sense to apply a general rule such as "Use the active voice" in all circumstances. For example, you may be expected to write a vigorous description of an event, detailing exactly what happened, but find that you need to use the passive voice when you do not know who was responsible for the event: Several of the campaign signs *were defaced*. Or, as another example, you may need to set aside the rule calling for Standardized English if you are writing dialogue in which the speakers use regional dialects. Analyzing your rhetorical situation, rather than always following general rules, will help you write sentences that are appropriate to you, your audience, and the specific context.

28 Sentence Unity

Effective academic and professional writing is composed of sentences that are consistent, clear, and complete. By carefully crafting your sentences, you demonstrate concern for your audience and an awareness of your rhetorical situation; thus, you have a better chance of achieving your rhetorical purpose. This chapter can help you

- choose and arrange details (**28a**),
- include necessary words (**28b**),
- revise mixed metaphors (**28c**),
- relate sentence parts (**28d**), and
- complete comparisons (**28e**) and intensifiers (**28f**).

28a Choosing and arranging details

Well-chosen details add interest and credibility to your writing. As you revise, you may occasionally notice a sentence that would be clearer and more believable with the addition of a phrase or two about time, location, or cause.

Missing important detail	An astrophysicist from the Harvard-Smithsonian Center has predicted a galactic storm.
With detail added	An astrophysicist from the Harvard-Smithsonian Center has predicted **that a galactic storm will occur within the next 10 million years.**

Without the additional information about time, most readers would wonder when the storm was supposed to occur. The added detail makes the sentence clearer.

Missing important detail	The cataclysm in the Milky Way will result in radiation levels capable of killing nearby organisms, but it will not affect Earth.
With detail added	The cataclysm in the Milky Way will result in radiation levels capable of killing nearby organisms, but it will not affect Earth, **which is 25,000 light-years away.**

The additional information in the second sentence about location helps readers understand why the Earth will be unaffected by a cataclysm in the Milky Way.

The details you choose will help your readers understand your message. If you provide too many details within a single sentence, though, your readers may lose sight of your main point. When you revise, be sure that the details you included in your first draft are still meaningful. The writer of the following sentence deleted the mention of her uncle as she revised because this detail was irrelevant to the main idea of her essay.

When I was only sixteen, I left home to attend a college in California ~~that my uncle had graduated from twenty years earlier~~.

When considering how much detail to include, you may sometimes want to write a long and fairly complex sentence. Just be sure that every detail contributes to the central thought, as in the following excerpt.

A given mental task may involve a complicated web of circuits, which interact in varying degrees with others throughout the brain—not like the parts in a machine, but like the instruments in a symphony orchestra combining their tenor, volume, and resonance to create a particular musical effect.

—**JAMES SHREEVE,** *Beyond the Brain*

By using parallel structures (see chapter **31**) and careful punctuation, this writer has created a long, yet coherent, sentence.

Besides choosing details purposefully, you also need to indicate a clear connection between the details and the main idea of your sentence.

Unrelated	Many tigers facing possible extinction live in India, **where there are many people.**
Related	Many tigers facing possible extinction live in India, **where their natural habitat is shrinking because of population pressure.**

Exercise 1

Rewrite the following sentences so that the details clearly support the main idea. You may need to combine sentences or add words.

1. Firefighting is a dangerous job, but there are many high-tech devices and fire-resistant materials.

2. Wildfires can trap firefighters. Fire shelters are being developed to withstand temperatures as high as 2,000 degrees.

3. NASA developed Uninhabited Aerial Vehicles. Firefighters need to get accurate information fast.

4. Firefighters have difficulty seeing through smoke. A thermal imaging camera detects differences in heat and distinguishes between humans and surrounding objects.

5. Opticom is a traffic-control system, so firefighters can get to a fire quickly. They can change a red light to green from 2,000 feet away.

28b   Including necessary words

When we speak or write quickly, we often omit small words. As you revise, be sure to include all necessary articles, prepositions, verbs, and conjunctions. Without the added article, the following sentence is incomplete.

The ceremony took place in ᵃⁿ auditorium.

Even though prepositions are sometimes omitted in speech, they should always be included in writing.

We discussed a couple ᵒᶠ issues at the meeting.

When a sentence has a **compound verb** (two verbs linked by a conjunction), you may need to supply a different preposition for each verb to make your meaning clear.

He neither **believes** ⁱⁿ nor **approves of** exercise.

All verbs, both auxiliary and main (27a(4)), should be included to make sentences complete.

She _{has} seen the movie three times.

Voter turnout has never _{been} and will never be 100 percent.

In sentences with two short clauses in which the second verb is exactly the same as the first, the second can be omitted.

The wind **was** fierce and the thunder [was] deafening.

Include the word *that* before a clause when it makes the sentence easier to read. Without the added *that* in the following sentence, a reader may stumble over *discovered the fossil* before understanding that *the fossil* is linked to *provided.*

The paleontologists discovered _{that} the fossil provided a link between the dinosaur and the modern bird.

That should always be retained when a sentence has two parallel clauses.

The graph indicated **that the population had increased** but **that the number of homeowners had not.**

TECH SAVVY

A grammar checker will sometimes alert you to a missing word, but it will just as often fail to do so. It may also tell you that a word is missing when it is not. You are better off proofreading your work yourself.

28c   **Revising mixed metaphors**

When you use language that evokes images, make sure that the images are meaningfully related. Unrelated images that appear in the same sentence are called **mixed metaphors.** The following sentence includes incompatible images.

As he climbed the corporate ladder, he _{incurred a large} ~~sank into a sea of~~ debt.

The combination of two images—climbing a ladder and sinking into a sea—could create a picture in the reader's mind of a man hanging onto a ladder as it disappears into the water. The easiest way to revise such a sentence is to replace the words evoking one of the conflicting images.

28d Relating sentence parts

(1) Mixed constructions are illogical.
A sentence that begins with one kind of grammatical structure and shifts to another is a **mixed construction.** To untangle a mixed construction, make sure that the sentence includes a conventional subject—a noun, a noun phrase, a gerund phrase, an infinitive phrase, or a noun clause. Prepositional phrases and adverbial clauses are not typical subjects.

Practicing
~~By practicing~~ a new language daily will help you become proficient. [A gerund phrase replaces a prepositional phrase.]

Her scholarship award
~~Although she won a scholarship~~ does not give her the right to skip classes. [A noun phrase replaces an adverbial clause.]

If you find a sentence that has a mixed construction, you can either revise the subject, as in the previous examples, or leave the beginning of the sentence as a modifier and add a new subject after it.

By practicing a new language daily, **you** will become more proficient.

Although she won a scholarship, **she** does not have the right to skip classes.

(2) Sentence parts are linked together logically.
When drafting, writers sometimes compose sentences in which the subject is said to be something or to do something that is not logically possible. This breakdown in meaning is called **faulty predication.** Similarly, mismatches between a verb and its complement can obscure meaning.

(a) Mismatch between subject and verb
The joining of a subject and a verb must create a meaningful idea.

Mismatch	The absence of detail screams out at the reader. [An *absence* cannot scream.]
Revision	The reader immediately notices the absence of detail.

(b) Illogical equation with *be*

When a form of the verb *be* joins two parts of a sentence (the subject and the subject complement), these two parts should be logically related.

Free speech
~~The importance of free speech~~ is essential to a democracy.
[*Importance* cannot be essential.]

(c) Mismatches in definitions

When you write a sentence that states a formal definition, be sure that the subject and the predicate (**21b**) fit together grammatically. The term being defined should be followed by a noun or a noun phrase, not an adverbial clause (**22b**). Avoid using *is when* or *is where*.

Ecology is ~~when you~~ the study of the relationships among living organisms and between living organisms and their environment.

Exploitative competition is ~~where~~ the contest between two or more organisms ~~vie~~ vying for a limited resource such as food.

(d) Mismatch of *reason* with *is because*

You can see why *reason* and *is because* are a mismatch by looking at the meaning of *because*: "for the reason that." Saying "the reason is for the reason that" is redundant. Thus, revise any sentence containing the construction *the reason is . . . because*.

The ~~reason the~~ old train station was closed ~~is~~ because it had fallen into disrepair.

(e) Mismatch between verb and complement

A verb and its complement should fit together meaningfully.

Mismatch	Only a few students used the incorrect use of *there*. [To "use an incorrect use" is not logical.]
Revision	Only a few students used *there* incorrectly.

To make sure that a relative pronoun in the object position is connected logically to a verb, replace the pronoun with its antecedent. Then check that the subject and verb have a logical connection. In the following sentence, *the inspiration* is the antecedent for *that*.

| **Mismatch** | The inspiration that the author created touched young writers. [To "create the inspiration" is not logical.] |
| **Revision** | The author inspired young writers. |

(3) Verbs used to integrate information are followed by specific types of complements.

Attributive tags are phrases used to identify sources of information (**11d(1)**). Most verbs in attributive tags are followed by a noun clause beginning with *that* or a *wh-* word (**21b(2)**). A few common verbs and their typical complements are listed below. (Some verbs such as *explain* fall into more than one category.)

VERBS FOR ATTRIBUTION AND THEIR COMPLEMENTS

Verb + *that* noun clause

| agree | claim | explain | report | suggest |
| argue | demonstrate | maintain | state | think |

Example: The researcher **reported** that the weather patterns had changed.

Verb + noun phrase + *that* noun clause

| convince | persuade | remind | tell |

Example: He **told** the reporters that he was planning to resign.

Verb + *wh-* noun clause

| demonstrate | discuss | report | suggest |
| describe | explain | state | wonder |

Example: She **described** what had happened.

Exercise 2

Revise the following sentences so that each verb is followed by a conventional complement.

1. The committee chair discussed that funding requests had specific requirements.
2. He persuaded that mass transit was affordable.
3. The two groups agreed how the problem could be solved.
4. Brown and Edwards described that improvements had been made to the old building.
5. They wondered that such a catastrophe could happen.

28e Completing comparisons

A comparison has two parts: someone or something is compared to someone or something else. As you revise your writing, make sure that your audience knows who or what is being compared. To revise incomplete comparisons, add necessary words, phrases, or clauses.

Printers today are quite different~from those sold in the early 1990s~.

His first novel was better~than the one just published~.

After you are sure that your comparisons are complete, check to see that they are also logical.

Her test scores are higher than ~those of~ the other students.

In the original sentence, *scores* were being compared to *students*. You could also rewrite this sentence as follows:

Her test scores are higher than the other students'.

Because *test scores* have already been mentioned, it is clear that *students'* (with an apostrophe) is short for *students' test scores*.

28f Completing intensifiers

In speech, the intensifiers *so, such,* and *too* are used to mean "very," "unusually," or "extremely."

> That movie was **so** funny.

In academic and professional writing, however, the intensifiers *so, such,* and *too* require a completing phrase or clause.

> That movie was **so** funny **that I watched it twice.**

> Julian has **such** a hearty laugh **that it makes everyone else laugh with him.**

> The problem is just **too** complex **to solve in one day.**

Exercise 3

Revise the following sentences to make them clear and complete.

1. By studying the villains' faces in the *Star Wars* movies can reveal popular notions about the look of evil.

2. To design the character of Darth Maul for *The Phantom Menace,* Iain McCaig started by illustrating a picture of his worst nightmare.

3. He drew generic male face with metal teeth and long red ribbons of hair falling in front of it.

4. Ralph McQuarrie sketched designs for R2D2 and Darth Vader, including his mask. McCaig wanted to create something scarier.

5. When after arriving at many dead ends, McCaig finally had an idea of what he wanted to do.

6. He designed a face that looked as though it been flayed.

7. The evil visage of Darth Maul was so horrible. To balance the effect, McCaig added elegant black feathers.

8. However, the need to add beauty was not shared by others on the production team, and the feathers eventually became small horns.

29 Consistency

Consistency in verb tense, point of view, and tone will help your readers to understand your message, your role in creating it, and their role as audience. This chapter will help you maintain consistency

- in verb tense (27a),
- in point of view (27b), and
- in tone (27c).

29a Verb tense

Every verb tense can be discussed in terms of time frame and aspect. *Time frame* refers to whether the tense is present, past, or future. *Aspect* refers to whether it is simple, progressive, perfect, or perfect progressive. (See the chart on page 617.) Consistency in the time frame of verbs, though not necessarily in their aspect, ensures that sentences reporting a sequence of events link together logically. In the following paragraph, notice that the time frame remains in the past, but the aspect may be either simple, perfect, or progressive.

past perfect

In the summer of 1983, I **had** just **finished** my third year of architecture

simple past   past perfect (compound predicate)

school and **had** to find a six-month internship. I **had grown** up and **gone**

past perfect

through my entire education in the Midwest, but I **had been** to New York

simple past simple past

City once on a class field trip and I **thought** it **seemed** like a pretty good place to live. So, armed with little more than an inflated ego and my school

simple past

portfolio, I **was** off to Manhattan, oblivious to the bad economy and the fact

past progressive

that the city **was overflowing** with young architects.

—PAUL K. HUMISTON, "Small World"

If you do need to shift to another time frame, you can use a time marker:

now, then, today, yesterday
in two years, during the 1920s
after you finish, before we left

For example, in the following paragraph, the time frame shifts back and forth between present and past—between today, when Edward O. Wilson is studying ants in the woods around Walden Pond, and the nineteenth century, when Henry David Thoreau lived there. The time markers are bracketed.

simple present   *simple past*

These woods **are** not wild; indeed, they **were** not wild [in Thoreau's day].

simple present

[Today], the beach and trails of Walden Pond State Reservation **draw** about

simple present

500,000 visitors a year. Few of them **hunt** ants, however. Underfoot and

simple present   *simple past*

under the leaf litter there **is** a world as wild as it **was** [before human beings

simple past

came to this part of North America].

—JAMES GORMAN, "Finding a Wild, Fearsome World Beneath Every Fallen Leaf"

On occasion, a shift in time is indicated implicitly—that is, without an explicit time marker. A writer may change tenses, without including time markers, (1) to explain or support a general statement with information about the past, (2) to compare and contrast two different time periods, or (3) to comment on a topic. Why do you think the author of the following paragraph varies verb tenses?

Thomas Jefferson, author of the Declaration of Independence, **is** considered one of our country's most brilliant citizens. His achievements **were** many, as **were** his interests. Some historians **describe** his work as a naturalist, scientist, and inventor; others **focus** on his accomplishments as an educator and politician. Yet Jefferson **is** best known as a spokesman for democracy.

Except for the two uses of *were* in the second sentence, all verbs are in the present tense. The author uses the past tense in the second sentence to provide evidence from the past that supports the opening sentence.

Before you turn in a final draft, check your verb tenses to ensure that they are logical and consistent. Revise any that are not.

The white wedding dress ~~comes~~ came into fashion when Queen Victoria

wore a white gown at her wedding to Prince Albert of Saxe. Soon after,

brides who could afford them bought stylish white dresses for their

weddings. Brides of modest means, however, ~~continue~~ continued to choose

dresses they could wear more than once.

Exercise 1

Determine whether the shift in tense in this passage is effective. Be prepared to state your reasoning.

[1]Life at North GRIP [Greenland Ice-Core Project], if not exactly comfortable, **is** at least well supplied. [2]Lunch the day I arrived **was** a fish stew prepared in a delicate tomato base. [3]In the midafternoon, there **was** coffee and cake; then, in the evening, cocktails, which **were** served in the chamber hollowed out of the snowpack, to relieve pressure on the drilling room. [The remaining verbs in this paragraph are all in past tense.]

—ELIZABETH KOLBERT, "Ice Memory"

Exercise 2

Revise the following paragraph so that it contains no unnecessary shifts in verb tense.

I **had** already **been walking** for a half hour in the semidarkness of Amsterdam's early-morning streets when I **came** to a red light. I **am** in a hurry to get to the train station and no cars **were** out yet, so I **cross** over the cobblestones, passing a man waiting for the light to change. I never **look** back when he **scolds** me for breaking the law. I **had** a train to catch. I **was** going to Widnau, in Switzerland, to see Aunt Marie. I **have** not **seen** her since I **was** in second grade.

29b Point of view

Whenever you write, you must establish your point of view (perspective). Your point of view will be evident in the pronouns you choose. *I* or *we* indicates a first-person point of view, which is appropriate for writing that includes personal views or experiences. If you decide to address the reader as *you*, you are adopting a second-person point of view. However, because a second-person point of view is rare in academic writing, avoid using *you* unless you need to address the reader (35d). If you select the pronouns *he, she, it, one,* and *they*, you are writing with a third-person point of view. The third-person point of view is the most common point of view in academic writing.

Although you may find it necessary to use different points of view in a paper, especially if you are comparing or contrasting other people's views with your own, be careful not to confuse readers by shifting perspective unnecessarily. The following paragraph has been revised to ensure consistency of point of view.

To an observer, a sleeping person appears passive, unresponsive, and

essentially isolated from the rest of the world and its barrage of stimuli.

While it is true that ^someone asleep is^ ~~you are~~ unaware of most surrounding noises ~~when~~

~~you are asleep,~~ ^that person's^ ~~our~~ brain is far from inactive. In fact, it can be as active

during sleep as it is ^in a waking state^ ~~when you are awake~~. When ^it is^ ~~our brains are~~ asleep,

the rate and type of electrical activity change.

For more information on the use of pronouns to indicate point of view, see **35d**.

29c Tone

The tone of a piece of writing conveys a writer's attitude toward a topic (**4a(3)**). The words and sentence forms (**22d**) a writer chooses determine the tone presented. Notice how the tone differs in the following two excerpts, which describe the same scientific experiment. The first paragraph was written for a book intended for the general public; the second was written for a journal article to be read by other researchers.

> Imagine that I asked you to play a very simple gambling game. In front of you, are four decks of cards—two red and two blue. Each card in those four decks either wins you a sum of money or costs you some money, and your job is to turn over cards from any of the decks, one at a time, in such a way that maximizes your winnings. What you don't know at the beginning, however, is that the red decks are a minefield. The rewards are high, but when you lose on red, you lose *a lot*. You can really only win by taking cards from the blue decks, which offer a nice, steady diet of $50 . . . payoffs. The question is: how long will it take you to figure this out?   —**MALCOLM GLADWELL**, *Blink*

> In a gambling task that simulates real-life decision-making in the way it factors uncertainty, rewards, and penalties, the players are given four decks of cards, a loan of $2000 facsimile U.S. bills, and asked to play so that they can lose the least amount of money and win the most (1). Turning each

card carries an immediate reward ($100 in decks A and B and $50 in decks C and D). Unpredictably, however, the turning of some cards also carries a penalty (which is large in decks A and B and small in decks C and D). Playing mostly from the disadvantageous decks (A and B) leads to an overall loss. Playing from the advantageous decks (C and D) leads to an overall gain. The players have no way of predicting when a penalty will arise in a given deck, no way to calculate with precision the net gain or loss from each deck, and no knowledge of how many cards they must turn to end the game (the game is stopped after 100 card selections).

> —ANTOINE BECHARA, HANNA DAMASIO, DANIEL TRANEL, AND
> ANTONIO R. DAMASIO, "Deciding Advantageously before Knowing the Advantageous Strategy"

In the excerpt from *Blink*, Malcolm Gladwell addresses the readers directly: "Imagine that I asked you to play a very simple gambling game." In the excerpt from the journal article, Antoine Bechara and his co-researchers describe their experiment from a third-person point of view. Gladwell also uses everyday words and expressions. For example, whereas the researchers use words such as "immediate reward" and "penalty," Gladwell conveys the same information informally: "wins you a sum of money or costs you some money." Finally, the researchers include a reference citation (the number one in parentheses) in their description, but Gladwell does not.

Neither of these excerpts is better than the other. The tone of each is appropriate for the given rhetorical situation. However, shifts in tone can be distracting. The following paragraph was revised to ensure consistency of tone:

Scientists at the University of Oslo (Norway) have evidence that ~~think they know why~~ the common belief about the birth order of children carries some truth. ~~kids has some truth to it.~~

Using as data IQ tests taken from military records, the scientists found that older children score significantly higher than their siblings. ~~have~~ ~~more on the ball than kids in second place.~~ According to the researchers, the average variation in scores is large enough to account for differences in college admission.

Exercise 3

Revise the following paragraph so that there are no unnecessary shifts in point of view or tone.

¹Many car owners used to complain about deceptive fuel-economy ratings. ²They often found, after they had already purchased a car, that their mileage was lower than that on the car's window sticker. ³The issue remained pretty much ignored until our gas prices started to rise like crazy. ⁴Because of increased pressure from consumer organizations, the United States Environmental Protection Agency reviewed and then changed the way it was calculating fuel-economy ratings. ⁵The agency now takes into account factors such as quick acceleration, changing road grades, and the use of air conditioning, so the new ratings should reflect your real-world driving conditions. ⁶Nonetheless, the ratings can never be right on target given that we all have different driving habits.

30 Subordination and Coordination

Subordination and coordination both refer to the joining of grammatical structures. **Subordination** is the linking of grammatically unequal structures (usually a dependent clause to an independent clause). **Coordination** is the linking of structures that have the same grammatical rank (two independent clauses, for example). By using subordination and coordination, you indicate connections between ideas as well as add variety to your sentences (chapter 33). This chapter will help you

- use subordination effectively (30a),
- use coordination effectively (30b), and
- avoid faulty or excessive subordination and coordination (30c).

30a Using subordination effectively

Subordinate means "being of lower rank." A subordinate grammatical structure cannot stand alone; it is dependent on the main (independent) clause. The most common subordinate structure is the dependent clause (22b(2)), which usually begins with a subordinating conjunction or a relative pronoun.

(1) Subordinating conjunctions
A **subordinating conjunction** specifies the relationship between a dependent clause and an independent clause. For example, it might signal a causal relationship.

The painters finished early **because they work well together.**

Here are a few of the most frequently used subordinating conjunctions:

Cause	*because*
Concession	*although, even though*
Condition	*if, unless*
Effect	*so that*
Sequence	*before, after*
Time	*when*

By using subordinating conjunctions, you can combine short sentences and indicate how they are related.

> *After the*
> ~~The~~ crew leader picked us up early on Friday~~.~~ *, we* ~~We~~ ate breakfast together at a local diner.

If the subjects of the two clauses are the same, the dependent clause can often be shortened to a phrase.

> *eating*
> After ~~we ate~~ our breakfast, we headed back to the construction site.

(2) Relative pronouns

A **relative pronoun** (*who, whom, which, that,* or *whose*) introduces a dependent clause that, in most cases, modifies the pronoun's antecedent (26a(2)).

> The temple has a portico **that faces west.**

By using an **adjectival (relative) clause**—that is, a dependent clause introduced by a relative pronoun—you can embed details into a sentence without sacrificing conciseness.

> *, which has sold well in the United States*
> Japanese automakers have produced a hybrid car.

An adjectival clause can be shortened, as long as the meaning of the sentence remains clear.

> The runner ~~who was~~ from Brazil stumbled just before the finish line.

CAUTION

A relative clause beginning with *which* sometimes refers to an entire independent clause rather than modifying a specific word or phrase. Because this type of reference can be vague, you should avoid it if possible.

     As   he should have

~~He is~~ a graduate of a top university,~~which should provide him with~~ many opportunities.

30b   Using coordination effectively

Coordinate means "being of equal rank." Coordinate grammatical elements have the same form. For example, they may be two words that are both adjectives, two phrases that are both prepositional, or two clauses that are both dependent or both independent.

a **stunning** and **satisfying** conclusion [adjectives]

in the attic or **in the basement** [prepositional phrases]

so that everyone would be happy and **so that no one would complain** [dependent adverbial clauses]

The company was losing money, yet **the employees suspected nothing.** [independent clauses]

To indicate the relationship between coordinate words, phrases, or clauses, choose an appropriate coordinating conjunction.

Addition	*and*
Alternative	*or, not*
Cause	*for*
Contrast	*but, yet*
Result	*so*

By using coordination, you can avoid unnecessary repetition and thus make your sentences more concise.

The hike to the top of Angels Landing has countless switchbacks. ~~It also~~ ~~has~~ long drop-offs.

                                                    and

MULTILINGUAL WRITERS

CHOOSING CONJUNCTIONS

In English, use either a coordinating conjunction or a subordinating conjunction, but not both, to signal a connection between clauses.

> Even though I took some aspirin, ~~but~~ I still have a sore shoulder.

> Because he had a severe headache, ~~so~~ he went to the health center.

Alternatively, the clauses in these two example sentences can be connected with coordinating conjunctions, rather than subordinating conjunctions.

> I took some aspirin, **but** I still have a sore shoulder.

> He had a severe headache, **so** he went to the health center.

Exercise 1

Using subordination and coordination, revise the sentences in the following paragraph so that they emphasize the ideas you think are important.

¹The Lummi tribe lives in the Northwest. ²The Lummis have a belief about sorrow and loss. ³They believe that grief is a burden. ⁴According to their culture, this burden shouldn't be carried alone. ⁵After the terrorist attack on the World Trade Center, the Lummis wanted to help shoulder the burden of grief felt by others. ⁶Some of the Lummis carve totem poles. ⁷These carvers crafted a healing totem pole. ⁸They gave this pole to the citizens of New York. ⁹Many of the citizens of New York had family members who were killed in the terrorist attacks. ¹⁰The Lummis escorted the totem pole across the nation. ¹¹They made stops for small ceremonies. ¹²At these ceremonies, they offered blessings. ¹³They also offered songs. ¹⁴The Lummis don't believe that the pole itself heals. ¹⁵Rather, they believe that healing comes from the prayers and songs said over it. ¹⁶For them, healing isn't the responsibility of a single person. ¹⁷They believe that it is the responsibility of the community.

30c   Avoiding faulty or excessive subordination and coordination

(1) Precise conjunctions enhance readability.

Effective subordination requires choosing subordinating conjunctions carefully. In the following sentence, the use of *as* is distracting because it can mean either "because" or "while."

~~As~~ *Because* time was running out, I randomly filled in the remaining circles on the exam sheet.

Sometimes you may need to add a subordinating conjunction to a phrase for clarity. Without the addition of *although* in the revision of the following sentence, the connection between being a new player and winning games is unclear.

Although Chen was a new player, ~~winning~~ *he won* more than half of his games.

Your choice of coordinating conjunction should also convey your meaning precisely. For example, to indicate a cause-and-effect relationship, *so* is more precise than *and*.

The rain continued to fall, ~~and~~ *so* the concert was canceled.

(2) Excessive subordination and coordination can confuse readers.

As you revise your writing, make sure that you have not overused subordination or coordination. In the following ineffective sentence, two dependent clauses compete for the reader's focus. The revision is clearer because it eliminates one of the dependent clauses.

Ineffective

Although researchers used to believe that ancient Egyptians were the first to domesticate cats, they now think that cats may have provided company for humans 5,000 years earlier **because** the intact skeleton of a cat has been discovered in a Neolithic village on Cyprus.

Revised

Although researchers used to believe that ancient Egyptians were the first to domesticate cats, they now think that cats may have provided company for humans 5,000 years earlier. They base their revised estimate on the discovery of an intact cat skeleton in a Neolithic village on Cyprus.

Overuse of coordination results in a rambling sentence in need of revision.

Ineffective

The lake was surrounded by forest, and it was large and clean, so it looked refreshing.

Revised

Surrounded by forest, the large, clean lake looked refreshing.

Exercise 2

Revise the following sentences to eliminate faulty or excessive coordination and subordination. Be prepared to explain why your sentences are more effective than the originals.

1. The Duct Tape Guys usually describe humorous uses for duct tape, providing serious information about the history of duct tape on their Web site.
2. Duct tape was invented for the U.S. military during World War II to keep the moisture out of ammunition cases because it was strong and waterproof.
3. Duct tape was originally called "duck tape" as it was waterproof and ducks are like that too and because it was made of cotton duck, which is a durable, tightly woven material.
4. Duck tape was also used to repair jeeps and to repair aircraft, its primary use being to protect ammunition cases.
5. When the war was over, house builders used duck tape to connect duct work together, and the builders started to refer to duck tape as "duct tape" and eventually the color of the tape changed from the green that was used during the war to silver, which matched the ducts.

31 Parallelism

Parallelism is the use of grammatically equivalent structures to clarify meaning and to emphasize ideas. Parallel structures often occur in a series.

> Their goals are **to raise awareness of the natural area, to build a walking path near the creek running through it,** and **to construct a nature center at the east end of the parking lot.**

This chapter will help you

- recognize parallel elements (**31a**),
- create parallelism by repeating words and grammatical forms (**31b**),
- use parallel elements to link sentences (**31c**),
- link parallel elements with correlative conjunctions (**31d**), and
- use parallelism for emphasis in introductions and conclusions (**31e**).

31a Recognizing parallel elements

Two or more elements are considered parallel when they have similar grammatical forms—for example, when they are all nouns or all prepositional phrases. Parallel elements are frequently joined by a coordinating conjunction (*and, but, or, yet, so, nor,* or *for*). In the examples that follow, the elements in boldface have the same grammatical form.

Words The dean is both **determined** and **dedicated.**

Phrases She emphasized her commitment to **academic freedom, professional development, cultural diversity,** and **social justice.**

Phrases	Her goals include **publicizing student and faculty research,** **increasing the funding for that research,** and **providing adequate research facilities.**
Clauses	Our instructor explained **what the project had entailed** and **how the results had been used.**
	He said **that we would conduct a similar project** but **that we would likely get different results.**
Sentences	When I interviewed for the job, <u>I tried not to sweat.</u> When I got the job, <u>I managed not to shout.</u>

Exercise 1

Write two sentences that illustrate each of the following structures: parallel words, parallel phrases, parallel clauses, and parallel sentences. Use the examples in this section as models.

31b Repeating words and grammatical forms

(1) The repetition of words often creates parallel elements.
By repeating a preposition, the infinitive marker *to,* or the introductory word of a clause, you can create parallel structures that will help you convey your meaning clearly, succinctly, and emphatically.

Preposition	For about fifteen minutes, I have been pacing in my office, hands **on** my hips, a scowl **on** my face, and a grudge **on** my mind.
	My embarrassment stemmed not **from** the money lost but **from** the notoriety gained.
Infinitive marker *to*	She wanted her audience **to remember** the protest song and **to understand** its origin.

Introductory word of a clause	The team vowed **that** they would support each other, **that** they would play their best, and **that** they would win the tournament.

(2) Parallel structures can be created through the repetition of form only.
Sometimes parallel structures are similar in form even though no words are repeated. The following example includes the *-ing* form (present participle) of three different verbs.

> People all around me are **buying, remodeling,** or **selling** their houses.

The next example includes a compound dependent clause (**22b**), each part of which has a two-word subject and a one-word predicate.

Whether	**mortgage rates rise** or **building codes change,** the real estate market should remain strong this spring.

31c Linking two or more sentences

Repeating a pattern emphasizes the relationship of ideas. The following two sentences come from the conclusion of "Letter from Birmingham Jail."

> **If I have said anything** in this letter <u>that overstates the truth and indicates an unreasonable impatience,</u> **I beg you to forgive me. If I have said anything** <u>that understates the truth and indicates my having a patience</u> that allows me to settle for anything less than brotherhood, **I beg God to forgive me.**
>
> —MARTIN LUTHER KING, JR.

Almost every structure in the second sentence is parallel to a structure in the first. To create this parallelism, King repeats words and uses similar grammatical forms. But the second sentence would still be parallel with the first even if more of its words were different. For example, substituting *written* for *said* and *reveals* for *indicates* ("If I have written anything that understates the truth and reveals my having a patience . . . ") would result in a sentence that was still parallel with the first sentence. Such changes, though, would lessen the impact of this particular passage because they would detract from the important substitution of "God" for "you" in the second sentence.

THINKING RHETORICALLY

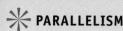 **PARALLELISM**

Parallel elements make your writing easy to read. But consider breaking from the parallel pattern on occasion to emphasize a point. For example, to describe a friend, you could start with two adjectives and then switch to a noun phrase.

My friend Alison is **kind, modest,** and **the smartest mathematician in the state.**

31d Using correlative conjunctions

Correlative conjunctions (or **correlatives**) are pairs of words that link other words, phrases, or clauses (**21a(7)** and **22c(2)**).

both . . . and
either . . . or
neither . . . nor
not only . . . but also
whether . . . or

Notice how the words or phrases following each conjunction in the pair are parallel.

He will major in **either** biology **or** chemistry.

Whether at home **or** at school, he is always busy.

Be especially careful when using *not only . . . but also*.

His team practices not only
~~Not only practicing~~ at 6 a.m. during the week, but ~~his team~~ also ~~scrimmages~~ on Sunday afternoons.

OR

does his team practice   it
Not only ~~practicing~~ at 6 a.m. during the week, but ~~the team~~ also scrimmages on Sunday afternoons.

In the first example, each conjunction is followed by a prepositional phrase (22a(4)). In the second example, each conjunction accompanies a clause (22b).

31e Emphasizing key ideas in introductions and conclusions

By expressing key ideas in parallel structures, you emphasize them. However, be careful not to overuse parallel patterns, or they will lose their impact. Parallelism is especially effective in the introduction to a paragraph or an essay. The following passage from the introduction to a chapter of a book on advertising contains three examples of parallel forms.

> While **men are encouraged to fall in love with their cars, women are more often invited to have a romance,** indeed an erotic experience, with **something closer to home, something that truly does pump the valves of our hearts**—the food we eat. And the consequences become even more severe as we enter into the territory of **compulsivity** and **addiction.**
>
> —JEAN KILBOURNE, *Deadly Persuasion*

Parallel structures can also be effective in the conclusion to an essay.

> **Because these men work** with **animals,** not **machines, because they live** outside in landscapes of torrential beauty, **because they are confined** to **a place** and **a routine** embellished with awesome variables, **because calves die** in the arms that pulled others into life, **because they go** to the mountains as if on a pilgrimage to find out what makes a herd of elk tick, **their strength** is also **a softness, their toughness, a rare delicacy.**
>
> —GRETEL EHRLICH, "About Men"

Exercise 2

Make the structures in each sentence parallel. In some sentences, you may have to use different wording.

1. Helen was praised by the vice president, and her assistant admired her.
2. Colleagues found her genial and easy to schedule meetings with.
3. When she hired new employees for her department, she looked for applicants who were intelligent, able to stay focused, and able to speak clearly.
4. At meetings, she was always prepared, participating actively yet politely, and generated innovative responses to department concerns.
5. In her annual report, she wrote that her most important achievements were attracting new clients and revenues were higher.
6. When asked about her leadership style, she said that she preferred collaborating with others rather than to work alone in her office.
7. Although dedicated to her work, Helen also recognized that parenting was important and the necessity of cultivating a life outside of work.
8. She worked hard to save money for the education of her children, for her own music lessons, and investing for her retirement.
9. However, in the coming year, she hoped to reduce the number of weekends she worked in the office and spending more time at home.
10. She would like to plan a piano recital and also have the opportunity to plan a family vacation.

32 Emphasis

In any rhetorical situation, some of your ideas will be more important than others. You can direct the reader's attention to these ideas by emphasizing them. This chapter will help you

- place words where they receive emphasis (32a),
- use cumulative and periodic sentences (32b),
- arrange ideas in climactic order (32c),
- repeat important words (32d),
- choose between active voice and passive voice (32e),
- invert word order in sentences (32f), and
- use an occasional short sentence (32g).

You can also emphasize ideas by using subordination and coordination (chapter 30), parallelism (chapter 31), and exact word choice (chapter 35).

32a Placing words for emphasis

Words at the beginning or the end of a sentence—especially the end—receive emphasis. Notice how the revision of the following sentence adds emphasis to the beginning to balance the emphasis at the end.

~~In today's society, most good~~ jobs require a college education.
Good _today_

You can also emphasize an important idea by placing it after a colon (41d) or a dash (41e).

At a later time [rocks and clay] may again become what they once were: dust.   —LESLIE MARMON SILKO, "Interior and Exterior Landscapes"

By 1857, miners had extracted 760 tons of gold from these hills—and left behind more than ten times as much mercury, as well as devastated forests, slopes and streams.

—REBECCA SOLNIT, *Storming the Gates of Paradise: Landscapes for Politics*

Exercise 1

Find the most important idea in each set of sentences. Then combine each set into one sentence so that the most important idea is emphasized. Be prepared to explain your changes.

1. Snowboarding is a new sport. It debuted at the Olympics in 1998. The Olympics were held in Nagano, Japan, that year.

2. Snowboarders came from around the world. Some competed in the giant slalom. Others participated in the halfpipe.

3. Snowboarding has increased in popularity. Each year, more and more people go snowboarding. It attracted 50 percent more participants in 2000 than it did in 1999.

4. Snowboarding is a fast-growing sport. The number of snowboards sold each year has increased dramatically.

5. However, the inventor of the snowboard is hard to identify. People have been sliding down hills on sleds for a long time.

6. Some sources credit M. M. "Jack" Burchet. Burchet tied his feet to a piece of plywood in 1929.

7. Sherman Poppen is most frequently cited as the inventor of the snowboard. His Snurfer went into production in 1966. (The name is a combination of the words *snow* and *surfer*.)

8. Poppen created the Snurfer for his daughter. He bound two skis together. He also fixed a rope at the front end.

9. Snowboarding originated as a sport for kids. It eventually became a competitive sport.

10. The United States snowboarding team won two medals in the 1998 Olympic Games. The team won seven medals in the 2006 Olympic Games.

32b Using cumulative and periodic sentences

In a **cumulative sentence,** the main idea (the independent clause) comes first; less important ideas or supplementary details follow.

> **The day was hot for June,** a pale sun burning in a cloudless sky, wilting the last of the irises, the rhododendron blossoms drooping.
> —ADAM HASLETT, "Devotion"

In a **periodic sentence,** however, the main idea comes last, just before the period.

> In a day when movies seem more and more predictable, when novels tend to be plotless, baggy monsters or minimalist exercises in interior emotion, **it's no surprise that sports has come to occupy an increasingly prominent place in the communal imagination.** —MICHIKO KAKUTANI, "Making Art of Sport"

Both of these types of sentences can be effective. Because cumulative sentences are more common, however, the infrequently encountered periodic sentence tends to provide emphasis.

32c Ordering ideas from least to most important

By arranging your ideas in **climactic order**—from least important to most important—you build up suspense. If you place your most important idea first, the sentence may seem to trail off. If you place it in the middle, readers may not recognize its full significance. If, however, you place it at the end of the sentence, it will not only receive emphasis but also provide a springboard to the next sentence. In the following example, the writer emphasizes a doctor's desire to help the disadvantaged and then implies that this desire has been realized through work with young Haitian doctors.

> While he was in medical school, the soon-to-be doctor discovered his calling: to diagnose infectious diseases, to find ways of curing people with these diseases, and **to bring the lifesaving knowledge of modern medicine to the disadvantaged.** Most recently, he has been working with a small group of young doctors in Haiti.

THINKING RHETORICALLY

 CLIMACTIC ORDER

Placing the least important idea at the end of the sentence can be effective when you are trying to be humorous, as in the following example:

> Contemporary man, of course, has no such peace of mind. He finds himself in the midst of a crisis of faith. He is what we fashionably call "alienated." He has seen the ravages of war, he has known natural catastrophes, he has been to singles bars.   —**WOODY ALLEN**, *Side Effects*

32d   Repeating important words

Although effective writers avoid unnecessary repetition, they also understand that deliberate repetition emphasizes key words or ideas.

> We **forget** all too soon the things we thought we could never **forget.** We **forget** the loves and betrayals alike, **forget** what we whispered and what we screamed, **forget** who we are.   —**JOAN DIDION**, "On Keeping a Notebook"

In this case, the emphatic repetition of *forget* reinforces the author's point—that we do not remember many things that once seemed impossible to forget. If you decide to repeat a word for emphasis, make sure that the word you choose conveys one of your central ideas.

32e   Choosing between the active voice and the passive voice

(1) Sentences in the active and passive voices differ in form.
A sentence in the **active voice** emphasizes an actor and an action by having the actor as the subject. The **passive voice** emphasizes the receiver or the result of the action, with the actor often omitted entirely (27d). If a reference to an actor is included in a passive sentence, this

reference appears in a prepositional phrase beginning with *by*. The verb phrase in the passive voice also differs from its active counterpart: it includes the auxiliary verb *be* and the past participle of the main verb.

Active   Bob Dylan wrote that song.

Passive   That song **was written by** Bob Dylan.

(2) Sentences in the active voice highlight actors and actions.

The author of the following excerpt uses the active voice to describe the passage of an airplane and the passengers inside it:

> [1]The tiny red light of an airplane **passes** through the sky. [2]It **soars** past a low cloud, the North Star, the bold white W of Cassiopeia—vanishing and reappearing, winking in a long ellipsis. [3]Inside, its passengers **read** glossy periodicals, **summon** flight attendants, and **unhitch** the frames of their safety belts. [4]They **gaze** from the panes of double windows and **float** away in a tight red arc.   —KEVIN BROCKMEIER, "Space"

Notice how much less effective the third sentence is when written in the passive voice, with the emphasis on the actors removed.

> Inside, glossy periodicals **are read,** flight attendants **are summoned,** and the frames of safety belts **are unhitched.**

(3) Sentences in the passive voice emphasize recipients or objects of actions.

In a paragraph from a government-sponsored Web page that warns against the use of illicit drugs, the passive voice is used to discuss the drug methamphetamine. Paragraphs on users and producers of the drug are written primarily in the active voice, but the paragraph about the drug itself and the various ways in which it is used is written in the passive voice. Drug users and producers are not mentioned in this paragraph because the drug itself is the focus.

> Methamphetamine **can be ingested, inhaled,** or **injected.** It **is sold** as a powder or in small chunks which resemble rock candy. It **can be mixed** with water for injection or sprinkled on tobacco or marijuana and smoked. Chunks of clear, high-purity methamphetamine ("ice," "crystal," "glass") **are smoked** in a small pipe, much as "crack" cocaine **is smoked.**
> —UTAH ATTORNEY GENERAL'S OFFICE

Because whoever or whatever is responsible for the action is not the subject of a sentence in the passive voice, such a sentence is often imprecise. Politicians sometimes favor the passive voice because it allows them to avoid responsibility by saying, for example, "Taxes will have to be raised" or "A few miscalculations were made."

TECH SAVVY

Grammar checkers flag all uses of the passive voice they find, usually suggesting that they be changed to the active voice. Be sure to determine for yourself whether the active voice or the passive voice is more appropriate for your rhetorical situation.

32f Inverting word order

Most sentences begin with a subject and end with a predicate. When you move words out of their normal order, you draw attention to them.

<u>**At the back of the crowded room**</u> sat **a newspaper reporter.**
[COMPARE: **A newspaper reporter** sat <u>**at the back of the crowded room.**</u>]

<u>**Fundamental to life in New York**</u> is **the subway.**
[COMPARE: **The subway** is <u>**fundamental to life in New York.**</u>]

A sentence with inverted word order will stand out in a paragraph containing other sentences with standard word order. Notice the inverted word order in the second sentence of the following passage.

[1]The Library Committee met with the City Council on several occasions to persuade them to fund the building of a library annex. [2]So successful were their efforts that a new wing will be added by next year. [3]This wing will contain archival materials that were previously stored in the basement.

The modifier *so successful* appears at the beginning of the sentence, rather than in its normal position, after the verb. *Their efforts were so successful that* . . . . The inverted word order emphasizes the committee's accomplishment.

MULTILINGUAL WRITERS

INVERTING WORD ORDER

English sentences are inverted in various ways. Sometimes the main verb in the form of a participle is placed at the beginning of the sentence. The subject and the auxiliary verb(s) are then inverted.

part ⌐ ⌐ aux ⌐ ⌐ s

Carved into the bench **were someone's initials.**
[COMPARE: Someone's initials were carved into the bench.]

An adjective may also begin a sentence. In this type of sentence, the subject and the linking verb are inverted.

adj ⌐ ⌐ link v ⌐ ⌐ s

Crucial to our success **was the dedication of our employees.**
[COMPARE: The dedication of our employees was crucial to our success.]

In other inverted sentences, the auxiliary verb comes before the subject. Sentences beginning with a negative adverb (such as *never, seldom,* or *rarely*) require this type of inversion.

neg adv ⌐ aux ⌐ s ⌐ v

Rarely have we experienced such bad weather!

32g   Using an occasional short sentence

In a paragraph of mostly long sentences, try using a short sentence for emphasis. To optimize the effect, lead up to the short sentence with an especially long sentence.

After organizing the kitchen, buying the groceries, slicing the vegetables, mowing the lawn, weeding the garden, hanging the decorations, and setting up the grill, I was ready to have a good time when my guests arrived. **Then the phone rang.**

Exercise 2

Add emphasis to each of the following sentences by using the strategy indicated. You may have to add some words and/or delete others.

1. (climactic order) In the 1960 Olympics, Wilma Rudolph tied the world record in the 100-meter race, she tied the record in the 400-meter relay, she won the hearts of fans from around the world, and she broke the record in the 200-meter race.

2. (periodic sentence) Some sports reporters described Rudolph as a gazelle because of her beautiful stride.

3. (inversion) Rudolph's Olympic achievement is impressive, but her victory over a crippling disease is even more spectacular.

4. (final short sentence) Rudolph was born prematurely, weighing only four and one-half pounds. As a child, she suffered from double pneumonia, scarlet fever, and then polio.

5. (cumulative sentence) She received help from her family. Her brothers and sister massaged her legs. Her mother drove her to a hospital for therapy.

6. (inversion) Her siblings' willingness to help was essential to her recovery, as were her mother's vigilant care and her own determination.

7. (periodic sentence) Her passions became basketball and track after she recovered, built up her strength, and gained self-confidence.

8. (climactic order) Rudolph set a scoring record in basketball, she set the standard for future track and field stars, and she set an Olympic record in track.

9. (active voice) Many female athletes, including Florence Griffith Joyner and Jackie Joyner-Kersee, have been inspired by Wilma Rudolph.

33 Variety

To make your writing lively and distinctive, include a variety of sentence types and lengths. Notice how the sentences in the paragraph below vary in length (short and long), form (simple, compound, and compound-complex), and function (statements, questions, and commands). This assortment of sentences makes this paragraph about pleasure pleasurable to read.

> Start with the taste. Imagine a moment when the sensation of honey or sugar on the tongue was an astonishment, a kind of intoxication. The closest I've ever come to recovering such a sense of sweetness was secondhand, though it left a powerful impression on me even so. I'm thinking of my son's first experience with sugar: the icing on the cake at his first birthday. I have only the testimony of Isaac's face to go by (that, and his fierceness to repeat the experience), but it was plain that his first encounter with sugar had intoxicated him—was in fact an ecstasy, in the literal sense of the word. That is, he was beside himself with the pleasure of it, no longer here with me in space and time in quite the same way he had been just a moment before. Between bites Isaac gazed up at me in amazement (he was on my lap, and I was delivering the ambrosial forkfuls to his gaping mouth) as if to exclaim, "Your world contains *this?* From this day forward I shall dedicate my life to it." (Which he basically has done.) And I remember thinking, this is no minor desire, and then wondered: Could it be that sweetness is the prototype of *all* desire?
>
> —**MICHAEL POLLAN**, *The Botany of Desire*

This chapter will help you

- revise sentence length and form (33a),
- vary sentence openings (33b), and
- use an occasional question, command, or exclamation (33c).

If you have difficulty distinguishing between various types of sentence structures, review the fundamentals in chapters 21 and 22.

(1) Combine short sentences.
To avoid the choppiness of a series of short sentences, consider using one of the following methods to combine some of the sentences into longer sentences.

(a) Use coordinate or correlative conjunctions.
Try combining ideas using coordinate conjunctions (*and, but, or, for, nor, so,* and *yet*) or correlative conjunctions (*both . . . and, either . . . or, neither . . . nor,* and *not only . . . but also*).

Simple sentences	Minneapolis is one of the Twin Cities. St. Paul is the other. They differ in many ways.
Combined	Minneapolis **and** St. Paul are called the Twin Cities, **but** they differ in many ways.
Simple sentences	The company provides health insurance. It also provides dental insurance.
Combined	The company provides **both** health insurance **and** dental insurance.

(b) Use relative pronouns or subordinating conjunctions.
The relative pronouns *who, which, whose,* and *that* can be used to combine simple sentences.

Simple sentences	Today, lawmakers discussed some new legislation. This legislation would promote the safety of rocket passengers.
Combined	Today, lawmakers discussed some new legislation **that** would promote the safety of rocket passengers.

You can also use subordinating conjunctions such as *because, so that,* and *even though* to join simple sentences. For a full list, see page 545.

Simple sentences	Legislation on space tourism has not been passed. Plans for a commercial rocket service are going forward anyway.

Combined	**Although** legislation on space tourism has not been passed, plans for a commercial rocket service are going forward anyway.

You may also decide to use both a subordinating and a coordinating conjunction.

Simple sentences	Private rockets have been involved in very few accidents. Legislators are discussing safety issues, though. They have not agreed on any regulations yet.
Combined	**Although** private rockets have been involved in very few accidents, legislators are discussing safety issues, **but** they have not agreed on regulations yet.

TECH SAVVY
Although a grammar checker will flag long sentences, it cannot determine whether they contribute to variety. You will have to decide whether you have used them effectively. See Using a Grammar Checker on page 507.

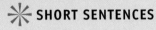 **THINKING RHETORICALLY**

⚹ SHORT SENTENCES

Occasionally, a series of brief sentences produces an intended effect. For example, a writer may have a rhetorical reason for conveying a sense of abruptness; therefore, what might seem choppy in one situation could be considered dramatic in another. The short sentences in the following passage capture the quick actions taking place as an accident is about to occur.

"There's a truck in your lane!" my friend yelled. I swerved toward the shoulder. "Watch out!" she screamed. I hit the brakes. The wheel locked. The back of the car swerved to the right.

Exercise 1

Convert each set of short sentences into a single longer sentence. Use no more than one coordinating conjunction in the revised sentence.

1. It was the bottom of the ninth inning. The score was tied. The bases were loaded. There were two outs.
2. A young player stepped up to the plate. This was his first season. He had hit a home run yesterday. He had struck out his last time at bat.
3. He knew the next pitch could decide the game. He took a practice swing. The pitcher looked him over.
4. The pitch came in high. The batter swung low. He missed this first pitch. He also missed the second pitch.
5. He had two strikes against him. The young player hit the next ball. It soared over the right-field fence.

(2) Avoid overusing coordinating conjunctions.

In early drafts, some writers overuse the coordinating conjunctions *and* and *but*, so the pattern of long compound sentences becomes tedious. The use of coordinating conjunctions can also be ineffective if the relationship the writer is signaling is vague. The following strategies should help you revise ineffective uses of coordinating conjunctions.

(a) Use a more specific subordinating conjunction or a conjunctive adverb.
You can often replace *and* with a more specific subordinating conjunction or a conjunctive adverb (22c).

I worked all summer to earn tuition money, ~~and I didn't~~ so that I wouldn't have to work during the school year.

OR

I worked all summer to earn tuition money, ~~and~~ ; thus I didn't have to work during the school year.

(b) **Use a relative clause to embed information.**

Seafood~~is nutritious, and it is low in fat, and it~~ has become available in greater variety.

, which is nutritious and low in fat, (inserted after "Seafood")

(c) **Allow two or more verbs to share the same subject.**

Marie quickly grabbed a shovel, ~~and then she~~ ran to the edge of the field, and ~~then she~~ put out the fire before it could spread to the trees.

(d) **Place some information in an appositive phrase.**

Karl Glazebrook ~~is a researcher in astronomy at Johns Hopkins University, and he~~ has questioned the conventional theory of galaxy formations.

, a researcher in astronomy at Johns Hopkins University, (inserted after "Glazebrook")

(e) **Place some information in a prepositional or verbal phrase.**

~~The snow was thick, and~~ we could not see where we were going.

In the thick snow, (inserted at beginning)

~~The plane pulled~~ away from the gate on time, ~~and then it~~ sat on the runway for two hours.

After pulling (at beginning) ... *the plane* (inserted before "sat")

OR

The plane, after pulling away from the gate on time, sat on the runway for two hours.

In the last example, the subject, *plane,* and the verb, *sat,* are separated. Although it is usually best to keep the subject next to the verb so that the relationship between them is clear, breaking this pattern on occasion can add variety without sacrificing clarity.

E x e r c i s e 2

Use any of the methods for revising the ineffective use of coordinating conjunctions to improve the following paragraph.

[1]Onions are pungent, they are indispensable, and they are found in kitchens everywhere. [2]China is the leading producer of this vegetable. [3]Libya is the leading consumer, and on average a Libyan eats over sixty-five pounds of onions a year. [4]One hundred billion pounds of onions are produced each year, and they make their way into a variety of foods. [5]Raw onions add zest to salads, but they also add zest to burgers and salsas. [6]Cooked onions give a sweetness to pasta sauces, and they can also be added to soups and curries. [7]The onion is a ubiquitous ingredient, yet its origin remains unknown.

33b Varying sentence openings

Most writers begin more than half of their sentences with the subject. Although this pattern is common, relying on it too heavily can make writing sound dull. Experiment with the following alternatives for beginning your sentences.

(1) Begin with an adverb or an adverbial clause.

Immediately, the dentist stopped drilling and asked me how I was doing. [adverb]

When the procedure was over, he explained that I should not eat or drink anything for an hour. [adverbial clause]

(2) Begin with a prepositional or verbal phrase.

In the auditorium, voters waited in silence before casting their ballots. [prepositional phrase]

To win, candidates need to convey a clear message to voters. [infinitive phrase]

Reflecting on the election, we understood clearly how the incumbent defeated the challenger. [participial phrase]

(3) Begin with a connecting word or phrase.

In each of the following examples, the connecting word or phrase shows the relationship between the ideas in the pair of sentences. (See also 4d.)

Many restaurants close within a few years of opening. **But** others, which offer good food at reasonable prices, become well established.

Difficulty in finding a place to park keeps some people from going out to lunch downtown. **However,** that problem may be alleviated with the construction of a new underground parking garage.

Independently owned restaurants struggle to get started for a number of reasons. **First of all,** they have to compete against successful restaurant chains.

(4) Begin with an appositive or an absolute phrase.

A town of historic interest, Santa Fe also has many art galleries. [appositive phrase]

History, art, and the color of the sky—these drew her to Santa Fe. [appositive series]

Her face turned to the sky, she absorbed the warmth of the sun. [absolute phrase]

(5) Begin with a direct object or a predicate adjective.

I was an abysmal football player. **Soccer,** though, I could play well. [direct object]

Vital to any success I had were my mother's early lessons. [predicate adjective]

Exercise 3

Rewrite each sentence so that it does not begin with a subject.

1. John Spilsbury was an engraver and mapmaker from London who made the first jigsaw puzzle in about 1760.
2. He pasted a map onto a piece of wood and used a fine-bladed saw to cut around the borders of the countries.
3. The jigsaw puzzle was first an educational toy and has been a mainstay in households all over the world ever since its invention.
4. The original puzzles were quite expensive because the wooden pieces were cut by hand.
5. Most puzzles are made of cardboard today.

33c Using questions, exclamations, and commands

When you have written a long series of declarative statements, you can vary the paragraph by introducing another type of sentence: a question, a command, or an exclamation (22e). The sentence that varies from the others will catch the reader's attention.

(1) Raise a question or two for variety.

> If people could realize that immigrant children are better off, and less scarred, by holding on to their first languages as they learn a second one, then perhaps Americans could accept a more drastic change. What if every English-speaking toddler were to start learning a foreign language at an early age, maybe in kindergarten? What if these children were to learn Spanish, for instance, the language already spoken by millions of American citizens, but also by so many neighbors to the South? —ARIEL DORFMAN, "If Only We All Spoke Two Languages"

You can either answer the question or let readers answer it for themselves, in which case it is called a **rhetorical question** (22e).

(2) Add an exclamatory sentence for variety.

> But at other moments, the classroom is so lifeless or painful or confused—and I so powerless to do anything about it—that my claim to be a teacher seems a transparent sham. Then the enemy is everywhere: in those students from some alien planet, in the subject I thought I knew, and in the personal pathology that keeps me earning my living this way. What a fool I was to imagine that I had mastered this occult art—harder to divine than tea leaves and impossible for mortals to do even passably well!
>
> —PARKER PALMER, *The Courage to Teach*

Although you can make your sentences emphatic without resorting to the use of exclamation points (chapter 30), the introduction of an exclamatory sentence can break up a regular pattern of declarative sentences.

(3) Include a command for variety.

> Now I stare and stare at people shamelessly. Stare. It's the way to educate your eye.   —WALKER EVANS, *Unclassified*

In this case, a one-word command, "Stare," provides variety.

Exercise 4

Explain how questions and commands add variety to the following paragraph. Describe other ways in which this writer varies his sentences.

¹The gods, they say, give breath, and they take it away. ²But the same could be said—couldn't it?—of the humble comma. ³Add it to the present clause, and, of a sudden, the mind is, quite literally, given pause to think; take it out if you wish or forget it and the mind is deprived of a resting place. ⁴Yet still the comma gets no respect. ⁵It seems just a slip of a thing, a pedant's tick, a blip on the edge of our consciousness, a kind of printer's smudge almost. ⁶Small, we claim, is beautiful (especially in the age of the microchip). ⁷Yet what is so often used, and so rarely recalled, as the comma—unless it be breath itself?

—PICO IYER, "In Praise of the Humble Comma"

U

USAGE

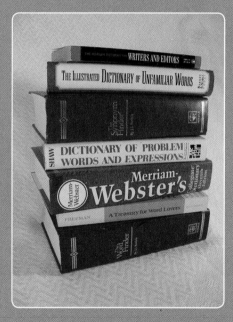

34 Good Usage 693

35 Exactness 707

36 Conciseness 719

Reference books can provide answers to questions about usage.

CHAPTER 34
Good Usage   693

34a Usage and the rhetorical situation   693
34b Clear style   694
34c Appropriate word choice   695
34d Inclusive language   696
34e Dictionaries   702
34f Thesauruses   706

CHAPTER 35
Exactness   707

35a Accurate and precise word choice   707
35b Evocative language   712
35c Idioms and collocations   713
35d First-person and second-person
pronouns   715
35e Clear definitions   717

CHAPTER 36
Conciseness   719

36a Eliminating wordiness and other
redundancies   719
36b Avoiding unnecessary repetition   723
36c Using elliptical constructions   723

34 Good Usage

Using the right words at the right time can make the difference between having your ideas taken seriously and seeing them brushed aside. In academic or professional writing, it is important to sound well informed and respectful. In conversation with friends, it is just as important to sound casual. Whatever the occasion, choosing the right words will help you connect with your audience. This chapter will help you

- understand how word choice is related to the rhetorical situation (34a),
- write in a clear, straightforward style (34b),
- choose words that are appropriate for your audience, purpose, and context (34c),
- use inclusive language (34d), and
- realize the benefits of dictionaries (34e) and thesauruses (34f).

34a Usage and the rhetorical situation

The words you use vary from situation to situation. How you talk to a loan officer differs from how you talk to your best friend. A discussion with a loan officer is likely to be relatively formal; a conversation with a friend will be less so. Understanding such differences in tone and making word choices that reflect those differences are essential in writing because readers cannot see your body language, hear the inflections of your voice, or interrupt to say that they are having trouble following you. Instead, readers respond to the words on the page or the screen. You can help them understand your ideas by choosing words that they know or that you can explain to them. When drafting, use words that come immediately to mind. Some of these words will be good choices. Others you can replace as you revise. Remembering your rhetorical situation will help you use the right word at the right time.

34b   Clear style

Although different styles are appropriate for different situations, you should strive to make your writing clear and straightforward. An ornate and wordy style takes more time to read and could make you seem stuffy or pretentious. To achieve a clear style, first choose words that your audience understands and that are appropriate for the occasion.

Ornate   The majority believes that achievement derives primarily from the diligent pursuit of allocated tasks.

Clear   Most people believe that success results from hard work.

When you write clearly, you show your readers that you are aware of the time and effort it takes to read closely. If you want readers to take your writing seriously, you must show them respect by not using obscure words when common words will do and by not using more words than necessary. Using words that are precise (35a) and sentences that are concise (chapter 36) can also help you achieve a clear style.

Exercise 1

Revise the following sentences for an audience that prefers a clear, straightforward style.

1. Expert delineation of character in a job interview is a goal that is not always possible to achieve.
2. In an employment situation, social pleasantries may contribute to the successful functioning of job tasks, but such interactions should not distract attention from the need to complete all assignments in a timely manner.
3. Commitment to an ongoing and carefully programmed schedule of physical self-management can be a significant resource for stress reduction in the workplace.

34c Appropriate word choice

Unless you are writing for a specialized audience and have good reason to believe that this audience will welcome slang, colloquial expressions, or jargon, the following advice can help you determine which words to use and which to avoid.

(1) Slang is effective in only a few rhetorical situations.

The term **slang** covers a wide range of words or expressions that are considered casual, facetious, or fashionable by people in a particular age group, locality, or profession. Although such words are often used in private conversation or in writing intended to mimic conversation, they are usually out of place in academic or professional writing. If your rhetorical situation does call for the use of slang, be sure that the words or expressions you choose are not so new that your audience will be unable to understand what you mean and not so old that your use of them makes you seem out of touch with popular culture.

(2) Conversational (or colloquial) words are usually too informal for academic and professional writing.

Words labeled *colloquial* in a dictionary are fine for casual conversation and for written dialogues or personal essays on a light topic. Such words are sometimes used for special effect in academic writing, but you should usually replace them with more appropriate words. For example, conversational words such as *dumb* and *kid around* could be replaced by *illogical* and *tease*.

 CAUTION

Because contractions (such as *you'll* for "you will" and *she's* for "she is") reflect the sound of conversation, you can use them in some types of writing to create a friendly tone. However, some of your instructors or supervisors may consider them too informal for academic or professional writing.

(3) Regionalisms can make writing vivid.

Regionalisms—such as *tank* for "pond" and *sweeper* for "vacuum cleaner"—can make writing lively and distinctive, but they are effective only when the audience can understand them in a specific context. Furthermore, they are often considered too informal for academic and professional writing.

(4) Technical words are essential when writing for specialists.

When writing for a diverse audience, an effective writer will not refer to the need for bifocals as *presbyopia*. However, technical language is appropriate when the audience can understand it (as when one physician writes to another) or when the audience would benefit by learning the terms in question.

Jargon is technical language tailored specifically for a particular occupation. Jargon can be an efficient shortcut for conveying specialized concepts, but you should use it only when you are sure that you and your readers share an understanding of the terms. *Splash,* for example, does not always refer to water or an effect (as in *making a splash*); the word also signifies a computer screen that can appear after you click on a Web site but before you view its opening page. Terms that originate as jargon sometimes enter mainstream usage because nonspecialists begin to use them. As computer use has grown, for example, technical terms such as *download* and *mouse* have become commonly used and widely understood.

34d Inclusive language

By making word choices that are inclusive rather than exclusive, you invite readers into your writing. Advertisers follow a similar principle when they choose images that appeal to a diverse audience. Prejudiced or derogatory language has no place in academic or professional writing; using it undermines your authority and credibility as a writer. Even if you are writing for one person you think you know well, do not assume that you know everything about that person. A close colleague at work might have an uncle who is gay, for example, or his sister might be married to someone of a different race or religion. Do not try to justify demeaning language on the grounds that you meant it as a joke. Take responsibility for the words you use.

UNITED COLORS
OF BENETTON.

NETTON

An inclusive advertisement appeals to a diverse audience. © The Advertising Archives.

(1) Nonsexist language indicates respect for both men and women.

Effective writers show equal respect for men and women. For example, they avoid using *man* to refer to people in general because they understand that the word excludes women.

Achievements [OR Human achievements]
~~Man's achievements~~ in science are impressive.

Sexist language has a variety of sources, such as contempt for the opposite sex and unthinking repetition of words used by others. Stereotyping can also lead to sexist language. Women, like men, can be *firefighters* or *police officers*—words that are increasingly used as gender-neutral alternatives to *firemen* and *policemen.*

TECH SAVVY

A grammar checker can find sexist words ending in *-ess (authoress)* or *-man (policeman)* and almost always flags *mankind.* Unfortunately, grammar checkers also erroneously identify as sexist many appropriate uses of the words *female, woman,* and *girl,* but not similar uses of *male, man,* and *boy.*

Being alert for sexist language and knowing how to revise it will help you gain acceptance from your audience, whatever its demographics. Use the following tips to ensure that your writing is respectful.

TIPS FOR AVOIDING SEXIST LANGUAGE

When you review your drafts, revise the following types of sexist language.

- **Generic _he:_** A doctor should listen to _his_ patients.

  A doctor should listen to **his or her** patients. [use of the appropriate form of _he or she_]

  Doctors should listen to **their** patients. [use of plural forms]

  By listening to patients, **doctors obtain important diagnostic information.** [elimination of _his_ by revising the sentence]

- **Occupational stereotype:** Glenda James, a _female_ engineer at Howard Aviation, won the best-employee award.

  Glenda James, an engineer at Howard Aviation, won the best-employee award. [removal of the unnecessary gender reference]

- **Terms such as _man_ and _mankind_ or those with _-ess_ or _-man_ endings:** Labor laws benefit the common _man_. _Mankind_ benefits from philanthropy. The _stewardess_ brought me some orange juice.

  Labor laws benefit **working people.** [replacement of the stereotypical term with a gender-neutral term]

  Everyone benefits from philanthropy. [use of an indefinite pronoun]

  The **flight attendant** brought me some orange juice. [use of a gender-neutral term]

- **Stereotypical gender roles:** I was told that the university offers free tuition to faculty _wives_. The minister pronounced them _man_ and _wife_.

  I was told that the university offers free tuition to faculty **spouses.** [replacement of the stereotypical term with a gender-neutral term]

  The minister pronounced them **husband** and wife. [use of a term equivalent to _wife_]

- **Inconsistent use of titles:** *Mr. Holmes* and his *wife,* Mary, took a long trip to China.

  Mr. and Mrs. [or Ms.] Holmes took a long trip to China. [consistent use of titles]

  OR **Peter and Mary Holmes** took a long trip to China. [removal of titles]

  OR **Peter Holmes** and **Mary Wolfe** took a long trip to China. [use of full names]

- **Unstated gender assumption:** Have your *mother make your costume* for the school pageant.

  Have your **parents provide you with a costume** for the school pageant. [replacement of the stereotypical words with gender-neutral ones]

Exercise 2

Make the following sentences inclusive by eliminating sexist language.

1. The ladies met to discuss the company's current operating budget.
2. The old boys run the city's government.
3. Mothers should read to their small children.
4. Some fans admired the actress because of her movies; others praised her for her environmental activism.
5. For six years, he worked as a mailman in a small town.

(2) Nonracist language promotes social equity.

Rarely is it necessary to identify anyone's race or ethnicity in academic or professional writing. However, you may need to use appropriate racial or ethnic terms if you are writing a demographic report, an argument against existing racial inequities, or a historical account of a particular event involving ethnic groups. Determining which terms a particular group prefers can be difficult because preferences sometimes vary within a group and change over time. One conventional way to refer to Americans of a specific descent is to include an adjective before the word *American: African American, Asian American, European American, Latin American, Mexican American, Native American.* These words are widely used; however, members of a particular group may identify themselves in more than one way.

In addition to *African American* and *European American, Black* (or *black*) and *White* (or *white*) have long been used. People of Spanish-speaking descent may prefer *Chicano/Chicana, Hispanic, Latino/Latina, Puerto Rican,* or other terms. Members of cultures that are indigenous to North America may prefer a specific name such as *Cherokee* or *Haida,* though some also accept *American Indians* or *Native People.* An up-to-date dictionary that includes notes on usage can help you choose appropriate terms.

(3) Writing about any type of difference should be respectful.

If a writing assignment requires you to distinguish people based on age, ability, geographical area, religion, or sexual orientation, show respect to the groups or individuals you discuss by using the terms they prefer.

(a) Referring to age

Although some people object to the term *senior citizen,* a better alternative has not been provided. When used respectfully, the term refers to a person who has reached the age of retirement (but may not have decided to retire) and is eligible for certain privileges granted by society. However, if you know your audience would object to this term, find out which alternative is preferred.

(b) Referring to disability or illness

A current recommendation for referring to disabilities and illnesses is "to put the person first." In this way, the focus is placed on the individual rather than on the limitation. Thus, *persons with disabilities* is preferred over *disabled persons.* For your own writing, you can find out whether such person-first expressions are preferred by noting whether they are used in the articles and books (or by the people) you consult. Be aware, though, that some writers and readers think that these types of expressions sound unnatural, and others maintain that they do not serve their intended purpose because the last word in a phrase can carry the greater weight, especially at the end of a sentence.

(c) Referring to geographical areas

Certain geographical terms need to be used with special care. Though most frequently used to refer to people from the United States, the term *American* may also refer to people from Canada, Mexico, and Central or South America. If your audience may be confused by this term, use *people from the United States* or *U.S. citizens* instead.

The term *Arab* refers to people who speak Arabic. If you cannot use specific terms such as *Iraqi* or *Saudi Arabian,* be sure you know that a country's people speak Arabic and not another language. Iranians, for example, are not Arabs because they speak Farsi.

British, rather than *English,* is the preferred term for referring to people from the island of Great Britain or from the United Kingdom.

(d) Referring to religion

Reference to a person's religion should be made only if it is relevant to your rhetorical situation. If you must mention religious affiliation, use only those terms considered respectful. Because religions have both conservative and liberal followers, be careful not to make generalizations about political stances (see 8i(12)).

(e) Referring to sexual orientation

If your rhetorical situation calls for identifying sexual orientation, choose terms used by the people you are discussing. The words *gay, lesbian,* and *bisexual* are generally used as adjectives. Their use as nouns to refer to specific people may be considered offensive.

CHECKLIST for Assessing Usage within a Rhetorical Situation

- Do your words convey the meaning you intend?
- Can your audience understand the words you have used?
- Do you explain any words your audience might not understand?
- Have you used any words that could irritate or offend members of your audience?
- Do any of your words make you sound too casual or too formal?
- Do your words help you to fulfill your rhetorical purpose?
- Are your words appropriate for the context in which you are writing?
- Are your words appropriate for the context in which they will be read?

34e   Dictionaries

A good dictionary is an indispensable tool for writers. Desk dictionaries such as *The American Heritage Dictionary* and *Merriam-Webster's Collegiate Dictionary* do much more than provide the correct spellings of words; they also give meanings, parts of speech, plural forms, and verb tenses, as well as information about pronunciation and origin. In addition, a reliable dictionary also includes labels that can help you decide whether words are appropriate for your purpose, audience, and context. Words labeled *dialect, slang, colloquial, nonstandard,* or *unconventional,* as well as those labeled *archaic* or *obsolete* (meaning that they are no longer in common use), are generally inappropriate for college and professional writing. If a word has no label, you can safely assume that it can be used in writing for school or work. But whether the word is appropriate depends on the precise meaning a writer wants to convey (35a). Because language is constantly changing, it is important to choose a desk dictionary with a recent copyright date. Many dictionaries are available—in print, online, or on CD-ROM. Pocket dictionaries, which are useful for checking spellings and definitions, omit important information on usage and derivation. The dictionaries incorporated into most word-processing programs are equivalent to pocket dictionaries and may provide insufficient information.

(1) Consulting an unabridged or specialized dictionary can enhance your understanding of a word.

An **unabridged dictionary** provides a comprehensive survey of English words, including detailed information about their origins. A **specialized dictionary** presents words related to a specific discipline or to some aspect of usage.

Unabridged Dictionaries

The Oxford English Dictionary. 2nd ed. 20 vols. 1989– . CD-ROM. 2005.

Webster's Third New International Dictionary of the English Language. CD-ROM. 2002.

Specialized Dictionaries

The American Heritage Dictionary of Idioms. 1997.
The American Heritage Guide to Contemporary Usage and Style. 2005.
The BBI Dictionary of English Word Combinations. 1997.
The New Fowler's Modern English Usage. 3rd ed. 2000.
Merriam-Webster's Dictionary of English Usage. 1994.

MULTILINGUAL WRITERS

DICTIONARIES AND OTHER RESOURCES

The following dictionaries are recommended for nonnative speakers of English.

> *Collins Cobuild New Student's Dictionary.* 2002.
> *Longman Advanced American English.* 2000.
> *Heinle's Newbury House Dictionary of American English.* 4th ed. 2003.

Two excellent resources for ESL students are the following:

> *Longman Language Activator.* 2003. (A cross between a dictionary and a thesaurus, this book supplies definitions, usage guidelines, and sample sentences.)
> Swan, Michael. *Practical English Usage.* 3rd ed. 2005. (This is a practical reference guide to problems encountered by those who speak English as a second language.)

(2) Dictionary entries provide a range of information.

Figure 34.1 shows sample entries from the tenth edition of *Merriam-Webster's Collegiate Dictionary.* Notice that *move* is listed twice—first as a verb, then as a noun. The types of information these entries provide can be found in almost all desk dictionaries, though sometimes in a different order.

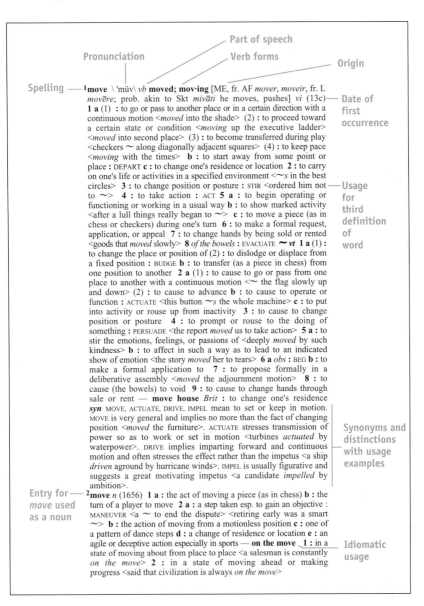

Part of speech

Pronunciation

Verb forms

Origin

Spelling

¹**move** \ 'müv\ *vb* **moved; mov·ing** [ME, fr. AF *mover, moveir,* fr. L
movēre; prob. akin to Skt *mivāti* he moves, pushes] *vi* (13c)
1 a (1) : to go or pass to another place or in a certain direction with a
continuous motion <*moved* into the shade> (2) : to proceed toward
a certain state or condition <*moving* up the executive ladder>
<*moved* into second place> (3) : to become transferred during play
<checkers ⁓ along diagonally adjacent squares> (4) : to keep pace
<*moving* with the times> **b** : to start away from some point or
place : DEPART **c** : to change one's residence or location **2** : to carry
on one's life or activities in a specified environment <⁓*s* in the best
circles> **3** : to change position or posture : STIR <ordered him not
to ⁓> **4** : to take action : ACT **5 a** : to begin operating or
functioning or working in a usual way **b** : to show marked activity
<after a lull things really began to ⁓> **c** : to move a piece (as in
chess or checkers) during one's turn **6** : to make a formal request,
application, or appeal **7** : to change hands by being sold or rented
<goods that *moved* slowly> **8** *of the bowels* : EVACUATE ⁓ *vt* **1 a** (1) :
to change the place or position of (2) : to dislodge or displace from
a fixed position : BUDGE **b** : to transfer (as a piece in chess) from
one position to another **2 a** (1) : to cause to go or pass from one
place to another with a continuous motion <⁓ the flag slowly up
and down> (2) : to cause to advance **b** : to cause to operate or
function : ACTUATE <this button ⁓*s* the whole machine> **c** : to put
into activity or rouse up from inactivity **3** : to cause to change
position or posture **4** : to prompt or rouse to the doing of
something : PERSUADE <the report *moved* us to take action> **5 a** : to
stir the emotions, feelings, or passions of <deeply *moved* by such
kindness> **b** : to affect in such a way as to lead to an indicated
show of emotion <the story *moved* her to tears> **6 a** *obs* : BEG **b** : to
make a formal application to **7** : to propose formally in a
deliberative assembly <*moved* the adjournment motion> **8** : to
cause (the bowels) to void **9** : to cause to change hands through
sale or rent — **move house** *Brit* : to change one's residence
syn MOVE, ACTUATE, DRIVE, IMPEL mean to set or keep in motion.
MOVE is very general and implies no more than the fact of changing
position <*moved* the furniture>. ACTUATE stresses transmission of
power so as to work or set in motion <turbines *actuated* by
waterpower>. DRIVE implies imparting forward and continuous
motion and often stresses the effect rather than the impetus <a ship
driven aground by hurricane winds>. IMPEL is usually figurative and
suggests a great motivating impetus <a candidate *impelled* by
ambition>.

²**move** *n* (1656) **1 a** : the act of moving a piece (as in chess) **b** : the
turn of a player to move **2 a** : a step taken esp. to gain an objective :
MANEUVER <a ⁓ to end the dispute> <retiring early was a smart
⁓> **b** : the action of moving from a motionless position **c** : one of
a pattern of dance steps **d** : a change of residence or location **e** : an
agile or deceptive action especially in sports — **on the move 1** : in a
state of moving about from place to place <a salesman is constantly
on the move> **2** : in a state of moving ahead or making
progress <said that civilization is always *on the move*>

Date of
first
occurrence

Usage
for
third
definition
of
word

Synonyms and
distinctions
with usage
examples

Entry for
move used
as a noun

Idiomatic
usage

Fig. 34.1. Examples of dictionary entries.

TYPES OF INFORMATION PROVIDED BY DICTIONARY ENTRIES

- **Spelling, syllabication (word division), and pronunciation.**

- **Parts of speech and word forms.** Dictionaries identify parts of speech—for instance, with *n* for "noun" or *vi* for "intransitive verb." Meanings will vary depending on the part of speech identified. Dictionaries also identify irregular forms of verbs, nouns, and adjectives: *fly, flew, flown, flying, flies; child, children; good, better, best.*

- **Word origin.**

- **Date of first occurrence.**

- **Definition(s).** Generally, the oldest meaning is given first. However, meanings can also be ordered according to frequency of usage, with the most common usage listed first.

- **Usage.** Quotations show how the word can be used in various contexts. Sometimes a comment on usage problems is placed at the end of the entry.

- **Idioms.** When the word is part of a common idiom (35c), the idiom is listed and defined, usually at the end of the entry.

- **Synonyms.** Some dictionaries provide explanations of subtle differences in meaning among a word's synonyms.

Exercise 3

Study the definitions for the pairs of words in parentheses. Then choose the word you think best completes each sentence. Be prepared to explain your answers.

1. Sixteen prisoners on death row were granted (mercy/clemency).
2. The outcome of the election (excited/provoked) a riot.
3. The young couple was (covetous/greedy) of their neighbors' estate.
4. While she was traveling in Muslim countries, she wore (modest/chaste) clothing.
5. The president of the university (authorized/confirmed) the rumor that tuition would be increasing next year.

34f   Thesauruses

A **thesaurus** provides alternatives for frequently used words. Unlike a dictionary, which explains what a word means and how it evolved, a thesaurus provides only a list of words that serve as possible synonyms for each term it includes. A thesaurus can be useful, especially when you want to jog your memory about a word you know but cannot recall. You may, however, use a word incorrectly if you simply pick it from a list in a thesaurus. If you find an unfamiliar yet intriguing word, make sure that you are using it correctly by looking it up in a dictionary.

35 Exactness

Make words work for you. By choosing the right word and putting it in the right place, you can communicate exactly what you mean and make your writing memorable. When drafting, choose words that express your ideas and feelings. Then, when revising, make those words precise and fresh. Use the words that you already know effectively, but add to your vocabulary regularly so that you can pick the exact words to suit your purpose, audience, and context. This chapter will help you

- master the denotations and connotations of words (35a),
- use fresh, clear expressions (35b),
- understand how to use idioms and collocations (35c),
- use the first- and second-person pronouns appropriately (35d), and
- compose clear definitions (35e).

35a Accurate and precise word choice

(1) A denotation is the literal meaning of a word.

Denotations are definitions of words, such as those that appear in dictionaries. For example, the noun *beach* denotes a sandy or pebbly shore. Select words whose denotations convey your point exactly.

Yosemite National Park ~~is really great~~. *astounds even an indifferent tourist like me.*

[Because *great* can mean "extremely large" as well as "outstanding" or "powerful," its use in this sentence is imprecise.]

The speaker ~~inferred~~ *implied* that the team attracted many new fans this year.

[*Imply* means "to suggest," so *implied* is the exact word for this sentence. *Infer* means "to draw a conclusion from evidence": From the figures before me, I *inferred* that the team attracted many new fans this year.]

The Glossary of Usage at the back of this book includes the definitions of many words that are commonly confused.

(2) A connotation is the indirect meaning of a word.

Connotations are the associations evoked by a word. *Beach,* for instance, may connote natural beauty, surf, shells, swimming, tanning, sunburn, and/or crowds. The context in which a word appears affects the associations it evokes. In a treatise on shoreline management, *beach* has scientific and geographic connotations; in a fashion magazine, this word is associated with bathing suits, sunglasses, and sunscreen. Most readers carry with them a wealth of personal, often emotional, associations that can influence how they respond to the words on a page. The challenge for writers is to choose the words that are most likely to spark the appropriate connotations in their readers' minds.

persistence
Mr. Kreuger's ~~relentlessness~~ has earned praise from his supervisors.

[*Relentlessness* has negative connotations, which make it an unlikely quality for which to be praised.]

aroma
I love the ~~odor~~ of freshly baked bread.

[Many odors are unpleasant; *aroma* sounds more positive, especially when associated with food.]

MULTILINGUAL WRITERS

CONNOTATIONS

Your ability to recognize connotations will improve as your vocabulary increases. When you learn a new word that seems to mean exactly what another word means, study the context in which each word is used. Then, to help yourself remember the new word, create a phrase or a sentence in which that word is used in the context you studied. If you are confused about the connotations of specific words, consult an ESL dictionary (see page 703).

(3) Specific, concrete words provide readers with helpful details.

A **general word** is all-inclusive, indefinite, and sweeping in scope. A **specific word** is precise, definite, and limited in scope.

General	Specific	More Specific/Concrete
food	fast food	cheeseburger
entertainment	film	*Ocean's Thirteen*
place	city	Atlanta

An **abstract word** refers to a concept or idea, a quality or trait, or anything else that cannot be touched, heard, or seen. A **concrete word** signifies a particular object, a specific action, or anything that can be touched, heard, or seen.

Abstract   democracy, evil, strength, charity

Concrete   mosquito, hammer, plastic, fog

Some writers use too many abstract or general words, making their writing vague and lifeless. As you select words to fit your context, you should be as specific and concrete as you can. For example, instead of the word *bad,* consider using a more precise adjective.

bad neighbors: rowdy, snobby, nosy, fussy, sloppy, threatening

bad meat: tough, tainted, overcooked, undercooked, contaminated

bad wood: rotten, warped, scorched, knotty, termite-ridden

To test whether or not a word is specific, you can ask one or more of these questions about what you want to say: Exactly who? Exactly what? Exactly when? Exactly where? Exactly how? In the following examples, notice what a difference concrete words can make in expressing an idea and how adding details can expand or develop it.

Vague	She has kept no reminders of performing in her youth.
Specific	She has kept no sequined costume, no photographs, no fliers or posters from that part of her youth.

—LOUISE ERDRICH, "The Leap"

Vague	I was struck by her makeup.
Specific	What foxed me was her makeup, which was on the heavy side and involved a great deal of peach-colored powder.

—DAVID SEDARIS, "This Old House"

As these examples show, sentences with specific details are often longer than sentences without them. But the need to be specific does not necessarily conflict with the need to be concise (chapter 36). Sometimes substituting one word for another can make it far easier for your readers to see, hear, taste, or smell what you are hoping to convey.

I ~~had an accident~~ while trying to ~~catch a fish.~~

fell out of a canoe ... *land a muskie.*

Writers use general and abstract words successfully when such words are vital to communicating ideas, as in the following sentence about what happens when a plague comes to an end.

> We expect a catharsis, but we merely find a transition; we long for euphoria, but we discover only relief, tinged with, in some cases, regret and depression.
> —ANDREW SULLIVAN, "When Plagues End"

(4) Figurative language contributes to exactness.

Figurative language is the use of words in an imaginative rather than a literal sense. Similes and metaphors are the chief **figures of speech.** A **simile** is a comparison of dissimilar things using *like* or *as*. A **metaphor** is an implied comparison of dissimilar things, without *like* or *as*.

Similes

He was **like a piece of rare and delicate china which was always being saved from breaking and finally fell.**   —ALICE WALKER, "To Hell with Dying"

When **her body was hairless as a baby's,** she adjusted the showerhead so that the water burst forth in pelting streams.
—LOIDA MARITZA PÉREZ, *Geographies of Home*

Metaphors

His **money was a sharp pair of scissors** that snipped rapidly through tangles of red tape.   —HISAYE YAMAMOTO

Making tacos is a graceful dance.   —DENISE CHÁVEZ, *A Taco Testimony*

Single words can be used metaphorically.

These roses must be **planted** in good soil. [literal]

Keep your life **planted** wherever you can put down the most roots. [metaphorical]

Similes and metaphors are especially valuable when they are concrete and describe or evoke essential relationships that cannot otherwise be communicated. Similes or metaphors can be extended throughout a paragraph of comparison, but be careful not to mix them (28c).

Exercise 1

Study the passsage below, and prepare to discuss the author's use of exact and figurative language to communicate her ideas.

¹The kitchen where I'm making dinner is a New York kitchen. ²Nice light, way too small, nowhere to put anything unless the stove goes. ³My stove is huge, but it will never go. ⁴My stove is where my head clears, my impressions settle, my reporter's life gets folded into my life, and whatever I've just learned, or think I've learned—whatever it was, out there in the world, that had seemed so different and surprising—bubbles away in the very small pot of what I think I know and, if I'm lucky, produces something like perspective.

—JANE KRAMER, "The Reporter's Kitchen"

Exercise 2

Choose five of the items below, and use them as the bases for five original sentences containing figurative language.

1. the look on someone's face
2. a cold rainy day
3. studying for an exam
4. your favorite food
5. buying textbooks
6. a busy street
7. waiting in a long line for a movie
8. the way someone talks

35b   Evocative language

Fresh expressions can capture the attention of readers, but when forced or overused, they lose their impact. Sometimes writers coin expressions as substitutes for words and phrases that have coarse or indelicate connotations. These expressions are called **euphemisms;** they occasionally become standardized. To talk about death or dying, for example, you might use words such as *pass away* or *being terminally ill.* However, although euphemisms may be pleasant sounding, they have a dark side. They can be used by writers who want to obscure facts or avoid negative reactions by others. Euphemisms such as *revenue enhancement* for *tax hike* and *collateral damage* for *civilian deaths during a war* are considered insincere or deceitful.

BEYOND THE RULE

DOUBLESPEAK

In his novel *1984*, published in 1949, George Orwell coined the term *doublespeak* to refer to language used intentionally to obscure the facts surrounding bad news. William Lutz has continued in Orwell's steps; his book *The New Doublespeak: Why No One Knows What Anyone's Saying Anymore* demonstrates the pervasiveness of doublespeak today.

The expressions *bite the dust, breath of fresh air,* and *smooth as silk* were once striking and thus effective. Excessive use, though, has drained them of their original force and made them **clichés.** Newer expressions such as *put a spin on something* and *think outside the box* have also lost their vitality because of overuse. Nonetheless, clichés are so much a part of the language, especially the spoken language, that nearly every writer uses them from time to time. But effective writers often give a fresh twist to an old saying.

> I seek a narrative, a fiction, to order days like the one I spent several years ago, on a gray June day in Chicago, when I took a roller-coaster ride on the bell curve of my experience.
>
> —GAYLE PEMBERTON, "The Zen of Bigger Thomas"

[Notice how much more effective this expression is than frequent references elsewhere to "being on an emotional roller coaster."]

Variations on familiar expressions from literature and history, many of which have become part of everyday language, can often be used to good effect.

We have met the enemy and he is us.   —WALT KELLY, Earth Day poster, 1970

[This statement is a variation on one made by American naval officer Oliver Hazard Perry during the War of 1812: "We have met the enemy and they are ours."]

Good writers, however, do not rely too heavily on the words of others; they choose their own words to communicate their ideas.

Exercise 3

From the following list of overused expressions, select five that you often use or hear and suggest creative replacements. Then, use each replacement in a sentence.

EXAMPLE

beyond the shadow of a doubt *undoubtedly* OR *with total certainty*

1. an axe to grind
2. hit the nail on the head
3. see the light
4. business as usual
5. climb the walls

6. eat like a pig
7. beat around the bush
8. bite the bullet
9. breathe down someone's neck
10. strong as an ox

35c   Idioms and collocations

Idioms are fixed expressions whose meanings cannot be entirely determined by knowing the meanings of their parts—*bear in mind, fall in love, in a nutshell, stand a chance.* **Collocations** are combinations of words that frequently occur together. Unlike idioms, they have meanings that *can* be determined by knowing the meanings of their parts—*depend on, fond of, little while, right now.* Regardless of whether you are using an idiom or a collocation, if you make even a small inadvertent change to the expected wording, you may distract or confuse your readers.

She tried to keep a ~~small~~ low profile.

They had ~~an invested~~ a vested interest in the project.

As you edit your writing, keep an eye out for idioms or collocations that might not be worded correctly. Then check a general dictionary, a dictionary of idioms (see page 703), or the Glossary of Usage at the end of this book to ensure that your usage is appropriate. Writers sometimes have trouble with the following collocations, all of which contain prepositions.

CHOOSING THE RIGHT PREPOSITION

Instead of	Use
abide **with**	abide **by** the decision
according **with**	according **to** the source
accused **for**	accused **of** the crime
based **off of**	based **on** the novel
bored **of**	bored **by** it
comply **to**	comply **with** rules
conform **of/on**	conform **to/with** standards
differ **to**	differ **with** them
in accordance **to**	in accordance **with** policy
independent **to**	independent **of** his family
happened **on**	happened **by** accident
superior **than**	superior **to** others

MULTILINGUAL WRITERS

UNDERSTANDING AND USING IDIOMS

The context in which an idiom appears can often help you understand the meaning. For example, if you read "When they learned that she had accepted illegal campaign contributions, several political commentators raked her over the coals," you would probably understand that *to rake over the coals* means "to criticize severely." As you learn new idioms from your reading, make a list of those you might want to use in your own writing. If you are confused about the meaning of a particular idiom, check a dictionary of idioms (see page 703).

Exercise 4

Write a sentence using each of the following idioms and collocations correctly.

1. pass muster, pass the time
2. do one's best, do one's part, do one's duty
3. in a pinch, in a rut, in a way
4. cut down, cut back, cut corners
5. make time, make sure, make sense

35d | First-person and second-person pronouns

Using *I* is appropriate when you are writing about personal experience. In academic and professional writing, the use of the first-person singular pronoun is also a clear way to distinguish your own views from those of others or to make a direct appeal to readers. However, if you frequently repeat *I feel* or *I think,* your readers may suspect that you do not understand much beyond your own experience or that you are more interested in talking about yourself than about your topic.

We, the first-person plural pronoun, is trickier to use correctly. When you use it, make sure that your audience can tell which individuals are included in this plural reference. For example, if you are writing a paper for a college course, does *we* mean you and the instructor, you and your fellow students, or some other group (such as all Americans)? The use of *we* can blind writers to differences of gender, race, religion, region, class, and sexual orientation. Readers sometimes feel excluded from works in which the first-person plural prounoun has been used carelessly. If you are using *we* in a memo to co-workers, are you intending to include the entire company, your group within it, or you and a specific individual? Because you may inadvertently use *we* in an early draft to refer to more than one group of people, as you edit, check to see that you have used the first-person plural pronoun consistently.

If you decide to address readers directly, you will undoubtedly use the second-person pronoun *you* (as has been done frequently in this book). There is some disagreement, though, over whether to permit the use of the indefinite *you* to mean "a person" or "people in general." Check with your instructor about this usage. If you are told to avoid using the indefinite *you,* recast your sentences. For example, use *one* instead of *you.*

Even in huge, anonymous cities, ~~you find~~ *one finds* community spirit.

However, owing to the formality of *one,* it might not always be the best choice. Changing the word order is another possibility.

Community spirit can be found even in huge, anonymous cities.

If you are unsatisfied with either of these strategies, use different words.

Community spirit arises even in huge, anonymous cities.

For additional advice on using pronouns, see chapter 26.

Exercise 5

Revise the following paragraph to eliminate the use of the first- and second-person pronouns.

¹In my opinion, some animals should be as free as we are. ²For example, I think orangutans, African elephants, and Atlantic bottlenose dolphins should roam freely rather than be held in captivity. ³We should neither exhibit them in zoos nor use them for medical research. ⁴If you study animals such as these you will see that, like us, they show emotions, self-awareness, and intention. ⁵You might even find that some use language to communicate. ⁶It is clear to me that they have the right to freedom.

35e Clear definitions

Because words often have more than one meaning, you must clearly establish which meaning you have in mind in a particular piece of writing. By providing a definition, you set the terms of the discussion.

> In this paper, I use the word *communism* **in the Marxist sense of social organization based on the holding of all property in common.**

A **formal definition** first states the term to be defined, then puts it into a class, and finally differentiates it from other members of that class.

> A *phosphene* [term] is **a luminous visual image** [class] that **results from applying pressure to the eyeball** [differentiation].

A short dictionary definition may be adequate when you need to convey a special meaning that may be unfamiliar to readers.

> Here, *galvanic* means **"produced as if by electric shock."**

Giving a synonym may also clarify the meaning of a term. Such synonyms are often used as appositives.

> *Machismo,* **confidence with an attitude,** can be a pose rather than a reality.

Writers frequently show—rather than tell—what a word means by giving examples.

Many homophones (such as *be* and *bee, in* and *inn,* or *see* and *sea*) are not spelling problems.

You can also formulate your own definition of a concept you wish to clarify.

Clichés could be defined as **thoughts that have hardened.**

When writing definitions, do not confuse readers by placing a predicate with a subject that is not logically connected to it (**28d**). Constructions that combine *is* or *are* with *when, where,* or *because* are often illogical because forms of *be* signify identity or equality between the subject and what follows.

Faulty   The Internet is when you look at text and images from across the world.

Revised   The Internet allows you to look at text and images from across the world.

E x e r c i s e   6

Using your own words, define any four of the following terms in full sentences.

1. collaboration   4. style
2. honesty   5. globalization
3. party   6. terrorism

36 Conciseness

To facilitate readers' understanding, effective writers generally convey their thoughts clearly and efficiently. This does not mean that they always write short sentences; rather, they use each word wisely. This chapter will help you

- make each word count (**36a**),
- avoid unnecessary repetition (**36b**), and
- use elliptical constructions (**36c**).

36a Eliminating wordiness and other redundancies

After writing a first draft, review your sentences to make sure that they contain only the words necessary to make your point.

(1) Redundancy contributes to wordiness.

Restating a key point in different words can help readers understand it. But there is no need to rephrase readily understood terms. If you do, your work will suffer from **redundancy**—repetition for no good reason.

Ballerinas auditioned ~~in the tryouts~~ for *The Nutcracker*.

Each student had a unique talent ~~and ability that he or she uses in his or her~~ for acting.

You should also avoid grammatical redundancy, as in double subjects (*my sister [she] is*), double comparisons ([*more*] *easier than*), and double negatives (*could[n't] hardly*).

MULTILINGUAL WRITERS

USING RELATIVE PRONOUNS

Review your sentences to make sure that no clause includes both a personal pronoun (26a(1)) and a relative pronoun (26a(2)) referring to the same antecedent (26c).

The drug **that** we were testing ~~it~~ has not been approved by the Food and Drug Administration.

The principal investigator, **whom** we depended on ~~her~~ for guidance, had to take a medical leave before the project was completed.

(2) Delete unnecessary words and recast wordy phrases.

One exact word often says as much as several inexact ones.

spoke in a low and hard-to-hear voice   **mumbled**

a person who gives expert advice   **consultant**

Some unscrupulous brokers are ~~taking money and savings from~~ ^{cheating} elderly people ~~who need that money because they planned to use it as a retirement~~ ^{out of their pensions.} ~~pension.~~

As you edit a draft, delete words that add no significant meaning to adjacent words, and replace wordy expressions with single words whenever possible.

^{If} ~~In the event that~~ taxes are raised, ~~expect complaints on the part of the voters.~~ ^{voters will complain.}

In addition, watch for empty or vague words such as *area, aspect, element, factor, feature, field, kind, situation, thing,* and *type.* They may signal wordiness.

^{Effective} ~~In an employment situation, effective~~ communication is essential at work.

USELESS WORDS IN COMMON PHRASES

yellow [in color]

at 9:45 a.m. [in the morning]

[basic] essentials

bitter[-tasting] salad

connect [up together]

because [of the fact that]

[really and truly] fearless

circular [in shape]

return [back]

rich [and wealthy] nations

small[-size] potatoes

[true] facts

was [more or less] hinting

by [virtue of] his authority

REPLACEMENTS FOR WORDY EXPRESSIONS

Instead of	Use
at this moment (point) in time	now, today
due to the fact that	because
in view of the fact that	because
for the purpose of	for
it is clear (obvious) that	clearly (obviously)
there is no question that	unquestionably, certainly
without a doubt	undoubtedly
beyond the shadow of a doubt	certainly, surely
it is my opinion that	I think (believe)
in this day and age	today
in the final analysis	finally

(3) The constructions *there are* and *it is* can often be deleted.

There or *it* followed by a form of *be* is an **expletive**—a word that signals that the subject of the sentence will follow the verb (21d(1)). Writers use expletives to create a sentence rhythm that emphasizes words that would not be emphasized in the typical subject-verb order. Notice the difference in rhythm between the following two sentences:

Three children were playing in the yard.

There were three children playing in the yard.

However, expletives are easily overused. If you find that you have drafted several sentences that begin with expletives, look for ways to revise a few of them.

Hundreds
~~There were hundreds~~ of fans _were_ crowding onto the field.

Joining the crowd
~~It was frightening~~ to join the crowd.

OR

I was afraid to join the crowd.

(4) Some relative pronouns can be deleted.

When editing a draft, check whether the relative pronouns *who, which,* and *that* can be deleted from any of your sentences. If a relative pronoun is followed by a form of the verb *be* (*am, is, are, was,* or *were*), you can often omit both the relative pronoun and the verb.

The change ~~that~~ the young senator proposed yesterday angered most legislators.

Bromo, ~~which is~~ Java's highest mountain, towers above its neighbors.

The Endangered Species Act, ~~which was~~ passed in 1973, protects the habitat of endangered plants and animals.

When deleting a relative pronoun, you might have to make other changes to a sentence as well.

handling
The Tsukiji fish market, ~~which handles~~ 2,000 tons of seafood a day, rates as the world's largest.

> **Exercise 1**
>
> Rewrite the sentences below to make them less wordy.
>
> 1. He put in an application for every job offered.
> 2. Prior to the time of the ceremony, he had not received an award.
> 3. The library is located in the vicinity of the post office.
> 4. The fans who were watching television made a lot of noise.
> 5. There was nobody home.
> 6. The release of certain chemicals, which are called *pheromones*, is a very primitive form of communication.
> 7. It is important to register early.
> 8. The road was closed because of the fact that there were so many accidents.

36b   Avoiding unnecessary repetition

Repetition is useful only when it contributes to emphasis, clarity, or coherence.

> We will not rest until we have pursued **every** lead, inspected **every** piece of evidence, and interviewed **every** suspect. [The repetition of *every* is effective because it emphasizes the writer's determination.]

The following sentences have been revised to remove needless repetition.

> ~~One week was like the next week.~~ Each week was as boring as the last.
>
> She hoped Alex understood that ~~the complaint she made did not mean~~ her complaint did not reflect her feelings about him.
>
> ~~she was complaining because she disliked him.~~

36c   Using elliptical constructions

An **elliptical construction** is one that deliberately omits words that can be understood from the context. In the following sentence, the word group *is* *the goal* can be taken out of the second and third clauses without affecting the meaning. The revised sentence is more concise than the original.

> Speed is the goal for some swimmers, endurance ~~is the goal~~ for others, and relaxation ~~is the goal~~ for still others.

Sometimes, as an aid to clarity, commas mark omissions in elliptical constructions.

> My family functioned like a baseball team: my mom was the coach; my brother, the pitcher; and my sister, the shortstop. [Be sure to use semicolons to separate items with internal commas (38b).]

As these examples show, parallelism (chapter 31) reinforces elliptical constructions.

Exercise 2

Revise this paragraph to eliminate wordiness and needless repetition.

> [1]When I look back on my high school career, I realize that I was not taught much about international affairs in the world in spite of the fact that improved communications, the media, the Internet, travel, trading with different foreign countries, and immigration have made the world smaller. [2]Nonetheless, because both international affairs and business interest me, I decided to major in political science now that I am in college and to study marketing as my minor. [3]There are advantages to this combination of a major and a minor in my job situation at work as well, for I am now currently working part-time twenty hours a week for a company that imports merchandise into the United States and exports products to other countries. [4]Eventually, at some future time, when I have graduated and received my bachelor's degree, I may go on to law school and pursue my interest in politics, unless, on the other hand, my supervisor makes the recommendation that I develop my skills in marketing by spending time overseas in one of the company's foreign offices. [5]The opportunity to work overseas would provide me with a knowledge, an understanding, and an appreciation of the world economy. [6]Such an understanding is essential for anyone hoping to succeed in business.

P

PUNCTUATION

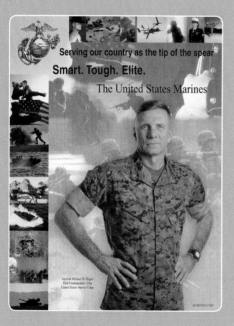

Serving our country as the tip of the spear

Smart. Tough. Elite.

The United States Marines

General Michael N. Hague
23rd Commandant of the
United States Marine Corps

MARINES.COM

The use of the period, a strong mark of
punctuation, with the words "Smart. Tough.
Elite." reinforces the strength of the image.

37 The Comma   727

38 The Semicolon   741

39 The Apostrophe   745

40 Quotation Marks   753

41 The Period and
Other Punctuation
Marks   760

CHAPTER 37
The Comma 727

37a Before a coordinating conjunction linking
     independent clauses 728
37b After introductory clauses, phrases, or
     words 729
37c Separating elements in a series 732
37d With nonessential elements 733
37e With geographical names and items in dates
     and addresses 737
37f With direct quotations 738
37g Unnecessary or misplaced commas 738

CHAPTER 38
The Semicolon 741

38a Connecting independent clauses 741
38b Separating elements that contain
     commas 742
38c Revising common semicolon errors 743

CHAPTER 39
The Apostrophe 745

39a Indicating ownership and other
     relationships 745
39b Marking omissions of letters or
     numbers 751
39c Forming certain plurals 752

CHAPTER 40
Quotation Marks 753

40a Direct quotations 753
40b Titles of short works 755
40c For ironic tone or unusual usage 756
40d With other punctuation marks 757

CHAPTER 41
The Period and Other Punctuation
Marks 760

41a The period 761
41b The question mark 761
41c The exclamation point 763
41d The colon 763
41e The dash 766
41f Parentheses 767
41g Square brackets 768
41h Ellipsis points 769
41i The slash 772

37   The Comma

Punctuation lends to written language the flexibility that facial expressions, pauses, and variations in voice pitch give to spoken language. For instance, a pause after *called* in the first of the following examples makes it clear that the spoken sentence refers to only two people: the recruiter and Kenneth Martin. In the second example, a pause after *Kenneth* lets the listener know that the sentence refers to three people: the recruiter, Kenneth, and Martin. In written text, the same meanings can be established by commas.

When the recruiter called, Kenneth Martin answered.

When the recruiter called Kenneth, Martin answered.

But pauses are not the most reliable guide for comma placement, because commas are often called for where speakers do not pause and pauses can occur where no comma is necessary. A better guide is an understanding of some basic principles of comma usage.

This chapter will help you use commas to

- separate independent clauses joined by coordinating conjunctions (37a),
- set off introductory clauses and phrases (37b),
- separate items in a series (37c),
- set off nonessential (nonrestrictive) elements (37d),
- set off geographical names and items in dates and addresses (37e), and
- set off direct quotations (37f),

as well as help you to

- recognize unnecessary or misplaced commas (37g).

37a Before a coordinating conjunction linking independent clauses

Use a comma before a coordinating conjunction (*and, but, for, nor, or, so,* or *yet*) that links two independent clauses. An **independent clause** is a group of words that can stand as a sentence (22b(1)).

INDEPENDENT CLAUSE,	**CONJUNCTION**	INDEPENDENT CLAUSE.
	and	
	but	
	for	
Subject + predicate,	nor	subject + predicate.
	or	
	so	
	yet	

The Iditarod Trail Sled Dog Race begins in March, **but** training starts much sooner.

In the 1960s, Dorothy Page wanted to spark interest in the role of dog sledding in Alaskan history, **so** she proposed staging a long race.

No matter how many clauses are in a sentence, a comma comes before each coordinating conjunction.

The race takes several days to complete, **and** training is a year-round activity, **but** the mushers do not complain.

When the independent clauses are short, the comma is often omitted before *and, but,* or *or.*

My friend races **but** I don't.

If a coordinating conjunction joins two parts of a compound predicate (which means there is only one subject), a comma is not normally used before the conjunction. (See 21b and 37g(3).)

The race starts in Anchorage and ends in Nome.

A semicolon, instead of a comma, precedes a conjunction joining two independent clauses when at least one of the clauses already contains a comma. (See also **38b**.)

When running long distances, sled dogs burn more than ten thousand calories a day**;** **so** they must be fed well.

Exercise 1

Combine each of the following pairs of sentences by using coordinating conjunctions and inserting commas where appropriate. (Remember that not all coordinating conjunctions link independent clauses and that *but, for, so,* and *yet* do not always function as coordinating conjunctions.) Explain why you used each of the conjunctions you inserted.

1. Dinosaurs lived for 165 million years. Then they became extinct.
2. No one knows why dinosaurs became extinct. Several theories have been proposed.
3. Some theorists believe that a huge meteor hit the earth. The climate may have changed dramatically.
4. Another theory suggests that dinosaurs did not actually become extinct. They simply evolved into lizards and birds.
5. Yet another theory suggests that they just grew too big. Not all of the dinosaurs were huge.

37b After introductory clauses, phrases, or words

(1) A comma follows an introductory dependent clause.
If you begin a sentence with a dependent (subordinate) clause (**22b(2)**), place a comma after it to set it off from the independent (main) clause (**22b(1)**).

> ### INTRODUCTORY CLAUSE, INDEPENDENT CLAUSE.

Although the safest automobile on the road is expensive, the protection it offers justifies the cost.

(2) A comma follows an introductory phrase.
Place a comma after an introductory phrase to set it off from the independent clause.

> ### INTRODUCTORY PHRASE, INDEPENDENT CLAUSE.

(a) Introductory prepositional phrases

Despite a downturn in the national economy, the number of students enrolled in this university has increased.

If you begin a sentence with a short introductory prepositional phrase (22a(4)), you may omit the comma as long as the resulting sentence is not difficult to read.

In 2009 the enrollment at the university increased.

BUT

In 2009, 625 new students enrolled in courses. [A comma separates two numbers.]

A comma is not used after a phrase that begins a sentence in which the subject and predicate (21b) are inverted.

With children came responsibilities.
[The subject of the sentence is *responsibilities*: Responsibilities came with children.]

(b) Other types of introductory phrases
If you begin a sentence with a participial phrase (22a(3)) or an absolute phrase (22a(6)), place a comma after it.

Having traveled nowhere, she believed the rest of the world was like her own small town. [participial phrase]

The language difference aside, life in Germany did not seem much different from life in the United States. [absolute phrase]

(3) A comma often follows an introductory word.

> **INTRODUCTORY WORD,** INDEPENDENT CLAUSE.

Use a comma to set off interjections, **vocatives** (words used to address someone directly), or transitional words.

Oh, I forgot about the board meeting. [interjection]

Bob, I want you to know that your design impressed everyone on the board. [vocative]

Moreover, the design will increase efficiency in the office. [transitional word]

When there is no risk of misunderstanding, some introductory adverbs and transitional words do not need to be set off by a comma (see also **38a**).

Sometimes even a good design is rejected by the board.

Exercise 2

Insert commas wherever necessary in the following paragraph. Explain why each comma is needed. Some sentences may not require editing.

[1]If you had to describe sound would you call it a wave? [2]Although sound cannot be seen people have described it this way for a long time. [3]In fact the Greek philosopher Aristotle believed that sound traveling through air was like waves in the sea. [4]Envisioning waves in the air he hypothesized that sound would not be able to pass through a vacuum because there would be no air to transmit it. [5]Aristotle's hypothesis was not tested until nearly two thousand years later. [6]In 1654 Otto von Guericke found that he could not hear a bell ringing inside the vacuum he had created. [7]Thus Guericke established the necessity of air for sound transmission. [8]However although most sound reaches us through the air it travels faster through liquids and solids.

37c | Separating elements in a series

A **series** contains three or more parallel elements. To be parallel, elements must be grammatically equal; for example, all must be phrases, not combinations of phrases and clauses. (See chapter 31.)

(1) Commas separate words, phrases, or clauses in a series.
A comma appears after each item in a series except the last one.

Ethics are based on **moral, social,** or **cultural values**. [words]

The company's code of ethics encourages **seeking criticism of work, correcting mistakes,** and **acknowledging the contributions of everyone**. [phrases]

Several circumstances can lead to unethical behavior: **people are tempted by a desire to succeed, they are pressured by others into acting inappropriately,** or **they are simply trying to survive**. [clauses in a series]

If elements in a series contain internal commas, you can prevent misreading by separating the items with semicolons.

According to their code of ethics, researchers must disclose all results, without omitting any data; indicate various interpretations of the data; and make the data and methodology available to other researchers, some of whom may choose to replicate the study.

THINKING RHETORICALLY

 COMMAS AND CONJUNCTIONS IN A SERIES

How do the following sentences differ?

We discussed them all: life, liberty, **and** the pursuit of happiness.

We discussed them all: life **and** liberty **and** the pursuit of happiness.

We discussed them all: life, liberty, the pursuit of happiness.

The first sentence follows conventional guidelines; that is, a comma and a conjunction precede the last element in the series. The less conventional second and third sentences do more than convey information. Having two conjunctions and no commas, the second sentence slows down the pace of the reading, causing stress to be placed on each of the three elements in the series. In contrast, the third sentence, with commas but no conjunctions, speeds up the reading, as if to suggest that the rights listed do not need to be stressed because they are so familiar. To get a sense of how your sentences will be read and understood, try reading them aloud to yourself.

(2) Commas separate coordinate adjectives.

Two or more adjectives that precede the same noun are called **coordinate adjectives.** To test whether adjectives are coordinate, either interchange them or put *and* between them. If the altered version of the phrase is acceptable, the adjectives are coordinate and should be separated by a comma or commas.

> Crossing the **rushing, shallow** creek, I slipped off a rock and fell into the water.
>
> [COMPARE: a rushing and shallow creek OR a shallow, rushing creek]

The adjectives in the following sentence are not separated by a comma. Notice that they cannot be interchanged or joined by *and*.

> Sitting in the water, I saw an **old wooden** bridge.
>
> [NOT a wooden old bridge OR an old and wooden bridge]

37d   With nonessential elements

Nonessential (nonrestrictive) elements provide supplemental information, that is, information a reader does not need in order to identify who or what is being discussed (see also 22b(2)). Use commas to set off a nonessential word or word group: one comma separates a nonessential element at the end of a sentence; two commas set off a nonessential element in the middle of a sentence.

> The Hilltop Folk Festival, **planned for late July,** should attract many tourists.

In the preceding sentence, the phrase placed between commas, *planned for late July*, conveys nonessential information: the reader knows which festival will attract tourists without being told when it will be held. When a phrase follows a proper noun (21a(2)), such as *The Hilltop Folk Festival*, it is usually nonessential. Note, however, that in the following sentence, the phrase *planned for late July* is necessary for the reader to identify the festival as the one scheduled for late July not for a different time.

The festival **planned for late July** should attract many tourists.

In the preceding sentence, the phrase is an **essential (restrictive) element** because, without it, the reader will not know which festival the writer has in mind. Essential elements are not set off by commas; they are integrated into the sentence (22b(2)).

(1) Commas set off nonessential elements used as modifiers.
(a) Adjectival clauses
Nonessential modifiers are often **adjectival (relative) clauses**—those clauses usually introduced by the relative pronoun *who, which,* or *that* (22b(2)). In the following sentence, a comma sets off the adjectival clause because the reader does not need the content of that clause in order to identify the mountain.

We climbed Mt. McKinley, **which is over 15,000 feet high**.

(b) Participial phrases
Nonessential modifiers also include **participial phrases** (phrases introduced by a present or past participle) (22a(3)).

Mt. McKinley, **towering above us**, brought to mind our abandoned plan for climbing it. [participial phrase beginning with a present participle]

My sister, **slowed by a knee injury**, rarely hikes anymore. [participial phrase beginning with a past participle]

(c) Adverbial clauses
An **adverbial clause** (22b(2)) begins with a subordinating conjunction signaling cause (*because*), purpose (*so that*), or time (*when, after, before*). This type of clause is usually considered essential and thus is not set off by commas when it appears at the end of a sentence.

Dinosaurs may have become extinct **because their habitat was destroyed.**

In contrast, an adverbial clause that provides nonessential information, such as an extra comment, should be set off from the main clause.

Dinosaurs are extinct, **though they are alive in many people's imaginations.**

(2) Commas set off nonessential appositives.

Appositives refer to the same person, place, object, idea, or event as a nearby noun or noun phrase but with different words (22a(5)). Nonessential appositives provide extra details about nouns or noun phrases (22a(1)) and are set off by commas; essential appositives are not. In the following sentence, the title of the article is mentioned, so the reader does not need the information provided by the appositive in order to identify the article. The appositive is thus set off by commas.

"Living on the Line," **Joanne Hart's most recent article,** describes the lives of factory workers in China.

In the next sentence, *Joanne Hart's article* is nonspecific, so an essential appositive containing the specific title of the article is integrated into the sentence. It is not set off by commas. Without the appositive, the reader would not know which of Hart's articles describes the lives of factory workers in China.

Joanne Hart's article "Living on the Line" describes the lives of factory workers in China.

If Hart had written only this one article, the title would be set off by commas. The reader would not need the information in the appositive to identify the article.

Abbreviations of titles or degrees after names are treated as nonessential appositives.

Was the letter from Frances Evans, PhD, or from Francis Evans, MD?

Increasingly, however, *Jr., Sr., II,* and *III* are considered part of a name, in which case the comma is omitted.

William Homer Barton, Jr.   OR   William Homer Barton Jr.

Exercise 3

Set off nonessential clauses, phrases, and appositives with commas.

1. Maine Coons long-haired cats with bushy tails have adapted to a harsh climate.
2. These animals which are extremely gentle despite their large size often weigh twenty pounds.
3. Most Maine Coons have exceptionally high intelligence for cats which enables them to recognize language and even to open doors.
4. Unlike most cats Maine Coons will play fetch with their owners.
5. According to a legend later proven to be false Maine Coons developed from interbreeding between wildcats and domestic cats.

(3) Commas set off absolute phrases.

An **absolute phrase** (the combination of a noun and a modifying word or phrase; see 22a(6)) provides nonessential details and so should always be set off by a comma or commas.

The actor, **his hair wet and slicked back,** began his audition.

The director stared at him, **her mind flipping through the photographs she had viewed earlier.**

(4) Commas set off transitional expressions and other parenthetical elements.

Commas customarily set off transitional words and phrases such as *for example, that is,* and *namely.*

An airline ticket, **for example,** can be delivered electronically.

Because they generally indicate little or no pause in reading, transitional words and phrases such as *also, too, at least,* and *thus* need not be set off by commas.

Traveling has **thus** become easier in recent years.

Use commas to set off other parenthetical elements, such as words or phrases that provide commentary you wish to stress.

Over the past year, my flights have, **miraculously,** been on time.

(5) Commas set off contrasted elements.

Commas set off sentence elements in which words such as *never* and *unlike* express contrast.

A planet, **unlike** a star, reflects rather than generates light.

In sentences in which contrasted elements are introduced by *not only . . . but also,* place a comma before *but* if you want to emphasize what follows it. Otherwise, leave the comma out.

Planets **not only** vary in size, **but also** travel at different speeds. [Comma added for emphasis.]

37e   With geographical names and items in dates and addresses

Use commas to make geographical names, dates, and addresses easy to read.

(1) City and state

Nashville, Tennessee, is the largest country-and-western music center in the United States.

(2) Day and date

Martha left for Peru on **Wednesday, February 12, 2009,** and returned on March 12.

OR

Martha left for Peru on **Wednesday, 12 February 2009,** and returned on 12 March.

In the style used in the second example (which is not as common in the United States as the style in the first example), one comma is omitted because *12* precedes rather than follows *February.*

(3) Addresses

In a sentence containing an address, the name of the person or organization, the street address, and the name of the town or city are all followed by commas, but the abbreviation for the state is not.

I had to write to **Ms. Melanie Hobson, Senior Analyst, Hobson Computing, 2873 Central Avenue, Orange Park, FL 32065.**

37f   With direct quotations

Many sentences containing direct quotations also contain attributive tags such as *The author claims* or *According to the author* (11d(2)). Use commas to set off these tags whether they occur at the beginning, in the middle, or at the end of a sentence.

(1) Attributive tag at the beginning of a sentence
Place the comma directly after the attributive tag, before the quotation marks.

> According to Jacques Barzun, "It is a false analogy with science that makes one think latest is best."

(2) Attributive tag in the middle of a sentence
Place the first comma inside the quotation marks that precede the attributive tag; place the second comma directly after the tag, before the next set of quotation marks.

> "It is a false analogy with science," claims Jacques Barzun, "that makes one think latest is best."

(3) Attributive tag at the end of a sentence
Place the comma inside the quotation marks before the attributive tag.

> "It is a false analogy with science that makes one think latest is best," claims Jacques Barzun.

37g   Unnecessary or misplaced commas

Although a comma may signal a pause, not every pause calls for a comma. As you read the following sentence aloud, you may pause naturally at several places, but no commas are necessary.

> Heroic deeds done by ordinary people inspire others to act in ways that are not only moral but courageous.

(1) A comma does not separate a subject and its verb or a verb and its object.

Although speakers often pause after the subject (21b) or before the object (21c) of a sentence, such a pause should not be indicated by a comma.

In this climate, rain at frequent intervals⤸produces mosquitoes. [no separation between the subject (*rain*) and the verb (*produces*)]

The forecaster said⤸that rain was likely. [no separation between the verb (*said*) and the direct object (the noun clause *that rain was likely*)]

(2) A comma does not follow a coordinating conjunction.

Avoid using a comma after a coordinating conjunction (*and, but, for, nor, or, so,* or *yet*).

We worked very hard on her campaign for state representative⁣,but⤸the incumbent was too strong to defeat in the northern districts.

(3) A comma rarely separates elements in a compound predicate.

In general, avoid using a comma between two elements of a compound predicate (21b).

I read the comments carefully⤸and then started my revision.

However, if you want to place stress on the second element in a compound predicate, you may place a comma after the first element. Use this option sparingly, or it will lose its effect.

I read the comments word by word, and despaired.

(4) Commas set off words, phrases, and clauses only if they are clearly nonessential.

In the following sentences, the elements in boldface are essential and so should not be set off by commas (37d).

Zoe was born⤸**in Chicago during the Great Depression.**

Perhaps⤸the thermostat is broken.

Everyone⤸**who has a mortgage**⤸is required to have fire insurance.

Someone⤸**wearing an orange wig**⤸greeted us at the door.

(5) A comma does not precede the first item of a series or follow the last.

Make sure that you place commas only between elements in a series, not before or after them.

She was known for⌒her photographs, sketches, and engravings.

The exhibit included her most exuberant, exciting, and expensive⌒ photographs.

E x e r c i s e 4

Explain the use of each comma in the following paragraph.

[1]Contrails, which are essentially artificial clouds, form when moisture in the air condenses around particles in jet exhaust. [2]Like ordinary clouds, contrails block incoming sunlight and trap heat radiated from Earth's surface. [3]This process reduces daytime highs and increases nighttime lows, narrowing the temperature range. [4]Multiple contrails can cluster together and obscure an area as large as Iowa, Illinois, and Missouri combined, magnifying the effect. [5]Although they may not alter the overall climate, contrails could still have environmental consequences.   —LAURA CARSTEN, "Climate on the Wing"

38   The Semicolon

The semicolon indicates that the phrases or clauses on either side of it are closely related. It most frequently connects two independent clauses when the second clause supports or contrasts with the first, but it can be used for other purposes as well. This chapter will help you understand that semicolons

- link closely related independent clauses (38a) and
- separate parts of a sentence containing internal commas (38b) but
- do not connect independent clauses to phrases or dependent clauses (38c).

38a   Connecting independent clauses

A semicolon placed between two independent clauses indicates that they are closely related. The second of the two clauses generally supports or contrasts with the first.

> For many cooks, basil is a key ingredient; it appears in recipes worldwide. [support]

> Sweet basil is used in many Mediterranean dishes; Thai basil is used in Asian and East Indian recipes. [contrast]

Although *and, but*, and similar words can signal these kinds of relationships, consider using an occasional semicolon for variety.

Sometimes, a transitional expression such as *for example* or *however* (24c(5)) accompanies a semicolon and further establishes the exact relationship between the ideas.

> Basil is omnipresent in the cuisine of some countries; **for example,** Italians use basil in salads, soups, and many vegetable dishes.
>
> The culinary uses of basil are well known; **however,** this herb also has medicinal uses.

A comma is usually inserted after a transitional word, though it can be omitted if doing so will not lead to a misreading.

> Because *basil* comes from a Greek word meaning "king," it suggests royalty; **indeed** some cooks accord basil royal status among herbs and spices.

38b   Separating elements that contain commas

In a series of phrases or clauses (chapter 22) that contain commas, semicolons indicate where each phrase or clause ends and the next begins.

> To survive, mountain lions need a large area in which to range; a steady supply of deer, skunks, raccoons, foxes, and opossums; and the opportunity to find a mate, establish a den, and raise a litter.

In this sentence, the semicolons help the reader distinguish three separate phrases.

Exercise 1

Revise the following sentences, using semicolons to separate independent clauses or elements that contain internal commas.

1. Soccer is a game played by two opposing teams on a rectangular field, each team tries to knock a round ball, roughly twenty-eight inches in circumference, through the opponent's goal.
2. The game is called *soccer* only in Canada and the United States, elsewhere it is known as *football*.

3. Generally, a team consists of eleven players: defenders (or fullbacks), who defend the goal by trying to win control of the ball, midfielders (or halfbacks), who play both defense and offense, attackers (or forwards), whose primary responsibility is scoring goals; and a goalkeeper (or goalie), who guards the goal.

4. In amateur matches, players can be substituted frequently, however, in professional matches, the number of substitutions is limited.

5. Soccer players depend on five skills: kicking, which entails striking the ball powerfully with the top of the foot, dribbling, which requires tapping or rolling the ball while running, passing, which is similar to kicking but with less power and more control, heading, which involves striking the ball with the forehead, and trapping, which is the momentary stopping of the ball.

38c Revising common semicolon errors

Semicolons do not set off phrases (22a) or dependent clauses (22b(2)) unless they contain commas. Use commas for these purposes.

We consulted Alinka Kibukian; the local horticulturalist.

Needing summer shade; we planted two of the largest trees we could afford.

We learned that young trees need care; which meant we had to do some extra chores after dinner each night.

Our trees have survived; even though we live in a harsh climate.

Exercise 2

Use a comma to replace any semicolon that sets off a phrase or a dependent clause. Do not change properly used semicolons.

1. Every morning I take vitamins; a multivitamin and sometimes extra vitamin C.
2. I used to believe that I could get my vitamins from a balanced diet; then I found out that diet may not provide enough of some vitamins, such as folic acid.
3. By eating a balanced diet, getting plenty of exercise, and keeping stress to a minimum; I thought I would stay healthy.
4. New research suggests that multivitamins are beneficial; when our diets do not provide all the recommended amounts of every vitamin every day; our health can suffer.
5. Although taking one multivitamin tablet a day is a healthy habit; we do not need to buy the most potent or most expensive vitamins available.

Exercise 3

Find or compose one sentence to illustrate each of the following uses of the semicolon.

1. To link two related independent clauses
2. To separate clauses in a sentence containing a transitional expression such as *however* or *for example*
3. To separate phrases or clauses that contain commas

39   The Apostrophe

Apostrophes serve a number of purposes. For example, you can use them to show that someone owns something *(my neighbor's television),* that someone has a specific relationship with someone else *(my neighbor's children),* or that someone has produced or created something *(my neighbor's recipe).* Apostrophes are also used in contractions *(can't, don't)* and in certain plural forms *(x's and y's).* This chapter will help you use apostrophes to

- indicate ownership and other relationships (39a),
- mark omissions of letters or numbers (39b), and
- form certain plurals (39c).

39a   Indicating ownership and other relationships

An apostrophe, often followed by an *s*, signals the possessive case of nouns. (For information on case, see **26b**.) Possessive nouns are used to express a variety of meanings.

Ownership	**Fumi's** computer, the **photographer's** camera
Origin	**Einstein's** ideas, the **student's** decision
Human relationships	**Linda's** sister, the **employee's** supervisor
Possession of physical or psychological traits	**Mona Lisa's** smile, the **team's** spirit
Association between abstractions and attributes	**democracy's** success, **tyranny's** influence

Identification of documents and credentials	**driver's** license, **bachelor's** degree
Identification of things named after people	**St. John's** Cathedral, **Valentine's** Day
Specification of amounts	a **day's** wages, an **hour's** delay

MULTILINGUAL WRITERS

WORD WITH APOSTROPHE AND S OR PHRASE BEGINNING WITH *OF*

In many cases, to indicate ownership, origin, and other meanings discussed in this chapter, you can use either a word with an apostrophe and an *s* or a prepositional phrase beginning with *of*.

Louise Erdrich's novels   OR   the novels **of** Louise Erdrich

the plane's arrival   OR   the arrival **of** the plane

However, the ending -*'s* is more commonly used with nouns referring to people, and a phrase beginning with *of* is used with most nouns referring to location.

my **uncle's** workshop, **Jan's** car, the **student's** paper [nouns referring to people]

the **end of** the movie, the **middle of** the day, the **front of** the building [nouns referring to location]

(1) Most singular nouns, indefinite pronouns, abbreviations, and acronyms require -'s to form the possessive case.

the dean's office [noun]   Yeats's poems [noun]

anyone's computer [indefinite pronoun]

the NFL's reputation [abbreviation]   OPEC's price increase [acronym]

Walter Bryan Jr.'s letter [To avoid confusion, no comma precedes *Jr.'s* here. *Jr.* is sometimes set off by a comma, however (37d(2)).]

To form the possessive of most singular proper nouns, add an apostrophe and an *s: Iowa's governor*. When a singular proper noun ends in *-s*, though, you will have to consult the style guide for the discipline in which you are writing. The *MLA Handbook for Writers of Research Papers* recommends always using *-'s*, as in *Illinois's legislature, Dickens's novels, Ms. Jones's address,* and *Descartes's reasoning*. The *Chicago Manual of Style*, however, notes some exceptions to this rule. An apostrophe without an *s* is appropriate in the following circumstances: (1) when a name ends in a syllable pronounced "eez" (*Sophocles' poetry*), (2) when a singular common noun ends in *-s (physics' contribution)*, and (3) when the name of a place or an organization ends in *-s* but refers to a single entity *(United States' foreign aid)*.

Possessive pronouns *(my, mine, our, ours, your, yours, his, her, hers, its, their, theirs,* and *whose)* are not written with apostrophes (26b(3)).

Japanese democracy differs from **ours.**

The committee concluded **its** discussion.

 CAUTION

Be careful not to confuse possessive pronouns with contractions. Whenever you write a contraction, you should be able to substitute the complete words for it without changing the meaning.

Possessive pronoun	Contraction
Its motor is small.	**It's** [It is] a small motor.
Whose turn is it?	**Who's** [Who is] representing us?

---

(2) Plural nouns ending in -s require only an apostrophe for the possessive form.

the boys' game   the babies' toys   the Joneses' house

Plural nouns that do not end in *-s* need both an apostrophe and an *s*.

men's lives   women's health   children's projects

 CAUTION

An apostrophe is not needed to make a noun plural. To make most nouns plural, add -s or -es. Add an apostrophe only to signal ownership, origin, and other similar relationships.

> protesters
> The ~~protesters'~~ met in front of the conference center.

> The protesters' meeting was on Wednesday.

Likewise, to form the plural of a family name, use -s or -es, not an apostrophe.

> Johnsons
> The ~~Johnson's~~ participated in the study.

> [COMPARE: The Johnsons' participation in the study was crucial.]

> Jameses
> The trophy was given to the ~~James's~~.

> [COMPARE: The Jameses' trophy is on display in the lobby.]

(3) To show collaboration or joint ownership, add -'s or an apostrophe to the second noun only.

In the examples below, the ending -'s follows the second singular noun (*plumber*). Just an apostrophe follows the second plural noun (*Lopezes*), which already ends in -'s.

> the carpenter and the **plumber's** decision [They made the decision collaboratively.]

> the Becks and the **Lopezes'** cabin [They own one cabin jointly.]

(4) To show separate ownership or individual contributions, add -'s or an apostrophe to each noun.

In the examples below, each plural noun is followed by an apostrophe, and each singular noun is followed by -'s.

> the **Becks'** and the **Lopezes'** cars [Each family owns a car.]

> the **carpenter's** and the **plumber's** proposals [They each made a proposal.]

(5) Add -'s to the last word of a compound noun.

my brother-in-**law's** friends, the attorney **general's** statements [singular]

my brothers-in-**law's** friends, the attorneys **general's** statements [plural]

To avoid awkward constructions such as the last two, consider using a prepositional phrase beginning with *of* instead: *the statements of the attorneys general.*

(6) Add -'s or just an apostrophe to a noun preceding a gerund.
Depending on its number, a noun that precedes a gerund takes either -'s or just an apostrophe.

Lucy**'s having** to be there seemed unnecessary. [singular noun preceding gerund]

The family appreciated the lawyers' **handling** of the matter. [plural noun preceding gerund]

MULTILINGUAL WRITERS

GERUND PHRASES

When a gerund appears after a possessive noun, the noun is the subject of the gerund phrase.

Lucy's having to be there [COMPARE: **Lucy** has to be there.]
The lawyers' handling of the matter [COMPARE: **The lawyers** handled the matter.]

The gerund phrase may serve as the subject (**21b**) or the object (**21c**) in the sentence.

       s

Lucy's having to be there seemed unnecessary.

                  obj

The family appreciated **the lawyers' handling of the matter.**

Sometimes you may find it difficult to distinguish between a gerund and a participle (22a(3)). A good way to tell the difference is to note whether the emphasis is on an action or on a person. In a sentence containing a gerund, the emphasis is on the action; in a sentence containing a participle, the emphasis is on the person.

Our successful completion of the project depends on **Terry's providing** the illustrations. [gerund]

I remember my **brother telling** me the same joke last year. [participle]

(7) Follow an organization's preference for its name or the name of a product; follow local conventions for a geographical location.

Consumers Union   Actors' Equity   Shoppers Choice   Taster's Choice

Devil's Island   Devils Tower   Devil Mountain

Whether an apostrophe is used in a brand name is determined by the organization that owns the name.

Exercise 1

Following the pattern of the examples, change the modifier after each noun to a possessive form that precedes the noun.

EXAMPLES

proposals made by the committee   *the committee's proposals*

poems written by Keats   *Keats's poems*

1. the day named after St. Patrick
2. a leave of absence lasting six months
3. the position taken by HMOs
4. the report given by the eyewitness
5. the generosity of the Lees
6. an article coauthored by Gloria and Alan
7. the weights of the children
8. the spying done by the neighbors
9. the restaurants in New Orleans
10. coffee roasted by Starbucks

39b   Marking omissions of letters or numbers

Apostrophes mark omissions in contractions, numbers, and words mimicking speech.

they're [they are]   class of '09 [class of 2009]

y'all [you all]   singin' [singing]

Contractions are not always appropriate for formal contexts. Your audience may expect you to use full words instead (for example, *cannot* instead of *can't* and *will not* instead of *won't*).

39c | Forming certain plurals

Although an apostrophe was used in the past to form the plurals of numbers, abbreviations, and words used as words, it is used only rarely for this purpose today. These plurals are generally formed by simply adding -s.

1990s   fours and fives   YWCAs   two *and*s   the three Rs

Apostrophes are still used, however, with lowercase letters and with abbreviations that include a combination of uppercase and lowercase letters.

x's and *y*'s   PhD's

The MLA differs from this style in recommending that apostrophes also be used to form the plurals of uppercase letters (*A*'s and *B*'s).

Exercise 2

Insert apostrophes where needed in the following sentences. Be prepared to explain why they are necessary.

1. Whose responsibility is it to see whether its working?
2. Hansons book was published in the early 1920s.
3. They hired a rock n roll band for their wedding dance.
4. NPRs fund drive begins this weekend.
5. Youll have to include the ISBNs of the books youre going to purchase.
6. Only three of the proposals are still being considered: yours, ours, and the Wilbers.
7. Few students enrolled during the academic year 06–07.
8. There cant be more *x*s than there are *y*s in the equation.
9. The students formed groups of twos and threes.
10. He is the only person I know who has two PhDs.

40   Quotation Marks

Quotation marks enclose sentences or parts of sentences that play a special role. For example, quotation marks can indicate that the words between them were first written or spoken by someone else or that they are being used in an unconventional way. This chapter will help you use quotation marks

- with direct quotations (40a),
- with titles of short works (40b),
- for words or phrases used ironically or unconventionally (40c), and
- in combination with other punctuation marks (40d).

40a   Direct quotations

Double quotation marks set off direct quotations, including those in dialogue. Single quotation marks enclose a quotation within a quotation.

(1) Double quotation marks enclose direct quotations.

Quotation marks enclose only the quotation, not any expression such as *she said* or *he replied*. When a sentence ends with quoted material, place the period inside the quotation marks. For guidelines on comma placement, see 40d(1).

> "I believe that we learn by practice," writes Martha Graham. "Whether it means to learn to dance by practicing dancing or to learn to live by practicing living, the principles are the same."

When using direct quotations, reproduce all quoted material exactly as it appears in the original, including capitalization and punctuation. To learn how to set off long quotations as indented blocks, see 13a(2).

(2) Quotation marks are not used for indirect quotations or paraphrases.
Indirect quotations and paraphrases (11d(3)) are restatements of what someone else has said or written.

> Martha Graham believes that practice is necessary for learning, regardless of what we are trying to learn.

(3) Single quotation marks enclose quotations within quotations.
If the quotation you are using includes another direct quotation, use single quotation marks for the embedded quotation.

> According to Anita Erickson, "when the narrator says, 'I have the right to my own opinion,' he means that he has the right to his own delusion."

However, if the embedded quotation appears in a block quotation, use double quotation marks. (Note that double quotation marks are not used to mark the beginning and end of a block quotation.)

Anita Erickson claims that the narrator uses the word *opinion* deceptively.

> Later in the chapter, when the narrator says, "I have the right to my own opinion," he means that he has the right to his own delusion. Although it is tempting to believe that the narrator is making decisions based on a rational belief system, his behavior suggests that he is more interested in deception. With poisonous lies, he has already deceived his business partner, his wife, and his children.

(4) Dialogue is enclosed in quotation marks.
When creating or reporting a dialogue, enclose in quotation marks what each person says, no matter how short. Use a separate paragraph for each speaker, beginning a new paragraph whenever the speaker changes. Narrative details can be included in the same paragraph as a direct quotation.

> Farmer looked up, smiling, and in a chirpy-sounding voice he said, "But that feeling has the disadvantage of being . . ." He paused a beat. "Wrong."
> "Well," I retorted, "it depends on how you look at it."
>
> —**TRACY KIDDER,** *Mountains Beyond Mountains*

When quoting more than one paragraph by a single speaker, put quotation marks at the beginning of each paragraph. However, do not place closing quotation marks at the end of each paragraph—only at the end of the last paragraph.

(5) Thoughts are enclosed in quotation marks.

Quotation marks set off thoughts that resemble speech.

> "His silence on this topic has surprised everyone," I noted to myself as I surveyed the faces of the other committee members.

Thoughts are usually marked by such phrases as *I thought, he felt*, and *she believed*. Remember, though, that quotation marks are not used with thoughts that are reported indirectly (40a(2)).

> I wondered why he didn't respond.

(6) Short excerpts of poetry included within a sentence are enclosed in quotation marks.

When quoting fewer than four lines of poetry, enclose them in quotation marks and use a slash (41i) to indicate the line division.

> After watching a whale swim playfully, the speaker in "Visitation" asks, "What did you think, that joy/was some slight thing?"

To learn how to format longer quotations of poetry, see 12e(4).

40b Titles of short works

Quotation marks enclose the title of a short work, such as a story, an essay, a poem, or a song. The title of a larger work, such as a book, magazine, newspaper, or play, should be italicized (or underlined if you are using MLA style). (See chapter 13.)

> "The Green Shepherd" first appeared in *The New Yorker*.

Short story	"The Lottery"	"The Fall of the House of Usher"
Essay	"Walden"	"Play-by-Play"
Article	"Small World"	"Arabia's Empty Quarter"
Book chapter	"Rain"	"Cutting a Dash"
Short poem	"Orion"	"Mending Wall"
Song	"Lazy River"	"The Star-Spangled Banner"
TV episode	"Show Down!"	"The Last Time"

Use double quotation marks around the title of a short work embedded in a longer italicized (or underlined) title.

Interpretations of "*Young Goodman Brown*" [book about a short story]

Use single quotation marks for a title within a longer title that is enclosed in double quotation marks.

"Irony in 'The Sick Rose'" [article about a poem]

MULTILINGUAL WRITERS

DIFFERING USES OF QUOTATION MARKS

In works published in Great Britain, you will notice that the use of quotation marks differs in some ways from the style presented here. For example, single quotation marks are used to set off the titles of short works, and a period is placed outside a quotation mark ending a sentence. When writing in the United States, follow the rules for American English.

British usage	In class, we compared Wordsworth's 'Upon Westminster Bridge' with Blake's 'London'.
American usage	In class, we compared Wordsworth's "Upon Westminster Bridge" with Blake's "London."

40c For ironic tone or unusual usage

Writers sometimes use quotation marks to indicate that they are using a word or phrase ironically. The word *gourmet* is used ironically in the following sentence.

His "gourmet" dinner turned out to be processed turkey and instant mashed potatoes.

CAUTION

Avoid using quotation marks around words that may not be appropriate for your rhetorical situation. Instead, take the time to choose suitable words. The revised sentence in the following pair is more effective than the first.

Ineffective He is too much of a "wimp" to be a good leader.

Revised He is too indecisive to be a good leader.

Similarly, putting a cliché (35b) in quotation marks may make readers conclude that you do not care enough about conveying your meaning to think of a fresh expression.

40d With other punctuation marks

To decide whether to place some other punctuation mark inside or outside quotation marks, identify the punctuation mark and note whether it is part of the quotation or part of the surrounding context.

(1) With commas and periods

Quoted material is usually accompanied by an attributive tag such as *she said* or *he replied*. When your sentence starts with such an expression, place a comma after it to separate the tag from the quotation.

> She replied, "There's more than one way to slice a pie."

If your sentence starts with the quotation instead, place the comma inside the closing quotation marks.

> "There's more than one way to slice a pie," she replied.

Place a period inside closing quotation marks, whether single or double, if the quotation ends the sentence.

> Jeff responded, "I didn't understand 'An Algorithm for Life.'"

When quoting material from a source, provide the relevant page number(s). If you are following MLA guidelines, note the page number(s) in parentheses after the final quotation marks. Place the period that ends the sentence after the final parenthesis, unless the quotation is a block quotation (13a(2)).

> According to Diane Ackerman, "Love is a demanding sport involving all the muscle groups, including the brain" (86).

CAUTION

Do not put a comma after *that* when it precedes a quotation.

Diane Ackerman claims that "[l]ove is a demanding sport involving all the muscle groups, including the brain" (86).

(2) With semicolons and colons

Place semicolons and colons outside quotation marks.

> His favorite song was "Cyprus Avenue"; mine was "Astral Weeks."
>
> Because it is repeated, one line stands out in "The Conductor": "We are never as beautiful as now."

(3) With question marks, exclamation points, and dashes

If the direct quotation includes a question mark, an exclamation point, or a dash, place that punctuation *inside* the closing quotation marks.

> Jeremy asked, "What is truth?"
>
> Gordon shouted "Congratulations!"
>
> Laura said, "Let me tell—" Before she could finish her sentence, Dan walked into the room.

Use just one question mark inside the quotation marks when a question you write ends with a quoted question.

> Why does the protagonist ask, "Where are we headed?"

If the punctuation is not part of the quoted material, place it *outside* the closing quotation marks.

Who wrote "The Figure a Sentence Makes"?

You have to read "Awareness and Freedom"!

She called me a "toaster head"—perhaps justifiably under the circumstances.

Exercise 1

Revise sentences in which quotation marks are used incorrectly and insert quotation marks where they are needed. Do not alter sentences that are written correctly. (The numbers in parentheses are page numbers, placed according to MLA guidelines.)

1. Have you read Nicholas Negroponte's essay Creating a Culture of Ideas?
2. Negroponte states, Innovation is inefficient (2).
3. However, he also believes that "without innovation we are doomed—by boredom and monotony—to decline" (2).
4. Negroponte suggests that new ideas are fostered by 'providing a good educational system, encouraging different viewpoints, and fostering collaboration' (3).
5. According to the author, "More than ever before, in the new "new economy," research and innovation will need to be housed in those places where there are parallel agendas and multiple means of support."
6. Peter Drucker, in Beyond the Information Revolution, discusses the potential of technological development by using historical references.
7. Drucker maintains, E-commerce is to the Information Revolution what the railroad was to the Industrial Revolution—a totally new, totally unprecedented, totally unexpected development (50).
8. Just as the railroad influenced a person's perception of distance in the nineteenth century, 'distance has been eliminated' through e-commerce in our own times, asserts Drucker (50).

41 The Period and Other Punctuation Marks

To indicate the end of a sentence, you can use one of three punctuation marks: the period, the question mark, or the exclamation point. Your choice depends on whether you want to express a statement, a question, or an exclamation.

Everyone passed the exam.

Everyone passed the exam? [informal usage]

Everyone passed the exam!

Within sentences, you can use colons, dashes, parentheses, square brackets, ellipsis points, and slashes to emphasize, downplay, or clarify the information you want to convey. (For use of the hyphen, see 42f.)

This chapter will help you use

- end punctuation marks (the period (41a), the question mark (41b), and the exclamation point (41c)),
- the colon (41d),
- the dash (41e),
- parentheses (41f),
- square brackets (41g),
- ellipsis points (41h), and
- the slash (41i).

To accommodate computerized typesetting, both CMS and APA guidelines call for only one space after a period, a question mark, an exclamation point, a colon, and each of the periods in ellipsis points. According to these manuals, there should be no space preceding or following a hyphen or a dash. The MLA style manual recommends using only one space after end punctuation marks but allows two spaces if they are used consistently.

41a The period

(1) A period marks the end of a sentence.
Use a period at the end of a declarative sentence.

Many adults in the United States are overfed yet undernourished.

Soft drinks account for 7 percent of their average daily caloric intake.

In addition, place a period at the end of an instruction or recommendation written as an imperative sentence (22e).

Eat plenty of fruits and vegetables. Drink six to eight glasses of water a day.

Indirect questions are phrased as statements, so be sure to use a period, rather than a question mark, at the end of such a sentence.

The researcher explained why people eat so much junk food.

[COMPARE: Why do people eat so much junk food?]

(2) Periods follow some abbreviations.

Dr. Jr. a.m. p.m. vs. etc. et al.

Only one period follows an abbreviation that ends a sentence.

The tour begins at 1:00 p.m.

Periods are not used with many common abbreviations (for example, *MVP, mph,* and *FM*). (See chapter 45.) A dictionary lists the conventional form of an abbreviation as well as any alternatives.

41b The question mark

Place a question mark after a direct question.

How does the new atomic clock work? Who invented this clock?

Use a period, instead of a question mark, after an indirect question—that is, a question embedded in a statement.

I asked whether the new atomic clock could be used in cell phones.

[COMPARE: Can the new atomic clock be used in cell phones?]

MULTILINGUAL WRITERS

INDIRECT QUESTIONS

In English, indirect questions are written as declarative sentences. The subject and verb are not inverted as they would be in the related direct question.

We do not know when ~~will~~ the meeting ^will^ end.

[COMPARE: When will the meeting end?]

Place a question mark after each question in a series of related questions, even when they are not full sentences.

Will the new atomic clock be used in cell phones? Word processors? Car navigation systems?

If a direct quotation is a question, place the question mark inside the final quotation marks.

Tony asked, "How small is this new clock?"

In contrast, if you include quoted material in a question of your own, place the question mark outside the final quotation marks.

Is the clock really "no larger than a sugar cube"?

If you embed in the middle of a sentence a question not attributable to anyone in particular, place a comma before it and a question mark after it.

When the question, how does the clock work? arose, the researchers described a technique used by manufacturers of computer chips.

The first letter of such a question should not be capitalized unless the question is extremely long or contains internal punctuation.

To indicate uncertainty about a fact such as a date of birth, place a question mark inside parentheses directly after the fact in question.

Chaucer was born in 1340 (?) and died in 1400.

41c The exclamation point

An exclamation point often marks the end of a sentence, but its primary purpose is rhetorical—to create emphasis.

Whoa! What a game!

When a direct quotation ends with an exclamation point, no comma or period is placed immediately after it.

"Get a new pitcher!" he yelled.

He yelled, "Get a new pitcher!"

Use the exclamation point sparingly so that you do not diminish its value. If you do not intend to signal strong emotion, place a comma after an interjection and a period at the end of the sentence.

Well, no one seriously expected this victory.

Exercise 1

Compose and punctuate brief sentences of the following types.

1. a declarative sentence containing a quoted exclamation
2. a sentence beginning with an interjection
3. a direct question
4. a declarative sentence containing an indirect question
5. a declarative sentence containing a direct question

41d The colon

A colon calls attention to what follows. It also separates numbers in parts of scriptural references and titles from subtitles. Leave only one space after a colon.

(1) A colon directs attention to an explanation, a summary, or a quotation.

When a colon appears between two independent clauses, it signals that the second clause will explain or expand on the first.

> No one expected the game to end as it did: after seven extra innings, the favored team collapsed.

A colon is also used after an independent clause to introduce a direct quotation.

> Marcel Proust explained the importance of mindfulness: "The true journey of discovery consists not in seeking new landscapes but in having fresh eyes."

 CAUTION

The rules for using an uppercase or a lowercase letter to begin the first word of an independent clause that follows a colon vary across style manuals.

MLA   The first letter should be lowercase unless (1) it begins a word that is normally capitalized, (2) the independent clause is a quotation, or (3) the clause expresses a rule or principle.

APA   The first letter should be uppercase.

CMS   The first letter should be lowercase unless (1) it begins a word that is normally capitalized, (2) the independent clause is a quotation, or (3) two or more sentences follow the colon.

Although an independent clause should always precede the colon, a phrase may sometimes follow it.

> I was finally confronted with what I had dreaded for months: the due date for the final balloon payment on my car loan.

All the style manuals advise using lowercase letters to begin a phrase following a colon.

(2) A colon may signal that a list follows.

Writers frequently use colons to introduce lists.

> Three students received internships: Asa, Vanna, and Jack.

Avoid placing a colon between a verb and its complement (**21c**) or after the words *including* and *such as*.

The winners were ⌒ Asa, Vanna, and Jack.

Many vegetarians do not eat dairy products such as ⌒ butter and cheese.

(3) A colon separates a title and a subtitle.
Use a colon between a work's title and its subtitle.

Collapse❙ *How Societies Choose to Fail or Succeed*

(4) Colons are used in reference numbers.
Colons are often used between numbers in scriptural references.

Psalms 3❙5   Gen. 1❙1

However, MLA requires the use of periods instead of colons.

Psalms 3.5   Gen. 1.1

(5) Colons have specialized uses in business correspondence.
A colon follows the salutation of a business letter and any notations.

Dear Dr. Horner❙   Dear Maxine❙   Enc❙

A colon introduces the headings in a memo.

To❙   From❙   Subject❙   Date❙

Exercise 2

Insert colons where they are needed in the following sentences.

1. Before we discuss marketing, let's outline the behavior of consumers consumer behavior is the process individuals go through as they select, buy, or use products or services to satisfy their needs and desires.
2. The process consists of six stages recognizing a need or desire, finding information, evaluating options, deciding to purchase, purchasing, and assessing purchases.
3. Many consumers rely on one popular publication for product information *Consumer Reports*.

(Continued on page 766)

(Continued from page 765)

4. When evaluating alternatives, a consumer uses criteria; for example, a house hunter might use some of the following price, location, size, age, style, and landscaping design.

5. The postpurchase assessment has one of two results satisfaction or dissatisfaction with the product or service.

41e   The dash

A dash (or em dash) marks a break in thought, sets off a nonessential element for emphasis or clarity, or follows an introductory list or series. The short dash (or en dash) is used mainly in number ranges (45g(2)).

TECH SAVVY
To use your keyboard to create a dash, type two hyphens with no spaces between, before, or after them. Most word-processing programs can be set to convert these hyphens automatically to an em dash.

(1) A dash marks a break in the normal flow of a sentence.
Use a dash to indicate a shift in thought or tone.

I was awed by the almost superhuman effort Stonehenge represents—but who wouldn't be?

(2) A dash or a pair of dashes sets off a nonessential element for emphasis or clarity.

Dr. Kruger's specialty is mycology—the study of fungi.

The trail we took into the Grand Canyon—steep, narrow, winding, and lacking guardrails—made me wonder whether we could call a helicopter to fly us out.

(3) A dash follows an introductory list or series.

If you decide to place a list or series at the beginning of a sentence in order to emphasize it, the main part of the sentence (after the dash) should sum up the meaning of the list or series.

> Eager, determined to succeed, and scared to death——all of these describe how I felt on the first day at work.

THINKING RHETORICALLY

 COMMAS, DASHES, AND COLONS

Although a comma, a dash, or a colon may be followed by an explanation, an example, or an illustration, is the rhetorical impact the same?

> He never failed to mention what was most important to him, the bottom line.

> He never failed to mention what was most important to him——the bottom line.

> He never failed to mention what was most important to him: the bottom line.

The comma, one of the most common punctuation marks, barely draws attention to what follows it. The dash, in contrast, signals a longer pause and so causes more emphasis to be placed on the information that follows. The colon is more direct and formal than either of the other two punctuation marks.

41f **Parentheses**

Use parentheses to set off information that is not closely related to the main point of a sentence or paragraph but that provides an interesting detail, an explanation, or an illustration.

> We might ask why affairs of state are classified as important and their discussants intelligent, while discussion of family and human interaction (what we disparagingly call "gossip") is dismissed as idle chatter.
>
> —ROBIN LAKOFF, *Language and Woman's Place*

In addition, place parentheses around an acronym or an abbreviation when introducing it after its full form.

> The Search for Extraterrestrial Intelligence (SETI) uses the Very Large Array (VLA) outside Sicorro, New Mexico, to scan the sky.

If you use numbers or letters in a list within a sentence, set them off by placing them within parentheses.

> Your application should include (1) a current résumé, (2) a statement of purpose, and (3) two letters of recommendation.

> For information on the use of parentheses in bibliographies and in-text citations, see chapters 13, 15, 17, and 19.

THINKING RHETORICALLY

✳ DASHES AND PARENTHESES

Dashes and parentheses are both used to set off part of a sentence, but they differ in the amount of emphasis they signal. Whereas dashes call attention to the material that is set off, parentheses usually deemphasize such material.

> Her grandfather—born during the Great Depression—was appointed by the president to the Securities and Exchange Commission.

> Her grandfather (born in 1930) was appointed by the president to the Securities and Exchange Commission.

41g   Square brackets

Square brackets set off additions or alterations used to clarify direct quotations. In the following example, the bracketed noun specifies what is meant by the pronoun *They*.

> "They [hyperlinks] are what turn the Web from a library of pages into a web" (Weinberger 170).

Square brackets also indicate that a letter in a quotation has been changed from uppercase to lowercase, or vice versa.

David Weinberger claims that "[e]ven our notion of self as a continuous body moving through a continuous map of space and time is beginning to seem wrong on the Web" (10).

To avoid the awkwardness of using brackets in this way, you may be able to quote only part of a sentence so that no change in capitalization is needed.

David Weinberger claims that "our notion of self as a continuous body moving through a continuous map of space and time is beginning to seem wrong on the Web" (10).

Within parentheses, square brackets are used to avoid the confusion of having two sets of parentheses.

People frequently provide personal information online. (See, for example, David Weinberger's *Small Pieces Loosely Joined* [Cambridge: Perseus, 2002].)

Angle brackets (< >) are used to enclose Web addresses in MLA works-cited lists (**13b**) so that the period at the end of an entry is not confused with the dot(s) in the URL: <http://www.mla.org>.

41h Ellipsis points

Ellipsis points indicate an omission from a quoted passage or a reflective pause or hesitation.

(1) Ellipsis points mark an omission within a quoted passage.

Whenever you omit anything from material you quote, replace the omitted material with ellipsis points—three equally spaced periods. Be sure to compare your quoted sentence to the original, checking to see that your omission does not change the meaning of the original. The following examples illustrate how to use ellipsis points in quotations from a passage by Patricia Gadsby.

Original

Cacao doesn't flower, as most plants do, at the tips of its outer and uppermost branches. Instead, its sweet white buds hang from the trunk and along a few fat branches, popping out of patches of bark called cushions, which form where leaves drop off. They're tiny, these flowers. Yet once pollinated by midges, no-see-ums that flit in the leafy detritus below, they'll make pulp-filled pods almost the size of rugby balls.

—PATRICIA GADSBY, "Endangered Chocolate"

(a) Omission within a quoted sentence

Patricia Gadsby notes that cacao flowers "once pollinated by midges . . . make pulp-filled pods almost the size of rugby balls."

(b) Omission at the beginning of a quoted sentence

Do not use ellipsis points to indicate that you have deleted words from the beginning of a quotation, whether it is run into the text or set off in a block. The opening part of the original sentence has been omitted in the following quotation.

According to Patricia Gadsby, cacao flowers will become "pulp-filled pods almost the size of rugby balls."

Note that the first letter of the integrated quotation is not capitalized.

(c) Omission at the end of a quoted sentence

To indicate that you have omitted words from the end of a sentence, put a space between the last word and the set of three spaced ellipsis points. Then add the end punctuation mark (a period, a question mark, or an exclamation point). If the quoted material is followed by a parenthetical source or page reference, the end punctuation comes after the second parenthesis.

Claiming that cacao flowers differ from those of most plants, Patricia Gadsby describes how "the sweet white buds hang from the trunk and along a few fat branches . . . ."
OR ". . . branches . . ." (2).

(d) Omission of a sentence or more

To signal the omission of a sentence or more (even a paragraph or more), place an end punctuation mark (usually a period) before the ellipsis points.

Patricia Gadsby describes the flowering of the cacao plant: "its sweet white buds hang from the trunk and along a few fat branches, popping out of patches of bark called cushions, which form where leaves drop off. . . . Yet once pollinated by midges, no-see-ums that flit in the leafy detritus below, they'll make pulp-filled pods almost the size of rugby balls."

If, in addition to omitting a full sentence, you omit part of another and that part ends in a comma, colon, or semicolon, place the relevant punctuation mark before the ellipsis points.

Patricia Gadsby describes the flowering of the cacao plant: "its sweet white buds hang from the trunk and along a few fat branches, . . . Yet once pollinated by midges, no-see-ums that flit in the leafy detritus below, they'll make pulp-filled pods almost the size of rugby balls."

(e) Omission of a line or more of a poem

To signal the omission of a full line or more in quoted poetry, use spaced periods covering the length of either the line above it or the omitted line.

The yellow fog that rubs its back upon the window-panes,

. . . .

Curled once about the house, and fell asleep.

—T. S. ELIOT, "The Love Song of J. Alfred Prufrock"

To avoid excessive use of ellipses, replace some direct quotations with paraphrases (11d(3)).

(2) Ellipsis points show that a sentence has been intentionally left incomplete.

Read aloud the passage that begins "The yellow fog . . ."

(3) Ellipsis points can mark a reflective pause or a hesitation.

Keith saw four menacing youths coming toward him . . . and ran.

A dash can also be used to indicate this type of a pause.

41i   The slash

A slash between words, as in *and/or* and *he/she,* indicates that either word is applicable in the given context. There are no spaces before and after a slash used in this way. Because extensive use of the slash can make writing choppy, consider using *or* instead. (If you are following MLA guidelines, avoid using *and/or, he/she, him/her,* and so on.)

A slash is also used to mark line divisions in quoted poetry. A slash used in this way is preceded and followed by a space.

> Wallace Stevens refers to the listener who, "nothing himself, beholds **/** Nothing that is not there and the nothing that is."

Exercise 3

Add appropriate dashes, parentheses, square brackets, and slashes to the following sentences. Be ready to explain the reason for each mark you add.

1. Researchers in an exciting field Artificial Intelligence AI are working on devices to assist the elderly.

2. One such device is Pearl a robotic nurse that helps around the house.

3. Another application is cooking software that checks for missing and or incorrect ingredients.

4. Researchers are even investigating Global Positioning Systems GPS as a way to track Alzheimer's patients' daily routines.

5. The actual cost of such devices expensive now but more affordable later is yet to be determined.

Exercise 4

Punctuate the following sentences with appropriate end marks, commas, colons, dashes, and parentheses. Do not use unnecessary punctuation. Give a justification for each mark you add, especially where more than one type of mark (for example, commas, dashes, or parentheses) is acceptable.

1. Many small country towns are very similar a truck stop a gas station a crowded diner and three bars

2. The simple life a nonexistent crime rate and down-home values these are some of the advantages these little towns offer

3. Why do we never see these quaint examples of pure Americana when we travel around the country on the interstates

4. Rolling across America on one of the big interstates I-20 I-40 I-70 I-80 or I-90 you are likely to pass within a few miles of a number of these towns

5. Such towns almost certainly will have a regional or perhaps an ethnic flavor Hispanic in the southwest Scandinavian in the north

6. When I visit one of these out-of-the-way places I always have a sense of well really a feeling of safety

7. There's one thing I can tell you small-town life is not boring

8. My one big question however is what do you do to earn a living in these towns

M

MECHANICS

"I won the spell — check bee."

42 Spelling, the Spell Checker, and Hyphenation   777

43 Capitals   787

44 Italics   798

45 Abbreviations, Acronyms, and Numbers   804

CHAPTER 42
Spelling, the Spell Checker, and
Hyphenation 777

42a Spell checker   777
42b Spelling and pronunciation   778
42c Words that sound alike   779
42d Prefixes and suffixes   780
42e Confusion of *ei* and *ie*   783
42f Hyphens   784

CHAPTER 43
Capitals   787

43a Proper names   788
43b Titles and subtitles   792
43c Beginning a sentence   793
43d Computer keys, menu items,
     and icon names   795
43e Unnecessary capitals   796

CHAPTER 44
Italics   798

44a Titles of works published or produced
     separately   799
44b Foreign words   800
44c Legal cases   801

44d Names of ships, submarines, aircraft,
     spacecraft, and satellites   801
44e Words, letters, or figures referred to as
     such and letters used in mathematical
     expressions   802
44f Words receiving emphasis   802

CHAPTER 45
Abbreviations, Acronyms, and
Numbers   804

45a Abbreviations with names   805
45b Addresses in correspondence   805
45c Abbreviations in source documentation   806
45d Acceptable abbreviations in academic
     and professional writing   807
45e Acronyms   809
45f General uses of numbers   810
45g Special uses of numbers   811

42 Spelling, the Spell Checker, and Hyphenation

When you first draft a paper, you might not pay close attention to spelling words correctly. After all, the point of drafting is to generate and organize ideas. However, proofreading for spelling mistakes is essential as you near the end of the writing process. Your teachers, employers, or supervisors will expect you to submit polished work.

You can train yourself to be a good proofreader by checking a dictionary every time you question the spelling of a word. If two spellings are listed, such as *fulfill* and *fulfil*, either form is correct, although the first option provided is generally considered more common. Whatever spelling you choose in such cases, use it consistently. You can also learn to be a better speller by studying a few basic strategies. This chapter will help you

- use a spell checker (42a),
- spell words according to pronunciation (42b),
- spell words that sound alike (42c),
- understand how prefixes and suffixes affect spelling (42d),
- use *ei* and *ie* correctly (42e), and
- use hyphens to link and divide words (42f).

42a Spell checker

The spell checker is a wonderful invention, though you must use it with care. A spell checker will usually flag

- misspellings of common words,
- some commonly confused words (such as *affect* and *effect*), and
- obvious typographical errors (such as *tge* for *the*).

However, a spell checker generally will *not* detect

- specialized vocabulary or foreign words not in its dictionary,
- typographical errors that are still correctly spelled words (such as *was* for *saw*), and
- misuses of words that sound alike but are not on the spell checker's list of words commonly confused.

The following strategies can help you use a spell checker effectively.

TIPS FOR USING A SPELL CHECKER

- If a spell checker regularly flags a word that is not in its dictionary but is spelled correctly, add that word to its dictionary by clicking on the Add button. From that point on, the spell checker will accept the word you added.
- Reject any offers the spell checker makes to correct all instances of a particular error.
- Use a dictionary to evaluate the alternative spellings the spell checker provides because some of them may be erroneous.

42b   Spelling and pronunciation

Many words in English are not spelled the way they are pronounced, so pronunciation is not a reliable guide to correct spelling. Sometimes, people skip over an unstressed syllable, as when *February* is pronounced "Febary," or they slide over a sound that is hard to articulate, as when *library* is pronounced "libary." Other times, people add a sound—for instance, when they pronounce *athlete* as "athalete." And people also switch sounds around, as in "irrevelant" for *irrelevant*. Such mispronunciations can lead to misspellings.

You can help yourself remember the spellings of some words by considering the spellings of their root words—for example, the root word for *irrelevant* is *relevant*. You can also teach yourself the correct spellings of words by pronouncing them the way they are spelled, that is, by pronouncing each letter mentally so that you "hear" even silent letters. You are more likely to remember the *b* in *subtle* if you pronounce it when spelling that word. Here are a few words typically misspelled because they include unpronounced letters:

condem*n*   foreign   lab*o*ratory   mus*c*le   solem*n*

Here are a few more that include letters that are often not heard in rapid speech, though they can be heard when carefully pronounced:

can*d*idate   diff*e*rent   enviro*n*ment   gover*n*ment   sep*a*rate

---

 **CAUTION**

The words *and, have,* and *than* are often not stressed in speech and are thus misspelled.

They would rather~~of~~ *have* written two papers~~then~~ *than* taken midterm~~an~~ *and* final exams.

42c   Words that sound alike

Pairs of words such as *forth* and *fourth* or *sole* and *soul* are **homophones:** they sound alike but have different meanings and spellings. Some words that have different meanings sound exactly alike (*break/brake*); others sound alike in certain dialects (*marry/merry*). If you are unsure about the difference in meaning between any two words that sound alike, consult a dictionary. A number of frequently confused words are listed with explanations in this handbook's Glossary of Usage.

Also troublesome are two-word sequences that can be written as compound words or as separate words. The following are examples:

Everyday life was grueling.	She attended class **every day.**
They do not fight **anymore.**	They could not find **any more** evidence.

Other examples are *awhile/a while, everyone/every one, maybe/may be,* and *sometime/some time.*

A lot and *all right* are still spelled as two words. *Alot* is always considered incorrect; *alright* is also considered incorrect except in some newspapers and magazines. (See the Glossary of Usage.)

Singular nouns ending in *-nce* and plural nouns ending in *-nts* are easily confused.

Assistance is available.   I have two **assistants.**

His **patience** wore thin.   Some **patients** waited for hours.

Contractions and possessive pronouns are also often confused. In contractions, an apostrophe indicates an omitted letter (or letters). In possessive pronouns, there is no apostrophe. (See also **26b** and **39a(1)**.)

Contraction	**Possessive**
It's my turn next.	Each group waited **its** turn.
You're next.	**Your** turn is next.
There's no difference.	**Theirs** is no different.

TIPS FOR SPELLING WORDS THAT SOUND ALIKE

- Be on the lookout for words that are commonly confused (*accept/except*).
- Distinguish between two-word sequences and single words that sound similar (*may be/maybe*).
- Use *-nts,* not *-nce,* for plural words (*instants/instance*).
- Mark contractions, but not possessive pronouns, with apostrophes (*who's/whose*).

42d   Prefixes and suffixes

When a prefix is added to a base word (often called the **root**), the spelling of the base word is unaffected.

necessary, **un**necessary   moral, **im**moral

However, adding a suffix to the end of a base word often changes the spelling.

beauty, beauti**ful**　　describe, descri**ption**　　BUT　　resist, resist**ance**

Although spellings of words with suffixes are irregular, they follow certain conventions.

(1) Dropping or retaining a final e depends on whether the suffix begins with a vowel.

- If a suffix begins with a vowel, the final *e* of the base word is dropped: bride, brid**al**; come, com**ing**; combine, combin**ation**; prime, prim**ary**. However, to keep the /s/ sound of *ce* or the /j/ sound of *ge*, retain the final *e* before *-able* or *-ous:* courage**ous,** manage**able,** notice**able.**
- If a suffix begins with a consonant, the final *e* of the base word is retained: entire, entire**ly**; rude, rude**ness**; place, place**ment**; sure, sure**ly**. Some exceptions are *argument, awful, ninth, truly,* and *wholly.*

(2) A final consonant is often doubled when a suffix begins with a vowel.

- If a consonant ends a one-syllable word with a single vowel or ends a stressed syllable with a single vowel, double the final consonant: stop, sto**pped,** sto**pping;** omit, omi**tted,** omi**tting.**
- If there are two vowels before the consonant, the consonant is not doubled: seat, seat**ed,** seat**ing;** remain, remain**ed,** remain**ing.**
- If the final syllable is not stressed, the consonant is not doubled: edit, edit**ed,** edit**ing;** picket, picket**ed,** picket**ing.**

(3) A final y is changed or retained depending on whether it is preceded by a consonant or a vowel.

- Change a final *y* following a consonant to *i* when adding a suffix (except *-ing*): lazy, laz**ily**; defy, def**ies,** def**ied,** def**iance** BUT defy**ing**; modify, modif**ies,** modif**ied,** modif**ier** BUT modify**ing.**
- Retain the final *y* when it follows a vowel: gray, gray**ish**; stay, stay**s,** stay**ed**; obey, obey**s,** obey**ed.**
- Some verb forms are irregular and thus can cause difficulties: *lays, laid; pays, paid.* For a list of irregular verbs, see pages 609–611.

(4) A final l is retained when -ly is added.

cool, coo**lly**　　formal, forma**lly**　　real, rea**lly**　　usual, usua**lly**

Exercise 1

Add the specified suffixes to the words that follow. Be prepared to explain the reason for the spelling of each resulting word.

EXAMPLE

-ly: late, casual, psychological   *lately   casually   psychologically*

1. -ing: put, admit, write, use, try, play
2. -ment: manage, commit, require, argue
3. -ous: continue, joy, acrimony, libel
4. -ed: race, tip, permit, carry, pray
5. -able: desire, read, trace, knowledge
6. -ly: true, sincere, normal, general

(5) A noun is made plural by adding -s or -es to the singular form.

- If the sound in the plural form of a noun ending in *f* or *fe* changes from /f/ to /v/, change the ending to *-ve* before adding *-s:* thief, thieves; life, lives BUT roof, roofs.
- Add *-es* to most nouns ending in *s, z, ch, sh,* or *x:* box, boxes; peach, peaches.
- If a noun ends in a consonant and *y*, change the *y* to *i* and add *-es:* company, companies; ninety, nineties; territory, territories. (See also 42d(3).)
- If a noun ends in a consonant and *o*, add *-es:* hero, heroes; potato, potatoes. However, note that sometimes just *-s* is added (photo, photos; memo, memos) and other times either an *-s* or *-es* suffix can be added (mottos, mottoes; zeros, zeroes).
- Certain nouns have irregular plural forms: woman, women; child, children; foot, feet.
- Add *-s* to most proper nouns: the Lees; the Kennedys. Add *-es* to most proper nouns ending in *s, z, ch, sh,* or *x:* the Rodriguezes, the Joneses BUT the Bachs (in which *ch* is pronounced /k/).

BEYOND THE RULE

WORDS BORROWED FROM OTHER LANGUAGES

Words borrowed from Latin or Greek generally form their plurals as they did in the original language.

Singular	criterion	alumnus, alumna	analysis	datum	species
Plural	criteria	alumni, alumnae	analyses	data	species

When a word with such an origin is in the process of changing, two different forms will be listed as acceptable in the dictionary: *syllabus/syllabuses, syllabi*.

Exercise 2

Provide the plural forms for the following words. If you need extra help, check a dictionary.

1. virus
2. committee
3. phenomenon
4. copy
5. delay
6. embargo
7. self
8. belief
9. foot
10. portfolio
11. cactus
12. census

42e   Confusion of *ei* and *ie*

An old rhyme will help you remember the order of letters in most words containing *e* and *i:*

Put *i* before *e*
Except after *c*
Or when sounded like *a*
As in *neighbor* and *weigh.*

Words with *i* before *e:* bel**ie**ve, ch**ie**f, pr**ie**st, y**ie**ld
Words with *e* before *i,* after *c:* conc**ei**t, perc**ei**ve, rec**ei**ve
Words with *ei* sounding like *a* in *cake:* **ei**ght, r**ei**n, th**ei**r, h**ei**r

Words that are exceptions to the rules in the rhyme include *either, neither, species, foreign,* and *weird.*

MULTILINGUAL WRITERS

AMERICAN AND BRITISH SPELLING DIFFERENCES

Spelling systems in the United States and Great Britain differ in a few minor ways. Although most words are spelled the same in both systems, there are some differences, including the following.

American	check	realize	color	connection
British	cheque	realise	colour	connexion

Use the American spelling system when writing for an audience in the United States.

42f Hyphens

Hyphens link two or more words functioning as a single word and separate word parts to clarify meaning. They also have many conventional uses in numbers, fractions, and measurements. (Do not confuse the hyphen with a dash; see 41e and 45f).

(1) Hyphens sometimes link two or more words that form a compound.
Some compounds are listed in the dictionary with hyphens (*eye-opener, cross-examine*), others are written as two words (*eye chart, cross fire*), and still others are written as one word (*eyewitness, crossbreed*). If you have questions about the spelling of a compound word, a dictionary is a good resource. However, it is also helpful to learn a few basic patterns.

- If two or more words serve as a single adjective before a noun, they should be hyphenated. If the words follow the noun, they are not hyphenated.

  You submitted an **up-to-date** report. The report was **up to date.**

  A **well-known** musician is performing tonight. The musician is **well known.**

- When the second word in a hyphenated expression is omitted, the first word is still followed by a hyphen.

  They discussed both **private-** and **public-sector** partnerships.

- A hyphen is not used after adverbs ending in *-ly* (*poorly planned event*), in names of chemical compounds (*sodium chloride solution*), or in modifiers with a letter or numeral as the second element (*group C homes, type IV virus*).

(2) Hyphens can be used to separate words into parts to clarify meaning.

- To avoid ambiguity or an awkward combination of letters or syllables, place a hyphen between the base word and its prefix: *anti-intellectual, de-emphasize, re-sign the petition* [COMPARE: *resign the position*].
- Place a hyphen between a prefix and a word beginning with a capital letter and between a prefix and a word already containing a hyphen: *anti-American, non-self-promoting.*
- Place a hyphen after the prefix *all-, e-, ex-,* or *self-: all-inclusive, e-commerce, ex-husband, self-esteem.* Otherwise, most words with prefixes are not hyphenated.

(3) Hyphens are frequently used in numbers, fractions, and units of measure.

- Place a hyphen between two numbers when they are spelled out: *thirty-two, ninety-nine.* However, no hyphen is used before or after the words *hundred, thousand,* and *million: five hundred sixty-three, forty-one million.*
- Hyphenate fractions that are spelled out: *three-fourths, one-half.*
- When you form a compound modifier that includes a number and a unit of measurement, place a hyphen between them: *twenty-first-century literature, twelve-year-old boy, ten-year project.*

Exercise 3

Convert the following word groups into hyphenated compounds.

EXAMPLE

a movie lasting two hours   *a two-hour movie*

1. a man who is fifty years old
2. a seminar that lasted all day
3. a street that runs only one way
4. history from the twenty-first century
5. roads that are covered by ice and snow
6. a paper that is well written

43 Capitals

When you look at an advertisement, an e-mail message, or even a paragraph in this book, you can easily pick out capital letters. These beacons draw your attention to significant details—for example, the beginnings of sentences or the names of particular people, places, and products. Although most capitalization conventions apply to any rhetorical situation, others are specific to a discipline or a profession. In this chapter, you will learn the conventions expected in most academic and professional settings. This chapter will help you

- use capitals for proper names (43a),
- capitalize words in titles and subtitles of works (43b),
- capitalize the first letter of a sentence (43c),
- use capitals for computer keys, menu items, and icon names (43d), and
- avoid unnecessary capitalization (43e).

BEYOND THE RULE

CAPITALIZATION STYLES

You may have noticed that different capitalization styles are used in various types of publications. For instance, the word *president* is always capitalized in documents published by the U.S. Government Printing Office, but it is capitalized in most newspapers only when it is followed by a specific name:

The delegates met with **P**resident Truman.

The delegates met with the **p**resident.

Advertisers frequently use capitalization to highlight
important words.

43a Proper names

When you capitalize a word, you emphasize it. That is why names of
people and places are capitalized, even when they are used as modifiers
(*Mexico, Mexican government*). Some words, such as *college, company,
park,* and *street,* are capitalized only if they are part of a name (*a university*
but *Oregon State University*). The following names and titles should be
capitalized.

(1) Names of specific persons or things

Zora Neale Hurston	Flight 224	Honda Accord
John Paul II	Academy Award	USS *Cole*
Skylab	Nike	Microsoft Windows

A word denoting a family relationship is capitalized only when it substitutes for the person's proper name.

I told **Mom** about the event. [I told Catherine about the event.]

I told my **mom** about the event. [NOT I told my Catherine about the event.]

(2) Titles accompanying proper names

A title is capitalized when it precedes the name of a person but not when it follows the name or stands alone.

Governor Peter Dunn	Peter Dunn, the governor
Captain Ray Machado	Ray Machado, our captain
Uncle Rory	Rory, my uncle
President Lincoln	Abraham Lincoln, the president of the United States

(3) Names of ethnic or cultural groups and languages

Asians	African Americans	Latinos/Latinas	Poles
Arabic	English	Korean	Spanish

(4) Names of bridges, buildings, monuments, and geographical features

Golden Gate Bridge	Empire State Building	Lincoln Memorial
Arctic Circle	Mississippi River	Grand Canyon

When referring to two or more geographical features, however, do not capitalize the generic term: *Lincoln and Jefferson memorials, Yellowstone and Olympic national parks.*

(5) Names of organizations, government agencies, institutions, and companies

B'nai B'rith	National Endowment for the Humanities
Phi Beta Kappa	Internal Revenue Service
Howard University	Ford Motor Company

When used as common nouns, *service, company,* and *university* are not capitalized. However, some institutions, such as universities or corporations, capitalize their shortened names.

> The policies of Hanson **U**niversity promote the rights of all individuals to equal opportunity in education. The **U**niversity complies with all applicable federal, state, and local laws.

(6) Names of days of the week, months, and holidays

> Wednesday   August   Fourth of July

The names of the seasons—spring, summer, fall, winter—are not capitalized.

MULTILINGUAL WRITERS

CAPITALIZING DAYS OF THE WEEK

Capitalization rules vary according to language. For example, in English, the names of days and months are capitalized, but in some other languages, such as Spanish and Italian, they are not.

(7) Designations for historical documents, periods, events, movements, and styles

> Declaration of Independence   Renaissance   Industrial Revolution

A historical period that includes a number is not capitalized unless it is considered a proper name.

> twentieth century   the Roaring Twenties
> the eighteen hundreds   the Gay Nineties

The name of a cultural movement or style is capitalized if it is derived from a proper name (21a(2)) or if capitalization distinguishes the name of the movement or style from the ordinary use of the word or phrase.

> Platonism   Reaganomics   New Criticism

Most names of cultural movements and styles are not capitalized.

> art deco   impressionism   realism   deconstruction

(8) Names of religions, their adherents, holy days, titles of holy books, and words denoting the Supreme Being

Buddhism, Christianity, Islam, Judaism

Buddhist, Christian, Muslim, Jew

Bodhi Day, Easter, Ramadan, Yom Kippur

Sutras, Bible, Koran, Talmud BUT biblical, talmudic

Buddha, God, Allah, Yahweh

Some writers always capitalize personal pronouns (26a(1)) that refer to the Supreme Being; others capitalize such words only when capitalization is needed to prevent ambiguity:

The Lord commanded the prophet to warn His people.

(9) Words derived from proper names

Americanize [verb]   Orwellian [adjective]   Marxism [noun]

When a proper name becomes the name of a general class of objects or ideas, it is no longer capitalized. For example, *zipper*, originally a capitalized trademark, now refers to a class of fastening devices and is thus written with a lowercase letter. A word derived from a brand name, such as *Xerox*, *Kodak*, or *Kleenex*, should be capitalized. If possible, avoid using brand names and choose generic terms such as *photocopy*, *camera*, and *tissue* instead. If you are not sure whether a proper name or derivative has come to stand for a general class, look up the word in a dictionary.

(10) Abbreviations and acronyms
These forms are derived from the initial letters of capitalized word groups:

AMEX   AT&T   CBS   CST   NFL   OPEC   UNESCO   YMCA

(See also 41a(2) and chapter 45.)

(11) Military terms
Names of forces and special units are capitalized, as are names of wars, battles, revolutions, and military awards.

United States Army	Marine Corps	Eighth Air Force	Green Berets
Russian Revolution	Gulf War	Operation Overlord	Purple Heart

Military words such as *army*, *navy*, and *war* are not capitalized when they stand alone.

My sister joined the navy in 2008.

STYLE SHEET FOR CAPITALIZATION

Capitals	No capitals
the West [geographical region]	driving west [compass point]
a Chihuahua [a breed of dog named after a state in Mexico]	a poodle [a breed of dog]
Washington State University [a specific institution]	a state university
Revolutionary War [a specific war]	an eighteenth-century war
U.S. Army [a specific army]	a peacetime army
Declaration of Independence [title of a document]	a declaration of independence
May [specific month]	spring [general season]
Memorial Day [specific day]	a holiday
two Democratic candidates [refers to a political party]	democratic procedures [refers to a form of government]
a Ford tractor [brand name]	a farm tractor
Parkinson's disease [a disease named for a person]	flu, asthma, leukemia
Governor Clay [a person's title]	the governor of our state

43b Titles and subtitles

The first and last words in titles and subtitles are capitalized, as are major words—that is, all words other than articles (*a, an,* and *the*), coordinating conjunctions (*and, but, for, nor, or, so,* and *yet*), prepositions (see the list on page 536), and the infinitive marker *to*. (For more information on titles, see 40b and 44a.)

From Here to Eternity

"To Be a Student or Not to Be a Student"

APA guidelines differ slightly from other style guidelines: APA recommends capitalizing any word in a title, including a preposition, that has four or more letters.

Southwestern Pottery from Anasazi to Zuni [MLA and CMS]

Southwestern Pottery From Anasazi to Zuni [APA]

MLA, APA, and CMS advise capitalizing all words in a hyphenated compound, except for articles, coordinating conjunctions, and prepositions.

"The Arab-Israeli Dilemma" [compound proper adjective]

"Stop-and-Go Signals" [lowercase for the coordinating conjunction]

However, when a hyphenated word containing a prefix appears in a title or subtitle, MLA and APA advise capitalizing both elements when (1) the second element is a proper noun (**21a(2)**) or adjective (*Pre-Columbian*) or (2) the word contains a doubled letter that could be hard to read (*Anti-Intellectual*). CMS recommends capitalizing the second element only if it is a proper noun or adjective.

"Pre-Columbian Artifacts in Peruvian Museums" [MLA, APA, and CMS]

"Anti-Independence Behavior in Adolescents" [MLA and APA]

"Anti-independence Behavior in Adolescents" [CMS]

43c Beginning a sentence

It is not difficult to remember that a sentence begins with a capital letter, but there are certain types of sentences that deserve special note.

(1) Capitalizing the first word in a quoted sentence

If a direct quotation is a full sentence, the first word should be capitalized.

When asked to name the books she found most influential, Nadine Gordimer responded, "In general, the works that mean most to one—change one's thinking and therefore maybe one's life—are those read in youth."

Even if you interrupt the quoted sentence with commentary, just the first letter should be capitalized.

"**O**ddly," states Ved Mehta, "**l**ike my earliest memories, the books that made the greatest impression on me were the ones I encountered as a small child."

However, if you integrate someone else's sentence into a sentence of your own, the first letter should be lowercase—and placed in brackets if you are following MLA guidelines.

> Nadine Gordimer believes that "[i]n general, the works that mean most to one—change one's thinking and therefore maybe one's life—are those read in youth" (102).

(2) Capitalizing the first word in a freestanding parenthetical sentence

If you place a full sentence inside parentheses, and it is not embedded in a sentence of your own, be sure to capitalize the first word.

> Lance Armstrong won the Tour de France a record-breaking seven times. (**P**revious record holders include Jacques Anquetil, Bernard Hinault, Eddy Merckx, and Miguel Indurain.)

If the sentence inside the parentheses occurs within a sentence of your own, the first word should not be capitalized.

> Lance Armstrong won the Tour de France a record-breaking seven times (**p**reviously, he shared the record with four other cyclists).

(3) Lowercasing or capitalizing the first word in an independent clause following a colon

According to *The Chicago Manual of Style*, if there is only one independent clause (22b) following a colon, the first word should be lowercased. However, if two or more independent clauses follow the colon, the first word of each clause is capitalized.

> The ear thermometer is used quite frequently now: **t**his type of thermometer records a temperature more accurately than a glass thermometer.

> Two new thermometers are replacing the old thermometers filled with mercury: **T**he digital thermometer uses a heat sensor to determine body temperature. **T**he ear thermometer is actually an infrared thermometer that detects the temperature of the eardrum.

The APA manual recommends capitalizing the first word of any independent clause following a colon. The MLA manual advises capitalizing the first word only if the independent clause is a rule or principle.

Think of fever as a symptom, not as an illness: It is the body's response to infection. [APA]

He has two basic rules for healthy living: Eat sensibly and exercise strenuously at least three times a week. [APA and MLA]

A grammar checker will flag a word at the beginning of a sentence that should be capitalized, but it will not be able to determine whether a word following a colon should be capitalized.

(4) Capitalizing the first word of an abbreviated question

In a series of abbreviated questions, the first words of all the questions are capitalized when the intent is to draw attention to the questions. Otherwise, such questions begin with lowercase letters.

How do we distinguish the legal codes for families? For individuals? For genetic research?

Did you remember to include your application? your résumé? your recommendations?

(5) Capitalizing a brand name that begins with a lowercase letter

A brand name such as *eBay* or *iPod* that begins with a lowercase letter should be capitalized if it is the first word in a sentence. However, a better choice is to recast the sentence so that the brand name occurs later.

Ebay attracts many shoppers.

Many people like to shop on eBay.

43d Computer keys, menu items, and icon names

When referring to specific computer keys, menu items, and icon names, capitalize the first letter of each.

To find the thesaurus, press Shift and the function key F7.

Instead of choosing Copy from the Edit menu, you can press Ctrl+C.

For additional information, click on Resources.

43e　Unnecessary capitals

(1) Unnecessary capitalization of common nouns

The same noun can be either common or proper, depending on the context. A **proper noun** (21a(2)), also called a proper name, identifies a specific entity. A **common noun** (21a(2)), which is usually preceded by a word such as *the, a, an, this,* or *that,* is not capitalized.

> a speech course in theater and television [COMPARE: Speech 324: Theater and Television]

> a university, this high school [COMPARE: University of Michigan, Bolton High School]

(2) Overusing capitalization to signal emphasis

Occasionally, a common noun is capitalized for emphasis.

> Some politicians will do anything they can for Power.

If you use capitals for emphasis, do so sparingly; overuse will weaken the effect. For other ways to achieve emphasis, see chapter 32.

(3) Signaling emphasis online

For online writing in academic and professional contexts, capitalize as you normally do. Be careful not to capitalize whole words for emphasis because your reader may think that you are SHOUTING—the term used to indicate the rudeness of this practice.

Exercise 1

Write a sentence using each of the following words correctly.

1. president	5. east	9. republican
2. President	6. East	10. Republican
3. company	7. street	11. river
4. Company	8. Street	12. River

Exercise 2

Edit the capitalization errors in the following paragraph. Be prepared to explain any changes that you make.

[1]Diana taurasi (Her teammates call her dee) plays basketball for the Phoenix mercury. [2]She has all the skills she needs to be a Star Player: She can pass and shoot, as well as rebound, block, and steal. [3]While playing for the university of connecticut huskies, she won the Naismith award twice and ranked in the majority of the big east's statistical categories. [4]Shortly after the huskies won their third straight ncaa title, taurasi was drafted first overall by the Phoenix mercury. [5]In april of 2004, taurasi played on the u.s. national team against japan, and, in the Summer of 2004, she made her olympic debut in Athens.

44 Italics

Italics indicate that a word or a group of words is being used in a special way. For example, the use of italics can clear up the ambiguity in the following sentence:

The linguistics students discussed the word stress.

Does this sentence mean that the students discussed a particular word or that they discussed the correct pronunciation of words? By italicizing *stress,* the writer indicates that it was the word, not an accent pattern, that the students discussed.

The linguistics students discussed the word *stress.*

This chapter will help you use italics for

- the titles of separate works (44a),
- foreign words (44b),
- the names of legal cases (44c),
- the names of ships, submarines, aircraft, spacecraft, and satellites (44d),
- words, letters, or figures used as such or letters used in mathematical expressions (44e), and
- words receiving emphasis (44f).

Word-processing programs make it easy to use italics. In handwritten or typewritten documents, you can indicate italics by underlining.

Edward P. Jones's novel <u>The Known World</u> won a Pulitzer Prize.

Although the use of italics instead of underlining is widely accepted in business writing, conventions for academic writing vary. MLA recommends underlining, but APA and CMS prefer italics.

TECH SAVVY
Remember that in e-mail and on Web pages, an underlined word or phrase often indicates a hyperlink. If you are not able to format your e-mail or other electronic text with italics, use an underscore before and after words you would normally italicize.

Edward P. Jones's novel _The Known World_ won a Pulitzer Prize.

44a **Titles of works published or produced separately**

Italics indicate the title of a work published or produced as a whole rather than as part of a larger work. A newspaper, for example, is a separate work, but an editorial in a newspaper is not; thus, the title of the newspaper is italicized (or underlined), and the title of the editorial is enclosed in quotation marks (40b). These differing conventions help readers recognize the nature of a work and sometimes its relationship to another work.

Helen Keller's "Three Days to See" originally appeared in the *Atlantic Monthly*. [an essay in a magazine]

The titles of the following kinds of separate works are italicized:

Books	*The Hours*	*Unaccustomed Earth*
Magazines	*Wired*	*National Geographic*
Newspapers	*USA Today*	*Wall Street Journal*
Plays, films, videotapes	*Death of a Salesman*	*Akeelah and the Bee*
Television and radio shows	*American Idol*	*A Prairie Home Companion*
Recordings	*Kind of Blue*	*Great Verdi Overtures*
Works of art	*American Gothic*	*David*
Long poems	*Paradise Lost*	*The Divine Comedy*
Pamphlets	*Saving Energy*	*Tips for Gardeners*
Comic strips	*Peanuts*	*Doonesbury*

When an italicized title includes the title of a separate work within it, the embedded title is not italicized.

Modern Interpretations of Paradise Lost

If the italicized title includes the title of a short work within it, both titles are italicized, and the short work is also enclosed in quotation marks.

Willa Cather's "Paul's Case"

Titles should not be placed in italics or between quotation marks when they stand alone on a title page, a book cover, or a newspaper masthead. Likewise, neither italics nor quotation marks are necessary for titles of major historical documents, religious texts, or Web sites.

The Bill of Rights contains the first ten amendments to the U.S. Constitution.

The Bible, a sacred text just as the Koran or the Torah is, begins with the Book of Genesis.

Instructions for making a cane-and-reed basket can be found at Catherine Erdly's Web site, Basket Weaving.

According to MLA and CMS guidelines, an initial *the* in a newspaper or periodical title is not italicized. It is not capitalized either, unless it begins a sentence.

The story was published in the *New York Times.*

Also recommended is the omission of an article (*a, an,* or *the*) at the beginning of such a title when it would make a sentence awkward.

The report will appear in Thursday's ~~the~~ *Wall Street Journal.*

44b   Foreign words

Use italics to indicate foreign words.

Japan has a rich store of traditional folktales, *mukashibanashi,* "tales of long ago." —GARY SNYDER, *Back on the Fire*

A foreign word used frequently in a text should be italicized only once—at its first occurrence.

The Latin words used to classify plants and animals according to genus and species are italicized.

Homo sapiens　　*Rosa setigera*　　*Ixodes scapularis*

Countless words borrowed from other languages have become part of English and are therefore not italicized.

bayou (Choctaw)　　karate (Japanese)　　arroyo (Spanish)

If you are not sure whether a word has been accepted into English, look for it in a standard dictionary (34e).

44c　Legal cases

Italics identify the names of legal cases.

Miranda v. Arizona　　*Roe v. Wade*

The abbreviation *v.* (for "versus") may appear in either italic or nonitalic type, as long as the style is used consistently. Italics are also used for the shortened name of a well-known legal case.

According to the *Miranda* decision, suspects must be informed of their right to remain silent and their right to legal advice.

Italics are not used to refer to a case by other than its official name.

All the major networks covered the O. J. Simpson trial.

44d　Names of ships, submarines, aircraft, spacecraft, and satellites

Italicize the names of specific ships, submarines, aircraft, spacecraft, and satellites.

USS *Enterprise*　　USS *Hawkbill*　　*Enola Gay*　　*Atlantis*　　*Aqua*

The names of trains, the models of vehicles, and the trade names of aircraft are not italicized.

Orient Express　　Ford Mustang　　Boeing 747

44e Words, letters, or figures referred to as such and letters used in mathematical expressions

When you refer to a specific word, letter, or figure as itself, you should italicize it.

The word *love* is hard to define. [COMPARE: They were in love.]

The *b* in *bat* is not aspirated. [COMPARE: He earned a B+.]

The *2* on the sign has faded, and the *5* has disappeared. [COMPARE: She sent 250 cards.]

Statistical symbols and variables in algebraic expressions are also italicized.

The Pythagorean theorem is expressed as $a^2 + b^2 = c^2$.

44f Words receiving emphasis

Used sparingly, italics can signal readers to stress certain words.

These *are* the right files. [*Are* receives more stress than it normally would.]

Italics can also emphasize emotional content.

We have to go *now*. [The italicized word signals urgency.]

If overused, italics will lose their impact. Instead of italicizing words, substitute more specific words (chapter 35) or vary sentence structures (chapter 33).

Exercise 1

Identify all words that should be italicized in the following sentences. Explain why italics are necessary in each case.

1. Information about museum collections and exhibits can be found in art books, museum Web sites, and special sections of magazines and newspapers such as Smithsonian Magazine and the New York Times.

2. The Web site for the Metropolitan Museum of Art has pictures of Anthony Caro's sculpture Odalisque and Charles Demuth's painting The Figure 5 in Gold.

3. The title page of William Blake's Songs of Innocence is included in Masterpieces of the Metropolitan Museum of Art.

4. This book includes a photograph of a beautiful script used in the Koran; the script is known as the maghribi, or Western, style.

5. The large Tyrannosaurus rex discovered by Sue Hendrickson in South Dakota is on display at the Field Museum.

6. The International Museum of Cartoon Art provides information about the designers of such comic strips as Blondie, Peanuts, Mutt and Jeff, and Li'l Abner.

7. The Great Train Robbery, It Happened One Night, and Grand Illusion are in the collection at the Celeste Bartos Film Preservation Center.

8. In 1998, the Songwriters Hall of Fame honored John Williams, who has written music for such movies as Jaws, Star Wars, and E.T.

9. The Smithsonian Institution's National Air and Space Museum houses an impressive collection of aircraft and spacecraft, including Spirit of St. Louis and Gemini 4.

10. The digital collection listed on the Web site Experience Music Project includes music from the albums Fresh Cream and Bluesbreakers with Eric Clapton.

45

Abbreviations, Acronyms, and Numbers

Abbreviations, acronyms, and numbers facilitate easy recognition and effective communication in both academic papers and business documents. An **abbreviation** is a shortened version of a word or phrase: *assn.* (association), *dept.* (department), *et al.* (*et alii* or "and others"). An **acronym** is formed by combining the initial letters and/or syllables of a series of words: *AIDS* (**a**cquired **i**mmune **d**eficiency **s**yndrome), *sonar* (**so**und **na**vigation **r**anging). This chapter will help you learn

- how and when to abbreviate (45a–45d),
- when to explain an acronym (45e), and
- whether to spell out a number or use numerals (45f and 45g).

Abbreviated brand names create instant recognition for products or services.

45a Abbreviations with names

The abbreviations *Ms., Mr.,* and *Mrs.,* and *Dr.* appear before names, whether given as full names or only surnames.

Ms. Gretel Lopez   **Mrs.** Marcus

Mr. Julio Rodriguez   **Dr.** Redshaw

Civil or military titles should not be abbreviated in academic writing.

Senator Larry Johnson   Captain James   Professor Sue Li

Abbreviations such as *Jr., Sr.,* and *MD* appear after names.

Samuel Levy **Jr.**   Deborah Hvidsten, **MD**

Mark Ngo **Sr.**   Erika C. Schuerer, **PhD**

In the past, periods were customarily used in abbreviations for academic degrees, but MLA and CMS now recommend omitting periods from abbreviations such as *MA, PhD,* and *MD.* The convention calling for a comma to set off *Jr.* or *Sr.* is also changing; these abbreviations are increasingly considered part of the names they follow and are thus not set off by commas.

Note that when two designations are possible, only one should be used.

Dr. Carol Ballou OR Carol Ballou, **MD** [NOT Dr. Carol Ballou, MD]

Most abbreviations of plural nouns end in *-s* alone, without an apostrophe: *Drs.* Ballou and Hvidsten. Exceptions are made when adding *-s* would create a different abbreviation, such as for *Mr.* and *Mrs.*

45b Addresses in correspondence

The names of states and words such as *Street, Road, Company,* and *Corporation* are usually written out when they appear in a letter, including in the address at the top of the page. However, they are abbreviated when used in the address on an envelope.

Sentence   Derson Manufacturing Company is located on Madison Street in Watertown, Minnesota.

Address   Derson Manufacturing Co.
200 Madison St.
Watertown, MN 55388

When addressing correspondence within the United States, use the two-letter state abbreviations established by the U.S. Postal Service. (No period follows these abbreviations.) If you do not know an appropriate state abbreviation or zip code, you can find it on the Postal Service's Web site.

45c   Abbreviations in source documentation

MLA, APA, and CMS all provide lists of abbreviations for writers to use when citing research sources in bibliographies, footnotes, and endnotes. Common abbreviations include the following (not all citation styles accept all of these abbreviations).

Bibliographies and Notes

anon., Anon.	anonymous, Anonymous
biog.	biography, biographer, biographical
bull.	bulletin
c. or ca.	circa, about (for example, *c. 1920*)
col., cols.	column, columns
cont.	contents OR continues, continued
et al.	*et alii* ("and others")
fig.	figure
fwd.	foreword, foreword by
illus.	illustrated by, illustrator, illustration
inc., Inc.	including; incorporated, Incorporated
intl.	international
introd.	introduction, introduction by
ms., mss.	manuscript, manuscripts
natl.	national
n.d.	no date
n.p.	no page number

Bibliographies and Notes (*continued*)

no., nos.	number, numbers
p., pp.	page, pages
P, Pr.	Press
pref.	preface
pt., pts.	part, parts
trans. or tr.	translation, translated by
U, Univ.	University

Computer Terms

FTP	file transfer protocol
HTML	hypertext markup language
HTTP	hypertext transfer protocol
MB	megabyte
MOO	multiuser domain, object-oriented
URL	uniform resource locator

Divisions of Government

Cong.	Congress
dept.	department
div.	division
govt.	government
GPO	Government Printing Office
HR	House of Representatives

For abbreviations of Latin terms used in writing, see 45d(6).

45d | **Acceptable abbreviations in academic and professional writing**

Abbreviations are usually too informal for use in sentences, but some have become so familiar that they are considered acceptable substitutes for full words.

(1) Abbreviations for special purposes

The names of months, days of the week, and units of measurement are usually written out (not abbreviated) when they are included in sentences, as are words such as *Street* and *Corporation*.

> On a Tuesday in September, we drove ninety-nine miles to San Francisco, California, where we stayed in a hotel on Market Street.

Words such as *volume, chapter,* and *page* are abbreviated (*vol., ch.,* and *p.*) in bibliographies and in citations of research sources, but they are written out within sentences.

> I read the introductory chapter and the three final pages in the first volume of the committee's report.

(2) Clipped forms

A word shortened by common usage, a **clipped form,** does not end with a period. Some clipped forms—such as *rep* (for representative), *exec* (for executive), and *info* (for information)—are too informal for use in college writing. Others—such as *exam, lab,* and *math*—have become acceptable because they have been used so frequently that they no longer seem like shortened forms.

(3) Abbreviations for time periods and zones

> 82 BC [OR BCE] for before Christ [OR before the common era]
>
> AD 95 [OR 95 CE] for *anno Domini,* "in the year of our Lord" [OR the common era]
>
> 7:40 a.m. for *ante meridiem,* before noon
>
> 4:52 EST for Eastern Standard Time

Words designating units of time, such as *minute* and *month,* are written out when they appear in sentences. They can be abbreviated in tables or charts.

> sec.   min.   hr.   wk.   mo.   yr.

(4) The abbreviation for the United States (U.S. or US) as an adjective

> the U.S. Navy, the US economy
> [COMPARE: They moved to the United States in 1990.]

The abbreviation *U.S.* or *US* should be used only as an adjective in academic and professional writing. When using *United States* as a noun, spell it out. The choice of U.S. or US will depend on the discipline in which you are writing: MLA lists US as the preferred form, but APA uses U.S., and CMS accepts either form.

(5) Individuals known by their *initials*

   JFK   LBJ   E. B. White   B. B. King

In most cases, however, first and last names should be written out in full.

   Oprah Winfrey   Tiger Woods

(6) Some abbreviations for Latin expressions

Certain abbreviations for Latin expressions are common in academic writing.

cf. [compare]	et al. [and others]	i.e. [that is]
e.g. [for example]	etc. [and so forth]	vs. OR v. [versus]

45e   Acronyms

The ability to identify a particular acronym will vary from one audience to another. Some readers will know that NAFTA stands for the North American Free Trade Agreement; others may not. By spelling out acronyms the first time you use them, you are being courteous and clear. Introduce the acronym by placing it in parentheses after the group of words it stands for.

The Federal Emergency Management Administration (FEMA) was criticized by many after Hurricane Katrina.

MULTILINGUAL WRITERS

USING ARTICLES WITH ABBREVIATIONS, ACRONYMS, OR NUMBERS

When you use an abbreviation, an acronym, or a number, you sometimes need an indefinite article. Choose *a* or *an* based on the pronunciation of the initial sound of the abbreviation, acronym, or number: use *a* before a consonant sound and *an* before a vowel sound.

A picture of **a UN** delegation is on the front page of today's newspaper. [*UN* begins with a consonant sound.]

I have **an IBM** computer. [*IBM* begins with a vowel sound.]

The reporter interviewed **a NASA** engineer. [*NASA* begins with a consonant sound.]

My friend drives **a 1964** Mustang. [*1964* begins with a consonant sound.]

Exercise 1

Place a check mark next to those forms that are appropriate for use in the sentences of a college essay. Correct those that are not.

1. after 8 p.m.
2. 457 *anno Domini*
3. on St. Clair Ave.
4. two blocks from Water Street
5. in Aug.
6. in the second mo. of the yr.
7. in Calif.
8. at the UN
9. Ms. Lydia Snow
10. for a prof.

45f   General uses of numbers

Depending on their uses, numbers are treated in different ways. MLA and CMS recommend spelling out numbers from one through one hundred (*nine employees, ninety-one employees*). If one of these numbers is followed by a word such as *hundred, thousand,* or *million,* it may also be spelled out (*nine hundred years, ninety-one million years*). A numeral is used for any other number, unless it begins a sentence.

The register recorded 164 names.

APA advises spelling out only numbers below ten. All three of these style manuals recommend using words rather than numerals at the beginning of a sentence.

One hundred sixty-four names were recorded in the register.
[Notice that *and* is not used in numbers greater than one hundred.
NOT One hundred and sixty-four names . . . .]

When numbers or amounts refer to the same entities throughout a passage, numerals are used.

Only 5 of the 134 delegates attended the final meeting. The remaining 129 delegates will be informed by e-mail.

In scientific or technical writing, numerals are used before abbreviations of measurements (2 L, 30 cc).

45g Special uses of numbers

(1) Expressing specific times of day in either numerals or words
Numerals or words can be used to express times of day. They should be used consistently.

4 p.m. OR four o'clock in the afternoon

9:30 a.m. OR half-past nine in the morning OR nine-thirty in the morning [Notice the use of hyphens.]

(2) Using numerals and words for dates
In a text, months are written as words, years are written as numerals, and days and decades are written as either words or numerals. However, 9/11 is an acceptable alternative to September 11, 2001.

May 20, 1976 OR 20 May 1976 [NOT May 20th, 1976]

the fourth of December OR December 4

the fifties OR the 1950s

from 1999 to 2003 OR 1999–2003 [Use an en dash, not a hyphen, in number ranges.]

TECH SAVVY
To create an en dash, press Option and the hyphen key simultaneously.

MULTILINGUAL WRITERS

DIFFERENT WAYS OF WRITING DATES

Many cultures invert the numerals for the month and the day: *14/2/2009* or *14 February 2009*. In publications from the United States, the month generally precedes the day: *2/14/2009* or *February 14, 2009*.

(3) Using numerals in addresses
Numerals are commonly used in a street address and for a zip code.

25 Arrow Drive, Apartment 1, Columbia, MO 78209

OR, for an envelope, 25 Arrow Dr., Apt. 1, Columbia, MO 78209

(4) Using numerals for identification
A numeral may be used as part of a proper noun (**21a(2)**).

Channel 10   Edward III   Interstate 40   Room 311

(5) Referring to pages and divisions of books and plays
Numerals are used to designate pages and other divisions of books and plays.

page 15   chapter 8   part 2   in act 2, scene 1 OR in Act II, Scene I

(6) Expressing decimals and percentages numerically

Numerals are used to express decimals and percentages.

    a 2.5 average   12 percent   0.853 metric ton

(7) Using numerals for large fractional numbers

Numerals with decimal points can be used to express large fractional numbers.

    5.2 million inhabitants   1.6 billion years

(8) Different ways of writing monetary amounts

Monetary amounts should be spelled out if they occur infrequently in a piece of writing. Otherwise, numerals and symbols can be used.

two million dollars	$2,000,000
ninety-nine cents	99¢ OR $0.99

MULTILINGUAL WRITERS

COMMAS AND PERIODS WITH NUMERALS

Cultures differ in their use of the period and the comma with numerals. In American usage, a decimal point (period) indicates a number or part of a number that is smaller than one, and a comma divides large numbers into units of three digits.

    7.65 (seven and sixty-five   10,000
    one-hundredths)   (ten thousand)

In some other cultures, these usages of the decimal point and the comma are reversed.

    7,65 (seven and sixty-five   10.000
    one-hundredths)   (ten thousand)

Exercise 2

Edit the following sentences to correct the usage of abbreviations and numbers.

1. A Natl. Historic Landmark, Hoover Dam is located about 30 miles s.e. of Las. Vegas, Nev.

2. The dam is named after Herbert Hoover, the 31st pres. of the U.S.

3. It is administered by the U.S. Dept. of the Interior.

4. Built by the fed. gov. between nineteen thirty-three and 1935, this dam is still considered one of the greatest achievements in the history of civ. engineering.

5. Construction of the dam became possible after several states in the Southwest (namely, AZ, CA, CO, NV, NM, UT, and WY) agreed on a plan to share water from the river.

6. The concrete used in the dam would have built a highway 16 ft. wide, stretching all the way from San Francisco to NYC.

7. 3,500 men worked on the dam during an average month of construction; this work translated into a monthly payroll of $500,000.

8. Spanning the Colorado River, Hoover Dam created Lake Mead— a reservoir covering 247 sq. miles.

9. A popular tourist attraction, Hoover Dam was closed to the public after terrorists attacked the U.S. on 9/11/01.

10. Today, certain pts. of the dam remain closed to the public as part of the effort to improve U.S. security.

Glossary of Usage

The term *usage* refers to the ways words are used in specific contexts. As you know from speaking and writing every day, the words you choose depend on your audience and your purpose. For example, you might use *guys* when you are at lunch with your friends but choose *people, classmates, employees,* or another more formal or precise word when you are writing a report. By learning about usage in this glossary, you will increase your ability to use words effectively. Many of the entries are context-specific; others distinguish between words that sound or look similar.

The definitions and guidelines in this glossary will help you write clear and precise prose. Nonetheless, you should be aware that the idea of standard usage potentially carries with it the assumption that words not considered standard are inferior. Words labeled "nonstandard" are commonly condemned, even though they may be words some people have grown up hearing and using. A better way to discuss usage is to label what is conventional, or accepted practice, for a specific context. Thus, words commonly used in one context may not be appropriate in another. The following labels will help you choose appropriate words for your rhetorical situation.

Conventional	Words or phrases listed in dictionaries without special usage labels; generally considered appropriate in academic and professional writing.
Conversational	Words or phrases that dictionaries label *informal, slang,* or *colloquial;* although often used in informal speech and writing, not generally appropriate for formal writing assignments.
Unconventional	Words or phrases not generally considered appropriate in academic or professional writing and often labeled *nonstandard* in dictionaries; best avoided in formal contexts.

Agreement on usage occurs slowly, often after a period of debate. In this glossary, entries are marked with an asterisk (*) when new usages have been reported by dictionary editors but may not yet be accepted by everyone.

a lot of   *A lot of* is conversational for *many, much,* or *a great deal of:* They do not have ~~a lot of~~ much time. *A lot* is sometimes misspelled as *alot.*

a while, awhile   *A while* means "a period of time." It is often used with the prepositions *after, for,* and *in:* We rested for **a while.** *Awhile* means "a short time." It is not preceded by a preposition: We rested **awhile.**

accept, except   The verb *accept* means "to receive": I **accept** your apology. The verb *except* means "to exclude": The policy was to have everyone wait in line, but mothers and small children were **excepted.** The preposition *except* means "other than": All **except** Joe will attend the conference.

advice, advise   *Advice* is a noun: They asked their attorney for **advice.** *Advise* is a verb: The attorney **advised** us to save all relevant documents.

affect, effect   *Affect* is a verb that means "to influence": The lobbyist's pleas did not **affect** the politician's decision. The noun *effect* means "a result": The **effect** of his decision on the staff's morale was positive and long lasting. When used as a verb, *effect* means "to produce" or "to cause": The activists believed that they could **effect** real political change.

agree on, agree to, agree with   *Agree on* means "to be in accord with others about something": We **agreed on** a date for the conference. *Agree to* means "to accept something" or "to consent to do something": The customer **agreed to** our terms. The negotiators **agreed to** conclude talks by midnight. *Agree with* means "to share an opinion with someone" or "to approve of something": I **agree with** you on this issue. No one **agreed with** his position.

all ready, already   *All ready* means "completely prepared": The rooms are **all ready** for the conference. *Already* means "by or before the time specified": She has **already** taken her final exams.

* **all right**   *All right* means "acceptable": The students asked whether it was **all right** to use dictionaries during the exam. *Alright* is not yet a generally accepted spelling of *all right,* although it is becoming more common in journalistic writing.

all together, altogether   *All together* means "as a group": The cast reviewed the script **all together.** *Altogether* means "wholly, thoroughly": That game is **altogether** too difficult.

allude, elude   *Allude* means "to refer to indirectly": The professor **alluded** to a medieval text. *Elude* means "to evade" or "to escape from": For the moment, his name **eludes** me.

allusion, illusion An *allusion* is a casual or indirect reference: The **allusion** was to Shakespeare's *Twelfth Night*. An *illusion* is a false idea or an unreal image: His idea of college is an **illusion**.

alot See **a lot of**.

already See **all ready, already**.

alright See **all right**.

altogether See **all together, altogether**.

a.m., p.m. Use these abbreviations only with figures: The show will begin at 7:00 **p.m.** [COMPARE: The show will begin at seven *in the evening*.]

* **among, between** To follow traditional usage, use *among* with three or more entities (a group): The snorklers swam **among** the fish. Use *between* when referring to only two entities: The rivalry **between** the two teams is intense. Current dictionaries also note the possibility of using *between* to refer to more than two entities, especially when these entities are considered distinct: We have strengthened the lines of communication **between** the various departments.

amount of, number of Use *amount of* before nouns that cannot be counted: The **amount of** rain that fell last year was insufficient. Use *number of* with nouns that can be counted: The **number of** students attending college has increased.

and/or This combination denotes three options: one, the other, or both. These options can also be presented separately with *or:* The student's application should be signed by a parent **and/or** a teacher. The student's application should be signed by a parent, a teacher, **or** both.

* **angry at, angry with** Both *at* and *with* are commonly used after *angry,* although according to traditional guidelines, *with* should be used when a person is the cause of the anger: She was **angry with** me because I was late.

another, other, the other *Another* is followed by a singular noun: **another** book. *Other* is followed by a plural noun: **other** books. *The other* is followed by either a singular or a plural noun: **the other book, the other books.**

anymore, any more *Anymore* meaning "any longer" or "now" most frequently occurs in negative sentences: Sarah doesn't work here **anymore**. Its use in positive sentences is considered conversational; *now* is generally used instead: All he ever does ~~anymore~~ **now** is watch television. As two words, *any more* appears with *not* to mean "no more": We do not have **any more** time.

anyone, any one *Anyone* means "any person at all": We did not know **anyone**. *Any one* refers to one of a group: **Any one** of the options is better than the current situation.

* **anyplace, everyplace, someplace** These words are becoming increasingly common in academic writing. However, according to traditional usage rules, they should be replaced by *anywhere, everywhere,* and *somewhere*.

as   Conversational when used after such verbs as *know, say,* and *see*. Use *that, if,* or *whether* instead: I do not know ~~as~~ whether my application is complete. Also considered conversational is the use of *as* instead of *who, which,* or *that*: Many of the performers ~~as~~ who have appeared on our program will be giving a concert this evening.

as, because   The use of *as* to signal a cause may be vague; if it is, use *because* instead: ~~As~~ Because we were running out of gas, we turned around.

* **as, like**   According to traditional usage, *as* begins either a phrase or a clause; *like* begins only a phrase: My brother drives too fast, just ~~like~~ as my father did. Current dictionaries note the informal use of *like* to begin clauses, especially after verbs such as *look, feel,* and *sound*.

assure, ensure, insure   *Assure* means "to state with confidence, alleviating any doubt": The flight attendant **assured** us that our flight would arrive on time. *Ensure* and *insure* are usually interchangeable to mean "make certain," but only *insure* means "to protect against loss": The editor **ensured** [OR **insured**] that the reporter's facts were accurate. Physicians must **insure** themselves against malpractice suits.

awhile   See **a while, awhile**.

bad   Unconventional as an adverb; use *badly* instead. The team played **badly**. However, the adjective *bad* is used after sensory verbs such as *feel, look,* and *smell*: I feel **bad** that I forgot to return your book yesterday.

because   See **as, because**.

being as, being that   Unconventional; use *because* instead. ~~Being as~~ Because the road was closed, traffic was diverted to another route.

* **beside, besides**   According to traditional usage, these two words have different meanings. *Beside* means "next to": The president sat **beside** the prime minister. *Besides* means "in addition to" or "other than": She has written many articles **besides** those on political reform. Current dictionaries report that professional writers regularly use *beside* to convey this meaning, as long as there is no risk of ambiguity.

better, had better   *Better* is conversational. Use *had better* instead: We ~~better~~ had better finish the report by five o'clock.

between   See **among, between**.

* **bring, take**   Both words describe the same action but from different standpoints. *Bring* indicates movement toward the writer: She **brought** me some flowers. *Take* implies movement away from the writer: He **took** my overdue books to the library. Dictionaries report that this distinction is often blurred when the writer's position is ambiguous or irrelevant: He **brought** [OR **took**] her some flowers.

bunch   Conversational to refer to a group: A ~~bunch~~ group of students participated in the experiment.

* **can, may**   *Can* refers to ability, and *may* refers to permission: You **can** [are able to] drive seventy miles an hour, but you **may** not [are not permitted to] exceed the speed limit. Current dictionaries report that in contemporary usage *can* and *may* are used interchangeably to denote possibility or permission, although *may* is used more frequently in formal contexts.

can't hardly, can't scarcely   Unconventional. Use *can hardly* or *can scarcely:* The students **can't hardly** wait for summer vacation.

capital, capitol   *Capital* means either "a governing city" or "funds": The **capital** of Minnesota is St. Paul. An anonymous donor provided the **capital** for the project. As a modifier, *capital* means "chief" or "principal": This year's election is of **capital** importance. It may also refer to the death penalty: **Capital** punishment is legal in some states. A *capitol* is a statehouse; the *Capitol* is the U.S. congressional building in Washington, DC.

censor, censure, sensor   As a verb, *censor* means "to remove or suppress because of immoral or otherwise objectionable ideas": Do you think a ratings board should **censor** films? As a noun, *censor* refers to a person who is authorized to remove material considered objectionable: The **censor** recommended that the book be banned. The verb *censure* means "to blame or criticize"; the noun *censure* is an expression of disapproval or blame. The Senate **censured** Joseph McCarthy. He received a **censure** from the Senate. A *sensor* is a device that responds to a stimulus: The **sensor** detects changes in light.

center around   Conversational for "to center on" or "to revolve around": The discussion **centered ~~around~~ on** the public's response to tax reform initiatives.

cite, site, sight   *Cite* means "to mention": Be sure to **cite** your sources. *Site* is a location: The president visited the **site** for the new library. As a verb, *site* also means "to situate": The builder **sited** the factory near the freeway. *Sight* means "to see": The crew **sighted** land. *Sight* also refers to a view: What an incredible **sight**!

climactic, climatic   *Climactic* refers to a climax, or high point: The actors rehearsed the **climactic** scene. *Climatic* refers to the *climate:* Many environmentalists are worried about the recent **climatic** changes.

coarse, course   *Coarse* refers to roughness: The jacket was made of **coarse** linen. *Course* refers to a route: Our **course** to the island was indirect. *Course* may also refer to a plan of study: I want to take a **course** in nutrition.

compare to, compare with   *Compare to* means "to regard as similar," and *compare with* means "to examine for similarities and/or differences": She **compared** her mind **to** a dusty attic. The student **compared** the first draft **with** the second.

complement, complementary, compliment, complimentary   *Complement* means "to complete" or "to balance": Their personalities **complement** each other. They have **complementary** personalities. *Compliment* means "to express praise": The professor **complimented** the students on their first drafts. Her remarks were **complimentary.** *Complimentary* may also mean "provided free of charge": We received **complimentary** tickets.

* **compose, comprise**   *Compose* means "to make up": That collection **is composed** of medieval manuscripts. *Comprise* means "to consist of": The anthology **comprises** many famous essays. Dictionary editors have noted the increasing use of *comprise* in the passive voice to mean "to be composed of."

conscience, conscious, consciousness   *Conscience* means "the sense of right and wrong": He examined his **conscience** before deciding whether to join the protest. *Conscious* means "awake": After an hour, the patient was fully **conscious.** After an hour, the patient regained **consciousness.** *Conscious* may also mean "aware": We were **conscious** of the possible consequences.

continual, continually, continuous, continuously   *Continual* means "constantly recurring": **Continual** interruptions kept us from completing the project. Telephone calls **continually** interrupted us. *Continuous* means "uninterrupted": The job applicant had a record of ten years' **continuous** employment. The job applicant worked **continuously** from 2000 to 2009.

* **convince, persuade**   *Convince* means "to make someone believe something": His passionate speech **convinced** us that school reform was necessary. *Persuade* means "to motivate someone to act": She **persuaded** us to stop smoking. Dictionary editors note that many speakers now use *convince* as a synonym for *persuade.*

could of   *Of* is often mistaken for the sound of the unstressed *have:* They could ~~of~~ **have** [OR might **have,** should **have,** would **have**] gone home.

couldn't care less   *Couldn't care less* expresses complete lack of concern: She **couldn't care less** about her reputation. *Could care less* is considered unconventional in academic writing.

council, counsel   A *council* is an advisory or decision-making group: The student **council** supported the new regulations. A *counsel* is a legal adviser: The defense **counsel** conferred with the judge. As a verb, *counsel* means "to give advice": She **counsels** people with eating disorders.

criteria, criterion   *Criteria* is a plural noun meaning "a set of standards for judgment": The teachers explained the **criteria** for the assignment. The singular form is *criterion:* Their judgment was based on only one **criterion.**

* **data**   *Data* is the plural form of *datum,* which means "piece of information" or "fact": When the **data are** complete, we will know the true cost. However, current dictionaries also note that *data* is frequently used as a mass entity (like the word *furniture*), appearing with a singular verb.

desert, dessert   *Desert* can mean "a barren land": Gila monsters live in the **deserts** of the Southwest. As a verb, *desert* means "to leave": I thought my friends had **deserted** me. *Dessert* refers to something sweet eaten at the end of a meal: They ordered apple pie for **dessert.**

device, devise   *Device* is a noun: She invented a **device** that measures extremely small quantities of liquid. *Devise* is a verb: We **devised** a plan for work distribution.

dialogue   Many readers consider the use of *dialogue* as a verb to be an example of unnecessary jargon. Use *discuss* or *exchange views* instead: The committee members ~~dialogued about~~ discussed the issues.

differ from, differ with   *Differ from* means "to be different": A bull snake **differs from** a rattlesnake in a number of ways. *Differ with* means "to disagree": Senator Brown has **differed with** Senator Owen on several issues.

different from, different than   *Different from* is generally used with nouns, pronouns, noun phrases, and noun clauses: This school was **different from** most others. The school was **different from** what we had expected. *Different than* is used with adverbial clauses; *than* is the conjunction: We are no **different than** they are.

discreet, discrete   *Discreet* means "showing good judgment or self-restraint": His friends complained openly, but his comments were quite **discreet.** *Discrete* means "distinct": The participants in the study came from three **discrete** groups.

disinterested, uninterested   *Disinterested* means "impartial": A **disinterested** observer will give a fair opinion. *Uninterested* means "lacking interest": She was **uninterested** in the outcome of the game.

distinct, distinctive   *Distinct* means "easily distinguishable or perceived": Each proposal has **distinct** advantages. *Distinctive* means "characteristic" or "serving to distinguish": We studied the **distinctive** features of hawks.

* **due to**   Traditionally, *due to* was not synonymous with *because of:* ~~Due to~~ Because of holiday traffic, we arrived an hour late. However, dictionary editors now consider this usage of *due to* acceptable.

dyeing, dying   *Dyeing* comes from *dye,* meaning "to color something, usually by soaking it": As a sign of solidarity, the students are **dyeing** their shirts the same color. *Dying* refers to the loss of life: Because of the drought, the plants are **dying.**

effect   See **affect, effect.**

elicit, illicit   *Elicit* means "to draw forth": He is **eliciting** contributions for a new playground. *Illicit* means "unlawful": The newspaper reported their **illicit** mishandling of public funds.

elude   See **allude, elude.**

emigrate from, immigrate to   *Emigrate* means "to leave one's own country": My ancestors **emigrated from** Ireland. *Immigrate* means "to arrive in a different country to settle": The Ulster Scots **immigrated to** the southern United States.

eminent, imminent   *Eminent* means "distinguished": An **eminent** scholar in physics will be giving a public lecture tomorrow. *Imminent* means "about to happen": The merger of the two companies is **imminent.**

ensure   See **assure, ensure, insure.**

especially, specially   *Especially* emphasizes a characteristic or quality: Some people are **especially** sensitive to the sun. *Especially* also means "particularly": Wildflowers are abundant in this area, **especially** during May. *Specially* means "for a particular purpose": The classroom was **specially** designed for music students.

etc.   Abbreviation of *et cetera,* meaning "and others of the same kind." Use only within parentheses: Be sure to bring appropriate camping gear (tent, sleeping bag, mess kit, **etc.**). Because *and* is part of the meaning of *etc.,* avoid using the combination *and etc.*

eventually, ultimately   *Eventually* refers to some future time: She has made so many valuable contributions that I am sure she will **eventually** become the store supervisor. *Ultimately* refers to the final outcome after a series of events: The course was difficult but **ultimately** worthwhile.

everyday, every day   *Everyday* means "routine" or "ordinary": These are **everyday** problems. *Every day* means "each day": I read the newspaper **every day.**

everyone, every one   *Everyone* means "all": **Everyone** should attend. *Every one* refers to each person or item in a group: **Every one** of you should attend.

everyplace   See **anyplace, everyplace, someplace.**

except   See **accept, except.**

explicit, implicit   *Explicit* means "expressed clearly and directly": Given his **explicit** directions, we knew how to proceed. *Implicit* means "implied or expressed indirectly": I mistakenly understood his silence to be his **implicit** approval of the project.

farther, further   Generally, *farther* refers to geographic distance: We will have to drive **farther** tomorrow. *Further* means "more": If you need **further** assistance, please let me know.

* **feel**   Traditionally, *feel* was not synonymous with "think" or "believe": I ~~feel think~~ that more should be done to protect local habitat. Dictionary editors now consider this use of *feel* to be a standard alternative.

fewer, less   *Fewer* occurs before nouns that can be counted: **fewer** technicians, **fewer** pencils. *Less* occurs before nouns that cannot be counted: **less**

milk, **less** support. *Less than* may be used with measurements of time or distance: **less than** three months, **less than** twenty miles.

* **first, firstly; second, secondly** Many college instructors prefer the use of *first* and *second*. However, dictionary editors state that *firstly* and *secondly* are also well-established forms.

foreword, forward A *foreword* is an introduction: The **foreword** to the book provided useful background information. *Forward* refers to a frontward direction: To get a closer look, we moved **forward** slowly.

former, latter Used together, *former* refers to the first of two; *latter* to the second of two. John and Ian are both English. The **former** is from Manchester; the **latter** is from Birmingham.

further See **farther, further.**

get Considered conversational in many common expressions: The weather ~~got better~~ improved overnight. I did not know what he ~~was getting at~~ meant.

go, goes Unconventional for *say(s), respond(s),* and other similar words: My friends say I'm strange, and I ~~go,~~ reply, "You're right!"

good, well *Good* is an adjective, not an adverb: He pitched ~~good~~ well last night. *Good* in the sense of "in good health" may be used interchangeably with *well:* I feel **good** [OR **well**] this morning.

had better See **better, had better.**

half A *half a* or *a half an* is unconventional; use *half a/an* or *a half:* You should be able to complete the questionnaire in **a half ~~an~~** hour.

hanged, hung *Hanged* means "put to death by hanging": The prisoner was **hanged** at dawn. For all other meanings, use *hung:* He **hung** the picture above his desk.

hardly See **can't hardly, can't scarcely.**

has got, have got Conversational; omit *got:* I **have ~~got~~** a meeting tomorrow.

he/she, his/her As a solution to the problem of sexist language, these combinations are not universally accepted. Consider using *he or she* and *his or her.* See **34d.**

herself, himself, myself, yourself Unconventional as subjects in a sentence. Joe and ~~myself~~ I will lead the discussion. See **26a(4).**

hopefully Conversational to mean "I hope": ~~Hopefully,~~ I hope the game will not be canceled.

hung See **hanged, hung.**

i.e. Abbreviation of *id est,* meaning "that is." Use only within parentheses: All participants in the study ran the same distance (**i.e.,** six kilometers). Otherwise, replace *i.e.* with the English equivalent, *that is:* Assistance was offered to those who would have difficulty boarding, ~~i.e.,~~ that is, the elderly, the disabled, and parents with small children. Do not confuse *i.e.* with *e.g.*, meaning "for example."

illicit See **elicit, illicit.**

illusion See **allusion, illusion.**

immigrate See **emigrate from, immigrate to.**

imminent See **eminent, imminent.**

* **impact** Though *impact* is commonly used as a verb in business writing, many college teachers still use it as a noun only: The new tax ~~impacts~~ affects everyone.

implicit See **explicit, implicit.**

imply, infer *Imply* means "suggest without actually stating": Though he never mentioned the statistics, he **implied** that they were questionable. *Infer* means "draw a conclusion based on evidence": Given the tone of his voice, I **inferred** that he found the work substandard.

in regards to Unconventional; see **regard, regarding, regards.**

inside of, outside of Drop *of* when unnecessary: Security guards stood **outside ~~of~~** the front door.

insure See **assure, ensure, insure.**

irregardless Unconventional; use *regardless* instead.

its, it's *Its* is a possessive form: The committee forwarded **its** recommendation. *It's* is a contraction of *it is*: **It's** a beautiful day.

-ize Some readers object to using this ending to create new verbs: *enronize.* Some of these new verbs, however, have already entered into common usage: *computerize.*

kind of a, sort of a The word *a* is unnecessary: This **kind of ~~a~~** book sells well. *Kind of* and *sort of* are not conventionally used to mean "somewhat": The report was ~~kind of~~ somewhat difficult to read.

later, latter *Later* means "after a specific time" or "a time after now": The concert ended **later** than we had expected. *Latter* refers to the second of two items: Of the two versions described, I prefer the **latter.**

lay, lie *Lay* (*laid, laying*) means "put" or "place": He **laid** the book aside. *Lie* (*lay, lain, lying*) means "rest" or "recline": I had just **lain** down when the alarm went off. *Lay* takes an object (to lay something), while *lie* does not. These verbs may be confused because the present tense of *lay* and the past tense of *lie* are spelled the same way.

lead, led As a noun, *lead* means "a kind of metal": The paint had **lead** in it. As a verb, *lead* means "to conduct": A guide will **lead** a tour of the ruins. *Led* is the past tense of the verb *lead:* He **led** the country from 1949 to 1960.

less, less than See **fewer, less.**

lie See **lay, lie.**

like See **as, like.**

literally Conversational when used to emphasize the meaning of another word: I was ~~literally~~ nearly frozen after I finished shoveling the sidewalk. *Literally* is conventionally used to indicate that an expression is not being used figuratively: My friend **literally** climbs the walls after work; his fellow rock climbers join him at the local gym.

lose, loose *Lose* is a verb: She does not **lose** her patience often. *Loose* is chiefly used as an adjective: A few of the tiles are **loose.**

lots, lots of Conversational for *many* or *much*: He has ~~lots of~~ many friends. We have ~~lots~~ much to do before the end of the quarter.

mankind Considered sexist because it excludes women: All ~~mankind~~ humanity will benefit from this new discovery.

many, much *Many* is used with nouns that can be counted: **many** stores, too **many** assignments. *Much* is used with nouns that cannot be counted: **much** courage, not **much** time.

may See **can, may.**

may of, might of See **could of.**

maybe, may be *Maybe* is an adverb: **Maybe** the negotiators will succeed this time. *May* and *be* are verbs: The rumor **may be** true.

* **media, medium** According to traditional definitions, *media* is a plural word: The **media** have sometimes created the news in addition to reporting it. The singular form is *medium:* The newspaper is one **medium** that people seem to trust. Dictionary editors note the frequent use of *media* as a collective noun taking a singular verb, but this usage is still considered conversational.

might could Conversational for "might be able to": The director **might** ~~could~~ be able to review your application next week.

most Unconventional to mean "almost": We watch the news ~~most~~ almost every day.

much See **many, much.**

myself See **herself, himself, myself, yourself.**

neither . . . or *Nor,* not *or,* follows *neither:* The book is **neither** as funny ~~or~~ nor as original as critics have reported.

not . . . no/none/nothing The use of multiple negative words is unconventional: I did **not** want ~~nothing~~ anything else. Multiple negation may be used for special effect (**25e**).

nothing like, nowhere near Unconventional; use *not nearly* instead: Her new book is ~~nowhere near~~ not nearly as mysterious as her previous novel.

number of When the expression *a number of* is used, the reference is plural: **A number of** positions **are** open. When *the number of* is used, the reference is singular: **The number of** possibilities **is** limited. See also **amount of, number of.**

off of   Conversational; omit *of:* He walked **off of** the field.

on account of   Conversational; use *because of:* The singer canceled her engagement ~~on account of~~ **because of** a sore throat.

on the other hand   Use *however* instead or make sure that the sentence or independent clause beginning with this transitional phrase is preceded by one starting with *on the one hand.*

other   See **another, other, the other.**

passed, past   *Passed* is the past tense of the verb *pass:* Deb **passed** the other runners right before the finish line. *Past* means "beyond a time or location": We walked **past** the high school.

per   In ordinary contexts, use *a* or *an:* You should drink at least six glasses of water ~~per~~ a day.

percent, percentage   *Percent* (also spelled *per cent*) is used with a specific number: **Sixty percent** of the students attended the ceremony. *Percentage* refers to an unspecified portion: The **percentage** of high school graduates attending college has increased in recent years.

perspective, prospective   *Perspective* means "point of view": We discussed the issue from various **perspectives.** *Prospective* means "likely to become": **Prospective** journalists interviewed the editor in chief.

persuade   See **convince, persuade.**

phenomena, phenomenon   *Phenomena* is the plural form of *phenomenon:* Natural **phenomena** were given scientific explanations.

plus   *Plus* joins nouns or noun phrases to make a sentence seem like an equation: Her endless curiosity **plus** her boundless energy makes her the perfect camp counselor. Note that a singular form of the verb is required (e.g., *makes*). *Plus* is not used to join clauses: I telephoned ~~plus~~ **and** I sent flowers.

p.m.   See **a.m., p.m.**

precede, proceed   To *precede* is to "go ahead of": A moment of silence **preceded** the applause. To *proceed* is to "go forward": After stopping for a short rest, we **proceeded** to our destination.

prejudice, prejudiced   *Prejudice* is a noun: They were unaware of their **prejudice.** *Prejudiced* is an adjective: She accused me of being **prejudiced.**

pretty   *Pretty* means "attractive," not "rather" or "fairly": We were ~~pretty~~ **fairly** tired after cooking all day.

principal, principle   As a noun, *principal* means "chief official": The **principal** greeted the students every day. It also means "capital": The loan's **principal** was still quite high. As an adjective, *principal* means "main":

Tourism is the country's **principal** source of income. The noun *principle* refers to a rule, standard, or belief: She explained the three **principles** supporting the theory.

proceed   See **precede, proceed.**

prospective   See **perspective, prospective.**

quotation, quote   In academic writing, *quotation,* rather than *quote,* refers to a repeated or copied sentence or passage: She began her speech with a ~~quote~~ quotation from *Othello. Quote* expresses an action: My friend sometimes **quotes** lines from television commercials.

raise, rise   *Raise (raised, raising)* means "to lift or cause to move upward, to bring up or increase": Retailers **raised** prices. *Rise (rose, risen, rising)* means "to get up" or "to ascend": The cost of living **rose** sharply. *Raise* takes an object (to **raise** something); *rise* does not.

real, really   *Really* rather than *real* is used to mean "very": He is from a ~~real~~ really small town. To ensure this word's effectiveness, use it sparingly.

* **reason why**   Traditionally, this combination was considered redundant: No one explained **the reason ~~why~~** the negotiations failed. [OR No one explained ~~the reason~~ **why** the negotiations failed.] However, dictionary editors report its use by highly regarded writers.

regard, regarding, regards   These forms are used in the following expressions: *in regard to, with regard to, as regards,* and *regarding* [NOT *in regards to, with regards to,* or *as regarding*].

* **relation, relationship**   According to traditional definitions, *relation* is used to link abstractions: We studied the **relation** between language and social change. *Relationship* is used to link people: The **relationship** between the two friends grew strong. However, dictionary editors now label as standard the use of *relationship* to connect abstractions.

respectfully, respectively   *Respectfully* means "showing respect": The children learned to treat one another **respectfully.** *Respectively* means "in the order designated": We discussed the issue with the chair, the dean, and the provost, **respectively.**

rise   See **raise, rise.**

sensor   See **censor, censure, sensor.**

sensual, sensuous   *Sensual* refers to gratification of the physical senses, often those associated with sexual pleasure: Frequently found in this music are **sensual** dance rhythms. *Sensuous* refers to gratification of the senses in response to art, music, nature, and so on: **Sensuous** landscape paintings lined the walls of the gallery.

shall, will   Traditionally, *shall* was used with *I* or *we* to express future tense, and *will* was used with the other personal pronouns, but *shall* has almost disappeared in contemporary American English. *Shall* is still used in legal writing to indicate an obligation.

should of   See **could of.**

sight   See **cite, site, sight.**

sit, set   *Sit* means "to be seated": Jonathan **sat** in the front row. *Set* means "to place something": The research assistant **set** the chemicals on the counter. *Set* takes an object (to **set** something); *sit* does not.

site   See **cite, site, sight.**

so   *So* intensifies another word when it is used with *that:* He was **so** nervous **that** he had trouble sleeping. Instead of using *so* alone, find a precise modifier: She was ~~so~~ intensely focused on her career. See **28f.**

someplace   See **anyplace, everyplace, someplace.**

sometime, sometimes, some time   *Sometime* means "at an unspecified time": They will meet **sometime** next month. *Sometimes* means "at times": **Sometimes** laws are unfair. *Some time* means "a span of time": They agreed to allow **some time** to pass before voting on the measure.

sort of a   See **kind of a, sort of a.**

specially   See **especially, specially.**

stationary, stationery   *Stationary* means "in a fixed position": Traffic was **stationary** for an hour. *Stationery* means "writing paper and envelopes": The director ordered new department **stationery.**

supposed to, used to   Be sure to include the frequently unsounded *d* at the end of the verb form: We are **supposed to** leave at 9:30 a.m. We **used to** leave earlier.

take   See **bring, take.**

than, then   *Than* is used in comparisons: The tape recorder is smaller **than** the radio. *Then* refers to a time sequence: Go straight ahead for three blocks; **then** turn left.

* **that, which**   *Which* occurs in nonessential (nonrestrictive) clauses: Myanmar, **which** borders Thailand, was formerly called Burma. Both *that* and *which* occur in essential (restrictive) clauses, although traditionally only *that* was considered acceptable: I am looking for an atlas **that** [OR **which**] includes demographic information. (For more information on essential and nonessential clauses, see **37d** and **37g.**)

* **that, which, who**   In essential (restrictive) clauses, *who* and *that* refer to people. We want to hire someone **who** [OR **that**] has had experience programming. Traditionally, only *who* was used to refer to people. *That,* as well as *which,* refers to things: He proposed a design **that** [OR **which**] will take advantage of solar energy.

their, there, they're   *Their* is the possessive form of *they:* They will give **their** presentation tomorrow. *There* refers to location: I lived **there** for six years. *There* is also used as an expletive (see **36a(3)**): **There** is no explanation for the phenomenon. *They're* is a contraction of *they are*: **They're** leaving in the morning.

theirself, theirselves   Unconventional; use *themselves.* The students finished the project by ~~theirself~~ themselves.

then   See **than, then.**

thru   *Through* is preferred in academic and professional writing: We drove ~~thru~~ through the whole state of South Dakota in one day.

thusly   Unconventional; use *thus, in this way,* or *as follows* instead: He accompanied his father on archeological digs and ~~thusly~~ discovered his interest in ancient cultures.

time period   Readers are likely to consider this combination redundant; use one word or the other, but not both: During this ~~time~~ period, the economy was strong.

to, too, two   *To* is an infinitive marker: She wanted **to** become an actress. *To* is also used as a preposition, usually indicating direction: They walked **to** the memorial. *Too* means either "also" or "excessively": I voted for her **too.** They are **too** busy this year. *Two* is a number: She studied abroad for **two** years.

toward, towards   Although both are acceptable, *toward* is preferred in American English.

try and   Conversational for *try to:* The staff will **try** ~~and~~ to finish the project by Friday.

ultimately   See **eventually, ultimately.**

uninterested   See **disinterested, uninterested.**

* **unique**   Traditionally, *unique* meant "one of a kind" and thus was not preceded by a qualifier such as *more, most, quite,* or *very:* Her prose style is ~~quite~~ unique. However, dictionary editors note that *unique* is also widely used to mean "extraordinary."

use, utilize   In most contexts, *use* is preferred to *utilize:* We ~~utilized~~ used a special dye in the experiment. However, *utilize* may suggest an effort to employ something for a purpose: We discussed how to **utilize** the resources we had been given.

used to   See **supposed to, used to.**

very   To ensure this word's effectiveness, use it sparingly. Whenever possible, choose a stronger word: She was ~~very satisfied~~ delighted with her new digital camera.

ways   Conversational when referring to distance; use *way* instead: It's a long ~~ways~~ way from home.

well   See **good, well.**

where   Conversational for *that:* I noticed ~~where~~ that she had been elected.

where . . . at, where . . . to   Conversational; omit *at* and *to:* **Where** is the library ~~at?~~ **Where** are you moving ~~to?~~

which   See **that, which** and **that, which, who.**

* **who, whom**   *Who* is used as the subject or subject complement in a clause: We have decided to hire Marian Wright, ~~whom~~ who I believe is currently finishing her degree in business administration. [*Who* is the subject in *who is currently finishing her degree in business administration.*] See also **that, which, who.** *Whom* is used as an object: Jeff Kruger, ~~who~~ whom we hired in 2007, is now our top sales representative. [*Whom* is the object in *whom we hired.*] Dictionary editors note that in conversation *who* is commonly used as an object as long as it does not follow a preposition. See **26b(5).**

whose, who's   *Whose* is a possessive form: **Whose** book is this? The book was written by a young Mexican-American woman **whose** family still lives in Chiapas. *Who's* is the contraction of *who is:* **Who's** going to run in the election? See **26b(3).**

will   See **shall, will.**

with regards to   Unconventional; see **regard, regarding, regards.**

would of   See **could of.**

your, you're   *Your* is a possessive form: Let's meet in **your** office. *You're* is a contraction of *you are:* **You're** gaining strength.

yourself   See **herself, himself, myself, yourself.**

Glossary of Terms

This glossary provides brief definitions of frequently used terms. Consult the index for references to terms not listed here.

absolute phrase   A sentencelike structure containing a subject and its modifiers. Unlike a sentence, an absolute phrase has no verb marked for person, number, or tense: *The ceremony finally over,* the graduates tossed their mortarboards in the air. See **22a(6)**.

acronym   A word formed by combining the initial letters or syllables of a series of words and pronounced as a word rather than as a series of letters: *NATO* for North Atlantic Treaty Organization. See **45e**.

active voice   See **voice.**

adjectival clause   A dependent clause, also called a **relative clause,** that modifies a noun or a pronoun. See **22b(2)**.

adjectival phrase   A phrase that modifies a noun or a pronoun.

adjective   A word that modifies a noun or a pronoun. Adjectives typically end in suffixes such as *-al, -able, -ant, -ative, -ic, -ish, -less, -ous,* and *-y.* See **21a(4)** and **25a. Coordinate adjectives** are two or more adjectives modifying the same noun and separated by a comma: a *brisk, cold* walk. See **37c(2)**.

adverb   A word that modifies a verb, a verbal, an adjective, or another adverb. Adverbs commonly end in *-ly.* Some adverbs modify entire sentences: *Perhaps* the meeting could be postponed. See **21a(5)** and **25a.**

adverbial clause   A dependent clause that modifies a verb, an adjective, or an adverb. See **22b(2)**.

alt tags   Descriptive lines of text for each visual image in an electronic document. Because these lines can be read by screen-reading software, they can assist visually impaired users. See **6d(3)**.

antecedent   A word or group of words referred to by a pronoun. See **21a(3)** and **26c.**

appositive   A pronoun, noun, or noun phrase that identifies, describes, or explains an adjacent pronoun, noun, or noun phrase. See **22a(5)** and **26b(4)**.

article   A word used to signal a noun. *The* is a definite article; *a* and *an* are indefinite articles. See **21a(4)**.

asynchronous forum   Online means of communication in which a period of time elapses between the sending and the receiving of a message. Internet newsgroups and electronic mailing lists are examples of asynchronous discussion groups. See **6b(1)**. COMPARE: **synchronous forum.**

attributive tag   Short phrase that identifies the source of a quotation: *according to Jones, Jones claims.* See **11d**.

auxiliary verb, auxiliary   A verb that combines with a main verb. *Be, do,* and *have* are auxiliary verbs when they are used with main verbs. Also called **helping verbs. Modal auxiliaries** include *could, should,* and *may* and are used for such purposes as expressing doubt or obligation and making a request. See **21a(1)** and **27a(4)**.

Boolean operators   See **logical operators.**

bulletin board   See **newsgroup.**

case   The form of a noun or pronoun that indicates the relationship of the noun or pronoun to other words in a sentence. Nouns and pronouns can be subjects or subject complements **(subjective case)**, objects **(objective case)**, or markers of possession and other relations **(possessive case)**. See **26b**.

claim   A statement that a writer wants readers to accept; also called a **proposition.** See **8d**.

clause   A sequence of related words forming an independent unit **(independent clause,** or **main clause)** or an embedded unit **(dependent clause** used as an adverb, adjective, or noun). A clause has both a subject and a predicate. See **22b**.

cliché   An expression that has lost its power to interest readers because of overuse. See **35b**.

clipped form   A word that is a shortened form of another word: *bike* for *bicycle.* See **45d(2)**.

collective noun   A noun that refers to a group: *team, faculty, committee.* See **21a(2)**.

collocation   Common word combination such as *add to, adept at,* or *admiration for.* See **35c**.

colloquial   A label for any word or phrase that is characteristic of informal speech. *Kid* is colloquial; *child* is used in formal contexts. See **34c(2)**.

common noun   A noun referring to any or all members of a class or group (*woman, city, holiday*) rather than to specific members (*Susan, Reno, New Year's Day*). COMPARE: **proper noun.** See **21a(2)**.

complement   A word or words used to complete the meaning of a verb. A **subject complement** is a word or phrase that follows a linking verb and categorizes or describes the subject. An **object complement** is a word or phrase that categorizes or describes a direct object when it follows such verbs as *make, paint, elect,* and *consider.* See **21c.**

complete predicate   See **predicate.**

complete subject   See **subject.**

complex sentence   A sentence containing one independent clause and at least one dependent clause. See **22d(3).**

compound-complex sentence   A sentence containing at least two independent clauses and one or more dependent clauses. See **22d(4).**

compound predicate   Predicate that has two parts joined by a connecting word such as *and, or,* or *but;* each part contains a verb: Clara Barton *nursed the injured during the Civil War* and *later founded the American Red Cross.* See **21b.**

compound sentence   A sentence containing at least two independent clauses and no dependent clauses. See **22d(2).**

compound subject   Two subjects joined by a connecting word such as *and, or,* or *but:* Students and *faculty* are discussing the issue of grade inflation. See **21b.**

compound word   Two or more words functioning as a single word: *ice cream, double-check.* See **42f(1).**

conditional clause   An adverbial clause (**22b(2)**), usually beginning with *if,* that expresses a condition: *If it rains,* the outdoor concert will be postponed.

conjunction   A word used to connect other words, phrases, clauses, or sentences. **Coordinating conjunctions** (*and, but, or, nor, for, so,* and *yet*) connect and relate words and word groups of equal grammatical rank. See **21a(7)** and **22c(1).** A **subordinating conjunction** such as *although, if,* or *when* begins a dependent clause and connects it to an independent clause. See **21a(7)** and **22c(3).** COMPARE: **conjunctive adverb.**

conjunctive adverb   A word such as *however* or *thus* that joins one independent clause to another. See **22c(4).** COMPARE: **conjunction.**

convention, conventional   Refers to language or behavior that follows the customs of a community such as the academic, medical, or business community.

coordinate adjective   See **adjective.**

coordinating conjunction   See **conjunction.**

coordination   The use of grammatically equivalent constructions to link or balance ideas. See chapter **30.**

correlative conjunctions, correlatives   Two-part connecting words such as *either . . . or* and *not only . . . but also.* See **21a(7)** and **22c(2).**

count nouns   Nouns naming things that can be counted (*word, student, remark*). See **21a(2)**. COMPARE: **noncount nouns.**

dangling modifier   A word or phrase that does not clearly modify another word or word group. See **25c(4)**. COMPARE: **misplaced modifier.**

dangling participial phrase   A verbal phrase that does not clearly modify another word or word group.

deductive reasoning   A form of logical reasoning in which a conclusion is formed after relating a specific fact (minor premise) to a generalization (major premise). See **8h(2)**. COMPARE: **inductive reasoning.**

demonstratives   Four words (*this, that, these,* and *those*) that distinguish one individual, thing, event, or idea from another. Demonstratives may occur with or without nouns: *This* [demonstrative determiner] *law* will go into effect in two years. *This* [demonstrative pronoun] will go into effect in two years.

dependent clause   See **clause.**

determiner   A word that signals the approach of a noun. A determiner may be an article, a demonstrative, a possessive, or a quantifier: *a reason, this reason, his reason, three reasons.*

direct address   See **vocative.**

direct object   See **object.**

direct quotation   See **quotation.**

ellipsis points   Three spaced periods that indicate either a pause or the omission of material from a direct quotation. See **41h.**

elliptical clause   A clause missing one or more words that are assumed to be understood. See **22b(2).**

essential element   A word or word group that modifies another word or word group, providing information that is essential for identification. Essential elements are not set off by commas, parentheses, or dashes: The woman *who witnessed the accident* was called to testify. Also called a **restrictive element.** COMPARE: **nonessential element.** See **22b(2)** and **37d.**

ethos   One of the three classical appeals; the use of language to demonstrate the writer's trustworthy character, good intentions, and substantial knowledge of a subject. Also called an **ethical appeal.** See **8f(1).** See also **logos** and **pathos.**

exigence   The circumstance compelling one to write. See **1b.**

expletive   A word signaling a structural change in a sentence, usually used so that new or important information is given at the end of the sentence: *There were over four thousand runners in the marathon.* See **21b(1).**

faulty predication   A sentence error in which the predicate does not logically belong with the given subject. See **28d(2).**

figurative language   The use of words in an imaginative rather than in a literal sense. See 35a(4).

first person   See **person.**

flaming   Heated, confrontational exchanges via e-mail. See 6c.

gender   The grammatical label that distinguishes nouns or pronouns as masculine, feminine, or neuter. In English, grammatical gender usually corresponds to natural gender. Gender also describes how people see themselves, or are seen by others, as either male or female. See 26c(2) and 34d(1).

generic noun   See **common noun.**

genre   A literary category, such as drama or poetry, identified by its own conventions. See 12a.

gerund   A verbal that ends in *-ing* and functions as a noun: *Snowboarding* is a popular winter sport. See 22a(3).

gerund phrase   A verbal phrase that employs the *-ing* form of a verb and functions as a noun: Some students prefer *studying in the library.* See 22a(3).

helping verb   See **auxiliary verb.**

homophones   Words that have the same sound and sometimes the same spelling but differ in meaning: *their, there,* and *they're* or *capital* meaning "funds" and *capital* meaning "the top of a pillar." See 42c.

idiom   An expression whose meaning often cannot be derived from its elements. *Burning the midnight oil* means "staying up late studying." See 35c.

imperative mood   See **mood.**

indefinite article   See **article.**

indefinite pronoun   A pronoun such as *everyone* or *anything* that does not refer to a specific individual, object, event, and so on. See 26c(1).

independent clause   See **clause.**

indicative mood   See **mood.**

indirect object   See **object.**

indirect question   A sentence that includes an embedded question, punctuated with a period instead of a question mark: My friends asked me *why I left the party early.* See 41a(1).

indirect quotation   See **quotation.**

inductive reasoning   The reasoning process that begins with facts or observations and moves to general principles that account for those facts or observations. See 8h(1). COMPARE: **deductive reasoning.**

infinitive   A verbal that consists of the base form of the verb, usually preceded by the infinitive marker *to.* An infinitive is used chiefly as a noun, less frequently as an adjective or adverb: My father likes *to golf.* See 22a(3) and 27b(6).

infinitive phrase   A verbal phrase that contains the infinitive form of a verb: They volunteered *to work at the local hospital.* See **22a(3)**.

inflection   A change in the form of a word that indicates a grammatical feature such as number, person, tense, or degree. For example, *-ed* added to a verb indicates the past tense, and *-er* indicates the comparative degree of an adjective or adverb.

intensifier   See **qualifier**.

intensive pronoun   See **reflexive pronoun**.

interjection   A word expressing a simple exclamation: *Hey! Oops!* When used in sentences, mild interjections are set off by commas. See **21a(8)**.

intransitive verb   A verb that does not take an object: Everyone *laughed.* See **21d**. COMPARE: **transitive verb.**

invention   Using strategies to generate ideas for writing.

inversion   A change in the usual subject-verb order of a sentence: *Are you* ready? See **21d**.

keywords   Specific words used with a search tool (such as Google) to find information. See **9b(1)**.

linking verb   A verb that relates a subject to a subject complement. Examples of linking verbs are *be, become, seem, appear, feel, look, taste, smell,* and *sound.* See **21a(1)** and **27d(1)**.

listserv   An online discussion forum consisting of a list of subscribers who share information about a specific subject by sending e-mail messages that are automatically distributed to all the other subscribers. See **6b(1)**.

logical operators   Words used to broaden or narrow electronic database searches. These include *or, and, not,* and *near.* Also called **Boolean operators.** See **9b(1)**.

logos   One of the three classical appeals; the use of language to show clear reasoning. Also called a **logical appeal.** See **8f(1)**. See also **ethos** and **pathos.**

lurk   To observe how users in a given online community write and conduct themselves in order to learn the conventions before joining their discussion. See **6b(1)**.

major premise.   See **premise.**

main clause   Also called **independent clause.** See **clause.**

minor premise.   See **premise.**

misplaced modifier   A descriptive or qualifying word or phrase placed in a position that confuses the reader: I read about a wildfire that was out of control *in yesterday's paper.* [The modifier belongs after *read.*] See **25c(4)**.

mixed construction   A confusing sentence that is the result of an unintentional shift from one grammatical pattern to another: When police appeared who were supposed to calm the crowds showed up, most people had already gone home. [The sentence should be recast with either *appeared* or *showed up,* not with both.] See **28d(1)**.

mixed metaphor   A construction that includes parts of two or more unrelated metaphors: Her *fiery* personality *dampened* our hopes of a compromise. See **28c**.

modal auxiliary   See **auxiliary verb.**

modifier   A word or word group that describes, limits, or qualifies another. See chapter **25**.

mood   A set of verb forms or inflections used to indicate how a speaker or writer regards an assertion: as a fact or opinion (**indicative mood**); as a command or instruction (**imperative mood**); or as a wish, hypothesis, request, or condition contrary to fact (**subjunctive mood**). See **27e**.

netiquette   Word formed from *Internet* and *etiquette* to name a set of guidelines for writing e-mail messages and listserv postings and for online behavior in general. See **6c**.

newsgroup   An online discussion group that is accessible to anyone and allows users to post messages related to a specific topic (or thread). Messages are kept on a server, organized by topic so that other users can search for, read, and respond to whatever has been discussed by the group. Also called a **bulletin board.** See **6b(1)**.

nominalization   Formation of a noun by adding a suffix to a verb or an adjective: *require, requirement; sad, sadness.*

nominative case   Also called **subjective case.** See **case.**

noncount nouns   Nouns naming things that cannot be counted (*architecture, water*). See **21a(2)**. COMPARE: **count nouns.**

nonessential element   A word or word group that modifies another word or word group but does not provide information essential for identification. Nonessential elements are set off by commas, parentheses, or dashes: Carol Murphy, *president of the university,* plans to meet with alumni representatives. Also called a **nonrestrictive element.** See **22b(2)** and **37d**. COMPARE: **essential element.**

nonrestrictive element   See **nonessential element.**

nonstandard, nonstandardized   Refers to speech forms that are not considered conventional in many academic and professional settings. See the Glossary of Usage.

noun   A word that names a person, place, thing, idea, animal, quality, event, and so on: *Alanis, America, desk, justice, dog, strength, departure.* See also **collective noun, common noun, count noun, noncount noun,** and **proper noun.** See **21a(2)**.

noun clause   A dependent clause used as a noun. See 22b(2).

noun phrase   A noun and its modifiers. See 22a(1).

number   The property of a word that indicates whether it refers to one (**singular**) or to more than one (**plural**). Number is reflected in the word's form: *river/rivers, this/those, he sees/they see.* See 26c(4) and 27f.

object   A noun, pronoun, noun phrase, or noun clause that follows a preposition or a transitive verb or verbal. A **direct object** names the person or thing that receives the action of the verb: I sent the *package.* An **indirect object** usually indicates to whom the action was directed or for whom the action was performed: I sent *you* the package. See 21c(1) and 21c(2). The **object of a preposition** follows a preposition: I sent the package to *you.* See 22a(4).

object complement   See **complement.**

object of a preposition   See **object.**

objective case   See **case.**

parenthetical element   Any word, phrase, or clause that adds detail to a sentence or any sentence that adds detail to a paragraph but is not essential for understanding the core meaning. Commas, dashes, or parentheses separate these elements from the rest of the sentence or paragraph. See 37d, 41e, and 41f.

participial phrase   A verbal phrase that includes a participle: The stagehand *carrying the trunk* fell over the threshold. See 22a(3). See also **participle** and **phrase.**

participle   A verb form that may function as part of a verb phrase (had *determined,* was *thinking*) or as a modifier (a *determined* effort; the couple, *thinking* about their past). A **present participle** is formed by adding *-ing* to the base form of a verb. A **past participle** is usually formed by adding *-ed* to the base form of a verb (*walked, passed*); however, many verbs have irregular past-participle forms (*written, bought, gone*). See 27a(1) and 27a(5).

particle   A word such as *across, away, down, for, in, off, out, up, on,* or *with* that combines with a main verb to form a phrasal verb: *write down, look up.* See 27a(3).

parts of speech   The classes into which words may be grouped according to their forms and grammatical relationships. The traditional parts of speech are verbs, nouns, pronouns, adjectives, adverbs, prepositions, conjunctions, and interjections.

passive voice   See **voice.**

past participle   See **participle.**

pathos   One of the three classical appeals; the use of language to stir the feelings of an audience. Also called an **emotional appeal** or a **pathetic appeal.** See 8f(1). See also **ethos** and **logos.**

person   The property of nouns, pronouns, and their corresponding verbs that distinguishes the speaker or writer (**first person**), the individuals addressed (**second person**), and the individuals or things referred to (**third person**). See 27b(1).

personal pronoun   A pronoun that refers to a specific person, place, thing, and so on. Pronoun forms correspond to three cases: subjective, objective, and possessive. See 26a(1).

phrasal verb   A grammatical unit consisting of a verb and a particle such as *after, in, up, off,* or *out: fill in, sort out.* See 27a(3).

phrase   A sequence of grammatically related words that functions as a unit in a sentence but lacks a subject, a predicate, or both: *in front of the stage.* See 22a.

point of view   The vantage point from which a topic is viewed; also, the stance a writer takes: objective or impartial (third person), directive (second person), or personal (first person). See 27b.

possessive case   See **case.**

predicate   The part of a sentence that expresses what a subject is, does, or experiences. It consists of the main verb, its auxiliaries, and any complements and modifiers. The **simple predicate** consists of only the main verb and any accompanying auxiliaries. See 21b and 21c. COMPARE: **subject.**

premise   An assumption or a proposition on which an argument or explanation is based. In logic, premises are either **major** (general) or **minor** (specific); when combined correctly, they lead to a conclusion. See 8h(2). See also **syllogism.**

preposition   A word such as *at, in, by,* or *of* that relates a pronoun, noun, noun phrase, or noun clause to other words in the sentence. See 21a(6).

prepositional phrase   A preposition with its object and any modifiers: *at* the nearby airport, *by* the sea. See 22a(4).

present participle   See **participle.**

primary source   A source that provides firsthand information. See 9a(3). COMPARE: **secondary source.**

pronoun   A word that takes the position of a noun, noun phrase, or noun clause and functions as that word or word group does: *it, that, he, them.* See 21a(3) and chapter 26.

proper adjective   An adjective that is derived from the name of a person or place: *Marxist* theories. See 43a(9).

proper noun   The name of a specific person, place, organization, and so on: *Dr. Pimomo, Fargo, National Education Association.* Proper nouns are capitalized. See 21a(2). COMPARE: **common noun.**

proposition   See **claim.**

qualifier   A word that intensifies or moderates the meaning of an adverb or adjective: *quite* pleased, *somewhat* reluctant. Words that intensify are sometimes called **intensifiers.**

quotation   A **direct quotation** (also called **direct discourse**) is the exact repetition of someone's spoken or written words. An **indirect quotation** is a report of someone's written or spoken words not stated in the exact words of the writer or speaker. See **11d(2)** and chapter **40**.

reflexive pronoun   A pronoun that ends in *-self* or *-selves* (*myself* or *themselves*) and refers to a preceding noun or pronoun in the sentence: *He* added a picture of *himself* to his Web page. When used to provide emphasis, such a pronoun is called an **intensive pronoun:** The president *herself* awarded the scholarships. See **26a(2)**.

refutation   A strategy for addressing opposing points of view by discussing those views and explaining why they are unsatisfactory. See **8e(2)** and **8g(3)**.

relative clause   See **adjectival clause.**

relative pronoun   A word (*who, whom, that, which,* or *whose*) used to introduce an adjectival clause, also called a **relative clause.** An antecedent for the relative pronoun can be found in the main clause. See **22b(2)**.

restrictive element   See **essential element.**

rhetorical appeal   The means of persuasion in argumentative writing, relying on reason, authority, or emotion. See **8f.**

Rogerian argument   An approach to argumentation that is based on the work of psychologist Carl R. Rogers and that emphasizes the importance of withholding judgment of others' ideas until they are fully understood. See **8f(2)**.

search engine   A Web-based program that enables users to search the Internet for documents containing certain words or phrases. Sometimes called a **search tool.** See **9d.**

secondary source   A source that analyzes or interprets firsthand information. See **9a(3)**. COMPARE: **primary source.**

sentence modifier   A modifier related to a whole sentence, not to a specific word or word group within it: *All things considered,* the committee acted appropriately when it approved the amendment to the bylaws.

simple predicate   See **predicate.**

simple subject   See **subject.**

split infinitive   The separation of the two parts of an infinitive form by at least one word: *to completely cover.* See **22a(3)**.

squinting modifier   A modifier that is unclear because it can refer to words either preceding it or following it: Proofreading *quickly* results in missed spelling errors. See **25c(3)**.

Standardized English   The usage expected in most academic and business settings. See the Glossary of Usage.

subject   The general area addressed in a piece of writing. See 3a. COMPARE: **topic.** Also, the pronoun, noun, or noun phrase that carries out the action or assumes the state described in the predicate of a sentence. Usually preceding the predicate, the subject includes the main noun or pronoun and all modifiers. A **simple subject** consists of only the main noun or pronoun. See 21b and 21d. COMPARE: **predicate.**

subject complement   See **complement.**

subjective case   See **case.**

subjunctive mood   See **mood.**

subordinating conjunction   See **conjunction.**

subordination   The connection of a grammatical structure to another, usually a dependent clause to an independent clause: *Even though customers were satisfied with the product,* the company wanted to improve it. See chapter 30.

syllogism   Method for deductive reasoning consisting of two premises and a conclusion. See 8h(2). See also **premise.**

synchronous forum   Online means of communication in which messages are exchanged in real time; that is, the receiver of a message sees it on the screen right after the sender completes it. Chat rooms are synchronous discussion groups. See 6b(2). COMPARE: **asynchronous forum.**

tense   The form of a verb that indicates when and for how long an action or state occurs. See 27b and 27c.

theme   The main idea of a literary work. See 12c(7).

thesis   The central point or main idea of an essay. See 3c.

tone   The writer's attitude toward the subject and the audience, usually conveyed through word choice and sentence structure. See 4a(3).

topic   The specific, narrowed main idea of an essay. See 3b. COMPARE: **subject.**

topic sentence   A statement of the main idea of a paragraph. See 4c(1).

Toulmin model   A system of argumentation developed by philosopher Stephen Toulmin in which a claim and supporting reasons or evidence depend on a shared assumption. See 8h(3).

transitions   Words, phrases, sentences, or paragraphs that relate ideas by linking sentences, paragraphs, or larger segments of writing. See 4d and 24c(5).

transitive verb   A verb that takes an object. The researchers *reported* their findings. See 21d. COMPARE: **intransitive verb.**

usability testing   The process of soliciting reactions from potential users of a Web site or other complex electronic document in order to improve the content or design of the document. See 6d(3).

verb A word denoting action, occurrence, or existence (state of being). See 21a(1) and chapter 27.

verb phrase A main verb and any auxiliaries. See 22a(2) and 27a(4).

verbal A verb form functioning as a noun, an adjective, or an adverb. See 22a(3). See also **gerund, infinitive,** and **participle.**

vocative Set off by commas, the name of or the descriptive term for the person or persons being addressed. See 37b(3).

voice A property of a verb that indicates the relationship between the verb and its subject. The **active voice** is used to show that the subject performs the action expressed by the verb; the **passive voice** is used to show that the subject receives the action. See 27d and 32e.

warrant According to the Toulmin model, the underlying assumption connecting a claim and data. See 8h(3).

Credits

These pages constitute an extension of the copyright page. We have made every effort to trace the ownership of all copyrighted material and to secure permission from copyright holders. In the event of any question arising as to the use of any material, we will be pleased to make the necessary corrections in future printings. Thanks are due to the following authors, publishers, and agents for permission to use the material indicated.

Text

p. 11: "Jaqui's Story" by David Hafetz from AUSTIN AMERICAN-STATESMAN, May 12, 2002. Copyright 2002 by Austin American-Statesman. Reproduced with permission of Austin American-Statesman in the format Textbook via Copyright Clearance Center.

pp. 22, 27: From GUNS, GERMS, AND STEEL: THE FATES OF HUMAN SOCIETIES by Jared Diamond. Copyright © 1997 by Jared Diamond. Used by permission of W. W. Norton & Company, Inc., and The Random House Group Ltd.

pp. 47–48: Austin Scaggs, "Ben Harper's European Vacation." ROLLING STONE (6 Sept. 2007); 83–84. © Rolling Stone LLC 2007. All Rights Reserved. Reprinted by permission.

pp. 50–51: Excerpt from "Credit Card Debt among College Students: Just What Does It Cost?" by Robyn Sylves. Reprinted by permission of the author.

p. 51: Jonathan Franzen, "My Father's Brain." Originally published in *The New Yorker.* Copyright © 2001 by Jonathan Franzen. Reprinted in *The Best American Magazine Writing* 2002, edited by American

Society of Magazine Editors, New York: Perennial, 2002, with permission by the Susan Golomb Literary Agency. 130–59. 151.1.

p. 62: From "Not Seeing the Forest for the Dollar Bills" by Donella Meadows as appeared in *Valley News,* June 30, 1990. Reprinted by permission of Sustainability Institute.

p. 63: Anna Quindlen, "Playing God on No Sleep: Isn't Motherhood Grand? Do You Want the Real Answer or the Official Hallmark-Card Version?" first appeared in *Newsweek,* 2001.

pp. 63–64: Excerpt from "September 11, 2001, Somewhere over Pennsylvania" by Randall Sullivan from *Rolling Stone,* 4/11/02. © Rolling Stone LLC 2002. All Rights Reserved. Reprinted by permission.

p. 70: Excerpt from "The Better Boss" by Larissa MacFarquhar as appeared in *The New Yorker* magazine, April 22 & 29, 2002, p. 86. Reprinted by permission of the author.

p. 103: FOR BETTER OR FOR WORSE © 2000 Lynn Johnston Productions. Dist. by Universal Press Syndicate. Reprinted with permission. All rights reserved.

Merriam-Webster's Collegiate Dictionary, Eleventh Edition © 2008 by Merriam-Webster, Incorporated (www.Merriam-Webster.com).

Photos and Illustrations

p. 6: © AFP/Getty Images.

p. 10: © AA Grapevine Inc. Permission to reprint the AA Grapevine, Inc., copyrighted material does not in any way imply affiliation with or endorsement of any of the material contained in the publication.

p. 16: © Image Source Ltd.

pp. 19, 23, 24: From GUNS, GERMS, AND STEEL: THE FATES OF HUMAN SOCIETIES by Jared Diamond. Copyright © 1997 by Jared Diamond. Used by permission of W. W. Norton & Company, Inc., and The Random House Group Ltd.

p. 34: © Jeremy Woodhouse/Photodisc/Getty Images.

p. 48: Courtesy of Maserati.

p. 49: © Mary Kate Denny/PhotoEdit.

p. 50: © Amy Etra/PhotoEdit, Inc.

p. 52: (left) M. L. King: © Flip Schulke; (right) Kennedy: © Time-Life Pictures/Getty Images

p. 53: © Scott T. Smith/Corbis.

p. 58: *Migrant Mother* by Dorothea Lange, 1936 Library of Congress, Farm Security Administration Office of War Information Collection.

p. 88: © 2003 Adobe Systems Incorporated in the US and/or other countries. Intel, Pentium, and the Pentium 4 processor logo are trademarks of Intel Corporation.

p. 98: "Coding for Corporate Survival." Courtesy of Jeff Pruchnic.

p. 99: "Coding for Corporate Survival"; "Discussion Papers." Courtesy of Jeff Pruchnic.

p. 113: Courtesy of *Columbia Journalism Review.* www.CJRdaily.org. Photo of protesters outside United Nations 2005 Summit 9/14/05 on the CJR Daily

Homepage © John Smock/AP Images.

p. 114: Google Beta Groups © Google Corporation. All Rights Reserved.

p. 115: Courtesy of Stacey Sheriff.

p. 118: Copyright © 2005 The Green Belt Movement.

p. 132: (advertisement) Green Team Advertising for Environmental Defense Fund; (photo of baby) © Stockbyte/Getty Images.

p. 133: Courtesy of Natural Resources Council of Maine.

p. 135: Poster courtesy of Faith Haney; (inset photo) University of Washington Libraries, Special Collections NA 815 and NA 134OF.

p. 138: © Creative Director: David Swope; Copywriter: Neil Levy; Photographer: Curtis Meyers.

p. 141: Courtesy of Canon USA, Inc. © 2005 Canon USA, Inc.

p. 145: Text by Anthony Cerretani and Abel Streep, Courtesy of *Outside Magazine*; photos (top right) © Jeffrey L. Rotman/Corbis; (center left) Courtesy of SUUNTO; (center right) © Matthew Wakem/Jupiter; (bottom left) © Jad Davenport. Text for "Red Sea," "Coral Sea," and "Beqa Lagoon" © Jad Davenport.

p. 146: Copyright © Scott K. Brown Photography, Inc.

p. 147: Firstgov.gov.

p. 148: © Barrel LLC/Tailor Made KSA.

p. 150: LIVE**STRONG**™ is a trademark of the Lance Armstrong Foundation.

pp. 151–152: Pew Charitable Trust.

p. 154: © Bruno Joachim/PhotoLibrary.

p. 168: © Bettmann/Corbis.

p. 191: © David R. Frazier/ Photo Researchers, Inc.

p. 197: © Danny Daniels/PhotoLibrary.

p. 199: University of Washington Libraries.

p. 203: Courtesy University Libraries, Pennsylvania State University.

p. 206: Screenshot from InfoTrac © Gale, a part of Cengage Learning, Inc. Produced by

Index

Numbers and letters in color refer to chapters and sections in the handbook; other numbers refer to pages.

a, an, 21a: 512–513, 514
  with abbreviations, acronyms, or numbers, 45e: 810
  omission of, from name of periodical, 13b: 295
a lot of, 815
a while, awhile, 816
abbreviated sentences, 23c: 560
abbreviation(s)
  in academic and professional writing, 45d: 807–809
  for addresses in correspondence, 45b: 805–806
  in APA documentation style, 15a: 346, 15b: 353, 355, 356
  in bibliographies, 45c: 806–807, 45d: 808
  capitalization of, 45a: 791
  clipped form as, 45d: 808
  for computer terms, 45c: 807
  in CSE documentation style, 19a: 454, 455, 456
  definition of, 45: 804
  of government divisions, 45c: 807
  indefinite articles with, 45e: 810

initials of well-known individuals as, 45d: 809
for Latin expressions, 45d: 809
in MLA documentation style, 13a: 276, 278, 13b: 298, 309–310
in online writing, 6c: 117
parentheses around, 41f: 768
for parts of speech, 21a: 508
periods with, 41a: 761, 45a: 805
plurals of, 39c: 752, 45a: 805
postal, 45b: 806
with proper names, 45a: 805
in source documentation, 45c: 806–807
for state names, 15b: 356, 17a: 406, 19a: 455
for time periods and zones, 45d: 808
of titles or degrees set off by commas, 37d: 735, 45a: 805
for *United States,* 45d: 808–809
for units of time, 45d: 808
absolute claim, 8d: 160
absolute modifiers, 25b: 579

absolute phrase, **22a**: 537,
    25c: 584, 831
  beginning sentence with, **33b**: 688
  commas with, **22a**: 537,
    37b: 730–731, **37d**: 736
  as sentence fragment, **23b**: 557
abstract
  in APA-style paper, **15c**: 369, 371
  in CSE-style paper, **19b**: 461, 462
  of journal article, **9c**: 202–203,
    14: 329, 330
  in laboratory report, **18d**: 442, 443
abstract nouns, **21a**: 510
  use of articles with, **21a**: 514
abstract word, definition of, **35a**: 709
academic degrees. *See* degrees
Academic Info, **9d**: 208
academic publishers, **10b**: 221
academic support services, **5b**: 100–102
academic writing. *See also* essay(s);
    research paper(s)
  abbreviations acceptable in,
    45d: 807–809
accept, except, 816
access date, **9d**: 209, **10d**: 228, **11b**:
    231, **13b**: 302–303, 304, 311,
    17a: 412, 413, **19a**: 457
accessibility, of Web site, **6d**: 124–125
accuracy
  in paraphrases, **11d**: 239–240
  of quotations, **11d**: 237
acronyms, 831
  capitalization of, **43a**: 791
  definition of, **45**: 804
  indefinite articles with, **45e**: 810
  parentheses around, **41f**: 768
  spelling out first usage of, **45e**: 809
ACS Style Guide, The (American
    Chemical Society), **18c**: 435
action
  calling for, **4b**: 63, **8d**: 161
  falling, **12c**: 256

action verbs, **21a**: 509, 510, **21c**: 521
active reading, and literary
    interpretation, **12b**: 251–253
active voice, **27d**: 628, 629,842
  and emphasis, **32e**: 677–678
  in writing in the humanities,
    16c: 385
  in writing in the social sciences,
    14c: 334
Ad*Access, **9d**: 211
ad hominem, **8i**: 178
address(es)
  abbreviations in, **45b**: 805–806
  commas in, **37e**: 737
  numerals in, **45g**: 812
  return, **20b**: 469, 471
Adflip, **9d**: 211
adjectival clause(s), **22b**: 540–542,
    25a: 576, **26a**: 591–592,
    30a: 663, 831
  agreement errors in, **27f**: 637
  as nonessential modifier, set off by
    commas, **37d**: 734
adjective(s), **21a**: 512–514,
    22b: 540, 831
  abbreviation for *United States* as,
    45d: 808–809
  beginning sentence with, **32f**: 680,
    33b: 688
  versus adverbs, **25a**: 572–573, 575,
    576–577
  comparative and superlative forms
    of, **25b**: 577–578
  as complements, **21c**: 522, 523
  coordinate, 831
  demonstrative pronouns as,
    26a: 592
  in idiomatic combinations,
    22a: 536
  order of, **25c**: 581
  participles as, **25a**: 573, 574
  pronouns as, **26a**: 588

adverb(s), **21a**: 514–515, **22b**: 542, 831
  versus adjectives, **25a**: 572–573,
    575, 576–577
  in attributive tags, **11d**: 237
  between auxiliary and main verb,
    21b: 520
  beginning sentence with, **32f**: 680,
    33b: 687
  comparative and superlative forms
    of, **25b**: 577–578
  conjunctive, **22c**: 545–546, **24a**:
    563–564
  following intransitive verb, **21d**:
    523, 524
  of frequency, **25c**: 582
  of manner, **25a**: 575
  relative, **22b**: 540
adverbial clause(s), **22b**: 542–543,
    25a: 576, 831
  beginning sentence with, **33b**: 687
  comma use with, **37d**: 734–735
  in mixed construction, **28d**: 650
adverbial conjunctions, **22c**: 545
advertisement(s)
  MLA documentation style for,
    13b: 302, 312
  as visual documents, **7a**: 131–132,
    7b: 138–139
  on Web sites, **9d**: 211
Advertising World, **9d**: 211
advice, advise, 816
affect, effect, 816
African American, use of, **34d**: 699, 700
African American literary criticism,
    12d: 261
afterword, MLA documentation style
    for, **13b**: 291
age, referring to, **34d**: 700
Age of Innocence, The (Wharton),
    12d: 260
aggregated databases, **9c**: 202
agree on, agree to, agree with, 816

agreement
  of pronoun and antecedent,
    26c: 599–602
  of subject and verb, **27f**: 634–641
AIP Style Guide (American Institute of
    Physics), **18c**: 435
aircraft names, italics for, **44d**: 801
Albert, Tanya, **10a**: 218
algebraic expressions, italics in, **44e**: 802
alignment, design principle of,
    7b: 135, 136
all ready, already, 816
all right, 816
all together, altogether, 816
Allen, Woody, **32c**: 677
Allison, Dorothy, **4a**: 58
allude, elude, 816
allusion, illusion, 817
alot. See a lot of
already. See all ready, already
alright. See all right
alt tags, **6d**: 125, 831
AltaVista, **9d**: 211, **10a**: 220
altogether. See all together, altogether
a.m., p.m., **45d**: 808, 817
AMA Manual of Style (American
    Medical Association), **18c**: 435
Amaki, Amalia, **16**: 378, 379
American Chemical Society, **18c**: 435
American Heritage Dictionary, The,
    34e: 702
American Indian, use of, **34d**: 700
American Institute of Physics, **18c**: 435
American Mathematical Society,
    18c: 435
American Medical Association, **18c**: 435
American Psychological Association
    (APA), **15**: 346. *See also* APA style
American Reference Books Annual
    (*ARBA*), **9b**: 201
Amnesty International, **3c**: 38
among, between, 817

amount of, number of, 817
ampersand, in APA documentation, **15a**: 347, **15b**: 352–353
an. See a, an
analogy, **3g**: 52
  false, **8i**: 180
analysis, **12b**: 253–254. *See also* cause-and-consequence analysis; process analysis
  in field report, **18d**: 438, 439
  of visual documents, **7a**: 131–133
Anaya, Rudolfo, **12d**: 260
and
  as conjunction, **21a**: 516, **21c**: 521, **27f**: 636
  as logical operator, **9b**: 199, 200
and/or, 817
Andrews-Rice, Kaitlyn, **12**: 249, **12f**: 266, 267
anecdote, opening essay with, **4b**: 61
Angier, Natalie, **10a**: 219
angle brackets, **13b**: 303, **41g**: 769
angry at, angry with, 817
annotated bibliography, **11c**: 235
annotation, of text, **2b**: 25, 26, 27
anonymous work
  APA style for citation of, **15a**: 348
  MLA style for citation and documentation of, **13a**: 277, **13b**: 290
another, other, the other, 817
antecedent(s), **21a**: 510–511, 831
  agreement of pronoun with, **26c**: 599–602
  clear pronoun reference to, **26d**: 603–605
  collective noun as, **26c**: 602
  indefinite pronoun as, **26a**: 593, **26c**: 600–601
  one as, **27f**: 637
  of relative pronoun in adjectival clause, **26a**: 591, **27f**: 637

anthology
  CMS documentation style for, **17a**: 410–411
  MLA documentation style for, **13b**: 291–292
anymore, any more, 817
anyone, any one, 817
anyplace, everyplace, someplace, 817
APA style, **15**: 346
  abbreviations in, **15a**: 346, **15b**: 353, 355, 356
  for abstract, **15c**: 369, 371
  for body of paper, **15c**: 369, 372, 376
  capitalization in, **41d**: 764, **43b**: 792–793, **43c**: 794–795
  for documentation of articles, **15b**: 352–356, 360–362, 364
  for documentation of books, **15b**: 352–361, 364–365
  for documentation of electronic or online sources, **15b**: 362–368
  for documentation of films and television programs, **15b**: 368
  for in-text citations, **15a**: 346–349
  italics in, **15b**: 354, 355, **44**: 798
  for reference list, **15b**: 349–350, 352, **15c**: 377
  sample paper in, **15c**: 368–377
  for spaces with punctuation marks, **41**: 760
  spelling out of numbers in, **45f**: 811
  for *that* versus *which,* **22b**: 541
  for title page of paper, **15c**: 369, 370
apostrophe
  forming certain plurals with, **39c**: 752
  indicating ownership and other relationships, **39a**: 745–751
  marking omissions of letters or numbers, **39b**: 751

appeal to tradition, **8i**: 178
appeals, rhetorical, **8f**: 167–170
application, letters of, **20e**: 480–482
applied sciences, **18**: 430
appositive(s), **22a**: 537, 831
  nonessential, set off by commas,
    22a: 537, **37d**: 735
  as sentence fragment, **23b**: 557
  synonym as, **35e**: 717
  for variety in sentences, **33a**: 686,
    33b: 688
appositive list, as sentence fragment,
  23b: 557
appositive pronouns, **26b**: 595–596
archetypes, **12d**: 263
Arem, Joel, **3g**: 54
arguable statement, **8b**: 157–158
argument, **8**: 154, **8h**: 175–176
  arrangement of, **8g**: 170–173
  avoiding rhetorical fallacies in,
    8i: 177–183
  evidence for, **8e**: 163–166
  fact and opinion in, **8c**: 158–159
  logic in, **8h**: 174–177
  purpose of, **8a**: 155–156
  rhetorical appeals in, **8f**: 167–170
  sample student, **8j**: 184–190
  topics for, **8b**: 156–158
argumentative writing, **1c**: 8,
  8: 154–155
Aristotle, **3d**: 42, **8f**: 167
arrangement
  of argument, **8g**: 170–173
  of ideas, **3d**: 41–42, **4c**: 68–71
  of Web document, **6d**: 119–120, 122
art
  MLA documentation style for,
    13b: 301–302, 311
  Web sites for, **9d**: 211
Artchive, The, **9d**: 211
articles (part of speech), **21a**: 512–514,
  26c: 601, **45e**: 810, 832

articles (publications)
  APA documentation style for,
    15b: 352–356, 360–362, 364
  CMS documentation style for,
    17a: 403–407, 411–414
  CSE documentation style for,
    19a: 454, 455–456, 458–459
  evaluating, **10b**: 222, **10c**: 224–225
  finding, **9c**: 202–206
  MLA documentation style for,
    13b: 293–297, 306–309
artist, MLA documentation style for,
  13b: 285–286
as, 818
as, because, 818
as, like, 818
Asian American, use of, **34d**: 699
assignment sheet, **5a**: 96, 99, 100
association, guilt by, **8i**: 181
assure, ensure, insure, 818
asterisks, in keyword search, **9b**: 198
asynchronous forums, **6b**: 112–113,
  115, 832
atmosphere, of literary work, **12c**: 257
attachments, to e-mail messages,
  20c: 474–475
attitude
  calling for change in, **4b**: 63
  in writing, **1e**: 15
attributive tags, **11d**: 236, 237,
  28d: 652, 832
  comma use with, **37f**: 738, **40d**: 757
  to divide quotations, **23d**: 527
audience(s), **1a**: 4, **1d**: 10–15
  netiquette and, **6c**: 116
  for online documents, **6a**: 110–111,
    6d: 117–118
  for periodicals, **10b**: 222
  purpose of argument and,
    8a: 155–156
  for research paper, **9a**: 196

(cont.)

audience(s) *(cont.)*
  revising and, **4a**: 56–57
  rhetorical appeals to, **8f**: 167–170
  visual documents and, **7a**: 131–133,
    7d: 146, 149
  for writing in the humanities,
    16a: 380–381
  for writing in the natural sciences,
    18a: 431–432
  for writing in the social sciences,
    14a: 331
author(s)
  APA citation style for, **15a**: 346,
    347–349
  APA documentation style for,
    15b: 352–353, 356–358, 360
  CMS documentation style for,
    17a: 403–404, 407–409
  credibility of, **1a**: 5, **10a**: 216–221,
    11a: 230
  CSE documentation style for,
    19a: 451, 454, 457–458
  MLA citation style for, **13a**: 274,
    275–276
  MLA documentation style
    for, **13b**: 285–286, 290–291,
    298, 299
  as narrator, **12c**: 256
  previewing and, **2a**: 20
  reasoning of, **11f**: 246
  references to names of, **12e**: 265–266
  sources for information about,
    10a: 217
  world view of, **10a**: 217–219
author-date system, **15**: 346
authority, false, **8i**: 180
authorship, in business writing,
    20: 467
auxiliary verb(s), **21a**: 509,
    21b: 519–520, **27a**: 613–615,
    28c: 648–649, 832
  adverbs of frequency with, **25c**: 582

do as, **27a**: 613, **27b**: 624
  in perfect progressive tenses,
    27b: 623–624
  in perfect tenses, **27b**: 621–622,
    623
  in progressive tenses, **27b**: 619–620
  in questions, **21d**: 525
  in simple future tense, **27b**: 619
  in verb phrases, **22a**: 530
awhile. See a while, awhile
axes, of line graph, **7c**: 140

background
  in argument, **8g**: 171
  opening essay with, **4b**: 62
  of Web document, **6e**: 127, 128
backing, in Toulmin model, **8h**: 176,
    177
backward S pattern, **7d**: 147
bad, 818
balance, of design elements, **6e**: 126
Balay, Robert, **9b**: 201
bandwagon, **8i**: 178
bar charts, **7c**: 141, 142
Bartleby.com, **9b**: 201
  base form, of verb, **27a**: 607,
    608, 609
be, **27a**: 613, **27b**: 628
  forms of, **27a**:611–612
  illogical equation with, **28d**: 651
  as main verb, **25c**: 582
be going to, **27b**: 619
Bearden, Romare, **16**: 378, 379, 380
because. See as, because
Bechara, Antoine, **29c**: 660
Bechdel, Laura, **8f**: 170
begging the question, **8i**: 178, 179
being as, being that, 818
Beloved (Morrison), **12d**: 261
Berry, Wendell, **21c**: 498
beside, besides, 818
better, had better, 818

between. See among, between
Bible. *See* sacred texts
bibliography. *See also* reference list;
 works-cited list
 abbreviations in, **45c**: 806–807,
  45d: 808
 annotated, **11c**: 235
 CMS style for, **17a**: 400, 402,
  404–407, **17b**: 428–429
 for literary interpretation, **12e**: 264,
  265
 for paper in the humanities,
  16c: 385, **17b**: 428–429
 previewing and, **2a**: 21
 working, **11c**: 234–235
bills, congressional, MLA-style
  documentation of, **13b**: 310
biographies, collections of, **9b**: 201
Black (or *black*), use of, **34d**: 700
Blackboard (courseware), **6b**: 113
Bless Me, Ultima (Anaya), **12d**: 260
block format, for letter, **20b**: 469
block quotation, **11d**: 237, **12e**: 265,
 13a: 279–280
blocks, of text, **7b**: 136, **7d**: 151
blog, **6b**: 112, 113
 APA documentation of posting to,
  15b: 365
 MLA documentation of posting to,
  13b: 314
body
 of APA-style paper, **15c**: 369,
  372–376
 of business letter, **20b**: 470, 471
 of business memo, **20c**: 472, 473
 of business report, **20h**: 491,
  496–500
 of critical analysis, **16d**: 394
 of historical research paper,
  16d: 388, **17b**: 416–425
 of oral presentation, **20g**: 487
Bolander, Anne E., **4c**: 69

book(s)
 APA documentation style for,
  15b: 356–361, 364–365
 CMS documentation style for,
  17a: 403–411
 CSE documentation style for,
  19a: 454, 455, 456, 457–458, 459
 evaluating, **10a**: 220–221, **10b**:
  221–222, **10c**: 224–225
 finding, **9b**: 198–201
 MLA documentation style for,
  13b: 290–293, 305–306
 numerals for pages and divisions in,
  45g: 812
 previewing, **2a**: 19–25
book publishers, **10b**: 221–222
book reviews
 APA documentation style for,
  15b: 362
 for assessing author's credibility,
  10a: 220–221
 MLA documentation style for,
  13b: 297
bookmark, **9d**: 209
Boolean operators, **9b**: 199, 836
Bostonians, The (James), **12d**: 260
both . . . and, **21a**: 516
brackets. *See* angle brackets; square
 brackets
brand names
 beginning with lowercase letter,
  43c: 795
 words derived from, **43a**: 791
bridges, capitalization of names of,
 43a: 789
bring, take, 818
brochure(s), **7a**: 131, 132–133,
 7d: 144, 149–153
 APA documentation style for,
  15b: 367
Brockmeier, Kevin, **32e**: 678
Brontë, Charlotte, **12d**: 263

Brooks, Gwendolyn, **12d**: 259
Brown, Jordana, **4b**: 63
building names, capitalization of, **43a**: 789
bulletin, MLA documentation style for, **13b**: 298
bulletin board, **6b**: 112–113, 114, 837
bullets, **7d**: 151
bunch, 818
business letters, **20b**: 469–471
 colon use in, **41d**: 765
business memos, **20c**: 472–474
business plans, **20f**: 482–486
business writing, **20**: 467. *See also specific types*
 conventions of language and organization in, **20a**: 467–469
 rhetorical situation for, **20**: 467, 468
bylines, **10b**: 222

call number, **9b**: 200
camera analogy, for focusing on topic, **3b**: 34
can, may, 819
can't hardly, can't scarcely, 819
capital, capitol, 819
capitalization
 of abbreviations, **43a**: 791
 of acronyms, **43a**: 791
 in advertisements, **43**: 788
 of company names, **43a**: 789–790
 of computer keys, menu items, and icons, **43d**: 795
 of days of week, **43a**: 790
 down-style, **7i**: 157
 of embedded question, **41b**: 762
 of first word of sentence, **43c**: 793–795
 following a colon, **41d**: 764, **43c**: 794
 of geographical features, **43a**: 789
 of government agencies, **43a**: 789
 of historical documents, periods, events, and movements, **43a**: 790
 of holidays, **43a**: 790
 of institutions, **43a**: 789–790
 of military terms, **43a**: 789–790
 of names of bridges, buildings, and monuments, **43a**: 789
 of names of ethnic or cultural groups and languages, **43a**: 789
 of organizations, **43a**: 789
 proofreading for, **4g**: 90
 of proper names, **43a**: 788–792
 of religions, their adherents, holy days, titles of holy books, and words denoting the Supreme Being, **43a**: 791
 of specific persons or things, **43a**: 789
 style sheet for, **43a**: 792
 styles of, **43**: 787
 of titles accompanying proper names, **43a**: 789
 of titles and subtitles, **15b**: 354, **17a**: 405, **19a**: 454, **43b**: 792–793
 unnecessary, **43e**: 796
 of words derived from proper names, **43a**: 791
capitol. See capital, capitol
captions, for illustrations, **7c**: 144, 145
Carey, Ken, **23c**: 559
Carroll, Margaret, **16b**: 383
cartoon, MLA documentation style for, **13b**: 302, 312
case, 832
 legal, MLA documentation of, **13b**: 298
 of pronouns, **26a**: 589, **26b**: 593–599
case study, **14d**: 341

catalog, online, 9b: 198–201

Catcher in the Rye, The (Salinger), 12d: 263

Cather, Willa, 12d: 262

cause(s)
  contributory versus primary, 3g: 50
  false, 8i: 181

cause-and-consequence analysis, 3b: 35, 3c: 38, 3g: 50–51

CD, MLA documentation style for, 13b: 301

CD-ROM, MLA documentation style for, 13b: 314

censor, censure, sensor, 819

center around, 819

Cepeda, Orlando, 3c: 39

chapter of book
  APA documentation style for, 15b: 355, 365
  CSE documentation style for, 19a: 458

character analysis, 12b: 254, 12c: 255

characters, in literary work, 12c: 254–255

chart(s), 7c: 140–142
  MLA documentation style for, 13b: 302, 312

chat rooms, 6b: 113

Chávez, Denise, 35a: 710

checklist, in survey question, 9e: 214

Chicago Manual of Style, The, 16c: 385, 17: 400, 39a: 747, 43c: 794. *See also* CMS style

Chicano/Chicana, use of, 34d: 700

Chodorow, Nancy, 12d: 262

choppy sentences, revision of, 22a: 532, 22b: 541

chronological order, 3g: 47, 4c: 69

chronological reading, 2: 18

chronological résumé, 20d: 475

chunks, of text, 7b: 136, 7d: 151

citation(s). *See* in-text citations

citation-name system, of CSE, 19a: 450, 452, 453

citation-sequence system, of CSE, 18d: 449, 19a: 450–451, 452, 453, 457, 19b: 461

cite, site, sight, 819

city
  of publication, 13b: 287–288, 296, 15b: 355–356, 17a: 406, 414, 19a: 455
  and state, comma separating, 37e: 737

Cixous, Hélène, 12d: 262

claim, 3c: 37, 832
  of argument, 8d: 160–162, 8e: 164–165
  in the humanities, 16b: 382, 16d: 389
  in Toulmin model, 8h: 176, 177

class-based literary theory, 12d: 261

classical arrangement, 8g: 171–172, 173–174, 16d: 389

classification, 3b: 35, 3g: 52–53

clause(s), 22b: 538, 832. *See also* adjectival clause(s); adverbial clause(s); dependent clause(s); independent clause(s)
  comma following introductory dependent, 37b: 729–730
  comma linking independent, 37a: 728–729
  comma separating series of, 37c: 732
  elliptical, 22b: 543, 25c: 583, 26b: 599, 834
  essential versus nonessential, 26a: 591–592
  including *that* before, 28b: 649
  integrating, 24c: 568
  linking of, 24c: 567, 569, 30a: 662–663, 665

(cont.)

clause(s) *(cont.)*
  as modifiers, **25a**: 576
  nominal, **22b**: 539
  noun, **22b**: 539–540, **27f**: 641,
    28d: 652
  parallel, **31a**: 669, **31b**: 670
  separating with period, **24c**: 567
cliché, 832
  definition of, **35b**: 712–713
  quotation marks for, **40c**: 757
climactic, climatic, 819
climactic order, **32c**: 676–677
climax, of plot, **12c**: 256
clip art, Web sites for, **9d**: 211
clipped form(s), **45d**: 808, 832
close reading, **12b**: 253
closing, of business letter, **20b**: 470, 471
CMS style
  for bibliography, **17a**: 400, 402,
    404–407, **17b**: 428–429
  for capitalization of titles, **17a**: 405,
    43b: 792–793
  for capitalization with colon,
    41d: 764
  for documentation of articles,
    17a: 411–414
  for documentation of books,
    17a: 403–411
  for documentation of interview,
    17a: 414
  for documentation of videocassette
    or DVD, **17a**: 414
  general documentation guidelines
    for: **17a**: 403–407
  italics in, **17a**: 406, **44**: 798,
    44a: 800
  notes in, **17a**: 400, 401
  sample paper in, **17b**: 415–429
  for spaces with punctuation marks,
    41: 760
  spelling out of numbers in,
    45f: 810–811

for use of *that* or *which*, **22b**: 541
coarse, course, 819
Cofer, Judith Ortiz, **3g**: 48, 49
Cohen, Emily, **20f**: 483, **20g**: 488
coherence
  of paragraphs, **4c**: 65, 68–71
  repetition of elements and, **7b**: 137
  transitional words or phrases for,
    4d: 72–73
  of Web document, **6d**: 120, **6e**: 128
collective noun(s), **21a**: 510, 832
  agreement of verbs with, **27f**: 639
  as antecedent, **26c**: 602
collocations, 832
  choosing right preposition in,
    35c: 714
  definition of, **35c**: 713–714
colloquial words, **34c**: 695, 832
colon
  in APA documentation, **15b**: 354,
    356
  in business correspondence, **41d**: 765
  capitalization following, **41d**: 764,
    43c: 794
  directing attention to explanation,
    summary, or quotation, **41d**: 764
  to emphasize words, **32a**: 674
  to join clauses, **24a**: 564, **24c**: 567
  quotation marks with, **40d**: 758
  in search path, **13b**: 303
  separating chapter and verse,
    13a: 277, **41d**: 765
  separating title and subtitle,
    41d: 765
  separating volume and page
    numbers, **13a**: 280
  signaling list that follows,
    41d: 764–765
color
  in visual documents, **7b**: 137,
    7d: 148, 149
  in Web documents, **6e**: 127–128

Columbia Guide to Online Style, The, **13b**: 305

Columbia Journalism Review, **6b**: 112, 113

columns, of text, **7b**: 136, **7d**: 151

comic strip, MLA documentation style for, **13b**: 302, 312

comma(s)
  with absolute phrases, **22a**: 537
  with adverbial clauses, **22b**: 542
  in APA documentation style, **15a**: 347, **15b**: 352–353, 354
  with conjunctive adverbs, **24a**: 564
  before coordinating conjunction linking independent clauses, **22c**: 544, **24a**: 563, **24c**: 567, **37a**: 728–729
  after direct object at beginning of sentence, **21d**: 526
  with direct quotations accompanied by attributive tags, **37f**: 738
  in divided quotation, **24d**: 570–571
  following transitional words, **38a**: 742
  with geographical names and items in dates and addresses, **37e**: 737
  between independent clauses, **24**: 562, **24a**: 564
  with interjection, **21a**: 517
  after introductory clauses, phrases, or words, **22a**: 532, **37b**: 729–731
  in MLA documentation style, **13a**: 275–276, 280
  with nonessential elements, **22a**: 531, 537, **22b**: 541, **37d**: 733–737
  with numerals, **45g**: 813
  quotation marks with, **40d**: 757
  semicolon separating elements that contain, **38b**: 742
  separating coordinate adjectives, **37c**: 733
  separating elements in series, **37c**: 732–733

  unnecessary or misplaced, **37g**: 738–740

comma fault, **24**: 562

comma splice(s), **24**: 562
  recognizing, **24b**: 565–566
  revising, **24c**: 567–569

command, for variety of sentences, **33c**: 690

commercial publishers, **10b**: 221–222

common ground, **1d**: 11, 13
  in argumentative writing, **8a**: 156, **8f**: 167, 168

common knowledge, **11e**: 241–242

common nouns, **21a**: 510, **43e**: 796, 832

company names, capitalization of, **43a**: 789–790

comparative form, of adjective or adverb, **25b**: 577, 578

comparatives, double, **25b**: 579

compare to, compare with, 819

comparison and contrast, **3b**: 35, **3g**: 51–52

comparisons
  completing, **28e**: 653
  effective, **25b**: 578–579

complement(s), **21c**: 521–523, 832–833
  mismatch of, with verb, **28d**: 651–652
  noun phrases as, **22a**: 528
  with verbs for attribution, **28d**: 652

complement, complementary, compliment, complimentary, 819–820

complete predicate. *See* predicate

complete subject. *See* subject (of sentence)

complex sentence, **22d**: 548, 833

compose, comprise, 820

compound-complex sentence, **22d**: 548–549, 833

compound noun, apostrophe use with, **39a**: 749

compound objects, **21c**: 521, 522, **26b**: 595

compound predicate, **21b**: 518, 833
avoiding comma between elements of, **37g**: 739
as sentence fragment, **23b**: 557

compound sentence, **22d**: 548, 833

compound subject, **21b**: 518, **26b**: 594, **27f**: 636, 833

compound verb, **28b**: 648

compound word, 833
hyphen in, **42f**: 784–785

comprise. See compose, comprise

computer. *See also* grammar checker; spell checker; word processor
organizing bibliographic entries with, **11c**: 235
organizing notes with, **11b**: 231–233

computer keys, capitalization of, **43d**: 795

computer screen, as rhetorical unit of email, **20c**: 474

computer terms, abbreviation of, **45c**: 807

concession, **8e**: 166, **8g**: 172, 173

conciseness
in business writing, **20a**: 469, **20c**: 472, 474
deleting *there are* and *it is* for, **36a**: 721–722
deleting unnecessary words for, **36a**: 720, 721
elliptical constructions for, **36c**: 723–724
redundancy and wordiness and, **36a**: 719
repetition and, **36b**: 723
replacing wordy expressions for, **36a**: 720, 721

using relative pronouns and, **36a**: 720, 722

conclusion
of argument, **8g**: 171, 172, 173
of business report, **20h**: 491, 501
of critical analysis, **16d**: 394, 399
effective, **4b**: 59, 62–64
of historical research paper, **16d**: 388, **17b**: 415–429
of oral presentation, **20g**: 487
parallelism in, **31e**: 672
in syllogism, **8h**: 175

concrete nouns, **21a**: 510

concrete word, **35a**: 709

condensed note form. *See* short note form

conditional clause, 833

conference papers, APA documentation style for, **15b**: 354

confirmation, in argument, **8g**: 171, 173

conflict, in literary work, **12c**: 255, 256, 258

conjunction(s), **21a**: 516, **22c**: 543–545, **30b**: 665, **30c**: 666, 833. *See also* coordinating conjunctions; correlative conjunctions; subordinating conjunctions
adverbial, **22c**: 545
combining short sentences with, **33a**: 683–684
for transitions within paragraph, **4d**: 72–73

conjunctive adverbs, **22c**: 545–546, 833
punctuation with, **24a**: 563–564
to replace coordinating conjunction, **33a**: 685

connecting word or phrase, beginning sentence with, **33b**: 688

connotation, **2b**: 26, **35a**: 708

Conrad, Joseph, 12d: 261
conscience, conscious, consciousness, 820
consensus building, 8f: 169–170
consequence(s), in cause-and-
consequence analysis, 3b: 35,
3c: 48, 3g: 50–51
consistency
in point of view, 29b: 658–659
in tone, 29c: 659–660
in verb tenses, 27c: 627,
29a: 655–657
Constitution, MLA documentation
style for, 13a: 278, 13b: 298
constraints, of rhetorical situation,
1a: 4–5, 1e: 15
Contemporary Authors, 12b: 253
contemporary sources, 10d: 228
content, reading for, 2b: 25–28
context, 1a: 4–5, 1e: 15–17
of online writing, 6a: 111, 6c: 117
context-based literary theory, 12d: 262
*continual, continually, continuous,
continuously,* 820
continuous pagination, of journal,
13b: 295, 296
contractions
versus possessive forms, 26b: 595,
39a: 747, 42c: 780
tone and, 34c: 695
contrast, 3g: 51. *See also* comparison
and contrast
of design elements, 6e: 127,
7b: 135, 136–137
contrasted elements, set off by commas,
37d: 737
contributory causes, 3g: 50
convention(s), 833
of business writing, 20a: 467–469
of writing about literature,
12e: 262–266
of writing in the natural sciences,
18c: 435–437
of writing in the social sciences,
14c: 334–337
conventional usage, 815, 833
conversational words, 34c: 695, 815
convince, persuade, 820
coordinate adjectives, 831
comma separating, 37c: 733
definition of, 37c: 733
coordinating conjunctions,
21a: 516, 22c: 543–544,
30b: 664, 665, 833
avoiding comma following,
37g: 739
avoiding overuse of, 33a: 685–686
to combine sentences, 33a: 683, 684
comma before, 37a: 728–729
in compound sentences, 22d: 548
joining independent clauses,
24a: 563, 24c: 567
joining parallel elements,
31a: 668
coordination, 30: 662, 833
avoiding faulty or excessive,
30c: 666–667
effective use of, 30b: 664–665
copyright
date, 13b: 288, 289
page, 13b: 289, 15b: 358
respect for, 9d: 210
corporate author
APA documentation style for,
15b: 353, 358
CMS documentation style for,
17a: 404
CSE documentation style for,
19a: 454, 458
MLA documentation style for,
13a: 276, 13b: 286, 290
correlative conjunctions (correlatives),
21a: 516, 22c: 544, 833
to combine sentences, 33a: 683
parallelism and, 31d: 671–672

Cosby, Bill, 8e: 165
could of, 820
couldn't care less, 820
council, counsel, 820
Council of Science Editors (CSE),
    18c: 435, 436, 437, 19: 450.
    See also CSE style
counsel. See council, counsel
count noun(s), 21a: 510, 834
counterarguments, 16d: 389, 390
country name
    in APA documentation style,
        15b: 356
    in MLA documentation style,
        13b: 288
course. See coarse, course
course syllabus. *See* syllabus
courseware, 6b: 113, 114
cover letter, 20e: 480
coverage, of research source,
    11f: 245–246
credentials, of authors, 10a: 216–217
credibility
    and argumentative writing, 8c: 158,
        8e: 166, 167, 168, 8i: 183
    of authors, 1a: 5, 10a: 216–221
    ethical appeals and, 8f: 168
    and online writing, 6c: 117
    of publishers, 10b: 221–222
    of research paper, 11a: 230
criteria, criterion, 820
critical analysis, 16d: 394–399
critical race theory, 12d: 260–261
critical review, 16d: 390–393
Cronin, Sarah, 14a: 332, 14d: 340
cropping, of image, 7c: 144
Crucible, The (Miller), 12d: 262
CSE style, 19: 450
    citation-name system of, 19a: 450,
        452, 453
    citation-sequence system of, 19a:
        450–451, 452, 457, 19b: 461

for documentation of articles,
    19a: 454, 455–456, 458–459
for documentation of books,
    19a: 454, 455, 456,
    457–458, 459
for documentation of electronic
    sources, 19a: 456–457,
    459–460
for end references list, 19a: 450,
    452, 460, 19b: 465–466
for in-text references, 19a: 450–452
name-year system of, 19a: 450, 451,
    452, 458, 460, 19b: 461
sample paper in, 19b: 461–466
cultural groups, capitalization of,
    43a: 789
cultural studies, 12d: 262
cumulative sentence, 30b: 631
currency, of sources, 11f: 245

Damasio, Antonio R., 29c: 660
Damasio, Hanna, 29c: 660
dangling modifier(s), 25c: 583–584,
    834
dangling participial phrase, 834
dash. *See also* en dash
    to emphasize words, 32a: 674
    following introductory list or series,
        41e: 767
    marking break in normal flow of
        sentence, 41e: 766
    quotation marks with, 40d: 758–759
    setting off nonessential element for
        emphasis or clarity, 41e: 766
    three-em, 17a: 402
data, 27f: 639, 820
data, in Toulmin model, 8h: 176
database
    CMS documentation style for work
        from, 17a: 413
    CSE documentation style for work
        from, 19a: 459–460

electronic, **9c**: 202–204

MLA documentation style for work from, **13b**: 307–309, 314

database subscription services, **9c**: 202

MLA documentation style for work from, **13b**: 307–309

date. *See also* access date; publication date

comma separating day and, **37e**: 737

cultural conventions for writing, **45g**: 812

numerals versus words for, **45g**: 811–812

uncertain, **41b**: 762

Davis, Lennard J., **4c**: 70

days of week, capitalization of, **43a**: 790

deadlines, managing, **5c**: 102–103

decimals, using numerals for, **45g**: 813

declarative sentence(s), **22e**: 550, 551

converting to questions, **21d**: 525

indirect question as, **41b**: 762

period following, **41a**: 761

thesis statement as, **3c**: 39

deductive reasoning, **4c**: 66, **8h**: 175, 834

definite article, **21a**: 512, 513

with abstract nouns, **21a**: 514

definition(s)

for exactness, **35e**: 717–718

formal, **35e**: 717

indefinite article in, **21a**: 513

mismatches in, **28d**: 651

as rhetorical method, **3b**: 35, **3g**: 53–54

Defoe, Daniel, **12d**: 261

degrees

abbreviations for, **45a**: 805

set off by commas, **37d**: 735

Delaney, Joseph F., **20d**: 476, 477

delivery, and Web document, **6d**: 119

Demmon, Mike, **18d**: 438, 439

demonstrative pronouns, **26a**: 592

demonstratives, 834

denotation, **2b**: 26, **35a**: 707–708

dénouement, **12c**: 256

dependent clause(s), **22b**: 539–543, **22c**: 544, **30a**: 662–664, 832

introductory, **37b**: 729–730

for revising sentence fragment, **24c**: 567–568

sentence form and, **22d**: 548–549

as sentence fragments, **23c**: 558–560

subjunctive mood in, **27e**: 632–633

description, **3b**: 35

in essay, **3g**: 48–49

in field report, **18d**: 438–439

spatial order and, **4c**: 69

descriptive language, **12c**: 255

desert, dessert, 821

design principles

for online documents, **6e**: 126–129

of visual rhetoric, **7b**: 134–137

detail(s), **3f**: 46

in descriptions, **3g**: 48–49

developing paragraph with, **3f**: 45–46

for sentence unity, **28a**: 646–647

determiner(s), 834

development, methods of. *See* rhetorical methods of development

device, devise, 821

dialogue, 821

dialogue, enclosing in quotation marks, **40a**: 754

Diamond, Jared, **2a**: 19, 22, 23, 24

diction, editing for, **4f**: 89

dictionaries, **2b**: 26, **4g**: 90, **34e**: 702–703

APA documentation style for entry in, **15b**: 366

MLA documentation style for entry in, **13b**: 297

(cont.)

dictionaries *(cont.)*
  parts of speech in, **21a**: 703–705
  range of information in,
      34e: 659–661
  specialized, **9b**: 200, 201, **27a**: 613,
      34e: 703
Didion, Joan, **32d**: 677
differ from, differ with, 821
different from, different than, 821
digital object identifier (DOI),
      15b: 362, 364
digital recordings, MLA
      documentation style for,
      13b: 300–301
dilemma, false, **8i**: 181
direct address. *See* vocative
direct discourse, 840. *See also* direct
      quotation(s)
direct object(s), **21c**: 521–522, 834, 838
  beginning sentence with, **21d**: 526,
      33b: 688
  with transitive verbs, **21d**: 523, 524
direct quotation(s), **11b**: 237–238,
      840. *See also* quotation(s)
directed freewriting, **3a**: 33
directness, in business writing,
      20a: 468–469, **20c**: 472, 474
directories
  previewing and, **2a**: 21
  subject, **9d**: 208
disability, referring to, **34d**: 700
discreet, discrete, 821
discussion group or forum. *See* online
      discussion group(s)
discussion section, in research report,
      14d: 341, 345, **18d**: 442, 448,
      19b: 461
disinterested, uninterested, 821
dissertation, MLA documentation style
      for, **13b**: 299
distinct, distinctive, 821
diverse audience, **1d**: 12–13

for online writing, **6a**: 111,
      6d: 117, 119
diverse views, argument and,
      8e: 165–166
divided quotations, **24d**: 570–571
division, **3b**: 35, **3g**: 52–53
do, **21d**: 525, **27a**: 613, **27b**: 624
document design. *See* design principles
documentation of sources. *See also*
      APA style; CMS style; CSE style;
      MLA style
  abbreviations in, **45c**: 806–807,
      45d: 808
  in natural sciences, **18c**: 437
  with paraphrase, **11e**: 242–243
  with quotation, **11e**: 243
Dogpile, **9d**: 207
DOI, **15b**: 362, 364
domain, **10c**: 223
Dorfman, Ariel, **33c**: 689
double negatives, **25d**: 585–586
doublespeak, **35b**: 712
Douglass, Frederick, **4b**: 61, **12d**: 260
draft(s)
  evaluating, **4e**: 75
  final, **4h**: 90–94
  first, **3e**: 44–44, **4e**: 77–82
  second, **4e**: 83–87
  submitting for review, **4e**: 76–77
drafting, **3**: 31
  of Web document, **6d**: 123–125
  of well-developed paragraphs,
      3f: 44–46
drama, **12a**: 251. *See also* play(s)
dramatic soliloquy, **12a**: 251
Drinkwater, Carol, **1c**: 7
due to, 821
DVD
  CMS documentation style for,
      17a: 414
  MLA documentation style for,
      13b: 300–301

DVD-ROM, MLA documentation style for, **13b**: 314
dyeing, dying, 821

Eagleton, Terry, **12d**: 261
EBSCO, **9c**: 203
    MLA documentation style for article from, **13b**: 309
-ed form of verb, **27a**: 608
edited work
    APA documentation style for selection from, **15b**: 359
    MLA documentation style for selection from, **13b**: 292
editing, **3**: 31, **4**: 55, **4f**: 87–89
edition of book
    APA documentation style for, **15b**: 359
    CMS documentation style for, **17a**: 410
    CSE documentation style for, **19a**: 454
    MLA documentation style for, **13b**: 291, 296
editor(s)
    APA documentation style for, **15b**: 353, 357
    CMS documentation style for, **17a**: 404, 409
    CSE documentation style for, **19a**: 454, 458
    MLA documentation style for, **13b**: 286, 290–291, 298, 305
editorial(s)
    evaluating, **10c**: 224–225
    MLA documentation style for, **13b**: 297, 307
effect. See affect, effect
Ehrlich, Gretel, **31e**: 672
either . . . or, **21a**: 516
either/or fallacy, **8i**: 180

electronic composition, **6d**: 119–121, 123–125
electronic database, **9c**: 202–204
electronic sources
    APA documentation style for, **15b**: 362–368
    CSE documentation style for, **19a**: 456–457, 459–460
    MLA documentation style for, **13a**: 278–279, **13b**: 302–304
electronic texts. *See* e-mail; instant messaging; online writing; Web documents
elicit, illicit, 821
Eliot, T. S., **41h**: 771
ellipsis points, 834
    for omission within quoted passage, **11d**: 237, **13a**: 280, **41h**: 769–771
    for reflective pause or hesitation, **41h**: 771
    to show sentence intentionally left incomplete, **41h**: 771
elliptical clause(s), **22b**: 543, **25c**: 583, 834
elliptical constructions, **26b**: 599, **36c**: 723–724
elude. See allude, elude
em dash. *See* dash
e-mail
    as form of business writing, **20c**: 472–475
    to instructor, **5b**: 101
    MLA documentation style for, **13b**: 313
    multiple audiences and, **1d**: 13
emigrate from, immigrate to, 822
eminent, imminent, 822
emoticons, **6c**: 117
emotional appeals, **8f**: 167, 169. *See also* pathos

emphasis
  climactic order and, **32c**: 676–677
  cumulative and periodic sentences
    and, **32b**: 676
  dash for, **32a**: 674, **41e**: 766
  exclamation point for, **41c**: 763
  intensive pronouns for, **26a**: 590
  inverting word order for, **32f**: 679–680
  italics for, **44f**: 802
  of negation, **25d**: 586
  overuse of capitalization for,
    43e: 796
  parallelism for, **31**: 668, **31c**: 670,
    31e: 672
  placing words for, **32a**: 674–675
  repeating words for, **4d**: 72,
    32d: 677
  short sentences for, **32g**: 680–681
  voice and, **27d**: 629, **32e**: 677–679
emphatic order, **4c**: 70
empirical evidence, **18b**: 434
en dash, **15b**: 355, **17a**: 407,
  45g: 812
encyclopedia(s)
  APA documentation style for entry
    in, **15b**: 366
  MLA documentation style for entry
    in, **13b**: 297, 306
  specialized, **9b**: 200–201
end punctuation, to identify sentence
  function, **22e**: 500
end references, in CSE style, **19a**: 450,
  452, 460, **19b**: 465–466
endnotes, CMS style for, **17a**: 400,
  401, **17b**: 426–427
ensure. See assure, ensure, insure
enthymeme, **8h**: 175
EPA, **18d**: 440, 441
equivocation, **8i**: 179
-er suffix, **25b**: 577, 578
Erdrich, Louise, **35a**: 709
ERIC, **9c**: 203, 205

MLA documentation style for article
  from, **13b**: 308
ESL students, usage resources for,
  34e: 703
especially, specially, 822
essay(s). *See also* writing
  arranging or outlining ideas in,
    3d: 41–43
  conclusion of, **4b**: 59, 62–64
  developing paragraphs for,
    3f: 44–46
  editing of, **4f**: 87–89
  evaluating draft of, **4e**: 75
  final draft of, **4h**: 90–94
  first draft of, **3e**: 43–44
  focusing topic of, **3b**: 34–36
  introduction of, **4b**: 59–62
  peer review of, **4e**: 74–82
  proofreading of, **4g**: 89–90
  revision of, **4a**: 56–59, **4c**: 65–71
  rhetorical methods of development
    for, **3g**: 47–54
  sample draft of, **4e**: 78–82, 83–87
  selecting subjects for, **3a**: 31–34
  thesis of, **3c**: 37–41
  transitions in, **4d**: 71–74
essay examinations, **5e**: 105–109
essential clause, **22b**: 540, 541,
  26a: 591, 592
essential element(s), **37d**: 734, 834
essential phrase, **22a**: 532
-est suffix, **25b**: 577, 578
et al., **13a**: 276, **13b**: 305, **15a**: 348,
  15b: 353, 357, **45d**: 809
etc., 822
ethical appeals, **8f**: 167, 168. *See also*
  ethos
ethnic groups
  capitalization of, **43a**: 789
  terms for, **34d**: 699–700
ethos, **8f**: 167, 170, **8i**: 177, 834
euphemisms, definition of, **35b**: 712

European American, use of, **34d**: 699, 700

evaluation
  of authors' credibility, **10a**: 216–221
  of literary work, **12b**: 254
  of online and print sources, **10c**: 223–226, **10d**: 227–228
  of publishers' credibility, **10b**: 221–222
  of Web site accessibility, **6d**: 124–125

evaluation claim, **8d**: 161

evaluation standards, for peer review, **4e**: 74–75

Evans, Walker, **33c**: 690

events, capitalization of, **43a**: 790

eventually, ultimately, 822

everyday, every day, 822

"Everyday Use" (Walker), **12**: 249, 250, **12c**: 256, 258, **12f**: 266, 267

everyone, every one, 822

everyplace. See anyplace, everyplace, someplace

evidence
  for argument, **8c**: 159, **8e**: 163–166, **8f**: 167
  in the natural sciences, **18b**: 434
  in the social sciences, **14b**: 332–334

evocative language, for exactness, **35b**: 712–713

exactness
  clear definitions for, **35e**: 717–718
  evocative language for, **35b**: 712–713
  figurative language and, **35a**: 707–711
  first-person and second-person pronouns for, **35d**: 715–717
  idioms and collocations for, **35c**: 713–715

examinations, essay, **5e**: 105–109

example(s), **3f**: 46

developing paragraph with, **3f**: 46, **3g**: 54

opening essay with, **4b**: 61

as supporting evidence, **8e**: 164, 165, **8h**: 175

except. See accept, except

exclamation point, **41c**: 763
  with interjection, **21a**: 517
  quotation marks with, **40d**: 758–759

exclamatory sentence, **22e**: 550
  for variety, **33c**: 690

executive summary, **20f**: 483

exigence, **1a**: 4, **1b**: 5–6, 834
  and research question, **9a**: 193–195

experiments, **14b**: 332

experts, as source for research, **9e**: 211–213, **10c**: 224–225

explanation, colon directing attention to, **41d**: 764

expletive, 834
  it as, **21b**: 519, **26d**: 605
  overuse of, **36a**: 721–722
  there as, **21b**: 519, **27f**: 637

explication, **12b**: 254, **16d**: 389

explicit, implicit, 822

exposition, of literary work, **12c**: 256

expository writing, **1c**: 7–8, **4c**: 70

expressive writing, **1c**: 7

external hyperlinks, **6d**: 121

fact(s)
  distinguishing from opinion, **8c**: 158–159
  as evidence, **8e**: 164, 164, **8h**: 175
  in opening of essay, **4b**: 60

fallacies, rhetorical, **8i**: 177–183

falling action, of plot, **12c**: 256

false analogy, **8i**: 180

false authority, **8i**: 180

false cause, **8i**: 180

false dilemma, **8i**: 180
farther, further, 822
faulty predication, **28d**: 650, 834
FedWorld, **9d**: 210
feel, 822
feminist literary theory, **12d**: 260
fewer, less, 822–823
fiction, definition of, **12a**: 251
field report, **14d**: 342, **18d**: 438–439
field research, **9e**: 211–215, **14b**: 332
field work, **18d**: 438
figurative language, **35a**: 710–711, 835
figures, **11d**: 237, **18c**: 437. *See also*
    graphics
figures of speech, **3g**: 52, **35a**: 710
film
    APA documentation style for,
      15b: 368
    MLA documentation style for,
      13b: 300
film review, MLA documentation style
    for, **13b**: 297
final draft, **4h**: 90–94
first, firstly; second, secondly, 823
first draft, **3e**: 43–44
first mention of noun, indefinite article
    with, **21a**: 513
first person, **26a**: 589, **27b**: 617, 839
    in academic and professional
      writing, **35d**: 715–717
    in writing in the humanities, **16c**: 385
    in writing about literature,
      12e: 263–264
    in writing in the social sciences,
      14c: 334
first-person pronouns, **26a**: 589
FirstGov, **9d**: 210
flaming, **6c**: 117, 835
Flaubert, Gustave, **12d**: 261
Fleck, Carole, **10a**: 218
flyers, **7d**: 144, 146–149

focal point, of poster or flyer, **7d**: 146,
    147, 148
focused questions, **9e**: 212, 213
focusing, on topic for essay, **3b**: 34–36
fonts, **6e**: 127, **7b**: 136–137
footnotes, CMS style for, **17a**: 400,
    401
foreign words, italics for, **44b**:
    800–801
foreword, forward, 823
foreword, MLA documentation style
    for, **13b**: 291
form, parallel structure through
    repetition of, **31b**: 670
formal definition, **28d**: 651, **35e**: 717
formatting, of business documents,
    20a: 469, **20c**: 472, **20d**: 475,
    476
former, latter, 823
Forster, E. M., **12d**: 261
forum. *See* online discussion group(s)
fractional numbers
    hyphens in, **42f**: 785
    using numerals for, **45g**: 813
fragment. *See* sentence fragment(s)
Franzen, Jonathan, **3g**: 51
freewriting, **3a**: 32–33, **9a**: 195
frequency, adverbs of, **25c**: 582
Freud, Sigmund, **12d**: 262
FrontPage, **6d**: 121, 122
full note form, **17a**: 400, 403–407
functional résumé, **20d**: 475
further. See farther, further
fused sentence(s)
    recognizing, **24b**: 565–566
    revising, **24c**: 567–569
future perfect progressive tense,
    27b: 624
future perfect tense, **27b**: 623
future progressive tense, **27b**: 621
future tense(s), **27b**: 616–624

Gadsby, Patricia, **41h**: 769–770

Gaebel, Alyssa, **4e**: 77–82

gender, 835

  agreement with respect to, **26c**: 600, 601

  usage and, **34d**: 697–699

gender-based literary theory, **12d**: 260

general words, **35a**: 709

generalization

  hasty, **8i**: 181

  in reasoning, **8h**: 174, 175

genre(s), 835

  of literature, **12a**: 249–251

  of visual documents, **7a**: 131, 133, **7d**: 144–153

geographical areas, referring to, **34d**: 700–701

geographical features, capitalization of, **43a**: 789

geographical names, commas with, **37e**: 737

gerund(s), 835

  possessive pronouns with, **26b**: 598

  verbs followed by, **22a**: 533, 534

gerund phrase, **22a**: 530–531, 835

  apostrophe use with, **39a**: 749–750

Gervais, Matthew, **14**: 329, 330, **14d**: 339–340

get, 823

Gladwell, Malcolm, **4c**: 66, **29c**: 659, 660

go, goes, 823

good, well, **25a**: 577, 823

Google, **9d**: 207, 211, **10a**: 220, **11e**: 242

Gorman, James, **29a**: 656

Gotthardt, Melissa, **4b**: 62

government agencies, capitalization of, **43a**: 789

government divisions, abbreviation of, **45c**: 807

government document or publication

  APA documentation style for, **15b**: 359

  CMS documentation style for, **17a**: 410

  MLA documentation style for, **13b**: 298, 309–310

grammar, **21**: 508

grammar checker

  capitalization errors and, **43c**: 795

  missing words and, **28b**: 649

  passive voice and, **27d**: 630, **32e**: 679

  in proofreading, **5d**: 104

  sentence length and, **33a**: 684

  sexist language and, **34d**: 697

  and tone of writing, **4a**: 59

Grapes of Wrath, The (Steinbeck), **12d**: 261

graphics, **7a**: 131

  as hyperlinks, **6d**: 120–121

  in research papers, **11d**: 237

  in visual documents, **7c**: 139–144, **7d**: 152

graphs, **7c**: 140–142, **14c**: 336–337

Green Belt Movement, **6a**: 11, **6d**: 117–119, 120

group author

  APA documentation style for, **15b**: 353, 358

  CMS documentation style for, **17a**: 404

  MLA documentation style for, **13b**: 286, 290

Guide to Reference Books (Balay), **9b**: 201

guilt by association, **8i**: 181

had better. See better, had better
half, 823
hanged, hung, 823
hardly. See can't hardly, can't scarcely
Harjo, Joy, **4d**: 72
Harris, Trudier, **3g**: 51, 52
has got, have got, 823
Haslett, Adam, **32b**: 676
hasty generalization, **8i**: 181
have, **27a**: 613, 615
Hayes, Jeff, **14d**: 338
he, generic, **34d**: 698
he/she, his, her, **26c**: 601, 823
heading(s)
    of business memo, **20c**: 472, 473
    previewing and, **2a**: 20
    in visual documents, **7b**: 137,
      7d: 150
    in writing in the humanities,
      16c: 385
    in writing in the natural sciences,
      18c: 436
    in writing in the social sciences,
      14c: 335
hearings, congressional, MLA
    documentation style for,
    13b: 309, 310
Heart of Darkness (Conrad), **12d**: 261
helping verbs, **21a**: 509. *See also*
    auxiliary verb(s)
Hemingway, Ernest, **12d**: 260
herself, himself, myself, yourself, 823
Hester, Nicole, **16d**: 388, **17b**: 415
hierarchical pattern, for Web site,
    6d: 122, 123
his or her, **26c**: 601
Hispanic, use of, **34d**: 700
historical documents, **43a**: 790,
    44a: 800
historical events, as exigencies, **1b**: 6
historical present (tense), **27b**: 618,
    27c: 627

historical research paper, **16d**: 387–388
Holden, Constance, **4d**: 71
holidays, capitalization of, **43a**: 790
holy days, capitalization of, **43a**: 791
home page, personal, MLA
    documentation style for,
    13b: 313
homophones, 835
    definition of, **42c**: 779
    proofreading for, **4g**: 90
    spelling of, **42c**: 779–780
hopefully, 823
Horne, Jed, **1e**: 16
Howard, Jennifer, **4b**: 60
however, **22c**: 546
HTML, **6d**: 121
Hulet, Kaycee, **16d**: 389
humanities, **16**: 378, **17**: 400
    audience and purpose for writing in,
      16a: 380–381
    conventions of language and
      organization in, **16c**: 384–385
    evidence, sources, and reasoning in,
      16b: 382–384
    rhetorical situation for writing in,
      16: 378–379
    samples of writing in,
      16d: 386–399, **17b**: 429
Humiston, Paul K., **29a**: 656
hung. See hanged, hung
Hurston, Zora Neale, **3g**: 51,
    12d: 260
hyperlinks, **6d**: 119–121,
    6e: 127–128, **44**: 799
hypertext, **6d**: 119, 120
hyphen
    capitalization with, **43b**: 793
    to clarify meaning, **42f**: 785
    linking two or more words that form
      compound, **42f**: 784–785
    in MLA documentation style,
      13a: 274, 280

in numbers, fractions, and units of measure, **42f**: 785
hypothesis, **14b**: 332–333, **18b**: 434

I. See first person
Ibid., **17a**: 401
Icon Browser, **9d**: 211
icon names, capitalization of, **43d**: 795
identification, numerals for, **45g**: 812
identity, and response to literature, **12b**: 252
idiom(s), 835
    definition of, **35c**: 713–714
    dictionary information on, **34e**: 705
    prepositions in, **22a**: 536
    understanding and using, **35c**: 715
i.e., 823–824
ignoring the question, **8i**: 182
illicit. See elicit, illicit
illness, referring to, **34d**: 700
illusion. See allusion, illusion
image(s)
    in combination with text, **7c**: 137–144
    concluding essay with, **4b**: 63–64
    from Internet sources, **9d**: 210–211
    MLA documentation style for, **13b**: 301–302
imagery, in literary work, **12c**: 255
immigrate to. See emigrate from, immigrate to
imminent. See eminent, imminent
impact, 824
imperative mood, **27e**: 631, 837
imperative sentences, **22e**: 550, 551, **23a**: 554
    period following, **41a**: 761
implicit. See explicit, implicit
imply, infer, 824
imprint, publisher's, **13b**: 288

in regards to. See regard, regarding, regards
in-text citations, **11e**: 243
    APA style for, **15a**: 346–349
    CMS style for, **17a**: 400
    CSE style for, **19a**: 450–452
    MLA style for, **13a**: 273–281
inclusive language, **34d**: 696–701
indefinite articles, **21a**: 512–513, 514
    with abbreviations, acronyms, or numbers, **45e**: 810
indefinite pronoun(s), **26a**: 593, **26c**: 600–601, 835
    agreement errors with, **27f**: 638–639
independent clause(s), **22b**: 538–539, 832
    colon following, **41d**: 764, **43c**: 794
    in compound, complex, and compound-complex sentences, **22d**: 548–549
    in fused sentence, **24**: 562
    joined by coordinating conjunction, **22c**: 544, **37a**: 728–729
    linked by conjunctive adverbs, **22c**: 545–546
    punctuation with, **24a**: 563–564, **21d**: 546, 548, **38a**: 741–742
    as simple sentence, **22d**: 547
index, previewing and, **2a**: 21
index cards, **11b**: 231, 234, **11c**: 234
indexes, print, **9c**: 204–205
indicative mood, **27e**: 631, 837
indirect object(s), **21c**: 522, 837
    with transitive verbs, **21d**: 523, 524
indirect question, **41a–b**: 761–762, 835
indirect quotation, 840
    no quotation marks for, **40a**: 754
indirect source
    APA documentation style for, **15a**: 349
    CMS documentation style for, **17a**: 411
    MLA citation style for, **13a**: 277

inductive leap, **8h**: 174
inductive reasoning, **4c**: 67, **8h**: 174–175, 835
infer. See imply, infer
infinitive(s), 835
    expressing time relations with, **27b**: 625–626
    pronouns with, **26b**: 598
    split, **22a**: 533
    verbs followed by, **22a**: 534
infinitive marker *to*, **22a**: 532, 533
    omitting, **22a**: 534, **27a**: 614
    repeating for parallel structure, **31b**: 669
infinitive phrase(s), **22a**: 532–534, 835
    as modifiers, **25a**: 576
inflection, 836
Infoseek, **9d**: 207
InfoTrac College Edition, **9c**: 203, 205, 206
    MLA documentation style for article from, **13b**: 309
-ing ending, **22a**: 530, 531
-ing form, of verb, **27a**: 608, 609
initials
    of authors, **13a**: 276, **13b**: 297, **15b**: 352–353, **17a**: 412, **19a**: 454
    individuals known by, **45d**: 809
inside of, outside of, 824
instant messaging, **6b**: 113, 115
institution names, capitalization of, **43a**: 789–790
institutional review boards (IRBs), **9e**: 214
instructions, in essay exams, **5e**: 105–106
instructor, academic support from, **5b**: 100–101
insure. See assure, ensure, insure
integration
    of clauses, **24c**: 568

of source material, **11d**: 235–241
of visual elements and text, **7c**: 143–144, 145
intended audience, **1d**: 10
intensifier(s). *See also* qualifier(s)
    adverbs as, **21a**: 515
    completing for sentence unity, **28f**: 654
intensive pronoun(s), **26a**: 590. *See also* reflexive pronoun(s)
interactive media, 797
interactive writing, **6**: 110
interjections, **21a**: 517, 836
interlibrary loan service, **9b**: 201
internal hyperlinks, **6d**: 121
Internet etiquette. *See* netiquette
Internet Public Library, **9d**: 208
interpretation, of literature. *See* literary interpretation
interrogative pronouns, **26a**: 592
interrogative sentences, **22e**: 550, 551. *See also* questions
interview(s)
    CMS documentation style for, **17a**: 414
    MLA documentation style for, **13b**: 299–300, 311
    as research source, **9e**: 211–213, **10c**: 224–225, **14b**: 332, 333
intonation, for questioning, **21d**: 526
intransitive verb, **21d**: 523, 524, 836
intriguing statement, as opening for essay, **4b**: 61
introduction
    of argument, **8g**: 171, 172
    of book, MLA documentation style for, **13b**: 291
    of business report, **20h**: 491, 494
    connecting conclusion with, **4b**: 64
    of critical analysis, **16d**: 394, 395
    effective, **4b**: 59–62

of historical research paper,
16d: 388, 17b: 415–429
MLA documentation style for,
12b: 281
of oral presentation, 20g: 487
parallelism in, 31e: 672
to questionnaire, 9e: 214
of research report, 14d: 342,
18d: 442, 443, 19b: 461, 463
introductory list, dash following,
41e: 767
introductory paragraph, 3c: 40
introductory participial phrase, 18c: 436
introductory series, dash following,
41e: 767
introductory clause, phrase, or word,
comma following, 37b: 729–731
invention, 836
inversion, 836
inverted word order
agreement errors and, 27f: 636
for emphasis, 32f: 679–680
in questions, 21d: 525–526
IRBs, 9e: 214
ironic tone, quotation marks for,
40c: 756–757
irregardless, 824
irregular verbs, 27a: 607, 609–612
is because/reason, mismatch of,
28d: 651
issue number(s), 13b: 295, 296,
15b: 355, 17a: 405, 19a: 456
issues, larger, in conclusion of essay,
4b: 63
it, 26d: 604
as expletive, 21b: 519, 26d: 605
deleting, 36a: 721–722
italics
for aircraft names, 44d: 801
for emphasis, 44f: 802
for foreign words, 44b: 800–801
for legal cases, 44c: 801

in mathematical expressions,
44e: 802
for satellite names, 44d: 801
for ship names, 44d: 801
for spacecraft names, 44d: 801
for submarine names, 44d: 801
for titles of works, 15b: 354, 360,
17a: 405, 44a: 799–800
underlining to indicate, 44: 798
for volume numbers, 15b: 355
word-processing programs and,
44: 799
for words, letters, or figures referred
to as such, 44e: 802
its, it's, 824
Iyer, Pico, 33c: 690
-ize, 824

James, Henry, 12d: 260
Jane Eyre (Brontë), 12d: 263
jargon, 1d: 13, 34c: 696
Jensen, Heather, 18: 430, 18a: 433,
18b: 435, 18c: 436, 437, 18d:
442, 443, 19b: 461, 27d: 629
journal(s), 13b: 293
APA documentation style for articles
from, 15b: 353, 354, 355, 360,
364
CMS documentation style for
articles from, 17a: 405, 406, 407,
411, 412–413
CSE documentation style for
articles from, 19a: 455–456,
458, 459
MLA documentation style for
articles from, 13b: 292,
293–296, 297
personal, 2e: 29, 3a: 32
reading, 2e: 29, 3a: 32
scholarly, 9b: 202, 10b: 222,
10c: 224–225
journalists' questions, 3a: 34

Jr., **15b**: 352, **37d**: 735, **45a**: 805
JSTOR, **9c**: 203
Jung, Carl, **12d**: 263

Kakutani, Michiko, **32b**: 676
Kelly, Walt, **35b**: 713
keyword search, **9b**: 198–199
keywords, 836
Kidder, Tracy, **40a**: 754
Kilbourne, Jean, **31e**: 672
kind of a, sort of a, 824
King, Martin Luther, Jr., **8e**: 166,
    8f: 168, 169, **31c**: 670
Kingsolver, Barbara, **3f**: 46
Klein, Melanie, **12d**: 262
Kolata, Gina, **18**: 430, 431
Kolbert, Elizabeth, **29a**: 657
Koster, Margaret, **16b**: 383
Kramer, Jane, **35a**: 711

labels, on illustrations, **7c**: 142,
    143, 144
laboratory experiments, in social
    sciences, **14b**: 332
laboratory report, **14d**: 342,
    18d: 440, 442
Lacan, Jacques, **12d**: 262
Lakoff, Robin, **41f**: 767
Lane, Pinkie Gordon, **12c**: 255
Lange, Dorothea, **4a**: 58
language(s)
    capitalization of names of,
        43a: 789
    descriptive, **12c**: 255
    inclusive, **34d**: 696–701
    SVO, SOV, and VSO, **21d**: 524
later, latter, 824
Latin American, use of, **34d**: 699,
    700
Latin expressions
    abbreviation of, **45d**: 809
    italics for, **44b**: 801

Latino/Latina, use of, **34d**: 700
law case. *See* legal case(s)
lay, lie, 824
layout, **7c**: 144, 145, **7d**: 149–151,
    153
lead, led, 824
least, **25b**: 577, 578
lecture, MLA documentation style for,
    13b: 299
lecture notes, APA documentation style
    for, **15b**: 365
Lederer, Richard, **4c**: 66
legal case(s)
    italics for, **44c**: 801
    MLA documentation style for,
        13b: 298, 310
length
    of e-mails and memos, **20c**: 474
    of introduction to essay, **4b**: 60
    of paragraphs, **3f**: 45
    previewing and, **2a**: 20
less, **25b**: 577, 578
less, less than. See fewer, less
letter
    of application, **20e**: 480–482
    business, **20b**: 469–471
    to editor, APA documentation style
        for, **15b**: 362
    of inquiry, **20b**: 470–471
    published, documentation of,
        13b: 299, **17a**: 411
LexisNexis, **9c**: 203
    MLA documentation style for article
        from, **13b**: 309
Librarian's Index to the Internet,
    9d: 208
library, and research, **9b**: 198–201,
    9c: 202–206
library research report, **14d**: 339–340
licensed databases, **9c**: 202
lie. See lay, lie
like. See as, like

line drawings, **7c**: 143
line graphs, **7j**: 164
linear pattern, for Web site, **6d**: 122
linking verbs, **21a**: 509, 512, 836
  with subject complements,
    21c: 522, **21d**: 523, 524, **25a**:
    576–577
links. *See* hyperlinks
list
  colon signaling, **41d**: 764–765
  dash following introductory,
    41e: 767
  for organizing essay exam response,
    5e: 106–107
  parentheses around numbers or
    letters in, **41f**: 768
  for planning and drafting essay,
    3d: 41, **3e**: 44
listserv, **6a**: 111, **6b**: 112, **9e**: 213,
  215, 836
listserv address, **9e**: 213
literally, 825
literary interpretation, **12b**: 251–254,
  258, **12d**: 259–263
  sample student, **12f**: 266–272
literary present (tense), **12e**: 264,
  27b: 618, **27c**: 627
literary theory, **12d**: 259–263
literature
  conventions for writing about,
    12e: 263–266
  genres of, **12a**: 249–251
  rhetorical situation for writing
    about, **12**: 249, 250
  vocabulary for writing about,
    12c: 254–258
literature review, **18d**: 437–438
live performances, MLA
    documentation style for,
    13b: 299–300
logic
  in argument, **8h**: 174–177
  in comparisons, **25b**: 579,
    28e: 653
  in humanities, **16b**: 384
logical appeals, **8f**: 167, 168. *See also*
    logos
logical operators, **9b**: 199, 200, 836
logical order, **4c**: 70–71
logos, **8f**: 167, 836
lose, loose, 825
lots, lots of, 825
lowercase letters, in APA
    documentation style, **15a**: 349,
    15b: 350
lurking, **6b**: 113, 115, 836
Lutz, William, **35b**: 712
-ly ending, **25a**: 575, 577
Lycos, **9d**: 207, **10a**: 220

Maathai, Wangari, **6d**: 118, 119,
  120
MacFarquhar, Larissa, **4c**: 70
Madame Bovary (Flaubert), **12d**: 261
magazine(s), **9c**: 202, **13b**: 293
  APA documentation style for articles
    from, **15b**: 353–354, 360, 364
  CMS documentation style for
    articles from, **17a**: 412, 413
  CSE documentation style for articles
    from, **19a**: 455–456, 458, 459
  evaluating, **10b**: 222,
    10c: 224–225
  MLA documentation style for
    articles from, **13b**: 295, 296, 307
main character. *See* protagonist
main clause, **22b**: 538, 832. *See also*
    independent clause(s)
main idea. *See also* theme
  revising and, **4a**: 56, **4c**: 65–68
main points
  in conclusion of essay, **4b**: 62
  in essay exam response,
    5e: 108–109

main verb, **22a**: 529–530

Mairs, Nancy, **4b**: 60

major premise, **8h**: 175, 839

man/mankind, as sexist usage,
  34d: 697, 825

Mandela, Nelson, **3g**: 52

manner, adverbs of, **25a**: 575

*Manual for Authors of Mathematical
  Papers, A* (American
  Mathematical Society), **18c**: 435

*Manual for Writers of Papers, Theses,
  and Dissertations, A* (Turabian),
  16c: 385, **17**: 400

manuals. *See* style manuals

manuscript page header, in APA-style
  paper, **15c**: 369, 370

many, much, 825

map, MLA documentation style for,
  13b: 302, 312

Marusak, Matthew, **16d**: 386, 390,
  391

Marx, Karl, **12d**: 261

Marx, Patricia, **4c**: 66

mathematical expressions, italics in,
  44e: 802

may. See can, may

may of, might of. See could of

maybe, may be, 825

McCourt, Frank, **3c**: 37, 40

McKibben, Bill, **22c**: 544

Meadows, Donella, **4b**: 62

meaning
  definitions and, **3g**: 53–54
  reading for, **2b**: 26–27
  symbols and, **12c**: 257–258

measurement words, agreement of
  verbs with, **27f**: 639

media, **27f**: 639

media, medium, 825

medium, as part of context, **1e**: 15

meeting software, **6b**: 113, 114

meetings, APA documentation style
  for, **15b**: 354

memos, **20c**: 472–474
  colon use in, **41d**: 765

menu items, computer, capitalization
  of, **43d**: 795

Merriam-Webster's Collegiate Dictionary,
  34e: 700, 703

message, in rhetorical situation, **1a**: 4

MetaCrawler, **9d**: 207, 211

metaphor(s), **3g**: 52, **28c**: 649–650,
  35a: 710–711, 837

meta-search engines, **9d**: 207

method, scientific, **18b**: 434,
  18d: 440

method section, in research report,
  14d: 342, 343, **18d**: 442, 444,
  19b: 461

Mexican American, use of, **34d**: 699

might could, 825

military terms, capitalization of,
  43a: 791–792

Miller, Arthur, **12d**: 262

minor premise, **8h**: 175, 839

misplaced modifiers, **25c**: 580–581,
  836

mixed construction, **28d**: 650,
  836–837

mixed metaphor(s), **28c**: 649–650, 837

*MLA Handbook for Writers of Research
  Papers,* **13**: 273, **39a**: 747

MLA International Bibliography, The,
  12b: 253

MLA style, **13**: 273, **16c**: 385
  abbreviations in, **13a**: 276, 278,
    13b: 298, 309–310
  for block quotations,
    13a: 279–280
  capitalization in, **24a**: 564, **41d**:
    764, **43b**: 792–793, **43c**:
    794–795

for citations of poetry, drama, and sacred texts, **13a**: 277–278, **41d**: 765

for documentation of articles, **13b**: 286–287, 293–297, 302–304, 306–309

for documentation of books, **13b**: 285–293, 302–306

for documentation of bulletin, **13b**: 298

for documentation of dictionary entry, **13b**: 297

for documentation of encyclopedia entry, **13b**: 297

for documentation of government publication, **13b**: 298

for documentation of images, **13b**: 301–302

for documentation of law case, **13b**: 298

for documentation of live performances and digital recordings, **13b**: 299–301

for documentation of online source, **13b**: 302–314

for documentation of pamphlet, **13b**: 298–299

for documentation of public law, **13b**: 298

for documentation of published dissertation, **13b**: 299

for documentation of published letter, **13b**: 299

for documentation of republished book, **13b**: 292

for documentation of sacred text, **13b**: 298

for documentation of translated book, **13b**: 292

for in-text citations, **13a**: 273–281

italics in, **44**: 798, **44a**: 800

for numbered notes, **13a**: 274

for punctuation in citations and quotations, **13a**: 280–281

for quotation marks, **40d**: 757–758

sample student paper in, **8j**: 185–190, **12f**: 267–274, **13c**: 315–328

for spaces following punctuation marks, **41**: 760

spelling out of numbers in, **45f**: 810–811

for title page of paper, **13c**: 315

for use of *that* or *which*, **22b**: 541

for works-cited list, **13a**: 273, **13b**: 281–282

modal auxiliaries, **21b**: 520, **27a**: 614–615, 832

moderate claim, **8d**: 160

Modern Language Association (MLA), **13**: 273. *See also* MLA style

modifier(s), **25**: 572, 837. *See also* adjective(s); adverb(s)

absolute, **25b**: 579

commas with nonessential elements used as, **37d**: 734–735

comparative and superlative forms of, **25b**: 577–579

dependent clauses as, **22b**: 540–543

as double negatives, **25e**: 585–586

infinitive phrases as, **22a**: 532–533, **25a**: 576

nouns as, **21a**: 512, **25a**: 575, **25c**: 585

placement of, **25c**: 580–585

prepositional phrases as, **22a**: 534–536

recognizing, **25a**: 572–577

verbal phrases as, **22a**: 530, 531, 532

monetary amounts, words versus numerals for, **45g**: 813

months
    abbreviation of, **45d**: 808
    capitalization of, **43a**: 790
monument names, capitalization of,
    43a: 789
mood, **27e**: 631–633, 837
more, **25b**: 577, 578, 579
Morrison, Toni, **12d**: 261
most, **25b**: 577, 578, 579, 825
motion picture. *See* film
movement, and design elements,
    6e: 126–127
movements, capitalization of, **43a**: 790
MSN Search, **9d**: 207
much. *See* many, much
multidisc work, MLA documentation
    style for, **13b**: 301, 314
multiple audiences, **1d**: 13–14
    for online writing, **6a**: 111
multiple-choice questions, **9e**: 214
multivolume work
    APA documentation style for,
        15b: 359
    CMS documentation style for,
        17a: 410
    MLA documentation style for,
        13a: 277, **13b**: 292–293
musical work, MLA documentation
    style for, **13b**: 310
My Ántonia (Cather), **12d**: 262
myself. *See* herself, himself, myself,
    yourself

names. *See* proper names
name-year system, for CSE
    documentation, **15a**: 375–377,
    383–384, **18c**: 437
narration, **3b**: 35, **3g**: 47–48,
    4c: 69
narrative, **3g**: 47, **12c**: 256
Narrative (Douglass), **12d**: 260
narrator, **12c**: 256

National Public Radio (NPR),
    10c: 226
Native American/Native People, use of,
    34d: 699, 700
Native Son (Wright), **12d**: 261
natural sciences, **18**: 430
    audience and purpose for writing in,
        18a: 431–433
    conventions of language and
        organization in, **18c**: 435–437
    evidence, sources, and reasoning in,
        18b: 434–435
    research questions in, **18a**: 433
    rhetorical situation for writing in,
        18: 430, 431
    samples of writing in,
        18d: 437–449
navigation, of Web site, **6d**: 118, 120,
    122, 126–127
n.d., **15b**: 353
near, as logical operator, **9b**: 199, 200
negation, **25d**: 585–586, **34a**: 644
negative adverb, **32f**: 680
neither . . . nor, **21a**: 516, **22c**: 544,
    27f: 636
neither . . . or, 825
netiquette, **6c**: 115–116, 837
NetMeeting, **6b**: 114
Netscape Composer, **6d**: 121
never, **37d**: 737
*New Princeton Handbook of Poetic
    Terms, The*, **12b**: 253
New York Public Library Picture
    Collection Online, **9d**: 211
newsgroup, **6b**: 113, 837
    APA documentation style for posting
        to, **15b**: 365
    for course, **5a**: 98
    MLA documentation style for
        posting to, **13b**: 314
newsletters, **7d**: 144, 149–153
newspaper(s), **9c**: 202, **13b**: 293

APA documentation style for article from, **15b**: 353–354, 362, 364

CMS documentation style for article from, **17a**: 413–414

CSE documentation style for article from, **19a**: 455, 456, 459

evaluating, **10b**: 222, **10c**: 224–225

MLA documentation style for article from, **13b**: 295, 296, 307

use of italics for, **44a**: 800

nominal clause, **22b**: 539

nominalization, 837

non sequitur, **8i**: 178

noncount noun(s), **21a**: 510, **22a**: 529, 837

none, agreement with, **27f**: 638, 639

nonessential clause, **22b**: 540–541, **26a**: 592

nonessential elements, 837
  definition of, **37d**: 733
  set off by commas, **22a**: 531, 537, **37d**: 733–737
  set off by dash or pair of dashes, **41e**: 766

nonnative speakers of English, dictionaries for, **34e**: 703

nonracist language, **34d**: 699–700

nonrestrictive clause, **22b**: 540–541

nonrestrictive element(s), **37d**: 733, 837. *See also* nonessential element(s)

nonsexist language, **34d**: 697–699

nonstandard, nonstandardized, 837

nonstandard usage, 815

nor
  joining antecedents, **26c**: 602
  joining subjects, **27f**: 636

not, as logical operator, **9b**: 199, 200

not . . . no/none/nothing, 825

not only . . . but also, **21a**: 516, **22c**: 544, **31d**: 671, **37d**: 737

notes. *See also* endnotes; footnotes
  abbreviations in, **45c**: 806–807, **45d**: 808
  in MLA-style paper, **12e**: 264, 271, **13a**: 274
  for research paper, **11b**: 231–234

nothing like, nowhere near, 825

noun(s), **21a**: 509–510, 837. *See also specific types*
  agreement of singular and plural in same sentence, **27f**: 640
  apostrophe use with, **39a**: 745–750
  as complements, **21c**: 521, 522, 523
  formation of plural of, **42d**: 782–783
  gerund phrases as, **22a**: 530
  in idiomatic combinations, **22a**: 536
  infinitive phrases as, **22a**: 532–533
  as modifiers, **21a**: 512, **25a**: 575, **25c**: 585
  -*s* ending to, **27f**: 639–640
  as subject of sentence, **21b**: 518
  types of, **21a**: 509–510
  verbal phrases as, **22a**: 530

noun clause, **22b**: 539–540, 838
  beginning with *what,* and verb agreement, **27f**: 641
  following verb for attribution, **28d**: 652

noun phrase, **22a**: 528–529, **22b**: 539, 838

noun strings, in writing in the sciences, **14c**: 334, **18c**: 436

n.p., **15b**: 365

NPR, **10c**: 226

number, **26a**: 589, 838
  agreement in, **22a**: 529, **25a**: 573, **26c**: 599–602, **27b**: 617, **27f**: 634

number of, 825–826

numbers. *See also* issue number(s);
    page number(s); volume
    number(s)
  in addresses, **45g**: 812
  call, **9b**: 200
  colons in, **41d**: 765
  to express decimals and percentages,
    45g: 813
  hyphens in, **42f**: 785
  for identification, **45g**: 812
  indefinite articles with, **45e**: 810
  for large fractional numbers,
    45g: 813
  with measurement abbreviations,
    45f: 811
  in MLA-style citations of poems,
    plays, and sacred texts,
    13a: 277–278
  for monetary amounts, **45g**: 813
  of paragraphs or screens in
    MLA-style citations,
    13a: 278–279
  parentheses around, **41f**: 768
  to refer to pages and divisions of
    books and plays, **45g**: 812
  referred to as such, **39c**: 752,
    44e: 802
  superscript, **13a**: 274, **17a**: 400,
    401, **19a**: 451, 452
  words versus, **45f–g**: 810–812

object(s), 838. *See also* direct object(s);
    indirect object(s)
  dependent clause as, **22b**: 539–540
  of preposition, **22a**: 528, 535,
    26b: 594, 595
  pronouns as, **26a**: 589, **26b**:
    594–595, 598
object complement, **21c**: 523,
    833
  following transitive verb, **21d**: 523,
    524

objective case, **26a**: 589, **26b**: 593,
    594–595, 598, 832
observation
  in humanities research, **16b**: 384
  in social science research, **14b**: 332,
    333
OCLC, **9c**: 203
off of, 826
omission
  apostrophe marking, **39b**: 751
  ellipsis points to mark, **41h**:
    769–771
  revising and, **4a**: 57
omniscient narrator, **12c**: 256
on account of, 826
on the other hand, 826
one, as antecedent of relative pronoun,
    27f: 637
online catalog, **9b**: 198–201
online discussion group(s),
    6b: 112–115, **9e**: 213
  MLA documentation style for
    posting to, **13b**: 313
  netiquette in, **6c**: 116–117
online peer reviewing, **4e**: 77
online résumé, **20d**: 476
online sources, **9d**: 207–211
  APA documentation style for,
    15b: 362–368
  CMS documentation style for,
    17a: 412–413
  CSE documentation style for,
    19a: 456–457, 459–460
  evaluating, **10c**: 223–226
  of information about authors,
    10a: 220
  MLA documentation style for,
    13b: 302–314
online writing
  capitalization in, **43e**: 796
  in discussion groups, **6b**: 112–115
  netiquette and, **6c**: 116–117

rhetorical situation for, **6a**: 110–112
visual elements with, **6e**: 126–129
open questions, **9e**: 212, 213, 214, 215
operators, logical (or Boolean), **9b**: 199, 200
opinion, distinguishing from fact, **8c**: 158–159
or
   joining antecedents, **26c**: 602
   joining subjects, **27f**: 636
   as logical operator, **9b**: 199, 200
oral presentations, **20g**: 487–490
organization
   as author, in CSE style, **19a**: 454, 458
   of data in tables, **7c**: 139–140
   of essay exam responses, **5e**: 106–108
   of information in the humanities, **16c**: 385
   of information in the natural sciences, **18c**: 436–437
   of information in the social sciences, **14c**: 335–336
   of notes, **11b**: 231–234
   of paragraphs, **4c**: 69–71
organizations' names, capitalization of, **43a**: 789
Orwell, George, **35b**: 712
other. See another, other, the other
outline
   for essay, **3d**: 41–43, **3e**: 43–44
   with MLA-style paper, **13c**: 315
oversimplification, **8i**: 181
ownership, apostrophe indicating, **39a**: 745–751
Oxford Companion to English Literature, The, **12b**: 253

page numbers
   APA style for, **15a**: 346, 347, **15b**: 355

CMS style for, **17a**: 407, 411
CSE style for, **19a**: 456
MLA style for, **13a**: 273, 274, **13b**: 291, 292, 293, 295, 306
pagination, of journal, **13b**: 295, 296, **15b**: 360
Palmer, Parker, **33c**: 690
pamphlet, MLA documentation style for, **13b**: 298–299
paragraph(s)
   coherence of, **4c**: 65, 68–71
   in dialogue, **40b**: 754
   drafting of, **3f**: 44–46
   examples for development of, **3f**: 46, **3g**: 54
   indents for, **13a**: 280
   location of thesis statement in, **3c**: 40
   numbers of, in MLA-style citations, **13a**: 278–279
   process, **3g**: 49–50
   revising of, **4c**: 65–74
   transitions within and between, **4d**: 71–73
   unity of, **4c**: 65, 67–68
parallelism, **31**: 668
   breaking from, **31c**: 671
   correlative conjunctions and, **31d**: 671–672
   in introductions and conclusions, **31e**: 672
   to link sentences, **31c**: 670
   recognizing parallel elements, **31a**: 668–669
   through repetition of form, **31b**: 670
   through repetition of words, **4d**: 72, **31b**: 669–670
paraphrase(s)
   creating, **11d**: 238–240
   documentation with, **11e**: 243
   to eliminate overuse of ellipsis points, **41h**: 771

(cont.)

paraphrase(s) *(cont.)*
  in Rogerian argument, **8f**: 169
  versus summary, **11d**: 240, 241
parentheses
  around acronyms and abbreviations, **41f**: 768
  in APA documentation style, **15a**: 347, **15b**: 353, 354, 355, 366
  with MLA-style citations, **13a**: 273–281
  for numbers or letters in list, **41f**: 768
  to set off information, **41f**: 767
parenthetical citations. *See* in-text citations
parenthetical element, 838
  set off by commas, **37d**: 736
parenthetical sentence, capitalization of first word of, **43c**: 794
participial phrase(s), **22a**: 531–532, 838
  in absolute phrase, **22a**: 537
  dangling, 834
  introductory, **18c**: 436, **37b**: 730
  as modifiers, **25a**: 576
  as nonessential modifier set off by commas, **37d**: 734–735
participle(s), 838. *See also* past participle(s), present participle(s)
  accompanied by auxiliary verbs, **27a**: 615–616
  as adjectives, **25a**: 573, 574
  beginning sentence with, **32f**: 680
  for time relationships, **27b**: 625, 626
particle, **21d**: 526, **27a**: 612–613, 838
parts of speech, **21a**: 508–517, 838.
  See also adjective(s); adverb(s); conjunction(s); interjection(s); noun(s); preposition(s); pronoun(s); verb(s)
  dictionary information on, **34e**: 705
  word groups as, **22**: 528

Passage to India, A (Forster), **12d**: 261
passed, past, 826
passive voice, **27d**: 628–630, 842
  to avoid *his or her*, **26c**: 601
  and emphasis, **32e**: 677–679
  of perfect subjunctive, **27e**: 632
past form, of verb, **27a**: 608, 609
past participle(s), **27a**: 608, 609, 838
  as adjectives, **25a**: 573, 574
  expressing time relations with, **27b**: 626
  in participial phrase, **22a**: 531
  in passive voice, **27d**: 628
past perfect progressive tense, **27b**: 623–624
past perfect tense, **27b**: 622
past progressive tense, **27b**: 620–621
past subjunctive mood, **27e**: 631–632
past tense(s), **27b**: 616–624
  in writing in the social sciences, **14c**: 334
pathos (pathetic appeal), **8f**: 167, 838
peer review, **4e**: 74–82
Pemberton, Gayle, **35b**: 712
per, 826
percent, percentage, 826
percentages, using numerals for, **45g**: 813
Pérez, Loida Maritza, **35a**: 710
perfect infinitive, **27b**: 625–626
perfect participle, **27b**: 626
perfect progressive tenses, **27b**: 616–617, 623–624
perfect subjunctive mood, **27e**: 632
perfect tenses, **27b**: 616–617, 621–623
performance, MLA documentation style for, **13b**: 299
period (punctuation mark)
  in abbreviations, **41a**: 761, **45a**: 805
  in biblical citations, **13a**: 277, 281, **41d**: 765

in divided quotations, 24d: 570

at end of sentence, 22e: 550,
41a: 761

with interjection, 21a: 517

with MLA-style citations, 13a: 280

with numerals, 45g: 813

quotation marks with, 40d:
757–758

to separate act, scene, and line
numbers in MLA-style citations,
13a: 277, 278, 281

to separate clauses, 24a: 564,
24c: 567

period (historical), capitalization of,
43a: 790

periodic sentence, 32b: 676

periodicals, 9c: 202. *See also* journal(s);
magazine(s); newspaper(s)

evaluating, 10b: 222

indexes to, 9c: 204–205

permission, to use image, 9d: 210

person, 26a: 589, 27b: 617,
27f: 634, 839

persona, 12c: 256

personal communication, APA
documentation style for,
15a: 349, 15b: 366

personal home page, MLA
documentation style for,
13b: 313

personal journal, 2e: 29, 3a: 32

personal pronoun(s), 21a: 511,
26a: 589–590, 839

personal response, to reading, 2d: 28–29

perspective, prospective, 826

persuade. See convince, persuade

persuasion, 8: 154

emphatic order and, 4c: 70

Petraglia, Richard, 3a: 33, 3b: 35–36,
4a: 58, 4e: 76, 77, 78, 82, 83,
87, 4h: 90, 91

phenomena, phenomenon, 826

photocopies, taking notes on,
11b: 231, 232

phrasal modals, 27a: 615, 27b: 619

phrasal prepositions, 21a: 516,
22a: 536

phrasal verb, 27a: 612–613, 839

phrase(s), 22a: 528, 839. *See also*
absolute phrase(s); participial
phrase(s); prepositional phrase(s);
transitional words and phrases

appositive, 22a: 537, 23b: 557,
831

comma following introductory,
37b: 729–731

comma separating series of,
37c: 732

as modifiers, 25a: 576, 25c: 583

nonessential, 21d: 525–526,
22a: 531–532

noun, 22a: 528–529, 22b: 539, 838

parallel, 31a: 668–669

as sentence fragments,
23b: 556–558

between subject and verb, 27f: 635

verb, 22a: 529–530

verbal, 22a: 530–534

pie charts, 7c: 140, 141

Pinter, Rachel, 14a: 332, 14d: 340

piracy, 11e: 242

plagiarism, 11d: 239, 11e: 241–243

planning

of essay, 3: 30

of Web site, 6d: 122, 125

play(s)

MLA documentation style for,
13a: 277, 278, 13b: 299

pages and divisions in,
45g: 812

quotations from, 12e: 265

plot, of literary work, 12c: 256

plural, 838. *See also* number, agreement in
  of abbreviations, **45a**: 805
  forming with apostrophes, **39c**: 752
  spelling of, **42d**: 782–783
plural verb forms, **27f**: 634
plus, 826
p.m. See a.m., p.m.
poetry, **12a**: 251
  explication of, **12b**: 254
  MLA citation style for, **13a**: 277, 278
  quotations from, **12e**: 265, **40a**: 755, **41h**: 771, **41i**: 772
point(s) of view, 839. *See also* person
  argument and, **8b**: 156–157, **8c**: 165–166
  consistency of, **29b**: 658–659
policy claim, **8d**: 161
Pollan, Michael, **33**: 682
Poniatowska, Elena, **4b**: 62
popular magazines, **9c**: 202
position paper, **16d**: 389–390
positive form, of adjective or adverb, **25b**: 577, 578
possessive case, **26a**: 589, **26b**: 593, 595, 598, 832
  apostrophe for, **39a**: 745–747
possessive determiner, **26c**: 600. *See also* possessive pronoun(s)
possessive forms, versus contractions, **26b**: 595, **42c**: 780
possessive pronoun(s), **26a**: 589, **26b**: 598, **26c**: 600
  confusion of with contractions, **42c**: 780
  no apostrophe with, **39a**: 747
post hoc, ergo propter hoc, **8i**: 180
postal abbreviations, **45b**: 806
postcolonial theory, **12d**: 261
posting date, **9d**: 209, **10d**: 228, **11b**: 231

PowerPoint, **20g**: 487–490
precede, proceed, 826
predicate, **21b**: 517–518, 519–520, 839. *See also* compound predicate
predicate adjective, beginning sentence with, **33b**: 688
predication, faulty, **28d**: 650, 834
preface, MLA documentation style for, **13b**: 291
prefix, spelling of words with, **42d**: 780
prejudice, prejudiced, 826
preliminary bibliography. *See* working bibliography
premise(s), **8h**: 175, 839
preposition(s), **21a**: 515–516, **22a**: 535–536, **28b**: 698, 839
  in collocations, **35c**: 714
  objects of, **22a**: 528, 535, **26b**: 594, 595
  phrasal, **21a**: 516, **22a**: 536
  repeating for parallel structure, **31b**: 669
prepositional phrase(s), **22a**: 534–536, 839
  in absolute phrase, **22a**: 537
  comma following introductory, **37b**: 730
  following linking verb, **21d**: 523, 524
  following indefinite pronoun, **27f**: 638
  as modifiers, **25a**: 576
  with passive voice, **27d**: 628
  as sentence fragment, **23b**: 557
  in simple sentence, **22d**: 547
  and variety in sentences, **33a**: 686, **33b**: 687–688
present infinitive, expressing time relations with, **27b**: 625
present participle(s), **22a**: 532, **26b**: 598, **27a**: 608, 609, 838

as adjectives, 25a: 573, 574
expressing time relations with,
    27b: 626
in participial phrase, 22a: 531
present perfect progressive tense,
    27b: 623
present perfect tense, 27b: 621–622
present progressive tense,
    27b: 619–620
present subjunctive mood, 27e: 631
present tense(s), 27b: 616–623
in writing about historical events or
    literature, 12e: 264, 27b: 618,
    27c: 627
in writing in the social sciences,
    14c: 334
presentation
    MLA documentation style for,
    13b: 299
    oral, 20g: 487–490
pretty, 826
previewing a text, 2a: 19–25
prewriting, 3: 31
primary audience, 1d: 13, 14
    for online writing, 6a: 111
primary cause, 3g: 50
primary consequence, 3g: 50
primary sources, 9a: 197, 839
    in the humanities, 16b: 382–383,
    16d: 388
    in the natural sciences, 18b: 435
    in the social sciences, 14b: 334
principal, principle, 826–827
print indexes, to periodicals, 9c:
    204–205
printouts, for taking notes,
    11b: 231
proceed. See precede, proceed
process analysis, 3b: 35, 3g: 49–50
process diagram, 7c: 142
progressive tenses, 27b: 616–617,
    619–621

pronoun(s), 21a: 510–511, 26a: 588,
    839. *See also specific types*
    as adjectives, 26a: 588
    agreement with antecedent of,
    26c: 599–602
    in appositives, 26b: 595–596
    cases of, 26b: 593–599
    clear references of, 26d: 603–605
    as complements, 21c: 521, 522,
    26b: 594
    first-person, 35d: 715–716
    as links between sentences, 4d: 71
    as objects, 26b: 594–595, 598
    point of view and, 29b: 658, 35d:
    715–716
    replacing gerund phrases, 22a: 530
    second-person, 35d: 715–716
    as subject of sentence, 21b: 518,
    23a: 554, 26d: 594
    types of, 26a: 589–593
pronunciation, misspelling and, 42b:
    778–779
proof, in argument, 8g: 171
proofreading, 4: 55, 4g: 89–90,
    5d: 104
    of essay exam responses, 5e: 109
proper adjective, 839
proper names
    abbreviations with, 45a: 805
    capitalization of, 43a: 788–792
    words derived from, capitalization
    of, 43a: 791
proper nouns, 21a: 509–510,
    26a: 592, 43e: 796, 839
proportion, of design elements, 6e: 126
proposition, 8d: 160, 8g: 171. *See also*
    claim
ProQuest, MLA documentation style
    for article from, 13b: 309
prospective. See perspective, prospective
protagonist, 12c: 254–255
protocol, in URL, 13b: 303

proximity
    design principle of, **7b**: 135, 136
    of image and related text, **7c**: 144
Pruchnic, Jeff, **5a**: 98, 99
psychoanalytic theories, **12d**: 262–263
PsycINFO, **9c**: 203
public domain, images in, **9d**: 210
public law, MLA documentation style
        for, **13b**: 298, 310
publication data
    APA documentation style for,
        15b: 355–356
    CMS documentation style for,
        17a: 406
    CSE documentation style for,
        19a: 455–456
    MLA documentation style for,
        13b: 287–288
publication date
    APA documentation style for,
        15a: 346, 347, 349,
        15b: 353–354, 358, 360
    CSE documentation style for,
        19a: 452, 455, 456, 457, 460
    MLA documentation style for,
        13b: 288, 295
*Publication Manual of the American
        Psychological Association,*
        14c: 334, **15**: 346
published dissertation, MLA
        documentation style for, **13b**: 299
published letter
    CMS documentation style for,
        17a: 411
    MLA documentation style for,
        13b: 299
publisher(s)
    in APA documentation style,
        15b: 356, 358
    in CMS documentation style,
        17a: 406
    credibility of, **10b**: 221–222

    in MLA documentation style,
        13b: 288–289
publishing software, **7d**: 149
Puerto Rican, use of, **34d**: 700
pull quotes, **7d**: 152
punctuation
    apostrophe as, **39a–c**: 745–752
    colon as, **41d**: 763–766
    comma as, **37a–g**: 727–740
    dash as, **41e**: 766–767
    ellipsis points as, **41h**: 769–771
    at end of sentence, **22e**: 550
    exclamation point as, **41c**: 763
    with independent clauses,
        24a: 563–564
    with MLA-style citations,
        13a: 279–281
    parentheses as, **41f**: 767–768
    period as, **41a**: 761
    proofreading for, **4g**: 90
    question mark as, **40b**: 753–759
    quotation marks as, **38a–d**: 710–716
    semicolon as, **38a–c**: 741–743
    slash as, **41i**: 772
    spaces with, **41**: 760
    square brackets as, **41g**: 768–769
purpose (rhetorical), **1a**: 4, 5, **1c**: 6–9
    of argument, **8**: 155, **8a**: 155–156
    of business writing, **20b**: 469,
        20f: 482
    and conclusion of essay, **4b**: 64
    of hyperlinks, **6d**: 121
    of online writing, **6a**: 111,
        6e: 126–127
    and paragraph organization, **4c**: 67
    of research paper, **9a**: 196–197
    revising and, **4d**: 74, **4e**: 75, 76
    tone and, **4a**: 57–59
    of visual document, **7a**: 131–133,
        7d: 146
    of writing in the humanities,
        16a: 380, 381

of writing in the natural sciences,
18a: 431, 433
of writing in the social sciences,
14a: 331

qualifier(s), 840
adverbs as, 21a: 515
in argument, 8h: 177
vague, 3c: 39
qualitative studies, 14b: 333,
18b: 435
quantitative studies, 14b: 332,
18b: 435
question(s), 22e: 550
and argument, 8b: 156–157
begging the, 8i: 178, 179
capitalization of abbreviated,
43c: 795
in essay examinations, 5e: 105–106
ignoring the, 8i: 182
interrogative pronouns in, 26a: 592
for interviews, 9e: 212
journalists', 3a: 34
opening essay with, 4b: 61
research, 9a: 193–195, 14a:
331–332, 16a: 381–382,
18a: 433
rhetorical, 22e: 551, 33c: 689
for survey, 9e: 213–214, 215
for variety, 33c: 689
word order in, 21d: 525–526
question mark
with quotation marks, 13a: 281,
40d: 758–759
use of, 41b: 761–762
questionnaire, 9e: 213–215
Quindlen, Anna, 4b: 63
Quinn, Timothy, 11a: 229, 230
quotation(s), 840
APA style for, 15a: 346, 347
attributive tags set off by commas in,
37f: 738

block, 11d: 237, 12e: 265,
13a: 279–280
capitalization of first word of,
43c: 793–794
colon directing attention to,
41d: 764
divided, 24d: 570–571
ellipsis points to mark omission in,
41h: 769–771
ending with exclamation point,
41c: 763
from literary works, 12e: 265
opening essay with, 4b: 61–62
questions as, 41b: 762
quotation marks for,
40a: 753–755
in research papers, 11d: 237–238,
11e: 243
square brackets for additions or
alterations to, 41g: 769–769
quotation, quote, 827
quotation marks
British usage of, 40b: 756
with commas and periods, 40d:
757–758
for dialogue, 40a: 754
for direct quotations, 11d: 237,
11e: 243, 40a: 753–755
for ironic tone or unusual usage,
40c: 756–757
with question mark, exclamation
point, or dash, 13a: 281,
40d: 758–759
with semicolons and colons,
40d: 758
for short excerpts of poetry, 38a: 712
single, for quotations within
quotations, 40a: 754
thoughts enclosed in, 40a: 755
for titles of short works, 13b: 287,
17a: 405, 40b: 755–756
quotes, pull, 7d: 152

race, referring to, **34d**: 699–700

race-based literary theory, **12d**: 260–261

radial pattern, for Web site, **6d**: 122, 124

radio program, MLA documentation style for, **13b**: 300, 311

raise, rise, 827

ranking scale, in survey question, **9e**: 214

reader-response theory, **12d**: 259

reading, **1a**: 4, 5, **2**: 18
  active, **12b**: 251–253
  of assignment sheet, **5a**: 96, 99–100
  close, **12b**: 253
  for content, **2b**: 25–28
  of examination instructions, **5e**: 105–106
  personal response to, **2d**: 28–29
  previewing in, **2a**: 19–25
  of syllabus, **5a**: 96, 97
  writing about, **2e**: 29

reading journal, **2e**: 29, **3a**: 32

real, really, 827

reason/is because, mismatch of, **28d**: 651

reason why, 827

reasoning
  deductive, **4c**: 66, **8h**: 175, 834
  examining author's, **11f**: 246
  inductive, **4c**: 67, **8h**: 174–175, 835
  in social sciences, **14b**: 332–333
  Toulmin model of, **8h**: 175–176, 841

reasons, in argument, **8e**: 163–164, **8g**: 173

rebuttal terms, **8h**: 177

recommendation section, of business report, **20h**: 491, 502

recursive process of writing, **3**: 32

recursive reading, **2**: 18

red herring, **8i**: 182

redundancy, **36a**: 719

reference book(s), **9b**: 198, 200–201
  APA documentation style for selection from, **15b**: 360
  criteria for evaluating, **10c**: 224–225
  for writing about literature, **12b**: 253

reference list
  APA style for, **15b**: 349–350, 352–368, **15c**: 377
  in business report, **20h**: 504
  CSE style for, **18c**: 437, **18d**: 449, **19a**: 450, 452, 460, **19b**: 461, 465–466
  in laboratory report, **18d**: 442, 449
  in social sciences, **14c**: 337

references (personal), **20d**: 479

reflection paper, **14d**: 338–339, **16d**: 386–387

reflective pause, ellipsis points for, **41h**: 771

reflexive pronoun(s), **26a**: 590, 840

refutation, **8e**: 165, **8g**: 171, 172–173, 840

regard, regarding, regards, 827

regionalisms, in academic writing, **34c**: 696

regular verbs, **27a**: 607–608

relation, relationship, 827

relative adverb, **22b**: 540

relative clause, **22b**: 540, **33a**: 686, 831. *See also* adjectival clause(s)

relative pronoun(s), **26a**: 591–592, **26d**: 604, 840
  to combine short sentences, **33a**: 683
  connection of, with verb, **28d**: 651
  deleting unnecessary, **36a**: 722

in dependent clause, **22b**: 539, 540, **30a**: 663–664

match of, with antecedent, **27f**: 637

omission of, **22b**: 541

redundant, **36a**: 720

relevance, of sources, **10d**: 227–228

reliability
  of information (evidence), **8c**: 158–159
  of periodicals, **10b**: 222
  of research findings, **11f**: 246

religion(s)
  capitalization of, **43a**: 791
  referring to, **34d**: 701

Renning, Adair N., **4c**: 69

repetition
  of design elements, **7b**: 135, 137, **7d**: 150
  for emphasis, **32d**: 677
  for linking sentences, **4d**: 72
  for parallelism, **31b**: 669–670
  unnecessary, **36b**: 723

reports, congressional, MLA documentation style for, **13b**: 310

reprinted works, MLA documentation style for, **13b**: 292

republished book, MLA documentation style for, **13b**: 292

rereading, **2c**: 28

research, **9**: 193
  field, **9e**: 211–215, **14b**: 332
  library resources for, **9b**: 198–201, **9c**: 202–206
  for literary interpretation, **12b**: 253
  online sources for, **9d**: 206–211
  rhetorical situation and, **9a**: 193–197

research paper
  in APA style, **15c**: 368–377
  in CMS style, **17b**: 415–429

in CSE style, **19b**: 461–466

rhetorical situation and, **11a**: 229–231

research question(s), **9a**: 193–195
  for writing in the humanities, **16a**: 381–382
  for writing in the natural sciences, **18a**: 433
  for writing in the social sciences, **14a**: 331–332

resolution
  congressional, MLA documentation style for, **13b**: 310
  of plot, **12c**: 256
  of position paper, **16d**: 389

resources, of rhetorical situation, **1a**: 4–5, **1e**: 15

respect, in writing about differences, **34d**: 700–701

respectfully, respectively, 827

response
  to literary work, **12b**: 252, **12d**: 259
  to reading, **2d**: 28–29
  to sources, **11f**: 244–246

restrictive clause, **22b**: 540

restrictive element(s), **37d**: 734, 834. *See also* essential element(s)

results section, of research report, **14d**: 342, 344, **18d**: 442, 445, **19b**: 461

résumés, **20d**: 475–479

return address, **20b**: 469, 471

review(s)
  of literary works, **12b**: 254
  MLA documentation style for, **13b**: 297, 307
  by peers, **4e**: 74–82

revision, **3**: 31, **4**: 55
  of choppy sentences, **22a**: 532, **22b**: 541
  of comma splices and fused sentences, **24c**: 567–569

(cont.)

revision *(cont.)*
  of double negatives, **25d**: 586
  of essay exam responses, **5e**: 109
  essentials of, **4a**: 56–59
  of faulty comparisons, **25b**:
      578–579
  of misplaced modifiers, **25c**: 581,
      582, 583–584
  of mixed metaphors, **28c**: 649–650
  peer review and, **4e**: 74–82
  of sentence fragments, **23b**:
      556–558, **23c**: 558–559
  of transitions within and between
      paragraphs, **4d**: 71–74
  for unified and coherent paragraphs,
      4c: 65–71
rhetoric
  definition of, **1**: 3
  visual, **7b**: 134–137
rhetorical appeal(s), **8f**: 167–170, 840
rhetorical fallacies, **8i**: 177–183,
      11f: 266
rhetorical methods of development,
      3b: 35, **3g**: 47–54
  for literary interpretation,
      12b: 252–253
rhetorical purpose. *See* purpose
      (rhetorical)
rhetorical question(s), **22e**: 551,
      33c: 689
rhetorical situation, **1a**: 4–5
  adjective use and, **25a**: 573
  adverb use and, **21a**: 515
  assessing usage in, **32d**: 657
  climactic order and, **32c**: 677
  gerund phrases and, **22a**: 531
  noun choice and, **21a**: 510
  noun phrases and, **22a**: 529
  in online environment, **6a**: 110–112,
      6b: 113, **6d**: 122
  and parallelism, **31c**: 671
  pronoun use and, **21a**: 511,
      26a: 590

research and, **9a**: 193–197
  of research paper, **11a**: 229–231
  sentence forms and patterns and,
      21b: 518, **21d**: 526, **22d**: 529
  sentence fragments and, **23c**: 559
  sentence style and, 645
  and short sentences, **33a**: 684
  tone and, **29c**: 659–660
  usage and, **21**: 508, **34a**: 693–694,
      34d: 701
  and use of commas and conjunctions
      in a series, **37c**: 732–733
  and use of commas, dashes, and
      colons, **41e**: 767
  and use of dashes and parentheses,
      41f: 768
  and use of images, **9d**: 210–211
  and use of slang, **42c**: 695
  verb choice and, **21a**: 509
  visual documents and, **7a**: 131–133
  for writing in business, **20**: 467, 468
  for writing in the humanities,
      16: 378–379
  for writing about literature,
      12: 249, 250
  for writing in the natural sciences,
      18: 430, 431
  for writing in the social sciences,
      14: 329–330
Rhys, Jean, **12d**: 261
rise. See raise, rise
Robinson Crusoe (Defoe), **12d**: 261
Rogerian argument, **8f**: 169–170,
      173, 840
Rogerian arrangement, **8g**: 172
Rogers, Carl R., **8f**: 169
root words, **42b**: 778, **42d**: 780
Rose, Mike, **4b**: 62
Roy, Jody M., **3g**: 53
run-on sentence, **24**: 562. *See also*
      fused sentence(s)
running head, in APA-style paper,
      15c: 369, 370

-*s* ending, **27f**: 635, 639
-*s* form, of verbs, **27a**: 607, 608, 609
Sacks, Oliver, **1d**: 13
sacred texts, **44a**: 800
    MLA documentation style for,
        13a: 277, 278, 281, **13b**: 298,
        310, **41d**: 765
Salinger, J. D., **12d**: 263
satellite names, italics for, **44d**: 801
Scaggs, Austin, **3g**: 47, 48
scanning pattern, for visual document,
        7d: 147
scholarly books, **9b**: 198, **10c**:
        224–225
scholarly journals, **9c**: 202, **10b**: 222,
        10c: 224–225
scientific method, **18b**: 434, **18d**: 440
scientific reports, **18c**: 436. *See also*
        specific types
Scientific Style and Format: The CSE
        Manual for Authors, Editors, and
        Publishers, **19**: 450
screen numbers, in MLA-style
        citations, **13a**: 278–279
scriptural references. *See* sacred texts
search, in online catalog, **9b**: 198–200
search engines (search tools), **9d**: 207,
        208, **10a**: 220, 840
search path, **13b**: 303, 309
second person, **26a**: 589, **27b**: 617,
        35d: 716
second-person pronouns, **26a**: 589,
        590, **35d**: 716
secondary audience, **1d**: 13, 14
    for online writing, **6a**: 111
secondary consequences, **3g**: 50
secondary source(s), **9a**: 197, 840.
        See also indirect source(s)
    CMS documentation style for,
        14a: 357–358
    in the humanities, **16b**: 383–384,
        16d: 388
    in the natural sciences, **18b**: 435

    in the social sciences, **14b**: 334
section, of newspaper, in MLA
        documentation style, **13b**: 296
Securities and Exchange Commission,
        10c: 223
Sedaris, David, **35a**: 709
Seife, Charles, **3c**: 41
Seitz, Anna, **8e**: 164, **8g**: 171,
        8j: 184, 185, **9c**: 204
semicolon
    in APA-style citations, **15a**: 348
    in compound sentence, **22d**: 548
    in CSE documentation style,
        19a: 451, 456
    between independent clauses,
        22c: 546, 548, **24a**: 563,
        24c: 567, **37a**: 729, **38a**:
        741–742
    in MLA-style citations, **13a**:
        276–277
    quotation marks with, **40d**: 758
    revising common errors in use of,
        38c: 743
    separating elements that contain
        commas, **37c**: 732, **38b**: 742
    separating links in search path,
        13b: 303
senior citizens, use of, **34d**: 700
sensor. See censor, censure, sensor
sensory details, **3g**: 48
sensory verbs, **21a**: 509, **21c**: 522
    adjective-adverb confusion and,
        25a: 576–577
sensual, sensuous, 827
sentence(s). *See also specific types*
    abbreviated, **23c**: 560
    capitalization in, **43c**: 793–795
    combining, **22a**: 532, **22b**: 541,
        22d: 549, **30a**: 663, **33a**:
        683–684
    conjunctions and conjunctive
        adverbs in, **21c**: 498–500

                                        (cont.)

sentence(s) *(cont.)*
    cumulative and periodic, **32b**: 676
    editing of, **4f**: 88
    effective, 645
    ending with preposition, **22a**: 535
    forms of, **22d**: 547–549
    functions of, **22e**: 550–551
    intentionally incomplete, **41h**: 771
    linking of, **4d**: 71–72
    omission marked by ellipsis points
        in, **41h**: 770–771
    parallelism and, **31a**: 669, **31c**: 670
    patterns of, **21d**: 523–526
    period at end of, **41a**: 761
    relating parts of, **28d**: 650–652
    run-on, **24**: 562
    short, **32g**: 680–681, **33a**: 683, 684
    subjects and predicates of, **21b**:
        517–520
sentence fragment(s), **23**: 553
    dependent clauses as, **23a**: 554,
        23c: 558–560
    phrases as, **23b**: 556–558
    recognizing, **23a**: 553–556
sentence modifier, **25c**: 584, 840
sentence structure, and paraphrasing,
    11d: 238–239
series
    book in, MLA documentation style
        for, **12b**: 283
    comma separating elements in,
        37c: 732–733
    dash following, **41e**: 767
setting, of literary work, **12c**: 257
sexist language, **26c**: 602,
    34d: 697–699
sexual orientation, referring to,
    34d: 701
shall, will, 827–828
ship names, italics for, **44d**: 801
Shipman, Pat, **1c**: 8

short note form, **17a**: 400, 403, 404,
    405, 408, **17b**: 426–427
should of. See could of
Shreeve, James, **28a**: 647
sidebars, **7d**: 152
sight. See cite, site, sight
signature, on business letter, **20b**: 470,
    471
Silko, Leslie Marmon, **32a**: 674
simile, **35a**: 710–711
simple future tense, **27b**: 619
simple past tense, **27b**: 619
simple predicate, **21b**: 518
simple present tense, **27b**: 617–618,
    27f: 635
simple sentence(s), **22d**: 547
    combining, **22d**: 549,
        33a: 683–684
simple subject, **21b**: 518
simple tenses, **27b**: 616–619
singular number, **26c**: 600–601, 838
singular verb forms, **27f**: 634
singular words, ending in -s, **27f**: 640
sit, set, 828
site. See cite, site, sight
site map, **6d**: 120
slang, **34c**: 695
slash, **12e**: 265, **41i**: 772
    in URL, **13b**: 303
slippery slope, **8i**: 182
"Slumber Did My Spirit Seal, A"
    (Wordsworth), **12b**: 254
Smithsonian Images, **9d**: 211
Snyder, Gary, **44b**: 800
so, 828
    versus *so that,* **22c**: 545
social sciences, **14**: 329
    audience and purpose for writing in,
        14a: 331–332
    conventions of language and
        organization in, **14c**: 334–337

evidence, sources, and reasoning in, 14b: 332–334
research questions in, 14a: 331–332
rhetorical situation for writing in, 14: 329–330
samples of writing in, 14d: 338–345, 15c: 370–377
social setting, 12c: 257
software
    meeting, 6b: 113, 114
    publishing, 7d: 149
    for résumé writing, 20d: 476
soliloquy, dramatic, 12a: 251
Solnit, Rebecca, 32a: 675
someplace. See anyplace, everyplace, someplace
sometime, sometimes, some time, 828
sort of a. See kind of a, sort of a
sound recording on CD, MLA documentation style for, 13b: 301
sources. *See also* citation of sources; documentation of sources; electronic sources; online sources; primary sources; secondary sources
    articles as, 9c: 202–206
    books as, 9b: 198–201
    coverage of, 11f: 245–246
    criteria for evaluation of, 10c: 224–225
    field research as, 9e: 211–215, 14b: 332
    indirect, 13a: 277, 15a: 349
    integrating into writing, 11d: 235–241
    questionnaires as, 9e: 213–215
    relevance and timeliness of, 10d: 227–228, 11f: 245
    reliability of, 11f: 246
    responding to, 11f: 244–246
    U.S. government documents as, 9d: 210

SOV (subject-object-verb) languages, 21d: 524
space. *See* white space
spacecraft names, italics for, 44d: 801
spatial order, 4c: 69–70
specialized audience, 1d: 10–12
    for brochure, 7a: 132–133
    for online writing, 6a: 111
specialized dictionaries, 9b: 200, 201, 27a: 613, 34e: 702, 703
specialized reference books, 9b: 200–201
specially. See especially, specially
specific word, definition of, 35a: 709
speech, online, MLA documentation style for, 13b: 311
spell checker, 42a: 777–778
    and proofreading, 4g: 90, 5d: 104
spelling
    British versus American, 42e: 784
    confusion of *ei* and *ie* in, 42e: 783–784
    of homophones, 42c: 779–780
    hyphens in, 42f: 784–785
    of monetary amounts, 45g: 813
    of numbers, 45f: 810–811
    of plural nouns, 42d: 782–783
    prefixes and, 42d: 780
    pronunciation and, 42b: 778–779
    proofreading for, 4g: 90
    spell checkers and, 42a: 777–778
    suffixes and, 42d: 781–782
    of words from other languages, 42d: 783
Spence, Gerry, 1c: 8
split infinitive(s), 22a: 533, 840
Spohn, Carla, 16d: 394, 395
sponsors, of Web sites, 10c: 223–226, 13b: 305, 15b: 366
square brackets, 11d: 237, 13a: 281, 15b: 368, 19a: 457, 41g: 768–769, 43e: 794

squinting modifier, 25c: 582, 840

stance, of writer, 1e: 15

Standardized English, 8e: 165, 645, 841

state name

in addresses, 45b: 806

in APA documentation style, 15b: 356

in CMS documentation style, 17a: 406

statement

arguable, 8b: 157–158

converting into question, 21d: 525

stationary, stationery, 828

statistical symbols, italics for, 44e: 802

statistics

opening essay with, 4b: 60

as supporting evidence, 8e: 164, 165

Steinbeck, John, 12d: 261

Stewart, Kristen, 10a: 218

storyboard, 6d: 122

Streetcar Named Desire, A (Williams), 12c: 257

style. *See also specific formats*

clarity in, 34b: 694

and online writing, 6c: 116–117

for writing in the humanities, 16c: 384–385

for writing in the natural sciences, 18c: 435–436

for writing in the social sciences, 14c: 334

style manuals

for writing in the arts and humanities, 13: 273, 16c: 385, 17: 400

for writing in the sciences, 18c: 435, 19: 450

for writing in the social sciences, 14c: 334, 15: 346

subject (of essay), 841

focusing of into specific topic, 3b: 34–36

selecting, 3a: 31–34

subject (of sentence), 21b: 517–519, 841

avoiding comma between verb and, 37g: 739

dependent clause as, 22b: 539–540

mismatch of, with verb, 28d: 650–651

noun phrase as, 22a: 528

pronoun as, 26a: 589, 26b: 594

in question, 21d: 525, 526

shared, 33a: 686

understood *you* as, 22e: 550, 23a: 554

verb agreement with, 27f: 634–641

subject complement, 21c: 522, 26b: 594, 27f: 640, 832–833

subject directories, 9d: 208

subject pronouns, dropping of, 23a: 554

subject searches, 9b: 198, 199–200

subjective case, 26a: 589, 26b: 593–594, 595, 832

subjectivity, of interpretation, 16c: 385

subjunctive mood, 27e: 631–633, 837

submarine names, italics for, 44d: 801

subordinating conjunction(s), 21a: 516, 22b: 539, 542, 22c: 544–545, 30a: 662–663, 30b: 665, 30c: 666, 833

to combine short sentences, 33a: 683–684, 685

introducing dependent clause, 22b: 539, 542, 22c: 544

subordination, 30: 662, 841

avoiding faulty or excessive, 30c: 666–667

effective use of, 30a: 662–664

subscription service, 9c: 202

MLA documentation style for work from, 13b: 307–309

subsequent mention, definite article and, **21a**: 513

substantiation claim, **8d**: 160, 161

subtitles
APA documentation style for, **15b**: 354
capitalization of, **43b**: 792–793
CMS documentation style for, **17a**: 405
CSE documentation style for, **19a**: 454
MLA documentation style for, **13b**: 287

suffix(es)
of adjectives, **25a**: 573
spelling and, **42d**: 781–783
of URL, **10c**: 223

Suggestions to Authors of the Reports of the United States Geological Survey (United States Geological Society), **18c**: 435

Sullivan, Andrew, **35a**: 710

Sullivan, Randall, **4b**: 64

Sullivan, Robert, **4c**: 71

summary
colon directing attention to, **41d**: 764
executive, **20f**: 483
of literary work, **12b**: 254
previewing and, **2a**: 20, 21
in Rogerian argument, **8f**: 169, 170
of source material, **11d**: 240–241

Sun Also Rises, The (Hemingway), **12d**: 260

superlative forms, of adjectives and adverbs, **25b**: 577–578

superlatives, double, **25b**: 579

superscript numbers, **13a**: 274, **17a**: 400, 401, **19a**: 451, 452

support, in argument, **8g**: 172

supposed to, used to, 828

Supreme Being, capitalization of, **43a**: 791

Suro, Roberto, **3c**: 38

surveys
questions for, **9e**: 214
in social sciences, **14b**: 332

Suslin, Marianne, **9c**: 204, **9d**: 210, **11b**: 231, **13c**: 316, 317

SVO (subject-verb-object) language, **21d**: 524

Swope, Sam, **3g**: 49, 50

syllabus, **5a**: 96–97, **5b**: 101

syllogism, **8h**: 175, 841

Sylves, Robin, **3g**: 50, 51

symbols, **12c**: 257–258

synchronous forums, **6b**: 113–115, 841

synonyms
as appositives, **35e**: 717
dictionary information on, **34e**: 705

synthesis, 802

Table function, **7d**: 149

table of contents, previewing and, **2a**: 21, 22

tables, **7c**: 139–140, 144, **14c**: 335–336, **18c**: 437

tags, attributive. *See* attributive tags

take. See bring, take

Tan, Amy, **4c**: 71

Tannen, Deborah, **3c**: 39

Tebbe, Michelle, **18a**: 433, **18b**: 435, **18c**: 437, **18d**: 437, **19b**: 461, 462

technical background report, **18d**: 440

technical words, audience and, **34c**: 696

television program
APA documentation style for, **15b**: 368
MLA documentation style for, **13b**: 300, 311

tense(s), 27b: 616–626, 841
  consistency of, 27c: 627,
    29a: 655–657
  in writing about historical events
    or literary works, 12e: 264,
    27b: 618, 27c: 627
  in writing in the social sciences,
    14c: 334
testimony, as supporting evidence,
  8e: 164, 165
Texas Department of Transportation,
  1d: 11
text, in relation to image, 7c: 137–139
text-based literary theory, 12d:
  261–262
textual hyperlinks, 6d: 120–121,
  6e: 127–128
than, then, 828
that
  omitting, 22b: 539–540,
    22c: 545, 28c: 649
  versus *which,* 22b: 541,
    26a: 592, 828
that, which, who, 26a: 591, 828
the, 21a: 512, 513, 514
  omission of, from name of
    periodical, 13b: 295
their, there, they're, 788
Their Eyes Were Watching God
  (Hurston), 12d: 260
theirself, theirselves, 829
theme, of literary work, 12c: 255,
  258, 841
then. See than, then
there, as expletive, 21b: 519, 27f: 637
  deleting, 36a: 721–722
  indefinite article with, 21a: 513
thesaurus, 34f: 706
  and tone of writing, 4a: 59
thesis, 3c: 37, 841
  for argument, 8b: 157
  assessing, 3c: 41

opening essay with, 4b: 62
  restating to conclude essay, 4b: 62
  for writing in the humanities,
    16b: 382
thesis statement, 3c: 37
  developing, 3c: 37–41
  placement of, 3c: 40–41, 8g: 170
  for response to essay exam question,
    5e: 107, 109
third person, 26a: 589, 27b: 617, 839
third-person pronouns, 26a: 589
thoughts, enclosed in quotation marks,
  40a: 755
thread, 6b: 113, 114–115
three-em dash, 17a: 402
thru, 829
thusly, 829
time designations
  abbreviation of, 45d: 808
  numerals versus words for, 45g: 811
time period, 829
time periods, abbreviations of, 45d: 808
time pressure, 5: 96
  and essay exams, 5e: 105
time zones, abbreviations of, 45d: 808
timeline, 3g: 50
timeliness, of sources, 6a: 111–112,
  10d: 227–228, 11f: 245
title(s)
  APA documentation style for,
    15b: 354
  capitalization of, 43a: 789,
    43b: 792–793
  CMS documentation style for,
    17a: 405
  colon separating subtitle and,
    41d: 765
  CSE documentation style for,
    19a: 454–455
  italics for, 44a: 799–800
  MLA documentation style for,
    13b: 286–287, 293–295

previewing and, **2a**: 20

quotation marks with, **40b**: 755–756

set off by commas, **37d**: 735

singular verb with, **27f**: 639

title of address, abbreviation of, **45a**: 805

title page

for APA-style paper, **15c**: 369, 370

of book, **13b**: 289, **15b**: 357

for CMS-style paper, **17b**: 415

for CSE-style paper, **19b**: 461, 462

for MLA-style paper, **13c**: 315

to, as infinitive marker, **22a**: 532, 533, 534, **27a**: 614, **31b**: 669

to, too, two, 829

tone, **4a**: 57, **34a**: 693, 841

consistency of, **29c**: 659–660

and contractions, **34c**: 695

of e-mails and memos, **20c**: 473–474

in introduction to essay, **4b**: 59–60

of literary work, **12b**: 256

and preposition at end of sentence, **22a**: 535

revising and, **4a**: 57–59

and sentence fragments, **23c**: 559

topic, 841

for argument, **8b**: 156–158

assessing, **3b**: 36

focusing of, **3b**: 34–37, **5c**: 103

in introduction to essay, **4b**: 59–60, 62

for literary interpretation, **12b**: 252–253

versus theme, **12c**: 258

topic sentence, **4c**: 65, 841

to express main idea, **4c**: 65–67

and paragraph unity, **4c**: 68

TotalNEWS, **9d**: 207

Toulmin, Stephen, **8h**: 175

Toulmin model of reasoning, **8h**: 175–176, 841

toward, towards, 829

Track Changes, **4a**: 56, **4e**: 78, 83

trade books, **9b**: 198, **10b**: 221–222, **10c**: 224–225

trade magazines, **9c**: 202, **10b**: 222

tradition, appeal to, **8i**: 178

Tranel, Daniel, **29c**: 660

transitional words or phrases, **2b**: 26, **5e**: 108

coherence and, **4d**: 72–73

commas following, **38a**: 742

to link independent clauses, **24c**: 569

in narration, **3g**: 47

set off by commas, **37d**: 736

types of, **4d**: 73

transitions, 841

within and between paragraphs, **4d**: 71–74

transitive verb, **21d**: 523, 524, **26d**: 587–588, 841

translated book

APA documentation style for, **15b**: 359

CMS documentation style for, **17a**: 409–410

MLA documentation style for, **13b**: 292, 305

truncation, **9b**: 198

try and, 829

Turabian, Kate L., **16c**: 385, **17**: 400

Turner, J. M. W., **27b**: 618

turning point, of plot, **12c**: 256

Turnitin, **11e**: 242

tutors, at writing centers, **5b**: 101, 102

typefaces. *See* fonts

ultimately. See eventually, ultimately

unabridged dictionaries, **34e**: 702

unconventional words, 815

underlining
  meaning of, **44**: 798–799
  in MLA style, **13b**: 286, 287
understood *you*, **22e**: 550, **23a**: 554
uniform resource locator. *See* URL(s)
uninterested. See disinterested,
  uninterested
unique, 829
unique noun, definite article with,
  21a: 513
United States, abbreviation for,
  45d: 808–809
United States Environmental
  Protection Agency (EPA),
  18d: 440, 441
United States Geological Society,
  18c: 435
units of measure
  hyphens in, **42f**: 785
  numerals with, **45f**: 811
unity
  of design elements, **6e**: 127
  of paragraphs, **4c**: 65, 67–68
  of sentences, **28**: 646
university presses, **10b**: 221,
  13b: 288, **15b**: 356
unlike, **37d**: 737
unpublished paper, APA
  documentation style for,
  15b: 354
unsigned article, MLA documentation
  style for, **13b**: 296
URL(s), **9d**: 208–209, **10c**: 223,
  13b: 302–304, 362, 365,
  17a: 412, 413, **19a**: 457
  angle brackets in, **41g**: 769
U.S. Constitution, MLA
  documentation style for,
  13a: 278, **13b**: 298
U.S. Courts, **9d**: 210
U.S. Government, as source of public
  information, **9d**: 210

U.S. Government Printing Office,
  9d: 210, **43**: 787
U.S. Postal Service, abbreviations of,
  45b: 806
usability testing, **6d**: 124, 841
usage, 815–816. *See also* word choice
  assessing, **42d**: 701
  and clear style, **34b**: 694
  conciseness in, **36a–c**: 719–724
  exactness in, **35a–e**: 707–718
  rhetorical situation and, **21**: 508,
    34a: 693–694, **34d**: 701
use, utilize, 829
used to. See supposed to, used to
Utah Attorney General's Office,
  32e: 678

vagueness, of thesis statement,
  3c: 39–40
values, and argument, **8**: 155, **8b**: 157,
  8e: 164
van Eyck, Jan, **16b**: 383
variety, in sentences, **33**: 682
  length and form and, **33a**: 683–686
  openings and, **33b**: 687–688
  type of sentence and, **33c**: 689–690
verb(s), **21a**: 509, 842. *See also* action
  verb(s); auxiliary verb(s); linking
  verb(s); tense(s)
  agreement of subject with,
    27f: 634–641
  for attribution and their
    complements, **28d**: 652
  in attributive tags, **11d**: 236
  avoiding comma between subject
    and, **37g**: 739
  compound, **28b**: 648
  consistency in tenses of,
    27c: 627
  followed by gerunds and/or
    infinitives, **22a**: 533–534
  forms of, **27a**: 607–616

in idiomatic combinations, **22a**: 536
irregular, **27a**: 607, 609–612
as key word in predicate,
    21b: 519–520
mismatch of, with complement,
    28d: 651–652
mismatch of, with subject,
    28d: 650–651
mood and, **27e**: 631–633
not used in progressive form,
    27b: 621
phrasal, **27a**: 612–613, 839
in question, **21d**: 526
regular, **27a**: 607–608
sentence patterns and types of,
    21d: 523–524
sharing same subject, **33a**: 686
taking indirect objects, **21c**: 522
tenses of, **27b**: 616–626, **27c**: 627,
    29a: 655–657, 841
voice and, **27d**: 628–630
verb phrase, **22a**: 529–530, 842
verbal, **22a**: 530, 842
verbal phrase(s), **22a**: 530–534
as sentence fragment, **23b**: 557
in simple sentence, **22d**: 547
and variety in sentences, **33a**: 686,
    33b: 687–688
very, 829
video, online, MLA documentation
    style for, **13b**: 311
videocassette, CMS documentation
    style for, **17a**: 414
visual documents, **7a**: 131–133
    design of, **7b**: 134–137
    genres and features of, **7d**: 144–153
visual elements, **7a**: 131
    in combination with text, **7**: 130,
        7c: 137–144
    previewing and, **2a**: 21, 23
    rhetorical purpose and,
        6e: 126–128, **7a**: 131–133

visual rhetoric, **7b**: 134–137
vivid image, concluding essay with,
    4b: 63–64
vocabulary, for literary interpretation,
    12c: 254–258
vocative, **37b**: 731, 842
voice, **27d**: 628–630, 842
    emphasis and, **32e**: 677–679
    in writing in the humanities,
        16c: 385
    in writing in the social sciences,
        14c: 334
volume number(s), **13a**: 277,
    13b: 293, 295, **15b**: 356,
    17a: 405, **19a**: 456
VSO (verb-subject-object) languages,
    21d: 524

Walker, Alan, **1c**: 8
Walker, Alice, **3c**: 40, **3f**: 45,
    46, **12**: 249, **12c**: 256,
    35a: 710
Walker, Marion A., **20**: 468
Wallin, Jason, **14**: 329, **14b**: 333,
    14c: 335–337, **14d**: 342
warrant, in Toulmin model, **8h**: 176,
    177, 842
ways, 829
we. See first person
"we real cool" (Brooks), **12d**: 259
Web address. *See* URL(s)
Web document(s). *See also*
    Web site(s)
    APA documentation style for,
        15b: 365–366
    composing, **6d**: 117–119
    designing, **6e**: 128–129
    drafting, **6d**: 123–125
    rhetorical situation for,
        6a: 110–112
Web Gallery of Art, **9d**: 211
Web log. *See* blog

Web site(s), **44a**: 800
  accessibility of, **6d**: 124–125
  arrangement of, **6d**: 118–119
  for course, **5a**: 97, 98, **5b**: 101
  CSE documentation style for,
    19a: 459
  evaluation of, **10c**: 223–226
  MLA documentation style for,
    13b: 312–313
  planning and developing of, **6d**: 125
  sponsors of, **10c**: 223–226,
    13b: 305, **15b**: 366
Web Studio, **6d**: 122
WebClipz, **9d**: 211
WebCrawler, **9d**: 207
WebCT, **6b**: 113
well. See good, well
Welty, Eudora, **4b**: 61
West, Cornel, **8d**: 163
Wharton, Edith, **12d**: 260
what, in noun clause, and verb
    agreement, **27f**: 641
where, 829
where . . . at, where . . . to, 830
  beginning dependent clause,
    30a: 664
which. See also that, which; that,
    which, who
  versus *that,* **22b**: 541, **26a**: 592
White (or *white*), use of, **34d**: 700
white paper, **18d**: 440, 441
  APA documentation style for,
    15b: 368
white space, **7b**: 136, **7d**: 147, 148
who, whom, **26a**: 592,
    26b: 596–597, 830
who, whose, whom, **26a**: 591
whoever, whomever, **26b**: 596–597
whose, who's, 830
Wide Sargasso Sea (Rhys), **12d**: 261
will. See shall, will
Williams, Tennessee, **12c**: 257

Williams, Terry Tempest, **4b**: 61
Wilson, David Sloan, **14**: 329, 330,
    14d: 339–340
wire service article, MLA documentation
    style for, **13b**: 296
with regards to. See regard, regarding,
    regards
word choice, **11d**: 238,
    34a: 693–694, **34c**: 695–696
word forms, dictionary information on,
    34e: 705
word order
  inverted, **21d**: 525–526, **27f**: 636,
    32f: 679–680
  in noun combinations, **25a**: 575
  of subject, verb, and object, **21d**: 524
word processor, **6**:110. *See also*
    grammar checker; spell checker
  for footnotes, **17a**: 401
  and graphs, **14c**: 337
  and italics, **44**: 798
  for superscript numbers, **13a**: 274
  for tables, **7c**: 139–140, **14c**: 336
  tracking revisions using, **4a**: 56
  for visual documents, **7d**: 149, 153
wordiness, **26d**: 605, **36a**: 719–722
words
  comma separating series of, **37c**: 732
  including necessary, **28b**: 648–649
  versus numerals, **45f–g**: 810–813
  placing for emphasis, **32a**: 674–675
  referred to as such, **39c**: 752,
    44e: 802
  repeating for emphasis, **32d**: 677
  repeating for parallelism, **31b**:
    669–670
  useless, **36a**: 721
Wordsworth, William, **12b**: 254
wordy expressions, replacements for,
    36a: 721
working bibliography,
    11c: 234–235

works-cited list, 13a: 273, 274,
    13b: 281–282
  sample student, 8j: 190, 12f: 272,
    13c: 327–328
world view, of author, 10a: 217–219
WorldCat, 9b: 201
would of. See could of
wrapping, of text, 7c: 144
Wright, Richard, 12d: 261
writer, in rhetorical situation, 1a: 4
writer's memo, 4e: 76–77
writing
  argumentative, 1c: 8
  choosing subjects for, 3a: 31–34
  expository, 1c: 7–8
  expressive, 1c: 7
  about reading, 2e: 29
  rhetorically, 1a: 4–5
writing centers, 5b: 101–102, 5d: 104
writing process, 4d: 74, 8: 155
  abbreviating, 5d: 103–104
  stages of, 3: 30–31

WWW Virtual Library, 9d: 208
WYSIWYG (What You See Is
    What You Get), 6d: 121

-y, changing to *i, 42d:* 781
Yahoo!, 9d: 208
Yamamoto, Hisaye, 35a: 710
year of publication, in APA-style
    citations, 15a: 346, 347,
    349
yes-or-no questions, 9e: 214
you
  addressing reader as, 26a: 590,
    29b: 658, 35d: 716
  understood, 22e: 550,
    23a: 554
your, you're, 830
yourself. See herself, himself, myself,
    yourself

Zanjani, Sally, 16b: 383

Chapter 21 Sentence Essentials

Article Usage 512

Abstract Nouns and Articles 514

Beginning a Sentence with *There* 519

Word Order 524

Inverting the Subject and the Verb in
Questions 526

Chapter 22 Phrases and Clauses in Sentences

Number Agreement in Noun
Phrases 529

Verbs Followed by Gerunds and/or
Infinitives 533

Prepositions in Idiomatic
Combinations 536

Chapter 23 Sentence Fragments

Subject Pronouns 554

Chapter 25 Modifiers

Adjective Suffixes in Other
Languages 573

Using Participles as Adjectives 574

Noun Modifiers 575

Ordering Adjectives That Modify
the Same Noun 581

Adverbs of Frequency 582

Negation in Other Languages 586

Chapter 26 Pronouns

Noun or Pronoun as Subject 594

Possessive Pronouns 600

Chapter 27 Verbs

Omission of Forms of *Be* in Other
Languages 612

Phrasal Verbs 613

Modal Auxiliaries and Main Verbs 614

Phrasal Modals 615

Signaling the Future with
Be Going To 619

Verbs Not Used in the Progressive
Form 621

Adding -s to Nouns and Verbs 635

Chapter 30 Subordination
and Coordination

Choosing Conjunctions 665

Chapter 32 Emphasis

Inverting Word Order 680

Chapter 34 Good Usage

Dictionaries and Other Resources 703

Chapter 35 Exactness

Connotations 708

Understanding and Using Idioms 715

Chapter 36 Conciseness

Using Relative Pronouns 720

Chapter 39 The Apostrophe

Word with Apostrophe and s or
Phrase Beginning with *of* 746

Gerund Phrases 749

Chapter 40 Quotation Marks

Differing Uses of Quotation Marks 756

Chapter 41 The Period and Other
Punctuation Marks

Indirect Questions 762

Chapter 42 Spelling, the Spell Checker,
and Hyphenation

American and British Spelling
Differences 784

Chapter 43 Capitals

Capitalizing Days of the Week 790

Chapter 45 Abbreviations,
Acronyms, and Numbers

Using Articles with Abbreviations,
Acronyms, or Numbers 810

Different Ways of Writing Dates 812

Commas and Periods with
Numerals 813

Assessing Audience. 14

Assessing an Author's Credentials 217

Assessing the Context. 17

Assessing Purpose 9

Assessing a Thesis 41

Assessing a Topic 36

Assessing Usage within a Rhetorical Situation 701

Comma Splices and Fused Sentences 569

Creating a Questionnaire 215

Designing an Online Document. 128–129

Determining an Author's World View. 219

Editing 88–89

Establishing Relevancy and Timeliness. 228

Evaluating a Draft of an Essay 75

Getting Help from Your Instructor. 101

Information in a Technical Background Report 440

Interpreting a Literary Work. 258

Planning and Developing a Web Site. 125

Previewing a Reading Selection 25

Proofreading 90

Reading an Assignment Sheet 100

Reading a Syllabus 97

Revising Paragraphs 73

Sources That Should Be Cited 243

Using a Course Web Site 98

Using Direct Quotations. 238